CONTENTS

FORTY-FIFTH REPORT

By the Select Committee appointed to consider European Union documents and other matters relating to the European Union.

ORDERED TO REPORT

TOWARDS A SINGLE MARKET FOR FINANCE: THE FINANCIAL SERVICES ACTION PLAN

Abstract

The Desirability of a Single Market in Financial Services

We, and our witnesses, agree that a single market in financial services would benefit the European Union and the United Kingdom. It should lower the cost of capital and borrowing, increase the range of choice for borrowers and investors and ought to provide protection for the investor/consumer.

The Financial Services Action Plan (FSAP)

The FSAP provides a major impetus towards the creation of an internal market but it raises many important issues. We recognise that deadlines are important to achieve political milestones but we do not believe that they should be the determining factor. Quality of legislation is vital. Financial markets carry an inherent *systemic* risk. Over-regulation could stifle innovation and lead to higher costs.

There will be major burdens for the Commission, the Committee of European Securities Regulators (CESR), Member States and Companies in transposing the framework regulation. We do not think that the extent of the potential burden has been fully recognised.

The Global Context

It is essential that any changes to the regulatory system in Europe take account of the global nature of financial markets. Business can move elsewhere. We think this must be a key criterion against which to test all proposed EU regulation.

The Position of London

London attracts envy and admiration in other Member States. There has been a misunderstanding about the nature of the financial markets located in London. They are not an exclusive UK asset. London is a global market not a national one; it should be regarded as a EU asset. If over-regulation or poorly drafted legislation drives business away from London, it will not go elsewhere in the European Union but to international markets where the regulatory touch is lighter.

The Investment Services Directive (ISD)

The Council decision on 7 October 2003, when the UK and four other Member States were outvoted, represents a step backwards. We urge the Government to make every effort to achieve an acceptable outcome.

Implementation and Enforcement

The Lamfalussy process is designed to accelerate the creation and subsequent implementation of framework legislation and to provide appropriate detail and guidance for industry. There is tension at the heart of this system between the light touch need for flexibility and the desire and intention of the regulators to achieve as much harmonisation as possible in order to bring about a level playing field.

Abstract (continued)

Parliamentary Accountability

We support a "call-back" requirement for legislation at Level 2 to be scrutinised by the European Parliament. The Lamfalussy process relies on comitology to accelerate the implementation of legislation but this must not be accompanied by a loss of parliamentary accountability.

A Single European Regulator

While the Lamfalussy process faces enormous challenges, we believe that it must be given time to see if it will work effectively in providing the regulatory framework that will enable a European single market to flourish. We found no support for the concept of a single European regulator.

Clearing and Settlement

Although not part of the Financial Services Action Plan there is a need for a Europe-wide, cross-border, efficient and effective clearing and settlement system. We did not examine this in detail and cannot make a recommendation for a specific means of achieving this. We support the Giovannini process. We urge the European Union at all levels to consider quickly whether legislation is required or whether the markets can create a pan-European, cross-border clearing and settlement system without the need for EU legislation.

International Accountancy Standards (IAS)

Negotiations on these are moving ahead and the International Financial Reporting Standards (IFRS) are due to be implemented in 2005. It is essential that the remaining difficulties (on IAS 32 and 39) be resolved soon and that mutual acceptability be achieved with other international systems such as the United States Generally Accepted Accounting Principles (GAAP).

CHAPTER 1: BACKGROUND

1. A single market in financial services has been an important part of the long-standing European Union objective of an Internal Market which ensures the free movement of people, goods, services and capital. At a time when the Commission is celebrating ten years of the European internal market[1], this report considers issues relating to a single market in financial services.

2. A single market in financial services means that a financial services provider authorised to provide financial services in one Member State is able to offer the same services throughout the EU competing on an equal basis within a regulatory framework that is consistent across the Union. On the other side, the consumer would have access to a wider range of more competitively priced products and would be able to shop with confidence and safety in the market place.

ORIGIN OF THE FSAP

3. The Commission published a Financial Services Action Plan (FSAP) in May 1999[2]. This Action Plan outlined three specific strategic objectives to improve the Single Market for financial services:

- **a genuine single market for wholesale financial services** including measures to enable corporate issuers to raise equity or debt on an EU-wide basis; to develop a common legal framework for integrated securities and derivatives markets; to work towards a single set of financial statements for listed companies; to provide legal security for cross-border securities trades; and to create a secure and transparent environment for cross-border restructuring.

- **open and secure retail markets** including measures to promote enhanced information, transparency and security for cross-border provision of retail financial services; to achieve speedy resolution of consumer disputes; and to develop balanced application of local consumer protection rules; and

- **clear, efficient prudential rules and supervision of financial services**.

---

[1] *The Internal Market – Ten Years Without Frontiers,* Commission paper.
http://europa.eu.int/comm/internal_market/10years/docs/workingdoc/workingdoc_en.pdf

[2] *Financial Services: Implementing the Framework for Financial Markets: Action Plan.*
http://europa.eu.int/comm/internal_market/en/finances/general/actionen.pdf

Political Endorsement

4. The Lisbon European Council in March 2000 gave new impetus to the Financial Services Action Plan as a key component of broader EU economic reform and as a means of making the EU the "most competitive and dynamic knowledge-based economy in the world"[3]. The Council reaffirmed the tight timetable for adopting FSAP measures by 2005 and set the deadline for the adoption of the Risk Capital Action Plan for 2003.

5. Successive European Councils have reiterated commitment to the FSAP and its deadlines. In its conclusion of the Brussels meeting on 16 and 17 October 2003, the European Council stated: "fully integrated and stable financial markets will play a crucial role in channelling savings into productive investment and enhancing economic growth". The European Council also "reiterates its call for rapid progress on all the outstanding components of the Financial Services Action Plan with a view to finalisation in accordance with the agreed timetable"[4].

The FSAP is only part of the Process

6. The FSAP is the main driver towards creating an internal market in financial services but it is only part of the process. For a market to function effectively, there also needs to be an unimpeded system for cross-border clearance and settlement. As the Bank of England points out (paragraph 18), legislation alone may be an ineffective instrument to secure changes in customer practice and FSAP measures have not always lived up to expectations whether in terms of their formulation or their implementation.

Progress to date

7. As we concluded this inquiry, thirty-five of the original forty-two measures outlined in the FSAP had been finalised[5]. The vast majority of the FSAP has therefore met the original deadline in the sense that they have been agreed in principle though most have yet to be implemented. It is uncertain whether all the FSAP measures can meet the 2005 deadline for implementation. There are three outstanding measures under negotiation at present: the Takeover Directive, the Investment Services Directive, and the Transparency Directive. The Proposals on the 10th and 14th Company Law Directives which cover cross-border mergers and allow companies to transfer their corporate seat to another Member State and the Directive on Risk-based Capital have yet to be brought forward by the Commission.

Implementation

8. The draft Directives issued by the Commission are subject to agreement between the Council of Ministers and the European Parliament under the co-decision procedure. Once agreement has been reached on a Directive, a date is stipulated for the measure to come into force. Member States are then given a period (usually 18 months) to implement the Directive by transposing the provisions into national law. To meet the stipulated deadline of 31 December 2005 and allow eighteen months for transposing the EU Directive into national law, the final date for adoption of measures at EU level is April 2004. This coincides with the end of the current European Parliament and elections for the new, post-enlargement Parliament. Such time pressure for the adoption and implementation of FSAP measures has led to claims that the "quality" of Directives is suffering. This report considers these claims in detail.

The Lamfalussy Process

9. The tight timeframe for adoption and implementation of FSAP measures agreed at the Lisbon Council in 2000 required a review of decision-making procedures for adopting EU legislation. In particular, the lengthy timetable for enacting previous legislation demonstrated that it would be difficult to review this round of primary legislation sufficiently quickly as and when circumstances change – as they inevitably will in such a fast-moving industry.

10. So a Committee of Wise Men was appointed, chaired by Baron Alexandre Lamfalussy, to address this problem. The Committee recommended a tiered decision-making process for EU legislation affecting securities markets[6] which was endorsed by the Stockholm European Council in March 2001. In December 2002, ECOFIN agreed to extend the Lamfalussy Process to apply not only to legislation on securities, but also to legislation on banking, insurance and financial conglomerates. The European

---

[3] Presidency Conclusions, Lisbon European Council, 23 and 24 March 2000.

[4] Presidency Conclusions, Brussels European Council, 16 and 17 October 2003.

[5] See Appendix 4 for a list of the expected timeline of key outstanding FSAP measures. *The EU Financial Services Action Plan: A Guide.* Paper prepared by HM Treasury, the Financial Services Authority and the Bank of England, 31 July 2003.

[6] The Regulation of European Securities Markets, February 2001.

Parliament has not yet agreed to this proposal because it wishes to ensure that it has full co-decision powers with the Council under the proposed Constitutional Treaty.

11. The Lamfalussy Process distinguishes several levels of decision-making. The first level of legislation adopted by the Council and the European Parliament following a Commission proposal under the co-decision procedure should only relate to framework principles and the definition of Commission implementing powers. Technical details for adopting Level 1 framework principles should be agreed at a second level by the Commission and Member State experts under the so-called Comitology procedure. Level 3 and Level 4 of the Lamfalussy procedure cover supervision of Member State implementation of the Directives (see Box 1).

Box 1

Lamfalussy Process

Level 1

Community legislation adopted by the Council and the European Parliament, upon a proposal by the European Commission, under the co-decision procedure: should be based only on **framework principles** and definition of implementing powers for the Commission

Level 2

Community legislation adopted by the **Commission** to lay down the technical details for the principles agreed at Level 1 under the so-called Comitology Procedure. Particular features:

- **Technical advice** prepared by the Committee of European Securities Regulators (CESR); following mandates issued by the Commission and based on consultation with market users;

- **Favourable vote of Member States** (qualified majority) as represented in the European Securities Committee (ESC);

- **European Parliament** may adopt resolutions a) within three months on the draft implementing measure; b) within one month after the vote of the ESC if level 2 measures go beyond implementing powers

Level 3

Committee of European Securities Regulators (CESR) in which the national supervisory authorities are represented, to facilitate consistent day-to-day implementation of Community law. CESR may issue guidelines and common, but non-binding, standards.

Level 4

Commission checks compliance of Member State laws with the EU legislation. If necessary, it takes legal action against Member States before the Court of Justice.

Source: Inter-Institutional Monitoring Committee, First Interim Report, May 2003.

Structure of this Report

12. In Chapter 2, we describe the major concerns which we seek to address in this Report. In Chapters 3, we examine specific themes, in Chapter 4 the outstanding Directives, and in Chapter 5 implementation and enforcement. In Chapter 6 we list our conclusions and in Chapter 7, our recommnendations.

Acknowledgements

13. We have received a heartening response to our Call for Evidence[7]. We are grateful to the many individuals and organisations who gave written and oral evidence[8]. In particular, we wish to thank the United Kingdom Permanent Representative to the European Union and his staff for helping us to meet witnesses in Brussels, and to H.M Ambassador and his staff at the British Embassy, Paris, for enabling us to meet a range of French witnesses. In Paris, we were particularly grateful to Senator Philippe Marini, the General Rapporteur of the Finance Committee in the French Senate, for making himself available to the Committee. Finally, we express our gratitude to our Specialist Advisers, Mr Graham Bishop, an independent consultant, and Mr Tom Troubridge, a partner in PricewaterhouseCoopers.

---

[7] See Appendix 2.

[8] See Appendix 3.

CHAPTER 2: A SINGLE MARKET IN FINANCIAL SERVICES

THE BENEFITS OF A SINGLE MARKET

14. A recent Report commissioned from London Economics by the European Commission[9], which looked exclusively at the integration of bond and equity markets, calculated that the creation of a single European Union financial services market would, by itself, lead to significant economic benefits. The Report suggested that full integration of EU financial markets would reduce the real cost of capital by 50 basis points for EU businesses, and result in a one off 1.1 per cent increase in GDP, or Euro130 billion in 2002 prices, over ten years for the EU as a whole.

15. Dr Friedrich Heinemann of the Zentrum für Europäische Wirtshaftsforschung (ZEW) in a report for the European Financial Services Round Table entitled "The Benefits of a Working European Retail Market in Financial Services", concluded that financial integration of retail financial markets between countries in the EU could result in an additional growth effect on EU GDP of at least Euro 43 billion annually (at 2002 prices).

16. The above research indicates substantial potential benefits from the full implementation of a single financial services market. The original Lamfalussy report itself concluded:

"it is not simple to quantify the net sum of these benefits, but potentially they are large".

17. Most of the evidence we received came from organisations facing the private costs of securing the wider benefits. EU economies in general are expected to experience a large collective benefit when a truly liberal internal market in financial services is achieved.

The Financial Services Action Plan

18. The Financial Services Action Plan (FSAP) is the vehicle intended to deliver these benefits by:

- reducing the costs of accessing capital and improving the efficiency of its allocation;

- giving retail consumers access to a wider range of more competitively priced products;

- promoting broader and more liquid equity and bond markets permitting greater investment diversification and reduce risk; and

- putting the financial services sector in a strong position to win market share outside the EU[10].

FSAP is only part of the process

19. However, the FSAP alone is only part of the process that will eventually lead to a single market in financial services. The Bank of England, for example, gives three reasons why the FSAP measures on their own are unlikely to deliver a single market in financial services (see paragraph 6):

- first, because legislation may not be an effective instrument to secure changes in customer practice;

- second, because the original FSAP does not cover some measures important to establishing a single market in financial services such as the removal of cross-border constraints on clearing and settlement (see paragraph 20 below); and

- third, because FSAP measures have not always lived up to expectations whether in terms of their formulation or their implementation[11].

Late Directives

20. Three elements of the FSAP have still to be brought forward by the Commission. They are:

- modernisation of the tenth and fourteenth Company Law Directives[12],

- a Directive which addresses the issue of corporate governance[13];

---

[9] Quantification of the macro-economic impact of integration of EU Financial Markets – November 2002. Study by London Economics, in association with PricewaterhouseCoopers and Oxford Economic Forecasting.

[10] Written evidence from HM Treasury – Page 156.

[11] Written evidence from the Bank of England – Pages 178 and 179.

[12] Written evidence from IMA – Page 204, written evidence from ProShare – Page 34, written evidence from FSA – Page 59 and written evidence from Prudential – Page 211.

- a revised Takeover Directive.

The Commission is currently working on a revised Directive embracing the tenth and fourteenth Company Law Directives and on a Directive on Corporate Governance, both of which are expected to be submitted to the Council and European Parliament by the end of this year. We discuss the problems surrounding the Takeover Directive in Chapter 3 (see paragraphs 69–75).

Other elements needed to create a single market

21. According to witnesses there are a number of other elements which are essential building bricks in the construction of an internal market:

- clearance and settlement[14],

- some form of common principles for taxation [Q. 137 and Q. 148] [15] (i.e. not rates of taxation) and;

- the proposed Directive on consumer credit [16] [Q. 74].

Clearance and Settlement

22. Clearance and real-time settlement systems for equities, corporate government bonds and exchange traded funds are essential elements of an internal market in financial services. The Commission was expected to issue a document in the summer of 2003 to identify what action was needed to establish an integrated settlement infrastructure. In the meantime, the governing Council of the European Central Bank (ECB), the Committee of European Securities Regulators (CESR) and Member States' central banks have set-up a joint Working Party to look at establishing standards for securities clearing and settlement systems.

23. There are, today, around twenty separate systems for fifteen domestic markets in the European Union compared to, effectively, one in the United States for a market of about the same size. The services of these systems are largely tailored to domestic settlement needs.

24. While domestic settlement is cheap and efficient, cross-border settlement is expensive and inefficient.

25. The European Parliament, calling on the Commission to impose a Directive on the clearing and settlement industry, suggested the separation of "core" and "value added" settlement services when performed by the same organisation.

26. One witness, CrestCo Ltd, part of the Euroclear Group which operates the settlement system for UK and Irish equities, corporate and (UK) Government bonds and exchange traded funds, state in their evidence that:

> "we are concerned that by forcing entities to separate "core" and "value added" services (however defined) the opportunity and momentum for delivering efficient structures to cope with the demands of cross-border settlement will be lost ……Furthermore, we do not believe that the case has been made for a specific Directive in this area. We believe that the implementation of the Giovannini recommendations, the work of the ESCB/CESR on strengthened and consistent regulatory standards across the clearing and settlement industry, and the presence of an active competition regulator should all help to create an efficient and low-cost market for settlement services in Europe without further intervention from legislators[17]".

Giovannini Committee

27. The Giovannini Group, chaired by Dr Alberto Giovannini, was set up in 1996 to advise the Commission on issues relating to EU financial integration and the efficiency of euro-denominated financial markets. Its two most recent reports have focused on cross-border clearing and settlement

---

[13] Written evidence from IMA – Page 204, written evidence from ProShare – Page 34, written evidence from FSA – Page 59 and written evidence from Prudential – Page 211.

[14] Written evidence from the London Stock Exchange – Page 3, written evidence from FESE – Page 110, written evidence from CrestCo – Page 187 and written evidence from Euronext – Page 133.

[15] Written evidence from Michel Prada – Page 207, written evidence from IMA – Page 203, written evidence from LSE – Page 3, written evidence from FESE – Page 110 and written evidence from FSPP – Page 196.

[16] Written evidence from Lloyds TSB – Page 205.

[17] Written evidence from CrestCo – Page 189.

arrangements in the EU securities markets. These reports found that EU infrastructure for clearing and settling cross-border transactions remained highly fragmented and were barriers to a single market in financial services. The Group's second report on EU cross-border clearing and settlements published in April 2003[18] identified three main areas for removing barriers through convergence:

- national differences in technical requirements and market practice
- national differences in tax procedures; and
- issues relating to legal certainty.

28. **The Committee did not examine these issues in detail in the course of this inquiry but we consider that an efficient and effective cross-border clearing and settlement system is a fundamental building block that has to be in place. We strongly support the work being done by the Giovannini Committee and we urge that an early decision be reached on whether EU legislation will be needed or whether the market alone could bring about a pan-European clearing and settlement system.**

International Accounting Standards (See Box 2)

29. International Accounting Standards, also known as International Financial Reporting Standards (IFRS), are currently being negotiated[19] and are a core objective of the FSAP. It is important that these standards should be in place in 2005. There are two difficult areas: IAS standards 32 and 39 (which cover hedging), which have run into significant opposition from the banking and insurance industries and in particular from France. The other unresolved issue is whether non-EU issuers will be allowed to use their own accounting standards to raise capital in the EU. It is important that compatible standards are achieved between the EU and the US. In this respect, we welcome the work being undertaken as a result of the Norwalk Agreement[20].

French concerns about aspects of IFRS

30. We heard evidence from the Deputy Governor of the Banque de France in which M Hannoun set out his concerns about IAS 32 and IAS 39 and the effect these standards might have on prudential supervision [Q. 425–428].

31. M Hannoun offered an illustrative example whereby a company in financial difficulties might seek to use the IAS 39 "fair value option" to calculate its liabilities and its debts. The company would show a reduction of the accounting value of its debt and a corresponding improvement in net income – an accounting sleight of hand that could confuse the market as to the company's true value. M Hannoun also had problems with consolidation and argued that the provisioning rules in IAS 39 had to be consistent with the Basel II Framework (See box 3).

32. We put his concerns to the Financial Secretary to the Treasury. Mrs Kelly said:

"international accounting standards may have an impact on financial stability but it is certainly not the only way in which this impact would be felt. They have a huge impact on investment opportunities in Europe as well, and it would be wrong to look at just one aspect of their impact without looking at the broader picture" [Q. 508].

---

[18] http://europa.eu.int/comm/economy_finance/publications/giovannini/clearing_settlement_arrangements140403.pdf

[19] Written evidence from ICAEW – Pages 197–201.

[20] **Norwalk Agreement**

This agreement was reached between the US based Financial Accounting Standards Board (FASB) and the UK based International Accounting Standards Board (IASB) in Norwalk Connecticut on September 18 2002. In this agreement both the FASB and the IASB pledged to use their best efforts to:

- make their existing financial reporting standards fully compatible as soon as is practicable; and
- to coordinate their future work programmes to ensure that once achieved, compatibility is maintained.

The agreement sets out as matters of priority to achieve compatibility:

- undertake a short-term project to remove variety of individual differences between US GAAP and International Financial Reporting Standards (IFRS, which include International Accounting Standards);
- remove other differences between US GAAP and IFRS still remaining on 1 January 2005 through coordination of future work programmes;
- continued progress on joint projects already underway;
- encourage their respective interpretive bodies to coordinate their activities.

Box 2

International Accounting Standards ("IAS")

IAS, or International Financial Reporting Standards ("IFRS") as they are now named, are accounting standards which have been evolving over many years. The intention is that IFRS should be used and accepted internationally by the world's capital markets. This is subject to acceptance by individual countries. IFRS is promulgated by the International Accounting Standards Board (IASB).

The European Parliament and Council of Ministers passed IAS 2005 regulation requiring endorsed IFRS for accounting periods commencing on or after 1 January 2005 for EU incorporated and EU listed companies.

The endorsement process involves a proposal to endorse each IFRS standard in each official language of Member States by the Accounting Regulatory Committee (ARC). The private sector sponsored the creation of the European Financial Reporting Advisory Group (EFRAG) to provide advice to the European Commission and to the ARC.

IAS 2005 regulation contained a requirement to endorse all existing IFRS by December 2002, which has not yet been completed. The delay is due to absence of all necessary translations plus concerns over the acceptability of IAS 39 which would restrict hedge accounting in particular by banks.

EFRAG has reviewed all current standards and has publicly recommended that the ARC adopt them in full.

The ARC have now endorsed all standards except IAS 32 and IAS 39 both relating to (financial instruments). These standards are undergoing significant revisions, particularly in the area of hedge accounting. The IASB has been consulting very widely and held round tables with constituents so that it could learn about the concerns face to face.

The IASB has a very full agenda and currently is targeting to issue many revised standards and some new standards by the end of March 2004. These will be all mandatory standards that will be in force at 31 December 2005. Examples include new standards on business combinations, insurance and share based payments. Revised standards include pensions and deferred taxes.

The implementation of IFRS is a core part of the FSAP as it will mean that all listed companies in the EU will prepare financial statements on the same basis for the first time.

Source: specialist adviser

---

33. We are grateful to the Banque de France for explaining their concerns but **we urge all parties to consider the importance of common accounting standards, not only in the interests of achieving an internal market in financial services in the European Union, but also in order to bring about compatibility of standards with the American and Asia-Pacific markets.**

Consumer Credit

34. Lloyds TSB Group say in their evidence:

> "the Commission did not consider this proposal [i.e. consumer credit] as a financial service issue but as a consumer protection issue. As a result, European parliamentarians generally believe this proposal is seriously flawed as it does not acknowledge sufficiently the practicalities of the markets"[21].

35. In his oral evidence, Mr Ian Mullen, Chief Executive of the British Bankers' Association acknowledged that the Consumer-Credit Directive was not part of the FSAP though it was allied to it. It was complicated by seeking to combine mortgages and financial services. He thought the Directive might be divided in two [Q. 74].

---

[21]   References to Lloyds TSB written evidence, paragraph 10.

36. This was not an area that we looked into.

Taxation

37. A number of witnesses argued that inherent in any effective cross-border trading within a single market in financial services was some form of agreement on the principles of taxation[22]. Again, the Committee did not examine this issue in this inquiry.

The Committee's decision to examine the FSAP

38. Nevertheless, even accepting the need for these additional measures, there is no doubt that the FSAP represents a considerable effort of political will on the part of the European Council, the Commission and the European Parliament to drive through the basic structure of a single market in financial services. Markets are dynamic and one witness argued that it was important to make the breakthrough in the form offered by the Financial Services Action Plan [Q. 136]. For this reason, the Committee concluded that it should concentrate on the progress achieved by the FSAP, consider the main issues that the process had thrown up, and ask whether or not these measures would be adopted on time.

MAJOR THEMES FROM OUR INQUIRY

Cultural Differences

39. We were struck by the different administrative traditions across Europe distinguishing between those Member States where state regulation of markets has been customary and those that have favoured flexibility and where the regulators have sought to maintain as light a touch as possible consistent with the need to protect investors. These cultural differences can be seen in a purely technical form in the tension between the need for maximum harmonisation in some Directives and for flexibility, or subsidiarity, in others. We discuss this balance in Chapter 5.

Wholesale/Retail

40. The division between these two sectors of the market is often blurred but does raise the question as to whether there is a need to regulate the wholesale capital markets in a different way from the regulation of the retail markets. There appears to be a consensus that the need for consumer protection measures is probably greater in the retail markets and that the creation of a single market will take longer in this area. All Member States have retail financial services; only a few are host to the global capital markets. **There is a problem, too, in that it is difficult to define what is meant by wholesale and retail in the context of financial services. More effort should go into seeking to clarify this distinction.**

41. The fear, particularly among UK witnesses, was that the EU might try to extend the comprehensive regulation desirable for the retail market to the wholesale market, where many contend there was less need for it and where the imposition of such regulation could easily stifle the wholesale capital markets. Some witnesses suggested that certain Members States saw close regulation of the retail *and* wholesale markets as a means of protecting national champions[23]. If this were to occur, the EU would be the loser because the cost of capital would fall more slowly and there would be a risk that non-EU issuers would move elsewhere. It is likely to take many years before a true single market in retail financial services emerges. In the meantime, we expect change to be driven by the markets and we remain optimistic that many of today's perceived cultural barriers in this field will be eroded by the force of economic advantage.

After the FSAP

42. The Commission has indicated [Q. 321] that its major task after the adoption of the FSAP will be to concentrate on monitoring implementation and enforcing the Directives. This is an area we address in detail in Chapter 4 where we also consider the case for a European Regulator -"EUROSEC".

SPEED VERSUS QUALITY AND THE 2004 DEADLINE

43. In support of their written evidence, the Association of Private Client Investment Managers and Stockbrokers (APCIMS) attached a list of twelve of the key measures affecting retail and wholesale markets in the FSAP which were outstanding. At the time the evidence was submitted – 26 June 2003 –

---

[22] Written evidence from Michel Prada – Page 207, written evidence from IMA – Page 203, written evidence from LSE – Page 3, written evidence from FESE – Page 110 and written evidence from FSPP – Page 196.

[23] Written evidence from LSE – Page 2 and written evidence from LIBA – Page 16.

not one of the measures had been adopted and implemented and the original deadline of 2003 for achieving the goals for wholesale markets had not been met. The Investment Management Association (IMA) thought that in terms of enacting FSAP legislation by 2005, it was likely that the programme would be met if not then, at least shortly afterwards.

> "However, IMA is concerned that this focuses too much attention on the *speed* with which legislation is enacted and insufficient attention on the *quality* of that legislation. In particular, we would not wish the quality of highly sensitive impending legislation to be compromised by an unnecessarily tight deadline (e.g. the Investment Services Directive, Capital Adequacy Directive, Transparency Obligations Directive, the Takeover Directive and Prospectuses Directive)".

44. This is a view echoed by other witnesses[24]. It was a question which the Committee addressed to witnesses whose oral evidence was heard[25]. The overall tenor of replies was that important legislation was being rushed. Some thought that because the FSAP was working to a politically-driven timetable[26], this was, perhaps, inevitable. Support for the timetable came from the users of the capital markets[27]. There was sense among UK witnesses that few other Member States were sufficiently close to the sophisticated capital markets to understand that bad legislation conceived to meet political deadlines could have serious repercussions and could impede the setting up of a single European market in financial services. **We were, therefore, pleased to hear the Financial Secretary to the Treasury argue robustly for quality of legislation, "we are very aware that it is much more important to get it right than to meet a deadline [Q. 494]". However, success remains a hostage to political fortunes as we have seen in the matter of the Investment Services Directive (paragraphs 53–55).**

45. Some witnesses attributed the slow start at the beginning of the process[28] to allegations of poor quality in the drafting of some of the earlier Directives combined with the Commission's failure to take expert advice [Q. 61] [29]. This was particularly the case for the Prospectus Directive. This was recognised and the Lamfalussy process was the EU's response. The Wise Men, in their report, underlined the paramount need for proper consultation. Lamfalussy is, in practice, just beginning its work in speeding-up the process of implementation. While some witnesses expressed doubts about whether or not the FSAP's current deadlines could be met, most thought that the important outstanding Directives, in particular, the Investment Services Directive, would go to the tape. It was not thought that delay on say, the Takeovers Directive, would substantively affect the outcome of the Financial Services Action Plan.

Commission's Resources

46. When we took oral evidence from the Director-General of DG Internal Market, Dr Alexander Schaub, he said that part of the problem for the uneven performance to date had been a lack of resources in his Directorate General. This lack of resources would become more acute when the Commission moved on to monitoring implementation and enforcing Directives. A surprising number of other witnesses also referred to what they considered to be a critical lack of adequate resources in DG Internal Market. These included Christopher Huhne MEP, the Secretary-General of the Federation of European Securities Exchanges, the Corporation of London, the FSA, Barclays Bank, London Investment Bankers Association, Aviva and the Institute of Chartered Accountants of England and Wales.

47. In her evidence, the Financial Secretary, while acknowledging that the issue of resource allocation was one for the Commission, said "we would argue pretty strongly that they should focus more resources on the implementation and enforcement procedure in the future, as well as thinking, as I said, about non-legislative ways of opening up opportunities for business across Europe." [Q. 525].

48. There would appear to be a serious matter of concern here which could affect how the single market in financial services develops. As Dr Schaub pointed out, the real key to success of the FSAP will come at the stage when Directives are implemented through transposition to national legislation and later in the matter of enforcement. **The Commission's Directorate General for the Internal Market will have an important role to play in monitoring implementation and enforcement and should be properly resourced to do the job effectively.**

---

[24] Written evidence from Prudential – Page 210, written evidence from Fidelity – Page 193, written evidence from the Corporation of London – Page 180 and written evidence from Stephen Revell –Page 214.

[25] Q.15, Q.60. Q.201, Q.219, Q.300, Q.329, Q.397, Q.434, Q.464 and Q494.

[26] Written evidence from FSPP – Page 195.

[27] Written evidence from European Financial Services Roundtable/Aviva – Pages 41 and 42 and written evidence from Unilever – Page 68.

[28] Written evidence from Lachlan Burn – Page 75

[29] Written evidence from QCA – Page 213, written evidence from the Bank of England – Pages 178 and 179 and written evidence from the London Stock Exchange – Pages 1 to 3.

Burden on companies

49. Finally, in a corollary to the issue of the pressure to complete the legislative process by the spring of 2004, the incoming Chairman of the United Kingdom FSA, Mr Callum McCarthy, reminded Government and the market of the existing and impending burden on companies as they scramble to adapt to the flood of legislation[30]. The Committee became aware of Mr McCarthy's speech late in the inquiry but in time for us to ask the Financial Secretary to the Treasury for her reaction to the issues Mr McCarthy had raised. Mrs Kelly said:

> "In a way, Callum McCarthy was making some very sensible points about the implementation process …… we are committed to particular Directives to which we have signed up, but obviously we want to see them implemented in a sensitive way" [Q. 529-530].

50. **We endorse the Minister's sentiments that the Directives should be sensitively implemented and that quality of regulation was more important than deadlines in the creation of a single market.**

---

[30] Mr McCarthy's speech at Ditchley Park. http://www.fsa.gov.uk/pubs/speeches/sp.154hmtl.

CHAPTER 3: THE REMAINING DIRECTIVES

What remains to be done?

51. Many witnesses have confirmed at various times during the course of this inquiry that the critical outstanding Directives are the Investment Services Directive, the Directive on transparency obligations for securities issuers – the "Transparency Directive", the Prospectus Directive (has since completed the Level 1 process, so it is no longer outstanding), the Capital Adequacy Directive[31] and the Takeover Directive[32].

52. The Commission has yet to bring forward its Capital Adequacy Directive, (in her evidence, the Financial Secretary to the Treasury suggested that this Directive did not form part of the FSAP[33] [Q. 499]), the new compromise on the Takeover Directive, a new Directive on Corporate Governance or the new Company Law Directive amending the 10th and 14th Company Law Directives. Most attention has, therefore, been focussed on the Investment Services Directive. This is because it is regarded as the "centrepiece of the FSAP" [Q. 524].

Investment Services Directive

53. A major concern for the UK has been to preserve the compromise reached in the European Parliament's first reading debate. In particular, Article 25 would allow major investment banks to continue to do business direct without having to use the local stock exchanges. The Committee visited Brussels the day that the Council (ECOFIN) voted to amend Article 25 by ten votes for and five against. The latter included the United Kingdom, Ireland, Luxembourg, Sweden and Finland. The dissenters included the largest equity capital market in Europe (the UK) covering about 40% of all EU business and the largest debt markets (UK and Luxembourg). This was a marked change from the normal way in which matters of this importance have been dealt with at ECOFIN [Q. 374]; it is rather as though the Agricultural Council had forced a vote on the European wine industry in the teeth of opposition from France, Spain, Portugal, Italy and Greece!

54. It is alleged that the Council amendment introduces covert protectionism by *requiring* investors to use exchanges by making obstacles to competition from investment banks sufficiently onerous as to dissuade them from doing off-exchange business as they currently do in London. In effect, the amendment reintroduces the pre-trade transparency requirement that was lost in the Commission proposal abolishing concentration rules [Q. 495]. Inevitably, this will raise costs. The Chief Secretary to the Treasury estimated the potential loss through less competitive pricing for institutional clients might be as much as around £300 million a year. A recent report[34] also suggested a similar figure of potential loss for institutional clients and questioned the true extent of off-exchange trading. The Financial Secretary wished to see the Council amendment to Article 25 reversed, although she noted that there had been important benefits secured through the ISD as it currently stood [Q495]. One witness thought that costs would be quite substantial [Q. 374]. Among the reasons said to have been given by the Presidency for proceeding to a vote on this occasion before a "common position" had been reached, was the need for the preliminary linguistic and juridical work to be put in hand in order to meet the spring 2004 deadline.

55. The Treasury Minister believed that much could still change between now and the adoption of the Directive [Q498], although other witnesses expressed doubt on that point [Q.374, 375 and 397][35]. **The Committee regrets that an issue of some importance was decided in ECOFIN by Qualified Majority Vote (QMV) in the face of opposition from important financial centres and urges the Government to make every effort to ensure that an acceptable outcome be reached.**

---

[31]   Written evidence from BBA – Page 24, written evidence from Barclays Bank – Page 48, written evidence from ACPIMS – Pages 173 and 174, written evidence from IMA – Page 202, written evidence from LIBA – Pages 14 and 15, written evidence from FESE – Page 110, written evidence from ICAEW – Page 199, written evidence from FSA – Page 58, written evidence from ProShare – Page 34, written evidence from Stephen Revell – Page 215, written evidence from HM Treasury – Page 159 and written evidence from Euronext – Page 133.

[32]   The Committee has reported earlier on EU Takeover legislation – *"Takeover Bids"* – 13th Report, 95–96, HL Paper 100 and *"If at first you don't succeed ...... Takeover Bids Again"*. 28th Report, 2002–03, HL Paper 128.

[33]   The Basel Committee's findings will be transposed into an EU Directive – Capital Adequacy Directive 3. The Basle timetable has slipped, so the timetable for CAD3 will too. Current target is that this Directive will be implemented by the end of 2006.

[34]   The Potential Impacts of ISD2, Article 25" - OC & C Consultants, August 2003.

[35]   See "Where next for the ISD" by Theresa Villiers, MEP, the Parliament Magazine, 3 November 2003

Capital Adequacy Directive

56. In its evidence, Association of Private Client Investment Managers and Stockbrokers (APCIMS) writes: "a financial company that falls within the Investment Services Directive also falls within the Capital Adequacy Directive which designates the amount of capital that a firm has to hold if it is to be allowed to operate. The amount of capital varies from type of firm to type of firm and is substantial"[36]. The Capital Adequacy Directive is now being revised (and also renamed as the **Risk-Based Regulatory Capital Directive**) to accommodate changes affected by the Basel II negotiations[37][38] (see Box 3). The Basel Committee is proposing to change the way internationally active banks assess risks and apply capital according to these risks. The European Commission proposes to take that work and apply it to every firm that falls within the Investment Services Directive (ISD). According to APCIMS, studies to date have shown that this could result in huge increases for investment firms wholly disproportionate to the amount of risks that they run. Other witnesses have observed[39]:

> "without substantial modification in European rules to take account of the risk profile of investment business, EU firms would need to hold significantly more regulatory capital than non-EU banks with a similar risk profile outside the EU, putting them" [i.e. the non-EU banks] "at a major competitive advantage".

57. The European Commission has still to bring forward the revised Directive. Dr Schaub, recognising that there had been concern, said that,

> "the Commission is technically ready for the necessary steps to be launched next spring" [Q. 313]".

---

[36] Written evidence from APCIMS – Page 173.

[37] See the article by the Chairman of the Basel II Committee, the Governor of the Bank of Spain – Financial Times, 30 October 2003.

[38] See the fears expressed by EUROCHAMBRES about implementing costs especially for SMEs – EU Reporter (27-31 October 2003).

[39] Written evidence from LIBA – Page 14.

Box 3

The Basel 2 Accord on Capital Adequacy

The Accord covers proposals for new requirements that improve banks' stability by tying their capital more closely to the risk of their assets.

The new accord's proposals are divided into three pillars:

1. minimum capital requirements;

2. supervisory review of capital adequacy and

3. public disclosure.

First Pillar: Minimum capital requirements:

The accord proposes:

- a new measure for calculating risk-weighted assets to provide improved bank assessments of risks and to make capital ratios more meaningful.

- introduces three distinct options for calculating credit risk and three others for operational risk to avoid a one-size fits all approach.

- introduces a requirement for explicit treatment of operational risk making the bank's capital ratio more reliable.

Second Pillar: Supervisory Review:

The second pillar of the new accord is based on a series of guiding principles for

- banks to assess their capital adequacy positions relative to their overall risks; and

- for supervisors to review and take appropriate actions in response to those assessments.

If there is a capital shortfall, supervisors may for example require a bank to reduce its risks so that existing capital resources are available to cover its minimum requirements.

Third Pillar: Market Discipline

The third pillar proposes a set of disclosure requirements that allow market participants to assess key information about a bank's risk profile and level of capitalisation. The New Accord places strong reliance on banks' internal methodologies which gives them greater discretion in determining their capital needs

---

Transparency Directive

58. One element in this Directive in particular has caused concern in London, namely the requirement for companies to make quarterly reports to the market.

> "The main issue with quarterly reporting is the need to ensure that companies announce material changes to the market. In the UK, this is a requirement placed upon companies right now in that they have to report immediately any information that is material to the share price. Such a requirement is not present in most European countries" [which have] "a phraseology about reporting to the market in terms such as "as soon as possible". The real concern, therefore, is that a transparency obligation that will improve reporting in some countries would actually reduce reporting in the UK"[40].

59. In fact, the obligation to report to the market is present in other European countries but is not practiced and enforced in the same way as it is in the UK. The real issue is a cultural one – the UK is used to reporting price sensitive information speedily whereas continental Europe is not.

60. APCIMS adds:

---

[40] Written evidence from APCIMS – Page 174.

"it needs to be noted that such reporting cannot be done without proper auditing as no company could afford to make a financial statement of this sort unless the numbers had been independently checked"[41].

61. We find this proposition questionable. Auditors do some sort of a review which might vary from private reporting to the Board of Directors to a formal review-style opinion which could be published. The point is that public reporting would require companies to prepare information to public reporting standards (with or without auditing) and to spend time communicating the results to the market (shareholders and analysts). There is also the question of liability which we address in paragraph XX below.

62. The Chairman of Euronext argued that when companies got used to it, quarterly reporting was not necessarily as onerous as feared and he did not accept that a requirement on companies to submit quarterly reports would lead to volatility and "short-terminism" or even accounting errors simply because people had to comply [Q. 478–479].

63. For the Commission, Dr Schaub said

"personally I believe that this is not a topic which requires a particular religious conviction. For me, it is typically a topic where we can live with diversity and see how the conviction within this integrated market will develop" [Q. 313].

64. The Committee found this to be a sensible approach. Mandatory quarterly reporting would not increase transparency in those markets where companies directed a regular flow of information to the markets but would increase costs. Quarterly reporting, however, would increase transparency in those markets where reporting was not currently frequent. **The obvious solution should be for a requirement for flexibility so that Member States could choose quarterly reporting or UK-type practice where existing national practice did not already require frequent reporting to the market. The objective of the Directive, after all, is transparency.**

Liability

65. One witness identified a potential problem that could arise from the Transparency Directive as it is currently drafted. Mr Lachlan Burn, a partner at Linklaters, introduced supplementary evidence covering this single point. He argued that:

"the draft Transparency Directive ("the Directive") significantly extends the established limitation in English case law on the civil liability of directors and auditors arising from the publication of a company's annual accounts and audit report. As a result, if implemented in its current form, the Directive would mean that directors and auditors would not only be liable to shareholders (as is presently the case) for any errors in the published financial information, but that they would also be liable to the general public. This substantial amendment to the current position on civil liability under English law is contrary to the Commission's stated intention that the Directive should not have such an effect in Member States".

66. Mr Burn's supplementary evidence goes into considerable detail on this point. The Committee were not in a position to take a view but when we spoke to the Director-General of the DG Internal Market, Dr Schaub admitted that it was not a point that had been raised to date [Q. 317]. Dr Schaub asked Baroness Cohen of Pimlico, a Member of our Committee who is also a non-Executive Director of the London Stock Exchange,

"is it your impression that the rules, as they are at present discussed in the Council and Parliament, would increase the degree of liability?"

67. Baroness Cohen answered that, she believed they did [Q. 318]:

"at the moment doctrine and practice are fairly clear in England. We are responsible to shareholders and only incidentally to the wider market, the people who can sue you - which, as a lawyer, is where I always look – are your shareholders. It looks as if the category of people who can sue you is being widened to anybody who might be a potential shareholder – to investors generally".

68. The Commission have yet to comment on Mr Lachlan Burn's supplementary evidence. **The Committee considers that it is important that the text of this Directive be clarified so that the degree of potential liability may be accurately identified. We therefore urge the Government to establish with the Commission the extent to which the liability of directors and auditors might be**

---

[41] Written evidence from APCIMS – Pages 173 and 174.

increased as a result of this Directive. If Mr Burn's interpretation of the effect of this Directive is confirmed, we wish to know how the Government will respond.

Takeover Directive

69. The Community has been struggling to agree a Takeover Directive for over 22 years. The last attempt failed in the European Parliament on 4 July 2001[42]. A further attempt failed in the Competitiveness Council on 19 May 2003. The Committee raised this issue with the Chair of the European Parliament, Economic and Monetary Affairs Committee, Dr Christa Randzio-Plath, who said:

> "I am very sorry I cannot give you a guarantee that at the end we will have a Directive but I can give you the impression that there is a positive approach to try to find reasonable compromises".

70. Asked what the sticking points were, Dr Randzio-Plath said,

> "the problems that you have are that you have the different cultures of the shareholders" [Q. 307-308].

71. Part of the European Parliament's difficulty lay in deciding where responsibility resided. Dr Randzio-Plath explained:

> "we deal with this Directive in three different Committees …… the Social Affairs Committee insists on the rights of the employees, there is also support in the Economic Affairs Committee. We do not know what the Legal Affairs Committee is doing" [Q. 304-308].

72. For the Commission, Dr Schaub said:

> "we believe that we need a Directive which eliminates at least some of the more unreasonable obstacles to cross-border takeovers" [Q. 313].

73. The two most difficult aspects of the Takeover Directive relate to articles 9 and 11. Article 9 proposes a ban on directors taking frustrating action, such as issuing new shares to a friendly party, when in receipt of a hostile bid. Article 11 would seek to override differential voting rights when an acquirer has more than 75% of the risk bearing capital of the target company. In this context, readers are invited to refer to the Committee's Report[43] published in June 2003 in which we examined the extent to which the potential advantages that the draft Directive would make available to UK companies/investors outweighed the potential disadvantages and the risk of increased litigation in the UK. The Government's Response sets out the Government's position in detail[44].

74. The Committee did not explore the nature of the new Portuguese compromise on the draft Directive nor whether it might succeed in attracting a majority in the European Parliament. Our concern was to determine how the failure to adopt this Directive within the deadline might seriously affect the FSAP. The Treasury witnesses believed that it would not [Q 499].

75. **It will be important for the capital markets that a level playing field in the regulation of takeovers emerges. The lack of an agreement on the Takeover Directive by the April 2004 deadline would not in itself seriously affect the ability of the EU to make progress with the other elements of the Financial Services Action Plan but such a failure could weaken the movement towards the efficient and effective operation of a single market in capital including that in existing companies. However, key provisions in the proposed Directive should not be diluted. There is, as we have said before[45], a clear UK interest in the Directive improving the position in other Member States, and in particular opening up markets for UK companies and making more secure the position of UK investors in Europe.**

---

[42] The Parliamentary vote split 273-273, but the vote was lost because of 22 abstentions. For a Directive to be passed, it must have a majority over those against and any abstentions – European Information Service (06/07/2001).

[43] "If at first you don't succeed …… Takeover bids again". 28th Report, Session 2002–03, HL Paper 128, Paragraph 80.

[44] Government Response.

[45] "If at first you don't succeed …… Takeover bids again". 28th Report, Session 2002–03, HL Paper 128, Paragraph 80.

CHAPTER 4: IMPLEMENTATION AND ENFORCEMENT

76. A key mechanism for implementation is the Lamfalussy process. The structure for this process is sketched in Box 1 but it is worth going back to the original task of the "Committee of Wise Men" chaired by Baron Alexandre Lamfalussy to see what that Committee was asked to do. The Committee was required:

- to assess the current conditions for implementing the regulation of the securities markets in the European Union;

- to assess how mechanisms for regulating the securities markets in the European Union can best respond to the developments underway on the securities markets; and

- in order to eliminate barriers and obstacles, to propose adapting current practices in order to ensure greater convergence and co-operation in day-to-day implementation and to take into account new developments on the markets[46].

Problems

77. The "Wise Men" identified the following key problems:

- the EU legislative system was too slow and there was no mechanism in place to adopt or update Directives in a timely manner in order to respond to developments in the market;

- too many delays occurred in the transposition and implementation of EU Directives by Member States. Member States faced a low risk of being sued for infringement;

- many of the Directives in the Financial Services field failed to distinguish between core principles and detailed provisions necessary to implement these principles. As a result, EU securities regulation had become inefficient and rigid with negative effects on European competitiveness. Many texts adopted were ambiguous allowing Member States to apply the same provisions in the treatment of business in different ways creating unnecessary cost. It also violated the requirement of the so-called "competitive neutrality" of supervision; and

- the existence of more than 40 public regulatory authorities concerned with regulating EU securities markets was far too many for an efficient system.

The Lamfalussy Solution

78. The response in the form of the Lamfalussy process, which was subsequently ratified and adopted, identified four levels.

Framework Principles and Implementing Measures

79. **Level 1,** the framework principles, consist of legislative acts, Directives or Regulations adopted by the co-decision process (Council of Ministers and European Parliament). **Level 2** would comprise technical implementing measures adopted by the Commission on the basis of powers delegated by Level 1 legislation.

80. The "Wise Men" recommended that Level 2 implementing measures should be used in order to ensure that technical provisions could be kept up-to-date with market and supervisory developments. Such amendments would be enacted according to a rule-making procedure using a "comitology" Committee. The newly established Committee, the European Securities Committee (ESC) would act in both advisory and regulatory capacities in the field of securities markets. A representative of the European Commission would chair the ESC which would be composed of Member State nominees representing the EU Economic and Finance ministries. In its *advisory* capacity, the ESC would advise the Commission on security issues relating to the adoption of proposed Directives or Regulations under the co-decision process. In its *regulatory* capacity, the ESC would vote on implementing measures proposed by the Commission (Level 2), though the ESC does not have a veto as such. In the absence of agreement, the matter would be referred back to the Council for decision (i.e. Level 1).

Committee of European Securities Regulators (CESR)

81. The Commission would also be assisted by a second Committee, the Committee of European Securities Regulators (CESR). CESR would comprise senior representatives of national regulatory

---

[46] Hertig/Lee 2003 paper.

agencies designated by Member States. CESR would act as an independent advisory group in the preparation of technical implementing measures (Level 2).

82. **Level 3** was designed to ensure consistent, timely, common and uniform implementation of Level 1 and 2 acts in Member States through enhanced co-operation and networking among EU securities regulators. Level 3 would be the responsibility of the Commission assisted by both the ESC and the CESR.

83. Finally, at **Level 4**, the Commission and the Member States would strengthen the enforcement of Community law.

Progress to Date

84. At Level 2, CESR has begun to develop implementing legislation for the Market Abuse and Prospectus Directives. The process is still in its infancy and, according to the London Stock Exchange, raised concern about the volume of implementing measures and the speed at which it was required to be processed[47]. Although most witnesses welcome the advent of the process, and believed that if properly applied, it would help speed the implementation of regulation, there was already a fear that the original objectives embodied in the four level structure were beginning to be lost. In particular, witnesses feared pressure on Level 2[48] exacerbated by extremely short timescales[49].

85. Other witnesses welcomed the fact that the Lamfalussy process firmly embedded consultation with practitioners and transparency into the policy-making process[50] but called for more clarity with regard to the specific competencies of Level 2 and Level 3[51].

86. One witness suggested that the Lamfalussy process and the creation of CESR should enable the EU to address differences in interpretation and transposition before they became embodied in national legislation or regulation. This would ensure that Directives were applied consistently across the EU[52].

87. UNICE, the Union of European Employers' Organisations expressed concern that,

> "all of the easy compromises have been made. We now have difficult ones to deal with......we feel that in some instances there has been too much regulation at Level 1, in other instances, there has been too little" [Q. 341].

88. Mr Paul Arlman, Secretary General of the Federation of European Securities Exchanges also had problems with the loading of responsibility at Level 2 – he called the process one of "*entassement*"– simply piling different national regulatory rules on top of each other. Nevertheless, he felt there was no going back – the Lamfalussy process had to be made to work [Q 354].

89. The Committee were privileged to have a private conversation with the Secretary-General of the Committee of European Securities Regulators (CESR), Mr Fabrice de Marigny. Mr de Marigny was accompanied by Mr Nigel Phipps who had been seconded to CESR's staff from the FSA. In spite of the difficulties that witnesses had pointed to, there was a sense that CESR was the beginning of an entirely new way of implementing EU legislation across the Union. The process of transparency and consultation with the practitioners in the marketplace had been formalised. This meant that in addition to the Council, Parliament and Commission legislating, the markets themselves were now part of the process of implementation. **The Committee concluded that this could only be to the good and that it was understandable given the complexity and magnitude of the task imposed by the FSAP, that progress should appear to many witnesses to be hesitant.**

90. **The Committee remains uncertain whether or not sufficient resources will be available to ensure smooth and effective implementation of legislation through the different levels of the Lamfalussy process. We have already recorded the Commission's concern on this point (paragraphs 46–48). We were struck by the modest size of the permanent cadre of CESR. We are also concerned that the process of implementation has yet to be costed. Deadlines set by the European Council are important to maintain the impetus towards integrated markets in financial services but there is still a lot to do. There is tension between those who want to keep regulation flexible at Level 2 and 3, primarily politicians, and CESR who want the same rules in each Member**

---

[47] Written evidence from the London Stock Exchange – Page 2, paragraph 12.

[48] Written evidence from LIBA – Page 15, B, paragraph 5c.

[49] Written evidence from Pricewaterhouse Coopers – Page 209, paragraph 3.

[50] Written evidence from FSPP – Page 196, paragraph 2.1.

[51] Written evidence from ICAEW – Page 200, paragraphs 24 and 25.

[52] Written evidence from Fidelity Investments – Page 194.

State. Inevitably, this will affect the way in which legislation is implemented and will pose problems in many Member States.

A European Regulator – EUROSEC?

91. One witness in particular doubted that the Lamfalussy process would succeed, although in oral evidence, Dr Ruben Lee did appear to mitigate this view. Nevertheless, he argued that eventually the system would prove impracticable and that there would be a need for some EU-wide, common regulator – EUROSEC[53]. This is a question which the Committee put to many of the witnesses[54]. None was inclined to support this proposition. The Committee had expected some support for this concept to have come from the French witnesses given the approach to regulation that has been associated with French administrative practice. However, all French witnesses we put the question to said that it was far too early even to think of such a proposition. **We agree with witnesses: there is no case for a European Regulator for as far forward as we can realistically see.**

Report of the Inter-institutional Monitoring Group (IIMG)

92. The Inter-institutional Monitoring Group (IIMG) for Securities Markets published its first interim public report on the Lamfalussy process in May 2003[55]. The IIMG consists of six experts nominated by the Commission, the Council and European Parliament and is expected to report bi-annually on the implementation of Lamfalussy. The May report stated that initial indications were that legislation was progressing faster than would otherwise be the case, that there had been positive joint working between all participants but that it was very early days and a more authoritative assessment would have to wait until more evidence was available[56]. **The Committee agrees that it is still too early to be able to judge the eventual success of the Lamfalussy process.**

The role of the Commission in monitoring implementation and enforcement

93. The Committee was encouraged by the enthusiasm shown by Director-General Schaub, for directing the Commission's resources into ensuring that implementation and enforcement become the focus of the Commission's activities (Q. 315). Dr Schaub stressed that the financial markets were special because inherent in them was the risk of *systemic* failure. Member States, the Commission and regulators had to be prepared to intervene should such a risk appear on the horizon. At the same time, European consumers and investors had to have confidence in the system.

94. In its recent communication "Internal Market Strategies Priorities 2003-2006" (IP/03/645) the Commission proposed a number of measures intended to increase the speed and consistency of transposition of internal market law including an "internal market compatibility test[57]" to assess whether specific regulations in specific Member States were compatible with internal market law; a recommendation on "best practices" to speed-up and improve the quality of transposition of internal market law; and a study on the different options for improving enforcement of internal market law[58]. **We welcome these proposals designed to increase the speed and consistency of transposing EU Directives into national law.**

Measuring the effectiveness of implementation and enforcement: the Commission's views

95. In his oral evidence to the Committee, Director General Schaub said:

"first we must make sure the rules are effectively and correctively transposed and that they are applied" [Q. 321].

96. Mr David Wright, Director of Financial Services in the Internal Market Directorate General spoke about the means:

- first, – the Commission needed resources;

- second, – from an economic point of view to look at market behaviour;

[53] The analogy is drawn with the US regulator – the SEC – which is a federal agency.

[54] Q.20, Q.52, Q. 83, Q. 108, Q, 151, Q.178, Q. 207, Q. 269, Q. 293, Q. 309, Q. 315, Q. 393–395, Q. 474, Q. 489, Q. 537.

[55] First Interim Report–Monitoring the New Process for Securities Markets in Europe (the Lamfalussy Process).http://europa.eu.int/comm/internalmarket/en/finances/mobil/docs/lamfalussy/2003-05-monitroingen.pdf

[56] Written evidence from HM Treasury –Page 158, paragraph 15.

[57] Written evidence from Prudential – Page 211, paragraph 17.

[58] Written evidence from Investment Management Association – Pages 202 and 203, paragraph 6.

- third, – to have scoreboards of Member States' performance in terms of implementing and enforcing Community rules;

- fourth, – for the Commission to publish guidance on how certain provisions of Directive should be implemented: [Q. 315].

97. Mr Wright went on to say that the private sector had been largely absent from helping the Commission to identify where Community Law was not being implemented and enforced properly, possibly through a fear of the commercial consequences of doing so:

"I think that ways have to be found and the private sector has to be more bold and imaginative in bringing such cases to us". [Q. 315].

98. **We agree with this view: the private sector has to be persuaded to identify cases of poor implementation or enforcement and to bring this information to the attention of the Commission.**

Measuring the effectiveness of implementation and enforcement: proposals from the London Stock Exchange

99. In supplementary evidence, the London Stock Exchange argued:

"despite the difficulties in measuring outcomes, it is essential for the Commission and policy-makers to set objectives for all legislative proposals and to keep sight of them throughout the process, at Levels 2, 3 and 4 of Lamfalussy, as well as during Level 1."

100. The London Stock Exchange suggested that one possible measure of success for the Prospectus Directive might be the number of cross-border issues of securities following implementation in 2005[59] and that the impact of the new Investment Services Directive might be assessed by surveying investment firms to see whether the Directive had affected their ability to operate from a centre elsewhere in Europe[60]".

Measuring the effect of the FSAP: Retail Markets: The Gyllenhammar Report

101. For the retail markets, a recent report for the European Financial Services Roundtable – the Gyllenhammar Report[61] – offered a more sophisticated analysis suggesting that the so-called "Sharpe ratio" measure of diversification – could be significantly increased by a Europe-wide diversification.

102. **The Committee was in no position to comment on whether or not these proposals would be effective though we recognise that some form of measurement of success after 2005 would help demonstrate the benefits that are expected to flow from a fully-liberalised market in financial services.**

Harmonisation versus Flexibility

103. It was clear to the Committee that while witnesses recognised the key importance of implementation and enforcement, there were inherent contradictions built into the system. Some Directives attempted maximum harmonisation even at the Level 1 Framework stage. Others sought to elaborate core principles and to allow flexibility in implementation though at Level 2, CESR appeared intent on securing maximum uniformity. There is no easy answer to this conundrum; inevitably the FSAP will be a mixture of both maximum harmonisation in some Directives and greater flexibility in others [Q. 521]. This will ensure that the process of implementation remains dynamic and will require all participants, Member States' Governments, the European Parliament, the Commission, the Regulators and the market practitioners to continue to co-operate in translating regulation across the European Union. **Given the uneven record of Member States in implementing Directives, we urge the Commission to engage at an early stage in the appropriate enforcement processes.**

Coherent Legislation

104. There are elements in the way in which the process is being managed that continue to give cause for concern. There is criticism of the lack of detailed cost-benefit analysis in the consultation stage of drafting Directives and there is no mechanism to measure the relative effect of Directives against the objectives of other Directives. Some witnesses argue that the overall aims of the single market may be

---

[59] Supplementary written evidence from LSE –Page 13, paragraph 18.

[60] Supplementary written evidence from LSE – Page 13, paragraph 24.

[61] Hynaman and Jopp, "The Benefits of a Working European Retail Market for Financial Services 2002".

served by one Directive and yet another Directive will, in effect, bring about a retrograde step[62]. There is also concern about how long it might take to change regulations to accommodate changes in the market[63]. One witness [Q. 344] suggested that the legislative process would take three years even if there was common agreement to make such changes, though the Lamfalussy Process is designed to allow changes to be made at Level 2 more quickly than at the level of primary legislation. **The Committee believes that there needs to be some review process and a mechanism to deal with fatal flaws that might emerge when Directives are transposed. We are glad to note that the Commission has set up four groups of market practitioners to assess the internal market for financial services and to help map out the next stage of the integration process following the completion of the Financial Services Action Plan.**

---

[62] Written evidence from Lachlan Burn – Page 76.
[63] The Times, 7 November 2003, Page 39.

CHAPTER 5: THE FSAP IN A GLOBAL CONTEXT

105. The degree of fragmentation in the European capital market still compares unfavourably with the US. In theory, the FSAP should encourage greater convergence and integration and, in time, competitiveness. But there is a careful balance to strike in regulating financial services. The FSAP may equally undermine the competitiveness of the European market if, for example, legislation hinders the development of some markets or drives them abroad[64].

106. The FSAP is essentially a European mechanism to bring about the creation of an internal market in financial services across the European Union – but in the nature of the global economy, whatever happens in Europe is bound to have repercussions in the major financial services markets elsewhere, most notably in the United States of America [Q. 520].

107. The three most important equity wholesale sectors are London, New York and Asia-Pacific (Tokyo/Hong Kong/Singapore). The most important debt markets are centred in London, New York and Luxembourg. Europe is also an essential time zone in the global economy. The most important retail financial industries can be found in those countries with high disposable incomes and an appetite for sophisticated products, for example, the United States. Continental Europe has lagged behind the UK in its appetite for equity investment in pension funds which is reflected in the relative sizes of the stock exchanges.

108. Many of the witnesses, particularly the UK witnesses, expressed concerns that there had not been a sufficient awareness of the global aspect among legislators, particularly from those Member States that had not traditionally been exposed to the international capital markets. Clearly, a Member State that has financial services primarily concentrated in the retail sector, will be less concerned with international capital movements than those Member States that participate actively in the global financial services markets.

109. **It is important that as Member States implement the measures constituting the FSAP, they should be aware, individually and collectively, of the need to remain competitive when measured against New York or the Asia-Pacific centres.**

EU/US Dialogue

110. The Commission was aware of the need to manage EU/US relations both at a political level and in the construction of a single market. In his written evidence to the Committee, the Commission's Internal Market Director noted that:

"therefore it is very important in parallel with the construction of a convincing European system to keep a clear eye on the transatlantic angle[65]".

The Sarbanes-Oxley Act 2002

111. Referring to the American reaction to the Enron scandal – the introduction of the Sarbanes-Oxley Act 2002, Dr Schaub said:

"the lesson to be learned from it is that we have to make sure that we do not ignore the transatlantic/global dimension but keep one eye on our internal process and, in parallel, work on the international prolongation" [Q. 320].

112. The Committee has already sought to monitor the impact of the US Sarbanes/Oxley Act in relation to the issue of reinforcing the statutory audit in the EU[66] and the need to register EU audit firms in the US. The Minister of State at the Department of Trade and Industry wrote

"our understanding is that a constructive dialogue is taking place but that it is too early to speculate on the outcome with confidence[67]".

113. In her evidence to the Committee, the Financial Secretary to the Treasury confirmed that the Government had sought to help establish and to promote a dialogue between the EU and the US in order to broaden and deepen discussion and to make it more forward-looking and proactive [Q. 516].

114. **The Committee is encouraged that the Government has been actively engaged in current discussions between the EU and the US and strongly supports the Commission's role in**

---

64 Written evidence from the Royal Bank of Scotland – Page 217, paragraph C3.

65 Written evidence from DG Internal Market – Page 94, paragraph 4.

66 Chairman of the Select Committee on the European Union's letter of 18 September 2003 to the Department of Trade and Industry – Doc 10739/03 Communication from the Commission: Reinforcing the statutory audit in the EU.

67 Letter from the Rt. Hon Jacqui Smith MP dated 7 October 2003 to Lord Grenfell.

encouraging a transatlantic dialogue. Inevitably, a single European market in financial services could provide a major challenge for New York. The dialogue will have to be handled carefully but the benefits to the global market in financial services are so great that any form of protectionism on either side of the Atlantic should be eschewed.

US Protectionism?

115. The Federation of European Securities Exchanges (FESE) was critical of the unilateral way in which the US had acted in the context of the transatlantic capital markets, in particular, in denying access to the United States of foreign trading screens. The FESE argued that the issue was essentially one of protectionism and a refusal on the part of the Americans to recognise the separate European regulatory authorities. Attempts to engage the United States in dialogue had, according to the FESE, only been partly successful [Q. 373].

The Position of London

116. The Committee also considered the consequences of FSAP legislation on the markets located in the City of London. We found that UK witnesses were mostly nervous fearing that the implementation of the FSAP would be slewed by political negotiation and that this would adversely affect the very large and vibrant capital markets that have emerged in London[68]. Witnesses also felt that the capital markets located in London were regarded by other Member States as a UK asset rather than as a resource that benefited EU industry as a whole and that, as a result, attempts were being made to use the legislative tools of the FSAP to "repatriate" business to other Member States[69]. Other witnesses thought that the FSAP's attempts to harmonise regulation would prove burdensome and have the effect of driving away non-EU business[70].

117. Continental witnesses tended to see things differently. Mr Michel Prada, Inspecteur Générale des Finances, Ministry of Economic and Financial Affairs, argued that:

"the City of London is old, strong and rich and open and innovative enough not to worry about the consequences of financial integration in Europe".

118. This is a view echoed by the Federation of European Securities Exchanges who thought that the removal of barriers to cross-border trades could only benefit those service providers (in the UK and elsewhere), who understood and implemented the play of competition better than others[71] – a view supported by a UK witness, ProShare[72].

119. We believe there has been increased awareness in other Member States about the importance of the London markets to the EU economy as a whole. Nevertheless, there are still, in part, residual, protectionist inclinations. These come more clearly to the fore in the Council rather than in the Commission or the European Parliament as was evident by the vote in ECOFIN on 7 October 2003.

120. We were heartened by the catalytic effect that CESR has had in the implementation process that has led to an increasing awareness of the different systems that need to be brought into some form of harmony. We gained the distinct impression from our discussions with witnesses in Brussels and Paris that the views expressed by some of the UK witnesses may well have applied in the early stages of the FSAP but that there had been, in the intervening period, a change in attitudes as the complexity of regulating these sophisticated markets was borne in on the national regulators and finance ministers in other Member States.

121. **The Committee recognises the fears of the practitioners in the UK market. London is, undoubtedly, successful and this attracts both admiration and envy from less successful markets. A single market in financial services can only be to the benefit of an efficient and competitive dominant market player. Nevertheless, it will be important for the Government and the financial services industry to monitor closely the implementation of Directives as the Lamfalussy process evolves and to be prepared to intervene at an early stage if EU legislative proposals contain elements that might seriously inhibit the ability of the markets in London to continue to attract non-EU issuers and participants.**

---

[68] CEBR–City's importance to the EU economy (Jan 2003).

[69] Written evidence from LSE – Pages 1 and 2, paragraphs 6 and 7; written evidence from Michel Prada – Page 208 and written evidence from Lachlan Burn – Page 77, paragraph 3.3.

[70] Written evidence from LIBA – Page 16, paragraph 11.

[71] Written evidence from FESE – Page 110.

[72] Written evidence from ProShare – Page 35, paragraph 16.

CHAPTER 6: ASSESSMENT AND CONCLUSIONS

An internal market for financial services

122. All the witnesses spoke strongly in favour of achieving a single, internal market in financial services. The benefits of such a market were evident. A truly liberal internal market in financial services would reduce the cost of capital and borrowing and increase the range of choice for savers and investors. It would broaden the market base, deepen liquidity and provide wider choice and adequate protection for the investor.

Financial Services Markets are Different

123. As Dr Schaub, Director-General for the Internal Market in the Commission rightly pointed out, financial services are different: there is an inherent risk of *systemic* collapse if the markets are not regulated with care.

The Global Context

124. It is essential for those involved in the process of regulating the financial markets to keep the global context firmly in view at all times. The European Union is not an island and business can and will go elsewhere[73]. The global context of every financial market reform should be a key criterion against which to judge the necessity for, and the impact of, proposed legislation and its implementation.

EU/US

125. In this context, it is vitally important for the development of globally competitive financial markets in the European Union that a dialogue be maintained with the world's largest capital markets – the United States of America and the Asia-Pacific markets which embrace Japan, Singapore and Hong Kong. We look forward to IFRS, planned for introduction in the EU in 2005 being accepted by markets globally and for other equivalent standards such as US GAAP being accepted in EU capital markets.

The Commission's Financial Services Action Plan (FSAP)

126. The FSAP can play a major part in achieving a single financial market within the European Union and we support the thrust of the Action Plan. However, its scope is large and timescale challenging. It would be foolish to ignore some of the potential problems, notably the balance to be achieved between speed of implementing legislation and the quality of that legislation.

127. The retrogressive vote at the ECOFIN Council meeting on 7 October 2003 on the Investment Services Directive was "justified" in part by the need to meet the administrative deadline set for the jurist/linguists within the political deadline for the Directive to be adopted. Not only was this vote a breach of the convention that agreement in ECOFIN should be sought by consensus but the vote effectively undid progress made in the European Parliament to keep the balance between a light, regulatory touch – particularly for the large, international investors - and retail investor protection measures. We regard this ECOFIN decision as possibly the most important signal to date that mishandling the FSAP could lead to a movement of financial services away from the EU and to a reduction in the availability of low-cost capital for EU industry. We trust that the decision to force a vote will not be repeated when other decisions on the single market in financial services are taken by ECOFIN.

Volume of Legislation

128. The volume of legislation, some of it yet to be agreed in principle, most of it yet to be agreed in detail, imposes substantial demands on businesses, on regulators, and on the Commission. In our view, the European Council and ECOFIN, the Commission and the Committee of European Securities Regulators (CESR) all need to recognise this and to consider a clear strategy to assess how realistic the 2005 implementation date is and to have a clear sense of priorities.

---

[73] It is interesting to compare this possibility with the reaction expressed by Mr Philippe de Buck, Secretary General of the Federation of European Employers Organisation (UNICE) in connection with the Commission's draft Directive on the European Chemical Industry – EU Reporter, Week 42, 13–17 October 2003.

The Role of London

129. The reason why London is currently the dominant wholesale capital market in Europe is in part because of the way in which the regulations have been drawn up and administered. London has welcomed foreign participants and has regulated with a light touch sensitive to the vagaries of the markets. However, there appears to be a widespread view in other Member States that the London-based markets are somehow a United Kingdom asset rather than an EU asset where profits are remitted to a Member State's companies or institutions. The wholly UK element is a very small proportion of this market. For example, the London Investment Banking Association lists 40 institutions which comprise its membership but of these, only 2 could be described as British and the British Bankers' Association has 272 members of which only 71 are UK institutions. A globally-efficient, low-cost financial market in London benefits both the EU industry and EU investors.

Lamfalussy Process

130. Effective consultation is at the heart of developing successful implementation of regulation. We welcome the fact that through this process the financial services industry itself has been formally integrated into the formulation of legislation. This was certainly not the case before in a number of Member States or at the European Commission and the earlier measures that constitute the FSAP were often marked by a lack of professional input.

131. We have also been impressed by the desire to consult, co-operate and to succeed at the heart of the Committee of European Securities Regulators. Witnesses have told us that the extent of consultation by national regulators now far exceeds that previously experienced. However, a much larger volume of work lies ahead, increased by the enlargement of the European Union to 25 Member States. Maintaining market responsiveness while achieving a large degree of harmonisation will be an enormous challenge to the whole process.

Harmonisation and Flexibility

132. A number of witnesses, both in the United Kingdom and France, expressed the hope that detailed legislation at the Lamfalussy process Level 2 and 3, would allow flexibility at Member State level. However, it is clear to us that CESR, in which the FSA plays an important role, is looking for maximum harmonisation and will face a real problem in seeking uniformity across 25 Member States. Some flexibility will undoubtedly be required. On the other hand, it will be important to ensure that the call for flexibility is not an excuse for non or slow implementation.

The Ability to respond to Changes in the Markets

133. It is important that the desire to achieve uniformity and harmonisation across 25 Member States does not result in sclerosis of the financial arteries of Europe. In spite of good intentions, detailed legislation at Level 2 could become inflexible and difficult to change quickly and it is vital that detailed legislation does not stifle financial innovation. By way of example, increased formal legislation is already slowing reaction times at national level. The listing rules on the London Stock Exchange used to be changed yearly. Now, to meet increased consultation through the FSA, it takes 18 months. Clearly, increased demand for consultation within 25 Member States and between 25 Member States will add a further drag on the flexibility of the regulatory system to respond rapidly to changes in the market[74].

Parliamentary Scrutiny

134. The major innovation in the Lamfalussy process is the introduction of the "comitology" procedure at Level 2. While this can lead to the more rapid implementation of regulations agreed under the Level 1 Framework principles, it also threatens the important principle of parliamentary accountability. We support the "call-back" provision which will require consultation with the European Parliament at Level 2.

Measures other than those proposed in the FSAP: Clearing and Settlement Systems

135. The FSAP alone cannot deliver a true internal market in financial services although it goes a considerable way towards creating a regulatory framework for such a market. There are elements which lie outside the formal corpus of measures which constitute the FSAP. One important example is the matter of cross-border clearing and settlement. This has been described by witnesses as the "plumbing system" of a single market in financial services. An efficient and effective cross-border single financial

---

[74] See the Editorial in the Times Business Section, 7 November 2003, Page 39.

market must have efficient and effective clearing and settlement systems. This is a fundamental building block that has to be in place. In this context, we strongly support the work being done by the Giovannini Committee and we urge that an early decision be reached at all political levels whether EU legislation will be needed or whether the market itself realistically, could bring about a pan-European effective and flexible clearing and settlement system.

International Accountancy Standards

136. We have already referred to the importance of international accountancy standards and mutual recognition with other accountancy standards such as the United States GAAP. Together with a clearing and settlement system, accounting standards constitute the basic tools for operating a true single market in financial services.

Redress

137. Many market players believe that there is a fundamental problem at the stage when regulation is implemented. How will the Commission obtain the detailed information and evidence required to take timely and effective enforcement action against a Member State before the European Court of Justice? [Q. 315]. Many believe that professionals and businesses will be reluctant to report their national regulator to the Commission for failing to enforce the FSAP. One witness suggested an informal method of resolving the difficulties – resort to an arbitrator or an ombudsman for professionals. This is a problem that needs to be addressed before 2005.

A Single European Regulator

138. Some observers have cast doubt on whether the Lamfalussy process will be able to cope with the enormous regulatory burden which is looming. We agree that there will be difficulties and we are not yet convinced of the commitment of all Member States to speed-up implementation. But in our view, the Lamfalussy process has to be given every opportunity to develop its role. We agree with the overwhelming majority of the witnesses that a single European Regulator is neither necessary nor desirable for as far ahead as we can realistically see.

CHAPTER 7: RECOMMENDATIONS

139. We list the various recommendations that we have made in the course of this Report.

- Clearing and Settlement: **The Committee did not examine these issues in detail in the course of this inquiry but consider that an efficient and effective cross-border clearing and settlement system is a fundamental building block that has to be in place. We strongly support the work being done by the Giovannini Committee and we urge that an early decision be reached on whether EU legislation will be needed or whether the market alone could bring about a pan-European clearing and settlement system (paragraph 28).**

- International Accounting Standards: **We urge all parties to consider the importance of common accounting standards, not only in the interests of achieving an internal market in financial services in the European Union, but also in order to bring about compatibility of standards with the American and Asia-Pacific markets (paragraph 33).**

- Wholesale Retail: **There is a problem, too, in that it is difficult to define what is meant by wholesale and retail in the context of financial services. More effort should go into seeking to clarify this distinction (paragraph 40).**

- Deadlines: **We were, therefore, pleased to hear the Financial Secretary to the Treasury argue robustly for quality of legislation, "we are very aware that it is much more important to get it right than to meet a deadline [Q. 494]". However, success remains a hostage to political fortunes as we have seen in the matter of the Investment Services Directive (paragraph 44).**

- Resources: Commission: **The Commission's Directorate General for the Internal Market will have an important role to play in monitoring implementation and enforcement and should be properly resourced to do the job effectively (paragraph 48).**

- Burden on Companies: **We endorse the Minister's sentiments that the Directives should be sensitively implemented and that quality of regulation was more important than deadlines in the creation of a single market (paragraph 50).**

- The Investment Services Directive: **The Committee regrets that an issue of some importance was decided in ECOFIN by Qualified Majority Vote (QMV) in the face of opposition from important financial centres and urges the Government to make every effort to ensure that an acceptable outcome be reached. (paragraph 55).**

- Transparency Directive: Quarterly Reporting: **The obvious solution should be for a requirement for flexibility so that Member States could choose quarterly reporting or UK-type practice where existing national practice did not already require frequent reporting to the market. The objective of the Directive, after all, is transparency (paragraph 64).**

  Liability: **The Committee considers that it is important that the text of this Directive be clarified so that the degree of potential liability may be accurately identified. We therefore urge the Government to establish with the Commission the extent to which the liability of a director or auditor might be increased as a result of this Directive. If Mr Burn's interpretation of the effect of this Directive is confirmed, we wish to know how the Government will respond (paragraph 68).**

- Takeover Directive: **It will be important for the capital markets that a level playing field in the regulation of takeovers emerges. The lack of an agreement on the Takeover Directive by the April 2004 deadline would not in itself seriously affect the ability of the EU to make progress with the other elements of the Financial Services Action Plan but such a failure could weaken the movement towards the efficient and effective operation of a single market in capital including that in existing companies. However, key provisions in the proposed Directive should not be diluted. There is, as we have said before[75], a clear UK interest in the Directive improving the position in other Member States, and in particular opening up markets for UK companies and making more secure the position of UK investors in Europe (paragraph 75).**

- Lamfalussy Process: Consultation with Market Practitioners: **The Committee concluded that this could only be to the good and that it was understandable given the complexity and magnitude of the task imposed by the FSAP, that progress should appear to many witnesses to be hesitant (paragraph 89).**

---

[75] "If at first you don't succeed ...... Takeover bids again". 28th Report, Session 2002–03, HL Paper 128, Paragraph 80.

Resources: **The Committee remains uncertain whether or not sufficient resources will be available to ensure smooth and effective implementation of legislation through the different levels of the Lamfalussy process. We have already recorded the Commission's concern on this point (paragraph 48). We were struck by the modest size of the permanent cadre of CESR. We are also concerned that the process of implementation has yet to be costed. Deadlines set by the European Council are important to maintain the impetus towards integrated markets in financial services but there is still a lot to do. There is tension between those who want to keep regulation flexible at Level 2 and 3, primarily politicians, and CESR who want the same rules in each Member State. Inevitably, this will affect the way in which legislation is implemented and will pose problems in many Member States (paragraph 90).**

- A European Regulator?: **We agree with witnesses: there is no case for a European Regulator for as far forward as we can realistically see. (paragraph 91).**

- Success of the Lamfalussy Process: **The Committee agrees that it is still too early to be able to judge the eventual success of the Lamfalussy process. (paragraph 92).**

- Commission's "Internal Market Strategies 2003–2006": **We welcome these proposals designed to increase the speed and consistency of transposing EU Directives into national law (paragraph 94).**

- The Private Sector and Enforcement: **We agree with this view: the private sector has to be persuaded to identify cases of poor implementation or enforcement and to bring this information to the attention of the Commission (paragraph 98)**

- Measuring the effectiveness of the FSAP proposals: **The Committee was in no position to comment on whether or not these proposals would be effective though we recognise that some form of measurement of success after 2005 would help demonstrate the benefits that are expected to flow from a fully-liberalised market in financial services. (paragraph 102).**

- Enforcement: **Given the uneven record of Member States in implementing Directives, we urge the Commission to engage at an early stage in the appropriate enforcement processes (paragraph 103).**

- Review Process: **The Committee believes that there needs to be some review process and a mechanism to deal with fatal flaws that might emerge when Directives are transposed. We are glad to note[76] that the Commission has set up four groups of market practitioners to assess the internal market for financial services and to help map out the next stage of the integration process following the completion of the Financial Services Action Plan (paragraph 104).**

- Global Context: **It is important that as Member States implement the measures constituting the FSAP, they should be aware, individually and collectively, of the need to remain competitive when measured against New York or the Asia-Pacific centres (paragraph 109).**

- EU/US Dialogue: **The Committee is encouraged that the Government has been actively engaged in the current discussions between the EU and the US and strongly supports the Commission's role in encouraging a transatlantic dialogue. Inevitably, a single European market in financial services will provide a major challenge for New York. The dialogue will have to be handled carefully but the benefits to the global market in financial services are so great that any form of protectionism on either side of the Atlantic should be eschewed (paragraph 114).**

- Position of London: **The Committee recognises the fears of the practitioners in the UK market. London is, undoubtedly, successful and this attracts both admiration and envy from less successful markets. A single market in financial services can only be to the benefit of an efficient and competitive dominant market player. Nevertheless, it will be important for the Government and the financial services industry to monitor closely the implementation of Directives as the Lamfalussy process evolves and to be prepared to intervene at an early stage if EU legislative proposals contain elements that might seriously inhibit the ability of the markets in London to continue to attract non-EU issuers and participants (paragraph 121).**

140. The Committee considers that the European Commission's Financial Services Action Plan raises important questions to which the attention of the House should be drawn and makes this Report to the House for debate.

---

[76] European Report 2815 – 28 October 2003, Page 11.2.

APPENDIX 1

Membership of Sub-Committee B

The Members of Sub-Committee B who conducted this inquiry were:

Lord Cavendish of Furness

Lord Chadlington

Baroness Cohen of Pimlico

Lord Faulkner of Worcester

Lord Fearn

Lord Howie of Troon

Lord Shutt of Greetland

Lord Skelmersdale

Lord Walpole

Lord Woolmer of Leeds (Chairman)

Declaration of Interests

Lord Cavendish of Furness	Director, Holker Holdings Ltd
	Director, Park Healthcare Ltd (Private Nursing Home)
	Director, United Kingdom Nirex Ltd
	Director, Burlington Slate Ltd
Lord Chadlington	Chairman, International Public Relations
	Director, Huntsworth Plc/Chadlington Consultancy/Oxford Resources Ltd
	Chief Executive, Quiller Consultants
Baroness Cohen of Pimlico	Non Executive Chairman, BPP Holdings Plc
	Non Executive Director, London Stock Exchange
	Non Executive Director, Management Consulting Group Plc
	Non Executive Director, Defence Logistics Org
Lord Faulkner of Worcester	Incepta Group Plc
Lord Fearn	Councillor, Sefton M.B.C
Lord Howie of Troon	Consultant, George S. Hall Ltd
Lord Shutt of Greetland	Self-employed Consultant (non-practising Chartered Accountant)
	Director, The Joseph Rowntree Reform Trust Ltd and subsidiary companies
	Trustee, The JRSST Charitable Trust
	Trustee, The Joseph Rowntree Charitable Trust
Lord Skelmersdale	Director, Broadleigh Nurseries Ltd
Lord Walpole	Landowner, retired Farmer, Gardener
	Active in countryside conservation since 1982
	Vice-President, Council for National Parks
	Director, Peter Beales Roses
	Member, Country Land and Business Association, National Trust
Lord Woolmer of Leeds	Partner, Halton Gill Associates
(Chairman)	Partner, Anderson McGraw
	Non Executive Director, Thornfield Properties Plc
	Non Executive Director, CourtCom Ltd
	Chairman, Energy Forum, Yorkshire and Humber Regional Development Agency (Yorkshire Forward)
	Member, Council of the Foundation for Management Education

APPENDIX 2

Call for Evidence

Sub-Committee B (Energy, Industry & Transport) of the House of Lords Select Committee on the European Union is undertaking an inquiry into the European Commission's *Financial Services Action Plan*.

On 11 May 1999, the Commission adopted an Action Plan which outlined a series of policy objectives and specific measures to improve the single market for Financial Services. The Financial Services Action Plan is to be implemented by 2005.

The Financial Services Action Plan outlined four strategic objectives:

- a genuine single market for wholesale financial services;

- open and secure retail markets;

- clear, efficient, prudential rules and supervision of financial services; and

- wider conditions for an optimal, single financial market

Evidence is invited on the following issues:

THE FINANCIAL SERVICES ACTION PLAN

- What progress has been made to date? Has this been beneficial or deleterious to UK interests? Has sufficient weight been given to the position and experience of UK financial services industry?

- What are the main outstanding matters that remain to be dealt with under the FSAP and what key issues will need to be resolved?

IMPLEMENTATION AND ENFORCEMENT

The success of setting up a single market in financial services will depend to a considerable degree on the way in which the regulatory Framework is implemented and enforced.

- How successful do you expect the Lamfalussy process to be? Are any changes needed?

- Who will be responsible for ensuring effective implementation and enforcement of the single market, after the regulatory Framework is in place? How successful do you expect this process to be? What will be the role of competition regulators at EU and Member State level?

- What issues will arise as the single market framework is implemented and enforced?

- What non-regulatory barriers might impede the effective functioning of a single market for financial services?

THE FUTURE

- How do witnesses see the future development of a single market in financial services following implementation of the FSAP? Are additional measures needed?

- Will the changes resulting from the FSAP proposals have an impact on the competitive position of London and EU markets as a whole in the global environment?

APPENDIX 3

List of Witnesses

The following witnesses gave evidence. Those marked * gave oral evidence.

* Mr Paul Arlman, (Federation of European Securities Exchanges)

  Association of British Insurers

  Association of Private Client Investment Managers and Stockbrokers (APCIMS)

  Bank of England

* Barclays Bank Plc

* British Bankers Association

* Mr Lachlan Burn (Partner, Linklaters)

  Corporation of London

  CrestCo Ltd

* Mr Richard Desmond (UNICE)

  Euronext

  European Investment Bank

  Fidelity Investments

* Financial Services

  Financial Services Practitioner Panel

* Mr Pehr Gyllenhammar (European Financial Services Round Table)

* Mr Hervé Hannoun (Banque de France)

* Mr Chris Huhne MEP

  Institute of Chartered Accountants in England and Wales

  Investment Management Association (IMA)

* Ms Ruth Kelly MP (HM Treasury)

* Mr Ruben Lee (Oxford Finance Group)

* Mr Jean-François Lepetit (Commission des Opérations de Bourse) [Evidence not printed at the witness's request]

  Lloyds TSB Group

* London Investment Banking Association

* London Stock Exchange

* Mr Philippe Marini (French Senate)

  Mr Michel Prada (European Commission)

  Pricewaterhouse Coopers

* ProShare

  Prudential Plc

  Quoted Companies Alliance (QCA)

* Ms Christa Randzio-Plath (Economic and Monetary Affairs Committee, European Parliament)

  Mr Stephen Revell (Freshfields Bruckhaus Deringer)

  Royal Bank of Scotland

* Dr Alexander Schaub, (DG Internal Market, European Commission)

* Mr Peter Skinner MEP

  Mr Luigi Spaventa

* Mr Jean- François Théodore (Euronext)

* Unilever

APPENDIX 4

List of FSAP Measures

Measures proposed but not yet adopted
(Legislative proposals in bold)

1. **Directive on transparency obligations for securities issuers. Commission proposal 26 March 2003.**
2. **Directive on investment services and regulated markets (upgrade Investment Services Directive). Commission proposal 19 November 2002 (COM (2002)625).**
3. **Directive on Takeover Bids. New Commission proposal adopted 2 October 2002 (COM(2002)534).**

Measures not yet proposed

4. Legal Framework for payments
5. **10th and 14th Company Law Directives**
6. **Risk-based Capital Directive**
7. **Third Money-Laundering Directive**

Measures adopted but not yet implemented

8. Directive on Insider Dealing and Market Manipulation (Market Abuse). Directive 2003/6/EC of 28 January 2003.
9. Amendments to the 4th and 7th Company Law Directives to allow fair value accounting: Directive 2001/65/EC adopted on 31 May 2001.
10. Regulation (EC)1606/2002 of the European Parliament and of the Council on the application of international accounting standards adopted on 19 July 2002.
11. Modernisation of the accounting provisions of the 4th and 7th Company Law Directives adopted 6 May 2003 (PE-CONS 3611/03, amending Directives 78/660/EEC, 83/349/EEC, 86/635/EEC, and 91/647/EEC on the annual and consolidated accounts of certain types of companies, banks and other financial institutions and insurance undertakings.
12. Directive on financial collateral arrangements. Directive 2002/47/EC adopted on 6 June 2002.
13. Political agreement on the European Company Statute. Directive 2001/86/EC and Regulation (EC)2157/2001 adopted on 8 October 2001.
14. Two Directives on UCITS. Directives 2001/107/EC and 2001/108/EC adopted on 21 January 2002.
15. Directive on the Prudential Supervision of Pension Funds adopted on 13 May 2003 (P5_TA (2003) 0086)
16. Directive on the Distance marketing of Financial Services. Directive 2002/65/EC adopted on 23 September 2002.
17. Directive on Insurance Mediation. Directive 2002/92/EC of 9 December 2002.
18. Adoption of the proposed Directive on the Reorganisation and Winding-up of Insurance undertakings. Directive 2001/17/EC adopted on 19 March 2001.
19. Adoption of the proposed Directive on the Winding-up and Liquidation of Banks. Directive 2001/24/EC adopted on 4 April 2001.
20. Adoption of the proposal for an Electronic Money directive. Directive 2000/46/EC adopted on 18 September 2000.
21. Amendments to the solvency margin requirements in the Insurance Directives. Directives 2002/12/EC and 2002/13/EC adopted on 5 March 2002.
22. Directive on the supplementary supervision of credit institutions, insurance undertakings and investment firms in a financial conglomerate. Directive 2002/87/EC of 16 December 2002.
23. Directive on Prospectuses. Decision on 3 July 2003. Directive (COM(2002)460).

Completed FSAP Measures

24. Amendment to the Money Laundering Directive. Directive 2001/97/EC adopted on 4 December 2001.
25. Commission Communication on the Application of Conduct of Business Rules Under Article 11 of the Investment Services Directive (ISD) (distinction between professional and retail investors). Issued on 14 November 2000, COM(2000)722.
26. Commission Communication on upgrading the ISD. Issued on 15 November 2000, COM(2000)729.
27. Commission Communication updating the EU accounting strategy. Issued on 13 June 2000, COM(2000) 359.

28. Commission Recommendation 2001/256 of 15 November 2000 on quality assurance of the statutory audit (C(2000) 3304).

29. Commission Recommendation 2001/6942 of 16 May 2002 on Statutory auditor's independence in the EU: A set of fundamental principles (C(2002)1873).

30. Implementation of the Settlement Finality Directive 98/26/EC of 19 May 1998. In the coming months the Commission will publish a report to modify the Settlement Finality Directive and the Directive stated under (11) to integrate the The Hague Convention in EU Law.

31. Review of EU corporate governance practices The final report of the Comparative Study was published on 27 March 2002 (available on DG Markt's website : http://europa.eu.int/comm/internal_market/en/company/company/news/index.htm).

32. Commission Communication on Funded pension Schemes. Issued on 11 May 1999 (Com (1999)134). This includes the Review of taxation of financial service products. This action has been taken care of in the context of the initiative on taxation of cross-border occupational pensions.

33. Commission Communication on clear and comprehensible information for purchasers. The work on the communication has been integrated in the context of the Commission Communication on an e-commerce policy for financial services (COM(2001)66 – 07/02/2001).

34. Commission Recommendation 2001/193 of 1 March 2001 to support best practice in respect of information provision (mortgage credit) (C(2001)477).

35. Commission report on substantive differences between national arrangements relating to consumer-business transactions. Discussions with industry ('Forum Group') and consumers are concluded. Information gathered is used for further Commission initiatives in the field of retail financial services.

36. Interpretative Communication on the freedom to provide services and the general good in insurance. Issued on 2 February 2000, C(1999)5046.

37. Commission Communication on a single market for payments. Issued on 31 January 2000, COM(2000)36.

38. Commission Action Plan to prevent fraud and counterfeiting in payment systems. Issued on 9 February 2001, COM(2001)11.

39. Commission Communication on an e-commerce policy for financial services. Issued on 7 February 2001, COM(2001) 66.

40. Commission Recommendation 2000/408 of 23 June 2000 on disclosure of financial instruments (C(2000) 1372).

41. Amendment of the Insurance Directives and the Investment Services Directive to permit information exchange with third countries. Directive 2000/64/EC adopted 7 November 2000.

42. Creation of two Securities Committees. Decision of 6 June 2001 setting up the European Securities Committee - ESC (C(2001)1493) and Decision of 6 June 2001 setting up the Committee of European Securities Regulators - CESR (C(2001)1501).

Based on European Commission *FSAP Eighth Progress Report* (3 June 2003) and Bank of England *EU Financial Services Action Plan: A Guide*, 31 July 2003.

APPENDIX 5
Glossary of Terms

Basel Committee	Basel Committee on Banking Supervision. This Committee is part of the Bank for International Settlements
Bond	A debt instrument issued by a borrower and promised a specified stream of payments to the purchaser, usually regular interest payments plus a final repayment of principal. Bonds are exchanged on open markets including, in the absence of capital controls, internationally, providing a mechanism for international capital mobility.
Capital Adequacy Directive	Directive that designates the amount of capital that a firm has to hold to be allowed to operate
CESR	Committee of European Securities Regulators comprising of senior representatives of national regulatory agencies designated by Member States
Clearance system	An arrangement among financial institutions for carrying out the transactions among them, including cancelling out offsetting credits and debits on the same account
Comitology	Secondary EU legislation
Debt Securities	IOUs created through loan-type transactions-commercial paper, bank CDs, bills, bonds, and other instruments
Derivatives	Contracts such as options and futures whose price is derived from the price of an underlying financial asset
DG Internal Market	European Commission department responsible for EU internal market in financial services
Equity	Ownership interest in a firm. Also, the residual value of a futures trading account, assuming its liquidation is at the going trade price. In a brokerage account, equity equals the value of the account's securities minus any debit balance in a margin account
European Securities Committee	Committee in charge of adopting technical implementation of FSAP framework principles. The Committee comprises of a representative from the Commission as chair and Member State nominees from Economic and Finance ministries
Eurosec	Term often used to describe the possible future single European financial regulator
FESE	Federation of European Securities Exchanges
FSAP	Commission Communication of May 1999 listing 42 measures for a single market in financial services
GAAP	Generally Accepted Accounting Principles
Giovannini Group	Committee set up in 1996 to advise the Commission on how to harmonise euro denominated financial markets
IAS	International Accounting Standards
IFRS	International Financial Reporting Standards
IIMG	Inter-institutional Monitoring Group responsible for reporting bi-annually on the implementation of the Lamfalussy process. The group consists of six experts from the Commission, the Council and the European Parliament.
ISD	Investment Services Directive

Lamfalussy Process	Tiered decision-making process for EU legislation on financial services
Liability	A financial obligation, or the <u>cash</u> outlay that must be made at a specific time to satisfy the <u>contractual</u> terms of such an obligation
Liquidity	A high level of <u>trading</u> activity, allowing buying and selling with minimum price disturbance. Also, a market characterized by the ability to <u>buy</u> and sell with relative ease. Antithesis of illiquidity.
Retail market	Market the deals with financial services for individual and institutional customers as opposed to <u>dealers</u> and <u>brokers</u>.
Risk	Often defined as the <u>standard deviation</u> of the <u>return</u> on total investment. Degree of uncertainty of return on an <u>asset</u>.
Risk-based capital ratio	Bank requirement that there be a minimum ratio of estimated total <u>capital</u> to estimated <u>risk</u>-weighted <u>asset</u>
Sarbanes-Oxley Act	US Act of law on corporate governance passed in reaction to the Enron scandal
Securities and commodities exchanges	<u>Exchanges</u> on which <u>securities</u>, <u>options</u>, and <u>futures</u> <u>contracts</u> are <u>traded</u> by members for their own accounts and for the accounts of customers.
Settlement	When payment is made for a <u>trade</u>
UNICE	Union of European Employers' Organisations
Wholesale market	Market the deals with financial services for <u>dealers</u> and <u>brokers</u>.

APPENDIX 6

Cost/benefit analysis of the European Commission's Financial Services Action Plan (FSAP)

Executive Summary

One of the major criticisms of the Financial Services Action has been that insufficient cost-benefit analysis has been carried out on the directives. For example, HM Treasury, the Financial Services Authority and the Bank of England wrote in ""The EU Financial Services Action Plan: A Guide", July 2003:

"Many market experts consider that the Commission should analyse in more detail the cost-effectiveness of proposed new FSAP measures, and the interaction between them. Their impact needs to be considered, not just on market behaviour and the efficiency of financial markets within the EU, but also on the EU 's global competitiveness, and in particular in relation to the US."

- The Commission's "impact assessments" for each measure are inadequately detailed, especially in financial terms.

- However, some detailed estimates have been made of the overall benefits of European financial integration. These add up to an annual benefit to the EU economy after 10 years of at least €189bn.

- To outweigh this public benefit, the annual private cost of each of the 40 measures would have to be nearly €5bn.

The consultancy OC&C estimates the cost to the EU of the currently proposed **Investment Services Directive** to be up to €450m per annum.

The Commission analyses make no attempt to estimate the costs involved in securing the assumed benefits.

Graham Bishop, Specialist Advisor

October 2003

The Benefits

The Lamfalussy report concluded the following benefits to EU financial integration:

Expected Benefits from an Integrated European Financial Services and Capital Market

I. Improving the allocation of capital in the European economy:
- More efficient, deeper, and broader securities markets enabling savings to flow more efficiently to investment.
- Reduced transaction costs and increased market liquidity.
- More diversified and innovative financial system.
- More opportunities to pool risk.

II. More efficient intermediation of European savings to investment:
- Intensified competition between financial markets and intermediaries.
- Economies of scale, scope and a reduction in inefficiency.
    - More economic cohesion.
    -

III. A strengthening of the EU economy, resulting in it becoming a more attractive location for inward investment

---

On the issue of the size of these benefits, the report concluded, "It is not simple to quantify the net sum of these benefits, but potentially they are large". However, recently two reports have attempted such quantification.

London Economics produced a "Quantification of the Macro-Economic Impact of Integration of EU Financial Markets" for the European Commission. Specifically, they investigated "the extent to which the merging of the presently still regionally-fragmented liquidity into a single liquidity pool would reduce the cost of equity and bond finance for businesses in Europe, help stimulate investment and expand productive capacity." So their focus was exclusively on integration of wholesale markets. Their conclusion was

"The level of EU-wide real GDP is raised by 1.1%, or €130 billion in 2002 prices, in the long-run. The press release states that "the long-run" is "defined as over a decade or so".

ZEW/IEP produced a report for the European Financial Services Round Table entitled "The Benefits of a Working European Retail Market for Financial Services". Their focus was exclusively on the retail side. Their conclusion was "World-wide cross-country samples show that differences in financial integration between countries amounting to one standard deviation of the relevant integration indicators can explain annual growth differences of 0.5 - 0.7 per cent. Although these results do not cover all present EU member states they indicate roughly the potential for growth through financial integration: in terms of the EU GDP of the year 2000 the lower per cent figure of 0.5 would mean an additional growth effect of 43 billion euro annually."

The benefits set out in the two reports are additive because the first report looks exclusively at the integration of bond and equity markets, while the second looks at retail markets. **The wholesale benefit is €130 billon after 10 years. The retail benefit (if we also express in 2002 prices) is €59-83 billion annually - with no timeframe given. But if we assume the same timetable, after 10 years the annual benefit is at least €189bn/ £134bn.**

Commission "impact assessments"

THE TEMPLATE

For each new proposal for a directive, the Commission is required to produce an assessment of the "impact on business with special reference to small and medium-sized enterprises". This involves providing answers to the following template of questions:

TITLE OF PROPOSAL

DOCUMENT REFERENCE NUMBER

THE PROPOSAL

1. Taking account of the principle of subsidiarity, why is Community legislation necessary in this area and what are its main aims?

THE IMPACT ON BUSINESS

2. Who will be affected by the proposal?
   – Which sectors of business?
   – Which sizes of business (What is the concentration of small and medium-sized firms)?
   – Are there particular geographical areas of the Community where these businesses are found?
3. What will business have to do to comply with the proposal?
4. What economic effects is the proposal likely to have?
   – On employment?
   – On investment and the creation of new businesses?
   – On the competitiveness of businesses?

5. Does the proposal contain measures to take account of the specific situation of small and medium-sized firms (reduced or different requirements etc)?

CONSULTATION

6. List the organisations which have been consulted about the proposal and outline their main views:

Sample of Commission Impact Assessments

Though the impact assessments conducted by the Commission are fairly short, they are too long to all be included in their entirety. Possibly the most important question in the Commission's Impact Assessment template is "4c", "What economic effects is the proposal likely to have on the competitiveness of business?" The following table sets out the answer for the 15 directives for which this analysis has been done. A spreadsheet is available from those who wish to read all the impact assessments.

PROPOSAL	What economic effects is the proposal likely to have on the competitiveness of businesses?
Market Abuse Directive	Prohibition and enforcement against insider trading reinforce the level playing field between market participants in access to issuer information, and so increase the fair competitiveness between these participants. Similarly, prohibition and enforcement against market manipulation reinforce the level playing field between market participants through transparency in market participant behaviours, thus contributing to the fair competitiveness between the participants.
Prospectus Directive	Positive impact can be expected due to the lower cost of raising capital and the existence of harmonised and comparable conditions, for all competitors, within the Union.
Investment Services Directive	On the industry. The proposal will increase of the confidence of investors in the fair functioning of the market due to the application of the market efficiency and investor protection oriented rules. This could well soar the European savings rate. In addition, it enhances the competitiveness of the financial industry as a whole. It creates a playing field which can adapt to the future evolution of the financial markets. It encourages innovation whilst taking due account of the interest that are to be protected. This openness will reinforce the European financial industry making it stronger and more adapted to the needs of its customers. Competitiveness, innovation and development will not only result in more employment in the financial sector but also in better shaped strategies towards investors. These will be able to get better risk-adapted financial products which should enhance the medium and long term returns of their savings.
Transparency Directive	Positive impact can be expected due to the lower cost of raising capital throughout the European Union and new robust Community disclosure requirements to which host Member States may not add further disclosure requirements. This does not prejudice other requirements for admission of securities to trading on a regulated market.
Collateral Directive	A sound and efficient legal regime for limiting credit risk will improve the stability of the European financial market. The increased possibilities for conducting cross-border business will create a more competitive market, which in macroeconomic terms are believed to enhance the potential for stronger growth in the gross domestic product and therefore also in job creation.
International Accounting Standards Regulation	Adoption of uniform, high quality financial reporting rules in EU capital markets will greatly enhance the comparability and transparency of financial information, thereby increasing the efficiency of the markets and reducing the cost of capital for companies.
Takeover Bids Directive	Although the proposal does not promote takeover bids as such, the harmonisation of the rules which govern takeover bids will contribute to improving the competitive position of companies in Europe. At the moment there are legal, economic and structural differences between the Member States with respect to defensive measures that can be put into operation in order to fight hostile takeover bids, so that companies in some Member States are more protected than companies in other Member States. The proposal will reduce these differences in several ways, without compromising the competitiveness of EU companies in relation to companies of third countries.

UCITS Directives	The fact that a wider range of investment funds would be covered by the Directive 85/611/EEC and that the units of such funds could be freely marketed throughout the EU, could increase the competition among management companies, thus improving the price/quality relation of these investment products.
Distance Marketing Directive	The text establishes Community rules which will facilitate the use of newtechnologies in distance selling. This may lead to these techniques being used moreoften by consumers in the internal market and consequently may have the effect ofincreasing employment and investment in these activities. Thecross-border possibilities may lead to an intensified competitiveness in retail business.
Pension Funds Directive	Positive effects can be expected. In the absence of any coordination at Community level, IORPs are the only major financial institutions unable to offer their services in a Member State other than their own. It has been calculated that, for a pan-European company, the cost of setting up separate occupational systems in each Member State is about EUR 40 million per year. Allowing IORPs to manage schemes for companies established in another Member State would result in economies of scale of several types: more efficient investment policies as a result of asset pooling, simplification of administration and compliance with the prudential and reporting rules of a single supervisory authority. Furthermore, labour mobility would become easier: workers could more easily take up a job in another Member State if they could remain members of the same IORP; multinationals would come up against fewer obstacles to moving their employees from one Member State to another.
E-Money Directive	The proposal, by establishing a legal framework for electronic money issuance, is likely to encourage further development and innovation in this field. This should have positive effects not only on the issuing institutions themselves but also on related enterprises associated with technological hardware and software development. Moreover, the proposal removes any legal uncertainty that may have been associated with cross-border issuance. It should, therefore, increase competition in the business of electronic money specifically and payment instruments generally. Electronic money also has the potential to reduce the costs of cash handling for enterprises generally.
Electronic Commerce Directive	The proposal again has a strong positive effect. By stimulating competition through facilitating entry in the market by small innovative firms, European electronic commerce suppliers will be internationally competitive in what is a truly global market.
Financial Conglomerates Directive	A single financial market will promote the competitiveness of the European economy and financial stability, and therefore will have a positive effect on investments and the creation of new business. The same goes for the competitiveness of business.

Taxation of Savings Income Directive	The present scope for non-taxation of cross-border interest payments results in a lossof tax revenue for Member States and may even force some Member States to reducetheir tax rates on domestic interest payments in order to avoid the risk of a furtheroutflow of savings. By ensuring effective taxation of cross-border interest payments, the Directive can contribute to Member States' efforts to restore the balance between the burden of taxation on the different factors of production and thereby to achieve areduction in the taxation on income from employment. This would be certain to havea positive effect on job creation and the fight against unemployment.
	The Directive should also have a favourable impact on the European financial area, because savers' decisions will no longer be determined by the possibility of avoiding tax but will instead be based on the intrinsic merits of the investments. This should help financial institutions, investment funds and other market operators to compete on equal terms.
	Since the scope of the Directive includes all cross-border interest payments, irrespective of the place of establishment of the issuer of the debt-claim giving rise to the interest, debtors established in the EU are not placed at a competitive disadvantage in relation to issuers outside the Community.
	Moreover, the scope of the Directive also includes income from investment funds established outside the Community when such income is paid in a Member State. The Directive should therefore not involve any particular risk of relocation of debt-issuing or investment fund activities to countries outside the Community. The risk of relocation of payingagent activities is reduced by the efforts that have been made to keep additional administrative costs to a minimum and by the continuing efforts to promote theadoption of equivalent measures at a wider international level.

Impact Assessments – A Private Sector Example

Ian McKenzie and Andy Sparks of OC&C Strategy Consultants published a study on "The Potential Impact of ISD2 Article 25" in August 2003. Its objectives were:

1. To identify and, to the extent possible, quantify the impact of the Article 25:

(i) As originally drafted (Note that this is the major thrust of this paper);

(ii) As per the compromise amendments that are emerging (as at mid-July)

2. To investigate the extent to which "off-exchange" trading is a likely to be detrimental to the effectiveness and efficiency of equity markets. We have addressed this by:

(i) Estimating the actual extent to which 'true' off-exchange trading currently occurs

(ii) Investigating the extent to which such principal trading can provide economic benefit to investors (as opposed to passing orders through to a central market on an agency basis)

Their main conclusions are:

- Overall, the model whereby Firms "smooth out" large institutional orders at one end of the order size spectrum and "aggregate" small, retail orders at the other end of the size spectrum is economically sound. Most of this apparently off-exchange trading activity does in fact end up in the central market as the potential for off-exchange crossing is actually quite limited.

- While the intentions seem honourable, many of the ISD2 proposals appear to be misguided in that they may well cause a withdrawal of liquidity from these principal trading roles which will increase costs and hurt investors through reduced liquidity, increased volatility and spreads, and worse prices.

In terms of quantifying the cost of the compromise proposals, OC&C conclude:

"While the narrowing of scope to the most active/systematic providers of principal execution appears a welcome step, the shift to normal/standard market size would move the impact of Article 25 directly onto the (core) institutional market. Without the ability to choose counterparties or the ability to price improve, those Firms who are caught by this provision will probably find it unattractive to continue to provide principal liquidity, This loss of liquidity would cause deterioration of prices for institutional clients (which might be worth **€375- 450m (around £300m) per annum**) and loss of price immediacy."

This last figure was cited by the Chief Secretary to the UK Treasury, Paul Boateng, in his argument against the political agreement reached by the European Council on the ISD on October 7th 2003.

APPENDICES

1.SUMMARY OF LONDON ECONOMICS REPORT

"Quantification of the Macro-Economic Impact of Integration of EU Financial Markets", November 2002

Financial services: integration of EU markets will boost growth, jobs and prosperity says new research

The integration of EU financial markets will bring significant benefits to businesses, investors and consumers. New research predicts that EU-wide real GDP will increase by 1.1% - or €130 billion in 2002 prices over a decade or so. Total employment will increase by 0.5%. Businesses will be able to get cheaper finance: integration of EU equity markets will reduce the cost of equity capital by 0.5% and a 0.4% decrease in the cost of corporate bond finance is expected to follow. Investors will benefit from higher risk-adjusted returns on savings. These are the main findings of new research conducted for the European Commission.

Internal Market Commissioner Frits Bolkestein said: "This economic evidence confirms what we have always said - that an integrated capital market in the EU will strengthen our economy. These results confirm the enormous prize that is up for grabs if we can finish off what we have started and drive through the remaining elements of the Financial Services Action Plan. I will do my utmost to achieve that and call upon the European Parliament and the Council to do likewise by taking the remaining difficult decisions that are necessary as quickly as possible. We must not miss this chance to put money in the pocket of every European. Furthermore these are the minimum gains they do not cover other major benefits such as wider choice, more innovation and easier finance for small companies. There could not be a better wake-up call to accelerate action.

The study is the first substantive piece of empirical research on the impact of financial integration on the cost of raising finance in Europe. The work began in late 2001. The consultants were invited to evaluate any impact of integrating EU equity and corporate bond markets on trading costs and the cost of capital. To the extent that a cost of capital impact could be discerned, they were asked to quantify any consequent impact on investment, GDP and employment.

This research highlights the powerful role that efficient and liquid financial markets can play in complementing bank-based finance to support growth and employment in Europe. It illustrates the need to complete the implementation of the EU's Financial Services Action Plan on schedule by 2005. The swift adoption of legislative proposals on Prospectuses, Market Abuse and Pension Funds, which are currently under negotiation in the Parliament and the Council, would be a decisive step in this direction.

The one measure which will do most to unleash these benefits will be the forthcoming Directive on investment services and regulated markets, due to be proposed shortly.

The estimates measure only the static effect of financial market integration on trading spreads (implicit trading costs). The research does not consider possible reductions in explicit trading costs (brokerage commissions or exchange fees) that can be expected to accompany increased competition between intermediaries and exchanges and lead to further economic benefits for EU citizens and business.

Furthermore, it does not measure the full dynamic benefits of financial integration. Related research including a further study to be published shortly by the Commission suggests that the deepening of financial markets resulting from integration can permanently boost output growth in manufacturing industry.

SUMMARY OF THE MAIN PROVISIONAL CONCLUSIONS OF THE STUDY

The cost of equity capital would fall, on average across Europe, by about 40 basis points, as a result of integration of EU financial markets.

There would be a further reduction of 10 basis points arising from reduced clearance and settlement costs, implying a total reduction in the cost of capital of, on average, 50 basis points across Member States.

The simulations performed as part of the study show that the combined reduction in the cost of equity, bond and bank finance, together with the increase in the share of bond finance in total debt finance should improve the equilibrium level of GDP and potentially also GDP growth:

- EU-wide real GDP is forecast to rise by 1.1%, or €130 billion in 2002 prices, in the long-run, defined as over a decade or so

- GDP per capita in current prices is forecast to be €600 higher in the EU and GDP per capita at 2002 prices €350 higher

- total business investment is forecast to be almost 6.0% higher and private consumption up by 0.8%

- total employment is forecast to be 0.5% higher.

These benefits will be shared by all Member States. There are no losers. Across the EU, the estimated increase in the level of real GDP stemming from integration of financial markets ranges from 0.3% to 2.0%. However, the majority of Member States show an increase in the range of 0.9% to 1.2%.

A breakdown of the contribution of the various changes in the user cost of capital shows that:

- the reduction in the cost of equity finance is the most important impact, accounting for 0.5 percentage points (or 45%) of the 1.1 percentage point increase in the EU-wide level of GDP in constant prices

the impact of the reduction of 40 basis points in the cost of bond finance alone is marginal, explaining a further 0.1 percentage point of the 1.1 percentage point increase in the EU-wide level of GDP in constant prices

The combination of the reduction in the cost of bond finance together with the increase in the share of bond finance in total debt finance, however, results in a more substantial boost to output. Together these two changes account for 0.3 percentage point of the 1.1 percentage point increase forecast in the EU-wide level of GDP in constant prices

Finally, the assumed reduction in the cost of bank finance of 20 basis points also explains 0.3 percentage point of the 1.1 percentage point increase forecast in EU-wide real GDP.

The results of the study do not take account of any dynamic effects that could raise output and productivity growth on a permanent basis. Thus, they can be said to be relatively conservative estimates of the likely impact of reductions in the user cost of capital brought about by deeper European financial market integration.

Moreover, European financial market integration will affect the EU economies through a number of additional channels (better portfolio allocations, greater access to finance, more innovation etc). Thus, the overall impact of European financial market integration is likely to be larger than reported in the research, which has focused on only one dimension of this integration process. A further study, to be published shortly by the Commission, supports this view by indicating the potential for permanently higher output growth in the manufacturing sector if all EU firms were to have access to more integrated and developed financial markets.

The full results are available on the Europa website:

http://europa.eu.int/comm/internal_market/en/finances/mobil/overview.htm

2.Executive Summary of ZEW/IEP report

"Benefits of a Working EU Market for Financial Services", November 2002

1.Introduction

In spite of considerable progress toward European capital market integration following the completion of the Single Market and the introduction of the Euro, national borders still constitute a considerable de facto barrier for retail financial markets. Direct cross-border business between financial service sup-pliers and end consumers is still the exception. Against this background this report addresses the following questions:

How powerful is the integrating effect of ongoing market trends like internet and cross-border mergers and acquisitions?

Which benefits could be realised if a higher level of integration could be achieved?

Which obstacles are mainly responsible for incomplete integration?

2.Deficits of retail market integration

Although stringent legal impediments to cross-border activities in banking and insurance no longer exist different indicators show a relatively low openness of national markets. The market shares of foreign banks in individual EU countries are relatively small compared to other wealthy industrial countries.

Entry into national banking markets is largely occurring through mergers and acquisitions (M&A). Case studies on multinational banks reveal that factors like high fixed costs of market entry make greenfield investment less attractive than M&A based access strategies.

The picture is not very different for the insurance sector where direct cross-border sales without physical presence in the target market play only a marginal role. Again, cross-border M&As are the predominant entry strategy. In addition, integration indicators show a markedly lower integration level for the life than for the non-life insurance market.

European fund market data on the number of registered foreign funds seems to indicate a larger degree of integration. However, since many of these "foreign" funds are of the Luxembourg or Dublin "round-trip" type, this indicator is misleading. Market shares of true foreign funds only reach significant levels in big markets like Germany while some small markets are effectively completely dominated by domestic fund suppliers.

The impact of the internet on the integration of retail markets for financial services does not meet optimistic expectations even in the case of the most developed e-finance market, the market for online brokerage. The analysis of price differences and direct cross-border activities dispells illusions: although the internet is increasingly becoming an alternative distribution channel it does not by itself overcome fragmentation of retail financial markets in the EU.

3.Potential integration benefits

The report advances the following arguments and quantified estimates on the beneficial consequences of further integration of financial services markets for consumers and the economy in the EU as a whole:

–*Product choice would increas*e, in particular for consumers in small countries who today suffer most from incomplete retail market integration. In these countries, the supply of available funds for example could be augmented by a factor between 10 and 20.

–There is considerable scope for falling prices resulting from a higher integration level in financial retail markets. Economies of scale could be realised. Calculations for the fund industry indicate a large cost savings potential: on the assumption that integration would lead to an average fund size in Europe similar to that of the US, there would be a *cost saving potential of about 5 billion Euro annually* given the present size of the EU fund industry.

These cost savings would be particularly helpful in the ongoing European reforms of pension systems since fund products will play an important role for funded old-age pensions.

– Private borrowers could benefit substantially through *lower interest rate*s. A simulation for the period of falling interest rates in the second half of the nineties shows: if competitive pressure in a more closely integrated financial market forced banks to adjust mortgage interest rates more quickly to falling market rates private borrowers would benefit. In terms of a 100,000 Euro mortgage loan these integration savings in interest payments would have amounted in the period 1995–1999 to annually 2,550 Euro in Italy, 1,690 Euro in Spain, 1,580 Euro in Portugal and 790 Euro in Ireland.

– Retail market integration would probably also reduce the well-known home bias in private investors' portfolios. Performance calculations for national, European and world portfolios show that investors could significantly in-crease the Sharpe ratios of portfolios. Often the Europe-wide diversification is already sufficient to harvest all the *benefits of international diversificatio*n.

–Furthermore, a larger degree of financial integration would be associated with *higher economic growt*h. Theoretical considerations and insights from the relevant empirical literature back the assumption of a significant link between financial integration and growth. World-wide cross-country samples show that differences in financial integration between countries amounting to one standard deviation of the relevant integration indicators can explain annual growth differences of 0.5 – 0.7 per cent. Although these results do not cover all present EU member states they indicate roughly the potential for growth through financial integration: in terms of the EU GDP of the year 2000 the lower per cent figure of 0.5 would mean an additional growth effect of 43 billion Euro annually. A quantification of potential employment effects associated with more financial integration is difficult to make. They crucially depend on the flexibility of labour markets and the progress in labour market reforms.

–Finally, more financial integration is rewarded by a growing *international role of the Euro* because the efficiency of a currency's financial markets is among the determinants of its global acceptance. A greater acceptance of the Euro could in turn lead to additional benefits due to higher seigniorage, falling liquidity premiums and transaction costs.

4. OBSTACLES

A number of obstacles impedes the development of unified financial retail markets in Europe. There are policy-induced obstacles like different taxation, consumer protection or supervision arrangements that are capable of alteration, and there are natural obstacles like differences in language and culture that can not realistically be addressed by national or European policymakers.

The impact of the different types of obstacles varies according to product type.

– For *insurance* products, a lack of confidence in the long-run reliability of unknown foreign suppliers is a particularly relevant obstacle. Furthermore, discriminatory tax practices and national differences in consumer protection due to different national policies and interpretations of the "general good" are important obstacles in the insurance business.

– The *internet-based* financial retail business is confronted with the following obstacles in cross-border activities: the need to design a variety of national marketing strategies, market peculiarities related to regulatory differences in consumer protection and supervision, the high costs of cross-border payments, the problems of cross-border identification of new customers, the heterogeneity of technical systems of stock exchanges and the consumer preference for "handshake", the physical meeting with the agent of a new supplier.

– Since successful management of asymmetric information problems is crucial for successful *credit business*, limited cross-border access to public credit registers and private credit buraux is a particular integration obstacle for the credit market.

– For *funds* the outdated definition of UCITS in the directives limits cross-border marketing of innovative fund products. In addition, the burden of registration in a target market raises the costs for entering a national market. Furthermore, host country responsibility for supervision of advertising and marketing together with tax discriminations hamper the emergence of a unified fund market. The problems are aggravated by distribution channels that are still biased in favour of domestic fund companies.

– There is the danger that new obstacles are created as a consequence of national pension reforms. The German example shows that very specific national requirements on new *pension products* can constitute additional barriers to entry for foreign suppliers.

5. SOME POLICY CONCLUSIONS

A strategy based on an attitude of "wait and see" is not justified because on-going market trends indicate that integration is unlikely to be completed without adjustments to the regulatory framework. The substantial potential benefits for consumers and economic growth clearly show that it is worthwhile to push hard for more integration of retail financial markets. Any integration strategy should aim to simplify direct cross-border contact between suppliers and consumers.

This contact would speed up convergence of prices and promote a wider product choice everywhere in the EU. The need for political action also comes from the delicate fact that the "costs of non-Europe" are higher in smaller and poorer member countries than in the bigger and richer ones. While the Financial Services Action Plan and other legal initiatives properly address a number of integration obstacles, more needs to be done. Proposals for reforms are listed below. This is not an exhaustive list of recommendations. It briefly addresses the most burning issues; a detailed specification of the reform options would certainly need further analysis.

It is important to devote more effort to ending *discriminatory tax practices* that currently shelter some national retail financial markets from foreign competition, and which do not conform with the EU Treaty. Examples concern the markets for life insurance and investment funds.

Differences in *consumer protection* rules among the 15 EU countries render a pan-European marketing strategy and standardised products impossible. This issue is a critical policy-induced obstacle and could best be addressed by the creation of a consistent uniform level of protection with harmonization on that basis. Three specific recommendations are:

– The debate on derogation from the principle of home country control in the e-commerce directive should be reopened.

– Furthermore, the interpretation of the "general good" provision should be harmonised and/or restricted.

– There is a need to arrive at a unified definition of pension products in order to improve the conditions for developing a pan-European market for this high potential market segment.

With FIN-NET the Commission has initiated an important infrastructure for creating *consumer confidence* in the legal safety of cross-border financial services. However, the existence of FIN-NET so far is not common knowledge.

An information campaign is necessary to make this network of European ombudsmen better known and better understood, at least to the financial media and the staff of banks and insurers.

With regard to *supervision*, there are short-, medium- and long-term options:

– In the short-run it would be helpful if the supervisory committees devoted more effort to the consistency of rule-books, the standardization of reporting requirements and the harmonisation of supervisory practice.

– In the medium-term a serious reform debate should be initiated, reflecting the possible advantages of a two tier supervisory system where multinational companies could opt for supervision on a European level.

– With a long-term perspective, more thought could be given to the possibility of establishing a single European supervisory authority, especially if effective cooperation among 25 to 30 national agencies after enlargement proves to become too difficult.

There is a huge gap between the *vision* of the EU as the most dynamic economy in the world and the *reality* of still fragmented EU-markets. In order to reduce this gap, the whole process of European regulation of financial services needs to be speeded up and member-states have to over-come their national policies of preserving market barriers or even re-establishing new ones. Otherwise it will be impossible to achieve the strategic objective of the Lisbon-process of a more deeply integrated European Union which will be able to match the challenges of globalization and to secure full employment by 2010.

Finally, while the study has shed light on important aspects of the enduring "cost of non-Europe" further analysis is required. Two issues deserve to be looked at more closely given their enormous complexity: First, the implication of national pension reforms for integration and second, the adjustment of consumer protection regulation to the changing needs of the internal financial retail market.

3.Summary of key findings of OC&C Report

"The Potential Impacts of ISD2 Article 25", August 2003.

Impact of Article 25 as Originally Drafted

1.Given that most Firms provide principal liquidity to their institutional clients across a broad range of equities, Article 25 would require them to publish continuous, firm, two-way prices in retail size for those equities – and to deal at these prices.

2.Article 25 would also appear to require Firms to deal via these retail-size prices with most "eligible counterparties" (which are defined by Member States). This implies that Firms would need to deal with a broader range of counterparties than they do today, with potential consequent increase to counterparty risk.

3.In broad terms Firms have four options in responding to this requirement:

(1) Offer competitive retail prices and seek retail business

(2) Offer uncompetitive prices so as to avoid having to execute retail business (though they may be restricted in their ability to do this on account of the requirement in article 25.3 for prices to reflect 'prevailing market conditions')

(3) Refrain from offering these retail-size prices and therefore have to withdraw from providing principal liquidity (in those stocks) to institutional customers

(4) Relocate trading operations outside the EU

Leaving aside the somewhat draconian option 4, and assuming that option 2 is possible, firms would be expected to make their decisions based on:

(i)   the costs involved in options (1) and (2) (including increased counterparty risk)

(ii) the revenue likely to be generated under option (1)

(iii) the impact of pulling out of principal, institutional trading under option (3).

(5) Assessing the likely revenue from option (1) – and the likely detriment from option (3) – is difficult. However, it is fairly clear that:

Firms with existing principal retail execution infrastructure (used at present largely for UK equities) would probably expand into the principal execution of retail order flow in Continental European equities with high traded turnover so as to be able to continue to offer principal execution to institutional clients. There would thus be an increase in principal trading activity at the retail level

Firms with or without existing principal retail execution would be likely to withdraw from principal trading in some less liquid (i.e., lower turnover) equities at the institutional level because principal trading at the retail level would be economically unattractive

(6) This withdrawal of liquidity at the institutional level is likely to cause spreads to widen on the affected stocks (from 5bp to 50bp depending on underlying liquidity). We estimate that this widening might cost European institutional investors around **£200m per annum** (about **EUR300**m) in worse prices, or simply discourage trading per se. The widening of spreads would be most notable at the smaller exchanges that might dent their ability to compete. The magnitude of this impact is very much determined by the scope of the stocks affected by the regulations.

(7) Total withdrawal of principal liquidity by Firms in the lowest traded stocks would expose institutional investors to increased market impact that might cause a further detriment of c **£50m** (about **EUR 75**m) **per annum**. Neither this, nor the effect set out in para -6 above, is a desirable outcome.

(8) Retail investors would also get worse prices under these new arrangements in that Firms would be reluctant to publish prices which included "price improvement" (as is currently the practice) for fear of being exposed to uncontrollable volumes and unwanted counterparties. This effect would cost retail investors an average 10% worsening of spreads.

Impact of Recent Compromise Proposals

(9) Recent (mid-July) compromise proposals seem to embody three major changes: (1) limiting the scope of Article 25's pre-trade price transparency requirements to Firms who "internalize on a systematic, regular and continuous basis", (2) expanding the scope of securities covered to "all listed securities" and (3) moving the published price requirement to "normal/standard market size". At the same time there is still debate around (i) whether to allow Firms to be more selective in their choice of counterparty and (ii) whether to allow Firms the ability to "price improve" their quotes on a client-by-client basis.

(10) While the narrowing of scope to the most active/systematic providers of principal execution appears a welcome step, the shift to normal/standard market size would move the impact of Article 25 directly onto the (core) institutional market. Without the ability to choose counterparties or the ability to price improve, those Firms who are caught by this provision will probably find it unattractive to continue to provide principal liquidity, This loss of liquidity would cause deterioration of prices for institutional clients (which might be worth **EUR 375- 450m (around £300m) per annum** and loss of price immediacy.

(11) Of all the provisions, the ability to price improve is probably the most important one as it provides the safety valve that would allow the other requirements to be workable.

The True Extent of Off-Exchange Trading

(12) The ISD2 legislation appears predicated on the assumption that off-exchange trading (internalisation) is both significant and detrimental. Our findings suggest that there is much confusion surrounding the definition of terms and that, in reality, 'true' off-exchange activity is neither overly large nor damaging.

(13) We have developed a framework for identifying the various different routes for the execution of client orders in the context of order-book equities and classifying them as on- versus off- exchange.

Based on indicative data from Firms, the key findings for order-driven stocks across Europe are:

- Pure agency trading is little used (4% of total traded value); instead major use is made of back-to-back risk-less principal trading (47%) which achieves the same end result and should be treated as on-exchange trading

- Extensive use is made of "worked risk-less principal trades" (23%) whereby the Firm smoothes the order into the market over time. Again we consider these to be on-exchange trades

- The remaining 26% of client trades is handled by Firms as "true principal trades" i.e., where the Firm provides liquidity and price immediacy for its clients. However around half of the resulting positions are actually still worked-off in central markets. Hence the only truly off-exchange trading is the circa 10% which the Firm 'crosses' between clients and the circa 4% which the Firm executes directly with other Firms (inter-investment firm market)

(14) We therefore conclude that off-exchange trading is rather less than some other data would lead one to believe. Consequently, the extent to which principal trading of equities by Firms 'fragments' liquidity is probably less than generally imagined.

The Economic Rationale for Firms to Undertake Principal Trading at both Institutional and Retail Levels

(15) Although still a widely debated issue, OC&C's view is that the 'fragmentation' of liquidity between different trading venues does not necessarily mean that overall market liquidity is diminished provided that there are some (investor) firms who can access across the different pools of liquidity. Rather, we would argue that principal trading by Firms is economically advantageous for certain kinds of orders (essentially very small orders and very large orders) with the result that overall liquidity is enhanced.

(16) Principal trading by Firms for large institutional orders offers advantages in that it can (i) mitigate "market impact" by "smoothing out" demand on the central market which helps avoid unnecessary price volatility (worth potentially 30-50bp), (ii) reduce transaction costs (given the lower cost involved in crossed trades) and (iii) provide price immediacy (which stimulates trading).

Given active competition between Firms, these benefits will largely accrue to investors.

(17) Principal trading at the level of retail order flow is also economically advantageous in that principal execution is inherently cheaper on account of (i) reduction in exchange fees and market-side clearing and settlement costs as the Firm only needs to go to the market (to flatten the net position) on a periodic basis; (ii) ability for Firm to capture spread through crossing of trades which allows the Firm to reduce/eliminate commission; (iii) potentially reduced clearing and settlement costs on the client-side as and when custody is shared.

(18) Finally, it is hard to argue that principal trading by Firms causes detriment to investors through lack of price transparency as (i) institutional investors are sophisticated and (ii) retail investors (trading via retail-facing intermediaries) are generally protected by best execution rules.

Conclusions

(19) Overall, the model whereby Firms "smooth out" large institutional orders at one end of the order size spectrum and "aggregate" small, retail orders at the other end of the size spectrum is economically sound. Most of this apparently off-exchange trading activity does in fact end up in the central market as the potential for off-exchange crossing is actually quite limited.

(20) While the intentions seem honourable, many of the ISD2 proposals appear to be misguided in that they may well cause a withdrawal of liquidity from these principal trading roles which will increase costs and hurt investors through reduced liquidity, increased volatility and spreads, and worse prices.

MINUTES OF EVIDENCE

Present:

Cavendish of Furness, L.	Howie of Troon, L.
Chadlington, L.	Shutt of Greetland, L.
Cohen of Pimlico, B.	Walpole, L.
Faulkner of Worcester, L.	Woolmer of Leeds, L.
Fearn, L.	(Chairman)

Memorandum by the London Stock Exchange

EXECUTIVE SUMMARY

1. The London Stock Exchange welcomes the Committee's inquiry and the opportunity to give written evidence. We look forward to the opportunity to supplement this with oral evidence if the Committee considers it appropriate.

2. Like many financial service providers, the Exchange has been actively engaged in the EU policy process. Since the inception of the Financial Services Action Plan (FSAP), the Exchange has devoted increasing levels of resource to monitoring developments, responding to consultations, preparing policy papers and campaigning in their support. While fully endorsing the objectives of the FSAP, the Exchange has been concerned that there are weaknesses in the decision-making process and in particular, that key directives will not lead to the best outcomes. In these debates, the Exchange has pursued two broad and related objectives:

— to promote the Exchange's interests as a commercial company in respect of individual proposals for legislation,

— to promote efficient capital markets,

  — in the interests of the Exchange (maximising the potential for competition);

  — for direct users of our markets (bringing benefits as providers compete on service and price); and

  — for the wider EU economy (lowering both the cost of capital for firms and the cost of financial products for consumers).

3. In addition, we have consistently communicated the strengths of London as an international financial centre. These include an intelligent approach to regulation, a skilled and flexible workforce and openness to international business. Building on those strengths means avoiding regulation that risks damaging the EU wholesale market based in London or reinforcing national market structures (at the expense of competition).

4. We welcome the UK government's initiatives to consult the City and to incorporate industry thinking in decision-making. However there is a concern that the interests of the EU wholesale market are not represented adequately in Council when other Member States have an exclusively retail focus.

A. THE FSAP

What progress has been made to date? Has this been beneficial or deleterious to UK interests? Has sufficient weight been given to the position and experience of UK financial services industry?

5. According to Commissioner Bolkenstein's last (and final) progress report[1], 34 of the 42 original measures have been finalised. "That means a final sustained effort by the Commission, the European Parliament and the Member States' institutions is necessary to reach compromise on the remaining measures" in the few months remaining before the hiatus in April 2004 caused by parliamentary elections and enlargement. We agree with the need to reach compromises, but the danger is that in the rush to complete the FSAP, the compromises either won't deliver the FSAP objectives or even worse, will take us away from the benefits of an efficient and competitive single market.

6. Given the importance of the City of London to Europe, it is difficult to distinguish "UK interests" from those of the wider European economy. As a financial centre, London delivers efficiency gains for the EU economy as a whole. Recent research estimates that London's critical mass of financial services contributed €33 billion of EU GDP per annum[2]. However, instead of being seen as a European asset, there is also a danger

---

[1] 8th Progress Report, 3 June 2003.
[2] CEBR—City's importance to the EU economy (Jan 2003).

that the financial services industry of City of London is assumed to be capable of being shared more equitably, by "repatriating" business to other Member States. This is based on a flawed assumption. As the research outlined above also makes clear, with London, 30 per cent of the business of the City would either migrate outside the EU to Switzerland or New York, or would cease to be transacted altogether. It's not a zero-sum game and London's loss isn't Paris or Frankfurt's gain.

7. We don't believe that this contribution and the folly of pursuing a policy of repatriation is acknowledged or fully understood either within the Commission itself or more important, among sufficient MEPs or Member States' governments to win the crucial votes. There is still a tendency to see financial services providers as "strategic" sectors of the economy and to protect them, rather to seek to capture the efficient gains and greater prosperity offered by a competitive single market for capital. This potential problem is exacerbated by the divergence in interests between the City, building on its global position, and many other Member States whose focus is retail and more inclined towards "fortress Europe".

What are the main outstanding matters that remain to be dealt with under the FSAP and what key issues will need to be resolved?

8. From the Exchange's perspective, the key outstanding issue is the Investment Services Directive (ISD), which sets the framework for the regulated markets of the securities industry. If no effective ISD is delivered, then the FSAP cannot be judged as anything other than a failure. Protracted negotiations in Parliament have yet to deliver amendments that will make into a workable directive and the risk is that policy makers will produce an outcome that although designed to protect retail investors, has the result of eroding liquidity in EU equity markets to the detriment of all investors.

9. The negotiations, and the preceding consultation, illustrate the difference in approach between the City and many continental markets that is proving difficult to reconcile. The first ISD regime, although important in effecting remote access for exchange members, was weakened by unevenness in implementation. It is essential that the new ISD does not lead to a similar outcome.

B. IMPLEMENTATION AND ENFORCEMENT

The success of setting up a single market in financial services will depend to a considerable degree on the way in which the regulatory Framework is implemented and enforced.

— *How successful to do you expect the Lamfalussy process to be? Are any changes needed?*

— *Who will be responsible for ensuring effective implementation and enforcement of the single market, after the regulatory Framework is in place? How successful do you expect this process to be? What will be the role of competition regulators at EU and Member State level?*

— *What issues will arise as the single market framework is implemented and enforced?*

— *What non-regulatory barriers might impede the effective functioning of a single market for financial services?*

10. While the Lamfalussy process is an interrelated set of four levels[3] of decision-making, crucial to its success is effective consultation before legislation is proposed. The first two directives after Lamfalussy's report, Prospectuses and Market Abuse, were rushed out with inadequate consultation and both were seriously flawed as a consequence. Since then, the Commission has strengthened consultation and made its procedures far more transparent for which it deserves credit.

11. The Parliament has also strengthened its role under co-decision and in the case of the Prospectus Directive agreed key amendments at First Reading response to a co-ordinated lobby of market interests led by the City of London. Unfortunately (or perhaps unsurprisingly in the light of the comments about protectionism above) key amendments to the Directive were removed in the Council (the only part of the EU institutional structure to retain its pre-Lamfalussy opacity!). Since then the second EMAC vote has rectified many of these weaknesses but this needs to be ratified in plenary and supported by the Commission and Council. Even with these improvements, the Prospectus Directive, instead of introducing a single market for listing equity, helps to institutionalise national structures and will lead to an increase in the cost of capital for many EU companies.

12. At level 2, CESR[4] has begun to develop implementing legislation for the Market Abuse and Prospectus Directives. The process, although still in its infancy, raises concern both about the volume of implementing measures (many hundreds of pages for Prospectuses alone) and the speed at which it is required to be processed.

---

[3] Level 1 Principles, Level 2 Implementation, Level 3 Co-operation, Level 4 Enforcement.
[4] The Committee of European Securities Regulators.

13. In addition to Levels 1 and 2 referred to above, Lamfalussy proposed a role for national regulators to co-operate in implementation (Level 3) and at Level 4 recommended a strong role for the Commission (in the shape of DG Competition) to ensure that directives are enforced. Since it is too soon to assess either the quality of peer pressure between regulators or the appetite of the Commission to enforce the objectives of directives, it is probably too soon to make a judgment about the Lamfalussy process. It is therefore also premature to consider the alternative of a single European regulator—a European SEC—in the event that the Lamfalussy process fails to deliver. Those of us who oppose the concept of a European SEC therefore have a real incentive to make Lamfalussy work.

14. In addition to regulatory barriers, there are other barriers that tend to restrict cross-border financial business, for example in investment. A recent report by the IMA[5] lists several such barriers. In taxation, all 15 Member States employ some form of discrimination against non-domestic investment funds. An earlier report suggested that not only has no Member State eliminated all such tax discriminations some have introduced or proposed new ones[6].

C. The Future

— *How do witnesses see the future development of a single market in financial services following implementation of the FSAP? Are additional measures needed?*

— *Will the changes resulting from the FSAP proposals have an impact on the competitive position of London and EU markets as a whole in the global environment?*

15. There is general agreement that the FSAP will not of itself deliver the single market. Particularly if the process of agreement of directives leads to anti-competitive outcomes, or national regulators or the Commission prove weak in implementation or enforcement. This is not an argument in favour of FSAP 2. On the contrary, the current raft of measures needs time to bed down and in particular, the Commission will want to assess Lamfalussy Levels 2 and 3 to see whether its intervention is required under Level 4 to enforce the well-established principles of EU competition law.

16. A key test of that commitment centres on the future of clearing and settlement of share trading. As the current investigation of Clearstream[7] by DG Competition has revealed, there are issues concerning fair access that need to be addressed. The Commission is currently considering its options but we recommend that issues of governance and competition should guide its actions.

17. The City's focus is increasingly global and London competes on that basis. The question that remains is whether the FSAP will enable Europe to do the same.

June 2003

Examination of Witness

Mr M Wheatley, Deputy Chief Executive, London Stock Exchange, examined.

Chairman

1. Good afternoon, Mr Wheatley. I apologise for keeping you waiting a little. I apologise secondly that we have reorganised the order of the questions but I am sure with your usual fleetness of foot and quick wittedness you will spot the relationship to the other questions. We aim to ask around eight questions and I should like to try to take round about five minutes per question; this is an indication of brevity in response and also brevity in question.
(*Mr Wheatley*) A challenge for all of us then.

2. It is much more important of course that we deal fully and properly with issues and if one senses that more time is needed, do be assured that we are more concerned to get full value from the oral session

rather than rushing matters. Thank you for coming today. Is there anything you would like to add to your written evidence by way of introduction?

A. Given your initial statements on brevity I would make just three points in advance. Firstly, we are at a reasonably advanced stage in terms of level one of the Financial Services Action Plan (FSAP) and we have heard various reports as to how successful it has been so far in terms of 34 of the 42 measures having been agreed. But real success can only be judged from the effect and we are urging and would urge you that there are three areas which are most important going forward, notwithstanding the very detailed articles. First, we think there have to be proper and sensible criteria for success; I do not think the Commission has adequately yet developed what those criteria are

---

[5] "Towards a Single European Market in Asset Management"—this study was commissioned by the Investment Management Association. The report—produced by ZEW (Centre for European Economic Research in Mannheim) under the direction of Doctor Friedrich Heinemann—examines the obstacles to greater competition in the provision of savings products by asset managers. Published Monday 19 May 2003.

[6] Discriminatory tax barriers facing the EU funds industry: A progress report—FEFSI and PricewaterhouseCoopers—20 January 2003.

[7] The Central Securities Depository owned by Deutsche Borse.

Chairman *contd.*]

and therefore how it will be judged. Secondly, it will only be properly implemented if the Commission is prepared to get tough on Member States. They did not last time round with the Investment Services Directive (ISD) and we still have certain Member States who have not implemented the original ISD or were very late in implementing it. Thirdly, even though level one is largely determined by this stage, there is still quite a lot to play for and the FSA needs to bear in mind that the UK position on the subsequent detailed levels needs every bit as much effort and scrutiny as we have put into this initial phase.

Lord Fearn

3. You say in paragraph 8 of your evidence, in connection with the Investment Services Directive ". . . the risk is that policy makers will produce an outcome that although designed to protect retail investors, has the result of eroding liquidity in EU equity markets to the detriment of all investors". What solution do you advocate to the problem of sufficient protection to retail investors—given that nothing can be total and perfect?

A. The London market starts from a position of being relatively *laissez-faire* in terms of how people do their business and the effectiveness of the market is a combination of the wholesale professional market, which largely sets the price, and the retail market, which accepts the price at which securities are traded. Our view of protection for investors is very simple: transparency. People ought to be able to see enough about the prices at which shares can be dealt, and have been dealt, so that they are capable and can judge whether, increasingly in real time on the number of websites that carry price information, or the next day in the press, whether they have got a good price. So the prices are carried and are very public, and the duty which sits on the person acting for the retail client to act in their best interests, which again the UK has always had to a strong degree. We have always had in the UK best execution requirements which ensure that, even though you may not have the access to information that a professional has, your broker, your agent, acting on your behalf, will act in your best interests. The combined effect of a transparent market and a best execution requirement, an agency duty on the broker to act to the best advantage of the client, are what protects the client. That has been our consistent line and the line actually has worked in London and has created a very successful retail market in London.

4. Will there be transparency in the EU?

A. There will be, but at the retail level they are doing something quite strange with transparency. At the moment in the UK—and we start from that model—when the first directive was implemented and it was finalised in 1993, we introduced a structure where all trades, whether it be for one million Vodafone or one hundred Vodafone, were available and public in real time to all investors. The European model has been that only certain trades are publicly available and that has been the continental model up until now and still exists. The trades which are publicly available are only those trades done within the electronic trading systems of exchanges. Those other trades, the very large trades, are opaque, they are done between banks, they remain opaque. One of the issues the directive is proposing is to make, at a Europeanwide-level, all trades visible. So on the one hand that is a positive, but it is not ruling as to how those trades may be made visible. As now there is one place, the London Stock Exchange or potentially a Reuters screen, where you would get access to all that information, it is not yet clear how the directive will ensure that, even though the trader has an obligation to publish the trades, they will be published in a form that everybody can see. We have some significant questions still over whether that degree of transparency will be achieved.

Chairman: You will not be surprised to hear that many of the people who have submitted written evidence have mentioned the Investment Services Directive (ISD) as a problem area. Lord Faulkner would like to take that up.

Lord Faulkner of Worcester

5. May I press you a bit on your assertion in your memorandum about liquidity and your fear that an ISD which is designed to protect retail investors would result in eroding liquidity in European equity markets? Why would that happen?

A. Liquidity is this slightly nebulous concept, but it is a combination of all of the client interests to trade at a particular point in time and the ability of the major banks to make their capital available. The inherent psychology of markets is that if you have a particular piece of information and you want to trade them in a particular way, you would usually not want all that information to be available to everybody else on the basis that the psychology is that if somebody knows there is a big buyer in the market then the price goes up and it is as simple as that. What you like to do is make that information available on a gradual basis. Some of the requirements within the ISD are such that even investors will not be able to manage their portfolios in the same way, or the banks themselves will have to disclose information in the way they have not done hitherto, which would make them less willing to make their capital available. Our judgment is that a healthy and effective market is one where you have the ability of liquidity providers to make their capital available in a market, as well as the ability of clients to make their interest available, but to do that in such a way that they can manage their impact on the market. The risk of the ISD is that it takes away the ability to manage that impact and the net result is that you would draw back from making information available.

6. May I put that back to you perhaps in a rather blunt and simple way?

A. Yes.

7. Is what you are saying that the opportunity for people to make money on the Stock Exchange comes from their having information which other people do not have and one of the effects therefore of the directive is to make information more freely available?

A. Anybody investing in a market usually tries to do so—I am not sure they are always successful—on

Lord Faulkner of Worcester contd.]

the basis that they have a different view of the stock from other people. So you take a view which says that actually the information I have, even if it is public, I have managed to interpret in such a way that I believe there is a buying opportunity here where other people may not think that. That is why people invest in stock markets. If there were not those differences of view, then you would have a very dull market, where actually prices did not particularly reflect the forward looking view of investors. It is true to say, however, that if you do have a view of the market and therefore you take a view that you want to buy a particular stock, you do not want that information to be shared by everybody until you have completed what you want to do. Then it is fine, it can be shared by everybody. There is an extent to which, whether you as an individual or a pension fund operating on your behalf, if you have information about a stock, which may be just your view or your particular analysis, you do not particularly want all the information related to that to be available to everybody else. That is the competitive advantage you have.

8. If there are already spreads between different markets in the same security, then surely people who are making the market will be working out how to make their profit out of that anyway.

A. Yes, they will, and the issue about the directive is less about whether they will work out how to make that profit, but the additional obligations which may be put on them to make prices available in the market and those additional obligations carry additional costs, which they do not bear today. If they are bearing additional costs, then the economics of operating in the market for them change against them.

9. Do you think that will inhibit the growth of liquidity?

A. I think it will and I think it is unnecessary.

Chairman

10. If you were an investor in Greece, or some of the accession states after next year, they may look at the problem of their securities, their savings, their investments and their ability to trade in a very different way to people with access to London. Being devil's advocate, it is perfectly understandable that the way in which they would like Investment Services Directives to be drawn up would be rather different to institutions and individuals used to dealing in a highly professional institutional liquid market.

A. Yes.

11. How can the two approaches and two perspectives be reconciled in a way which does not damage our liquid markets?

A. There is nothing inherently different in the investor in Greece—let me take Greece; careful what country, but let us choose Greece; or any country—than the investor in the UK. You want to know, one, that the price at which you have dealt is a reasonable price, the best price available at that particular time; two, that the title you have bought will indeed remain yours and not go through the problems of somebody buying in the Russian market a few years ago when

you thought you had bought the stock and you found you had not; three, that the company itself operates to reasonable standards of corporate governance and transparency. In all of those things, it does not matter whether you are a major institution in the UK or a small investor, all of those things are equally important to you, but the directive is doing something quite different to that and it is effectively requiring that the Greek person buying Greek shipping stock, it depends what the stock is, be careful about the nationality but the person buying stock, is doing that within a local market regime, whereas what we have been arguing is that you should have the ability to do that in the most effective regime within Europe, which may be the Greek market, it may be the London market, it may be the German market. One of our complaints is that the effect of one of the elements of the Investment Services Directive, but also of the Prospectuses Directive, is that it is building blockages around free and open competition in Europe. Our core hypothesis is that if you want a more efficient capital market in Europe, you have to have easier competition, freer competition, which will mean that the more efficient suppliers will win at the cost of the less efficient suppliers. The problem that smaller exchanges and smaller banks have is that they know some of the most efficient suppliers of financial services and capital markets and capital are London based suppliers and it is why the political agenda has been to deny the true ability of the Financial Services Action Plan to allow open competition between markets.

Chairman: I promise you we shall return to that theme, because it is a key issue coming up time and again in evidence to us. Lord Cavendish wants to have a look at the Lamfalussy process.

Lord Cavendish of Furness

12. In paragraph 10 of your written evidence you draw attention to the welcome improvement in the Commission's consultation process after a bad start. Is there anything further you feel needs to be done first?

A. It was a bad start. The Lamfalussy process, which was founded on the concept of consultation (full and widespread consultation) was not properly adopted with the first two directives which came out of it and they were very messy as a result. We think you can only really assess it once things have got to level four effectively. We had seen some early signs and some very, very positive signs come out of it, but actually we will only really understand by the final stage whether it (Lamfalussy) is working. That is probably all I can say. It is early days.

13. On a similar theme, in the last paragraph of your memorandum, paragraph 17, you say "The City's focus is increasingly global and London competes on that basis. The question that remains is whether the FSAP will enable Europe to do the same". If the plan is finally declared to be successful, would it help or hinder London's ability to compete globally? Is it in London's interest to do everything they can to make it a success?

Lord Cavendish of Furness *contd.*]

A. You posited that with an "if"; if it is seen to be successful. One of the points I made right at the start is that the criteria for success are poorly drafted. The EU currently has some criteria which suggest measuring composition of a portfolio, how far it has moved away from being just a home biased portfolio (home bias in the structure of the financial centre). I would say that one of the key criteria for success is about the cost of capital within Europe and benchmarking that against the cost of capital in the US. If the criteria for success are drawn broadly enough, and therefore we can say it is successful because the cost of capital has come down, but we can take as a benchmark the US, has the cost of capital improved against the US, then Europe and London will have gained. If the criteria for success are relatively narrowly drawn, as they are today, my fear is that you could have a big tick which says yes, it has been successful, but in practice it has made Europe and our position less competitive world wide.

14. Do I get the feeling that you feel there is a lack of sophistication.

A. Yes; very strongly so. It is too simplistic.

Chairman

15. What at this late stage can be done about that?

A. It is easy to play a numbers game: there are 42 FSAP measures, have they all been passed? That is the D-G Internal Market's wish, because then they can go on and do something else, but I do think there is still time to go back to the Commission and seek for those to be further elaborated. It has to take account of things like the quality of markets, not just the quantity, so have they all been passed and have portfolios widened? It has to be to do with things like the quality of the market overall, and cost of capital. Importantly, not just whether they have all been ticked off at level one, but whether they are successfully implemented and being enforced at levels three and four. I referred earlier to the initial Investment Services Directive and we had something which was drafted in a form which could have allowed significant progress in Europe back in 1993. It did not go into so much of the detail. We have a lot of detail in the current directives but ISD 1 did not go into detail, left a lot to local interpretation and that local interpretation was, by and large, not to implement fully the directive. In effect, what we had was a directive where the box was ticked, but one of the key elements of the directive was about the common passport, that you could use your passport in one country to operate in another. Until 1999, or maybe even 2000, you still could not do that in Milan and you cannot do that in Madrid still, today, ten years later, after the directive has been implemented. Enforcement and implementation are what success is about, not just ticking the boxes that they have all been achieved at the political level.

16. We shall return to that theme too. In your written evidence I do not think—forgive me if I cannot recall every word—you made quite as much of this issue of criterion for success. If I am wrong, forgive me. Could you send us a brief note on what you would regard as the desirable statement of the criterion for success?

A. Okay. At the moment, almost the only success is that Bolkestein's final progress report talks about 34 of the 42 original measures having been finalised. When we say "finalised" that means it has received some political support. What we have not done is see those finalised directives—and those that are still are not finalised—turned into operation and we have not seen the Commission's attempt to test whether that operation is actually meeting the original objectives. We are very comfortable with the original objective of the Financial Services Action Plan and have said so throughout. Where we are concerned is that they have not currently got measures of success which would allow us, the UK, or any other regime, to say it is successful other than in a box-ticking sense. Our message to you and to MEPs and to others is let us have some real criteria for success, which are matched back to the original objectives of the Financial Services Action Plan.

17. I am inviting you and your colleagues, if you have time, to send us a supplementary note on what you would regard as the criteria for success, as I am sure that would be extremely helpful.

A. Certainly.

Lord Shutt of Greetland

18. In paragraph 11 of your memorandum you suggest that differences between the Council and the European Parliament over the Prospectuses Directive, ". . . instead of introducing a single market for listing equity, helps to institutionalise national structures and will lead to an increase in the cost of capital for many EU companies". Has the recent agreement by the European Parliament on the Prospectuses Directive solved the problems for AIM? Is that cost effective?

A. Two elements to that really, if I may? Firstly, the question of choice. Until now, indeed still today, we have been arguing that companies may have their investor needs better met by different markets from their home markets. To give you a specific example, we created two markets in the UK, one of them is AIM, which is a market for very small companies and one of them is techMARK, which is a market aimed specifically at hi-tech companies and we have also created a biotech sector[1]. We have been marketing, both locally and around Europe, that certain types of companies will find an appreciative analyst audience or ready investor base, because the investor base already understands them. So for techMARK we have had some success in countries such as Israel, which has a high technology component of these companies without a developed capital market. We have been successful in winning a number of companies from there. We have been successful in winning companies from for example Australia and Canada to AIM, because AIM has a particular bias for certain types of companies. What the directive does for those markets is two things. Firstly, the Prospectuses Directive requires that a company wishing to access a public market must first do so through its home authority. We can no longer go to

---

[1] *Note by the witness*: The biotech sector of techMARK is called techMARK mediscience.

Lord Shutt of Greetland contd.]

the hi-tech company or the internet company in Madrid or Milan and say "Come to London for all of your needs". They are required to go through their home market first. That removes an element of what we had hoped was going to be efficient competition in Europe and it embeds across Europe, today 15, by next year 25 separate competent authorities, which is 25 potential costs which might not otherwise have been needed. For general competition in Europe, we believe the Prospectuses Directive was a step backwards. The specific issue of last week[2] for AIM was that the directive will now allow delegation of certain types of activity. It will allow delegation of pre-vetting, subject to the consent of the local competent authority. What differentiates AIM, which is unique in global markets, is that it is probably the only successful small company market currently existing. NeuerMarkt, the German market closed, the French version closed, NASDAQ is going through significant problems in the US and its European company closed. AIM is a hugely successful market. We have something like 700 companies on AIM at the moment. One of the distinguishing features for AIM is what we call the NOMAD, the nominated adviser, who has the responsibility for submitting the prospectus. It does not go through the competent authority. The concession which has been allowed in the directive is that the competent authority may delegate those powers. So we have the ability for the FSA, UKLA, to delegate powers which could allow AIM to go forward. We now have to complete the process by ensuring that UKLA does indeed delegate those powers. It has shifted the problem from Brussels. Brussels have said they have a solution for us. We now have a UK issue which is between us, the Treasury and the UKLA, agreeing the structure which will work for AIM. We do not have a problem with Brussels now. It is a domestic issue as such; we have to agree how it works locally.

19. Is that solvable?
A. It is solvable but it is not solved.

Lord Walpole

20. One of the things I have noticed in a lot of the written evidence we have had is that politicians do not seem to understand financial services. I am certainly one of those, I am on a steep learning curve at the moment and you are being very helpful so far. In paragraph 13 of your written evidence you say "Those of us who oppose the concept of a European SEC . . . have a real incentive to make Lamfalussy work". Why do you oppose the establishment of a European SEC?
A. Our issue is that we do not yet have, in fact we are quite a long way from, common standards of regulation across Europe. The Financial Services Action Plan may take us to common standards; I say "may" because there is still a huge amount of water to go under the bridge before we genuinely have those standards operating in the different states. The fact that ten years ago we had the first ISD, which still

is not fully implemented, makes us concerned for the process. If the process this time round is accompanied not just by proper interpretation at each national level but enforcement and supervision at European Commission level, then we will start to move towards standards which look as though they are the same in each market and if, by offering a service in one market, you can offer a similar service in another market. Our concern is, given that we are so early in that process, that the imposition of a Europe-wide SEC would be trying to fit a single regulatory regime across Europe, which is too early for it to be effective. Our view is: let us see the Lamfalussy process work; let us see implementation and enforcement at level three and four; let us see us get towards a common mode of operating a capital market. If you move to a EuroSEC too early, then the danger is that you try to fit a single standard, a single approach across Europe, before Europe is ready for it. The issue we struggle with constantly is that the UK, being such a diverse market, being a wholesale capital market as well as a retail market, has a diverse set of needs. If the European SEC were to come along now or in the near future trying to apply a common standard, it would run some of the risks that the directives run, of taking the view that actually equity markets are all retail, because in most European markets they are retail. That is why we say now is not the time; maybe at some time in the future, but certainly not now.

21. What specific failure of the Lamfalussy process would make a European SEC likely or probably a political response?
A. If the Financial Services Action Plan fails and fails in the narrow sense of not getting political agreement to the directives. If the remaining directives, of which the ISD is probably the most contentious, do not get to that level of agreement, then there will be a call which says, we are not able to agree that at political level within the Commission, let us now create a European SEC and give it a mandate for imposing a standard across Europe.

22. The standards will of course refer to all the other members when they join.
A. Yes; absolutely.

23. How many financial services are available in the eastern bloc?
A. Very few. Most countries within the old eastern bloc have created exchanges and tried to kick-start a capital market. In the case of Poland, large parts of the public sector were transferred into designated organisations which were investors, with the hope that they would subsequently transfer them to private individuals. Poland is probably the more developed of the European markets. Most of the other markets are very, very small and at a very early stage and are not at this stage significant sources of funding for growth in those countries.

Lord Chadlington

24. In your written evidence you say that in considering the FSAP, one of the objectives of the exchange has been to promote efficient capital markets for the wider EU economy, lowering the cost

---

[2] *Note by witness*: On 2 July the European Parliament voted to approve certain amendments to the Directive.

Lord Chadlington *contd.*]

of capital for firms and the cost of financial products for consumers. I have two questions about that. First of all, while one accepts these are laudable aims, does it not mean a continued reduction in the spread that financial intermediaries can charge, so raising the competitive pressures within the financial system? Secondly, do you think that will force a higher degree of finance to be provided through issuing securities—securitisation—so enhancing the importance of financial markets rather than banks? Will those trends increase the problem of many continental systems where small banks play a much larger, almost social role, in implementing the FSAP and adapting to its consequences?

A. Let me deal with the first question first, which is what creates the more efficient market, more attractive capital. Inevitably part of the benefit we see of greater competition is taking cost out of the system and the fact that there are 25 equity exchanges in Europe means that there are 25 sets of costs to bear, 25 chief executives to pay, 25 systems to develop and implement, 25 networks to operate. Our view, very simply, is yes, one of the pressures will be to reduce the profitability of exchanges and reduce the number of exchanges in Europe. The same holds true for the intermediaries. If it is more competitive across borders, the less efficient will be forced out at the cost of the more efficient, who will be the players who survive. Our belief is that we, both at the London Stock Exchange and the players who operate in our market, are at the efficient end of the scale and will be major beneficiaries as Europe opens up and as the boundaries become more open to competition. To answer your question: it does mean a reduction in spread, a reduction in profitability, but we hope and expect that will force out the less efficient and the more efficient will be the survivors.

25. Does that have anything to do with size?

A. Yes; economies of scale do operate in our markets so some of it is to do with size. If you have the scale to operate and provide a service across borders, there are certain economies of scale in some parts of the operation, not all. There are some parts of the operation of trading specifically where huge economies of scale come from size and some other parts of the operation, which are advising or more specialist skills, where you will tend to continue to need niche players and you will operate at a local level in the different markets because you are much closer to the information.

26. So you are squeezing out of the medium.

A. Probably; yes. The medium is probably the wrong term, a squeezing out of the less efficient and the less efficient, almost by definition, have not grown to be the major players. That is a good thing for the effectiveness of Europe's capital markets and that implies not just at the bank end but at the exchange end as well. Your second point, which was the securitisation of the financial system, is again quite an important one and an important part of the philosophy. UK companies have funded their growth largely through equity funding; that has been the story of the UK for the last 100 years. Much of continental Europe has largely funded its growth through bank spending and they have been moving to securitisation through equity over the last four or five years. It has taken a bit of a step back, as the markets have become much more difficult, but our long-term belief is that that is the best and most appropriate way for you to access risk capital: investors who can make intelligent choices about risk and therefore price that into the price at which they make capital available to you rather than bank lending, which tends to make much narrower choices about what risk it is prepared to take, therefore the cost of finance tends to be higher.

Lord Howie of Troon

27. In your written evidence, you were alarmed at the rush to complete the action plan and you thought certain consequences would arise from the rush. Can you give precise examples where the planned measures would actually reduce the existing benefits? If more time were taken, what could be done to avoid that?

A. One of the existing benefits which I mentioned, which is removed in the Prospectuses Directive, is very simple: a company no longer has the choice, if it believes a better equity market will suit its needs, that it can go to that equity market as part of its initial process through the competent authority. It has removed a choice from companies which was there and some companies were exercising that choice. You now have to go through your own market regulator. So that is a specific element of choice which exists today and which is being removed. Other opportunities are being missed. Some of the opportunities revolve around transparency. I come back to the earlier question about how a Greek private investor gets confidence. He largely gets confidence through availability of information and that information being available to him on a very quick and open basis. The UK model has evolved to do that, so companies release information in real time, if they have news which could affect their share price and all trades are published in real time and are available to anybody real time for a price, or indeed anybody for free, if they are prepared to take a 15-minute delay. Those things exist today. Two of the elements of the directives are changing that. One is a general push towards companies releasing information on a quarterly basis and being able to release that information not just through our structure, which is electronically pushing it out to as many people as possible, but on occasion through publication in a national newspaper. For us that is a missed opportunity; it could have been that the very transparent model for company information — in real time and electronically — became available. The opportunity was that that could be available across Europe. In terms of trade prices the opportunity which is being missed is to force all trades to be available in real time through common quality standards and through generally accessible gateways. That is an opportunity which has been missed because it is allowing firms to publish information, potentially without the quality threshold, potentially through slightly obscure channels. Some things have been taken away and we believe some opportunities are potentially going to be missed.

Lord Howie of Troon *contd.*]

28. So in a sense transparency means immediacy.

A. It is both, yes. Transparency means full information immediately available to the widest possible range of individuals and governments.

29. That brings me to a comment you made right at the beginning, when you spoke about the psychology of the market, if a market can have such a thing.

A. It can.

30. I seem to remember—tell me if I am right—that about 60 or 70 years ago the Stock Exchange was described as a casino. Tell me whether that was right or wrong and if it was right are not a good deal of these efforts just whistling in the wind?

A. You are right in the sense that it was said. I cannot remember who said it, but I have read it. That is correct. Markets operate best if they are very transparent, with information very widely available. That is understood by us, it is understood by the companies which operate in the market, it is understood by the firms who operate broking activities within the market. That is what brings customers to the market and gives confidence. In terms of whistling in the wind, there is a general acceptance that we have evolved to a standard operation of a market which is very efficient, very open and provides good protection. There is a general will to see the standards which have evolved in the most evolved market within Europe, which is the UK, applied at a European level. The frustration is that we are missing an opportunity to take those standards and apply them at a broader level.

Lord Howie of Troon: That reminds me of the days when I used to play pontoon, where transparency and immediacy were paramount.

Baroness Cohen of Pimlico

31. May I start by declaring an interest both to the Committee and to the audience? I am a director of the London Stock Exchange and as such partly instrumental in having forced Mr Wheatley into an evidence-giving position in front of us.

A. Thank you very much.

32. What I am trying to tease out of this, is that I think what you are saying to us is that the reason the FSAP is going to work rather better on the retail market than it is going to work on the wholesale market is presumably because there are many other countries in Europe which do not have that much experience of a wholesale market because they finance through bank lending rather than through securitisation. Is this right roughly? If so, what can we do? I know that the London Stock Exchange have always complained that they tend to find themselves carrying the banner on this with the government being absolutely useless.

A. I do not think we ever said "absolutely useless"; hopefully when we see the minutes that will be correctly transcribed. You are absolutely right on the first point. European companies have primarily been financed through bank lending and debt in some other form. The London market has been an equitised market for at least the last 100 years. European markets which have started to get exposure to equity have largely been either at the retail end, this was particularly the case in Germany with the NeuerMarkt where there was a massive rush of retail into equity products, or, where there has been a wholesale requirement, much of that requirement has been serviced from the London-based houses, since London has been the wholesale market for many of the European markets. That is why the risk is that the regulator in the local markets have only had experience of regulating largely retail business on an equity level. In terms of what we can do about it, we are obviously some way down the line in the process of evolving the particular, explicit directives at least at level one, at the political level. What we can do about it, is ensure that the UK government understands that the game is not over when we have ticked all 42 boxes. The real game starts then and what we can do about it is force the Commission to come up with a set—and we will provide you with some suggested wording—of real quality measures for success and, secondly, ensure that the Commission takes its responsibilities seriously in terms of enforcement and is properly resourced in terms of enforcement across markets. They are the things we can still do, notwithstanding the fact that we may have all 42 boxes ticked quite quickly, certainly by early next year.

Chairman

33. Both yourself and other people too have hit this common theme in that London is really a European asset, it is a European institution, a European asset. There is a danger still that a lot of the other Member States really see financial services sector institutions as strategic sectors of their economy. They really want to build around and protect their own financial market, their own financial institutions, rather than look more widely both across Europe, the single European capital market, but also globally. So this theme which has come across time and time again to us, that it is exceptionally difficult to get the weight, not of London in the sense of part of the UK, but the London financial market as part of Europe and part of the global market, to have its appropriate impact on all these regulations and directives and so on, because essentially so many of the Member States are really looking at it from the point of view of all those mini-fortresses; in a strategic sense, they must have their own institutions, they must have their own stock exchange and so on and so forth. Do you think that it is inevitable that over five, 10, 15 years that will be broken down by the force of competition, by the Commission and so on enforcing and implementing? Do you think that will be broken down or do you think that we are going to be going through this FSAP in a way which will damage London, because that balance has not been struck at the time the FSAP is being driven through? Has HMG done enough to support that position? The French have looked after their farmers very well indeed for year, after year, after year. I do not mean the UK government looking after London as a UK asset but looking after them as a global and European asset. Has that message got through as strongly as it should have done?

Chairman *contd.*]

A. I think the message is understood but the willingness to act on it is not there, the political will is not there. London has today probably on average 25 to 40 per cent of the flow into every single European market and it developed that from about 1979 when we abolished exchange controls. We have had that very strong position in all the European markets. When that was first recognised by the other European exchanges—and now I am talking about the more mature ones rather than the newcomers— they set out and revolutionised their exchanges from about the mid-1980s onwards and their government supported them. One of the things which it will not surprise you to know is that most of the exchanges had stamp duty in place and their governments removed stamp duty in response to London's competitive threat and that happened from about 1985 to 1990. They created a number of exchanges and financial centres which were more attractive. What then happened was that it was not the London firms doing the business in London, it was London firms doing the business and routing a fair bit of it to the continental exchanges, which is pretty well the situation today. The risk we run is exactly as you say:

the financial centre is seen as a major part of the nation's status in much the same way as an airline is. We have seen that the airline industry has been supported and protected in a way which is not the most efficient operation of the market. The risk is that that is exactly what we are seeing currently within exchanges.

34. You have been extremely patient and have been far briefer than we could reasonably have expected you to be and I do appreciate that and the Committee does too. Is there anything you think we have missed that we really ought to make sure we reflect upon when we come to reach our conclusions?

A. The one thing we have not specifically focused on, but which is very important to us, is the particular importance and role of MEPs in this process. We are talking to this House today; we talk to government. One of the things which I think is critically important is that we use our MEPs in the way that we see other countries using their MEPs, which tend to use them much more as a political tool than the UK has done.

Chairman: Thank you very, very much again. We are indebted to you.

Supplementary memorandum by the London Stock Exchange

"CRITERIA FOR SUCCESS"

EXECUTIVE SUMMARY

Since the FSAP was launched, various estimates have been made of the benefits of the single market that it was designed to deliver. These (mostly macro-economic) measures have been useful in creating political will to support the project and to give momentum to the process of regulatory reform. In their report proposing a new procedure to speed up the legislative programme, the Lamfalussy Committee used the great economic prize on offer to help make the case for their recommendations[8].

The high-level objectives for the FSAP, "to cut the cost of capital", "to make the EU more competitive[9]" are easy to support. What is more difficult is estimating the impact that any single directive will have in moving towards the over-arching goal of creating a more efficient market. This process of separating cause from effect becomes even more complex during what is currently a time of great change in capital markets—the introduction of the euro, new technology and consolidation among financial services providers can all bring benefits in the efficient allocation of capital and give users more opportunity to choose between competing offers.

Despite the difficulties in measuring outcomes, it is essential for the Commission and policy makers to set objectives for all legislative proposals and to keep sight of them throughout the process, at levels 2, 3 and 4 of Lamfalussy, as well as during level 1.

Although level 1 for most FSAP directives[10] is now complete, there is still much to play for in levels 2, 3 and 4. The Commission is committed to a process of review of outcomes and parliamentarians, national and European, are well placed to participate and to hold the Commission to account and to ensure that benefits of directives are not lost by poor implementation or weak enforcement.

In June[11], Internal Market Commissioner Frits Bolkestein said: "The clock is ticking. We have nine months to deliver the remaining parts of the Financial Services Action Plan. Most of the Commission proposals are on the table: It is now up to the European Parliament and the Member States to ensure that European businesses and consumers can reap the benefits of financial integration. There is a huge economic prize out there estimated at a direct windfall gain of at least 130 billion euros[12] for the financial services sector, not to

---

[8] Lamfalussy Report Chapter 1 "The benefits of European financial integration".

[9] The central conclusion of the Lisbon Summit—to become the world's most competitive and dynamic economy by 2010.

[10] Although important work on Level 1 remains on the Investment Services and Transparency Directives in particular.

[11] Press Release accompanying the Commission's 8th and Final Progress Report, 2 June 2003.

[12] London Economics 12 November, 2002.

mention the knock on effects of cheaper capital for Europe's businesses. The end result will be renewed confidence, more economic growth and more jobs. We must not let that slip."

INTRODUCTION

1. The Financial Services Action Plan (FSAP) was launched at a time of significant change in global capital markets. New technology allows markets and service providers to interconnect systems and market participants to access them from remote locations. As securities trading becomes increasingly electronic, unit costs are falling and a significant number of exchanges continue to report record volumes of activity. In the EU, the introduction of the single currency removed a major barrier to investment by sector in the eurozone. The consequent rebalancing of portfolios was itself a significant driver of growth in the level of transactions. In the financial services industry, securities houses and exchanges are engaged in a process of consolidation and rationalisation.

2. The programme of liberalisation of regulation launched by the Commission therefore has to be seen against a background of other important drivers that will bring efficiency gains that should benefit EU GDP. This makes it difficult to measure cause and effect.

POSITION OF THE LONDON STOCK EXCHANGE

3. In the process of regulatory change in global capital markets, it is possible to discern two broad types of response. The first sees the process of liberalisation as an opportunity to compete across borders—indeed to render the concept of "cross-border" redundant in the EU context. A signal that the single market for financial services has been created might be that "cross-border" finally means EU to US, not UK to France or Germany. The London Stock Exchange has positioned itself as being at the forefront of the drive to open up competition and like many financial services providers in the City of London we believe that we are well-placed to benefit from the removal of barriers. The other perspective sees liberalisation as a potential threat to domestic players and may try either to dilute the positive impact on competition from the directives that are agreed or (for example in the case of takeovers) to prolong negotiations *ad infinitum*.

4. This presents the Commission with a dilemma: to propose directives that are designed to deliver the most effective and competitive outcomes, or to accept the political realities of co-decision and try to reconcile a set of competing national interests as expeditiously as possible. Faced with the demands of Heads of Government as expressed at Council Meetings to get the reform agenda agreed and the limited time and scarce resources it has in which to deliver it, there is a danger that the Commission might be forced to follow the path of least resistance rather than take the route towards maximum benefits.

BENEFITS OF THE FSAP

5. Since the Financial Services Action Plan (FSAP) was launched, various attempts have been made to quantify the benefits it is expected to deliver—frequently characterised in terms similar to Commissioner Bolkestein above as "a huge economic prize". These benefits are usually expressed in broad macro-economic terms. They are difficult to calculate and even harder to disprove.

APPROACH OF THE UK GOVERNMENT

6. In papers on the development of EU economic reform and the FSAP, the UK Government identified[13] two tests that any FSAP measure should pass. Wholesale market measures should cut the cost of capital for European firms; and retail measures should reduce the costs of financial products to EU consumers.

7. In the context of Europe's broader reform agenda, the Government recommended that the EU should identify specific measures of success against which progress can be monitored—for example by measuring depth and liquidity of capital markets and calculating price differentials for standard financial services products. They recommend benchmarking the EU's financial services market against "the best in the world" and propose the following measures:

— equity market capitalisation as percentage of GDP (EU 106 per cent; US 181. percent).

— dependence on debt as a source of corportate finance (EU 50 to 70 per cent US 20 per cent).[14]

---

[13] These tests were referred to by the UK Treasury in their 2002 paper "Completing a dynamic single European financial services market: A catalyst for economic prosperity for citizens and business across the EU".

[14] 1999 figures.

— price differentials for basic retail products[15] for example credit cards financing can differ by a factor of three between Member States).

8. We agree that such a benchmarking of these indicators will be helpful to measure progress towards delivering the Lisbon agenda.

CECCINI REPORT

9. The first major quantitative study into the single market for financial services was part of the analysis of the impact of a fully established EC Internal Market by 1992. In 1988, the Ceccini Report on the costs of "non-Europe" estimated that the benefits of the liberalisation of financial services would contribute 1.5 per cent of the 4.5 per cent of GDP that would accrue on completion of the Internal Market.

RETAIL MARKETS

10. Although seen more as propaganda than authoritative analysis by many commentators, the Ceccini Report helped to galvanise support for the 1992 project. A recent update for the European Financial Services Roundtable—the Gyllenhammar Report[16]—used a similar methodology but claimed to be a much more sophisticated analysis.

11. Gyllenhammar estimated the positive impact of an efficient retail market at 0.5 to 0.7 per cent of EU GDP[17]. Among the other benefits identified was around €5 billion annually from the economies of scale that would be achieved as the average fund size is expected to increase to US levels and the suggestion that retail market integration would probably reduce the "home market bias" in investment portfolios. Better diversification from a wider spread of investments tends to boost returns and lower risk. The so-called "Sharpe ratio"—a measure of diversification—could be significantly increased by a Europe-wide diversification. This is particularly the case for countries like France and Germany, where home bias persists in portfolios, but less so for the UK where investors have tended to invest more in non-domestic companies.

12. We recommend that the Commission undertake to test the Gyllenhammar analysis once the single market measures have been agreed and implemented and that the Sharpe ratio is periodically calculated as an indicator of diversification. Unless retail investors have confidence to invest in non-domestic securities, the single market will not have achieved its objectives.

WHOLESALE MARKETS

13. For wholesale markets, a recent London Economics report[18] sponsored by the Commission, predicted a 1.1 per cent increase in EU GDP over the next 10 years from the integration of capital markets. This includes a reduction in the cost of equity capital by 0.5 per cent and 0.4 per cent in the cost of corporate bond finance. Although described as the first substantive empirical research on the impact of financial integration on the cost of raising finance, the study does not measure the full dynamic benefits of integration. Further research from the Commission (not yet published) is claimed to demonstrate that "the deepening of financial markets resulting from integration can permanently boost output growth in manufacturing industry".

A MICRO APPROACH

14. In addition to these broad measures, the Commission has set objectives for individual FSAP directives. Two examples are below.

PROSPECTUS DIRECTIVE

15. According to the Commission, the Directive will make it easier and cheaper for companies to raise capital throughout the EU on the basis of approval from a regulatory authority ("home competent authority") in one Member State.

16. It will reinforce protection for investors by guaranteeing that all prospectuses, wherever in the EU they are issued, provide them with the clear and comprehensive information they need to make investment decisions. The Commission cites issuers and investment banks as critics of the existing regime—directives on listing particulars (1980) and prospectuses (1989)—"had not achieved the aim of facilitating the raising of capital across borders in Europe". ·

---

[15] Sources: European Commission 1998; OECD 2000.

[16] Heinemann and Jopp, the Benefits of a Working European Retail Market for Financial Services 2002.

[17] At 2000 figures 0.5 per cent of EU GDP would mean an annual growth of £43 billion.

[18] Study on the "quantification of the macro-economic impact of integration of EU financial markets, 12 November 2002.

17. It is still the case that there are almost no pan-European issues, although in several Member States—particularly smaller markets—issuers are likely to try to attract support for an IPO by encouraging participation by non-domestic (often UK) institutional investors.

18. One possible measure of success for the Prospectus Directive therefore might be the number of cross-border—in the sense of pan-European—issues of securities following implementation in 2005.

19. For an individual IPO, it might be assumed that under the new regime the cost of the IPO should fall as a proportion of the capital raised. For example, under the current regime the host country authority, in the case of recognition of a prospectus, is authorised to require additional information related to the domestic market (including translation into the host country languages)[19].

20. Unfortunately the Prospectus Directive is likely to raise costs in other areas, for example by requiring companies to seek approval in their home country first. This means that the benefits of real single market for listings are less likely to be captured because once they have been admitted to the official list in a particular Member State, issuers are more likely to seek admission to trading to a regulated market in that Member State. Indeed the additional requirements imposed on smaller companies are likely to increase their costs of capital overall and given that many of the costs of an IPO are fixed, may make the decision to access a public equity market less attractive for smaller companies.

21. Principally for these reasons, the London Stock Exchange is currently consulting on how to move its AIM[20] market beyond the scope of the Directive to preserve the current nexus between AIM companies and their nominated advisers "nomads". Under this system of regulation, it is the nomad who endorses a company's decision to join AIM, rather than the UK Listing Authority. We are confident that agreement will be reached whereby AIM becomes an MTF under the new ISD (see paragraph 23 below).

INVESTMENT SERVICES DIRECTIVE

22. The main objective of the new Directive is to update the current regime to help investment firms operate EU-wide while at the same time protecting investors. The existing Investment Services Directive, dating from 1993, relies heavily on mutual recognition and has not proved sufficient in practice to ensure investment firms can operate EU-wide on the basis of authorisation in their home country.

23. The new ISD seeks to establish a comprehensive regulatory framework governing the organised execution of investor transactions by exchanges, other trading systems and investment firms. Two types of markets are envisaged—regulated markets and multi-lateral trading facilities or MTFs.

24. A test of the impact of the new ISD might be to survey investment firms to see what impact they believe the directive has had on their ability to operate from one centre in Europe after it has been implemented. If such firms have a working passport (as is the declared intention) the need to have a physical presence in more than one Member State should be reduced. This is particularly important as the EU grows to 25 Member States.

CONCLUSION

25. Given the range of variables and the background of significant change that is sweeping through the financial sector, none of the above measures can be relied upon in isolation. All are probably capable of being partially discounted or otherwise explained away.

26. In these circumstances, and as the process of regulatory reform continues, it is important that policy makers agree some measures of success in advance of legislating and that the objectives for each directive are clearly stated. These should be kept firmly in sight during the implementation phase and during levels 3 and 4 of Lamfalussy.

27. The Commission is committed to a programme of review for FSAP directives and we believe that national parliamentarians and MEPs are well-placed to participate in that process and to ensure that these commitments are fulfilled.

Memorandum from the London Investment Banking Association

I attach LIBA's response to the Sub-Committee's request for evidence. I draw the Sub-Committee's attention in particular to the following points:

— The danger to London's international proportionately regulated wholesale markets from over-detailed and interventionist European legislation.

---

[19] Under the present system, mutual recognition is granted only to prospectuses (for listing or public offer) that set out the information specified in the Listing Particulars Directive (80/390/EEC) and approved by the competent authorities.

[20] Alternative Investment Market for smaller companies.

— In particular, the need to ensure that the Prospectuses Directive, Investment Services Directive, and proposed Risk-Based Regulatory Capital Directive do not harm wholesale markets.

— The need to improve European consultation practices further to achieve a genuine dialogue between legislators, regulators, and interested parties.

— The need to bring European authorities' practice more closely into line with the "spirit" of the Lamfalussy Report to improve legislative quality and relieve resource constraints.

— The need to develop a coherent body of fundamental principles of financial services regulation as a foundation for both legislation and enforcement, as recommended by the Lamfalussy Committee.

I also attach as background to our evidence three publications which provide recent statistical information and analysis of the importance of the London markets to both the EU and the world:

— "International Financial Markets in the UK", published by International Financial Services London, May 2003 (http://www.ifsl.org.uk/uploads/RP_IFM_2003_05.pdf)

— "The City's Importance to the EU Economy", published by the Corporation of London, January 2003 (http://www.cityoflondon.gov.uk/business_city/research_statistics/pdf/city2eu03.pdf)

— "Sizing up the City", published by CSFI and the Corporation of London, June 2003 (http://www.cityoflondon.gov.uk/business_city/research_statistics/pdf/sizing_up_the_city.pdf)

A. THE FINANCIAL SERVICES ACTION PLAN

What progress has been made to date? Has this been beneficial or deleterious to UK interests? Has sufficient weight been given to the position and experience of UK financial services industry? What are the main outstanding matters that remain to be dealt with under the FSAP and what key issues will need to be resolved?

1. Measured by number of measures completed, substantial progress, with significant pressure to complete FSAP by April 2004. However the number of measures adopted is not the best gauge of the FSAP's success. Moreover, passing a measure does not necessarily make it good. Many of the most significant and controversial measures for UK and European financial services are not completed: Investment Services Directive Proposal; proposed Risk-Based Regulatory Capital Directive; Prospectuses Directive Proposal.

2. Sufficient weight has not been given, in the case of particular measures, to the particular characteristics and experience of the international financial services industry concentrated in London, the key role it plays in the European and international capital markets, and the benefits it brings to Europe as a whole and to Europe's ambitions on the world stage. The dominance of London in European wholesale markets[21] is much greater than UK representation in Council or European Parliament or CESR, where quite properly, FSA has been seeking a leadership role.

3. Some other Member States tend to determine policy by reference to the needs of their own domestic financial services industry, in particular the retail sector, rather than the EU's wholesale markets, where the bulk of cross-border business, and of value of industry's capital-raising, is concentrated. The resulting compromises sometimes risk significant harm to the ability of London and the EU to compete with other major financial centres worldwide. There it too much emphasis on "maximal harmonisation" of rules at a detailed level, and not enough emphasis on "mutual recognition" of national regulation based on agreed minimum standards, but tailored to national market characteristics.

4. Main outstanding matters and key issues include (see also Section C, para 14):

(a) Investment Services Directive Proposal: intrusive and restrictive regulation of capital market structure based on administratively-guided market models, and unbalanced emphasis on protecting small and retail investors, risks major harm and disruption to flexible, diverse, innovative, competitive yet effectively regulated international wholesale capital markets in London.

(b) Proposed Risk-Based Regulatory Capital Directive: European Commission proposes to apply the revised Basel Accord (designed for, and likely to be applied outside Europe only to major internationally active banks) to securities firms and fund managers as well. Although securities firms and banks share a number or risks, their overall risk profile can be very different. Until now a common framework for all sectors has been tenable, but the revised Accord has concentrated on a wholly banking perspective. Hence, the impact of the revised Accord will differ substantially depending on the balance of the risks of the firms. Without substantial modifications in European rules to take account of the risk profile of investment business, EU firms would need to hold significantly more regulatory capital than non-banks with a similar risk profile outside the EU, putting them at a major competitive disadvantage.

---

[21] See "The City's Importance to the EU Economy", published by the Corporation of London, January 2003, particularly Chapter 2, London's international financial markets are almost without exception the largest by far in the EU, and many account for a majority of the EU's activity.

(c) Prospectuses Directive Proposal: Discriminates imprudently against non-EU businesses; constrains rather than liberalises markets; weakens Europe's and London's Euromarket dominance.

(d) Takeovers Directive Proposal: Provides insufficient clarity to facilitate cross-border transactions and insufficient protection for investors.

B. IMPLEMENTATION AND ENFORCEMENT

How successful do you expect the Lamfalussy process to be? Are any changes needed? Who will be responsible for ensuring effective implementation and enforcement of the single market, after the regulatory Framework is in place? How successful do you expect the process to be? What will be the role of competition regulators at EU and Member State level? What issues will arise as the single market framework is implemented and enforced? What non-regulatory barriers might impede the effective functioning of a single market for financial services?

5. The Lamfalussy process is in principle the right way forward for legislative and regulatory development in the financial services single market. In practice it has yielded some important improvements too, but significant problems remain to be solved before it meets its full potential, eg:

(a) welcome improvements in consultation practice have still to be turned into a genuine dialogue between legislators and interested parties;

(b) providing more time and resources to ensure that haste does not undermine legislative quality (tight implementation deadlines for particular directives and the imminent 2004–05 FSAP deadline are particular and very serious problems at present, but need not always be);

(c) better use of the multi-level Lamfalussy approach to distinguish, as originally intended, between high-level principles and detailed application. So far, contrary to Lamfalussy's central objectives, legislative proposals have become more detailed, thus making the resource shortage referred to in (b) even worse. There is also a need to avoid using the Lamfalussy potential for "Level 2" legislative measures too widely, simply because the option exists, in order to try to harmonise more regulatory detail than strictly necessary.

6. The Member States are responsible for implementing, and the Commission for enforcing (at Lamfalussy Level 4) the single market. The Commission has recently published its proposed enforcement approach in its "Internal Market Strategy 2003–2006". The signal of a new willingness to enforce existing legislation rather than trying to solve problems largely by yet more legislation is welcome. It remains to be seen how effective the Commission's proposed strategy will be, which relies on co-operation from Member States. The poor level of co-operation from some Member States in the past suggests that this may not be an easy task for the Commission.

7. Experience already reveals some of the main difficulties likely to arise as the single market framework is implemented and enforced:

— some Member States' resistance to implementing properly or fully measures which threaten perceived national interests, and exploitation of ambiguous wording to the same end;

— politically expedient agreement on legislative texts that are too inflexible for the needs of innovative and diverse markets (a particular problem is the tendency to over-regulate professional and institutional markets);

— tension between the regulatory control over a cross-border service of the "country of origin" regulator and the "country of recipient" regulator.

8. Non-regulatory barriers include widely divergent market cultures and underlying assumptions about the role of governments and regulators in markets. These differences underlie many of the political disagreements over primary legislation, and can be expected to persist in detailed implementation.

9. Because the participants in wholesale markets are very professional, and the market mechanism manages relations between them efficiently, regulation of wholesale markets needs to be "light touch" and market-oriented, focusing on where the market mechanism does not control excesses. By contrast, the administratively-guided approach applied across much of Europe puts restrictions in place for precautionary reasons, regardless of the market's record, or its ability to control malpractice.

10. Discriminatory taxation or simply differentially structured tax systems can also act as significant barriers to cross-border services.

C. THE FUTURE

How do witnesses see the future development of a single market in financial services following implementation of the FSAP? Are additional measures needed? Will changes resulting from the FSAP proposals have an impact on the competitive position of London and EU markets as whole in the global environment?

11. There are several threats to the future development of a single financial services market, even if the FSAP measures are completed and implemented. For example, we fear detailed bureaucratic harmonisation around standards which are more appropriate for retail and administrative-guided markets than for diverse wholesale markets. This risks driving wholesale business away from London and the EU to more effectively regulated markets elsewhere, and making the EU market less attractive for updating regulation will diminish market innovation and diversity. We also fear that protectionist regulation and uneven implementation of "harmonised" measures will distort the competitive position, and damage London in particular.

12. Some of what the FSAP is intended to bring about could be achieved by more efficient enforcement of existing Community legislation. This underlines that the emphasis should now turn from legislation to enforcement. Further legislative and regulatory change, where needed, should take place where possible at Lamfalussy Level 2 or 3. Further new legislation or substantial change to Directives should be avoided unless this is the only feasible way to remedy serious problems.

13. Any further legislation, and continuing implementation and enforcement of the FSAP/Lamfalussy structure, should take place in a context of agreed fundamental objectives for financial services legislation (as recommended by Lamfalussy). Such a coherent body of principles will be needed even after the FSAP is complete.

14. Changes resulting from the FSAP measures could well have a significant impact on the competitive position of both London and EU markets in the global environment. Key examples include:

— the Prospectus Directive, where despite substantial improvements to the treatment of bond markets, the constraints on regulation of equity and third country issuers' prospectuses are likely to harm London and EU markets' attractiveness to issuers in the EU and worldwide;

— the Investment Services Directive, where possible constraints on market structure and transparency obligations could reduce liquidity and thereby drive substantial institutional business away from London and the EU;

— the proposed Risk-Based Regulatory Capital Directive, where inappropriate treatment of investment business lines could expose firms undertaking a significant proportion of investment business to punitive regulatory capital obligations.

15. The cumulative impact of such regulatory constraints, in a market where margins are already very thin and market intermediaries are increasingly mobile, could well be extremely serious.

16. EU savers and investors deserve access to investments worldwide. Outward-looking investment firms facilitate these demands by bringing investment opportunities to EU citizens. The focus of the FSAP on an attempt to create a single market for the EU by regulatory fiat and administrative action neglects the outward-looking nature of EU investors and the markets that serve them, and sometimes discriminates, for no good reason, against the rest of the world. It risks replicating the regulatory constraints that have limited outward investment from, and inward investment to, other markets (one reason why £800 billion of overseas money is managed from London), and restricting the access to global markets that EU investors demand.

25 June 2003

Examination of Witnesses

SIR ADAM RIDLEY, Director-General and MR T BAKER, Director, London Investment Banking Association, examined.

Chairman

35. Welcome, Sir Adam and Mr Baker. I apologise that we are behind schedule. You will have gathered we have done our best to catch up a little and we should really like to try to aim at concluding at around six thirty, if that is agreeable to you. Is there anything you would like to say by way of introduction today?
(*Sir Adam Ridley*) Thank you, I should like to make one personnel point and then three very small points by way of introduction. First of all, I should explain who Mr Baker is. He is not just any old

common or garden director of LIBA. He has been working non-stop on European issues, but particularly negotiating on the Investment Services Directive (ISD) more or less 24 hours a day for much of the last six months. Therefore he is extremely well informed on every aspect of that very tortuous business. So much for him and I hope you will hear from him shortly as well as from me. Second, a point about LIBA. LIBA is the London Investment Banking Association by name, but in substance we are very much more international, as I hope the list of members attached to our evidence indicated. Not only do we have a very widespread international

Chairman *contd.*]

membership not just from Europe. We work increasingly closely with large numbers of international associations or European associations and, as such, therefore try to reflect in our political activity the nature of the very heterogeneous international economy which you were discussing a little while ago with Mr Wheatley. The other point I would make is that, as far as your own deliberations go and what we from our point of view see as important, some of what we are talking about is still very much to play for. Much of the FSAP has been legislated for and is going down the line probably into uncontrollable detail. This really makes things like the Investment Services Directive or the Capital Adequacy Directive, which you have not touched on today, very much to play for. We as an association welcome the interest you are taking and look forward to the impact you will be able to have on the negotiations we are involved in.

Chairman: May I say that we found your written evidence extremely helpful, very focused and hitting nails right on the head every time. I do thank you for that and it was very, very clear, right to the point and was certainly very helpful to us. May I invited Lord Howie to start the questions?

Lord Howie of Troon

36. May I begin by saying how glad I am that Mr Baker is so expert in these matters since I am not and I shall listen carefully to what he says? In paragraph 3 of your written evidence you say that there is not enough emphasis on mutual recognition and too much on maximal harmonisation. As a novice, I should like you first of all to explain these two terms to me and then go on to give some practical examples of how your ideas would work and why they would improve the goal of a single market for financial services?

(*Sir Adam Ridley*) May I take a non-economic parallel first for mutual recognition? You might say that we would be happy in this country to allow in doctors who had been trained elsewhere. If I might just push the thought, you will see what I mean . . . We accept the validity of someone else's medical qualifications and allow the doctor to practise here and conversely they do ours. What we are talking about therefore in the economic or commercial areas is much the same thing. If I might just follow the logic of it through, what is abundantly clear, is if you were simply to say, against a general background of removing manifest obstacles, each of us will control the business originating from our own economies; we will have acceptable minimum standards, to do with things like fraud and all the rest of it; and then we will say that there will be good information for investors, so they can choose properly between the different services on offer. Under those circumstances, a great deal of mutual trade can take place, without any of us having to adopt one single harmonised rule, apart from the minimum standard. For everything else, we accept their doctors and they accept ours, as it were. That is infinitely easier to promote, even between two countries, than it is to standardise. The more you multiply the number of interlocutors and bargainers and negotiators and members of the Community, the

more you multiply the confusion and the complexity. It will not be a linear process, it will grow as a square of the numbers of countries. When we move shortly to 25, possibly more, Member States, you can just imagine how fiendishly difficult it will be to harmonise. That is the principal point we would make. There is one other element that it would be appropriate to stress. Financial services come in an enormous variety of shapes and sizes, markets come in an enormous variety of shapes and sizes, and so do their legal regulation and legislation. If you try to put them together, it is very difficult, for just that reason, not that the underlying processes are fundamentally very different, but that the apparatus we have evolved to deal with financial services is unique to each country. To integrate is a painfully slow process. *Ergo,* once again, mutual recognition is so much easier.

(*Mr Baker*) The great danger is one of homogenisation of rules at a very detailed level and harmonisation of rules involves some countries becoming more sophisticated, but some countries, including potentially the UK, having to change rules in a way which actually damages a mode of regulation which has evolved to meet the needs of a more sophisticated market.

Chairman

37. Is the pass sold on that or is that something which in implementation can be overcome?

(*Mr Baker*) The pass is not sold, in fact the European Commission has made a number of steps towards this mutual recognition approach in other areas such as the Electronic Commerce Directive, which provides what we think is a very good precedent, based on what is called the country of origin approach. The Investment Services Directive itself is based primarily upon home country regulation. There are some areas though, particularly in relation to the regulation of branch business, where it is not quite right yet. Many of our members operate as branches from London and that could cause problems. The main problem is the level of detail.

Lord Howie of Troon

38. I noticed in the paper today that some people involved in investment banking earn very large salaries, talk of millions, which I find inconceivable, but good luck to them in a manner of speaking. Does this mean that large sums of money are siphoned off quite legally by individuals and do not reach the parts that other things do not reach?

(*Sir Adam Ridley*) I think the process of siphoning is not something which is bringing much benefit to the coffers of our modest Investment Banking Association; would that it were. Putting that minor problem on one side, one of the essences of the process we are all talking about is increasing the number of our competitors and increasing the degree of competition. That manifestly has the effect of putting pressure on the excess margins, which then act as a kind of honeypot for the extravagant or for the aggressive individual, who then tries to persuade

Lord Howie of Troon *contd.*]

his employers he is so essential that he needs this kind of bonus. Coming from an investment banking background myself, at one time one of the very interesting things was watching us, the merchant banks, destroy part of our franchise by over-rewarding ourselves and then finding that all sorts of riff-raff came in and attacked us and competed with us, people like the accountants, which was really very demeaning and shocking!

Chairman: I have to tell you that the inquiry is going down channels even I had not imagined, but then Lord Howie always takes me down channels I do not expect.

Lord Chadlington

39. I am extremely glad I am not an accountant. You mention in your written evidence that there is a threat to the wholesale market caused by regulation more appropriate to retail markets. Could you please suggest some measures which could improve that position?

(*Sir Adam Ridley*) We are talking principally about the Investment Services Directive and picking up some of the points you have already had. There are also aspects of the Prospectuses Directive and the Capital Adequacy Directive. I shall just ask Tim Baker to say a few words about the ISD and then I will say a little about the others.

(*Mr Baker*) There are three particular problems with the ISD, some of which Mr Wheatley referred to earlier on. First of all, it would cause liquidity providers to become retail market makers; that may be partly to do with bad drafting, but that would be its effect. Secondly, it would limit the ability of investors to determine how they wanted their trading interest to be disclosed to the market by imposing "mandatory pre-trade transparency" provisions. Thirdly, the point I mentioned in response to the previous question about the need for an approach to country of origin regulation, which means that there is no overlap of requirements with different authorities in different countries trying to regulate the same piece of business. The problems arise because of the attempt to legislate at too detailed and interventionist a level and the solution to those problems needs to be to rise to a higher level of framework principles, so that all European markets can be accommodated. There are fears in a number of European markets, as was discussed earlier, about the effect of a mutual recognition approach upon the relative competitive position of different markets and that is perhaps something we need to recognise by going to a higher level of framework principles.

40. I am seduced by that argument, as I was a moment ago. What I cannot get at is practically what one does to raise it. Do you see what I mean? Once you have got into the minutiae of things, my experience is that it is very difficult to get people back to principles, because the process has already been advanced too far. What can one do practically, if others like me are seduced by the force of your argument?

(*Mr Baker*) It is a very good question. We are very much into the minutiae of the legislation. At the moment, there is little that can be done, because,

both in the Council and in the Parliament, legislation is being carried forward at such a level of detail. There is a deadline of April 2004 when the Financial Services Action Plan is supposed to be wrapped up and it may be that at a later stage the solution will be perceived to be to go back to a higher level of generality and principle.

41. I hope you are right, because, as Sir Adam said earlier on, when we end up with 25 and more the problem gets worse and in a mathematical progression which must be quite alarming.

(*Sir Adam Ridley*) May I just add one tiny homily which may be little more than an effort to deploy Ockham's razor, which is something we all love but none of us likes to use. At the top level, you should only put in those principles which are going to be enduring and timeless. The test is that it always needs to be there. At the next level down, level two, you put in those things which are needed now and which need to be harmonised and uniform, such as they are, but which may well change. If you take stock exchanges, there was the dealing system of open outcry 15 or 20 years ago, people standing around on the floor, dressed in their decorative clothes. Then that fell away and it all became electronic within one stock exchange. Now there is a third phase coming, which is international communication between exchanges. That is an example of something which requires a series of change in the rules at level two. At the third level, you say that is something which should be for the individual countries to do, and you should not write in too much detail. That theory is then confronted by the institutional reality that if you put these 15 nationalities in one room, who scarcely know one another and are just learning to get on, then they write in every possible personal and nationally-oriented exception. In these respects we are in the very, very early days. What we have to do, if I may reinforce what Mr Baker said, is be willing to go back repeatedly and push these difficult issues, because it is remarkably difficult in practice to see how it will happen. We would urge you to urge it on us.

(*Mr Baker*) The level two draft legislation for the Prospectuses Directive included a proposed prospectus for Greek shipping companies, to pick up on your discussions earlier.

Chairman

42. At the very beginning, the stated intention was to stick to high level principles. In practice more and more detail has gone into directives. Are you saying you believe that when it comes to the process of implementation and so on, in your view it must and will be possible to evolve a situation where we go back to higher level principles and have more flexibility in the system? Effectively the idea of starting from basic broad principles rather than lots of details was always the intention, but that is not what is happening, is it?

(*Sir Adam Ridley*) If you say "it must do", undoubtedly that would be an injunction and a precept of good behaviour that we have to support. Whether it will do, is going to depend on the extent to which we attempt to do the impossible. If I might

Chairman contd.]

just identify one really pathological problem, or possibly two which come into play here, you will perhaps see what I mean a bit more clearly. If we seek to achieve agreement where it is barely possible, and the only way you can do it is by a very elaborate system of derogations and exceptions, then we have designed by the very process of seeking agreement a method of building a Christmas tree. So we often find ourselves pushing too far, too fast and therefore we have no choice, simply because of the intrinsic technical complexity. The other alternative—and these are not mutually exclusive—is that we do not trust someone; indeed sometimes none of us trusts anybody, to take the most extreme possibility. In that case you prescribe down to the last detail precisely what should be done, so that there is no latitude left for some outrageous group of regulators in some other country simply not to apply the Directive. In other words, there is an enforceable right which gives you some hope. If we attempt to go either politically in an unrealistic direction or technically or both, as sure as eggs are eggs, we will get Christmas-tree-like legislation, and that is what we have.

43. May I add a grace note to that? It seems to me that what I am taking from this exchange is that the more detail into which we go, the more potential damage we would do to our own national market. Is that a reasonable conclusion?

(Mr Baker) Yes; in the legislation. What we need to do is push much more down to what is called level three, which is the regulators learning in a much less pressured way how to reconcile national differences.

(Sir Adam Ridley) The answer is yes, is it not?

Chairman: I assure you we will revisit that before the afternoon is up.

Lord Faulkner of Worcester

44. May I press on with this question of the ISD and the other things which you say in paragraph 4 where you are very critical, you do not mince your words at all? You use words like "intrusive" and "restrictive" and "major harm" and "disruption" and "insufficient clarity" and so on relating to the ISD and then on the Takeovers Directive proposal. Do you have any solutions for solving these sorts of problems?

(Sir Adam Ridley) I shall just make one comment which is to go back to what I said earlier, that if you see part of the difficulty with the ISD is seeing that there is no underlying deal to be done on certain elements, then—

45. You tear it up.

(Sir Adam Ridley) Not the whole thing. You quite simply say that there is a provision here and a provision there where the views of the important members are so far apart that it is simply neither prudent nor necessary to proceed now. That would be one solution, which is to duck the issue. A second one would be to leave it subject to review. A third might be to say that, though we will seek to implement it in some way or other, we will leave a degree of discretion to the local regulators and you devolve into a lower level. I do not mean that in a bad way. However, I think that the best of all these answers, analytically, is to go back to what Mr Baker

just said. Instead of leaving it devolved to the regulators in the present structure analytically you really ought to go straight back to the top level. Those are some quick answers.

46. I understand that. Would you make the same points about the Takeovers Directive as well?

(Sir Adam Ridley) The Takeover Directive is notorious for having two features which offer total contradictions between different parts of the European industrial community and arguably it would be better to duck both of those issues. However, the danger is, if the heart of the directive is being put on one side, you are left with such a poor creature that you wonder whether it is worth bothering with at all in that case.

Chairman

47. That is a very important issue.

(Sir Adam Ridley) Sometimes maybe you should reculez pour mieux sauter, in some way; you have to hold back and stop to think whether you have done your reconnaissance, exploration and analysis properly.

48. May I pose two questions which have come up time and again? Firstly, do you think that the rush, the pressure, to get agreement on directives, by spring of next year should be resisted? In other words, is it better not to finish up with these last critical, important directives? Is it better that we do not get agreement by April to avoid a poor agreement, or should we still aim at April 2004? Secondly, if there were no agreement on some of these critical last directives, would that not blow a hole right through a single financial market, if you do not have things like an ISD, Takeovers Directive, Prospectuses Directive?

(Sir Adam Ridley) May I offer you a personal opinion, because LIBA has not really adopted a policy view on this? My own view with 20:20 hindsight is that your question is very persuasive. We went into the FSAP as a set of different financial and industrial interests, as a government, a set of bureaucracies and regulators, without analysing adequately what we were going to do. Having set off down the road, like every other member of the Union, we failed to do our homework adequately. We then found insufficient bureaucratic resources to do the job properly and we did not set up the right consultative procedures until very late in the day. If ever there were an example of a monumental hash-up, this is it. Under such circumstances therefore, one is very tempted, and I say this as much as a one-time Treasury official as I do as a representative of a trade association, to say if something looks like going seriously wrong, why not hold back? To which the answers are two-fold. One you identified, which was that you are perhaps leaving behind a very big hole. There is no way of telling, we do not know enough. The other alternative is to say, yes, it is a hole, but if dealing within it is so desirable, probably people will find another way of filling it. In some cases it may be—I have not thought it through—that existing legislation could do much of the business required, if it were enforced and pursued properly. In that line of thought, I think Mr Wheatley was hinting early on in

Chairman *contd.*]

his remarks to you that much of the so-called single passport for an integrated European economy for single users could be achieved with adequate enforcement which exists today.

(*Mr Baker*) As Sir Adam has said, we do have an ISD. The question you posed as to whether it would be better to have a directive or not, depends on what kind of directive we are able to achieve over the next few months. Certainly there are intensive efforts in both the Council and the Parliament to improve what the Commission has come up with. It depends what we end up with.

49. Do you feel the politicians are determined to reach agreement, even if that leaves some major problems for London? Are they going to reach agreement by 2004 come what may? Do you feel that way.
(*Mr Baker*) Yes, there is certainly huge pressure to reach political agreement.

Lord Shutt of Greetland

50. In paragraph 5 you refer to significant problems in implementing the Lamfalussy process and in particular too much prescription at level two. Are you suggesting that a lot of the detail could be filled in by Member States—I think you are—rather than being drafted by CESR, but where do you draw the line?
(*Sir Adam Ridley*) There is no single simple answer, but as a rule you are back to the same issue that we had when discussing the heartland of the directive itself. It is not possible or sensible, with a community of 10 or 15, to be too specific about exactly what each element in the regulatory or legal process should be. Therefore you have to adopt a procedure which will accommodate within reasonable limits the idiosyncrasies of the different legal systems of the members. In some areas of national financial life, there should not be much variation: in others there will be a great deal. I cannot offer a single standard formula, it will be a matter of case by case. That is a fairly irritatingly tautological response. Tim Baker has thought about this more and may be able to help reinforce me.
(*Mr Baker*) May I just mention that there are some areas where there is not enough harmonisation, so it is not always a case of too much harmonisation? Examples of that are the treatment of what are called "eligible counterparties" in the ISD, where firms are dealing with very large companies who are as expert as themselves and not owing customer obligations to their counterparty. That is an area which is very much up in the air in the Investment Services Directive.

Lord Cavendish of Furness

51. On the question of costs, do you feel that the benefits are going to justify the cost of this operation? As a secondary question, of which you will not have had notice, what is your personal view as to the political drive behind FSAP? To me it is absolutely mysterious how there could be this tremendous rush, other than the accession countries, to have such a major reform in such a tight timescale. One is left

perhaps with the suspicion that the ascendancy of the London market is regarded with some jealousy by others.
(*Sir Adam Ridley*) I believe that the benefits of the integrated market would be very large in the long run. The benefits which have been illustrated in the calculations undertaken recently by Oxford Economics and publicised by the Commission, are not unreasonable, just as I believe there were very substantial benefits initially from liberating trade when the Community was created 40 years ago. Unfortunately we are not talking about doing very much to bring about those changes. We are not opening up many bits of the marketplace with the measures which have been proposed. Indeed, as was suggested both by Mr Wheatley and Mr Baker, we are closing some bits down. So my own instinct is that at this stage, while we are creating a machine which could produce progressively more market integration, I do not see a great deal arising which would not have been coming anyway. I am agnostic about it, but I suspect that it is unlikely that there is an enormous net tangible benefit attributable to the measures which are currently coming through. That is not to say they could not follow later. I see this therefore as desirable as part of a much longer run process, of which this stage is a first and rather unsatisfactory failure. If you look at the history of the United States, you will find that it took them hundreds of years to get some of these things. If I might address the issue of the timing in relation to the accession countries, I suspect that the accession countries issue is just an accident of history. We have a timetable fixed for the FSAP which reflects the earlier failures of a succession of integration proposals for the financial markets which goes back to Lord Cockfield, 20 years or something like that. It was reactivated, very properly, in the late 1990s, and I do not think that at that time people thought it would take us long. Therefore when it failed and we had Lamfalussy, we suddenly realised, that there would be an interaction between the end of the FSAP, the accession and a new European Parliament and everything seemed to point to this terrible rush. I see it as just an accidental sequence of events which rings things; as it happens three cars collide at a crossroads.

Lord Walpole

52. In paragraph 12 of your written evidence you refer to the need to shift the emphasis from legislation to enforcement. Do you have a view on how enforcement will work and the balance between local and central enforcement? Do you believe a EuroSEC is likely? Would you support it and, if not, what is the best way of overcoming this problem by making local legislation work?
(*Sir Adam Ridley*) Like the Stock Exchange, we think this is a very important and neglected area and I think many others observing the scene do so. It is in a sense an extremely important stage, too, because Commissioner Bolkestein and his new Director General, Alexander Schaub, have just published in their new strategy review the first serious document recognising the need to pay attention to this area, so

Lord Walpole *contd.*]

it is a very fruitful moment for us to be musing on it. May I take a step back? There are many issues lurking here. The first is that there is something odd about introducing legislation and regulation when what you are really doing is trying to remedy the unenforceability or the lack of enforcement of existing regulation. What we have been saying in relation to the ISD is that it is not being enforced or it is difficult to enforce. We are then having, piling Pelion on Ossa another great armful of regulation and legislation. This is not an anti-bureaucracy or an anti-regulation point, it is just a matter of plain logic. One can go a little further than that, though. If you look at what has to happen when you introduce very complex rules in the financial sector, you have to ask who is going to ensure that rules, when implemented notionally, are actually put into practice. We can see a hierarchy, with the European institutions themselves at the top, then governments, then trade associations, then firms and citizens and consumer groups and retail organisations. Having produced very complex legislation in the financial area, the Commission has not, for the most part, had a consistent policy, as we understand it, of having any follow-through. In some areas such as electronic communications, they do have a unit actively pursuing implementation, in others they do not. So there is a big gap there and they, poor things, have a tremendous pressure on their staff and resources. Outsiders always tell them that they are employing too many people and asking why they do not cut back, when actually they may need a lot more to do this properly. What should the role of individual national governments be? Interesting question. Manifestly there is a possibility, and I think the Commission recognise this, that when you produce a piece of community legislation, you need to ask how it is going to be transposed or translated into domestic rules and regulations or indeed self-regulation come to that. This process is now being debated and thought about by the team in D G Internal Market, but it has not really got very far. Some of those who have commented on the Lamfalussy report—and I am thinking of one of your distinguished specialist advisers –have also been picking up some of these issues. You can then go a little lower down and ask what the job of the trade associations is. The trade associations, if told that they have this task, could add it to the truly Titanic list of things they have to do, but what else we have on our plate has to be borne in mind and I will just illustrate it from LIBA's point of view. This year LIBA took off the web the details of the FSA's consultation documents and at the beginning of the year we counted 85, of which probably we would need to deal with 45, nearly one a week, on each of which we would need to consult our very busy members on in the middle of their working days. We already have between 12 and 15 major Community directives and consultations to work on and they will roll and roll and roll. We also have minor matters in the United States and I could go on. You see the point. With a staff of six directors, the likelihood that we could get involved in looking at the implementation and enforcement end of even one directive is very, very small. When you get to the level of the individual firms, they do not like to complain about the incompetence of governments in marketplaces in which they wish to perform, because they feel, not unsurprisingly, that if they go to the Italian regulator, or the French regulator, or the Dutch regulator and say they are discriminating against them, they will not be very popular. This is an insight which does not seem to have penetrated the minds of quite large numbers of people. I am not referring to our distinguished Houses of Parliament; but it is a very real problem. This rather long development of my answer leads you towards what we think is a particularly important area. None of us has done enough thinking about it, whether it be the Commission, the trade associations, the Treasury, the FSAs of this world. There is no point in cascades of even good rules and good legislation coming through, if we have not worked out how to put it into effect. May I just comment briefly on the EuroSEC issue? If you start from the hypothesis which I articulated at the beginning, there is an immense variety of different ways of skinning the cat in financial services markets; lots of different, funny markets and all sorts of different laws and legal structures. In some countries they regulate the banks this way, in others they do it that way. Some leave a big role to the stock exchanges, others have integrated FSAs. These realities should lead you to recognise very quickly that it would be impossibly difficult to create a unified regulator across the board, a unified FSA for Europe. That is not to say that analytically one could not imagine something much more narrow and focused. I have in my ill-spent past spent time dealing with the Lloyds insurance market, and in the light of that could see advantages in having a degree of international regulation for the insurance world. That is a rather special case; but anything broad is just unimaginable and I think it would explode under its own weight.

Lord Howie of Troon

53. Is your graphic phrase Pelion on Ossa is not unlike whistling in the wind?
(*Sir Adam Ridley*) The two have a lot in common, but I am afraid my Greek leaves me at this stage.

Lord Fearn

54. In paragraph 14 of your written evidence you refer to the threat to the attractiveness of the EU to non-EU issuers. Can you expand on this threat and whether the proposed measures will make the EU a more expensive place to raise capital compared with the US for instance? Could you explain whether by "issuers" you mean third country issuers?
(*Mr Baker*) Certainly there are major issues for third country issuers. Taking some examples, the major damaging effects of the Prospectuses Directive on the bond markets have been avoided as a result of very significant efforts by the UK government and by the European Parliament. Mr Wheatley described the fact that in the equity market there are still problems about the ability of issuers to choose where the competent authority is that approves the prospectus. There is a particular issue for third party issuers because a third party issuer essentially has to

Lord Fearn contd.]

choose which country he goes through. At least he has the choice to start with, but once he has chosen a country, he has to stick with that. So that is a respect in which third country issuers are at a disadvantage. On the ISD, it is much more a case of imposing restrictions upon the ability of intermediaries to operate within the market, which make it a less attractive market to operate in at a secondary market level. So the loss of flexibility in the secondary market has potentially a knock-on effect on the willingness of issuers to bring issues to the primary market in Europe.

(*Sir Adam Ridley*) May I take one illustration very quickly from the Prospectuses Directive, which graphically shows this, but I am not absolutely certain that this finally got voted. Suppose that you say to a non-EU company that, to issue a security, you must produce a prospectus containing accounts drawn up according to the European accounting standards. Suppose also that that company prepares its accounts to some other standards, for example American ones. Suppose that it costs them $10 million to do the preparation of the accounts to European standards, rather than the normal $250,000 for their domestic standards. This is a point cited to me by my colleagues in the International Primary Markets Association. It would be highly discouraging to anybody from outside the European company environment. That was a very serious risk which caused some acute anxiety during the negotiations for the Prospectuses Directive. That is just one good example.

55. So it is a real threat.

(*Sir Adam Ridley*) Yes and just to give you an illustration of how serious it was, the Treasurer of the General Electric Company in the United States, which is one of the biggest single private issuers of capital in the world and responsible for something like 60 or 70 billions of euro market debt, came to Paris to explain this problem to the CESR and a number of scales fell from eyes as a result. If General Electric Company chooses to issue debt in other parts of the world, then that will be business lost to us, probably in substantial measure. It is a very big burden if we get it wrong.

Baroness Cohen of Pimlico

56. I should perhaps repeat my declaration of interest for anyone who was not here. I am a director of the London Stock Exchange. LIBA, like the London Stock Exchange, carries a very heavy representational burden. We always feel we are carrying more representational burden than is wholly reasonable and I am sure you do too. Given that we are really the custodians of the expertise on how you run international markets, do we have enough of a team negotiating this? Is the central government team fully on side? Are there enough of them? Is there some way that the central government team, whatever I mean by that, some combination of ministers and Treasury, could be more useful?

(*Sir Adam Ridley*) I would put the thing this way. Historically this country was always slightly odd in not having a very well designed single focus for financial sector policy. This is not an ideological issue. To the extent that the successive governments of the day chose to think about it, you were never quite sure whether it was in the Treasury or the Bank of England or DTI or some other places, or whether it reposed with an individual expert, who might be brought in to do a study like Lord Bullock in the 1970s. When the FSA was created, that swept away a great deal of the expertise, quite properly if you like, and brought it together to the one institution, but with a very circumscribed clearly defined perimeter. That happened to be at much the same time as the enormous surge of importance of international policy as the Financial Services Action Plan was just beginning in 1997–98. At that stage the Treasury also faced the fact that it was introducing the Financial Services and Markets Bill here, which, you will recall, did take a certain amount of their time, indeed it probably nearly killed more than one of them. Looking at it as an ex-Treasury official, what I vividly recall is the great difficulty for the Chancellor of ever getting enough people for anything, because he had to be purer than driven snow, he never could really have as many people as he privately believed he needed. So to have had the expansion simultaneously in people on the domestic side for the FSMA and on the international side for the FSAP would have been incredibly difficult. I just do not know whether ministers and officials perceived the real need or not; even if they had perceived it, I doubt whether they could have achieved it. What we have seen subsequently was a sharp and significant response in staff in the recent year and a half. There has been a dramatic increase in the number of people and that, coupled with a lot of sophisticated work in the FSA, has kept our national and industrial noses just out of the water. So I give the Authorities a lot of compliments for what they have done recently, but I then end up rather wistfully and sadly saying we are only just able to swim forward even so. I think I can say from my own position that there has to be a sustained and continuing effort, whether or not this FSAP comes to anything. We have to recognise that in European Policy making the degree of complexity of the issues, combined with the complex sequence of political and semi-political and semi-technical negotiations, is of a different order of magnitude compared to domestic policy where we just go down to the FSA; or come in here to your Lordship's House, to commend to you some amendment that would preserve the Chinese wall, to give a quaint example which some of you may recall, in the Financial Services Markets Act.

Chairman

57. Sir Adam and Mr Baker, you have been extraordinarily patient with us. Your oral evidence today has been splendidly clear and very, very helpful to us. Is there anything you would like to add where you feel we have not touched on something or not quite got the emphasis right that we ought to bear in mind in our deliberations?

(*Sir Adam Ridley*) One very focused comment on what the markets at issue are. This picks up from something Martin Wheatley said. If we get these policies badly wrong, quite often we are actually

Chairman *contd.*]

working to weaken a world marketplace. Certainly we are damaging the relationships between many of the most important members of the Community. Not only are we are probably differentially damaging London and its wholesale business, but I suspect that we often fail to sit down and think of the rest of the world. This is the bit we have the least perception of. I would merely say of that importance, that it is very difficult for us to say anything without it sounding boastful.

58. I have to say that this is something I picked up at the end of our discussions with the Stock Exchange and we are very mindful of the strong way in which you express that in your written evidence. Given that, and we now take the point here, in practical terms in what way could we in our deliberations, in due course our report and discussions in Europe with MEPs and institutions and investors and so on, help to achieve better progress on those issues and that weight of importance of London in a global environment, a better balance, over the ensuing months? In other words, what remains to be done which has not been done or you fear may not be done?

(*Sir Adam Ridley*) That is a difficult question. We are quite a long way down the road as far as much of the immediate FSAP work is concerned. I suspect what I would say is looking a bit beyond that. We, as an organisation, dealing with highly intelligent businesses by all standards, very well organised, constantly discover how little we know, any of us, about anything outside our own immediate parish. The same is true even of the top lawyers who come to work with us from the big City houses, from the FSA or from wherever. So the first point I am making is the overwhelming value and significance of a well thought out consultative procedure. If you do not get the consultations on the technicalities right, you are slaughtered, and the results would be catastrophic and you have no idea what you end up doing. That is

one area where a lot of progress has been made, but it is very patchy and, dare I say it, Europe has a great deal to learn from the UK here. The FSA, with this government's help, has been sticking to some extremely good consultative standards; they are not perfect but we have to build round that. If you do not have them in Europe, then that is much worse. The second area is much more difficult because it is the politics, the perception of whose interests these policies serve. I would merely say, looking at it from our point of view, with our small staff and small working groups, trying to run something like a piece of concerted international diplomacy on about five or six issues at once and probably in two continents—I am referring to the United States as well as the Investment Services Directive—that it is quite impossible. We have to find ways of addressing these issues and find ways of organising ourselves so that we both get more representation; a more dispassionate representation and ensure it is not wrongly badged as the worst kind of Union Jack promotion. We can do a certain amount. The third bit is to go on building on the increasingly effective partnership with Whitehall and the FSA, which has been really getting very much better. I think the interest you all take helps immensely and the questions which have been asked in your Lordships' House, as well as in the House of Commons, in recent months and years have helped a lot.

59. Do you want to add anything, Mr Baker?
(*Mr Baker*) I always let Sir Adam have the last word.
(*Sir Adam Ridley*) A self-refuting comment.
Chairman: You may think that I say this to every witness but I assure you I do not, not with the same warmth. Thank you very much indeed for today's evidence.

MONDAY 14 JULY 2003

Present:

Cohen of Pimlico, B.   Walpole, L.
Fearn, L.   Woolmer of Leeds, L.
Shutt of Greetland, L.   (Chairman)

Memorandum from the British Bankers' Association

1. The British Bankers' Association has been closely involved in lobbying on behalf of its members in relation to key FSAP measures and also in the creation of the Lamfalussy process, the Securities Committee and the Committee of European Securities Regulators (CESR). We have made many individual submissions to the EU institutions and others.

2. We have deliberately kept our responses short in view of the request in the Call for Evidence.

A. The Financial Services Action Plan

3. Progress to date has been reasonably good if measured by the number of pieces of legislation passed. However (1) some of the most difficult measures have been left until last eg the Investment Services Directive (2) there are issues about the quality of some of the legislation.

4. It is difficult to judge whether progress to date has, overall been beneficial or deleterious. The biggest threat to UK interests is the threat that some of the legislation is too narrowly European in focus and potentially could damage the competitiveness of global markets based in the City of London.

5. The development of the Lamfalussy process is improving the weight being given to UK experience of financial services. A significant negative factor, however, is the fact that many EU Member States have predominantly retail financial services markets and do not always appreciate the importance of global wholesale markets.

6. The main outstanding matters under the FSAP are: Implementation of the Basel Accord through a Regulatory Capital Directive, the Investment Services Directive, the Transparency Obligations Directive and the Prospectus Directive—although the latter is nearing completion. There are a range of key issues which will need to be resolved including (1) market structure and best execution issues in the ISD (2) quarterly reporting in the Transparency Obligations Directive and (3) issues of timing of adoption, consistency of supervisory approach and flexibility of legislation and rule-making under the Regulatory Capital Directive.

B. Implementation and Enforcement

7. It is too early to reach a definitive view but there are many positive signs (see Michael McKee's letter of 13 Feb 2003 to the Commission on the Lamfalussy process) attached. The Lamfalussy process should be seen as an evolving process. Changes will need to be made as the stakeholders gain more experience of the process.

8. The Commission will be responsible for effective enforcement and implementation. It is planning to work more closely with Member State governments on implementation issues. We support this in principle. It is too early to say how successful this new approach will be—but if properly resourced it should be more effective than current practice. Competition regulators will have a continuing role in helping to break down inappropriate barriers within the internal market. Once the current reorganisation within DG Competition has been completed we would expect that DG Competition would continue to have an important role working closely with DG Market.

9. It is impossible to give definitive views about issues which will arise as the single market framework is implemented and enforced. One could expect, however, that closer attention to enforcement could produce resistance in some areas due to a wish to protect sectors or institutions which may be regarded as economically vulnerable in a truly integrated single market.

10. there are a range of non-regulatory barriers which have been identified in the past—different cultural attitudes and expectations are among the most significant, administrative inertia and lack of knowledge of community law are also important.

C. The future

11. It is extremely important to avoid a flood of new EU legislation. The FSAP measures which are being adopted and will soon be implemented will create a heavy burden of change on EU financial institutions. We would oppose significant new measures. We note that, in any event, substantial work will soon be done in relation to company law under the EU's Company Law Action Plan.

12. The changes resulting from the FSAP will have an impact on the competitive position of London and EU markets. Much of the BBA's work is directed towards ensuring that the changes either have a positive impact, or minimise any negative impacts. We consider that the laws most likely to have a significant impact on London and on EU competitiveness have not yet been passed. They include the Investment Services Directive and the Regulatory Capital Directive.

9 June 2003

Annex

BBA comments on Lamfalussy process

The BBA has participated in dialogue with the Commission and the Lamfalussy Wise Men Group since the inception of the Wise Men's mandate. Since the implementation of the Lamfalussy process the BBA has participated at all levels of the Lamfalussy process—inputting amendments and proposals at Level 1 in relation to Lamfalussy style Directives, submitting consultation responses to CESR, participating in a CESR Consultative Working Group (Market Abuse), attending and presenting at CESR open meetings and discussing with the Commission a range of aspects of the Lamfalussy process. In addition, as a member of the European Banking Federation, the BBA has been an active participant in the EBF's work on Lamfalussy and has input its views into the EBF's submission to the IIMG.

In the context of the proposal to extend Lamfalussy we submitted a substantial paper which contained many comments on the current Lamfalussy process which we consider to be of use to the IIMG. We have already submitted this paper to you separately but, for convenience, we attach a fresh copy. (Not printed)

In view of this we are confining our additional comments to a small number of salient points.

Lamfalussy in General

We have the impression that a range of institutions are putting forward a variety of criticisms of Lamfalussy in action to date. We do not consider Lamfalussy to be perfect but we consider that criticisms should be seen in context. We continue to consider that Lamfalussy is the right approach for the present and immediate future for the EU.

The context is as follows:

— Lamfalussy has only just begun and all the parties involved are feeling their way with the process. Any criticism of performance to date must be seen in this light. Longer experience may show such criticism to be valid—but equally experience may result in modifications which improve the position.

— At present, as the deadlines for the Financial Services Action Plan approach quickly, a highly artificial situation has been created whereby the Lamfalussy process is being operated within unrealistic timeframes. This inevitably squeezes the time available for good quality industry consultation.

Our comments, therefore, must be seen in this context. They are as follows:

Lamfalussy Level 1

We do not consider that either the Market Abuse Directive or the Prospectus Directive Proposals can be regarded as genuine Lamfalussy Level 1 Proposals. Both were largely drafted before the Lamfalussy process was approved and are, in essence, old style Directives with some Lamfalussy type provisions providing for Level 2 implementing measures grafted on.

Consequently the first genuinely Lamfalussy style Proposal is the Investment Services Directive Proposal of November 2002.

This Proposal has benefited greatly from an extensive consultation process of around 18 months and this is positive evidence of the Lamfalussy process working well. Overall the text of the Proposal is much more acceptable than some of the early consultation proposals.

However, there were some significant last minute changes made at the political level just prior to publication of the Proposal. There is an issue about the right balance between technical consultation and political decision making. The provisions which were inserted at the last moment are fairly impractical and would have benefited from technical expertise in their drafting.

Two other general points are noteworthy in the ISD Proposal. The first is that the Proposal is very detailed for a framework Directive. There are a number of areas of the Proposal where we would consider that much of the detail is excessive for a Level 1 framework Directive. In part we consider that this may be due to the Commission drawing upon CESR work intended for use at a lower level (say Level 2 or Level 3) and including it in Level 1 text. Examples would include some of the provisions of Article 19 on best execution and much of the detail of Article 18 on conduct of business requirements.

We recognise that in the early stages of the Lamfalussy process it is necessary for the European Parliament and the Council to gain confidence in the process and that, in consequence, it is not necessarily appropriate to provide for too many Level 2 implementing measures. However, notwithstanding this we consider that the balance could be improved.

The second point is that, nonetheless, the Proposal does contain a large number of provisions calling for Level 2 implementing measures and we consider that a smaller number of provisions would be more appropriate. There is a real danger that if the law made at Level 1 and Level 2 is overly detailed that the result is an excessively rigid straitjacket for investment firms limiting market flexibility, innovation and economic growth. More consideration should be given to subsidiarity and the use of either CESR standards or rules made by national regulators on a co-ordinated basis to ensure a higher degree of flexibility.

Lamfalussy Level 2

Level 2 has been characterised by very short timeframes within which CESR has to deliver technical advice to the Commission. These timeframes are in part engendered by the deadlines set by the Council for the Financial Services Action Plan but we have a sense that the Commission is shortening the deadlines more and more as the 2005 deadline looms closer. The only logic for this is meeting the deadlines and the result is that the time for CESR to consult with the industry is inappropriately short. The more complex the legislation and the mandate the more inappropriate this is. Consequently a difficult timetable for the Market Abuse first mandate has turned into an almost impossible timetable for the Prospectus first mandate (if quality technical advice is the desired outcome).

We would advocate a better balance to give more chance of a better quality product. Ideally CESR should have one year to deal with a complex mandate—this would allow two rounds of consultation—a longer first round and a shorter second round. We consider that this would considerably improve the quality of the technical advice.

We also notice that the quality of the technical advice is greatly improved where the issue is one which CESR has previously consulted upon prior to a mandate. So, for example, the stabilisation aspects of the Market Abuse first mandate had been the subject of previous CESR consultation and were much improved in consequence.

By way of contrast much of the Prospectus Directive mandate had not previously been consulted upon. Consequently we would advocate, where possible, preparatory work by CESR involving industry consultation.

We would also suggest that CESR could improve its "expectation management" by giving better advance notification of what the industry can expect in terms of meetings and consultation. Towards the end of the first market abuse mandate CESR released some draft text of proposed technical advice just ahead of an open meeting which was a last opportunity for the industry to comment.

This fell far short of a second round consultation but, in the context of the deadline given by the Commission it was a genuine attempt by CESR to give the industry some text to inform the discussion at the open meeting. As such it is something which we support.

However, CESR did not explain this to the industry or to attendees at the open meeting and, consequently, many attendees had the impression that CESR was seeking to shut down discussion and debate and give limited opportunity for analysis of the draft technical advice.

While the industry would still have been concerned about the limited time available there would have been greater understanding of the constraints facing CESR and the attempts which CESR were making to give meaningful feedback to the industry.

IIMG approach to analysis of Lamfalussy process

One thing which has become apparent to us through our involvement with Lamfalussy work is that many market participants, trade associations and EU institutional participants are still relatively unfamiliar with the Lamfalussy process and how it operates in practice. At times this leads to unrealistic expectations of what a particular part of the process can be expected to produce.

We would suggest that it would be helpful for the IIMG first report to reiterate the outline of the process set out in the Lamfalussy report of 2001 and to describe how the Lamfalussy process actually operates in practice today. This approach of benchmarking the process against the report would assist understanding of the process and could also form the basis for some comments upon the extent to which the current process is appropriate and a practical implementation of the ideals of the report.

Michael McKee
Director
Wholesale & Regulation

13 February 2003

Examination of Witnesses

MR IAN MULLEN, Chief Executive and MR MICHAEL MCKEE, Executive Director, British Bankers' Association, examined.

Chairman

60. Welcome to you both, Mr Mullen and Mr McKee. Thank you for your evidence, in which you have very cleverly managed to be exceptionally brief and yet managed to include quite a lot, a great skill. We have read them all with great interest and our questions will touch upon, as you know, two or three of the elements of the submission. Is there anything you would like to open the batting with before we go to the questions?

(*Mr Mullen*) Yes, I think so, my Lord Chairman, perhaps a little bit of context as to who we are and what we are about. The British Bankers' Association, as the name would suggest, represents the industry in the UK. However, of our 250 members—the large banks that are present in the UK—only some 70 of those are actually British and that reflects the fact that many of the banks that are here in the UK are here because of London and the wholesale market and, depending on the criteria you use, of course, London is 25-35 per cent of the wholesale financial services in Europe. So of those members, when I say that 71 are British, many of those 71 are focused primarily on the wholesale markets also. Therefore, the focus of regulation and law, one would say on the wholesale markets, tends to be of a prudential regulatory focus whereas with the retail markets it is conduct of business. Some 60-70 per cent of our law and regulation now comes to us by way of Brussels and, therefore, at the British Bankers' Association a great deal of our attention and focus is placed on Brussels, particularly so with regard to the European Banking Federation, which is a Federation consisting of the 15 EU countries, plus the Norwegians, the Swiss and the Icelanders. When I first took on this role just over two years ago I thought that the European Banking Federation was perhaps an association of associations with maybe a bridge too far. In fact, in its 40 years the European Banking Federation has proved itself to be very effective; the reason being that time and again it comes up with a consensus view on matters of financial law and regulation. The Commission and the Parliament, as they become more important, will almost always listen to the pan-European industry voice than they will the special pleading of a pressure group or a sovereign state. At the moment I am pleased to say that I am the Chairman of the Executive Committee of the European Banking Federation and will be for a couple of years; it takes up a great deal of our time.

61. Thank you very much. Let us start where you finished. If that is the case, why is it that a number of witnesses have said to us this whole business of the Action Plan got a long way down the line before proper and further consultation really started to happen, because this has been a recurring theme? If they listen very carefully to you, why were they not listening in the early days?

(*Mr Mullen*) Let us start on two things. One is the Financial Services Action Plan, and concurrently there was the decision to implement the Lamfalussy process. Should we describe that? I think you are fairly aware of them. The speed with which the implementation of the Financial Services Action Plan commenced, I think, took everyone somewhat by surprise, and just the weight of legislation going through a fairly hard pressed Commission caught both the Commission and the industry by surprise. Michael, would you like to come in?

(*Mr McKee*) Yes. Maybe if I could add some other points to that. I think historically Europe has not tended to consult much. The Commission has always had an informal open ear to associations like ours, to the European Banking Federation, et cetera, but formal consultation is not something that has tended to be the norm either from the Commission itself, and even more particularly from other Member States in Europe. The consultative process the UK has developed has, of course, itself predominantly developed most strongly over, say, the last five to ten years and does not tend to be the norm in other Member States, although some do have consultative processes. There has been an element of conforming to what would have been seen as the European norm of less consultation; that has been one issue there. The other thing is it is correct to say that Lamfalussy began in and around the same time as the Action Plan, but it did follow a little bit behind. So certainly we saw the creation of the Lamfalussy group as an opportunity to encourage Europe to be stronger in the consultative side. I think that a number of trade associations and others who made representations to the Lamfalussy group were extremely successful in inculcating a better consultative approach, and that is why it has developed more with the latter directives rather than the original directives.

Chairman *contd.*]

62. In your evidence in paragraph four you said that you cannot yet judge if progress has been "beneficial or deleterious" because of the risk that legislation may be too "narrowly European" and it could damage the competitiveness of the global markets based in the City of London. As you appreciate, we want to appraise negative risks but, equally, we want to make sure that we do not fail to see the beneficial opportunities. Can you give specific examples where you think there appears to be the possible risk of damage?

(*Mr Mullen*) I think the Regulatory Capital Directive is a case in point. Here you have a large and important piece of legislation to our industry. In fact, as you would all know, this finds itself born not of the EU, it is a global initiative through the Basel Committee, and this is Basel 2. Basel 1 has served us well in regulating, or allowing capital to be dispersed across the industry in an effective way. The requirement is now that capital be better apportioned according to the risk, and there is a danger in this that the Basel Accord itself is too complex and too prescriptive. Also, the Basel Accord was designed for large international banks and there was an initiative by the G12 particularly that it should be applied universally to all banks. As you may now know, the US has decided that they will, in fact, only apply it to large complex banks whereas in Europe, we have decided to implement the Capital Adequacy Directive—which is the application of the Basel Accord—not only to all 10,000 banks but also to the broader financial services industry. This is a huge undertaking. It is particularly of concern where the Capital Adequacy Directive is being implemented where the Americans have taken another route. One of the dangers that we will have, I am sure, in implementation is a tendency for sovereign nations to look at special pleading for their own particular areas of concern. One that has been widely publicised would be the Germans and their concern with the Mittelstam, their middle to medium-sized markets. So that is an area where that particularly important part of the Financial Services Action Plan could have long and deep concerns to us.

(*Mr McKee*) One of the things there is, of course, that is looking forward and that is one of the reasons why we cannot be certain yet whether the Action Plan is a positive or a negative, looking at it right across the board. The Capital Adequacy Directive or, indeed, the Capital Directive that, together with the Investment Services Directive and possible action in relation to clearing and settlement, those are three very critical pieces of European action. I say action because it is not clear whether the work in clearing itself will be legislative or not at this stage, so we cannot tell how they will work out. We are hoping that they will work out in a positive fashion, but we are not certain on that. You have asked let us look at the positive side. There are some Action Plan pieces of legislation which I think we could definitely be positive about. The Pensions Directive, for example, I think we do look at that and say this will make it easier to develop a more pan-European pensions market. That has got to be good for Europe as a whole and it will make other Member States more flexible in their pension arrangements. It probably will not make our UK arrangements any more flexible, but the positive thing is that there is nothing really detrimental which has come out of the legislation *vis-à-vis* the UK pensions market and, because it makes the European regime generally much more flexible, we see that as positive. Also, the Collateral Directive is a positive piece of legislation, although I think its impact overall is in many respects smaller, in that a lot of work had already been done to work around some of the problems that the Collateral Directive fixes. Nonetheless, that is a useful directive because it underpins the operation of the wholesale markets in relation to refills, for example. Overall, I think when you look at the Action Plan it is primarily a plan that helps bring many other Member States up to a higher standard than their legislation previously was at. That is not to say that the UK is by any means perfect in a European context. We have had very well-developed financial services and financial markets and, to that extent, often the difficulty is that certain Member States want to preserve a particular part of their market, or a particular legal area of significance within their own legislation. They then translate that, or seek to translate that on a pan-European basis, and that then can create problems for the way the London markets work.

63. We will return to that issue, I can tell you.
(*Mr Mullen*) Yes.
Chairman: Forgive me if I gee you up a bit. Lady Cohen?
Baroness Cohen of Pimlico: Can I just have a quick unpick of the Capital Adequacy Directive?
Chairman: This is where Lord Shutt is coming in. Lord Shutt is going to cover not merely that but the various elements you have covered. Your question was more detailed, was it not?

Lord Shutt of Greetland

64. Yes, my Lord Chairman. In the document that you have sent to us, on the first page A3, you talk about issues of the quality of some of the legislation. Then you set out in paragraph six the main outstanding matters, and there are three outstanding matters: market structure and best execution issues; quarterly reporting; timing of adoption, consistency of supervisory approach versus flexibility of legislation and so on. Can you tell us, briefly, what the risks are from poor decisions—because you are talking about quality—and then balance that with comments on benefits which might flow from good decisions?

(*Mr Mullen*) Yes. Again, if we look at the Capital Adequacy Directive and I focus on that because of its huge impact on our business. As I said earlier, a decision has been taken to apply the directive to financial services firms generally within the EU and this is an enormous undertaking, and as I say, exacerbated by the fact that the US has decided to follow a different route—what you might call Basel 1 with US characteristics. What we may have is excessive lobbying from sovereign states in seeking to apply the directive within their own countries in a way that is protectionist, and this is a real risk.

(*Mr McKee*) The benefit that flows, if we get it right, is that by prompt implementation and putting

Lord Shutt of Greetland *contd.*]

it through the legislative process quickly and giving adequate flexibility, we can get the benefits that are intended to flow from the Basel Accord. On the one hand, in particular for smaller banks there is the possibility that, for example, you are lending to small and medium-sized enterprises who will be treated better than under the current Accord, so that would be a potential benefit to flow for smaller banking institutions or for, in fact, bigger ones lending to SMEs. On the other hand, you have the internal ratings based approach and that can give you significant benefits if you are sophisticated in your risk management and utilise that well.

(*Mr Mullen*) Yes. There will be winners and losers in this and those who might not benefit as much are remaining strangely silent but, as the Accord is applied, I think that you will see some considerable tension arising.

(*Mr McKee*) Yes. Maybe then if we move to another piece of legislation, one that no doubt you will have heard about before is the Investment Services Directive and, in particular Article 25, which is the mandatory code disclosure provision. Now there has been a lot of tension and discussion and negotiation around this Article. In general, the proponents of Article 25 and, indeed, those who are trying to strengthen it further, broadly speaking, Franco-Italian, their approach, I think, in our view, is likely to prevent the proper development of a genuine pan-European market in equities because it will tend to encourage business to continue to be done on-exchange in other countries and, indeed, may well encourage business that is already being done off-exchange in the UK to be done on national exchanges in other countries. We feel that is not positive. The reason for that being that the off-exchange business that is really generated, particularly in the wholesale sphere, is generally done at better prices and cheaper for the consumers. In the UK the retail service provider network, which has been created in the UK context, is also doing business with retail brokers at prices that are inside the London Stock Exchange and, therefore, our concern is that Article 25 could damage some of that business. We are concerned as well that liquidity may move outside of the European market—that is a risk at any rate—because the business cannot be done as profitably in Europe as it can be done in the US, or in Asia; so that is the downside. The upside would be that if Article 25 were deleted—and I am not suggesting that necessarily is what will happen; the state of negotiations currently do not necessarily suggest that will definitely happen—if it did happen, we believe that would encourage more of a drive towards competition and towards more genuinely pan-European markets. One of the consequences would be that some of the smaller markets might well disappear and, of course, if those markets are located in particular Member States, then naturally they have an interest in seeking their preservation.

(*Mr McKee*) It is an emotive issue. I remember the head of the Spanish Exchange saying to me that this was the market where the value of his country's assets was established, and it was anathema to him that this would move outside the sovereign state. One can understand this.

Chairman

65. Yes. We have come across this many times in evidence and the problem of the stock exchange being a bit like state airlines and other securities.
(*Mr Mullen*) Yes.

Baroness Cohen of Pimlico

66. I would just like to have a go at the Capital Adequacy Directive because I think I understood the point you were making there. I used to do capital adequacy and there are rules. I cannot see, applying the same rules which you apply to a big group to a little group, how good can come?
(*Mr Mullen*) There are graduations of application. There is the standard method, which is an improved Basel 1 approach. Basel 2 then has the IRB approach the Internal Ratings Based approach—which is a methodology that allows large banks that have developed their own credit and market and operational risk methodology to convince the regulator of the efficacy and effect of that, and then benefit by a lower capital weighting.

67. Everything we do in America is dead safe, therefore, we do not need to have the same structure. It is share one capital come whatever.
(*Mr Mullen*) I would say probably in Britain we are the leader of the risk-based approach, but it tends to be the more sophisticated investment banks, yes.

68. What are the objectives saying—that we in the British bank companies are not really sophisticated enough to do that, so we are going to be disadvantaged?
(*Mr Mullen*) They are not at a disadvantage. If you apply proper financial risk theory, then because you have a broad distribution of risk across the Mittelstam or, indeed, with ourselves with our large retail markets here in the UK, then these organisations will benefit considerably.
If there is to be a bias towards who would benefit from Basel 2, then it will tend to be those banks who have a strong retail presence, and particularly within the mortgage markets, whereas those with a large operational risk and complex products will be those where the risk is looked at far more keenly.

69. Right.
(*Mr Mullen*) So you are apportioning the risk to where it is most keenly felt.

70. I understand. The Clerk has reminded me that effectively, I have an interest to declare, which I expect you knew, I am a director of the London Stock Exchange.
(*Mr Mullen*) Yes.

71. I should properly have declared it and I am sorry I did not in the first place. Against that background, what precisely is going wrong with the Capital Adequacy Directive, because I do know that something is?
(*Mr Mullen*) There is concern that in an effort to apply risk more completely and more effectively that there is over-prescription, and with over-prescription you get a complexity that what one might hear is that the Quants have taken over. The boardrooms and, indeed, executive committees of banks have been

Baroness Cohen of Pimlico *contd.*]

very aware of what has been happening for some time now and their input is coming in, and the need to have a cost benefit effect from Basel is now an issue well voiced and being taken care of.

Lord Fearn

72. In paragraph C12 you say that the changes resulting from the FSAP will have an impact on the competitive position of the London and EU markets. You were beginning to touch on them in answer to Lord Shutt's question. Do you have a view on the most important level at which these "laws" may have an impact? There are arguments that key elements should be pushed down to Level 3. Is there a risk that such legislation would be open to manipulation by national regulators to protect national interests?
(*Mr Mullen*) My legal colleague will answer.
(*Mr McKee*) Yes. I think our view is very much that, on the one hand, Level 1 at present is still more detailed than it needs to be. In many ways the whole principle behind Lamfalussy Level 1 is that the enduring principles should be kept in Level 1. Now one of the practical problems—and it is a practical political problem—has been that the European Parliament is somewhat cautious, shall we say, about the whole Lamfalussy process. From their own institutional perspective they have reasons to be cautious, because some matters that otherwise would be dealt with in the primary legislation are being moved down through the Lamfalussy process to Level 2. Because of that concern and the fact that the Parliament has not really signed up fully to the idea of Lamfalussy in the long term at this point in time, the result is the legislation that is currently being drafted is still at Level 1, probably close to being as detailed as it was before Lamfalussy. So that is Level 1, and I would say it is too detailed. Level 2, it is difficult for anybody to say much about Level 2 at this stage. I am on the Consultative Working Group of the Committee of European Securities Regulators, which has been looking at the Market Abuse Directive and the Level 2 implementing measures to be made under that Directive. Those are the first sets of implementing measures to be made at all through the Lamfalussy process and none have yet been made. The first set has just been, as it were, to use our terminology "laid" before the European Securities Committee and the Parliament a few days ago. It looks like that will be relatively detailed legislation. One of our concerns is, although it is difficult to tell at present, that too much Level 2 detail may come in, because if Level 1 is fairly detailed you then get a little more detail at Level 2. Our concern is really that in the UK a lot of rules that would be made by FSAP rules will, in fact, be made effectively as Level 2 legislation, or maybe even Level 1 legislation in the European context. We do see that as a concern and we do think that more could be done at Level 3. One of the practical problems we have at present is the Financial Services Action Plan deadlines mean that everybody in the European legislative process is working at a very fast speed to try and get the current legislation through. That means that CESR has not had a proper chance to consider how Level 3 will operate, and the national regulators are really only at

an early stage in thinking about what does Level 3 in Lamfalussy really mean. I think we see it as being at two levels. In my view, there is a CESR level—although CESR may or may not agree with that—where CESR could have a role in ensuring greater co-ordination, and harmonisation, and convergence across Europe at that level by setting standards perhaps. Also, there is a role for each national legislator and each national regulator in adapting some of these European standards for their own national conditions.

73. So could it be manipulated then?
(*Mr McKee*) I think there is always going to be a tension here between the need to develop greater convergence on a pan-European scale and the fact that notwithstanding that need, nonetheless, there are local factors which require adaption. The classic example here is what happens to those financial institutions who only want to do business in their own country? What happens to those consumers who only want to buy products within their own country? Now the pan-European legislation often will affect those institutions, those consumers, even though they have no interest in cross-border business. So you do have a problem there that a lot of purely domestic business is currently being affected, and additional costs are being incurred in implementing it in relation to legislation which is really designed for cross-border business.
(*Mr Mullen*) One would make the distinction between prudential regulation and conduct of business. Prudential regulation, particularly as it applies to the wholesale markets, quite obviously and normally is effective when you attempt to apply it to the pan-European basis. What is less obvious—and we are beginning to see this as we move into the retail markets—is that pan-European retail services are really quite product-specific. For instance, cards—both debit and credit cards—clearly have a pan-European future, the economies of scale and scope; similarly, with some insurance products and the uses of the Directive as well. Where you are looking at retail banking because of language, tax and custom, there tends to be a deep rooted predisposition with the consumer to maintain within their own locale. Unless there is—a personal opinion—more merger and acquisitional activity, the pan-European initiative in retail financial services will be less obvious. This has manifested itself too in this somewhat understandably parochial attitude towards conduct of business regulation.
Chairman: That has come neatly, if not, in fact, half-way through the question that Lady Cohen was going to raise with you.

Baroness Cohen of Pimlico

74. I do not think I have got really much more to ask about that one, except insurance companies. Where we have had British insurance companies maintain they are blocked from the German markets, is the FSAP generally going to assist that process? I cannot really get a feel for it never having known very much about selling retail products.
(*Mr Mullen*) Yes, I think it will. The area where we will see the Directive and where we will be able to

Baroness Cohen of Pimlico *contd.*]

gauge this is the Consumer Credit Directive, which is again a very large piece of legislation. It is not part of the Financial Services Action Plan but it is allied to it. Unfortunately, it is complicated by the fact that the Directive involves both mortgages and other financial services products, and what we might see is that directive becomes two; I think that is an important distinction. What will be manifest is the predisposition of, shall we say, southern European countries towards a Napoleonic code approach to legislation, particularly conduct of business. That means that they are more policy optimistic, shall we say, whereas our markets are more markets optimistic. They will look more at prescriptive consumer protection, whereas in our markets we are more disposed towards self-regulation. When I say "ours", it is not just the UK, it tends to be Northern Europe.

Chairman

75. Some evidence to us has rather implied criticism that other parts of the EU give more attention to approaching things from "a protecting the investor's" point of view, almost exactly what you said. If you were somebody who had got endowments, or life assured policies and so on—I am thinking of some well-known life assurer's business—do you not think that they might think our talk about self-regulation financial institutions being better than a small European country putting cautious rules down to the best advice might not be a good idea? It does ring a bit untrue in the light of the behaviour and the outcome of some British financial institutions recently, does it not?

(*Mr Mullen*) I think it depends, my Lord Chairman. If you take a spectrum of risk and at one end there is the widows and orphans issue—we will steal an insurance expression, *uberrimae fidae*, utmost good faith—and at the other end you have *caveat emptor*, depending upon the product, the level of where *caveat emptor* comes in will vary. If you take current accounts, the level of current account activity, the customer is more focused on convenience than he is on price. The longer the length of the product, whether it be a mortgage, a debt product, a lending product of greater length or an investment product, then you tend towards protection for the individual. The markets are so gauged that in the UK within our current account and, shall we say, the market that looks after the individual's working capital, that is self-regulated. Dr DeAnne Julius' lengthy report came out saying that our self-regulation was an exemplar of it, whereas it has been felt that with longer investment products there is need to have more statutory regulatory intervention. That would seem a sensible way of moving forward. In Europe, where you would default to statutory regulation, in the long run that is not good for the markets, but our business is about innovation and innovation will always front-run the regulator and if there is a default to statutory regulation, as has happened, then you will have innovation stifled, so therefore our self-regulation is that which stands between innovation and the late arrival of the regulator.

76. It did not do people who bought split trusts any good. I am just trying to understand from a wider point of view and looking at some of the record in the United Kingdom institutions, just taking another example and the way in which people had a lot of trust and faith in self-regulation of United Kingdom financial institutions, and how they have been deeply badly let down in split investment trusts.

(*Mr Mullen*) And the industry has injured itself because of this, because our business depends upon trust.

Baroness Cohen of Pimlico: It is well served in the mortgage market, however, perhaps, Chairman. Deregulating mortgages did a lot of good.

Chairman: I am just trying to balance how one sees this.

Lord Shutt of Greetland

77. In the papers that you have sent us we have your notes of your meeting at the Guildhall on 6 March where you end up by saying, "There are two issues on which it is particularly important that the EU institutions listen. The EU institutions need to pay more attention to ensuring a high quality of law". Now, there is a sense in which the law is the law but what do you mean by this "high quality of law"? Is this exceedingly detailed, or is this high quality law masterly vague? How do you define it? What is this quality? We are taking evidence later from the Financial Markets Law Committee but we need to know what you mean by this high quality law.

(*Mr Mullen*) What we mean is that in its application it can be properly enforced. Much of the legislation that is going through at the moment—and this is something that DG Markt and Director General Shaub is focusing on—has a general acceptance that much more attention will have to be focused on implementation and enforcement of the law and regulation. This is particularly the case—I see it myself starkly—as we bring these ten accession countries into the EU, and over the last seven years that they have been associates of ours, helping them educatively and in many other ways, there is a pressing need for them—and indeed for all of us—to realise that these directives as they are applied to local law and regulation can be enforced, and that is what I mean by good law.

78. So high quality law is an enforceable law? That is what you are really saying?

(*Mr Mullen*) Indeed.

(*Mr McKee*) Could I maybe add something? One of the things we mean as well by better quality law is law which is grounded in the reality of how the financial markets work. For example, when the Prospectus Directive proposal first came out it bore no relationship whatsoever to how the financial markets behaved in terms of the issuance of capital and new issuance, either in the equities markets or in the debt markets, so a significant element has to be how does this cohere with how the financial markets are working. That is one element. The other thing is that it has to be sufficiently flexible—in other words, at a sufficiently high enough level—to allow the capital markets to continue to grow, so there is an element of our earlier point saying that Level 1 needs

Lord Shutt of Greetland *contd.*]

to be high level, and even Level 2 should not be too detailed. This is critical because if it is too detailed there is a significant risk that the way in which different markets and different parts of the EU work will be constricted. We are not just talking here about the United Kingdom financial markets but equally the German financial markets and the French. That is a significant risk and it is a risk that is a concern right across the different banking associations that are involved in the European Banking Federation.

(*Mr Mullen*) The ability to have equivalence of action across the EU is of utmost importance. It is not part of the Financial Services Action Plan but anti money-laundering.

Chairman

79. In some of the evidence we have had, and I think you yourself touched on it, Mr Mullen, there is a concern that there has been a rush and that that has been affecting the quality and eventually the law will come out. We touched in question two on a number of issues that you said remain the key issues to be addressed.

(*Mr McKee*) That is right.

80. Yet the Commission is apparently hell bent and rushing to get these things completed by next April.

(*Mr Mullen*) Yes.

81. Is there compatibility between achieving high quality law and those timescales on those key issues? If so, would you on balance prefer to see the resolution of those matters taking more time even if deadlines are missed?

(*Mr Mullen*) That is the view of the British Bankers' Association and, indeed, the 4100 banks of the European Banking Federation. What we would like to see is the quality rather than the quantity of regulation and legislation improved.

(*Mr McKee*) I think what we would also recognise, though, is that the deadlines that have been set are deadlines set by the Council and therefore by all fifteen Member States, and the Commission in that respect—you are right—is hell bent on meeting those deadlines and it will say it is hell bent on meeting those deadlines because they have been set by the Council so I do not think that is going to give or change. Equally, however, our comments on quality are not just directed towards the current state of play on the deadlines but also towards the longer term and the situation once those deadlines have passed.

82. It is just possible we might want to return with a brief bit of correspondence on that but we will try to avoid it if we can.

(*Mr Mullen*) Not at all.

Lord Walpole

83. Can I ask you about your Hertig and Lee critique of the Lamfalussy process, and incidentally Dr Lee is appearing before us. I must say I think your opening sentence to the paper is one of the best sentences I have read for years: "It has been said that 'In Ireland the inevitable never happens and the unexpected constantly occurs'. The same is true of the European Union as a whole"—I think that is a

superb remark! In your summing up you cite the evidence for political will existing in the EU institutions—in other words, the Commission, the Council and the Parliament—but if it turns out to be insufficient to enforce these directives, do you foresee the political will to create a European SEC instead?

(*Mr McKee*) Thank you very much. Firstly I would say definitely that there would be no political will to return to the status quo before Lamfalussy, so that is unquestioned. If Lamfalussy were seen to fail at some point in the future, I think you would be into a new paradigm. Does that mean there would necessarily be a European SEC? It is extremely difficult to read the rules on that because you are in a situation where the Lamfalussy process we will certainly be working with and towards for several years to come and it seems to me it is a dynamic process and not something that is staying still. It has already developed considerably from the original Lamfalussy report. It is now in practice and, as it is developing, a whole range of us are contributing comments, criticisms and feedback—Mr Bishop among others is sitting on the Institutional Monitoring Group, so a lot is changing—and in itself it may transmogrify into something different from the original idea. So that is one possibility—that Lamfalussy may not be supported in its current form, for example, by the European Parliament but might change into something different and it is not clear what that might be. Will there be a European single regulator? I think it is very difficult to judge on that and I think it would be impolitic for me to say "Yes" or "No" to that. What is clearly the case is that there are some people in Europe who are already advocating that and will push it. On the other hand, as I have said in my paper and I think it is fairly clear at the moment, all the evidence suggests that Member States and their regulators are not in favour of that. Now is not the right time, and I would agree with that. I do not think that now—or indeed the next three, four or five years—would be the right time. There is too much diversity in Europe, both in terms of the financial markets and in terms of even the powers of individual regulators, for that to be a realistic outcome. From our point of view, the key thing would be that whatever comes out four or five years hence is that from a perspective of the London markets they are best regulated by somebody who is geographically close to them. That is absolutely critical so that is the key thing one way or the other from a United Kingdom perspective.

Baroness Cohen of Pimlico

84. I have a very short supplementary: if this whole process is being pushed too fast, is there some suggestion in your evidence that perhaps the outcome has to be an SEC in the end? What happens if you push through fast and end up with rather a mess? Is a European SEC possibly the default position?

(*Mr McKee*) I would say not necessarily. The big question for a start is what is the European SEC? For a start the SEC itself in the US is simply a regulator predominantly of the cash, equities and bonds market; you have the CFTC which regulates the

Baroness Cohen of Pimlico contd.]

derivatives market; you have the Federal Reserve Bank and the OCC regulating the banks; you have fifty different states regulating the insurers. Some people talk about the US SEC as though it were the FSA and I do not think that sort of a regulator could live or survive in a 25 country—perhaps 27 country—EU.

Baroness Cohen of Pimlico: Yes. That was the better question, or the answer to the question I did not quite ask!

Chairman

85. I suspect enforcement will probably be of more significance than regulation, but that leads me to one last short question to which I would like a short answer. By what date do you anticipate or expect at the current rate of progress there will be a single financial market in Europe?

(*Mr McKee*) I think in the wholesale markets we can confidently look forward to a pan European market in 2010.

86. And for retail would you care to have a guess?

(*Mr McKee*) The retail market I think is dependent upon mergers and acquisition, rather than cross-border activity.

(*Mr McKee*) I would draw a distinction between the wholesale market and bonds, which I think is pretty well here already, and in equities where to some extent some of the comments I made about the Prospectus Directive suggest to me that we would have a completely pan European equities market by 2010.

(*Mr McKee*) You will have local exchanges but the value transfer networks, the clearing and settlement, will consolidate across boundaries.

Chairman: We have already taken more time than we should have asked of you, and we are exceptionally grateful to you. Thank you so much for coming. I did indicate that there may be just one item we might want to exchange correspondence on, but I promise you we will avoid it if we can because you have already had more than enough on these matters. Thank you for coming.

Memorandum from Proshare

A. THE FINANCIAL SERVICES ACTION PLAN

What progress has been made to date? Has this been beneficial or deleterious to UK interests? Has sufficient weight been given to the position and experience of the UK financial services industry?

1. ProShare supports the principle of a single European market in financial services. We see considerable benefits for the private investor in having easy access to a well-regulated European securities market as well as considerable benefits from a single market for the UK companies raising capital and for The City of London as the most important financial centre in Europe.

2. The Financial Services Action Plan ("FSAP") is an extremely ambitious project with a demanding timetable. Of the 42 measures contained within, 35 are said by the Commission to have been completed. However, to complete the remainder of the Plan within the deadline of April 2004 will require an exceptional level of political agreement. Even then, no measure has yet been implemented and a great deal of work remains to be done to produce the second level of regulation essential to support the framework measures.

3. From our perspective, the progress made to date on the FSAP has generally not been beneficial to the UK private investor. In a number of regards (see below for details) we face the prospect of both less customer choice and higher charges. In addition, we are not convinced that protection for the private investor will be enhanced by measures in the FSAP and that they could well result in a reduction in the current levels of investor protection that we enjoy in the UK.

4. The UK financial services industry is perhaps unique in Europe as it includes both a world-ranking wholesale market as well as a long-established and large retail market. While we support the need for investor protection in the retail markets, increased regulation of the wholesale market is potentially damaging to both the UK and the EU's external financial activities.

5. In our experience, we think that this industry has been well represented by HM Treasury and the FSA. This is a difficult role, because despite the UK's role and experience, we are one Member State in a Community of 15. To lobby effectively, the UK must find allies among other Member States and for a variety of reasons, not just political ones, this is often difficult.

6. In addition, the UK financial services industry has, in our view, suffered from a lack of co-ordination and focus on the key issues and as a result has not always been effective in its lobbying.

What are the main outstanding issues that remain to be dealt with under the FSAP and what key issues will need to be resolved?

7. There are five areas that need to be resolved:

— Investment Services Directive—the key issues here are the potential threat to execution-only trading and changes to the Best Execution rules. Proposed changes requiring the introduction of suitability tests whenever an individual buys or sells a security will remove the current choice available to UK investors, many of whom prefer to use a straightforward execution-only service rather than pay for advice. In our experience, investors using these services understand that they take full responsibility for their decisions and adding a layer of protection is unnecessary and will ultimately lead to increased charges.

Agreement needs to be reached on this point and the new rules for Best Execution.In our view, investors are broadly content with the existing UK rules where the market operates automatically to find the best practice and many would find the proposal that would require investors to choose their execution venue quite baffling and overly bureaucratic.

— Prospectus Directive—in principle this should be of considerable benefit in creating a level playing field across the EU when shares are initially offered to the private investor. However a key area for ProShare has been the treatment of employees who are offered shares in their employer. At present UK companies are exempted for the requirement to issue a prospectus in this case. Other Member States have different rules and practices and these differences form a major barrier to the development of cross-border employee share plans. The latest draft of the Directive contains an exemption, but the wording is extremely vague and will not cover either unlisted companies or non-EU listed companies, such as US or Swiss companies. As these companies will in future have to bear the cost of producing a full prospectus when they issue shares to employees, this is likely to result in an overall reduction in financial participation in the EU.

— Market Abuse Directive—again this Directive, when completed, should be of great benefit to private investors across the EU in clamping down on insider trading or the misuse of relevant information. However in the UK we have a fairly new Code of Market Conduct introduced by the FSA. The main issue that remains to be resolved therefore is the extent to which the code will be subsumed by the MAD and there will be a "levelling down" of its powers and reach. This appears to be still a matter of considerable uncertainty.

— Transparency and Obligations Directive—The two key issues here are quarterly reporting and the dissemination of information to the market. We are not against the principle of quarterly reporting—many large UK companies and companies across the EU already report on this basis—but we would be very concerned if this was seen as anything but a supplement to the current FSA rules for the dissemination of market-sensitive information which work extremely well and add immeasurably to openness and transparency in the UK market.

— Modernising Company Law and Corporate Governance—this is an extremely important subject in terms of safeguarding shareholder rights and improving the very differing standards of governance that currently exist in the EU. Yet has only just appeared as a Commission Action Plan and the main proposals fall well outside the timetable of the FSAP. The aims of the FSAP cannot be achieved until significant improvements have taken place in this area.

B. Implementation and Enforcement

How successful do you expect the Lamfalussy process to be? Are there any changes needed?

8. In theory the process is a good idea. It introduces more expertise into the process and is open and consultative. However, the dominance of the process by CESR, the European association of national regulators has, in our view, not always produced new thinking but reinforced national approaches to regulation, often leaving the UK isolated. Commission officials, to give them their due, are approachable and will listen to concerns, but often lack the detailed industry knowledge and will therefore follow closely the CESR advice.

Who will be responsible for ensuring effective implementation and enforcement of the single market, after the Regulatory Framework is in place? How successful do you expect this process to be? What will be the role of competition regulators at EU and Member State level?

9. As this will presumably fall initially to a number of bodies—EU institutions, CESR, national governments and regulators, it will require exceptional co-ordination, co-operation and flexibility if this is to be successful. Moreover, there will need to be a focus on, and common understanding of, the "European vision" rather than nationalistic concerns. Given the number of bodies involved, there is every chance of

effective implementation and enforcement slipping between these various fingers. There is also an increased risk of non-compliance by Member States for their own domestic reasons and no effective sanctions.

10. A single EU financial services regulator could resolve these issues, but we think this is a long way off and will require a significant degree of political agreement and support form the Member States.

11. In the meantime, competition regulators could have an important role to play in exposing and challenging existing rules that, often unwittingly, discriminate against other players entering a particular market. A good example would be the legal requirement in France that allows only a French-domiciled mutual fund to hold savings collected from French employees.

What issues will arise as the single market framework is implemented and enforced?

12. Please see paragraph 9 above. In addition, a key issue will be the flexibility that Member State governments will introduce in the process that will allow the creation of not only a common floor of standards through the EU that will be enforced by local regulators but also preserve the right for bodies such as the London Stock Exchange to impose additional standards as it sees fit. At the same time, the flexibility should be so wide as to allow Member States to avoid compliance with the underlying Directive etc.

What non-regulatory barriers might impede the effective functioning of a single market for financial services?

13. These are significant and include:

— Lack of investor knowledge about cross-border securities and how to access this market.

— Lack of information on EU companies due to differing reporting and governance standards, differing attitudes to the dissemination of price-sensitive information.

— Cost issues—including trading charges, clearing and settlement fees, custody and currency (for non eurozone Members).

— Language

C. THE FUTURE

How do witnesses see the future development of a single market in financial services following the implementation of the FSAP? Are additional measures needed?

14. We believe there will be little impact on the private investor in the short to medium term. It has taken a generation for the UK consumer to become comfortable with the idea of buying, say, a German car, and while it may not take as long for him or her to become comfortable with the idea of buying a share in the German car company, we are still a long way from this. This will require a rebuilding of investor confidence generally as well as a much greater awareness by EU companies of private investor needs and how to service these effectively.

15. In particular, some Member States have a long way to go still to build an equity culture and the promotion of an awareness and understanding of the risks and rewards of direct and indirect equity investment by the general public is a major omission from the FSAP. This concentrates exclusively on investor protection and ignores investor education. In our experience, this is a critical factor in creating any healthy and vibrant retail investment market.

Will the changes resulting from the FSAP proposals have an impact on the competitive position of London and EU markets as a whole in a global environment?

16. The benefits of the FSAP in terms of financial harmonisation, together with the increasing role of the euro, should make Europe more competitive globally in raising capital in the wholesale markets. In addition, we think that London will still retain its position as the dominant financial centre in the EU. Aside from regulation, London benefits from an attractive corporate and individual tax regime (with the exception of stamp duty) and an unequalled environment in terms of the concentration of skills and experience contained within the City of London.

27 June 2003

Examination of Witness

MR MICHAEL SAVORY, Chairman, ProShare, examined.

Chairman

87. Good afternoon, Mr Savory.
(*Mr Savory*) Good afternoon.

88. You have been very patient.
A. It was interesting to hear the questions being put to my colleagues from the BBA.

89. We are going to ask you some different ones! Is there anything you would like to say by way of an opening remark? As you know, we have many questions to ask you.
A. I think it might be helpful for your Committee to know my credentials for being here and setting the scene because I am a stockbroker who has served the retail community now for some 40 odd years and I remain a stockbroker with HSBC, one of our biggest banks. I have also been engaged with one of our trade bodies, Atkins, in sitting on their European Committee studying particularly the Investment Services Directive but also the impact on the brokers providing services to the retail sector, but it is of course in my capacity as Chairman of ProShare that I am here today and, although I know your Committee has had a brief on ProShare, we would try and say that we do speak for the retail community. It is very hard to get a voice for retail investors anywhere in Europe but I would suggest that the United Kingdom is rather better placed with an organisation like ProShare and the activities that we undertake. Perhaps that introduction might help set the scene.
Chairman: If I may say so I thought the paper you submitted to us was exemplary, particularly the first two paragraphs. I remember an old professor of mine always drew a little hammer and a nail, and if you got exactly the point he would always have the hammer hitting the nail. If I could draw a hammer and a nail I would on the first two paragraphs!

Lord Fearn

90. You say that FSAP has generally not been beneficial to the United Kingdom private investor. Many commentators observe that FSAP has placed too much emphasis on retail investor protection, yet you think that the FSAP measures could result in a reduction in the current levels of investor protection that we enjoy here. Could you expand on your concerns and suggest what can be done at this stage?
A. I think we must not lose sight of the real aims of the FSAP which was investor protection in the first instance. The wholesale markets effectively can look after themselves. Our concerns really stem from some of the individual articles in individual directives and if I could just point to examples of that, if we take the Investment Services Directive, in particular Article 18 which attempts to comprise every provider of financial services with an obligation to give suitable advice to the retail investor. None of us would argue that you would otherwise want to give but suitable advice, but in so doing you have to have a financial understanding of the individual's ability to (a) understand the advice you are giving him and (b) also the detail of his knowledge of the alternatives that are available. Now, that requirement specifies for every

type of investor and yet there is a very large body of investors in this country who have already made up their own mind; they have sufficient experience to conduct their own business without seeking advice and certainly without giving background information in such depth. It is in that context that additional expenses will be incurred. To capture a full financial CV of every individual before you give advice or before you give a service is very expensive, and the market we are well known for, which is execution-only services, would be constrained by the additional costs associated with that clause. If you move to an area such as market abuse, we already have in this country a very high regime of controlling market abuse set by the Financial Services Authority, and to have a new directive whose standards are not necessarily as high but will have certain articles of compliance will add again to regulatory cost to the extent that the private investor will have to pay more for the services they get. Illustrations such as the Prospectus Directive and Transparency Directive all contain conditions of disclosure of information, standards of disclosure, which are more onerous on the provider of services and on each occasion that you apply those tests of regulation you are adding the burden of regulatory cost. That is what we are worried about, and that cost will have to be recovered by increasing the charges to the end user, the retail investor.

91. So will the situation improve or deteriorate?
A. A lot depends on the level to which this regulation is imposed. We are already seeing a lot of detail in Level 1 and in Level 2 and it is the extent of that detail that is worrying. Remember, beyond that we also have to go to the conduct of business rules. That is the detailed fine print. None of that is yet available. We are hoping that the conduct of business rules that the Financial Services Authority impose on us here in the United Kingdom will become a good model for other regulators around Europe—indeed, it is true to say that many regulators in some other countries do not have rules anything like those and hopefully they will use those as good examples. But whatever the circumstances we are going to have to re-impose new conduct of business rules which will inevitably lead to additional compliance expense within firms providing retail services.

92. In a nutshell, through you, Chairman, what is Article 18?
A. Article 18 is what is known as the suitability test. It deals with the applicable advice, the applicable service that you are delivering, and the competence of the investor to understand what you are delivering. Frankly, I would argue that it is quite a good clause if I was wearing strictly my training hat as an educator, because I believe in fact investors are better protected by understanding products than by not understanding them.

Baroness Cohen of Pimlico

93. I should declare an interest before I begin: I am a director of the London Stock Exchange. Your evidence says that increased regulation of the

Baroness Cohen of Pimlico *contd.*]

wholesale market is potentially damaging to both the United Kingdom and the EU's external financial activities. I do not think I disagree but could you expand on this comment, and are you talking about the impact on non EU issuers, or the impact on EU issuers?

A. One should start with the work the Corporation of London undertook in asking Sir Nigel Wicks to review the implications of the FSAP on the London wholesale market. The conclusions drawn from that review were quite clear: that more constraint, more rule and more regulation will lead to loss of flexibility, loss of creative planning, of new instruments and new methods of capital fund raising. There is a strong culture of innovation in the City of London, something which has been fostered over many decades and which has, in fact, led to the City itself being a very successful area geographically for attracting foreign investment and capital raising. The European example is one more of dissemination of those skills across other financial capitals within Europe by means of regulation, and it is the worry that this regulation will drive business away and drive creative thinking away. In today's terms of conducting business electronically you can really operate almost anywhere nationally around the world and the fiscal constraints are not there. Fortunately, however, we have the benefits of time zones and benevolent regulation and taxation, and these are all ingredients to encourage the wholesale markets to prosper in London.

94. That does apply equally to non EU issuers as well us, so that would be threatened?

A. If you look at the quantity of capital raised through London by non EU issuers it is very pronounced. The London Stock Exchange lists a whole wide variety of companies from Asia, Europe to emerging Eastern European states as well. They will go to where capital is available and London is an important source: they will remain in London until such time as other factors diversify. If fund management diversifies abroad, as could easily happen, capital fund raising will go with it in time.

Baroness Cohen of Pimlico: Of course. Thank you.

Chairman

95. In paragraph 7 of your written evidence you refer to the potential threats in the Investment Services Directive. You have touched already on some of that, particularly in relation to execution only trading and best execution rules. How can these problems be resolved? How would you like to see the Investment Services Directive changed in a way that would avoid those problems but still provide the investor protection that you, I am sure, would want to have in place?

A. The ISD itself has two polarised articles—I have referred to Article 18. I think it is true to say that by negotiation with our European counterparts and by persuading them of the merits of a diverse range of products we are winning that argument. We have taken that argument to Europe and we have put our case very strongly and I think we are close to getting agreement that certain carve-outs will be permitted allowing execution-only to be regulated as it is at the present time, without the full suitability clause to which I referred earlier. One of the more contentious clauses is Article 25 which deals with pre and post trade transparency or, as some will say, on-exchange trading—the concentration rule process whereby all transactions have to be functioned through a recognised exchange—and this process is well established in Europe but in the United Kingdom it has become very diverse. We have exploited all the alternative methods of price formation, particularly electronic transmission of information, and in that way we have been able to deliver services very cost effectively. One of the drawbacks of Article 25 would be to virtually eliminate the competitive options available by diverse means of price formation—imposing effectively exchange rules on anybody who operates an electronic platform. We do not feel that there is full understanding of the benefits of this across Europe. Again, it is one of the issues which engages us in trying to communicate to the practitioners how successful it has been for us and, indeed, showing illustrations of how successful it has been in the United States in driving costs down. If one just uses the United States as an illustration, transaction costs in the United States are less than one half than here in the United Kingdom, and we are significantly lower than the cost of executing trades on exchange in Europe. There is, however, an associated factor and that is experience. Europe does not have the same degree of wider share ownership that we have enjoyed in the last twenty years and, if you do not have large numbers of your population directly investing themselves, you do not have a need to develop the systems to support them and everything I have just described has come about through the benefits, if one can say that, of wider share ownership from privatisation.

96. So what is the solution that you would be putting forward to enable us to use our flexibility that has grown up over time?

A. We would like to see, of course, wider share ownership throughout Europe. We feel that participation by employees in their companies through all share employee schemes and more privatisation is the way forward.

97. Meanwhile, in this year's negotiations?

A. In the negotiations we keep putting our case and try to demonstrate how successful we have been. We are against one or two countries, though, who preserve the *status quo* because the charges are proportionally very much higher, and we do recognise that if you drive our model through Europe it will lead to job losses in the financial services industry and that is unpalatable.

98. Which countries, for example?

A. Italy and France are very pronounced in wanting Article 25 preserved as it currently is.

Lord Shutt of Greetland

99. I would just like to pursue this a little. You mentioned the electronic age and we also have the credit card age and so on. Most products that we want to buy we can go and buy. If you want to buy a motor car you cannot quite get it on credit card but

Lord Shutt of Greetland *contd.*]

not far off with some of the figures on credit cards these days. I am just trying to understand the nature. If I come off the street and see you are a stockbroker and come to your office, and say, "I woke up this morning and I see you have developed very well at your bank but I am not going to buy your stock, please get me 10,000 Deutsche Bank", and you do not know me from Adam, what are the problems and what makes this worse in terms of being able to execute that deal?

A. The key problem we have had up to now has been the lack of common trading platforms and settlement agencies to which we can adhere our service to meet that particular need and we sincerely hope that through market forces a lot of those issues will go away. We are already seeing integrated exchanges: we are seeing integration of settlement agencies and clearing houses. All of that is removing practical barriers. The truth, though, is that it has been a cultural problem up to now. There has been very little appetite by United Kingdom investors to invest into Europe and conversely from Europe into the United Kingdom. It is worth illustrating that there are amongst the top fifty companies in Europe only seven that are British, and that means that the remaining 43 should be sources of investment activity by United Kingdom investors but they do not participate; they simply do not involve themselves in that, and that lack of practical demand has meant that British institutions, British retail stock broking businesses, have not been adventurous. They have not gone to Europe and developed their services or capability there to execute from their customers in the United Kingdom and, vice versa, they have not sought investment activity in Europe. Now clearly the aim of the FSAP will be to break down those barriers, those passports, of entry. We already had it with the first Investment Services Directive. Theoretically that did allow you to conduct your business in Europe but nobody took the opportunity to exploit it. One of the practical reasons for that was simply there was too much business going on in local markets to even worry about going abroad.

100. But in the practical position of somebody saying here, "I want to buy this stock", does this make it worse or not?

A. It does not make it worse; it improves it but it improves it with a high degree of regulatory control which in itself makes it more expensive than probably to do it today.

101. But does it mean you have to spend a month finding out something about me and whether I have life insurance policies and all that sort of stuff?

A. Under Article 18, unless it is reformed, the answer is yes, we would have to go through a very extensive questionnaire to evaluate your financial circumstances in order to give you guidance as to what you can do. Hopefully that would not apply.

102. So it could be worse in that I could buy a car from a showroom but to buy this stock it could take a long time before all this information is processed?

A. In theory, yes. Hopefully the carve-out will be agreed and that problem will go away but as it stands, if you want specific advice, we would have to go through that detailed questionnaire and that process will have to be renewed certainly on a fairly regular basis and that will add to your delay—your choice.

103. And the price has gone?

A. The price may well have gone.

104. The question that I also want to ask is you have said that we cannot get much further with FSAP until company law modernisation and corporate governance is brought up to scratch. What are the problems on this, the practical implications of not making progress in those areas, and what has to be pushed forward as a matter of urgency?

A. I think we have to look at the experiences of the last four or five years and the failure in certain areas of corporate governance, particularly in North America, to realise that one of the key directives would have been a directive on corporate governance. It is not part of the FSAP. It is being tackled potentially at a later date by further directives and certainly by increased accounting standards that will be coming in. As it stands at the moment there are a number of areas that concern us—for example, voting rights. It is not standard practice across Europe to have equal voting rights for all shareholders. Transparency on directors' remuneration and benefits is not apparent from an annual report of certain countries in Europe, and unless you get transparency on a common basis of financial information it leads investors to distrust the information they have to hand and it makes comparative judgment also very difficult, so there are some very practical elements of corporate governance that need to be introduced before investors' confidence is established.

Lord Fearn

105. You refer to the United Kingdom being isolated within CESR and the dominance of national approaches rather than developing a new European approach. Can you give examples of where the United Kingdom has lost out as a result of this?

A. As ProShare we have been at the forefront encouraging wider share ownership through equity participation by employees in companies. This is a somewhat unusual practice from a purely European perspective. Very few companies in Europe adopt all-share schemes, and we have been very fortunate in persuading the government in this country not only to give a beneficial tax regime to this type of investor but also to encourage companies to stimulate wider share ownership amongst their employees. We do not have that cultural structure in the FSAP. There is no provision for extending wider share ownership through all-share employee schemes across Europe. That is a major problem that we have attempted to address in drawing it to the attention of Commission and CESR, but it is not one seen by European counterparts as particularly important so we feel that is a drawback for the United Kingdom.

106. So should there be more efforts by the United Kingdom regulator to make our position better?

A. The United Kingdom regulator, the Financial Services Authority, as a member of CESR is aware of the range of services that we have for investors and

Lord Fearn *contd.*]

shareholders—I have no doubt that in the right quarter they have been making comment—but this is a minor issue in their overall armoury of concern. But it is very important to us, with the huge range of public share ownership that we have through participation schemes, that we do not want to see anything that constrains that and certainly, when it comes to the Prospectus Directive. We would wish to see complete flexibility given to companies to issue shares to their employees without having to go through the whole gambit of issuing a new prospectus each time which under the current plan they would have to do. That would be a massive discouragement to companies undertaking such schemes.

107. So if we had an effective single market how would that benefit the United Kingdom?

A. From our perspective, to get wider share ownership across employees of companies who are multi continental, businesses who have employees right across Europe jointly participating in their business' success, would be an enhancement to cross-border trading, undoubtedly. It would lead to shareholders wanting to trade in local and in national share ownership in Europe.

Lord Walpole

108. I want to see whether you agree with the two gentlemen earlier. You referred to the risks of effective implementation and enforcement slipping between various fingers, and that a single EU regulator could resolve these issues. Do you regard a Euro SEC as inevitable, or what do you think of the criteria of success on implementation and enforcement areas so that various people can get together as they described and use national regulators? They went for the national regulators; which do you think will happen?

A. The reality will be that we will have multi-tier regulation. As the FSAP comes into force we will not only have regulation at a national level but also the imposition of a code of conduct from CESR and from the Commission, and of course each national regulator will have to impose those rules on the conduct of their businesses in their jurisdiction. The issue we are concerned about is areas that are cross-border related. For example, take the illustration of the United Kingdom investor who wants to go and buy Mercedes Benz shares, does so through a German stockbroker, and then finds some dissatisfaction with the service they receive. Where do they lodge their complaint? Where do they go for redress if they lose money? We do not have a unified proposal for a common Ombudsman across Europe. Do they go and complain to the local German regulator and, if so, where can they get compensation? Those will be practical issues that we would like to see introduced to bring harmonisation to the process. There is therefore an enormous risk in the early years of lack of co-ordination and in time this may well devolve. The Wicks review made a strong plea for some co-ordination and for a review from time to time by the Commission of the way local rules are implemented. Now there is a dichotomy, in my view, here. You have on one count the need to harmonise and establish uniform rules of conduct and, on the other, you have local national interest saying, "But we do things differently in this country, therefore we want exemption".

Chairman

109. Is that not what we all say? Is that not the argument?

A. This is the problem, is it not? Everybody is saying, for protectionist reasons, "We do it better than you. We do it for cultural reasons this way, therefore give us room to impose local rules and local conducts of business that tailor our own needs". Of course that is not achieving the objective of harmonisation and it seems to me this is not going to happen overnight: we do need to move gradually to bring recalcitrants to book if they are not imposing the regulations as they should and it does lead to difficulties when you get down to the very small print in the directives. One of the complaints that can be levied is that the directives ought to establish very high levels of principle without too much detail and allow detail at Level 2, Level 3, and ultimately conduct of business rules to impose the operation of processes. I , however, do not totally adhere to that. I believe you must have at Levels 1 and 2 some degree of detail in order to set the overall tone and what matters is how that will be implemented in the years to follow.

Lord Walpole

110. Going back to your Mercedes point, if I wanted to buy some Mercedes shares would I have to use a German stockbroker?

A. No, you would not, and indeed, hopefully, you would use a United Kingdom based stockbroker, but in the harmonised market you should have complete free choice and it should be perfectly possible to use a German stockbroker who has his operations either on the internet and therefore available to you electronically or who may have a branch office in your home town. There should be openness of access both ways. The difficulty is one of recompense at the moment.

Lord Walpole: That has been very helpful.

Baroness Cohen of Pimlico

111. In paragraph 15 you are suggesting that the FSAP concentrates far too much on investor protection and not enough on investor education. I am not very sure about investor education. Can you give examples where successful investor education programmes have been promulgated by regulators or the law? What measures would you like to see in the FSAP in respect to investor education?

A. Some of us, Lady Cohen, will remember the famous advertising programme of Sid promoting British Gas...

112. Yes.

A. . . . and the success of the privatisation programme during the early and mid-1980s did more to educate investors about direct investment in this country than any efforts by stockbrokers or regulators. It raised awareness of capital share

Baroness Cohen of Pimlico *contd.*]

ownership and the opportunity for participating directly in the stock market. The education was done by advertising; it was done by media communication; there were a whole host of ways by which the average man in the street became cognisant of not only the mechanisms but also the benefits. That, of course, led to a lot of misunderstanding. Investors subsequently lost money in activities they entered into because that education process did not continue. I was hearing earlier the allusion to split capital investment trusts, and here is a classic example of where the investors went in without really understanding the instruments they were buying. It could also be said that those promoting the instruments did not understand them either! Whatever way you go, the fact is that investors are far better protected if they can understand what they are buying and they have a knowledge of what they are buying than if it is simply something on the shelf to be picked off. If you just take the illustration of smoking, it is only as a result of the education that "Smoking Kills" that people understand the risks they take when they enter into it, and just simply to have a rule which says "Buying shares may endanger your financial wealth, they can go up and down" is not good enough. We are unusual in this country in that our regulator is the only regulator I am aware of through Europe which by law has an obligation to educate. I have to say critically it is not fulfilling that obligation . . .

113. It is not doing that.
A. Absolutely, not as it should, and my belief is that not only should regulators be obliged to educate but also obliged to ensure that the practitioners of the services also educate themselves.

114. The examples you have given of education, however, were not education as altruism but because people wanted to sell you something.
A. The Government, yes!

115. Or the company, indeed, might have wished to sell you something. I have half a feeling that those might be the only people really going to bother to do the education and perhaps the reason the FSA does not is because it comes out too dry, and lacking a specific example.
A. There is no question that it does come out dryly but equally if you look at other products—not just stocks and shares—like the house mortgage industry, this has involved educating investors as to the nature and variations of mortgages on offer and most of the providers contain in their literature a great deal of descriptive background of the products they are offering, and it is by the dissemination of that information that investors become educated. I should say that the role of ProShare starts very much younger than that. We start educating in schools. We believe it should be part of the school curriculum and, indeed, we are very successful—not at getting it into the formal curriculum but into the voluntary sector which not only stimulates interest but helps young people grow up with an understanding of balancing budgets and household bills and so forth, as well as direct investments in the stock market.

Chairman

116. I asked the previous witnesses this question: do you think that nationals and other European states looking at United Kingdom financial service industry—looking at the failure of many companies fully to fund company pensions, at split investment trusts, at pension companies like Equitable Life and so on badly letting down people—mean that the appeal of self-regulation and the virtues of the United Kingdom system of self-regulation is a convincing case?
A. Chairman, we have gradually seen the erosion of self-regulation. When I first started there was no regulation . . .

117. Is it any surprise, with that kind of experience?
A. It is normal reaction by legislators when something goes wrong to throw another law in the hope of solving the problem and preventing it from happening again. Experience also shows that fraudulent activity will get round whatever regulation you put in place.

118. I must put on the record that none of the cases I gave you then, as far as we know, involved fraudulent activity.
A. But this is always the concern—that malpractice will lead to misunderstanding by investors and they will subsequently lose money. The answer is that at the end of the day regulation will progressively get tighter and tougher—that is the inevitable way that life evolves. I heard you ask earlier whether this would lead to the establishment of an EU SEC and I think inevitably in time we will see European regulation become more harmonised and centralised. Hopefully we can make a pitch to have the EU SEC located in London—we have all the experience here!

119. I think the French have already made moves in that regard! Lastly, shortly, on the retail side particularly, when do you think there will be a meaningful single market in which you can see people buy Italian shares from German stockbrokers on the internet at competitive prices?
A. In the descriptive terms that you would like, I would say it would be a lifetime away! I say that simply because I do think it is a very cultural aspect. You have to get used to buying something that is abroad. We buy more American shares than we buy British shares and it is compatibility of language, currency, practice, conduct—there are a whole host of issues. I do genuinely believe it will take many years. It is not going to happen overnight.

120. Do you think not being in a single currency makes it more difficult, or has no impact?
A. It is certainly an issue, there is no question of that. If you are making a judgment about buying something you are adding an extra dimension to that decision, and there is no question that a harmonised currency would be one benefit that would stimulate cross-border trading.

121. Mr Savory, you have been a model of brevity and precision. Thank you very much.
A. Thank you.

MONDAY 8 SEPTEMBER 2003

Present:

Cavendish of Furness, L.   Howie of Troon, L.
Chadlington, L.   Shutt of Greetland, L.
Cohen of Pimlico, B.   Walpole, L.
Fearn, L.   Woolmer of Leeds, L. (Chairman)

Memorandum submitted on behalf of European Financial Services Round Table

1. I am responding on behalf of the European Financial Services Round Table (EFR), which I chair. (I am also Chairman of Aviva, the leading UK insurer.) CEOs and chairmen from a number of leading European banks and insurers formed the EFR in 2001. The members of the EFR believe that completion of a single European market for financial services will bring substantial benefits to customers, including increased competition and greater innovation. These benefits will help to drive down prices and deliver a wider and better choice of financial products to customers. For ease of reference, my comments follow the structure of the Sub-Committee's Call for Evidence.

A. THE FINANCIAL SERVICES ACTION PLAN

2. Creation of a single market for financial services would have positive economic consequences for citizens of the UK and for other EU member states. The strong economic case has been restated recently, in research published by both EFR and the Commission.

3. The Financial Services Action Plan (FSAP) is a programme of measures which will contribute to the achievement of this objective, and should therefore be welcomed. There are important FSAP measures still to be completed before the effective deadline of 2004, such as the Takeover Directive. However, it must be recognised that much further work will then be needed, especially in respect of retail markets.

4. The interests of the UK financial services industry will be best served by completion of the single market. Its interests and capabilities have been taken sufficiently into account during the development of FSAP. The Treasury, the Financial Services Authority and the UK financial services industry itself have all been active and influential in the development of the FSAP agenda and individual measures. The European Commission is generally recognised also to have made strong efforts to strengthen its processes for consultation on proposed initiatives with market participants and other stakeholders, although this remains a key challenge.

B. IMPLEMENTATION AND ENFORCEMENT

5. The 2004 enlargement of the Union will pose additional challenges for the speed and effectiveness of decisionmaking. The role of the European Commission as the champion of the single market will remain crucial. The increased emphasis which the Commission has placed on consistent implementation and more effective enforcement action against breaches of Member States' obligations is therefore to be welcomed.

6. The implementation of the Lamfalussy process for securities, and its planned extension to the banking and insurance sectors, should simplify the legislative process and increase the speed of response to evolving market requirements. Important challenges include the development of consistent implementation by Member States, improved cross-sector coordination (including regulation of the increasingly important financial services groups which undertake both banking and insurance business) and effective management of the process (for example in terms of target setting and provision of adequate resources).

7. There are clearly non-regulatory barriers to the full functioning of a single market, including linguistic and cultural preferences. These may not change rapidly, but they do not constitute a reason to delay the implementation of the required regulatory framework.

8. Taxation, which remains the responsibility of Member States, is crucial to the design of some financial products, such as private pensions. EFR published in 2002 research arguing that it would be very desirable to establish greater consistency between Member States on the tax treatment of pension products during both the saving and the retirement phases. However, different national rates of taxation would not prevent the creation of a single market for funded private pensions. Such a market would make an important contribution to the major challenge of funding Europe's pensions.

C. THE FUTURE

There are several areas where extensive further work will be required to complete a single market.

9. In the retail markets, national "consumer protection" measures have often had the effect of protecting local providers from new competitors based in other Member States. This has typically been at the expense of local consumers' interests, with higher prices and reduced choice the consequences. Good consumer protection is essential, but there is no reason for retention of diverse national regimes.

10. Supervision of institutions should be undertaken on a consistent basis across sectors and national boundaries. Today, there are in many Member States several supervisory bodies addressing specific market sectors. Coordination of over 30 agencies' positions is of course very complex. Further institutional changes may ultimately be necessary to promote genuine convergence of rules and practice.

11. The adoption of consistent accounting standards across Europe (and more widely) is necessary, but the development of adequate IAS standards for banking and insurance business has not yet been achieved and this may block the planned adoption of IAS reporting in 2005 for the European financial services industry.

12. Successful implementation of both FSAP and the other measures required to complete a single market for financial services will have a positive impact on the global competitiveness of the EU financial services industry, including the London based institutions.

26 June 2003

Examination of Witness

MR PEHR G GYLLENHAMMAR, Chief Executive Officer, Aviva; Chairman, European Financial Services Round Table, examined.

Chairman

122. Good afternoon, Mr Gyllenhammar, I do apologise that we have kept you waiting. Could I first of all thank you for the paper we received that we have read with interest, which is outwardly brief but to the point, and you know that we are going to ask you some questions largely arising from that evidence. Before we go into the evidence I will ask in a moment if there is anything you would like to add by way of a preamble to the questions. Before we do, we have a convention in the House, as you will know, to declare any interests and I have an interest to declare that amongst a whole number of pension policies that I hold, some of them are with Aviva.

(*Mr Gyllenhammar*) Should I extend my apologies, my Lord!

Baroness Cohen of Pimlico: Indubitably!

Chairman: Does anyone else have any interests to declare?

Baroness Cohen of Pimlico: I am a director of the London Stock Exchange.

Lord Chadlington: My company is an adviser to a number of financial institutions although I am personally involved with only one, namely Agon (?).

Lord Walpole: I am a customer of what I shall call Norwich Union.

Baroness Cohen of Pimlico: We are all that surely.

Chairman

123. Thank you very much. Is there anything you would like to start off with by way of introduction?

A. I have really nothing to add, my Lord, except perhaps one parallel. The longest part of my business career has been in the manufacturing industry and I think that the creation of the single market, which works rather well for goods, has been to the benefit of both the customers and the most competitive firms in the market, and the market itself has helped to create a convergence, the same rules, (for example you buy the same vehicles across the European Union), which was not the case say 15 or 20 years ago where you had almost one specification for each country as a Member of the European Union. We are looking to the same result in financial services.

Chairman: That is an extremely helpful observation, I may say. You yourself represent a number of companies who are key players through the Round Table and obviously your own business, too, is important. So far the comments and witnesses we have had have focused largely on capital markets but we are acutely aware obviously of the importance of investors as well as issuers and your group and your own wider interests cover both of those, so we are particularly interested in your evidence today. Baroness Cohen would like to start the questions.

Baroness Cohen of Pimlico

124. You have highlighted the economic case for implementing the Financial Services Action Plan to benefit citizens but you went on to say that much more is going to need to be done for retail investors even after the action plan is completed. Could you give us some examples of what is needed—I know that insurance companies are rather at the front of this—and some examples of how long all this might take?

A. I wish I could answer that, Baroness Cohen.

125. Have a shot.

A. Well, I will have a shot at it. I think the Lamfalussy process, which has been widely applauded as a quick route to achieving results, maybe is a very good process, but it takes an enormous amount of time and rather few things have happened. That started really to concentrate on the capital markets and I think that a single market for capital is extremely important as an avenue to an

Baroness Cohen of Pimlico contd.]

open retail market. We have mainly taken an interest in a retail market that works across the European Union and there, Baroness, we are nowhere. There are a couple of obstacles that I mentioned in my brief paper. One is consumer protection which I think is a snake pit in the European Union. Every government wants to be the champion of the consumer whereas we who work in the market think that the consumer is the champion if the market works. So we have at least 15 different sets of legislation to protect the consumer in 15 Member countries and we will have another ten. We have discussed this with legislators and we realise that most countries think that they have the best consumer protection legislation. A second is of course supervision, that we have more than 15 because some countries do not have, as we have, the FSA. They have separate regulators for banks and for insurance companies respectively, so we are probably up to about between 20 and 25 regulators. Then we have the additions, the central bankers who are no longer central bankers (namely in the euro zone) who are, in my opinion—and I do not want to sound arrogant or snooty—under-employed. They would like to have a supervisory role and then we have the European Central Bank who thinks they should play a particular role in supervising banks. So on supervision and regulation we have a wide array of possible solutions and we do not necessarily need one, but I think we need one set of principles as with consumer protection. So those are two of the difficult areas where I think it takes a lot of goodwill, tolerance and a liberal view to say that we are not that different among the 15.

126. I take it that all this goodwill and tolerance is not really going to be extended by your competitors?

A. I do not know. The members of our little club are prominent representatives of very important companies and I think in most cases we share the same objectives and I hope that we will all stand up and be counted when it comes to saying and being convincing in saying that we would like the process to move forward much, much faster. Finally, if I may add something on the timetable. When there are 25[1] it will not be easier than when we have 15, particularly as ten come from entirely different circumstances and have to be brought up-to-date. They are still undergoing training and all the present Members are providing that training and sharing experiences but it will take a long time. To have them participate in the deliberations of consumer protection will be a very long process, so we need to be ready by the end of 2004, in my opinion.

Chairman

127. Could you just give one example of a financial product where you feel that businesses like yourself are hampered in selling into other Member States of Europe because of over-protective consumer regulation.

A. We can start and try to see what happens if we are going to just sell a product that we have designed here into any other European Union Member State. First of all, they do not know the product so it has to

go direct over the counter, which is very difficult, or through their brokers or financial advisors. They will not recognise the product, they may wish to protect their own market. They will deny knowledge of the product because the products are different, they are tailored to national customs, savings patterns, tax systems and consumer protection. What we would like to see is the possibility that we cannot be stopped by any of those barriers but we can design a product here or anywhere. In Spain, where we also operate on a fairly large scale, and say we think "this is a good product for the consumers across the European Union and we would like to trade it". It stops now partly with supervision and regulation, consumer protection and, of course, the cultural differences. But that is not a trade barrier, that is our problem and we cannot blame anyone for different practices and different traditions.

Baroness Cohen of Pimlico

128. For example, a term life policy, that is difficult? I was trying to think of the most straightforward financial services product.

A. And the term product is very simple, both in concept, design and execution. I think we would have to sell it through our subsidiaries in France or in Spain. We can theoretically sell it but I think it would be very difficult to sell it from the United Kingdom into any European Union Member State.

129. Even something as straightforward as that you would be selling through a subsidiary?

A. Yes.

Lord Chadlington

130. You clearly believe that the completion of a market from the financial services industry's point of view would be greatly to their advantage in the UK. I wonder whether you feel at the moment that the UK financial services industry is making the most of the opportunities as they fall out and develop? Secondly, I am wondering whether, when it is all completed, you think there might be any damage to the UK industry? Can you see anything which perhaps they cannot get over when everything is completed and, if so, give me some examples?

A. As regards the first part of your question, an open market for retail in the European Union would be of great benefit, I think, to companies only working in the United Kingdom that have not got the resources or have not had the opportunity to invest outside the United Kingdom in subsidiaries, or establish subsidiaries. That requires size, scale that is, and financial means. If you had a completely open retail market, there would be nothing to prevent a medium sized provider, or even small provider, in the United Kingdom selling throughout the European Union. Today they are excluded, not least because they have not got the means and the resources to establish subsidiaries or to acquire companies. When it comes to potential damage to the United Kingdom and the financial services industry here, I think the damage that will be done is probably well deserved. That sounds cruel but it means to weed out the weakest and develop the strongest. I think in general

---

[1] Union members.

Lord Chadlington contd.]

terms this market is one of the most sophisticated in the European Union and in many cases the most advanced which means that I think we have a competitive advantage vis à vis many of our competitors around Europe. We are strong in the design of products, in the exchanges in this country and the biggest exchange in the whole European Union, the ease of dealing with transatlantic relations and doing business with the United States. I think there is a competitive advantage to the United Kingdom of having an absolutely open, transparent market and a level playing field.

131. And it will only be the weak who are damaged in your judgment?

A. Which always happens in a market economy, my Lord. If the weak disappear it makes the stronger, stronger.

Lord Cavendish of Furness

132. Turning to part B of your paper, implementation and enforcement, you speak of benefits of the Lamfalussy process and its extension from securities to banking and insurance. The essence of the Lamfalussy process is consultation and you state that the Commission is recognised as having made great strides in its approach. Do you believe that all the other participants are playing their appropriate roles fully in commenting on the draft proposals from bodies of people like CESR?

A. In my paper we are rather complimentary of the European Commission because I think they do make efforts. At times they fail, and there are bitter complaints where they have failed, and that is why they do a better job of consultation in the next phase. The consultation process is very difficult because you have so many interested parties in every European Union member country. If you take the number of players here who are consulted and who wish to be heard, it is a very heavy process. I think the balance for the Commission is between speed and to consult meticulously with everybody. I do not think that in this market we always have done the best job. There are so many complaints about details and so many detailed counter-proposals. I would be absolutely whimsical if I was in the Commission. I would say, "We have started this consultation process and we have got so many complaints and counter-proposals, where do we start? If we now interrupt we will make enemies in the market in almost every country". I do not envy them the task of having a consultation process. I think that the time for consultation on each and every proposal should be very short, very concentrated, not to allow too much noise to develop over time and then everybody being unhappy with the proposals. It is not possible to make everybody happy with the proposals. They need to speed it up.

133. Just so I can get a bit of the flavour, what sort of commitment does the Commission make in this process? How many people are involved?

A. One thing I must say to explain how I see the Commission's dilemma is they have very few people. In spite of the fact that we say it is a terrible bureaucracy and it is awful and overmanned, if you look at the Commissioner for Financial Services, Mr Bolkenstein, he has very few associates. One of their problems is that they have not got the capacity to develop some of these proposals. They have to go to the industry or to outside advisors who they cannot even pay for. That creates its own problems because it is the people who are extremely good at lobbying and who are willing to commit the resources who may come out and talk. It is more of a problem in the United States, I think, but we are building that problem now in Europe. They say that it is very difficult to get more resources because they are under budget constraints, which we also understand.

Lord Chadlington

134. I wonder whether you feel that the lack of resources, that analysis you have made, means that these proposals are tested to the degree that you would like them to be? Are they rigorously interrogated to the degree that you would like them to be?

A. My Lord, yes, I think they are and that is where the consultation process comes in. The temptation for the Commissioner is to say, and if I were a Commissioner I would say, "Look, you have to have a time limit", but because their resources are pretty slim they are tested in the consultation process and then I think it is very difficult for the Commission to counter all the experts that appear in almost every single market but we have a lot of experts here.

Lord Shutt of Greetland

135. Bearing all that in mind, are you satisfied that the process will bring consistent implementation by Member States?

A. The implementation by the Member States, my Lord, of course is another story because if we look at the Stability Pact, which is at the highest level of political decision-making one can see that the implementation was supposed to have been done but one does not really live up to the commitments, so implementation goes at different speeds in different countries. There are rather good statistics of what has happened in the past, ie countries that are always slow and sometimes hardly ever get there and countries that are very meticulous with implementation. I think this is something one perhaps has to tolerate in a Union of 15 or perhaps 25 Members. If we just get this on track, even if the implementation is uneven and slow, I think the market will correct that over time. I may have a naive belief, my Lord, in the market but I think that once we get going the market forces are extremely powerful and the consumers are quite intelligent and smart.

136. Will there not in these circumstances be an element that is left to the discretion at the national level?

A. The discretion at national level is the problem. I happen to believe, and I think that view is shared by most of our members, that if on both consumer protection and supervision we can agree on common principles, that is a way forward. That was the success of the single market in other areas—mutual recognition based on common principles and then you hope for convergence through the market forces.

Lord Shutt of Greetland contd.]

But there are those who suggest one single regulator for banks and insurance companies throughout the European Union and also one set of legislation for consumer protection. Some of us think that would be a very long wait and could be almost an excuse to prevent common standards in the market. I therefore am a firm believer in common principles and then national implementation which means that you will have a divergence, my Lord. But it is better to get on to that route quickly and hope for the convergence through the market forces than to wait. Nobody knows how long for one common set of standards and legislation for the whole union.

Chairman: I am sure we will return to that theme. Let me push on but I would like to return to that point myself later. Lord Howie?

Lord Howie of Troon

137. Since these are financial matters I have no personal things to declare! You draw attention to taxation especially relating to pensions in your paper and we know that there is no common attitude towards the treatment of taxation and pensions throughout the Member States, although this is obviously a fairly important matter (or perhaps it goes beyond the main aspects of the action plan). How could the Member States set about creating a sufficiently unified tax treatment given that the veto on tax matters is jealously guarded by the Member States?

A. My Lord, our departure point is that pensions' portability is very important within a political union because freedom of movement for people is one of the main principles of the union. You can study wherever you choose, you can live and work wherever you choose, you can retire wherever you choose, but that means very little if in a climate where pensions are going to be a big problem for most countries within the Community you cannot move with your pension. The worst example is of course where you have entirely different tax treatment. We are not talking about tax rates, we do not think that there is any chance or any willingness on our part to have a debate on tax rates but this concerns tax treatments and principles, and we suggest that the 15 should agree on what we call EET, which we also had in the report about pensions that the Round Table published. That is: Exemption from contributions, Exemption from investment returns during the accumulation period and Taxable income upon retirement. If you move from one country that does it another way to a country that has EET you will lose twice and if you are dependent upon your pension you will never be able to afford to move, which deprives you of one of the basic rights on which the European Union was founded. So we think as a minimum countries should be able to agree upon this EET taxation principle which many of the members already have. As we know, in France the government has declared themselves that they will be insolvent in 2007, in four years' time, unless they do something about their pension scheme (government sponsored of course), Italy have hardly touched their own problem and country after country, apart from the United Kingdom and Holland, which I think is

the best funded of all, will face this problem of an ageing population where you have to ask people to work longer, pay more and get less, or any combination of the three. We think therefore that private savings (and everybody agrees who studies this problem) will be more and more important and facing the growth in private savings we have to have common principles across the union otherwise we will, as I said, be deprived of many of the basic rights on which the union was founded.

Lord Cavendish of Furness

138. If EET fails to win approval universally, based on what you said earlier about the power of the market in a beneficial sense, would that not have the same effect ultimately?

A. It will not have the same effect if countries cannot agree. For example, if you want to move from country A to B and you come from an EET, or rather you have the opposite protection of principles, you will lose both ends. You could also gain but that is really not the purpose of the system. So we are not talking about tax harmonisation when it comes to VAT or tax rates but the same types of principles which one should be able to agree upon in a civilised society.

Lord Howie of Troon

139. But has not the recent excitement over pensions in the last year or so been caused more by the vagaries of the stock market than anything else? How would you help to avoid that?

A. We cannot avoid it, my Lord. If you talk to me as the chairman of the pension provider and a provider of financial products, the choice for the consumer/the customer is really, "Would you like to invest your money yourself with our help?", that is you give us instructions on exactly how to invest it in a so-called unit-linked product, or you do not think you have the expertise or the time so you ask us to manage the investment. Those are, in principle, the two variations on how to save and if we help the customer and use our expertise and judgment and the market goes down we may perform slightly better or worse than the market, but if it goes down, it goes down and there is very little we can do about it. Over time you hope there will be a progression and you will come out better than you started. There is no guarantee and no-one can give that guarantee. State sponsored schemes have tried to give that guarantee only to see that the schemes go bankrupt.

Lord Fearn

140. Your comments on the cost to consumers of consumer protection, they are pretty powerful—section nine. As this is an area where attention will have to be focused in the future, could you give some ideas on how to tackle this?

A. Coming back to what I said earlier, we are working on a report on consumer protection, which will only be our first preliminary report and then we will have to continue and refine it, which is to base consumer protection around the European Union on

Lord Fearn *contd.*]

common principles. Eventually, perhaps, there will be European-wide legislation, but as I said we think that will take a long time and there will be an enormous fight before you achieve it. Therefore, an acceptance of common principles and mutual recognition, leaving this partly to the discretion of the members, is perhaps the most practical way forward.

141. The report that you have just mentioned, when is that due?
A. It is due later this autumn. We hope to be able to publish the report some time in November, if we can agree on the proposals.

142. Who is working on that?
A. It is our members and their associates. The work is led by the Chairman of Banque Nationale de Paris, BNP, Mr Pebereau, and he has a group of both members and associates at his disposal.

143. How does the local provider come into this?
A. The local provider does not come into this. We have made it easy for us, my Lord. We are a private club, so people cannot demand an entry, they can only be invited. It is a private club because we think that everything else is so complicated. We allow ourselves the privilege to publish reports, and there we are absolutely transparent, and influence the debate. That is what we are doing.

Chairman

144. When we touched upon the question of taxation you set out very neatly the principles.
A. Yes.

145. I well understand the report is in process on consumer protection but could you share with us today your thoughts at this moment about the key principles that might be an approach to the consumer protection problem?
A. I cannot, my Lord, because the principles underlying almost every set of consumer protection legislation that we have seen are more or less the same, namely "we are the champion of the consumer". Whether you buy a television set, you buy a radio or you buy a car or you buy a financial services product, it is based on very much the same principles. The problem lies in the detail into which consumer protection legislation goes when it comes to different classes of product. When it comes to financial services I think we have gone far and in our club we are all in favour of extensive consumer protection, but there is a limit beyond which you can hardly go because you start to design the products of the industry. I must say that in the insurance industry in this country the regulators are close to designing our products and I think that is a breach in the credo that the market, after all, is a miraculous provider of the best and the worst. One hopes that consumer protection legislation will weed out the worst but leave the best to develop.

146. A lot of pension fund holders might wonder whether the market has been a very good servant for people holding pension funds, including in the UK. A lot of people might say UK pension providers have not been very good servants of the consumer.

A. My Lord, that is partly justified. There are several things one should not be very proud of. On the other hand, to say that a product does not perform to the expectations of the customer, is designed and sold in bad faith, is something I would not accept. I think that the so-called mis-selling is an exception to the rule. Without saying too much about Aviva, the company I chair, I must say that we have had very little mis-selling but we would still have a number of dissatisfied clients. It is also about the perception. A client who has seen a product, or the value of a product or pension, grow every year and who is suddenly faced with losing the bonus, seeing the value of their investment go down, if they were under the misconception there was a guarantee they could pay back their mortgage with their insurance—there was not any guarantee in most cases—they are then displeased. I think that is an absolutely natural reaction, but much of that is really because of the precipitous decline in the markets over the last two or three years. I am not defending the whole industry but I am suggesting, my Lord, that the market is a very powerful driver of development of better practice and that the bad practice has to be weeded out.

147. I diverted from the principal thrust of what I was asking, which was to do with principles. When you talked earlier about the problems of consumer protection you said that you thought the best way to approach the myriad 15/25 Member States' different approaches was not to have or seek a common single regulatory framework of consumer protection across the whole of the Union but rather to seek to develop some common principles.
A. Yes.

148. That was what I was asking you about. In relation to taxation you have put forward some common principles: not tax rates, common principles to approach the problem of taxation and pensions. In relation to consumer protection, what is the thinking of you and your organisation at present, subject to the report, about the key principles, the common principles, that you feel would avoid this attempt to have single European-wide consumer protection law that you said, quite rightly, could take years to get agreement on? What are the principles that you are looking for there?
A. My Lord, on taxation it is easier because consumer protection is such a wide area, so even if we talk in terms of principles it would be a fairly large document. Some of the basic principles are transparency, as far as possible complete transparency on what you sell and what the conditions are under which you sell it and the rights for the consumer, not only to test the transparency but also to go to an ombudsman or the like and have the possibility to be heard. And for the company to stand corrected on what they have offered or what they seem to have guaranteed. I think those are two very important principles in any consumer protection legislation. In some countries you do not have that. I could go further but then I would have to go into quite some detail and I am not sure that would be interesting.

Chairman *contd.*]

149. I will leave it at that point for the other questions but you and other people on the retail side have made a great deal about the difficulties raised by consumer regulation at Member State level arguing that that is burdensome, it raises problems of ease of protection by Member States of their industries, time and time again it is raised, and you yourself said a way forward in that is to establish some common principles.

A. Yes.

150. When I press you on that you are not really able to tell us much about it. I have to say that leaves us as a Committee with a difficulty. If you as an industry cannot say what is the way around it, then I fear the answer is that Member States will continue to use consumer protection to thwart the single market.

A. The reason I am not giving an extensive answer, my Lord, is that we are working on exactly this. I do not want to pre-empt my colleagues who are working on it. Let me say that if we pick one set of legislation in any of the 15 that would be a blessing—perhaps not a blessing for every consumer—because as most of these consumer protection legislation competences are fairly well advanced I do not think it matters all that much, the problem is to have 15 or 25, not one. When it comes to supervision, it is the same thing. If we had one supervisory body to deal with that would be so, but now we have to deal with one in every country where we operate and many of them are based on the same principles, it is just that the procedures are totally different.

Lord Walpole

151. You mention that "further institutional changes" may be necessary to achieve the convergence of regulatory rules under point ten. That might be just an evolution of the Lamfalussy process but some observers argue that the process is likely to fail and so a EuroSEC will become necessary. Would you like to see that happen or do you think that we are likely to be forced down that route whether we like it or not?

A. First of all, the Lamfalussy process was a well thought through effort on getting a consensus on how to proceed with greater speed. Unfortunately, for whatever reason, we have not seen the speed. We have seen the process and we understand how it works but we have not seen the speed.

152. Also did you touch on the common accounting standards and the like?

A. I did not actually, no. I do not know when the legislators, both the Commission who proposed the legislation or the Parliament or the Council, will recognise that speed is of the essence and that the processes are less interesting and important than the result. Again the deadline it seems to us in our club is December 2004. After that, with a new treaty or a new constitution, whatever they would like to call it, and new voting rules in the European Union, we may sit here in ten or 15 years and discuss exactly the same problems.

153. I think really what I am asking is whether you think individual countries can in fact look after themselves or whether you need overriding bodies like EuroSEC to keep an eye on them?

A. As I said earlier—

154. —You just touched on it earlier.

A. In our club there are different views. There are those who believe that one single regulator is the solution and that that will provide clarity and that will provide simplicity and lower the costs. If that can be achieved it may be a good solution. Some of us are slightly more pragmatic (without priding ourselves on being pragmatic) in saying that can be very hard to achieve. Where would the regulator be? What type of rules should they follow? Some of us just fear that that will take precedence over the efficiency and limited size of that regulatory body and that perhaps with common principles and mutual recognition we could do rather well in the European Union.

Chairman: Has anybody any more questions?

Lord Chadlington

155. I am very struck by the points you have been making about pensions and job mobility, which seem to me to be essential to the whole success of the scheme. Maybe you have said all you want to say about this subject. Is there anything that we could see or read or you would refer us to which would help us get an even bigger insight into that little bit of what you said? It just struck so many chords with me.

A. We have published two reports but with a fairly limited distribution. One is on the advantages of having a single market for financial services and there we used outside institutes to do the report for us. That was the first report on the subject in Europe and the Commission and the European Union did their work later. We had more striking results in our projections than they did. We said additional growth of between 0.5 and 0.7 percentage points a year and they had about 1.5 per cent in 10 years, which we thought was pretty modest. The other report we did in our group was on pensions. My Lord, if it is acceptable I could have these reports distributed to this distinguished group.

Lord Chadlington: Thank you very much indeed, if you could.

Chairman

156. That would be extremely helpful. Is there anything you would like to add in conclusion that we may have missed or perhaps misinterpreted?

A. You are very kind. There is only one thing I would like to underline and that is that having worked internationally I think that the United Kingdom and its government and Parliament has nothing to fear when it comes to an absolutely wide open, transparent market in this area of financial services. We have champions here and the country *per se* is also a champion in that field and it should be seen as a great opportunity to have an open and transparent market and therefore should not lobby too intensely on specific items so that one obscures the goals of being a good partner welcoming the opening of the market. To go back to the

Chairman contd.]

consultation processes I mentioned earlier, I think London was a difficult place to deal with when it came to some of the consultation processes, for example on one single prospectus. The champions made it clear that they understood better than anyone else and I think that upset some European members. It is not my advice to the members but if the industry would listen that would be my advice: do not be too smart in lobbying on detail, be smart in getting the open and transparent market in the United Kingdom.

Chairman: Thank you for your wise words.

Lord Shutt of Greetland

157. I am sorry to come back to this but you have made several references to "the club". Are we clear that we have got the aim and purpose of the club that was referred to? Are we clear about that?

A. If I may then, my Lord, send the two reports and the simple objectives of the club and the membership.

Lord Shutt of Greetland: Thank you very much.

Chairman: You have been helpful to the very last moment. Thank you very much.

Memorandum from Barclays Bank Plc

A. THE FINANCIAL SERVICES ACTION PLAN

The eighth report on progress with the FSAP produced by the Commission on 3 June shows that in terms of actions delivered considerable progress has been made. However, this hides the fact that those measures which remain to be delivered are in fact the most controversial and important not only for the UK but for European Financial Services at large. These are the Investment Services Directive, the Capital Adequacy Directive and the Prospectus Directive. The Commission's report highlights the fact that there are "nine months left to deliver the FSAP" with the result that the tension between delivering to time and delivering to quality has dramatically heightened.

In addition the FSAP had deadlines of 2003 for wholesale and 2005 for retail issues. Clearly there is no hope of the 2003 deadline for wholesale issues being met because even if all the outstanding directives were passed this year, there would still be an implementation process of some 18 months before they could be expected to be seen in Member State legislation. The position for the retail market is not much better.

It is really too early to say whether the progress to date has been beneficial to the UK, particularly as the most influential areas have yet to be decided let alone implemented at Member State level. What has been lacking however is a clear benchmark contained in the preparation for the legislation against which success can be empirically measured.

Considering that the UK Financial Services industry, particularly in wholesale but also in some areas of retail represents the bulk of EU Financial Services activity, then clearly insufficient weight has been given to its position and experience. Representation in the Council and European Parliament on these issues is not determined by market share or activity but by the general rules attached to voting procedures.

The UK Government's approach can be contrasted to that of some other Member States which specifically set out to protect their industry from the force of truly competitive markets.

The key issues to be dealt with are:

The Investment Services Directive

Much debate has been around the approach to the structure of the wholesale markets but equally there are issues in respect of execution only and direct offer services which are critical to the way retail investment products are offered at reasonable cost to consumers in the UK.

The Prospectus Directive

Ostensibly aimed at liberalising markets. The current effects appear to be in the other direction with fundamental threats to the Eurobond Market driven by disproportionate attempts to protect retail consumers.

Capital Adequacy Directive

This will be based on the, to be agreed, Basle Accord and the threat is that EU implementation will begin to unpick the carefully crafted compromise of the Accord.

B. IMPLEMENTATION AND ENFORCEMENT

We are hopeful that the Lamfalussy process will be a success because it does offer a sensible method for creating greater flexibility and a speedier EU process. It is however being significantly strained by the deadlines imposed by the FSAP. This has generated considerably more legislative initiatives at one time than were, perhaps, originally envisaged when the proposals were put forward.

This FSAP timeline has meant that consultations have run in series and to very short timeframes which is less than optimal. The other areas where improvement might be seen are in terms of more feedback from CESR on why it has reached its decisions and to date the framework directives have still contained significantly more detail than one might have imagined was envisaged by the Lamfalussy proposals.

Member States will be responsible for ensuring effective implementation and enforcement of the legislation. In addition, the Commission has a role in ensuring that the Member States do implement and enforce correctly. There are signs that the Commission is now more willing to turn its attention to enforcement rather than writing new legislation but this will require significant cultural change within the Commission and to the extent that past performance is a guide to future activity, much remains to be done to convince the market that this will occur. There needs to be proper co-ordination between DGs Market and Competition.

One perceived problem around implementation and enforcement is the true level of political will within Member States to implement and enforce wholeheartedly. Where the legislation threatens perceived national interests, then there is, in some cases, an understandable, if not desirable, reluctance to implement and enforce with full vigour.

In terms of non-regulatory barriers, then beyond language, culture, tax regimes and often the need for physical presence, there are also the differences in philosophical approach between Member States, for example in terms of the degree to which a truly free market is embraced and in the consumer field, the freedom to be given to individuals to be able to make their own mistakes—*Caveat emptor*.

C. THE FUTURE

One issue which will certainly come to the fore is whether or not there is a need for a single Regulator/Supervisor. Proposals in the Convention's work would appear to make this a more likely possibility. Our view is that it is too premature to consider such a move because regulation is best done near the markets which remain, in a physical sense, very much nationally based. The other area of development will be in relation to the retail market which the FSAP has in the main ignored. Any further initiatives must contain clear measures of success based upon a proper understanding and identification of the barriers or problems. The approach of full harmonisation should not be the only one on the agenda, mutual recognition should prevail wherever possible. Greater recognition of other factors which impede cross border activity beyond differences in legislative approach (for example with the Consumer Credit Directive the importance of positive data in opening up markets has not been addressed), should be considered.

The changes driven by FSAP proposals will undoubtedly have an impact on the competitive position of London. For example, they may be too prescriptive in terms of market structure eg Article 25, of the ISD, and looking forward, possible proposals in relation to Clearing and Settlement. Legislation which is overly prescriptive of market practices, at least at the wholesale end, is more likely to stifle innovation and competition than to promote it. A marketplace which is unable to adapt because of regulatory constraints will undoubtedly be at a disadvantage in a global marketplace.

The FSAP should not be seen in isolation, it must be regarded as part of a wider EU project. This should be aimed at producing a globally competitive marketplace rather than a constrained EU tradeblock. This will require more flexible labour markets and a more liberal approach to global free trade issues in the round. Should Member States not face up to the new realities and adapt accordingly, then there will be disadvantageous knock on effects in the UK.

June 2003

Examination of Witness

MR WILLIAM ELDRIDGE, Public Affairs Director, Barclays Bank plc, examined.

Chairman

158. Thank you, Mr Eldridge for waiting. I am aiming to conclude around five minutes past six just to give you and also members of the Committee a feel. Thank you again for your written evidence which we have all read with interest and for coming this afternoon, we are very grateful to you for your time. Is there anything you would like to add by way of introduction?

(*Mr Eldridge*) I think perhaps a short preface. I am sure everybody here knows Barclays. We are beginning to see ourselves very much more as a European bank rather than just a UK bank. We have made it clear in our strategy that we have clear objectives for expansion in Europe and you may have seen our recent acquisition in Spain which is starting to bring that about. We have also been involved in the Brussels process for much more than a decade and indeed I do not think any other UK bank devotes quite so much time and effort to it as we do. Overall we see the financial services action plan as a real opportunity rather than a threat and generally we are supportive of what the Commission is trying to achieve, so if I could put those points in my opening remarks against which to put the rest of my case.

Chairman: Indeed you can. That is very helpful to us.

Lord Chadlington

159. Good afternoon, Mr Eldridge. In your paper you refer on several occasions to the notion of benchmarking and whether or not we could establish benchmarks that we might be able to measure success and failure against. I find that quite attractive. I wonder if you could expand upon what those benchmarks might look like?

A. Yes, I think so. At a very high level the overall objectives, to paraphrase the Financial Services Action Plan, are to create deep and liquid capital markets but if there is actually a clear definition of what "deep and liquid" is, it has now escaped me and has been obscured by the detail of each of the individual Directives and by the actions which go to make up the Action Plan. I would suggest that probably at the outset there was no clear numerical objective against which to look at the plan and, similarly, each Directive in its turn has not had clear numeric type objectives in it. Perhaps I could give you a specific example: if we take the Prospectus Directive, which is more or less through the process now, to fit with the thrust of the FSAP its objectives might have been to generate more and cheaper cross-border issuing activity, so that could have been its overall objective, and we would need a start point, we would need to understand what are the current volumes, what does current pricing look like, and then to think about what are the trends that we have seen, so what are the market trends anyway, because what we want to measure is the dynamics of the effect of the Directive rather than where was the market going anyway. You could perhaps break that down into targets like number of companies quoted on what to them are overseas exchanges, number of

issues that are being made across borders, number of investors buying those issues, targets for the lower cost of each of those issues, greater choice of investors and so on. For each Directive you could think of a set of specific measures to measure them against. I think you might also want to put in something about perceptions as well because that is as important as some of the straightforward numbers. What it really requires is much more clarity about what is the impact that the legislators would want a particular Directive to achieve. If there was that clarity then perhaps some of the political discussions would come to conclusions more easily. To be fair, the Commission has started to do some work in this area. They have got a working paper[2] out but it is at a much more macro level rather than looking at individual Directives and their effects. The economic ministers have asked for a further and updated report to be produced at the beginning of next year but, again, that is much more general rather than looking specifically at each individual Directive.

160. I just about got that bit and then I sort of staggered to two conclusions and I did not like them very much. The first was that on the individual Directives if you set numerical targets or benchmarks there seem to me to be so many other things that are coming into play that you cannot really just take it and say "that is because of the Directive" because so many other things might have come into play to affect the targets you have established. Could you comment on that? Secondly, I thought it was easier to do the more you went after individual Directives. In other words, the bigger the thing you take, the harder it is to produce numerical benchmarks which actually become really defensible. If I can put it back to you and say what does "deep and liquid" actually mean? Give me some numbers which you would be prepared to live with which are benchmarks.

A. I think to take the second one first, I agree with you that the bigger the objective then the harder it is to produce a set of numerics that might describe it unless and until you have broken that down into all the individual Directives which then tot themselves back up to make the overall plan. To turn to the first question, "are there not lots of other things which will impact it"? Yes, there are but in terms of setting benchmarks, if you looked at trends in the marketplace at the moment and where they were taking you, you would iron out some of those. If you think that it is impossible to measure the effect of any piece of legislation you might wonder why you bothered with it in the first place.

161. That is precisely the problem this current Government has on the number of targets. All I am arguing is I think what you are saying feels good but I am not sure when we get down to the practicalities of it that it can deliver what you are promising. That is really what I am asking. I do not want to get too carried away with it because I do not think it is absolutely central to what you are saying but it is seductive, I think.

---

[2] SEC (2003) 628—26/5/03.

Lord Chadlington *contd.*]

A. I would not want to drive down the depth of some of these targets with numerics to a finite degree but I think it would be worth having some clear objectives in the Directive before you set out to craft it and draft it.

Lord Shutt of Greetland

162. In the paper that you sent us there seems to be a fair bit of scepticism about it. If you look at the pre-penultimate paragraph on the first page, you say: "The UK Government's approach can be contrasted to that of some other Member States which specifically set out to protect their industry from the force of truly competitive markets." Then if you turn over the page to the penultimate paragraph you then, again, are talking about implementation and enforcement and you seem sceptical about that. Are you saying that you welcome the UK Government's approach and more should be done to prevent other Member States from preventing the conditions for competition across the European Union, or do you think the UK Government should be doing that? Have you got some firm examples where other Member States have been successful in protecting their industries?

A. Yes, I am saying that the UK Government has got the right approach in terms of a desire to produce a competitive marketplace. I think a competitive marketplace is what industry should thrive best in. Yes, I am saying that they have got the right approach. Examples of where other Member States have successfully protected their industry: there are the Germans with their Landesbanks, which were receiving state aid for many years and they have now finally done a deal with the Commission which will see that state aid phased out over a number of years, but that is a very clear example of where Member States have done it. To take a different marketplace, the French have successfully protected their electricity markets from open competition. The Italians did quite a good deal for their farmers with milk quotas and they brought that into a piece of financial services legislation on tax, so they were quite happy to bring two dossiers that had nothing to do with each other together to produce results to protect their interests. There are three examples.

163. What are you fearful of in this?

A. What I am fearful of? That Member States will continue to find ways of protecting their companies from true open market competition. You might say that there is one example in the Investment Services Directive which is being looked at in the way that exchanges are being protected from competitive threats from investment services companies which can put trades together on their own books rather than going through an exchange. The Italians introduced that quite late in the day into the Commission's paper at the end of all the consultation, so it was put in at last minute and they acted in that sense to protect their domestic interests.

Baroness Cohen of Pimlico

164. Barclays is one of our biggest banks but where else are you coming from on this? Are you direct sellers of financial service products as in life insurance, house insurance, and heaven knows what? All you guys have been in and out so much I am not quite sure where Barclays presently stands.

A. The bulk of the insurance products we sell are under an arrangement with Legal & General. We do write some of our own insurance but not a great deal. Different parts of the business sell investment products on different bases but you are right that we do approach this market in different ways.

165. Are you a member of Mr Gyllenhammar's club?

A. We are. I am not sure we would describe it as a club.

Lord Howie of Troon

166. What would you describe it as, a conspiracy?

A. Not at all, no, because as Mr Gyllenhammar did say, the output of the group is always made public so in that sense . . .

Baroness Cohen of Pimlico: . . . it cannot be much of a conspiracy.

Lord Howie of Troon: The best kind!

Baroness Cohen of Pimlico

167. My specific question is under the Investment Services Directive. You are talking about issues around "execution only" and "direct offer" services within the Investment Services Directive. Could you be more specific about those. I did not quite understand how they affected the UK and what changes you want.

A. Are you all familiar with what is meant by "execution only" and "direct offer"?

168. Yes.

A. Okay. The Investment Services Directive as proposed by the Commission would have required that before any sale or purchase was entered into by a customer that they had been advised about the suitability of that transaction for them. Obviously with execution only stockbroking or direct offer sales, usually done with a leaflet or possibly out of an advertisement, it is the consumer who makes up their mind whether they want to buy or sell (particularly in execution only) a set of shares. They contact the company they want to deal with and say, "Buy me or sell me whatever", and that is it and they pay a relatively cheap price to do that. Most execution only service providers will also offer advice but at a price and different levels of advice with different prices attached. The danger we saw from the Commission's initiative is that it would force UK consumers who have shown themselves to be more than happy to deal on an execution only basis to have advice for which they would then have to pay, which seems rather odd to us.

169. You would end up unable to carry on with the UK practice?

Baroness Cohen of Pimlico *contd.*]

A. That is right and indeed it would run counter to the Sandler proposals which are currently on the table which talk about "cheap to offer" products. It also runs contrary to some of the other initiatives that the Commission has put forward which look to provide more information about a company's activities to consumers/investors so that they are better informed so that they can make their own decisions. If they are having to have advice about their decisions in a sense they do not need the information.

170. And how are you getting on with this one, are you making any progress on keeping execution only?

A. We are making progress. I am pleased to say Theresa Villiers, the MEP, who is the rapporteur for this in the Economic and Monetary Affairs Committee in the European Parliament did listen to what UK industry had to say and did come up with some compromise amendments which would enable the UK's practices to continue, but that is only in committee, it still has to go to plenary, it still has to be looked at by Council, so it is by no means over and done yet and the support we have had so far from the Treasury has been very helpful and I would hope that they will continue with that.

Lord Cavendish of Furness

171. Still with the implementation and enforcement section of your evidence, on the Lamfalussy process you point out that the framework Directives have contained significantly more detail than one might have expected (level one) and that there could be more feedback from CESR on level two measures and how they have reached their decisions. Do you think the market participants understand the split between level one and two? Are there lessons to be drawn from your comments when the process moves on to levels three and four?

A. I think in terms of "do the participants understand it", it depends how far you go down. I am sure the people on the trading floor have not a clue, but why should they? I think those who are more intimately involved with the process do understand it. As the process goes on there is more literature available. The inter-institutional monitoring group produced a very good report which lays out exactly what each level is supposed to do and how it fits with the next level, so in a sense there is no real excuse for anybody who wants to know not being able to find out. Added to that those of us involved in the process are learning by experience. The process is not very old. It would be amazing if everybody thought they were experts already. Do I think there are things to learn from what we have experienced so far when it comes to levels three and four? I think certainly level four is slightly different because that is more about the Commission taking action to enforce against Member States and it is rather hard to see how consultation could come into that. It is difficult to see how the Commission could hold a consultation that says, "Please tell us which Member States are not enforcing", because many market participants have learnt to their cost that it is probably not one of the world's greatest ideas to stand up and say, "This regulator is not applying this legislation properly and

I am the victim of their wanting to enforce it against me." But in terms of level three where it is CESR working on guidelines for implementation, then I think there probably is quite a lot of room for consultation, not least to make sure that market participants understand what the guidelines mean before they are promulgated. Thus I think there is plenty to be learned for level three, probably less for level four.

Lord Howie of Troon

172. In your submission you bring up the question of the level of political will among Member States to implement and enforce, as you put it, wholeheartedly. How serious a problem is this and could that lead to the failure of the action plan?

A. How serious a problem is it? Mr Gyllenhammar touched briefly on it and said there were various facts and figures. I cannot remember all the facts and figures but I have written some of them down. The Commission regularly researches and publishes where individual countries are in terms of implementing Directives and implementing them properly. These are just a few numbers from their last report[3] which was published in May this year. The UK has 23 outstanding Directives, which is exactly in line with the Commission's target of allowable outstandings, the French have more than twice that with 50, the Italians even more with 59, and there were only four countries who have fewer to transpose than the UK. The position is just as bad with infringements where France has 220, Italy 200 and the UK only 121. The Commission's comment on this is: "It is particularly worrying that the transposition deficit for internal market Directives has worsened considerably", and I can only say "Amen" to that. There is plenty of evidence there that transposition is not going ahead as well as it should and some countries seem to be pretty bad both at transposing and transposing correctly. Would it cause the Financial Services Action Plan to fail? In part the answer to that is it depends how slow people really are to transpose. You can be behind on the Commission's numbers but if you have got things in train it is not as bad as the figures perhaps first show. Coming back to where we started, in a sense, if we have no clear benchmarks of what success looks like it is going to be pretty hard to tell whether the Plan has actually succeeded or failed in any event. It might be easy to spot particular glaring errors and omissions but taken as a whole it might be much harder and one person's success will be seen as another's failure, depending on what your objectives really were. Just one other thing that I might add. The UK has got the Presidency of the Council in the second half of 2005, which coincides quite nicely with the original deadline for completing the Financial Services Action Plan, and it might be an area that the UK would like to put at the heart of their Presidency to do with implementation and enforcement of the Directives in the Action Plan.

173. You cannot be terribly happy with the situation when one of the big players in the Union

---

[3] Internal Market Scoreboard No.12 5/5/03.

Lord Howie of Troon *contd.*]

transgresses and infringes more than twice as much as the British do. Is there any way that you can suggest to minimise this disparity?

A. I think it has got to be around peer group pressure. It has got to do with the Commission being given more encouragement to enforce rather than just legislate. If we think about what the Commission was set up to do, it was set up to produce legislation and it is possibly only DG Competition which has a real enforcement role. Its problem is not just that it does not have very many members of staff but also that they have been recruited to write legislation, not to enforce it.

174. Quite. But if the Commission writes legislation which it is unable to enforce, do you not think it would be a good idea to stop writing any more until it is able to enforce something or do we wait until Chirac goes?

A. No. I think undoubtedly it would be beneficial if the Commission were to think about how things were going to be enforced, that goes without saying. To say that should mean they should stop legislating now just because they have not necessarily been able to enforce everything previously is probably rather too drastic. In my nightmare moments I would probably agree with you but realistically I do not think you can just say "we will stop all future legislation because we have not been able to enforce everything else 100 per cent". The outstandings and the infringements, in a sense, are evidence that the Commission does put effort into making sure that things are transposed and where they are not transposed properly it does seek to get Member States to toe the line. I think it is about speeding up that part rather than turning all hands from A to B.

Lord Howie of Troon: I put it a little starkly perhaps. Of course, the same thing happens here in that legislation goes through without everybody realising really whether or not it is working. This is not new in politics. I will leave it at that.

Chairman

175. In our previous discussions with Mr Gyllenhammar the issue of consumer protection came up, as you will have observed from the gallery there. In your view, in the retail markets is the differing approach of 15 and then 25 Member States in consumer protection likely to be an area that in retail financial services does pose problems in making progress in the single market?

A. I think so. I can give a number of specifics. Quite a long time ago, so it is history, Barclays wanted to pay interest on current accounts in France. We were prevented from doing it because you cannot do that in France. That is a difference between a product type which is totally acceptable in one country and not at all acceptable in another and that is quite difficult to rationalise. Similarly, with one of our recent products, Open Plan, which is a mortgage which is then put together with current accounts and savings accounts so you do not pay as much, we had to build a different product to fit with the Spanish regime. Effectively it does the same thing at the end but it is not the same. Those are two specifics where

we have encountered difficulties. The only pan-European product is a thing that rejoices in the name of the UCITS, which to everybody else is a unit trust, and they are hedged about with what qualifies as a UCITS. You can sell them across borders but the way you market and advertise them is then subject to local rules. So even though you have got a product that will travel, how you market it and how you advertise it is then subject to different rules in each Member State. Those are the practical difficulties that we all face. Different companies approach it in different ways. Some set up subsidiaries in the individual countries and just take on board whatever the local requirements are and do that. Clearly it does not allow for a pan-European provision other than on a Member State by Member State basis.

176. What is your view about how to approach that particular area of problem for retail of financial services? Do you put a lot of faith in the 25 countries who agree a set of common principles that they will apply in domestic legislation?

A. I think if what we started from was a greater acceptance of mutual recognition, which means that if you have complied with the rules that are in the country that you set off from then you do not have to comply again when you get to the country that you are wanting to sell in, that would be a great start. In a sense, the advantage of that is that you do not have to go right down to the nth degree of harmonising everything but you could agree on some principles and the principles might include, for example, that customers have to be given enough but not too much information.

177. It is difficult to disagree with that as a proposition but what does it mean?

A. I think what it means is the information that they have has to be sufficient to enable them to understand what are the key elements of the product, what is the nature of the risks they are taking on, what is the nature of the price they are going to pay and what are the main service elements that they can expect to receive. Another area that we might all agree on as a principle is that they have a right to withdraw, that they have a right to be able to complain not just to the company but through an ombudsman system and then to the courts if necessary, but that they do not have to go to court because it is jolly expensive to go to court. This is possibly more from the suppliers' side, that regulators should not attempt to regulate the detail of the product because if they do that then they are going to stymie any kind of development because you have to build your product inside what the rules say and if there is regulation more around how you sell it and to whom you sell it then that should provide adequate protection. I think those are a number of principles that you could start to build agreement on and then Member States' legislation could be tested against those principles to see whether it was reasonable.

Lord Walpole

178. I think we have got ourselves separated from the flow. If we go back to the last question, the consequence of the point that you were referring to

Lord Walpole *contd.*]

in the previous question was the formation of a single regulator, EuroSEC, to ensure common standards of enforcement throughout the EU. You say you are against this. Why?

A. I do not think it is necessary to have a single regulator (certainly at this stage) to produce a single market. If you look at other areas where we have got single markets then they do not necessarily have their own regulator either. I think that we should devote the relatively scarce resources that we have got into more immediate problems rather than something which is a long-term solution which we may or may not need. There is more to be had by getting regulators to talk to each other, as they do under the Lamfalussy process, particularly at level three, to agree how they are going to implement it.

179. You mean the different national regulators?

A. Yes, the different national regulators. I perhaps should say supervisors rather than regulators. Any supervisor to supervise effectively needs to be close to their market to understand what is going on here. It is quite hard to see how that could be done with one supervisor sat wherever when you have still got a European market characterised by market-places in the main financial centres and other financial centres as well. So I think there are those practical reasons around "we have got bigger fish to fry now" and I am not sure that I am convinced it is a necessary thing even in the longer term.

180. So you think you can make the national supervisors more effective?

A. I think that is right, yes.

181. I think that answers the question. I was not quite sure whether the last person in your chair agreed with you or not, even though he is in the same club.

A. Sometimes he clearly spoke for Aviva and sometimes he clearly spoke for the EFR.

182. I know he was talking about insurance rather than banking but I think he was also clear that he did not see that as the immediate solution, at least that is what I heard him say, and that he could see it as a possibility for the future but not something that was necessary for the future. Do you think there is a possibility it will be needed in the future? You still say no, do you?

A. To say never—If the other ways of making sure that regulators do regulate in a similar fashion, if the market as a whole does not begin to coalesce, if we tried the other ways and they have not worked, then an alternative must be a single regulator. Whether it is an alternative of choice is another matter altogether and it is not my alternative of choice.

183. Is there a danger that the supervisors or regulators (and I think you prefer supervisory bodies) might become captured by their respective industries and become protective of them?

A. I am not sure certainly in the UK that we would regard the FSA as being captured by the industry at all.

184. Elsewhere in Europe do you think this is a possibility?

A. Do I think in other countries that the regulators have been captured by their industry? Not necessarily. I think there are other countries where the national psyche is different, that it sees its collective objective as preserving national champions, if you will, whereas the United Kingdom psyche is more directed towards producing an open competitive market place and if actually the square mile is not occupied by UK firms but UK plc as a whole is getting a great deal out of it, so be it.

185. This is an important issue. If you want to argue against a EuroSEC then it is enormously important that Member States all have their own supervisory bodies, that they are not in fact acting as protective devices for their own industries but actually they are doing what we would regard as a supervisory role to ensure a competitive environment for the best interests of the consumer eventually.

A. That is true, but their start point is always the Directive on which they are working. If the Directives are crafted in such a way that it is more than possible for a regulator to interpret them one way or the other then that is exactly what they will do and that has been a political decision at some point in the legislative process which again, I think, goes back to this issue about if we were all clear about what the objectives were, even if we did not put numbers round them, then producing a legislation to achieve that objective would be easier or at least the political decisions would be more transparent.

Baroness Cohen of Pimlico

186. You do not mean if we are all clear, you mean if we are all agreed. If I wanted to have national champions and other people wanted to have competitive markets there is not a great deal of meeting of minds possible.

A. There is not, which is a very fair push back, but if you look at where the Financial Services Action Plan comes from, it is not about making life easier for financial services companies at all, it is about making life better for industry and consumers, the ones who use finance, and that was agreed at the highest political level even if it is now somewhat discredited, but heads of state did sign up to that at Lisbon as their objectives, so there was at one point political agreement about what was going to be achieved.

Baroness Cohen of Pimlico: On a rather broad motherhood and apple pie basis.

Lord Chadlington: If Mr Eldridge's position is going towards establishing objectives rather than numerical objectives then I am much closer to his position than I was when we started.

Chairman: Lord Fearn, would you like to take us on on that happy note?

Lord Fearn

187. You refer to the dangers to London of the FSAP proposals, and indeed to the wider EU, if the Financial Services Action Plan is not aimed at producing a globally competitive marketplace. What are your views on a cost/benefit analysis of FSAP?

A. Again, taking the Plan as a whole, going back to how we talked about objectives, I am not sure that it was ever possible to do a cost/benefit analysis for the Plan as a whole. I do think that, taking individual

Lord Fearn *contd.*]

initiatives, more work about the cost and benefits could have been, and should have been, done. That is not saying anything new, the Commission is charged with producing a cost/benefit analysis before it comes forward with any piece of legislation. I am not saying we should be doing anything new there.

188. Should they be charged?
A. They are.

189. They are actually doing it?
A. They are charged with doing it.

190. Has it a degree of accuracy about it?
A. Sometimes.

191. That is very cautious.
A. But often not.

192. So what is the use of doing it?
A. The cost/benefit analysis that they do is more often paying lip service to what they should be doing rather than what one might wish to see by way of cost/benefit analysis.

193. So if they embark on it, it could really be disadvantageous to any country or our country?
A. It could be disadvantageous to any country, we are not necessarily sure at the moment which. In a sense what is more important is have they done a piece of work to show that the cost/benefit analysis for the EU as a whole produces a positive result because if we were to go back and say "We will only participate in this if it produces a benefit to the UK" then we would be doing all those things which I have railed against other Member States doing in terms of protecting their industry. I think you would have to take it in the round but I am not convinced it has been carried out in the round either.

194. So it is a useless exercise?
A. What they have done is not terribly good at the moment but I think, to be fair to them, it is not an easy thing to do because the nature of the Action Plan is very wide and in many ways until you have got to the end of the Directive and you know what all the costs to the suppliers are you cannot do that side of the equation. You can probably have a good idea what the benefits to industry might be, but until it is finally agreed and we understand what all the mechanisms are that the financial services industry has to go through it is actually quite difficult to work out the costs and that is why the Commission finds it so difficult.

Lord Fearn: Thank you very much.

Lord Walpole

195. Very very briefly, what about the new members to the EU, what is your feeling about them and whether they are going to be able to regulate themselves and whether you will understand what they are up to because their institutions are all very new, are they not?
A. Yes they are. The accession countries have made great strides to get themselves in line to adopt the existing legislation which exists in the EU, the *acquis.* I am sure that some of them will be better at implementing financial services legislation than other legislation and we have already seen that in the sense that different countries are further forward in getting themselves in line with the *acquis.* Within the EU as it stands there have always been countries that people have pointed to—and I am not going to name them—and said, "Well, I would not fancy any products from that country ending up being sold to our retail customers", but I think the real issue is that if there is proper communication between the regulators and proper peer group pressure then changes can and will be made but I am not going to be tempted into being critical overall of any of the accession countries.

Chairman

196. Thank you very much for your succinct and extremely helpful answers during the course of the session. You have enabled us to keep almost to time, and it is not your fault if we have not. Is there anything you would like to add by way of final remarks?
A. I think there are just three main points. The action plan should be motivated by a need to generate more competition and more open markets. I still think greater clarity about the objectives of each piece of legislation and then a follow-up to see that it is achieving those would be beneficial. Also without proper implementation and enforcement all of that which comes beforehand is really irrelevant. Those are the three key points.

Chairman: I can tell you that whatever our views on the first two points are, on the third point you have the unanimous support of the Committee and we have not even got to the draft report yet. Thank you for coming, we enjoyed your evidence and thank you for your time.

Supplementary memorandum from Barclays

ADVERSE IMPACTS OF FSAP ON LONDON/EU WITHIN CONTEXT OF GLOBAL MARKETS

Two types of adverse consequences:

— EU legislation imposed additional (net) burdens on EU financial service providers, or on some of them, compared to service providers operating outside EU;

— deliberate or unintended extra-territorial impacts of FSAP generate reprisals from other countries.

In more detail

1. Examples of where EU operators would be disadvantaged:
— CAD3;

Possible application to EU asset managers who operate globally will disadvantage them compared to US competitors where Basel II will only be applied to banks. This will raise costs for EU providers in a business that operates on thin margins.

— Transparency Obligations Directive.

Requirements for non-EU issuers to produce "equivalent" financial information would increase their costs. This would discourage use of EU-regulated markets by non-EU issuers. As a consequence EU investors would have a reduced choice or have to go to, say, the USA to invest. EU-based arrangers (banks etc) would have fewer clients to service in the EU and hence would employ fewer people in the EU.

2. Extra-territorial impacts

The Financial Conglomerates Directive has been quoted by US firms as requiring them to make unnecessary structural charges.

There are also difficulties with Data Protection legislation. On the other hand the US authorities have placed requirements on non-US firms, most notably with the Sarbanes-Oxley legislation.

There is a danger that without better dialogue between US and EU legislation then more such cases could occur. A second danger is that the disagreements degenerate into a tit for tat dispute which exacerbate rather than improve relations.

24 September 2003

MONDAY 15 SEPTEMBER 2003

Present:

Cavendish of Furness, L.	Fearn, L.
Cohen of Pimlico, B.	Walpole, L.
Faulkner of Worcester, L.	Woolmer of Leeds, L. (Chairman)

Memorandum from the Financial Services Authority

INTRODUCTION

1. The FSA is the single statutory regulator directly responsible for the regulation of deposit taking, insurance, investment business and exchanges. It is an independent non-government body which exercises its statutory powers under the Financial Services and Markets Act 2000 (FSMA). The FSA is a company limited by guarantee, financed by levies on the industry. It receives no funds from the public purse. It is accountable to Treasury Ministers and, through them, to Parliament.

2. The FSMA requires the FSA to pursue four objectives:

— to maintain confidence in the UK financial system;

— to promote public understanding of the financial system;

— to secure the appropriate degree of protection for consumers whilst recognising their own responsibilities; and

— to reduce the scope for financial crime.

The legislation applies these objectives directly to specific FSA activities—making rules, preparing and issuing codes, giving advice and guidance and determining the general policy by which it acts.

3. In carrying out these activities the FSA is also required to take into account a number of factors, which we refer to as "principles of good regulation". These are:

— using its resources in the most economic and efficient way;

— recognising the responsibilities of regulated firms' own management;

— being proportionate in imposing burdens or restrictions on the industry;

— facilitating innovation;

— taking into account the international character of financial services and the UK's competitive position; and

— facilitating, and not having an unnecessarily adverse effect on, competition.

4. The EU agenda on financial services issues continues to present a challenging set of risks and opportunities for the FSA's statutory objectives and the principles of good regulation. Since EU legislation effectively determines UK law in this area, failure to engage effectively with the EU's single market programme would pose a threat to the FSA's ability to achieve its objectives and uphold its principles of good regulation.

5. The Financial Services Action Plan (FSAP) is due to be completed by 2005. Discussions on the post-FSAP agenda are already under way, not least since 2010 is the deadline set by the Council of Ministers for the EU to be recognised as the world's most competitive economy. The Commission and a growing number of Member States seem to accept that a more committed approach is required to achieving the single market across all financial sectors if this objective is to be met.

6. The FSA works closely with HM Treasury in pursuit of UK objectives on FSAP measures. We provide technical support to HMT in the Council negotiations on FSAP directives and help analyse the impact of these measures on UK legislation, the financial services industry and consumers. We also, together with HMT, organise regular specialist drafting and more general update meetings with trade associations and other relevant bodies on current dossiers.

7. Our answers have been kept deliberately brief. More detail may be found in the recent speeches by Howard Davies (Chairman) and David Green (Head of International Policy Co-ordination and EU Affairs).

A. Financial Services Action Plan

8. The primary objective of the FSAP, agreed in 1999, is to facilitate the creation of a single market in financial services. 42 separate initiatives form the FSAP, which aims to deliver a fully operational single market for securities by 2003, and for banking and insurance by 2005. It is unlikely that all the measures will be agreed and implemented by these deadlines.

9. However, the fact that most of the FSAP measures have already been agreed should be seen as a considerable achievement. It is far from easy for EU Member States with very different national histories, economic structures and political constraints, to adopt common policies. Since all agreements reached will inevitably be compromised, it is unsurprising that not all the adopted legislative measures are fully in line with preferred UK policy. Together with HMT, the FSA works to ensure that proposed EU legislation will provide net benefits to consumers, firms and markets in the UK. We place much emphasis on cost-benefit analysis to evaluate the expected impact on proposed regulatory policies. We seek also to use this approach in the negotiations on the FSAP measures and to get it accepted more widely in Brussels, where a Better Regulation Action Plan is now being implemented. Consultation of consumers and firms is an important part of our regulatory impact analysis. It is a helpful means of ensuring that the competitive position of the UK is properly taken into account in EU negotiations.

10. Some 34 of the 42 planned FSAP initiatives have been agreed. A significant number of these have already been implemented by Member States and work is well under way on the others—a Regulation on International Accounting Standards, the Financial Groups Directive and the Distance Marketing Directive. Of the eight or so which have still to be agreed, the most important for FSA are the Risk-based Capital Directive for banks and investment firms, the wide-ranging revision of the Investment Services Directive (ISD) and the Transparency Directive (TD).

11. Agreement of the first of these may be facilitated by its close connections with the revised Basel Accord, although some would argue that this could also still serve to inject some tension into the negotiations at EU level. On the ISD, serious effort is being invested by the Commission and Presidency in identifying the most important issues for Member States in a bid to secure agreement on the most controversial issues as soon as possible. Several rounds of consultation based on the Lamfalussy approach of actively seeking the views of all relevant parties preceded publication of the formal draft TD. But there is a good deal still to play for in the Council negotiations on all of these and the European Parliament is expected to continue to take a close interest in these measures.

12. While activity on all these measures continues, a range of other issues have begun to compete for attention and resources. These include the need for the development of regulatory networks to provide effective regulation of the single market, better enforcement action, the EU corporate governance and retail agendas, the respective roles of legislative and non-legislative options and the content of the Constitutional Convention and Treaty negotiations. In assessing the relative importance of these, it is becoming increasingly important to look beyond 2005 and consider the priorities for action once the FSAP is completed.

B. Implementation and Enforcement

13. We welcome the application of the Lamfalussy approach to the regulation of the securities sector, and the decisions to apply this approach to banking, insurance and pensions, conglomerates and UCITs by the end of this year.

14. The Lamfalussy approach is a major initiative to improve the quality of the European legislative process in the area of financial services. The four-level approach of the process (i) framework legislation agreed by Commission, Council and Parliament, (ii) technical implementing measures, (iii) regulatory networks, and (iv) enforcement by regulators and the Commission, should help to ensure that EU legislation is drafted, consulted on, agreed, implemented and enforced in the most effective way.

15. At the highest level of the Lamfalussy structure, ECOFIN has set up an EU Financial Services Committee (FSC). The FSC is to give political advice on financial market issues to ECOFIN. It should thus fill the potential gap between the high-level political and the technical, regulatory levels, and provide for cross-sectoral strategic reflection, separate from the legislative process.

16. Experience to date in the securities sector has shown that the legislative process is now more open. A good example of this was the consultation process organised by the Commission on the revision of the ISD. What some call the "Prodi amendment", which introduced a last minute change to the proposed Directive, may come to be considered an accident along the road towards greater transparency. Another example of the improved consultation is the public document on consultation agreed by the Committee of European Securities Regulators (CESR) and the practice that has followed it. It is planned that the regulatory committees of the other financial sectors will imitate CESR's good practice in the area of consultation.

17. But the role of CESR and the other committees of regulators is not confined to technical advice. The Lamfalussy report proposed that level 3 should also cover strengthened co-operation and networking between national regulators with a view to ensuring consistent transposition of level 1 and level 2 legislation.

Greater emphasis on the convergence of regulatory and supervisory practice is another area where the Lamfalussy approach is expected to make an improvement on what went before. It is important to ensure that it can continue to develop as desired despite the immense pressure on the resources of regulators, practitioners, finance ministries and the Commission resulting from the consultation process on level 2 implementing measures.

18. The major responsibility for enforcement falls on the European Commission. But Member States, regulators and the private sector also need to provide information to the European Commission about areas where problems exist or are likely to arise. Trade associations and other representative bodies can be very useful in this respect as individual market participants are often reluctant to step forward. The work recently overseen by the Association of British Insurers on the remaining barriers to the single market in financial services, and the report organised by the Investment Management Association on the main problems facing the development of a single market in asset management are excellent examples of what can be achieved.

19. Competition authorities can be expected to have an important role to play in the process. Their expertise will be particularly helpful in identifying the remaining barriers to cross-border business and ways of overcoming them. Relying more on competition policy would also be preferable to the traditional tendency simply to produce more EU legislation to tackle barriers to the completion of the single market.

20. The Inter-Institutional Monitoring group (comprising two representatives nominated by each of the Commission, the Council and the Parliament) recently published its interim report on the Lamfalussy process. The report is favourable and underlines that good progress has been made while recognising that the process is still in a "learning by doing" phase and that further improvements are necessary. Generally it is accepted that the effectiveness of the Lamfalussy process cannot properly be assessed until it has had time to settle down and all four levels are functioning as intended. In our view, there are no ready alternatives to the Lamfalussy process in the short-term. Calls for a single regulator are premature and raise questions relating to the legislative framework for enforcement in individual Member States of federal regulator's rules and the identity of a "rescuer of last resort". There are also differences concerning the underlying philosophy of such a central authority, and more practical issues such as the choice of location and staffing.

21. Tax and market structure are examples of significant non-regulatory barriers to a single market. The first is considered by many to be a major obstacle to cross-border business. Barriers linked to market structure, such as asymmetries of information and sunk costs can, to a large extent, be addressed by competition authorities.

C. THE FUTURE

22. Although it is now generally accepted that there is no need for a second FSAP, this does not mean that the process of European law-making will stop for financial services. Several additional legislative measures are already in the pipeline: new solvency requirements for insurance companies (the "Solvency 2" Directive) which should provide for a risk-based approach to capital requirements; plans for a fast track procedure for reinsurance to bring this sector in line with the rest of insurance regulation; and, a recently published Corporate Governance Action Plan is likely to give rise to some further legislation in that area.

23. Otherwise the forward-looking programme for financial services is likely to be characterised by three main themes:

(i) improving enforcement of existing legislation, including more effective assessment (using meaningful indicators) of the progress achieved so far.

(ii) a fresh emphasis on non-legislative options including competition policy.

(iii) greater emphasis on the international dimension of the single market (including the rapidly growing EU/US agenda and the role of both the Commission and individual Member States in progressing that).

24. There have been concerns that the series of measures coming out of the FSAP and related initiatives could severely strain a number of firms which will have to comply with the new rules. We are aware that the scale of the change is enormous and that there is a risk that the domestic reform agenda in the financial services industry combined with the European one could create some bottlenecks. The FSA takes these concerns very seriously and works with firms and consumers to ensure that what is agreed makes sense and what is implemented is manageable.

25. The changes resulting from the FSAP are expected to bring changes to the profile of competition in the UK and across the European Union. Increased competition should be one of the main benefits of the single European market for financial services. This is expected to bring significant benefits to financial firms, investors and consumers. A recent study by London Economics suggested that, as a result of the Action Plan, EU-wide real GDP will increase by 1.1 per cent or €130 billion (in 2002 prices) over a decade or so. While precise figures of this kind must be treated with caution, even with a margin of error the prospects for growth as a result of the FSAP are encouraging.

26. Firms and consumers must avoid being reactive only to unwelcome initiatives, instead of being proactive. It is important that they take the initiative in the policy area they are most concerned with and lobby in Brussels to make their voice heard.

27. The impact on the overall competitive position of the UK and the European Union is expected to be positive. To a large extent it will depend on firms' reaction to the new opportunities that open up. Because of the well-developed nature of London's financial markets, UK firms have an advantage in a number of financial areas. But we need to continue to ensure that legislation primarily suited to the regulation of retail markets (which predominate in the other Member States) is not inappropriately applied to wholesale markets, the main examples of which are located in London. Meanwhile, UK firms need to accept that greater competition will mean that there will be losers as well as winners. The global impact of the FSAP and wider liberalisation elsewhere depends on the degree of enhanced competition achieved within the EU. The stronger this effect, the more likely it is that firms are competitive in the EU market will also be able to play a significant role in global markets. But the impact on the global competitive position of the EU will also depend on the way international standards that are linked to some of the FSAP Directives (eg on accounting, and on capital requirements for banks and insurance companies) are implemented and enforced.

27 June 2003

Examination of Witnesses

MR DAVID GREEN and MS DIANE MOORE, International Policy Co-ordination and EU Affairs, Financial Services Authority, examined.

Chairman

197. Mr Green, thank you for coming this afternoon and for the paper that you kindly circulated in advance. As you know, I met with you some long time ago now and you gave me an excellent steer and good advice at that stage, too. Through you, may I thank the FSA for their assistance to us. We are aiming for the impossible, which is something like 40 minutes in total, because we have another witness to try to get back on schedule. This does not mean that we care less about the issues, but we are just trying to keep things to order. If there is anything you would like to add before we start, please do, and then we will go straight to questions.
(*Mr Green*) No, thank you, Chairman. We are happy to take the questions as they arise.

Lord Cavendish of Furness

198. You note in your introduction that the EU agenda on financial service continues to present a challenging set of risks and opportunities for the FSA as statutory objectives and principles of good regulation. Could you enlarge on these a bit and develop what can be done about the risks, what they are and what are the principal opportunities?
(*Mr Green*) I think the risks come in three broad categories. There are risks in relation to process, risks in relation to substance of policy, and risks in relation to implementation. On process, the risk for the FSA, and indeed for the various parts of the official sector in the UK involved in this, are that we are unable to get our voice heard in the way that we would wish. We are, as you know, and as we said in our paper, required by the Financial Services and Markets Act to follow various objectives, statutory objectives, and principles of good regulation. It is obviously important for us that we can promote those principles within a framework that allows us to be heard, so that it is important that the kinds of evolution in the committee structure with which you

are familiar, the so-called Lamfalussy committees, proceeds smoothly. There is still some way to go on that. It is important that in the overall legislative process proper consideration is given to the kind of statutory objective Parliament has given us in the UK. There are risks of being edged out of the process in various ways, but I think we are dealing with that by being very active ourselves, working with the Treasury and with industry and being out in the institutions themselves through secondments to try to make sure that we are actively involved in the process. On the substance, the danger is that different visions of the future of the EU Single Market, different from ours, may make progress in ways that we find difficult to resist. There is a risk of pressure for total standardisation of regulation, which is a theme that runs through the whole of this debate. While that has certain advantages, it could also have enormous costs if not applied in the right places and at the right time. There is a risk that in any individual venture, and there are a lot of them, there may be steps taken which undermine the kind of objectives that have been agreed so recently with Parliament here.

199. On opportunities, is the structure of the FSA unique, and does its uniqueness present special problems, which do not apply to other Member States?
(*Mr Green*) It is almost unique, if that is not perhaps a contradiction in terms. The integration of the Banking Securities and Insurance Regulation, which seemed quite new in the United Kingdom at the time, although not completely original, has actually spread over quite a lot of Europe now, and that has made our task easier in structural terms. The Germans have a single regulator, as do the Austrians. The Belgians are about to have one. The Irish have one. The Swedes and Danes have always had one. There are partial mergers in some other countries. The intention in the UK reform to integrate the approach to regulation is one where structures elsewhere in Europe are supportive, by and large.

Lord Cavendish of Furness *contd.*]

What we do not have elsewhere are the kinds of objectives and principles in the prospectuses of the individual regulators and we have continued to press on that. It is too late for the individual regulators but we continue to press at the European level to promote those objective, and indeed those same principles appear in Lamfalussy's own report, perhaps not entirely by accident. I should just mention that there is a risk simply of overload from the implementing of all the objectives. That is a risk that we can mitigate by careful planning, looking at those areas of legislation where there is some scope for rephrasing if that becomes necessary, and by generally continuing to keep the industry alert, if there is a slip, to these dangers. The opportunities for the FSA are perhaps themselves difficult to distinguish from the opportunities for the UK economy more widely, in that the creation of a sensibly functioning Single Market ought to make it easier for us to fulfil our objectives in relation to protecting consumers, for instance. If we have a better crafted and better understood set of rules for cross-border business, which is part of the objective of the plan, then it should be the case that consumers will be better protected in the UK than they otherwise would have been. That is an example of the kinds of opportunities.

Chairman

200. On that last point, is there not a problem that each Member State has its own view on how consumers are best protected? Some of the evidence given to us is that that can introduce certain difficulties, inflexibilities, difficulties in the market place for a single market in practice.

(*Mr Green*) That is indeed correct. One of the big continuing debates is about the best way of protecting consumers. It is quite interesting in the Financial Services Action Plan itself that the single wholesale market, the single capital market, has very clear objectives and is rather more cautious than the tone that was adopted in relation to the retail market. There are, to caricature greatly, two broad views in relation to consumer protection. One is that you can really only protect the consumer by allowing the consumer to be offered safe products and that if the product is save, that is really all you can do because the consumer will never be very well equipped to judge on the safety and soundless of a product. By and large, that approach is quite widely held in a large number of other Member States. The alterative approach is to allow great liberality in the production of products, whether they are savings products or borrowing products, but to equip the consumer with protection in the form either or both of a duty on the supplier of the financial services product to consider the suitability of the product for the purchaser of the product and a duty to offer advice, with a selection of rules about how the price may be given. You can see that in a rather fundamental sense those are quite different approaches. I think the reality is that in many countries there is a rather mixed approach, and indeed in the UK we have seen, as a result of the various difficulties which have arisen over the last

few years, some kind of a move to suggest that we have rather more structured products. These are the kinds of recommendations that were made, which do not need a whole paraphernalia of advice or should not need it. I think you have more of a convergence on a rather less clear middle ground. That debate goes on all the time, so that it would not be correct to say that there were fundamental differences of view between Member States, but in relation to any particular issue, there can be quite a number of different views on the table. I do not know whether that is a sufficiently clear answer to your question. It is a rather muddy situation.

Chairman: If we have time, I may return to it. If not, perhaps I could write to you a brief note on it.

Lord Fearn

201. You are generally positive on the status of FSAP and how much has been achieved, and you note that 34 of the 42 objectives have been agreed. However, other witnesses we have seen are less positive and point to important directives, such as those mentioned in paragraph 10 of your evidence—the Capital Directive, the Investment Services Directive and the Transparency Directive—all of which have to be completed by May 2004 when Parliament changes. My first question is: do you not accept that important aspects of FSAP are seriously behind schedule? What impact will rushed or delayed legislation have on FSAP and the UK Financial Services sector in particular?

(*Mr Green*) In relation to the general question, how well are we doing, it is certainly the case that there are some important measures, which have not been completed. I think most of the measures in the plan are more or less on track. There is some slippage but, and this relates to part of your question, there is also an appreciation that it is still better to have good legislation rather than rushed legislation. I think there has been a tension throughout this process between the need to set rather demanding timetables, because otherwise you would never get there, and the need to get the legislation right. In relation to the overall structure of the plan, one of the features of it is that beneficial effects will not come through in some areas until all the parts are there. In the way that the plan has traditionally been presented, if you like, the vision of the final product is not clear. In relation to capital market measures for instance, there are different measures scattered throughout the plan, but the underlying concept is that you have common accounting standards, a common process for issuing securities, common prospectuses, common rules for wholesale market behaviour, common rules of market abuse, common rules for infrastructure, and you have a common approach to the selling of investments to retail investors. In a way, all those have to be in place before you get the benefits of it. Somebody suggested to me that here was an analogy to be made with the construction of a motorway, that you have a bridge built here and a bit of road built there, but it all looks a mess and is completely unusable until every

Lord Fearn *contd.*]

single bit is in place. I think there is some virtue in that analogy in relation to the capital markets agenda. It has, I think, been in some respects more difficult to make progress than was generally expected in that the sheer diversity of arrangements in the Member States was probably not appreciated by anybody, and we are still struggling with that. Some kind of delay in some areas is perhaps inevitable. There is a recognition that it will be important to get it right rather than rushed. You will be familiar with the debate about whether the capital adequacy arrangements for banks that are being, if you like, generated in Basle, now to be carried over into the EU, are exactly right. Clearly, it would be desirable to get a proper international agreement on that rather than sticking to a rigid timetable, but there is a balance between needing to get all the bits in place before you get any results and making sure that the measures are fit for purpose. I do not know whether that really answers your question and all the points in it.

202. Yes, apart from the fact that the UK financial services will be affected more than any other.

(*Mr Green*) I think that is quite difficult to say. Certainly to the extent that the existing wholesale capital markets are by and large based in London, the measures at the wholesale level are more disciplined than in some other countries which do not actually have wholesale capital markets in the same sense and you can say that the UK is more affected. At the same time, those measures, to the extent that they do produce a more efficient capital market overall, may mean that the markets in London are much better placed to exploit the opportunities that are opening up than are other countries, which may either have no wholesale market that they can develop or have a rather poor, uncompetitive wholesale market, the protection of which will be either eliminated or reduced by these measures. In a sense, if you have a country with a small equity market at present, if you look at the numbers, there may be no great effect, but it is possible that this kind of opening of a single market will actually eliminate quite a lot of the players, or indeed the exchanges, so that for that country the effect looks rather powerful.

203. You also referred to a number of issues which have begun to compete for attention and resources, such as the development of regulatory networks, better enforcement action, and the EU corporate governance and retail agendas, amongst others. The implication is that these will be priorities post-2005. Are these now key aspects of FSAP which need to be in place before 2005?

(*Mr Green*) The answer to that is that some of them do need to be in place, but I think it is also fair to say that quite a lot of work is currently under way on them. On the regulatory networks, a lot of work has been done to build on existing networks. In some cases, all that is happening is that existing structures are being enhanced. The reality of the networks is probably more advanced than the formal agreement to their final shape. Enforcement is something which clearly can only follow on after you have got the legislation agreed. People are

starting to think about that. The Commission is hoping to use the co-ordinates legislative activity next year, as you have the new European Parliament and the new Commission. It is hoping to use that force to work up its agenda for enforcement. In practice, the results of that will probably not be given good effect until 2005, but if our evidence suggested that these were issues that either were being delayed or could be delayed, perhaps we did not draft it carefully enough.

Chairman

204. You did not touch there upon issues of pan-European clearance and settlement systems. Is that not a problem for at least the equity markets and retail markets?

(*Mr Green*) It is certainly the case that the current clearing and settlement arrangements are quite diverse across the EU. Certainly in the equity markets, until quite recently, they have been very departmentalised. As the Committee will be aware, there have been quite a lot of connections made of varying degrees of stringency between a number of the exchanges and a number of the market infrastructure players, both on the clearing and on the settlements side.. My own current feeling is that, provided we can be certain that there is overall sound supervision of these arrangements, then we should continue to allow market forces to play out in the competition between these various pieces of machinery, if you like, rather than trying to impose a model on them. There is, as I am sure you will be aware, Chairman, a proposition that if you have a sort of utility of clearing and settlement, a lot of the costs which currently can be identified in the structure might be reduced, but utilities always raise question about regulation and competition. At least for the time being, I think, broadly speaking, to allow the market players to see how best they think they can provide a service in the clearing and settlement is the best way forward, always provided that there are not barriers to reasonable steps in that direction. Does that take you far enough in an answer?

Chairman: In the time available, I think it is as far as we can go. It does leave some interesting issues to discuss.

Lord Walpole

205. You have just touched on it a moment ago and in fact you do state in your very useful memorandum at paragraph 18 that the responsibility for enforcement really does fall on the European Commission. How will the Commission discharge its responsibility and will the approach be any different from enforcement in previous directives where there is still a high level of non-compliance amongst Member States? Indeed, do you agree that effective enforcement is a key to the success of the implementation of FSAP, and what recommendations would you have to have to achieve success in this area?

(*Mr Green*) It is the case still that the Commission is the body formally responsible for enforcement of

Lord Walpole contd.]

directives. In the financial services area, the Commission themselves are quite clear that, unless there is adequate enforcement, the benefits for the wider economy, which this rather extensive project is designed to achieve, will not emerge. They are clear about that and they have said so. At the same time, these are very complex markets with a great deal of technical detail, which is quite difficult for the Commission officials themselves to grasp, and they acknowledge this. They will be looking for help from market participants and from the regulators in identifying those areas where implementation is deficient and also, in that process, identifying where the priorities are for implementation. I think we have in the City a number of trade associations, both in isolation and collectively, which have been working hard at trying to produce their shopping list for implementation, but it will be very necessary for the market participants to work out the ones that really make a difference rather than those that are just a nuisance. There will also be a role for the networks of regulators, which already exist, though some in more formal shape than others, themselves to look at whether implementation has been sufficiently comprehensive and, if necessary, to point the finger to where the Commission can use its own pressure. It will be a difficult task but not only we but also the Commission would subscribe to your proposition that without effective implementation, the benefits are not going to be derived from the project.

206. Do you feel that the ten new Members are going to be able to cope with regulation in their own countries?

(Mr Green) It so happens that I was talking to the Commission this morning about our enforcement effort. Of course, making sure that the ten acceding countries are up to scratch is one of the things that will be particularly important for the Commission. They have drawn certainly on other regulators in the work that is being done prior to accession to highlight the key areas that are necessary, and the FSA has participated in those efforts. We continue, within the scope of our own resources, to help from time to time in giving advice to the acceding countries, but that is a large call on the Commission's resources. I think we can expect that the relevant parts of the Commission will themselves be saying, once the priorities for enforcement become clear, that they need more staff themselves, as well as getting assistance from others.

Lord Faulkner of Worcester

207. Would it not be a whole lot easier if there were a single regulator?

(Mr Green) I think it would be very expensive for all 25 countries to change their rule books into one on which it had been possible for a collective decision to be reached. It comes back to the tension that we were talking about earlier about standardisation. There is quite a lot of reservation at this stage as to whether absolutely all parts of regulation could or should be standardised. Certainly, standardising the existing 25 rule books, depending on the area you are trying to look at, and

you may be looking at banking or much wider, will be a huge practical task. In a number of areas, particularly at the retail level, there will be a question about whether it is even sensible to have standardised regulation. In terms of developing a structure, it is easier to see a case for unifying regulation as much as possible in relation to the wholesale capital markets. On some versions of the single regulated proposition, that is all that is being talked about. There are other variations, one of which is that you should have a euro-FSA. Of course, in the ordinary course, we might be flattered that that examples was held up. In relation to both those kinds of model, one a sort of conduct of business model for the wholesale market and the other a prudential regulator for banking and insurance as well, there are generic difficulties in relation to the legal framework that will be necessary for this because, of course, the current arrangements are that we have no federal legislation and we have no federal courts. You would need to have legislation that had the force of law uniformly across the countries.

208. If that were in place—

(Mr Green) If that were in place, and also you had courts which would be able to enforce that legislation uniformly, federal courts, if you like—and this is the analogy to the other countries that have federal systems—I think those would be necessary conditions for that to work. In relation to prudential regulation, safety and soundness of banks and insurance companies, there are additional sets of issues, which come into play in that government and parliaments tend to have rather strong views about the way in which prudential regulation is constructed because if it goes wrong, they have to pay for the consequences with bank bail-outs or insurance company bail-outs or by the governments if such were to be called on. The arrangements for accountability in the European context between a federal regulator—I say federal in order to be clear as to what we are talking about—possibly the federal central bank, and of course within the eurozone there is such a bank, and the sources of public money to deal with rescues are quite difficult. We have in the UK arrangements established to deal with this elaborated under the Financial Services and Markets Act: the relationship between Treasury, the Bank of England and the FSA. That can be done in a single jurisdiction but if you are dealing with a federal regulator with its own federal budget, then the relationship between the responsibility for supervision and the provision of public money to deal with that is quite a difficult one, which I think none of such proposals as there are around at present for a single regulator can deal with.

209. You do not feel, from what you are saying, it is likely that we are going to be forced down that road?

(Mr Green) I do not think we shall be forced down that within the immediate foreseeable future. It will continue to be discussed because, going back to what I was saying much earlier on, there are economies for certain players to be had out of standardisation. If all the rules were the same

Lord Faulkner of Worcester *contd.*]

everywhere, and I was a banking group or an insurance group, then I could save loads of money in compliance costs and reporting costs. The case will continue to be put that there should be one set of rules for whatever it is. The debate, in that sense, would continue. For the legal and accountability reasons I mentioned, a federal regulator is not likely to be a serious runner within the immediately foreseeable time frame.

(*Ms Moore*) There will be a day of reckoning. It is currently done by the institutional monitoring group looking at the Lamfalussy report. Basically, that report says that by the end of 2004 you should be able to determine whether the system of regulatory networks is working sufficiently effectively to continue. The group has produced an interim report which is basically positive, but when you think you have 15 different regulators all doing different things, it has actually made a lot of progress over the short time of its life so far. There is a lot to do. In that regulatory network, you have what a single regulator did not have, namely the ability of competent regulators to come together to discuss what their differences might be, different approaches to enforcement and so on.

Chairman: I do apologise to you, Diane Moore. I am very remiss in not introducing you. You have been sitting there but I was not clear what your name was. Please forgive me for the discourtesy.

Baroness Cohen of Pimlico

210. I should declare an interest. I am a Director of the London Stock Exchange, as I expect you knew. You said at paragraphs 25 and 27 that you expect the United Kingdom financial services firms to have an advantage in a number of financial areas if markets opened up. That is not necessarily quite what everybody else has said to us. Are the United Kingdom firms doing enough to position themselves for the opportunities post-2005 or are they mainly worrying about whether they will be able to comply with the new regulations?

(*Mr Green*) They are certainly worrying about whether they will be able to comply with the new regulations. Going back to an earlier point, some of them may not even be worrying enough about that. I think the position varies as between the firms. United Kingdom firms of course can mean British-owned firms, and that can mean firms based in the UK. That is sometimes a distinction on which it is worth reflecting. I think some firms are certainly looking very much at how they may be able to expand their business across Europe and very often will be thinking, for a variety of reasons, that they will continue to base a number of features of their operations and perhaps their brain, if you like, their management, in London. That will certainly apply to a number of non-EU firms characteristically headquartered in London. With the British-owned firms, there are really quite marked differences. Some of them have been very actively considering whether the reduction in barriers made possible by the programme that we are describing, which continues an earlier opening up of markets, provides them with opportunities to move

physically into other parts of the EEA. You must remember that this is not just the EU; it also includes Norway and Iceland and so on. Some of them will be looking at whether they can market their products more effectively on a pan-European basis. Others may be starting to be afraid that there will be firms based elsewhere in Europe which are going to start offering products to British consumers, perhaps over the internet. There has been quite a lot of publicity over the last few months about some firms based elsewhere in the EU targeting UK consumers with bank accounts and so on. There is quite a varied picture of sponsors. I have to say that there are probably more firms based within countries elsewhere in Europe that are thinking about exploiting the Single Market as a whole. It is also fair to say that the pressure for doing that comes also from the use of the common currency, which is noted in the joint paper put out by the Treasury, the FSA and the Bank, which you may also have seen. For those firms, the common currency zone removes one of the barriers to cross-border business that they might otherwise have seen. The picture is quite varied. It is almost impossible to generalise.

211. Is it possible to generalise as far as expecting the FSAP network to be beneficial?

(*Mr Green*) I think it is almost impossible to generalise about that. A lot will depend on the way that the various players respond. Of course, we are not just talking about either the financial services firms or infrastructure providers. We are talking about the users of financial services, the borrowers. I know that you are going to be taking evidence from the corporate sector and consumers. You may find the competition that results produces a better deal. The whole project is, of course, for the benefit of the economy as a whole. Some parts of the financial services sector will, if they are unable to deal with the competition which emerges, individually almost certainly come under pressure. If there were not some parts of the financial services sector complaining about the risk of this extra competition, then it would not be working. It is not possible to know in advance how all this will come out. Adding up the costs and benefits of all the different players is quite difficult.

212. Is there a particular sector that is whingeing particularly or that feels itself threatened?

(*Mr Green*) No, I do not think there is. It varies from time to time. One of the peculiarities of this debate—and it relates to an issue that we have not really teased out here, the structure of legislation—comes back to the issue about the framework directives and how detailed you make legislation. Characteristically, any one group of players will say they want framework directives, but they really want lots of detail for everybody else to make sure they are not cheating. In areas where they think they might be at risk themselves, they want lots of detail to make sure that they can mount a defence. Against that general background, the grumbles tend to move around according to the issue of the moment. Is that fair?

(*Ms Moore*) That is fair comment.

Lord Cavendish of Furness

213. You said that the project is for the benefit of the economy as a whole. I have forgotten, and perhaps I should know this, but is that actually not a total generalisation itself? An economy is the sum total of the players, is it not?

(*Mr Green*) Yes, it is. Is it written down somewhere? I think it will be in the decisions made by the European Council when launching the action plan. I would need to come back to the Committee on that. The proposition, generally speaking, is that it is very strange that an area like Europe, with so many people so close together, should have this extraordinary plethora of barriers in the way of doing financial services and undertaking financial services business with their neighbours and that a reduction in those barriers almost certainly will contribute to economic welfare as a whole.

(*Ms Moore*) In the preamble to the Financial Services Action Plan, which is on the Commission website, there is quite a reasonable text on what their objectives are. It may be too general but it gives the gist.

214. Was that one of them, that the projects would benefit economies as a whole?

(*Ms Moore*) Yes. They delve into more detail, if I recall, about deeper and more liquid markets, flexibility of competition, benefits for consumers, those sorts of things.

Chairman

215. You comment in paragraph 23 of your memorandum to us on the need for greater emphasis on the international dimension of the single market. Could you just expand on that? You touched on it in paragraph 27.

(*Mr Green*) Yes. Clearly, the regulation of the markets in Europe will affect the attractiveness and competitiveness of those markets in relation to other financial centres, and indeed the users of financial markets in other countries. One of the objectives that we have in relation to this is to make sure—and it is consistent with the FSA's own objective under the legislation—that there is regard to the UK's competitive position. I think one of the concerns that we have had in these debates within Europe is that there is a risk that some kind of legislative solution that squared all the circles within Europe may nevertheless damage the competitiveness of such markets in the EU to attract foreign participants. The largest of those markets—and there are several different ones—are in London, and so it has been important to make sure that we have not damaged, in the course of these negotiations, the existing international attractiveness of markets in the EU and where possible enhanced them. An example of the risk of damage has been in the Prospectus Directive where some of you will know there was at one time a concept that any issuer of bonds would need to get their prospectus better in their own country, which is not the current practice in relation to international bond markets. As a result of heightening consciousness of it, that position was preserved. You could say that it might have been desirable if we had been able to make the position

the same in equity markets and say that prospectuses, issuers of equity, could be vetted anywhere. I think that was a bridge too far in the current circumstances. I think that gives an example of at least preserving the kind of features of the European markets which attract non-EU players where possible, and a number of these measures will make for greater efficiency, to make sure that these are enhanced. The consciousness that in particular there may be greater benefits to be had from closer integration of EU and US markets is a subject that I has been increasingly touched upon. The Chancellor has paid quite a bit of attention to this. The Commission themselves are engaged on a dialogue to try to make sure that where integration is beneficial, that can be progressed further.

216. Does the majority of the larger EU states, other than the UK, share that particular perspective?

(*Mr Green*) I think they are probably less sensitive to it in some aspects because their own marketplaces are not necessarily ones that are visited by non-EU users, whether as borrowers or investors. Certainly, the firms located in an number of the major EU centres—Germany, France, the Netherlands, Sweden—will certainly be very conscious that they attract a lot of their own business from outside the EU. I think we can expect that they will be reminding their own government that keeping markets open, and indeed expanded, for them is an important issue as well. I think that consciousness is there.

Lord Cavendish of Furness

217. I think you implied that you were concerned that the UK strength is not being undermined by the final outcome. There may be conspiracy here, but is there a suggestion sometimes that other Member States would like to weaken it in certain respects where it seems to have a flow position?

(*Mr Green*) I think there has been a feeling in some other Member States that the UK must in some way have cheated in order to get this premium position in the financial markets and they will have been told that flexible regulation is the answer to this. Can flexible regulation really be serious regulation is a question that is being asked. Maybe some time ago there were suggestions that if regulation could be standardised in some kind of way, this would prevent any possibility that the UK might be cheating in the ways that they suspect might be the case. I think that has moved on a little bit, for a number of reasons that we have already touched upon, partly I think that a number of other Member States would have realised that some of the most important and most successful of their own financial services firms actually benefit from the flexible regulation. One of the great advantages that has come out of this much closer dialogue, in the construction of the market in the discussions between finance ministries but also in this network of regulators, is that there has been a clearer understanding of how regulation in London works. Quite a lot of times there have been misapprehensions. Recently, Sir Howard Davies and I were having discussions with another European securities regulator who suddenly said, "Ah, I just did not understand how that worked. Now I

Lord Cavendish of Furness *contd.*]

understand it, maybe this makes sense". This discussion between the regulators about exactly how each other's systems work, which are not necessary terribly easy to grasp if you are coming from a different mind set, has been one of the most useful things that has taken place. I would say that your proposition, which certainly I would say had something to it a while ago, has been diluted simply by engagement in the debate from both directions.

Chairman

218. Thank you very much indeed. That was extremely helpful.

219. (*Mr Green*) We have been delighted to assist.
Chairman: Thank you for your attendance and for your thorough and positive responses to us this afternoon. Thank you, Ms Moore.

Memorandum from Unilever

Unilever's Perspective

1. Unilever is pleased to provide its views on the Financial Services Action Plan (FSAP). We consider the move towards a European Single Market in financial services to be a key deliverable of the Lisbon Summit Agenda. During the European Summit in 2000, government leaders agreed on the ambitious goal for Europe to become the most competitive, dynamic, knowledge-based economy by 2010. The FSAP covers a wide range of policy initiatives to further this goal.

2. Our submission will focus mainly on the debt capital markets. We will do this from the perspective of a large international company with strong credit ratings that give us global access to both short-term and long-term debt capital markets. We are able to tap those markets that give us the most efficient access to the debt capital we need at any particular time. The principal markets that we access are the euromarket and the US domestic market. We also selectively access other national domestic markets, eg the Swiss capital market.

3. Unilever's balance sheet strength and credit rating give it ready access a wide range of European and global short-term and long-term debt capital markets. Companies with lower credit ratings or no rating at all may be more restricted in their access to the capital markets and may, typically, be limited to their national markets, which may not give them the flexibility and depth of capital market access. The domestic market available to US companies is much larger than those domestic markets available to their European counterparts.

4. In our view, one of the key challenges for the FSAP is to support the development of a much larger and more liquid debt capital market in Europe. It should facilitate efficient access to a wide source of funds from short to very long maturities whilst being subject to the relatively light touch regulation and low cost of the euromarkets. It should not only do this for companies with strong credit ratings, but also for other companies at rates and conditions commensurate with the character and strength of their businesses. Wider use of credit ratings would aid the development of the European debt market.

5. In relation to this, we see the introduction of the euro as a major milestone. It has removed one of the most important remaining non-tariff barriers to the provision of financial services. The euro has had a significant impact in increasing the range of investors that Unilever can access with a single debt offering by pooling together the "home currency" investor bases of the eurozone countries. This has resulted in much bigger bond issues, significantly improving the efficiency of the market.

Unilever's Funding Arrangements

6. Unilever seeks to access, in the most effective way, the widest possible range of investors that are interested in meeting our funding needs across a wide range of currencies and maturities.

7. Unilever's principal funding programmes for short-term debt are our US domestic commercial paper (CP) programme (strategically important because we can raise large amounts in a matter of days if needed) and our multicurrency euromarket CP programme (competitive with US domestic CP for ongoing funding but does not match the size and liquidity of the US market if larger amounts were to be required). For long-term debt the equivalent programmes are the US "Shelf" programme (for accessing the US domestic market and for global bond issues) and our multicurrency euromarket "Debt Issuance Programme" (DIP).

8. Each programme has a set of pre-agreed, standard documents detailing the terms and conditions of any debt instrument issued within that programme. This enables specific debt instruments to be issued quickly and efficiently, with the minimum of additional document preparation needed. The US Shelf is registered with the SEC in the United States. Unilever's recent global bond issues off the Shelf have been listed on the

Luxembourg Stock Exchange. The DIP is listed with both the UKLA and Euronext Amsterdam. Issues off the US Shelf use the DTC (Depository Trust Company) clearing system, whilst issues off the DIP are cleared through Euroclear and Clearstream, Luxembourg.

9. The US long-term market has substantially greater depth than the euromarket, particularly at longer maturities. In addition, by comparison with the eurobond market, it tends to remain liquid even when there is significant global financial uncertainty and turbulence. The eurobond markets have made good progress in terms of both depth and available maturities in recent years following the introduction of the euro, but there is still a long way to go to match the US domestic market.

POSSIBLE IMPROVEMENTS

10. The FSAP could bring significant improvements in the following areas:

Access to investors, ease and costs

11. Although we can access the largest investor pools with a small number of debt programmes, there are investors falling outside this scope. The Prospectuses and Investment Services Directives could facilitate access as it provides for a single EU prospectus, the harmonisation of certain exemptions from the prospectus requirements and a definition of a "qualified" (ie professional) investor. In general we expect the FSAP to enhance access to a broader range of investors. It is important that implementation takes place in a manner that does not make this access more difficult or expensive. Indeed, reducing the costs associated with market participation (such as dealing costs, stamp duties and withholding taxes) would improve the liquidity of capital markets in Europe.

Equity Issuance

12. Unilever has not issued ordinary equity for many years. However, some general comparisons between capital raising via debt and equity can be made. The equity markets are currently structured in such a way that they do not maximise the ability of companies to access as broad a range of equity investors as debt investors.

13. Unilever expects that the Prospectuses and the Investment Services Directives will work towards a more harmonised and cost efficient regime for the issuance of and dealing in all securities. We furthermore welcome the fact that the Company Law Action Plan will also address these issues. However, the costs incurred in cross-border share trading are a significant impediment to the effective functioning of a single European market for equities and will remain so until a pan-European settlement system is established that enables cross-border share dealing to be conducted as cheaply as domestic share dealing.

ENSURING FSAP's CONTRIBUTION TO THE LISBON COMPETITIVENESS AGENDA

14. Progress on the FSAP should be measured against the Lisbon competitiveness agenda. This means that the criteria should be the quality rather than the quantity of measures adopted. With much of the FSAP adopted, it is now of key importance that the effectiveness of the policy is assessed. We welcome the Commission's plans to focus on monitoring implementation and enforcement. Consistent implementation and enforcement of harmonised regulations can be as important as the regulations themselves.

15. We also strongly support the Commission's efforts to define economic indicators to measure progress and the extent the FSAP contributes to Europe's competitiveness. The guiding principle behind legislative and policy objectives should be the contribution they make to raising the EU's GDP.

16. To achieve high quality legislation, new measures should meet the needs of market participants and be subject to a rigorous impact assessment. If measures are rushed through or compromised because of short-term protectionist and anti-competitive national forces, there is a real risk that these may add to the costs companies incur when operating on the financial markets, or even limit the functioning and development of the market itself, rather than provide the expected benefits.

17. Regulation should, above all, strive for transparency and security of the markets. This means, *inter alia* appropriate investor protection, but new measures should also take into account the different nature of risks that different types of market participants face. It is important to distinguish between the level of protection appropriate to "retail" investors and that appropriate to "wholesale" investors.

18. It is for this reason that Unilever is pleased that the Lamfalussy procedure foresees extensive consultation with market participants. To ensure that a comprehensive assessment of the impacts of proposed changes can be made, users of financial services should be consulted at all stages and should be represented in the relevant advisory bodies. This also includes representation in the Level 2 Market Participants Advisory

Committee, as the representation of issuers' and investors' needs should not be left to the providers of financial services. As the matters dealt with are often of a complex nature with far-reaching implications, Unilever considers that deadlines for responses should be extended as they are currently too tight.

THE GLOBAL CONTEXT

19. Europe's ability to compete at a global level also depends strongly on the ability to agree common approaches and regulatory standards globally, and in particular with the US. Improving the transatlantic relationship should be one of the EU's most important cross-sector priorities and will aid the development of a more efficient European and global capital market. Unilever supports the work to agree International Accounting Standards (IAS), leading towards convergence between the various accounting standards (especially IAS and US GAAP) and greater transparency in accounting for derivatives.

20. The health and efficiency of the financial derivatives markets (for example, the interest rate and currency swap markets) is very important to Unilever's (and many other companies') use of the debt markets. Derivatives can enable companies to source funds more efficiently from the cheapest market (eg raising euro to meet a sterling need) and to manage separately liquidity exposure (ie when debt matures and needs to be refinanced) and interest rate exposure (ie how much of our debt is kept at a fixed rate and how much is kept at a floating rate). Important to this is the current discussion on a new accounting standard for derivatives (IAS 39).

21. There are, however, important practical difficulties in the proposed IAS 39 that are likely to impose significant additional costs on companies without evident increased clarity for the users of financial statements. These additional costs arise from two sources. First, the administrative burden. We will have to extensively document numerous relationships between our loans and derivatives, which will also require major adjustments in our reporting and transaction systems. Second, a bias towards less efficient financial management that results from certain combinations of underlying debt and overlaid derivatives having the derivative element marked to market every quarter through the P&L, causing an unacceptable level of volatility in the reported accounts. This may bias companies against the use of derivatives, even when they are important to sourcing debt at the lowest cost (such as raising funds in one currency and swapping them into another where this provides lower cost funding), because of the difficulty in explaining the volatility in reported results to equity investors.

CONCLUSIONS

22. We expect that the FSAP will make a significant impact on European financial integration, with tangible benefits not only for big players such as Unilever, but also for smaller companies. The Prospectuses Directive is likely to improve access to investors in a significant way. As a global player, the FSAP will make an important contribution to Unilever's aims, particularly as it is likely to facilitate a considerably deeper EU debt market.

23. In more general terms, the FSAP implementation deadline of 2005 constitutes in our view one of the most important milestones of the Lisbon competitiveness strategy. The quality, market and customer orientation as well as the global compatibility of the regulatory measures will determine the extent to which they will help expected GDP growth resulting from financial integration to materialise.

24. Most of the legislation adopted under the FSAP has not yet come into force, while the Lamfalussy procedure has not yet been fully tested. The monitoring of the implementation and enforcement of FSAP legislation, as well as the functioning of the Lamfalussy procedure—taking into account the views of industry, alongside those of financial services providers—will be of key importance.

25. Looking forward, Unilever considers that the important issue of pension reform should be one of the key priorities in the coming years. Further development of the European Pension Fund Directive to achieve the effective removal of investment restrictions imposing limits for pension funds within the EU on their equity, corporate bond and non euro denominated investments would mark an important step in the development and deepening of a key investor base in the European capital markets.

4 September 2003

Examination of Witnesses

Mr Rudy Markham and Dr Kevan Greene, Unilever, examined.

Chairman: Thank you for your written evidence, which was to the point and extremely helpful. A number of Members of the Committee will depart at various times, depending upon how long we go on for. You have been very kind and said you will stay as long as the Committee is able to continue and I am grateful.

Baroness Cohen of Pimlico

220. I should declare an interest. I am a director of the London Stock Exchange. You have highlighted in your evidence that the FSAP is one of the key deliverables of the Lisbon Process so presumably serious delays would look like a setback, given your view that the 2005 implementation deadline is an important milestone. In paragraph 14 you say you would rather have quality than quantity and point to the risks of rushed legislation. Do you feel the balance is being struck correctly at present or can you point to any specific instances where adverse results have already happened, especially ones that might have damaged the UK final system's interests?

(*Mr Markham*) I represent an international company which is headquartered in Europe. About 40 per cent of our business is in Europe. We run it in a global context. Secondly, we are significant users of the debt market and occasionally the equity market. We are substantial investors in pension fund assets in Europe. Thirdly, for performance terms, particularly for competitive financial performance, we look for a level playing field with our US, Swiss and Japanese competitors. We need common standards and we assume, when they are established, adherence and, where necessary, enforcement. To respond to your specific questions, we believe the fulfilment of the ambitions of the Lisbon aim is urgent but of course they have to be implementable and enforceable. We believe that we need the necessary time for consultation with market practitioners to enable effective, practical legislation but that should be balanced with the principle or process which seeks to harmonise the minimum number of common principles, to adopt mutual recognition of principles across the European Union, where appropriate, and to commence as rapidly as possible with implementation. Put another way, the prize is high so we see it as an imperative to get it done but it has to be done such that it can be implemented practically and therefore flexibly across Europe. We see the opportunity for that as lying above all in the consultation phase with practitioners and then some rapid conclusions on the minimum elements of law which should be harmonised in order to enable effect to be given to those intentions.

221. Your school of thought is of mutual recognition rather than trying to harmonise?

(*Mr Markham*) Harmonisation is the first prize. Mutual recognition is the second prize.

222. It would do, would it not?

(*Mr Markham*) Indeed.

223. Have we any bad signs, adverse results beginning to show anywhere, from your point of view?

(*Mr Markham*) As we showed in our submission, in the area, for example, of accounting standards there are some understandable delays occurring. We believe it is important that they are resolved. Generally though we are comfortable with the process and very happy to engage in the consultation and, from our perspective, this is a particularly welcome opportunity.

(*Dr Greene*) We are at a certain stage in the process and there are lots of important directives, like the Takeover Directive, which are still to be formulated. We are unable to say we are satisfied. There is a lot to be done from here. There are a lot of important measures to be agreed and we obviously have concerns about the time we have to implement things properly.

224. Do you see alarm bells ringing anywhere?

(*Mr Markham*) Not yet.

Chairman

225. There is a political imperative apparently to get any remaining issues resolved and in place by April or so of next year. You just mentioned the Takeover Directive. Are you content that the right balance will be struck between getting it right, getting it through?

(*Mr Markham*) We could get into the specifics of individual directives. On a number of them we have a position as to how far progress is being made. My basic contention would be we are very supportive of the directives and the progress being made and we are comfortable we are contributing our part to the individual detail of those legislations.

226. Do you feel that the views of users are adequately and properly being taken into account and playing their part in the consultations?

(*Mr Markham*) I pause to comment on the position of all users. I am certainly comfortable that, as an international company active in a number of markets, our voice is heard. Therefore, there is the opportunity for those who formulate the detail of the directives to take account not only of our views but perhaps of our practical experience of operating in debt and equity markets across the world.

Baroness Cohen of Pimlico: I observe that if Unilever's views are not being heard it would be a strange thing.

Chairman

227. Do you think that the Prospectus Directive will lower or raise the costs of issuance for a company such as Unilever?

Chairman *contd.*]

(*Mr Markham*) In one sense, the straight cost of issuing, I do not expect any notable additional costs from the introduction of the directive. Its overall intent is to deliver a larger and deeper pool of capital, accessible by more and more players and all of the experience in practical economics shows that that reduces the cost of equity and raises the efficiency of attracting it. That has to be good for business and for investors.

228. You may not have heard the evidence of the FSA who felt that in relation to the clearing and settlement, which you touched on in the equities element of your paper, they were content to allow market forces to resolve that. How long do you think market pressures will take to resolve those issues and do you think that is quick enough?

(*Mr Markham*) As long as the direction is clear and we are moving to the implementation of a directive across Europe, the necessary priority of resolving the outstanding issues by the various institutions will be accorded. The one follows from the other.

Baroness Cohen of Pimlico: I do not think that is what the London Stock Exchange thinks.

Lord Fearn

229. Consultation and transparency are the watch words, reading through your document, for the process and you seem pleased about that, in paragraph 18. In particular, you say that consultation should not be left just to the providers of financial services. How does Unilever play its role in participating in the consultation procedures? Do you leave it to bodies in the UK or elsewhere in the EU? Which ones do you use?

(*Mr Markham*) We participate in a number of fora, both in this country and in the Netherlands, which is our other parent company head office, and in a number of bodies in Europe. In this country, we participate directly and indirectly in the CBI. We participate in the equivalent organisation in the Netherlands. In terms of European organisations, we are a member of the European Round Table. We contribute to the thinking of UNICE. We provide input directly both in terms of view and in terms of practical experience of implications to the Accounting Standards Board in this country and to the International Accounting Standards Board. I would stress that our input is twofold. It is a view from our perspective as business people, so limited by our own interest; and secondly, some assessment of the practical implications of introducing whatever rules or changes are proposed, and some things people may not have seen simply because of the complexity of the legislation.

230. You also mentioned the need for the FSAP to broaden the markets to enable retail investors to become more involved. How should their views be incorporated?

(*Mr Markham*) Let me explain why one of the objectives in which we are most interested is that the FSAP is broadening the pool of available capital and making it more comparable with the capital markets in the United States of America. One of the features of the American market is the wide variety of institutional capital and also of private or retail capital. To do that, you need to ensure that there is both protection for retail investors and also much greater transparency in terms of accounting and reporting. Collecting their views is a lot harder and I am probably not the person to contribute a proposal as to how you best seek their views, but probably through shareholder bodies of one form or another or institutions that particularly look after the interests of small shareholders. There are, for example, numbers of bodies in the Netherlands that I am aware of. I am less aware of them in this country.

Lord Faulkner of Worcester

231. In your paragraph 14 you are singing the praises of consistency: "Consistent implementation and enforcement of harmonised regulations can be as important as the regulations themselves." Is there not a danger that, whilst the regulations are consistent, they may be inflexible and the loss of flexibility will make them less effective and remove national discretion?

(*Mr Markham*) Yes indeed. There is always a balance between legislation which is consistent and applied and the level of flexibility. That is why I argued a little earlier for a minimum level of regulation necessary to ensure a level playing field at the highest level across Europe, and for the flexibility within that to adapt to local circumstances which could reflect differing stages of development of economies, of capital markets, of retail versus wholesale, as an example.

232. How long do you think it will be before we can judge whether the FSAP is working in the way intended?

(*Mr Markham*) That is a question I am probably least qualified to answer. Maybe I could suggest that the European Union, in setting up their ambitions in the Financial Services Action Plan, set a goal of lowering the cost of equity and debt by roughly half a percentage point and by a contribution to the GDP growth of in the region of something like 1 per cent.[1] Those are very high level macro indicators but nevertheless they seem to me to be indicators worth tracing, not least because if you look at the valuation of companies in Europe they tend to be structurally lower in like for like sectors than those in America which has something to do with differences in the cost of capital in that market compared with Europe, and therefore a greater alignment between the market valuation of companies in Europe and those in North America would provide an indicator of progress towards the achievement of this plan.

---

[1] *Note by witness*: Unilever does not have its own estimate of the potential benefits; our source for these estimates is the Eurofi Preliminary Report on "An Integrated European Financial Market", 26 November 2002 (page 5) that quotes figures of the European Commission.

Baroness Cohen of Pimlico

233. As the Financial Services Action Plan moves towards completion, its goals include a broader and deeper bond market and you say that much has been achieved; yet there is still a long way to go to match the US domestic market, to quote you at paragraph nine. Do you think there are some additional measures that should be proposed or should we be patient and just wait for the full results of the FSAP? Where are you on that and if you do think there are more measures what should they be?

(*Mr Markham*) If I look at the differences, the US market is characterised by much greater size. It has five or six times the European market for debt and equity[2] and it is characterised secondly by a greater level and breadth of maturity and, thirdly, by a much higher level of turnover, so greater liquidity. The intentions of the Financial Services Action Plan in the aggregate will stimulate, I believe, both the expansion of the market, the broadening of maturity and the increase in liquidity. A lot of the need to reinforce changes in pension legislation allowing a greater flexibility in the way in which pension funds across Europe invest their funds in a variety of instruments will stimulate that. Clarity and consistency of accounting principles will make it easier for investors to compare the offerings of one company with those of another. The continued progress that the euro is making as a common currency is simply making it easier for people to compare prospectus. All of these elements reinforce one another and I believe, in the aggregate, they are sufficient to achieve the goals set out in the Action Plan.

234. Is the EU doing enough to encourage funded retirement savings, perhaps in the form of pension funds, because you are running a huge pension fund. Would that flow of capital help to provide the impetus to match the effectiveness of US bond markets?

(*Mr Markham*) There are two issues with regard to pensions. Again, there is a limit to the contribution I and our company can make to the general policy. First is the development of savings to provide for retirement in whatever form and the legislation which stimulates and encourages both employees and employers in a tax efficient way to do that. There are significant differences in the tax efficiency with which post-employment provisions for money are made available. A harmonisation there would be of significant importance, both in terms of tax legislation and secondly in terms of freedom of investment choice. The second is the provision of those benefits, having established the entitlements. There, a greater liberalisation in terms of instrument that can be applied and within Europe, in terms of the markets where people may invest. For example, the creation of the euro suddenly made available for a number of countries the opportunity to invest in a euromarket, and not just in their own domestic capital market, particularly for small countries in population terms

where the capability of the capital markets to offer the resilience they need for, for example, long term pension investment, the emergence of a pool of European money has made the opportunity a lot better and therefore contributes significantly to improving the outlook for pension investment as you go forward, all independent of the evolution of debt and equity markets, but it enables them to function better. It is not really my place to comment on whether I think the European countries individually are doing enough but I have indicated perhaps from our perspective where we look to areas of efficiency and improvement in going forward.

Chairman

235. You touch on the euro issue quite positively in your memorandum. Do you think the UK not being in the euro, in the new, single, liberalised, financial markets in Europe will have any significance at all?

(*Mr Markham*) The existence of one stable currency and the breadth of that supports the evolution of a common capital market and a common debt market. The UK as a participant in that is a benefit. The important element for us is the relationship between the countries which are within the euro and those that are not. The thing for any capital raiser, for any business operating in that environment, is that differences in currencies, if they reflect differences in economic policy and differences in economic direction, can lead to volatility. Volatility in an investment framework is essentially an additional cost.

236. You talked earlier of the macro estimates of benefits, whether in terms of a half per cent reduction in borrowing costs or one per cent growth in GDP, which is a pretty solid return on a half per cent reduction in borrowing costs.

(*Mr Markham*) It is impressive.

237. It does not entirely add up on my arithmetic but I will take it at face value. Do you feel that this high level of macro analysis is adequate or should there be quantified benchmarks for gains from each particular directive? Time and time again in this Committee we look at directives or proposed directives and the hard nosed thinking about costs and benefits, whether financial directives or other directives, often is not as rigorous as the macro assertions of benefits. I wonder what you think about that. Do you think that what I will call a more hard nosed attitude towards quantifying benchmarks would be helpful? Have you any practical suggestions of what might be done in that regard?

(*Mr Markham*) I hesitate to presume to advise this Committee on something as complicated as this but I would share from our own business an approach we have taken to targeting something for our whole business—in our case quite a large business but nevertheless small compared with the affairs you are considering. We have opted in our business, in order to change the performance level and our expectations, for a very simple expression of performance improvement which we have translated into two or three key metrics which apply

---

[2] *Note by witness*: The five or six times factor was intended to refer to the debt markets; for the equity markets, we believe the factor is more like two to three times.

Chairman contd.]

to the business as a whole. For an operator sitting in one of our operating units, serving a local market, they may seem too macro, too far removed, but what we have found is that, through their understanding of what our ambition was and the scale of our ambition and the routes we were seeking to achieve those ambitions, they have translated that in their own environment in a way which enables them to contribute to the overall achievement of our objective. If I were to translate that as an answer, I would say a very limited number of necessarily high level benchmarks, coupled with your expectations of the routes through which those benefits will be delivered, are the key to enabling users of the market place to understand how they best can capitalise on the opportunity and deliver the benefits that you are seeking and believing are there.

238. How would you apply that thinking to the Takeover Directive that is yet to be resolved?

(Mr Markham) I was thinking of the easy one, Chairman. You will have to seek a minimum number attached to the particular directives that you are seeking. I would suggest that maybe not each of the directives has to have a specific target in its own right because in aggregate they contribute to the achievement of what we want, which is a significantly deeper pool of capital more efficiently and economically available to retail and institutional investors in Europe which will increase our competitiveness vis a vis the United States, Switzerland and Japan. That would be reflected, amongst other things, in the valuation of companies in Europe and that in itself may be a contributor of greater value from takeovers which may happen in Europe or which European companies may take elsewhere because they have higher valuations to justify taking other companies over.

239. The problem is that that is exactly the answer that a bureaucrat would give and not you. They would say all this hangs together as a whole and we cannot separate out one bit. It is the whole Action Plan that will make the difference. When you come to look at the individual directives and to say precisely how is this going to contribute to that and what are the costs of doing this, tell us exactly what the benefits would be, in the real world, you cannot be exact but you could at least have a stab at the way in which you would assess their success or otherwise. It is sometimes jolly difficulty to see these things.

(Mr Markham) That is why I opt for a structural reduction in the cost of equity and a structural reduction in the cost of debt. That, for me, is the most important.

Lord Walpole

240. I am not sure I can understand this question, let alone what the answer might be, but you do make trenchant criticisms of the costs involved in reporting under IAS 39 in paragraph 21. These may be administrative costs but perhaps more significantly real economic costs may be incurred by moving away from optimal debt management techniques. However, the International Accounting Standard project is very much a transatlantic, even global, project that you welcome in principle in paragraph 19. Do you believe that it is only a governance failure of the standard setting process that may impose these costs? How would the governance be improved to avoid this in the future?

(Mr Markham) As I said in our memorandum, we attach great weight to a convergence of accounting standards between Europe and north America, which is what the IAS seek to do. Much of what we have seen evidences that. We recognise they have made great progress with the areas of least contention and as they move into the areas of greater contention so the speed of progress slows down a little. I think that is manifest in the debate and discussion around the proposed IAS 39, which is understandable in intent and complex in application and, like a broad net, sometimes catches fish you would rather not have caught. That is the way I look at it. As a company, we have been invited to provide our views and an understanding of the implications, both directly to the IASP and through the various bodies, so I have no issue with the consultation process. I regard the consultation process as not yet finalised. My understanding is that that is indeed the case, so I do not take any issue with the governance of it. I recognise it is a difficult issue in order to satisfy the intent of the standard bearers and those who need to operate in accordance with the standards, because there is a clear risk which we have tried to highlight in the paper that a slavish adoption of the standard could lead to uneconomic behaviour in order to avoid, as some people may see it, volatile earnings which they would have greater problems with in terms of dealing with their shareholders. That I think is a very unfortunate side effect. I remain hopeful that the parties involved, the IAS and those with whom they are consulting, will find rapidly a solution which is workable, practicable, achieves the aims they seek but also avoids uneconomic behaviour.

Chairman

241. How much debt finance did you raise short, medium, long, in the last 12 month financial period?

(Mr Markham) We had at the beginning of this year debt of around 17 billion.

242. Outstanding?

(Mr Markham) This is 31 December 2002. It is down from a peak of 26 billion at the end of 2000. That was on the back of a very substantial acquisition in north America. We funded that acquisition for about two-thirds of the money in the United States and about one-third in Europe.[3] We have had good experience with raising capital on broadly competitive terms in both of those markets. We would have raised more in Europe if the debts had been there and if the maturities had been there. That has been the biggest shortfall. In terms of costs, our experience with the euromarket has been very positive. Our costs of debt raising are about a third of the US costs. That is the reason we have

---

[3] *Note by witness:* By mistake, Europe and United States quoted the wrong way round.

Chairman *contd.*]

such great confidence that, as this Action Plan gets traction, we can see a lot more opportunity as we get a more liquid market here and as we get greater maturity.

Baroness Cohen of Pimlico

243. The difference in costs? I am a little startled.
(*Dr Greene*) We are not talking about the interest rates. We are talking about the costs of the process.

244. I presume also you raised your debt as to a third in the United States because that is where your income was? Were you matching debt to where the income arose?
(*Mr Markham*) No. Our policy is to tap whichever capital market provides capital with the greatest flexibility and then hedge across, which is what we did.
Chairman: In simple terms, if the hoped for saving in costs for raising capital by the FSAP had been in place for the last five or 10 years, how much would that have reduced your annual costs for raising capital and servicing your debt?

Baroness Cohen of Pimlico

245. They are two different questions.
(*Mr Markham*) On 18 billion, that is about 90 million per annum in terms of income[4]. The second fact is the valuation of the company because if the cost of capital is reduced by half a per cent the market valuation will be significantly higher. The return to investors who invest in our shares will be that much better so the pension returns will be better etc.

Chairman

246. If it turns out your figure is in haste, in error, it would be helpful if you could drop us a note for the record afterwards but at the moment you say around £90 million a year?
(*Mr Markham*) Euros.

247. Say £60 million per annum in the costs of raising capital. That would translate in the value of the shares to the stockholders and so on.

---

[4] *Note by witness*: The EUR 18 billion leading to EUR 90 million pa was quoted by way of illustration for that magnitude of debt if it had all been raised in Europe with a saving of half a percent pa as suggested by the previously referenced European Commission report (Unilever does not have its own estimate of the likely reduction in cost of capital following full implementation of the FSAP). In fact, at the end of the year 2000 following Unilever's acquisition of Bestfoods, Unilever's net debt was EUR 26 billion reducing to EUR 23 billion at end 2001 and EUR 17 billion at end 2002 (prior to year 2000, Unilever's debt was relatively low). Also, as stated above, much of the debt was raised outside Europe. It is difficult to say what the proportion raised in Europe would have been if this fund raising had taken place at a time after full implementation of FSAP. As a consequence, it is difficult to give a meaningful figure for what would have been the actual savings for Unilever. Clearly the savings would have been substantial but rather less than EUR 90 million pa as this would require a saving of half a percent on EUR 18 billion of debt raised fully in Europe.

(*Mr Markham*) Indeed.

248. That is quite significant, potentially?
(*Mr Markham*) Certainly.

249. It is bringing home the fact that we have not perhaps concentrated enough on the practical benefits to the customers, as opposed to how this affects this financial institution or that. It is rather like bothering about who makes the car as opposed to does the customer really like it and get the benefit. Do you think that Italian, Spanish and German companies and so on will share your views about the benefits of this FSAP? You are a multinational, international company. What is the feeling across Europe like in the European industry more generally?
(*Mr Markham*) This is speculation but having listened anecdotally to them you would have to differentiate between those companies that operate in a big field, some of the large car companies, for example, that are therefore exposed to and able to access the capital markets and the euromarkets. I would be surprised if their views were very different from my own in terms of looking for a greater cost efficiency. I would expect that the bigger opportunities with smaller companies which do not have access to broad, capital markets, with start-up companies which may have to use more traditional forms of finance and therefore, as a measure, the broadening of the capital markets, would be of particular relevance to smaller companies which have still to prove themselves, and therefore have the necessary energy and creativity to do that. This broadening and deepening of the market will genuinely be a significant advance to that in whichever country they sit. In this country that must be an important additional incentive for start-up companies and smaller companies.

Lord Walpole

250. What about companies in the ten new Members or are there no companies where this is relevant at this stage? There will be, will there not?
(*Mr Markham*) Yes. I guess again the same principle ought to apply. As entrepreneurs see the access to a broader and deeper pool of capital, a more clearly regulated pool of capital and greater transparency in its use, and investors have the opportunity to make those judgments, that will catch on quite quickly. I would be fairly positive without knowing the specifics of individual companies that need it. Cheapening money and making that available to people who can use it to add economic value has generally worked in almost every environment that I have had anything to do with.

Chairman

251. You have been very patient with us and we are extremely grateful to you. If you feel there is anything we have missed or an emphasis we have not got quite right, would you like to add any concluding remarks?

Chairman *contd.*]

(*Mr Markham*) I have talked rather a lot and I apologise. As we have indicated, we are very much in support of this initiative and, like most companies that are seeking opportunities to improve, we are hungry to get on with it and get the benefits.

Chairman: It has been invaluable for us to hear your evidence and we are genuinely grateful. Thank you.

MONDAY 6 OCTOBER 2003

Present:

Cohen of Pimlico, B.   Shutt of Greetland, L.
Fearn, L.   Walpole, L.
Howie of Troon, L.   Woolmer of Leeds, L. (Chairman)

Memorandum submitted by Mr Lachlan Burn—Partner, Linklaters

1. BACKGROUND

Over the last few years, I have been closely involved in commenting on a number of the EU Financial Services Action Plan Directives. These include, in particular, the Prospectus Directive, the Transparency Directive, the Market Abuse Directive and the Collateral Directive.

I have worked closely with the International Primary Market Association and (in relation to the Prospectus and Transparency Directives) with the Treasury and Financial Services Authority negotiating teams as a member of their drafting advisory group. In the case of the Collateral Directive, I was a member of the Bank of England's advisory group; and I am currently a member of the City of London Solicitors' Company working group, which is considering the measures necessary to implement the Directive in the United Kingdom.

I am also a member of the Listing Authority Advisory Committee and the Primary Markets Group of the London Stock Exchange and have discussed many of the FSAP Directives in meetings of those bodies.

My involvement has focussed mainly on the effect of these Directives on the international capital markets. This market includes international debt securities (US$1.4 trillion of new issues in 2001)[22] of which roughly 60 per cent[23] were managed out of London. The majority of issuers (63 per cent)[24] in this market were based outside the EU.

2. EVIDENCE

2.1 *What progress has been made to date?*

Progress has been slow and difficult. One of the main objectives of the FSAP—the creation of a pan-EU securities market—should have been relatively easy to achieve. The current impediments to the creation of this market are well known, consisting mainly of the cost and time implications resulting from translation requirements for prospectuses and the requirement to include tax disclosure in the prospectus for each jurisdiction in which securities are sold.

However, instead of simply eliminating or modifying these barriers, the FSAP has been used by some Member States and their authorities as an opportunity to introduce new concepts, driven by consumer protectionism and, in some cases, a desire to preserve or re-establish national markets. Many of these new concepts would have a potentially damaging effect on existing markets—particularly the wholesale markets— and on the creation of a pan-EU market, and have consequently been strenuously resisted, notably by those representing the United Kingdom. The ensuing search for compromise has led to the slow and difficult progress referred to above.

Examples of this include:

— Denial of choice. Currently, an issuer is free to decide where it lists any of its securities and where it seeks approval of its prospectuses. Under the Prospectus Directive, where the securities are shares or (under the current draft) convertible bonds, there is no choice. The issuer has to seek approval for its prospectus in its country of incorporation. Various arguments have been produced to justify this approach but at the heart of the proposal is the desire of certain national authorities to retain control over their own companies and to protect their domestic markets.

— Failure to recognise needs of wholesale markets. Some participants in the negotiations appear to think that there is no such thing as a listed institutional market. In other words, once a security is listed, it is available to any retail investor; and therefore the initial and continuing disclosure requirements should be the same for all issuers, whether their securities are bought only by institutions or not. Accordingly disclosure standards for securities that are bought only by

[22] BIS Quarterly Review December 2002.
[23] International Financial Services London Report May 2002.
[24] International Financial Services London Report May 2002.

institutions are unnecessarily burdensome. This is consumer protectionism operating to the detriment of the wholesale markets.

— Exclusion on non-EU issuers. Non-EU issuers comprise the greater part of the international debt markets. Yet the Prospectus and Transparency Directives take little account of them. For example, companies that do not produce accounts to a "true and fair" standard will have to produce additional disclosure, which is likely to involve reconciling their accounts to International Accounting Standards. The intention in the minds of some is to enable retail investors to make an accurate comparison between the attractions of the various EU and non-EU issuers in the market—consumer protectionism again. But the effect is to impose huge additional costs on non-EU issuers and potentially deter them from seeking an EU listing. There is insufficient thought for institutional investors, who are well able to understand, for example, US accounting standards.

Other factors that have made progress slow and difficult include:

— Insufficient expert input into the design and drafting of the legislation. There is little involvement of people who have real knowledge of how international markets work in the formation of policy or the production of drafts. Offers to provide such people to perform these services have been rejected, on the basis that the process must not be seen to be unduly influenced by any particular segment of the markets. But the concern should be less about influence and more about knowledge. Without detailed knowledge, it is impossible to legislate effectively.

— Poor technical drafting of Directives and subordinate legislation, resulting in uncertainty as to the intended result and potential effect of the law.

— Inadequate consultation procedures, with insufficient time being given for consultation and insufficient consideration being given to the relative importance of the respondents. Small domestic markets appear to be given the same weight in the argument as large international markets.

— Poor feedback. Arguments are often rejected with little or no explanation. When an explanation is given, it is often difficult to follow and fails to address the point.

— A negotiating process that is Byzantine in its complexity and is concerned more with achieving agreement on a Directive than in ensuring that the Directive works properly.

— A desire on the part of national authorities to preserve the concepts they are familiar with their own domestic markets, whether or not these are appropriate to a cross-border market.

— A fear of the United Kingdom—some Member States appear to fear that London will become to the EU what New York has become to the United States in the financial markets, coupled with a belief that this can (and should) be controlled through the FSAP.

— The absence of any proper cost/benefit analysis of the proposals. For example, the explanatory memorandum to the Transparency Directive states several times that its overall effect will be to reduce the cost of capital. This, indeed, should be the intended and actual result; but the proposals will not achieve it. Instead, by imposing annual and semi-annual prospectus style reports, they will increase the cost of capital.

However, despite the difficulty of the process, the United Kingdom has been reasonably successful to date in achieving satisfactory compromises in many areas.

2.2 *Has this been beneficial or deleterious to UK interests?*

If its stated objective is achieved, the FSAP should be beneficial to the United Kingdom. A true pan-EU financial market should, through the operation of market forces, enhance the position of the United Kingdom as an international financial centre. As indicated above, it is the fear that this might happen that has, in part, influenced the way in which some have reacted to the FSAP. The EU has (even before enlargement) a larger population than the USA. Coupled with this, the demographic trend in many EU countries will lead to a significant change in favour of private funding of pensions, which in turn will fuel the financial markets. As a result, it is likely that the EU financial markets will prosper over the medium to long term and that the United Kingdom will (if market forces are allowed to operate properly) benefit from this.

Whether it will in fact do so depends, however, on how the FSAP continues to develop and how it is implemented. Some people see a borderless financial market-place as a threat to their national interests. The challenge is to convince them that this is not so or, if they prove to be beyond persuasion, to defeat their attempts to disrupt the creation of such a market.

The treatment of non-EU issuers is of particular concern. If they are put off seeking an EU listing by the new regime, there will be a drop in listing fees for the UK. But, perhaps even more significant, many EU institutional investors are restricted in their ability to invest in non-EU listed securities. If non-EU issuers stay away from EU markets, such investors will be deprived of investment opportunity; and if non-EU issuers de-list their existing securities, such investors may have to sell their holdings of those securities, resulting perhaps in a depression of bond prices.

On balance, though, I remain hopeful that the FSAP will be beneficial overall to the United Kingdom rather than deleterious.

2.3 *Has sufficient weight been given to the position and experience of the UK financial services industry?*

No. Anyone seeking to create a pan-EU financial market would logically look to see whether anything of the sort already existed—(it does, in London)—and then adopt its better elements as a model. In many ways, the opposite has happened. Little notice is taken of the UK's experience, when policy is determined or when legislation is drafted. In negotiations, the impression is sometimes given that what is bad for the UK is good for other EU Member States. It is clear that some representatives of Member States believe that the United Kingdom has stolen part of their market and look forward to that part being repatriated as a result of the FSAP.

2.4 *What are the main outstanding matters that remain to be dealt with under the FSAP?*

There is much to be done and little time to do it in. The Prospectus Directive is nearing completion; but the subordinate legislation is still in preparation. Many very important areas remain in doubt—including the way in which medium term note programmes (the preferred method for issuing debt securities) will operate and how non-EU issuers will be able to access the EU markets. The Transparency Directive has yet to receive its first reading in the European Parliament and its text is currently highly unsatisfactory. These Directives (and their subordinate legislation) will have to be implemented into English law. The Listing Authority will have to amend its rules to comply with them. And everything will have to be completed by 2005. The closer that deadline comes, the less realistic it becomes.

3. SOME CONCLUSIONS

Some important battles have been won. Some have been lost. Some remain to be fought. But overall, despite a very poor start reasonably good progress has been made, although more slowly and with the expenditure of greater effort than should have been necessary.

I thought that I should set out some thoughts, in conclusion, as to how matters could be improved.

3.1 *More influence, earlier*

In this area, the pen is undoubtedly more powerful than the sword. Once the person doing the drafting has laid down the pen, whatever has been written is very difficult to change. The secret is either to be the draftsman, or to be at his elbow as he writes. The United Kingdom needs to ensure that it has a much more active involvement at this level.

3.2 *Greater awareness and involvement*

The FSAP does not exist in a vacuum. It is about the markets; and it is intended to benefit the markets. The markets consist of three basic elements—users of capital (issuers); providers of capital (investors); and financial intermediaries. The problem is that the FSAP is being designed without proper involvement of people who are from the market. And participants in the markets (with honourable exceptions, particularly among the financial intermediaries) are unaware and largely uninterested in what is being done. The absence of a coordinated and coherent involvement by investors and issuers is hugely damaging to the negotiating process. Many market participants are too busy earning their daily bread to inform themselves as to what is going on. They should be encouraged to do so, though. When the world's computers were threatened by the turn of the millennium, a very successful campaign was launched in the United Kingdom to increase awareness and ensure that avoiding action was taken. Something of the same sort would be extremely beneficial in relation to the FSAP.

3.3 *Education*

There is widespread ignorance throughout the EU as to what the markets actually do and how they benefit the EU as a whole. For example, there is already a very large international debt market that operates largely from London and provides inexpensive funding to most of the EU's leading companies. Its default record is extremely good. Yet it is seen in many countries as being a threat and its significant benefits are largely ignored. The market based in London is seen as being a UK market—whereas most of the major participants are non-UK institutions, including most of the large continental European banks. In short, London is already a pan-EU market with pan-EU participants; but many in the EU are unaware of the fact. It already provides many of the benefits to the EU that are sought under the FSAP—relatively inexpensive capital, job creation and so on—but again many are unaware of the fact. People need to be made more aware of what they already have, if they are to be persuaded not to damage it.

3.4 *Continental alliances*

There is little doubt that, until attitudes change, the best way of influencing the FSAP is to win alliances with continental European market participants and authorities. With a qualified majority voting Directive, the United Kingdom's vote alone can do nothing. We need to build systematic links and alliances with those in other Member States who can assist us in our quest to build genuine, borderless EU financial markets.

25 June 2003

Examination of Witness

MR LACHLAN BURN, Partner, Linklaters, examined.

Chairman

251. Good afternoon, Mr Burn. Our apologies for keeping you waiting. We have about forty minutes, which is never long enough, the implication is that we must keep our questions brief and to the point and it would be extremely helpful if you could keep that in mind. First of all could I thank you for your paper . . .

(*Mr Burn*) It is a pleasure.

252. . . . it was extremely helpful and useful in focusing our minds and we shall certainly be referring to it in our questions. If there is anything you would like to add briefly at the start by all means do, and I will give you an opportunity at the end to add anything in writing later by nuance or substance, then we will go straight into questions.

A. I think the only introductory remark I would like to make is that I am a number of things. I am a partner in a law firm and I am a member of various committees but all that I say here will represent my own views and not those of anybody else.

Lord Shutt of Greetland

253. Good afternoon, we have received a letter from Lord Browne-Wilkinson of the Financial Markets Law Committee in which he mentioned that some element of legal uncertainty is inevitable in the type of markets that we are considering. He went on to say that Community law may not be as effective when aimed at business dealings within the wholesale markets as it is in other areas of activity. Do you agree with these observations? Are some of your criticisms simply reflecting this fundamental problem and if so what can be done about it or will we just have to live with a less precise legal framework than users of English commercial law are used to? How do continental countries cope with this problem?

A. There are a number of issues there. As a proposition, yes, I agree that legal certainty is very difficult to achieve when dealing with very complex markets. What I think we are dealing with in a number of the Financial Services Action Plan Directives is not so much legal uncertainty as uncertainty as to what is required in terms of disclosure. I think it should be possible to make it clear what companies who are coming into markets should be required to disclose and what the expectations of them are. To fail to make that clear creates uncertainty in the market, which is highly undesirable and it is likely to put off a number of issuers, both in the EU and outside. I agree with the statement although I think what we are talking about is less legal uncertainty and more uncertainty as to what the words on the page mean. A lot of the Directives are written in a language which is opaque, difficult to understand and in some cases has a meaning which is broader off the page than I think the people who wrote the words intended. That is undesirable and one should expect better of European draftsmen.

254. There should be disclosure and clarity.

A. Yes, absolutely.

Baroness Cohen of Pimlico

255. Mr Burn, can I start by saying I am a Director of the London Stock Exchange so that we start on equal terms, as it were. You made the familiar point that in 2001 about 60 per cent of debt issuers are managed outside of London and 63 per cent of the issuers of international debt are outside of the EU. You go on to list examples of the threats posed to the role of EU financial markets, including London, starting with denial of choice, failure to recognise the needs of the wholesale markets and the exclusion of non-EU issuers. These are familiar points to us but could you elaborate with some detail on these instances so that we can ask for responses?

A. Yes. I think the clearest example of a deterrent to non-EU issuers is the accounting issue. From a consumer protection point of view it is understandable that European authorities should want to create a single playing field so that anyone looking at investing in the markets should be able to take a number of companies' accounts and compare them, which indicates that there should be a single set of accounting standards and a single set of auditing standards underpinning them. Of course the world is populated by people who live by different accounting standards and the way the Directives have been written, both the Prospectus Directive and the Transparency Directive, they require international accounting standards and auditing standards and even the United States of America will not meet that.

Baroness Cohen of Pimlico contd.]

The accounts will have to produce a true and fair view and of course in the United States they have a different standard. If you go further afield, if you go to Asia, you will find all sorts of issuers that are currently bought and listed in the EU, bought by EU institutions, who will be excluded. Japanese issuers obviously spring to mind. Japanese accounting and auditing standards clearly would not comply with the directives. That is a good example how a lot of existing issuers will be put off by all this. Other examples are the requirements for wholesale debt issuers to put in their capital expenditure requirements over the next few years pretty much regardless of materiality, what the currency of the capital expenditure is, how they are going to fund it—getting close to cash-flow requirements over future years—and requirements to disclose how the audit committees work, which is irrelevant to a debt investor. I think those sort of things are way over the top. All of those were proposed by CESR at level two, the initial proposals that they put forward. Fortunately they have been persuaded to cut those back, so the current proposals for wholesale debt are relatively anodyne. I do not think we should be lulled into a false security by that because of course level two is only part of the process. You have the Directive at level one, whereas level two is the Committee of European Security Regulators advising the Commission when the Commission implements regulations. Then there is level three, which is what I worry about, where we will I suspect see a lot more detail coming out of CESR in terms of guidance, maybe even detailed rules, all designed to achieve harmonisation across the EU. I think that we will see some of this issue of consumer protectionism coming back in.

256. Can I ask you to generalise, how seriously do you assess the threat posed to the market as these Directives actually emerge and the underlying political attitudes? Since London has most of the market how serious is the threat to us?
A. I would like to address that in two ways. The first is a sort of view from outer space, if I may be that general. I think that any successful financial market needs a financial centre. The fact that in the United States the market is based in New York is not an accident, it is a function of financial gravity. I think London ought to fulfil that role in relation to the pan-European market. I think that that is going to be the role that we aspire to because we are the biggest capital market in Europe. We have more issues listed on London than anywhere else. Luxembourg is our nearest rival. I think that the threat is more to London than anywhere else. If you go to some of the continental exchange authorities the only people listed there are their nationals. If the Asian issuers delist from the European markets they will be de-listing from Luxembourg and London.

257. Do you see this as likely?
A. Yes, I do. I can give you concrete examples of that. Historically Japanese companies listed a lot of their convertible bonds on the London Stock Exchange but they are going to move their listings to Singapore because of the threats, particularly of the Transparency Directive but also the Prospectus Directive.

Chairman

258. Can I just follow up on that, in your evidence you say that one of the main objectives of the FSAP to create a pan-European securities market should have been relatively easy to achieve, this is outlined in paragraph 2.1 of your evidence as the kind of things that are required to help it on its way. You go on to say that instead of doing simple things, modifying what could have been done, the FSAP has been used by some Member States and their authorities as an opportunity to introduce new concepts driven by consumer protectionism and in some cases a desire to preserve or re-establish national markets. Many of these matters are a potential threat. How widely are your concerns shared by issuers, lenders and financial intermediaries from outside the EU and within it, because it is the market that should really be pretty concerned about these things?
A. Financial intermediaries are very concerned. Issuers, I think, have yet to wake up to some of these threats. It is very, very difficult to get them to pay attention when they are busy running their companies and doing the things that directors of companies have to do. One of the major problems with the whole debate at the moment is the fact that the real users of the market, the issuers and the investors, have been relatively silent, they have not spoken up. In most cases that is because they have not been sufficiently well informed of the issues and that is despite the efforts of the market to prepare briefing notes which have gone out to these issuers. It is partly due to the fact that the really important debate has to be had between the continental issuers and investors and their own regulators and authorities. In many countries on the Continent of Europe there is no culture of people answering back to their regulators and authorities. For example in Germany, German institutions and German banks are very reluctant to disagree with what has been proposed by the authorities. In the absence of that debate too often when the issues are raised they come forward with a United Kingdom label attached and too often it is seen as the United Kingdom being difficult again and although it does affect other issuers they are too often silent.

259. In 2.1 you went on to say that the consequence of this way of looking at it by other Member States is that it will have a damaging effect on existing markets, especially wholesale markets and on the creation of a pan-European market. Do you think there is any shared understanding of these concerns with other Member States in the EU?
A. I think very little. It is one of the things that has concerned me for some time. There is fairly general ignorance about the international markets that happen to be located in the United Kingdom. There is a sense that it is a United Kingdom dominated market and it is United Kingdom institutions that dominate it. People are not sufficiently aware that there are actually very few United Kingdom players in the market. Too often people are ignorant of what the market involves. For example one relatively senior official in the Commission was heard to say about a year ago that he thought the euro markets were the markets for issues denominated in euro. It

Chairman *contd.*]

was explained to him there were 19 currencies and the euro was just one of them and that the dollar was also an important currency. I think that level of ignorance is very damaging. We really do need to educate people as to the benefits to Europe as a whole of the relatively cheap funds available through international channels. If the markets are damaged non-EU issuers are going to go away. The nightmare scenario is that they will not only not come with their new issues but they will delist their existing issues. We are different from other major capital markets in that a lot of our institutional investors can only buy and hold securities in volume if they are listed in the EU. Those institutional investors will have to sell and, because a lot of selling has a downward effect on the price, we will see the bond market contracting and prices cut, which would be disastrous.

260. I have always had some difficulty with appointing the Transparency Directive, if you take your concept of a listed institutional market, where you say that disclosing standards are an unnecessary occurrence, but in the US there is nothing burdensome in the SEC rules, apart from accounting disclosures, is there anything else that you have in mind as being particularly burdensome and particularly prone to driving people away? How are institutional investors going to exercise their fiduciary responsibility if they do not have the information or is there some other route whereby private investors get private information?

A. There is a huge institutional market which is unlisted. An awful lot of securities are sold without a listing in the United States. To a very large extent the wholesale markets there are unlisted whereas in the EU, for reasons I have given, they have to be listed. In the current CESR proposal I think at level two the best example is the accounting and auditing requirement. There are two separate issues there, a lot of Japanese companies have US GAAP accounts but they are not based on international audit standards. I think a lot of detail has been taken out, for example in relation to asset-backed securities; but it will come back. I am sure it will come back at level three. We should not be lulled into a false sense of security by what we currently see.

261. Your contention is that really it does not matter in terms of disclosure because in some sense these are wholesale securities?

A. I think it does matter. An efficient market is well informed. I think the Directives themselves recognise that wholesale investors are very important. A lot of these institutional investors have their own research departments and they go to see the issuers and talk to them. They also have the benefit of research through the banks. They also have the benefit of ratings. So with all that together they do not need so much mandated disclosure. But they do need some disclosure. The secret is to develop a balance so that disclosure is optimal. If you ask people, "how much disclosure do you want, do you want this, this and this?" They will say, "I want everything". It is only when you start saying what the cost of that will be and how much it will add to the cost of their investment that they start saying, "actually on that basis I do not need this, this and this". There is too much of, "retail investors need this disclosure, why

should wholesale investors not get it too"? There is not enough thought about the cost implications of that and whether given the cost there is a benefit which outweighs the cost.

262. Possibly not enough understanding that retail investors do not really buy it?

A. In the United Kingdom that would be perfectly true. In some continental countries some retail investors do buy debt securities. At the level of the Directive the decision has been taken, it is 50,000 euro denominations or higher and that is deemed to be a wholesale security. I could buy one but I do not have the protection of the Directive.

Baroness Cohen of Pimlico: Thank you.

Lord Fearn

263. We have heard much evidence about the absence of proper cost benefit analyses, however the Finance Director of Unilever told us that he was far more interested in the final rate of interest that he paid than the cost of legal accounting work (although he certainly wanted to minimise that) do you have any suggestions on how to separate these two factors? What would you wish to see considered in the analyses? Should there be high level comments on the whole FSAP or on each Directive?

A. The cost benefit analysis is about more than how much you pay the lawyers. I think if I were an issuer the sort of things I would worry about would be the expenditure of management time in preparing transparency information, preparing quarterly reports and semi-annual reports and the liability issues. The whole concept of liability for on-going reporting of the Transparency Directive is changing English law as it is currently written. We will probably have to abolish the case which says, when you are preparing your Annual Report, you are preparing it for the shareholders to enable them to exercise their rights in shareholders' meetings. You are not preparing the report for investors to enable them to take investment decisions. The way the Transparency Directive is written it says that the purpose of the report is to inform the public. There has to be responsibility for the report. If the report is aimed at the public presumably the responsibility has to be to the public. The public in that context I think means not just the United Kingdom public but the European public. If you are a director who signs a responsibility statement you are taking responsibility to the European public and if anything goes wrong, you are liable to suit in many different jurisdictions. It is one of the major issues of transparency directive.

Chairman

264. How would you resolve that at this stage that FSAP have got to?

A. I think if you look at the back of any of these Directives you will find an impact statement. In the case of the Transparency Directive it says not once but three or four times that the effect of it is going to be to reduce costs. I think all of that is based on a report done by London Economics a number of years back. I am not an economist but I did try to trawl through this thing. I am quite sure that the

Chairman contd.]

assumptions on which that report was based did not take account of the fact that for example every six months, under the Transparency Directive, the directors of the company have to sit down and write a mini prospectus which discloses what has happened and what is going to happen, for which they are liable to the public. That was not taken into account and obviously that is going to have a significant effect on the process. Companies are going to have to spend more time doing this and they are going to have to employ advisers and they are going to have to pay substantial sums of money. I am not talking about lawyers here. I am talking about accountants A lot of this is going to have to be reviewed and that will cost a lot of money.

Baroness Cohen of Pimlico

265. What you are saying is that all of us who are directors of companies are going to end up responsible for prospective investors instead of just the people who actually own our shares?
A. Yes.

266. The interim statement will be a whole new exercise.
A. Yes. Also by law under the Transparency Directive it is not just the financial statements but there is a management report that goes in front of them, a report that is akin to a prospectus. The third part is a responsibility statement. If you add all that together with the liability you have a very nasty situation.

Lord Howie of Troon

267. Towards the end of your paper you talk about ignorance as to what the markets actually do, and I have to say that includes me, and later on you talk about continental alliances, I would like to know how can the United Kingdom authority persuade market participants that they should get involved and what should we be doing to demonstrate to our continental neighbours that open and efficient capital markets could help their economies?
A. I think that the market does need to explain itself better to all concerned. I think that we need to dispel this delusion that the London market is populated by London institutions and is a British attempt at world domination. I think that what we need to do is to make it clear that the users of international markets include EU companies that access relatively cheap capital and that comparing the wholesale markets to the cost of capital in the States, there are significant differences. I think cheap capital is good thing provided it is combined with protection. That is the trick. It is to give proper protection through disclosure, but not just disclosure. It not just putting things in prospectuses. It is also about proper investor protection through things like conduct of business rules to make sure that when you are selling to Granny Smith, whoever is selling to her is properly authorised and has to comply with rules about best execution and to ensure that the nature of the investment is clear. I think it is balancing those things. I suspect the more disclosure you have the more cost you are driving into the process and you are not achieving proper protection in terms of protecting Granny Smith because Granny Smith will throw out a 100 page management report with accounts attached. It is a balance. There is a risk that in the wholesale markets we will find there is too much disclosure and it drives up cost and it drives out issuers and the results will be bad for all. As to continental alliances, I said earlier that too much of the comment for the market comes with a United Kingdom label attached to it. The trick with qualified majority voting is to make sure that the same sort of questions come to a number of Member States at the same time so that when the people get to the working groups they are all carrying the same message from their constituents and the United Kingdom is not the only person raising a particular point. Too often people say it is just the United Kingdom. Continental alliances are very important. How do we mobilise people? This is something that has been exercising me for over a year now and I do not know the answer. I know that it is worth trying to capitalise on the fact that in the United Kingdom we have an international community, an international market, international intermediaries. And some of the major investors are in the United Kingdom. We have people who have contacts on the Continent and what we need to do first of all is to build up a network of people who are are in key positions. I would have thought that if someone like the Governor of the Bank of England wrote to the chairman of international banks or to the institutional investors, and so on, then perhaps we could get a directory of people who are in key positions. That would be a start. Having got those people's names one could use them as a two-way process to inform the comment process and also to go out and convince their counterparts on the Continent of Europe to raise their voices. If you take a United Kingdom corporate most of them will have operations in France or Germany, they will know their French and German counterpart and using that network might be helpful.

268. Would that network reach Granny Smith and would it actually matter if it did not?

A. No, it would not. Granny Smith's voice is going to be heard through consumer protection lobby. What I am mainly concerned about is not so much retail offerings. In retail offerings you will always have the kitchen sink thrown in. What I am mainly concerned about is separation of wholesale markets and retail markets. We have a great threat to this separation. Of course on the Continent in many countries there is no separation; they do not have a wholesale market, they have one market. For example, when the issue of the definition of a wholesale market was being discussed someone came up with the denomination of 50,000 euro and France said "retail investors can still buy. We have rich retail investors and they still need protection". There is a great risk in the assimilation of two markets. If we lose the wholesale market we lose the cost efficiencies from reduced disclosure.

Lord Howie of Troon: I can just see a glimmer of knowledge.

Lord Walpole

269. Many of the witnesses have talked about the risk of an EuroSEC, given the problems identified by the FLMC and your own comments about the motivation of some countries do you feel that this would solve all of the difficulties and be a complete panacea?

A. I think a European SEC is plan B. If this does not work that is what we will have. I hope I will not be seen as a cynic if I say that I think a European SEC would be a complete disaster. The reason I say that is that I suspect a European SEC would be founded on good European principles. There would a member for every Member State and they would all bring relative degrees of knowledge to the debate. The reason the US SEC works reasonably well is that there are people who understand the market, they are informed about it. What you do not have in the US is a representative from every state. But I am afraid that is what we would get if there was a EuroSEC and the result would be to weight everything in favour of those people who do not believe in wholesale markets and have no particular feel for the international market, who do not care about non-EU issuers, and so on, and all would be lost.

Chairman

270. Let me conclude with this, in your paper and today again you tended to say there were some serious problems and then at the end of that the exact opposite, you say that subsequent discussions have gravely modified this, so really there are denied. Do problems remain?

A. What we have seen is a series of battles in a war. The war goes on. Some of the battles have been fought and they have been—I can speak from bitter personal experience—exhausting but fortunately the market has managed to make its voice heard and concessions have been won. The Prospectus Directive is largely workable. It is by no means ideal, it still has a number of major issues in it which need to be sorted out, but it is workable. It is not the end of the story. The Directive is level one. At level two there are a number of issues which still remain outstanding. Again if you compare the first draft to the current draft, the current draft is a lot better. When we go on there will be level three, which is guidance. My fear is that in the search for maximum harmonisation, which is a phrase used a lot in the context of the Prospectus Directive, we will end up before long with a European set of listings rules,

detail rules. There is one in London several hundred pages long and I fear we may well end up with that at a European level. There are a number of battles to come, we should not be complacent. We have won several, but the battles to come will still have to be fought.

271. Later this week we are going to Brussels and Paris and to Frankfurt next week, what two major issues do you think we should raise?

A. Is this with the Commission?

272. The Commission and various other institutions.

A. I think one of the things I would say to the Commission is that they need to get their focus back on to the objective, which is to create an efficient capital market. I think recently they have had their attention diverted by trying to get a Directive through in a very short time scale. That is one thing I would say to the Commission, we want to see more focus on the objective and less focus on reaching a compromise which keeps different Member States happy.

Baroness Cohen of Pimlico

273. We are going to see the Deputy Governor of the Bank of France; Jean Francios le Petit for International Relations; the Secretary General; Jean Francois Theodore of Euronext, and I guess it is going to be difficult to put some of this to him and Mr Philippe Marini of the Senate, that is not quite the audience for this.

A. It is difficult. I am not sure I have any messages for those gentlemen.

274. Except to say, "rally, lads, or we all lose out on the stock markets".

A. They would say that they do not really have an international stock market.

Baroness Cohen of Pimlico: The Bank of France would say that it is wonderful.

Chairman

275. Mr Burn, thank you very much. Is there anything you want to add?

A. No, I do not think so.

Chairman: Can I thank you again for your evidence and for coming to see is this afternoon we are very grateful.

Supplementary Memorandum from Lachlan Burn, Partner, Linklaters

SUBMISSION ON THE DRAFT TRANSPARENCY DIRECTIVE (2003/0045 (COD))

The draft Transparency Directive (the "Directive") significantly extends the established limitation in English case law on the civil liability of directors and auditors arising from the publication of a company's annual accounts and audit report. As a result, if implemented in its current form, the Directive would mean that directors and auditors would not only be liable to shareholders (as is presently the case) for any errors in the published financial information, but that they would also be liable to the general public. This substantial amendment to the current position on civil liability under English law is contrary to the Commission's stated intention that the Directive should not have such an effect in Member States.

BACKGROUND

Articles 4, 5 and 6 of the Directive require issuers of securities on regulated markets to disclose to the public an annual financial report (Article 4), a half-yearly financial report (Article 5) and certain quarterly financial information (Article 6).

By virtue of Articles 4 and 5, both the annual and half-yearly financial reports must include a statement made by the directors (or by other responsible persons within the issuer) that the information contained in these report is, to the best of their knowledge, in accordance with the facts and that the reports make no omission likely to affect their import.

Under Articles 4 and 5 the audit report for the annual financial report (and, if one exists, for the half-yearly financial report) must also be disclosed in full to the public with the financial report.

Article 7(2) is the provision which in our view unintentionally extends the boundaries of civil liability in England and Wales. It states:

> "Member States shall ensure that their laws, regulations and administrative provisions on civil liability apply to those persons responsible for the information disclosed to the public in accordance with Articles 4, 5 and 6."

Article 7(2) should be interpreted in the light of Recital 10 to the Directive, which sets out the policy underlying this provision:

> "Investor confidence should be reinforced by ensuring that, under national law, a company and its administrative, management, or supervisory bodies bear responsibility and civil liability as far as annual and interim financial reporting is concerned. This is the most effective way to enforce the requirement that issuers provide the public with accurate and reliable information. Each Member State should ensure such responsibility and liability under its national law or regulations."

CIVIL LIABILITY—THE PRESENT POSITION UNDER ENGLISH LAW

Existing English case law clearly limits the extent to which the directors and auditors of a company may be liable in respect of negligent misstatements in the company's financial statements and audit reports.

This limitation was established in the leading case of Caparo Industries plc v Dickman[25], in which the House of Lords held that the purpose of statutory accounts was to enable shareholders to hold to account those responsible for running the company by the exercise of their shareholder rights in general meeting. Accordingly the purpose of statutory accounts is not to inform shareholders' investment decisions, and nor is it to inform the investment decisions of the wider public. In the ordinary course of events, therefore, the directors in preparing the accounts and the auditors in auditing the accounts owe no duties of care to potential investors or to the public at large to ensure that the accounts are accurate.

In light of the decision in Caparo, under English law the civil liability of directors and auditors is currently limited to (i) losses suffered by shareholders as a result of their actions as shareholders in reliance on the misstated accounts, and (ii) losses arising in certain other narrower or exceptional cases, for example where accounts are provided to particular investors (or to other third parties, such as lenders) in circumstances where the directors or the auditors know that the recipients will rely on the accuracy of the accounts or audit report. Beyond these two categories of civil liability the directors and auditors have no liability to a member of the general public.

CONCERNS

It seems relatively clear that the intention of the current wording of Article 7(2) of the Directive (particularly when interpreted in the light of Recital 10), is to require Member States to ensure that under their law, civil liability should attach to the company, its directors and others responsible for information in company accounts. It also seems relatively clear in the context that civil liability means the payment of damages to investors or others who have suffered loss. The "trigger" for potential liability (based on the wording in Article 7(2) of the Directive) is disclosure to the public. It is implicit in the wording of Article 7(2) and Recital 10 that such civil liability should also be to "the public" to whom the accounts or other information has been disclosed as required by the Directive.

Whilst "the public" is not a defined term in the Directive, we believe that it is likely to mean the European public rather than merely the UK public: this is particularly so once the broader context of the Financial Services Action Plan and the related directives such as the Prospectus Directive are taken into account.

If under the Directive, the intention is to ensure issuers, directors and others responsible for accounts are liable for civil damages to investors, or the public generally, for losses caused by inaccurate or unreliable information in those accounts, this represents a significant extension of the current position under English

---

[25] [1990] 2 AC 605.

law. As explained above, the current extent in English law of the directors' civil liability for the accounts (and therefore whether any compensation is payable by the directors at all) is limited by the Caparo doctrine described above.

Accordingly it is apparent that the impact of Article 7(2) on English law is to broaden very significantly the liability of a company and its directors and auditors: they would not only be exposed to liability arising from civil actions brought by shareholders (as is currently the case in light of Caparo), but they would also potentially be liable to the public or investors as a whole. The rule in Caparo is thus probably inconsistent with our interpretation of Article 7(2) and Recital 10.

JURISDICTION

It is also unclear from the drafting of the Directive how the jurisdictional issues arising from the new provisions will be resolved. If "public" does indeed mean "European public", will the remedy be available against the company and its directors only before the courts and under the law of the home state of the company? Or will the company and directors be capable of being sued under the local law and before the local court of the state where the shares are offered, bought or held? Or alternatively, will the company or directors be capable of being sued under the local law and before the local court of any EU state?

The provisions thus raise the possibility of a French or German issuer being sued by a UK-based investor here in the UK for financial statements made in France/Germany. It also raises the possibility of forum shopping to find the most advantageous law to sue under, unless the jurisdictional issue is adequately addressed in this or another Directive.

3 October 2003

Memorandum from Ruben Lee* Managing Director, Oxford Finance Group

The development of an integrated market in financial services in the EU has been a long time coming. The latest legislative project to seek to implement it is the Financial Services Action Plan (FSAP), a program the Commission adopted in 1999 containing over 40 legislative measures that are divided into four broad areas: retail markets; wholesale markets; prudential rules and supervision; and other aspects necessary for an optimal single financial market. The key legislative procedure by which it is hoped to implement the bulk of the FSAP is the Lamfalussy Process. Its goals are to reduce barriers to integration in the single market for financial services, and to allow European governments a fast track to implement changes in the regulation of financial services within the EU. Unfortunately, the Lamfalussy Process will fail in delivering these goals, and in response some form of Pan-European securities markets regulator is likely to be established.

The Lamfalussy Process has certainly enhanced the transparency of, and consultation procedures in, the EU legislative process, thereby significantly improving the mechanism for creating EU law. It will not succeed, however, in reducing the barriers to integration in the single market for financial services, because of its failure to address two fundamental issues: national protectionism and bureaucratic inertia. This failure will make increased harmonisation and some centralisation of supervision inevitable.

The comitology-oriented institutional reforms adopted as part of the Lamfalussy Process will neither reduce delays in regulatory implementation, nor improve substantive flexibility and certainty of EU financial services legislation. National protectionism and bureaucratic inertia will not be constrained, institutional power struggles between the Commission, Council and Parliament, will continue as previously, and enforcement of EU law will remain weak.

In addition, the Lamfalussy reforms will be blamed even for those regulatory deficiencies that are not directly related to them. In particular, market participants will consider the Lamfalussy Process to be the cause of the likely outcome of the FSAP, namely the quick delivery of bad law, even though such delays do not arise as a direct result of the Lamfalussy recommendations. Similarly, some Member states will blame the Lamfalussy Process for any form of regulatory arbitrage they find unpalatable, even though they originally agreed that it should expressly aim at facilitating mutual recognition—and, thus, regulatory competition. Finally, the practical realities of European enlargement will make the Lamfalussy Process irrelevant, as regulatory strategies will aim at maximum harmonisation and centralisation, rather than minimum harmonisation and mutual recognition.

The combination of the failure of the Lamfalussy Process on the one hand, and the unacceptability of strengthening mutual recognition and regulatory competition in the EU on the other hand, will both reduce

---

* The views presented here are those of the author alone, and do not necessarily represent those of any institutions with which the author is affiliated, the Oxford Finance Group, or any of its clients. The opinions presented here draw on "Four Predictions about the Future of EU Securities Regulation", co-authored with Gerard Hertig, forthcoming, Journal of Comparative Law Studies (2003). A draft version of the article is available at http:/papers.srn.com/sol3/papers.cfm?abstract-id = 376720£Paper Download.

objections to, and generate sufficient political support for, the establishment of some form of Pan-European securities markets regulator. Notwithstanding current opposition to the establishment of a Pan-European securities regulator, there will be a European Securities and Exchange Commission. There will be no apparent alternative.

Examination of Witness

DR RUBEN LEE, Managing Director, Oxford Finance Group, examined.

Chairman

276. I apologise that we are running a little behind schedule. We are aiming to take round forty minutes, we may stray a little over that but we will do our very best not to, I apologise if we do. I believe you might want to say a few words before we begin. Do bear in mind the time we have. Can I thank you for your written evidence to date. We are looking forward to discussing these matters with you. By all means do start with your introductory remarks.

(*Dr Lee*) Thank you. Can I repeat the disclaimer beforehand that the I words I am going to say are my own and not those of the Oxford Finance Group, which I run, my customers, the European Parliament, which I advise, nor Gérard Hertig my co-author. May I also thank you for inviting me. I have a few very brief words, I want to say that I think that the Committee's inquiry is very, very timely and also very important because it provides one of the few broad overviews of this issue that is possible, because most people are stuck in the trenches fighting particular issues. On that basis I wanted to outline a few key things which I would bear in mind. The key one has already been alluded to here, and I have read in the previous evidence, which is that in my view the FSAP is over-archingly a political exercise, not a legal concern and not an economic exercise but over-archingly a political exercise. That determines a range of different factors, it determines how you assess it and what responses you have to it. I think there are three big questions that need to be addressed with regard to this political exercise. The first is, what is the current political response to it, not in the United Kingdom but throughout the rest of Europe because it is this that the United Kingdom needs to respond to? The second, in light of that and given the objectives we all have, which is promoting the United Kingdom, and in this instance I think we are in the very happy situation that what is good for the United Kingdom is good for Europe, big question is, what policies should the United Kingdom authorities be following? The final big issue is, given acceptance of these policies what strategy should we be following? I would be delighted to answer these or some of the questions that you have put down before me.

277. That is extremely helpful. In your evidence that you put before us you said that unfortunately the Lamfalussy Process will fail in delivering these goals and in response some form of pan-European securities markets regulator is likely to be established. Are you suggesting that all aspects of the Lamfalussy Process will fail or are you principally saying that level four will fail?

A. I think we need to examine both the objectives which Baron Lamfalussy and his Wise Men laid out in his report and also the wider objectives. He had many goals, including establishing a mechanism to be able to update Directives in a timely fashion, responding to the slow transposition and implementation of European Directives in international law, the lack of enforcement, the fact that we had framework Directives that were too detailed, they should be more principle-based and he also used the words inefficiency, ambiguous, and a lack of transparency and consultation. Those are the broad objectives that Lamfalussy discussed. Then there are the wider objectives of the FSAP, which are making our capital markets better. I do not think that the whole Lamfalussy Process will fail and indeed I think with the evidence to date we are seeing a range of areas where significant advances are being shown compared to what has happened. In particular we are seeing much more transparency and we are seeing much more consultation. It is not sufficient and there are particular instances where we have seen major flaws in this and this is, as many people have said, a learning-by-doing a process, but I think we have seen a lot of benefits there. I could point to the weaknesses if you want to. I think that the workings of CESR have also been widely praised for the fact that they are bringing a network of people and allowing the various regulators round Europe to consult much more, and that is increasing education round the regulatory market, if you will, and I think that is to all of our advantage. On the other hand there are some key failures. We have recently seen that there continues to be poor implementation of Directives and I think that will continue. There has been widespread criticism that the Directives are still too detailed. Most important I think that the two key causes of the problems which Lamfalussy identified namely national protectionism and bureaucratic inertia are not being sufficiently addressed and these will continue to give rise to the other problems Lamfalussy identified, such as the inefficiency, rigidity, ambiguity and so on and so forth.

278. That is helpful. If one puts aside the process and concentrates on the substance do you have a view on whether the substance which has emerged actually provides the appropriate objectives?

A. I want to make a range of different comments on that. The first is that the FSAP has already been in existence for some time and most of the Directives have already been passed. We have, as you know, only a few more to go through, which may or may not be delivered by next year. I think revisiting what might have been in those forty or above Directives is pointless at the moment because we have them, and we need to deal with them. That does raise a question as to whether there should be an FSAP 2, if you will, if there is a lack of concrete building blocks in the current situation. My view, akin to many in the

Chairman *contd.*]

United Kingdom, and indeed round Europe is that we would do much better not to have a vast new range of Directives filling in the missing blocks. There may be specific Directives which are required after detailed consultation and, as many people have said, there should be much greater focus on enforcement. That is what was in the FSAP and what might be in a hypothetical second one. Now if we look examine the issue of what was hoped for and what was delivered in terms of the substance of the various Directives my view is that we have seen some major advances but where national interests are—or will be—seriously threatened the response in the current raft of Directives will be the same as in the past. In particular, this will lead to some form of political ambiguity as a means of achieving a deal or worse than that pure protectionism, and one could interpret aspects of the Investment Services Directive and a range of other aspects of other Directives. I think that those incentives on the part of national governments remain and to the extent they have the powers, I think they still do, this will become evident in the substance of relevant Directives

Chairman: I may return to that a little later.

Lord Howie of Troon

279. I wonder if I misheard what you said in reply to the Chairman's question, did you say that the Lamfalussy Process would not fail?

A. I wrote an article in which I specifically stated that it will fail. Here what I outlined were some aspects of the Lamfalussy Process as a process which have achieved successes and which are beneficial but I outlined a range of problems within it which I previously outlined in the article and which I continue to believe will lead effectively to its failure.

280. You say very clearly in the conclusion to your paper that the Lamfalussy Process will not work, have I missed something?

A. No, I do not think you have and I think what I just said confirms that. It will and it is working in parts but overall I would judge it in the future to lead to a failure. That is how I can put it.

281. Thank you. I was trying clarify my mind. Your paper suggests, and you did refer to this in your earlier comment, that national protectionism and bureaucratic inertia will not be constrained as the process goes forward, does the United Kingdom financial services industry arising from that, including wholesale and retail, stand to be winners or losers if the FSAP goes forward? Would that matter?

A. It certainly does matter. Let me give you two responses to that, we have a long and fine tradition in the United Kingdom of being open, of allowing foreign firms access to all the various elements of our financial services and in that sense I think that the United Kingdom authorities have behaved, if I can say, very well. I think that their actions have promoted competition in the United Kingdom which has led to a better financial services industry in the United Kingdom and to enhance delivery of capital markets for the benefit of corporates and consumers. That is purely focusing on the United Kingdom. The question then arises as to whether the proposed liberalisation, which is one key thrust in the FSAP,

will materialise in the rest of Europe. To the extent that national protectionism stops this will be against the interests of our financial services industry, which would seek to provide services to those countries again in which protectionism is being practised. It will also lead to the disadvantage of the wider constituencies in those countries, which responds rather specifically to a general concern that you raised earlier on, which is how do we get people on our side and motivate people. I have a longer response to that broad question which I think is important.

282. Suppose the FSAP does go ahead what do you think the impact would be on issuers and investors both here and in the rest of the Union?

A. There a rhetoric reality gap. If it goes ahead in the sense that competition is promoted and markets are liberalised with the appropriate protection of consumers and so on and so forth that will be to the benefit of the United Kingdom financial services industry because we will be able to sell our services abroad. As I indicated I think that will also be to the benefit of many constituencies in all of those different countries that are part of this process. That is the rhetoric. The question is, does the reality match the rhetoric? I would argue that there are strong incentives and a range of different contexts where it does not.

283. Thank you.

A. For example there are issues to do with competition clearing settlement and other issues, the ability of corporates to chose prospectus, location—

Lord Howie of Troon: You almost remind me of a comment in the film *Fort Apache* where it was said, "if the truth conflicts with the legend, print the legend".

Chairman: Dr Lee, you keep leaving us on the edge of pressing issues, I am going to do my very best to return to them.

Lord Fearn

284. You say that market participants will consider the Lamfalussy Process to be the cause of the likely outcome of the FSAP, namely the quick delivery of bad law, even though such delays do not arise as a direct result of the Lamfalussy recommendations. Can you explain what you mean by this statement where you refer on the one hand to the quick delivery of bad law and on the other hand to delays (this appears to be a contradiction). Are your concerns over quick delivery of bad law motivated by how much more does need to be delivered before the European Parliament elections in May 2004 when the FSAP effectively needs to be completed?

A. In the paper, Gérard Hertig and I noted two different types of that outcome might arise, either the quick delivery of poor law or the slow delivery of better law, and both of those would lead to the Lamfalussy Process being questioned. We could see examples of both; and in that sense their combined pressure would not be contradictory. I have a couple of comments on the timing, namely that it should be delivered by 2004, 2005. As always, a balance needs to be drawn by giving people an incentive to make

Lord Fearn *contd.*]

laws and allowing for appropriate disclosure and there is no right answer to that. In the middle and towards the end of a long process of legislation, it is unsurprising that people are getting legislative fatigue, if I can say that, and it is also unsurprising we are seeing some problems with rapid results. On the other hand, in some senses I applaud having a timetable so that we get some results, so I am not so worried that the last, more difficult, ones would not be passed by the proposed timetable, we will deal with them later.

285. Are they going to be bad laws? You used that phrase.

A. Whether they will be bad law or not will be dependent on a range of different factors. It will be dependent, as I indicated before, upon both the extent to which nations are able to protect their interests and pursue those national interests in the wider European interests through the process; it will also be dependent upon the extent to which there is appropriate consultation through the Lamfalussy Process. That second issue, consultation and transparency, is getting better although I think there are still flaws and there have been particular instances of problems with it. The first one has not been addressed and Lamfalussy does not deal with it and I see that as being a real problem with the process.

Chairman

286. In your paper you predict the arrival of a EuroSEC which you say will initially focus on corporate disclosure issues with soft enforcement powers. In your view, should that come about? Would a EuroSEC focus on both the wholesale and retail markets?

A. As we note in the paper, my co-author and I disagree on this issue. I believe the existence of a EuroSEC would not be beneficial for the most part, in the sense that (a) it would be staffed by people who have less practical knowledge of the markets than the SEC—again quoting Lachlan—and (b) I think the reason it will be promoted is to promote national interests. It would not be created to further competition in the markets, so that is why in my view the existence of a EuroSEC would not be beneficial. However, that said, what I think is absolutely critical for the Committee to appreciate is the extent to which there is in my view a relatively wide political support amongst a range of different types of constituencies and nations for the existence of such a body. So what that means is, however much we rant against it in the UK, we need to be aware that there is a growing constituency for such a body. Of course, saying there will be a EuroSEC does not specify what it will do, how it will be financed, who will staff it and all the details, but I would argue that the political constituency regards those details just as that, details to be solved later, and not as problems that should stop the creation of such a body. That is a long response to a short question, the summary is, in my view the creation of a EuroSEC would not be beneficial and we should seek to promote our various objectives, competition, consultation and so on and so forth, under the current structures, but we need a

twin-track strategy in order to respond to what I see as a growing political constituency for a EuroSEC and that political process needs to follow a range of different areas, again leaving it open to subsequent discussion should we wish to.

287. That appears to be saying, if I can see my way through that . . .

A. Sorry.

288. Not at all . . . that in reality the FSAP is being largely driven by political imperatives to secure the perceived individual interests of Member States rather than efficient, lowest cost wholesale capital markets, and that in your view a likely outcome is that the same political interests will see a EuroSEC as a figleaf to overcome perceived problems of bureaucracy, inertia, protectionism. The very institution you are predicting will itself be scarcely better than the problems it was meant to be resolving—I think I have got you right there—whereas, as you heard from our previous witness, Mr Burn, and I do not think he would disagree with you on that, EuroSEC might be of value if it was largely market driven rather than politically driven, representing all Member States' interests, seeking to get the lowest common denominator, compromise and protect interests. In your view, is it possible to conceive realistically of a EuroSEC which might be the result of market pressure and market interests which would be of value? How else do market interests really get borne out? How does the market rule?

A. Yes, it is possible in my view for the UK—and I am answering this directly—to help shape the agenda of what such an institution might be. As I indicated, I think the UK should be following a twin-track strategy, making the best of the current situation through CESR, through the Commission and so on and so forth, but recognising what might come about and following the appropriate political process to best influence the outcome so that were a EuroSEC to come about it would enshrine some of the objectives which Lamfalussy himself put out but which have not been, if you will, implemented in the process, and indeed to be more market-friendly than an alternative vision of EuroSEC. So I am responding yes. Even if you think there might be a EuroSEC, as I think is relatively likely, it does not mean its structures are pre-specified and I think there is room for UK authorities to exert significant influence on what structure might come about.

289. Can you imagine the French and the German Governments agreeing to a EuroSEC based in London?

A. I think the question of the euro is at issue here.

290. EuroSEC?

A. Yes, and I am responding by saying I think the question of the euro is at issue here. I think a response to that is initially no, but if you ask me—

291. What do you mean "initially no"? If EuroSEC is based in Paris, it is not going to shift five years later.

A. Forgive me. I absolutely agree with that. What I mean by initially no is, if you go up and ask a politician in Paris or Germany, would they allow a EuroSEC in London, they would respond initially no. However, if you ask me, is it beyond the talents

Chairman *contd.*]

and the skills of our politicians to influence the debate in order to get it based in London, notwithstanding that initial no, then I would say, no, it is not beyond the skills and talents of our politicians, it is within their powers to do so. That requires skilful politics.

Chairman: We must move on, we have much to talk about.

Lord Fearn

292. The ESEC model you put forward appears to rely on a more litigious model like perhaps the US model to make it work, ie the ESEC provides the ammunition for the lawyers to fire. Surely this requires a major change in European culture which will take years. Who will fund the ESEC? Why should Member States agree to fund ESEC as well as their own national regulators? This will increase costs in the European financial services industry which the FSAP is trying to reduce.

A. A couple of comments on that. In our paper, the prediction that there would be a EuroSEC was not dependent on the existence of US-style litigation in Europe; that was one minor element of the analysis. I do think however that notwithstanding the fact it is not European culture right now to have a very litigious process, I think things can change in unexpected ways. Here I would quote my co-author who talks about the Swiss experience, where currently Swiss directors are facing liability litigation, possibly for hundreds of millions of euros, where two or three years ago this would not even have been conceivable, so what is inconceivable today is common practice tomorrow. One should not think that culture is completely unchangeable; I think it is possible. In terms of the details of who will fund the SEC and so on and so forth, I would regard these as details to which we do not have answers and neither does anybody else, but I would not regard them as issues which would be determinative in not allowing the existence of a EuroSEC. I would make one further comment on that which is that when I travel around Europe giving speeches—for example I was in Paris just a few days ago—people in the industry come up and say to me, "We would much rather have one set of rules than 15 sets of rules because it is so difficult dealing with them all", and, yes, how will the EuroSEC be funded is one issue but the cost faced by the industry is another issue and that is an indication of at least some constituencies which would like to create a EuroSEC.

Lord Walpole

293. I am still totally confused because I am much more used to things like the Environment Agency which does not consist of representatives from absolutely everywhere who know nothing about it, it consists of experts who do things properly, and whenever I ask questions about the EuroSEC that is what I have in my mind, do you think that is not going to happen and it will be purely representational and political? That is not the question I was meant to ask I know.

A. What I think you are saying, just so I interpret it, is that I envisaged a body which would be purely representational but you have experience with bodies which are constituted with people who have expertise in the relative area or inquiry, whatever it may be. I would respond in a somewhat similar manner to the Chairman. There are a range of different responses but the first is, do I think it is possible for a EuroSEC to have market representatives and indeed to be facing the market, and the answer is I think it is possible but to do that will require a great deal of wise and skilful politics and I look forward to seeing that. Do I think, however, on the other hand, that initially the creation of such a body would in many continental Europeans' minds be staffed by official representatives, and I would say yes to that too. I would point to either the European Bank or to the existence of CESR which to my mind would probably be a proto-European SEC which contains representatives of authorities around Europe.

294. What I want, as a person who is going to invest or not, or will consider what to invest in, is what you have just said about the people in France, I want the whole thing to be an even playing field wherever it is, so if I want to go and invest, because I happen to like a Saab, in something Swedish, or perhaps I prefer a BMW and want something German, it should be easy for me to do it whichever it is, wherever it is.

A. My response to that is I would agree. Now place yourself in the context of a hypothetical continental European authority which has its national interests at stake and which may not view consumer interests being their prime national interests, but may rather seek to protect specific banks or its national stock exchange, whatever it may be, so in order to create such a body you need to convince such a continental national authority to structure a body which may not promote the interests which it perceives initially to be in its national interests. So that is where the skilful politics is required, that is where the building of alliances and the support from different constituitences is needed, that is where appropriate discussion, education, persuasion and trade-offs are required. That is the political agenda.

295. You refer to the "combination of the failure of the Lamfalussy Process on the one hand, and the unacceptability of strengthening mutual recognition and regulatory competition in the EU on the other hand". How will the creation of this body, ESEC, your predictive model, result in market forces lowering the cost of capital for European issuers and promote economies of scale across the EU thus reducing the number of players, eg stock exchanges and intermediaries? Could the outcome not in fact be a reduction in GDP and an increase in the cost of capital?

A. Yes, it could be. Suppose a EuroSEC were to come about, the issue is, will it promote legislation and regulation, if you will, which deepens and makes more liquid the capital markets in Europe, or will it seek to protect national interests? The very notion in your question that there might be losers in this competition is threatening to a range of national interests. Of course, I as a pro-competitive Briton would say that competition is beneficial and let the

Lord Walpole *contd.*]

losers take the hindmost, and we have had many winners and losers in the UK. The issue is, will such a structure be able to accommodate that view, or will it be structured not to accommodate that view expressly, and I think that there is a probability, at least a 50 per cent probability, that it might be structured so as not to promote competition. That is the key area which I think our twin-track political approach needs to be addressing; on the one hand, promoting the best we can under the current FSAP and the Lamfalussy Process and, on the other hand, responding to what I perceive to be a growing political constituency across a range of countries and a range of different areas of the industry for the existence of such a body. Although it may perhaps be frustrating for the authorities to be looking at such a question, given they already have a process, nevertheless I would view it as being essential.

Lord Howie of Troon

296. You make a number of predictions in your paper but I do not think you have distinguished between wholesale and retail markets at all. We do know that most wholesale markets are in only one or two Member States rather than in the majority of them, do you think that the Lamfalussy Process could work out successfully for wholesale markets but not for retail markets?

A. I think the question of evaluating the Lamfalussy Process depends upon who is asking and what criteria they use for assessing the success of the process. I think that the Lamfalussy Process itself does not make strong distinctions between wholesale and retail and so in that sense many people looking at it will not be able in their minds to say, "This bit of it is successful and that bit of it is not successful." From the UK's point of view, given that we have the biggest wholesale market in Europe, one strategy which we have been pursuing is to try and distinguish wholesale and retail and get the so-called light touch with the wholesale market. There are two issues there: whether it will be possible to get such a light touch in the outcome of the Lamfalussy Process and whether it will be possible for, as again my friend was talking about, some continental European regulators to accept that distinction as many of them do not. So I think we should be pushing as much as we can to have that distinction but be realistic that we may not be that successful in getting it, if you will.

Chairman

297. Could I turn to the question of wholesale markets. In the written evidence of Mr Burn, which we quoted in the oral hearing, he reminds us on the

international debt securities market there is some nearly 1.5 trillion US dollars of new issues, 60 per cent managed out of London and 63 per cent of the market based outside the EU. After next year there will be 25 Member States in the EU, all shapes and sizes. How can a process based, or apparently based, so much on Member States seeking to protect their own perceived local interests reasonably, transparently, facilitate the efficient operation and hopefully the growth of the role of London in such markets? Very, very few of the 25 Member States have any experience whatsoever of that kind of market, is this not a problem? Or is this paranoia on the part of the UK? Are we worried about something here which other Member States would say to us if we talked to them, "We are not seeking to constrain that"?

A. This is a complicated area and I have written on the strategies of EU accession countries' stock exchanges, so it is an area in which I am interested. I would have two broad comments here. The first is, and again this goes back to the twin-track political strategy I was talking about, that what the UK needs to do is to make clear in this context that what is good for the UK is good for Europe, which is a difficult but possible sale. So I think to the various new countries which are acceding and indeed to many of the existing countries, the promotion of capital markets in the UK should be promoted as beneficial to Italian corporates and French investors and so on and so forth, and my view is that this reality needs to be sold strongly. The second response is to disagree in part with what you hinted at, and that is that many of the new countries may be more pro-competitive than in fact some of the existing Member States, so actually, as in a range of other contexts, we might see more allies there than opponents.

298. Back to coalition of interests. I promised we would finish by 6.15, is there anything you would like to say by way of conclusion?

A. I would like to repeat what I said before, which is that we in the UK, whatever our preferences with regard to the EuroSEC, need to appreciate the political reality of what is going on on the Continent and to have an appropriate response to it.

299. If in the event there are one or two matters we want to follow up by correspondence—we try to avoid that if we can—we may write to you; you raised intriguingly a number of matters we have left in the air. Thank you so much for your evidence today and for your written evidence.

A. Thank you very much.

WEDNESDAY 8 OCTOBER 2003

Present:

Cohen of Pimlico, B.   Walpole, L.
Fearn, L.   Woolmer of Leeds, L.
Shutt of Greetland, L.   (Chairman)

Examination of Witness

Ms Christa Randzio-Plath, Chairman, Economic and Monetary Affairs Committee, European Parliament, examined.

Chairman

300. First of all, I am extremely grateful to you for fitting this in. We know how busy you are and we appreciate this. If I may, we have a whole range of matters to discuss with you but we have narrowed it down to a smaller number of questions. Our principal reason for being here today is in relation to the Financial Services Action Plan. If I may, I would like to start with a question to you on that. So far there has been a substantial measure of political agreement at Level 1 but some of the more difficult Directives remain to be resolved, and Level 2 and Level 3 are less advanced. What, as a politician, is your view of the real status of the FSAP? Do you think that the political deadline of spring 2004 will be met? Do you think that it is leading to rushed legislation? Are decisions sometimes perhaps not of the quality that one ought to have? What is your view of how things are going?

(Ms Randzio-Plath) We have now passed 36 of the 42 measures and it was a heavy workload for the European Parliament, but I cannot see that there are any qualitative arguments against the work we have done. However, we of course have a big problem with the legislation within the framework of this Financial Services Action Plan. The first problem is that we, as Parliament, negotiated in order to get a compromise text. There is a political will to get this legislation through, but we do not have the impression that the co-legislator always has the same ambition. Because of different national financial cultures, there are vested interests and often they do not help to promote the procedures in the co-decision process. We are always under time pressure, because the Commission can wait as long as it wants to present a draft proposal and the Council can also wait for 20 years if the Council wants before they give their opinion. As you know, the takeover bids took 16 years. We try to organise pressure by having good-quality legislation so that we can tell the Council, "What we are doing as the European Parliament, you could also do". It also depends on the priorities of the different EU presidencies—and every six months there is somebody else to negotiate with—as to whether this ambition is shared, not only by the European Parliament but also by the Council. We were therefore rather astonished, in a positive way, that yesterday there was political agreement on ISD. This compromise goes very much in the direction of the Parliament's position concerning transparency. Our tough negotiations, with different points of view, do not represent pure ideology either from one side

or the other, because we know that we can only get a text if there is a reasonable text which can be understood, and where you have taken into consideration the interests not only of the professionals but also the non-professionals, the consumers, the industry, and so on. I do not think that we have to be anxious about the quality of the legislation. I would also underline that, from the beginning as the chair, I said that I wanted the political groups to agree as to who would deal with each report, so that our rapporteurs could be prepared before receiving the draft proposal. This was helpful. I also proposed having an expert panel. I was the chair of the Subcommittee on Monetary Affairs during stages 2 and 3. Because there were so many problems to deal with, it was clear that it was necessary for all members of the committee, whatever their professional background, to have the same information and knowledge. These experts on the monetary panel helped us develop skills, expertise and knowledge. This panel also contributed to the opinion-building of the EMAC members, which was also very helpful. We were not helpless, therefore, when being approached by so many lobbyists. You can imagine how many lobbyists are active in this field. The number has only been surpassed by the lobbyists in relation to the reconstruction of British churches—because I am rapporteur on reduced VAT, where we are only at the start and I have already received 200 letters.

Chairman: You touched upon the question of a lot of vested interests, lobbying and so on. I will invite Lord Shutt to develop that.

Lord Shutt of Greetland

301. One of the objectives of the FSAP is greater competition, with resulting benefits to users of capital and consumers in their role as savers. However, the implications of this objective, applied properly, will be the demise of the weaker and the less efficient players in the financial services industry. Do you agree with that conclusion? If so, do you think this outcome will be politically acceptable amongst Member States, or will Member States protect their own industries, thus frustrating one of the objectives?

A. I cannot see that Member States are protecting. Of course, the interests of the City of London are different from other financial places. Every government tries to structure the environment to the extent that their industry can be successful. What we have to do, however, is to look at the standards,

Lord Shutt of Greetland *contd.*]

rules, regulation and supervision which will make it clear that there are equal conditions and that there is fair rather than unfair competition. I think that the Financial Services Action Plan goes exactly in that direction. Whether that is enough has to be proved, because we do not have the experience of a single market in the European Union. We are just realising the single market on financial services. We have also asked ourselves whether it would not be better to see if there is a necessity to streamline the European legislation and the American legislation. I have tried to contact my colleagues in Congress in order to ventilate these questions, because it is not only our companies that are concerned by the Sarbanes-Oxley Act and other questions: Americans could also be concerned by measures we take within the Financial Services Action Plan. This is therefore very important. Our concern is also to protect the savers and consumers. One of our objectives, therefore, was to promote transparency and confidence. With this legislation we looked to see that there were not too many risks in the Supplementary Pension Directive. We tried to protect the employees and not give the funds the possibility of having investment which was too risky—given the experience you have had in the United Kingdom with pension funds, for example, where people who have worked up to the age of 65 are now obliged to continue working because there is no special reassurance by the government. The transparency aspect is in all Directives—concerning market abuse or, now, good corporate governance, or prospectuses. We are focussing on the saver and on the small investor, because there has to be protection. The last point is the ISD point, with pre-trade transparency—where the City of London's interest is not to include the professionals. We now have a compromise situation, with competition between the industry and also the stock exchange. It is not a satisfactory compromise for you or for some others, but it is a compromise and may also be a good one. There is a problem for the Parliament that I have not mentioned. In order to accelerate decision-making, we agreed that for a certain period there would be a special procedure, the Lamfalussy Process. Up to now, I have not had the experience that this helps to accelerate legislation. The acceleration of legislation is more a matter for political will to decide than the expertise of experts. I do not think that it has been proved. We can see that CESR is working very hard and that they are also trying to be very transparent, which is very good. However, they are also giving us work again. We have now passed the Market Abuse Directive and CESR had to look at definitions. There is a borderline between political decision-making and technical experts. We now have to say to the Commission, "We think that the three additional Directives you want to implement are in the framework and scope of the Directive we voted for". There is therefore continuous pressure for Parliament to deal with the original Directive and to look at whether the delegated legislative power to the Commission respects the original political decision. It is a lot of work. We will have an evaluation, not only by the committee but we will also invite Mr Lamfalussy to look into this process, and we shall organise a hearing before the end of the legislature—

given the fact that the finance ministers would like to extend this procedure to the banking and insurance legislation. It might even go to other committees, where technological aspects, environmental aspects, the question of food safety, telecommunication, or other issues are included. I think that this is very necessary. Otherwise, we could not say that we have taken into account the citizens'—the savers and the consumers—interests. You do not know whether the experts are taking account of that interest, or are just looking to the development of new financial products.

Baroness Cohen of Pimlico

302. I think that I am a representative of one of the vested interests. I am a director of the London Stock Exchange. I listened to the emphasis placed on the importance of consumers, but of course one of the key criteria for success is whether the cost of capital in Europe will stay at US levels or below, because that is what will bring non-EU issuers to European markets. Do you think that we will be able to achieve this objective of keeping the cost of capital down to US levels or below and, if so, by when?

A. I cannot predict that, of course. You also have to realise that there has been an integrated financial services market in the United States since the 1930s, and there are still problems with diverse approaches. I would say that the Financial Services Action Plan addressed a lot of the crucial problems. I would also say that it is now a lot to implement on the national level. We have to look at whether there is also a harmonised approach in the implementation process. If you have such an ambitious plan, I am not so much in favour of always having Directives. I would have been more in favour of regulation, because they could then enter into force immediately even if you do not yet have the transformation process from a Directive to national legislation. There can sometimes be very small formulations of crucial importance, which make the financial markets function in a different way. I am therefore looking with interest, if we have no other compromise for the takeover bids, at applying the principle of subsidiarity under Articles 9 and 11. Then I think you will see that there is no really integrated market. On whether or not it is harmful for attracting capital, however, I could not give my final judgment. When we introduced the euro, our argument was that you attract more capital to the single market with a single currency. However, if there are barriers like different legislation, a different degree of protection, different formalities, different formulas that have to be given to a stock exchange and other authorities, and so on, these are not very attractive for foreign capital. Even the German market is too small. We are the biggest country, but nevertheless the German market is too small. We prefer to use the strength of the single market with, next year, 450 million people. We have to look to the strength of the single European market.

303. Do we think that there will be sufficient mutual recognition of other large markets, such as the US, to attract capital or will the political arguments that exist between the various parts of

Baroness Cohen of Pimlico contd.]

Europe lead to more barriers to cross-border activity? I suppose this is a question about how optimistic you are about the whole opening up of the market.

A. This is a principle of the single market—that you want to open the market but also, at the same time, to have regulation and correct supervision. Otherwise you cannot guarantee. Even in the States there is now more regulation, and there is also a call for more regulation. I do not think that we have over-regulation here. We may have to look at what is the best regulation. This is the key question. The Financial Services Action Plan tried to go that way.

Lord Fearn

304. The Takeover Directive is a crucial part of the plan to improve the productivity of the EU's capital stock by introducing an effective market in corporate control, so that corporate assets can be moved into the hands of those who can make the most productive use of them. Do you expect a Directive to be enacted that meets this criterion? Will the Commission simply withdraw any proposal that would be an inadequate Directive?

A. Everything is now under negotiation. There is no agreement yet in the Council. Maybe the Portuguese compromise is a compromise. One cannot really see whether there is a compromise which will achieve the majorities needed. It is pure speculation in the actual debate, judging what will be the outcome of our legislation. I am very sorry, I cannot give you a guarantee that at the end we will have a Directive, but I can give you the impression that there is a positive approach to try to find reasonable compromises.

305. That is your expectation?

A. Yes. As a chair, I am also responsible for doing my utmost to reach a compromise.

306. Will that be difficult?
A. Yes.

Chairman

307. What are the sticking points? What are the problem points?

A. The problems are that you have the different cultures of the shareholders. For example, in Sweden or Germany we have the golden share principle. Should this be allowed or allowed only for a transitional period? If we say that there should be a framework for takeover bids, could one or could one not leave out the specificities of, for example, France, Sweden and Germany? There is also the question of the rights of the employees if there is a hostile takeover. This is also the right for information and consultation.

Lord Fearn

308. So will it be consultation, or will there be a vote in the end?

A. We deal with this Directive in three different committees, and of course every committee has a priority. The Social Affairs Committee insists on the

rights of the employees, and there is also support in the Economic Affairs Committee. We do not know what the Legal Affairs Committee is doing. There are the negotiations on the golden share, or the Portuguese proposal, or the question of whether or not we enter a grandfather clause. It was also very difficult to predict the last vote when, by one vote, we killed the Directive in the European Parliament. We are in a very difficult situation of negotiation. We have to be very careful in the words we use, because it could then destroy negotiating positions.

Chairman: We have been conducting an inquiry in the House of Lords into these issues and have had various witnesses before us, reflecting different views, as you would expect. Lord Walpole would like to ask the last question that reflects just one strand of what we heard from those witnesses.

Lord Walpole

309. We have had some witnesses before us who have suggested that the Lamfalussy Process will in fact fail and be replaced by a "EuroSEC". What areas give you the most concern about the future of the Lamfalussy Process and therefore the ultimate goal of an effective single financial market and what can be done about your problems? I know that you have touched on some of them, but if these problems are really a reflection of a lack of political will to create a genuinely single financial market, could you envisage the necessary political will to set up something that is as substantial as a EuroSEC? In fact, I am not quite clear from the various witnesses exactly who would be a EuroSEC. Could you explain that as well?

A. There is no mandate to have a EuroSEC, not even in the Treaty. If you look at the Draft Treaty on the Constitution, there is no mandate to do anything like that. So how can you create it if there is no legal base for it? So many Member States have so many different solutions that I do not see it. When the finance ministers proposed having the Lamfalussy group, I think that it was the idea of Lamfalussy and the others also to deal with this subject, but the finance ministers excluded the subject from their mandate and gave them a completely different one, which had more to do with inter-institutional relationships than with SEC. It was strange that, besides Sir Nigel Wicks, no one had experienced this inter-institutional relationship; nevertheless, we were obliged to respect the result. I do not see this developing, therefore. We also had a report on supervision in the European Union—prudential control and so on. We are very much in favour of trying to have the same standards and structures in the Member States, following the same line in the application of the standards. It is premature to judge what an SEC at a European level could be like. The Lamfalussy Process has nothing to do with the setting up of the SEC, because it is on the legislation side. The SEC in the United States does not have a delegated power to legislate. They are given a different mandate. Under the framework of Article 35 of the Treaty, we could not give the mandate to a European SEC. That would not be possible. I do not see that there is any legal base in the Treaty, not even

Lord Walpole *contd.*]

in the draft Constitution Treaty, which allows that. My personal opinion is that you do not have to streamline everything. I do not know whether the British system is really the best. There are countries where the central banks have traditionally done and are doing a very good job. In my opinion, central banks always have to be included because they have to contribute to financial stability. This is in the ECB's mandate. However, one could not interpret the definition of that mandate—i.e. the ECB contributing to financial stability—as meaning that they could also supervise. This is therefore an unsolved question, and no one has wanted to deal with it.

Chairman

310. I should hasten to add that our own Committee has not taken any view on the question of a EuroSEC. I suspect that the views you have expressed will find widespread support. We are here airing a view that some witnesses have expressed to us, but I have to say that it does not find a lot of favour with me. May I ask one last question? Do you think that the distinction between wholesale markets and retail markets is sufficiently strong for a drive to secure a single market in wholesale markets to be a greater priority in timescale than that in retail

markets? Being practical as a politician, in 20 to 30 years' time, who knows? In the next few years, however, do you think that wholesale markets are really where the single market is likely to make the most rapid progress?

A. If I look back at the development of free movement of capital, services, and so on, that is probable. We had that experience there, so why should it be different with financial products? However, one must not forget the development of an ageing society. This changes a great deal. We have the three pillars and, as you know, the first pillar is no longer able to secure the pension age. We also know that there is a development in the supplementary pension system. In some Member States 90 per cent of employees have an additional pension, and in almost all Member States people are invited to do something for themselves in order to secure their pension age. This could impact more on the retail market. The demographic situation has changed, and I think that the retail market will therefore become more and more important.

Chairman: You lead us into interesting territory but I suspect that time has run out. It is a good note on which to end, and I look forward on another occasion perhaps to discussing that with you. Thank you for your time.

Memorandum from the European Commission's Internal Market DG

INTRODUCTION

The Internal Market Directorate-General is grateful for the opportunity to submit evidence on the FSAP to the Committee's inquiry. Most of the regulatory initiatives taken by this DG in the last four years to create an integrated EU financial services market are FSAP measures.

A. ECONOMIC BENEFITS FROM INTEGRATED EUROPEAN FINANCIAL MARKETS

1. Integration of EU financial markets is central to the economic reform agenda launched by EU Heads of State and Government at Lisbon in 2000. Deep, integrated and liquid capital markets with the widespread use of the euro will link companies looking to raise capital to invest and develop, with consumers and investors looking to save and make the best returns. Successive EU Councils have recognised that the objective of making the EU the most competitive, dynamic knowledge-based economy in the world by 2010 cannot be achieved without such integration. The integration process is being carried out in an open, transparent way—based on encouraging as much pan-European cross-border competition as possible, coupled with the necessary prudential and consumer safeguards.

2. Conversely, fragmented markets act as a major barrier to successful economic performance, hindering legitimate economic activity. Despite all the efforts made under the Single Market programme of the 1980s, the level of cross-border investment and capital raising has remained stubbornly low. British businesses, markets and investors are unnecessarily held back.

3. As the Lamfalussy Report underlined, if this fragmentation can be tackled, the potential benefits of open and competitive EU financial markets are huge[26] and will be felt right across sectors and in all Member States. 18 million businesses and 450 million consumers stand to benefit from the higher overall growth potential, lower cost of capital, employment expansion and a smoother absorption of volatility[27]. This even underestimates the impact on an enlarged EU of 25 Member States. If anything, as the largest financial market in the EU, the City of London stands to benefit disproportionately from this.

---

[26] See the Sixth and Seventh FSAP Progress reports (http://europa.eu.int/comm/internal market/en/finances/actionplan/index.htm).

[27] Although financial services represent "only" about 6 per cent of EU GDP and 2.45 per cent of EU employment, London Economics (2002) estimate that integrated equity and corporate bond markets could reduce trading costs and thereby boost overall EU GDP by 1.1 per cent and employment by 0.5 per cent.

4. European businesses need those benefits now, rather than in 20 years time. EU Heads of State and Government have responded to those concerns by calling for the completion of the FSAP by 2005 and the integration of the EU securities market by the end of this year: a demanding, but necessary, timetable. Such integration is not only essential: in a modern global financial environment, it is unavoidable. The unforeseen damaging consequences on British and EU companies and auditors of the attempts from the US to tackle corporate governance through the 2002 Sarbanes-Oxley Act have underlined this. What happens in one jurisdiction can and will have impacts on others. It is therefore increasingly unrealistic to rely on regulation by national authorities or exchanges alone. International (and particularly EU) regulators must converge and co-operate effectively on the basis of high and equivalent standards.

B. DELIVERING THE FINANCIAL SERVICES ACTION PLAN

5. Effective and complete delivery of the FSAP is the only way to achieve such integration. Its 42 original measures tackle all the major areas of weakness. Nevertheless, in coming forward with individual measures or proposals, the Commission has consistently focused on delivering real results on the ground that will contribute to an integrated financial market. In bringing forward these proposals, the Commission has acted on a pragmatic and case-by-case basis. It has also worked to establish consensus and compromise. More specifically, in proposing measures, it has looked to strike a balance between a range of competing pressures:

— allowing markets to innovate and giving investors and consumers sufficient protection;

— ensuring that large financial institutions or companies are adequately regulated, and that smaller ones are not overburdened;

— introducing regulation suitable for large financial centres and also for much smaller ones;

— the often different views and cultures of individual Member States as to what constitutes good regulation;

— the different interests of companies, investors, exchanges and service providers;

— pressures for maximum harmonisation giving greater legal certainty on the one hand versus an alternative minimum harmonisation approach giving greater flexibility to individual regulators to tailor implementation to local specificities.

6. In striking this balance and in ensuring that legislation delivers real benefits on the ground, the Commission has followed the Lamfalussy recommendations and moved to regular and systematic consultation of all interested parties on all proposals and emerging policy thinking. For example, before adopting a proposal on investment services, it carried out no fewer than three extensive public consultations. There have been many more in other areas. In carrying out such consultations, the Commission has striven to get the right balance between giving sufficient time and opportunity for comment and renewed consultation, and the tight timetable set by EU Heads of State and Government.

7. In examining responses to these consultations, Member States governments and industry have constantly supported the FSAP. To further integrate the EU financial markets we need to look for the best characteristics of all different approaches applied and combine them in a fruitful compromise. The Commission has actively taken account of the importance of the UK financial services industry for the EU financial markets and for the overall EU's economic performance as well, because—although not perfect—the UK financial markets have undoubtedly proven to function effectively over the past decades.

8. At the same time the Commission is aware some of the concerns expressed in the UK that EU harmonisation might be inconsistent with the traditional UK approach, incompatible with the needs of the markets, overly prescriptive and protectionist in motivation. If anything, the Commission has sometimes—unfairly—been criticised by some observers in other Member States for paying excessive attention to British interests. Over the last years it has become more and more clear that to bring the EU—and thus the City of London—a big step forward, a European capital market cannot emerge or be efficient on the basis of 15 different sets of rules, soon to be 25 with enlargement of the Union next year.

9. As progress has been made in delivering the measures in the FSAP, framework legislation alone will not deliver the benefits aimed for. The Commission was the first EU institution to endorse the Lamfalussy recommendations for regulatory reform; a judicious combination of framework legislation, adaptable implementing measures, day-to-day regulatory and supervisory co-operation and convergence, and effective implementation and enforcement. It is based on intensive and continuous cooperation between supervisory authorities, underpinned by binding obligations to ensure coherent enforcement throughout the EU. Once the process matures, decision making will accelerate and the quality will improve.

10. Whilst there have inevitably been teething problems in getting the new approach up and running, the approach is already showing its worth in the securities area. The first measures in the area of market abuse should be adopted around October/November this year. All 15 Member States and the Commission agree that the approach is needed in the banking, insurance and occupational pensions, and investment funds areas, to strengthen financial stability, ensure effective implementation and enforcement and cut complaint costs for EU businesses. The Commission is coming forward with a package of four Decisions and a proposal for a

Directive. At the same time, the Commission recognises that more needs to be done to ensure effective oversight of the process and an institutional balance between the Council and European Parliament. As recommended by the Commission, the draft EU Convention seeks to address these concerns.

11. Building a fully integrated market is an ongoing process requiring constant effort, vigilance and updating. The FSAP approach has proven successful: it introduced clear deadlines and created broad commitment. Much has been achieved since adoption in 1999. The EU is close to establishing a comprehensive framework which enshrines effective single market freedoms and common regulatory objectives in principles-based rules. However, the EU is still at a relatively early stage in unlocking the benefits: the legislation is not yet complete, and implementation and enforcement have only just begun, let alone EU businesses making full use of the opportunities created. It is therefore totally unrealistic to expect all the benefits to have fed through yet.

12. However, there is growing evidence that the combination of the euro and the FSAP is enabling a profound restructuring of the EU financial landscape. At the time of writing, 36 out of 42 FSAP measures have been adopted, with others close to adoption, including major pieces of legislation of real benefit to European (and thus British) businesses, markets and investors. This represents an unprecedented achievement in European terms. To give just a few examples:

— The two UCITS Directives and the Pension Funds Directive, giving investment and pension fund managers much greater freedom to invest and operate on a cross-border basis.

— The regulation moving EU listed companies to International Accounting Standards by 2005, cutting costs for businesses and allowing investors to compare the results of companies on a like with like basis.

— The Financial Conglomerates Directive, ensuring that cross-border conglomerates are regulated and supervised effectively and efficiently.

— The Market Abuse Directive, giving investors from the UK and other Member States the confidence that markets will be effectively policed against manipulation or abuse of any kind.

— The Prospectus Directive, replacing 15 (and effectively 25) sets of requirements with a single set of documents, valid across the EU.

13. Getting agreement on these measures has been achieved thanks to a consensual approach. In legislative terms, there has been a major acceleration in the rate of progress. To give one example, even the relatively controversial Prospectus Directive took only two years from proposal to adoption, compared to eight and a half years for its predecessor, the Public Offers Directive. The Commision welcomes the fact that HM Government supported the emerging agreements in the Council of Ministers on every single proposal in the area of financial services; a sign that all significant concerns were adequately addressed.

C. What Remains to be Done?

14. As the Lamfalussy Report pointed out, significant barriers (tax, legal, cross border acquisition) will remain. Whilst these are important though, they require a considerably longer-term approach to tackle. It is essential to remove regulatory barriers first. Therefore, looking forward, the first priority must be agreement on the remaining FSAP measures already on the table: ISD, Transparency, Take-Over bids, the resolving IAS 32/39 debate, which are central to an integrated EU financial market, and perhaps as a result are proving to be the most difficult. The Commission is committed to getting the ISD and Transparency Directives adopted before the end of this year. Furthermore, the Commission has shown its willingness to work towards an acceptable compromise on Take-Over Bids. Unfortunately, this willingness is not yet being reciprocated by some Member States, holding up the finalisation of this file.

15. Next year, the Commission is also coming forward with legislative proposals on Cross-border Mergers, Company Seat Transfer, Money Laundering and Terrorist Financing; the capital framework for banks and investment firms; Reinsurance Supervision and the EU Legal Framework for Payments. Whilst in many cases such measures were not in the original FSAP, they are natural (and necessary) developments if the objective of an integrated market is to be met.

16. A second and no less important priority must be ensuring that all measures are effectively implemented and enforced. The Lamfalussy arrangements will play a vital role in the continuous monitoring of the effectiveness of implementation and enforcement. Although the main responsibility for ensuring effective implementation and enforcement of EU legislation lies with the Member States, where perceived national interests make them reluctant to implement and enforce effectively, the Commission—as guardian of the Treaty—will play a role as well.

17. In the end of last year, the Commission adopted a Communication on the better application and enforcement of Community law. This foresees more than 10 preventive measures to ensure correct transposition. A novel and alternative mechanism for solving individual cases of misapplication of Community law has also been established ("SOLVIT"). Market participants must also play their role—by bringing dubious transposition faulty enforcement or infringements to the attention of the Commission. The

Commission itself is committed to applying the same energy to ensuring effective implementation as it has to the legislative phase itself. The Commission will not hesitate to pursue infringements even to the EU Court of Justice if necessary.

18. A third and final priority is to take stock of the state of EU financial integration and look at what will needs to be done in the coming years. The Commission believes that there is much to be gained by launching a wide-ranging, transparent and bottom-up assessment, which maps out the state of integration of the EU financial markets following completion of the legislative phase of the FSAP. For key financial segments, this assessment should point out the principal regulatory, supervisory, administrative, and other public policy impediments to the undertaking of cross-border business. It should undertake preliminary reflections on areas where there may be added value from further action, but also where action is not necessary or counter-productive. Where costs will outweigh benefits, action should not be attempted. The Commission is beginning its reflections in these areas, along with others.

19. In conclusion, the benefits for the European Union, its businesses, its citizens and enhanced global influence of an integrated, competitive and open capital market is a huge prize to aim for. It will strengthen sustainable economic growth and contribute a major boost to European economic reform.

4 September 2003

Examination of Witnesses

DR ALEXANDER SCHAUB, Director-General, and MR DAVID WRIGHT, Director of Financial Markets, DG IV Internal Market, European Commission, examined.

Chairman

311. Good morning, Dr Schaub and Mr Wright, and thank you for meeting with us.

(*Dr Schaub*) We are very pleased to have you here. It is not every day that we have a group of very eminent members from the House of Lords. We are also grateful and appreciative that you are following our business closely. We are very much aware that what is happening here in the business of financial services in Europe is a slightly revolutionary process. We are trying—and by "we" I mean the Member States of the European Union together with the institutions—to develop a single capital market in Europe. We are doing this not just as a *l'art pour l'art* exercise, because we want to harmonise everything, but because we believe that, without the support of a very strong European integrated capital market, European industry will have a handicap if our companies are trying to compete worldwide. This level playing field with other global players is much more difficult today, when we have much more worldwide business and when competing companies have, if they come from the US, a very dynamic, creative and modernising, reform-orientated capital market. We had therefore better get our act together and create something of at least the same competitive quality. That is the adventure on which we are embarked. We have sent you a text as a sort of written evidence, and we are very pleased to discuss with you further. I was told that I should make some introductory remarks, but I am really in your hands in terms of how we proceed.

312. First of all, thank you again for your kindness in meeting us. Can I say initially that we would wholeheartedly share the sentiments you have just expressed. Our questions are simply to probe areas where we see some problems, but not because we do not agree with the thrust of the policy. I am sure that you will understand that is the context. Clearly one concentrates on the problems from time to time because those are what have to be resolved. What we will try to do is go through a number of questions that we would particularly like to cover. First, a great

deal of agreement has been reached to date, but obviously there remain some difficult Directives still to resolve. What is your view in the Commission now on the position that the FSAP has reached? Do you think that the political deadline of spring 2004 will be met with all of the outstanding Directives, or do you think that there is a danger that the Commission may run out of time to get Level 1 measures enacted, so that CESR has time to give proper, considered advice? What is your judgment?

(*Dr Schaub*) First of all I should say that the formal deadline is later than spring 2004, because the five years which were foreseen will go to the end of 2004. However, we know that in the real world there are several months—six, seven or eight months—which may be inoperative because Parliament is being renewed, is going into an election campaign, and then has to be organised again. The Commission is being renewed. This is happening in a unique way. Eleven new Commissioners arrive on 1 May and we will have not only a total quantitative but also a qualitative change within the institution. Then, on 1 November, a new Commission for an enlarged Community will start. This will require adjustments, political selection and confirmation processes, which inevitably will distract attention from our business here and which may make it impossible to take forward the normal rule-making process and the co-decision procedure. So *de facto* we have until probably the end of March/April and, in an extreme constellation, we may have until the end of next year—if it is about additional formal steps. Is it possible to achieve everything? My view is that, seen from today, it is not impossible. I would say additionally that, if we just count the measures—and we are very much aware that it is one thing to count legal acts, but it would be naive to believe that the world has changed because legal acts have been adopted—the more important question after that is, "And what have these legal acts achieved?".

313. Yes, we will be coming to that.

(*Dr Schaub*) We are not yet there. It is much easier to count. The figures are that 42 measures were

Chairman *contd.*]

foreseen; 36 have been adopted, and there is also the chance that the remaining ones can be achieved. I would say that there are two, or perhaps three, particularly difficult areas. You know what they are. The first one is in the press everywhere today—the Investment Services Directive. I do not believe that it will be a real problem to come to a conclusion. I am more worried about the way in which this Directive is being adopted. It is not optimum and, if you are interested, we can come back to it. However, there is little doubt that it will be adopted. The second one— also a very famous title—is the Takeover Directive. That is a story that goes back over the last 22 years. We believe—but probably only because we are incorrigible optimists in this place—that there is a chance to come to a conclusion by next March/April. That will depend to a large extent on the German Government. They have taken a rather emotional interest in this business here, for reasons which have more to do with German internal politics, the close link between the German Chancellor and the *Land* of Lower Saxony and a little company in his *Land* which is also politically influential. At present we feel that there is a willingness to contribute to a conclusion which, after 22 years, could be seen as not shameful. In other words, we believe that we need a Directive which eliminates at least some of the more unreasonable obstacles to cross-border takeovers. If it does not eliminate them completely in one courageous stroke, then at least the more dynamic companies should have the possibility of entering into an exercise where they can make clear that they feel strong enough not to work with rather old-fashioned, defensive mechanisms. The moment of truth in this matter will probably only come towards the end of this year and we shall have to see what the situation is then. The situation has been changing dramatically—upwards, downwards and upwards again—but we are convinced that it is a possibility. The third, which is also under permanent debate, is the capital adequacy—the Basle II implementation—within the European Union. You will know that there has recently been a new outbreak of nervousness, worry and uncertainty; nevertheless, we believe that it remains possible to get to grips with this. The Commission is technically ready for the necessary steps to be launched next spring, and then we will have to see how far we get. There is also, for instance, the Cross-Border Mergers Directive, which is not easy but, apart from a particular German problem again, linked to German heritage of a postwar enthusiasm—the *Mitbestimmung* topic– we believe that it can be done. We have the Transparency Directive, which creates limited agitation about the question of whether companies should present quarterly reporting and, if so, what should be in it; should it be compulsory or should there be a choice. Personally, I believe that this is not a topic which requires a particularly religious conviction. For me, it is typically a topic where we can live with diversity and see how the conviction within this integrated market will develop. We then have another topic which in some ways is comparable to the Basle II process, namely the International Accounting Standards convergence on which we are working. Here we have the rather exceptional situation where practically all players admit that it is highly desirable and largely beneficial to have a single set of standards for auditing worldwide, because this would greatly facilitate the life of companies and would considerably increase the credibility of the process. At present, companies active worldwide are obliged to produce their accounts, sometimes in two, three or four versions. If they are active on different continents and in different countries and all have different standards, they have to produce exactly the same economic story in four versions. The four versions may come to completely conflicting, incompatible conclusions, so that in one continent they have several hundred millions of benefit and, in the next country, applying the next country's standards, they make a loss in that year. Even if the high priest of this science explained that to you, I do not believe it is a way of inspiring confidence amongst the participants of the marketplace. They will remain puzzled as to why the same company is so good in one system and so bad in another system. There is therefore broad convergence that we need this. At this stage there is, not surprisingly, quite a spectacular quarrel about some of the standards which are being developed by the IAS Board. We have been working very hard to encourage the protagonists of the two sides to increase their efforts to come to a common approach. That is not so easy, because the people who are involved are not used to working together and have to learn that it is worthwhile investing more serious efforts and to find common ground, because if this process fails it will be a major setback for all those who are convinced that we need this common base. It would mean a major setback for everybody. Importantly, we are also aware that this is not a political process. Standard-setting is not something that political leaders should be deciding; it is for the professionals to agree. We are not telling them how they should do it; we are influencing the process by telling them, "Please make a further effort. Can you not sort out your differences? Can you not listen more to the objections? Can you not come up with compromise proposals which would allow common ground?". However, we have abstained, and I can assure you that we will abstain, from trying to tell them how to do it. That is not our business and that would create more damage than advantage. Mr Bolkestein has engaged in this a great deal personally. He has met several times, and will continue to meet, Sir David Tweedie and his people. He has met, and will meet again when we go to Washington next week, Paul Volcker, who is the head of the board of trustees of this enterprise. In November there will be another meeting, where people will try to find common ground. Paul Volcker will come to Brussels and we will have a working dinner with him. So the efforts are underway and there is a chance. One cannot guarantee it because it is complicated, but the evidence that we must reach common ground is so overwhelming that I cannot believe that it will fail in the long term. The people working on the IAS Board also have to understand that it is one thing to produce the most beautiful standards, it is another thing if no one in Europe is prepared to apply these standards. The whole of the work is then done for nothing. It is *l'art pour l'art*, and I believe that they

Chairman contd.]

will understand this. As I have said, it is a picture where complete success is possible; where a number of the missing items still create many difficulties, but where all the main players are working towards success. So, in a particularly happy constellation, all things could fall into place; in a less favourable constellation, some may not fall into place by the earlier date of April. However, even if one, two or three items went into early 2005, it would not be a disaster. The main thing is the credibility of the process, which until now has been quite considerable. You will not find many phases in the development of the European Union where a totally new project, like an integrated capital market, has proceeded so efficiently and smoothly with such a large number of important legislative Acts.

Chairman: That is extremely helpful and I will certainly want to come back on some of the detailed points you have mentioned. You take us to the point where Level 1 is out of the way and, hopefully, moving towards Level 2. Then comes implementation. Perhaps we might spend a little time looking at that phase.

Lord Shutt of Greetland

314. One of the objectives of the FSAP is greater competition, with the resulting benefits to users of capital and consumers in their role as savers. However, the implication of this, if applied properly, will be the demise of the weaker and less efficient players in the financial services industry. Do you agree with this conclusion? If so, do you think that this outcome will be politically acceptable amongst Member States, or will Member States protect their own industries, thus frustrating one of the objectives of the FSAP?

(Dr Schaub) I think that you have posed the problem perfectly correctly. Whenever you have structural change—and we are talking here about very significant cross-border, structural adjustments—there are people who will win, we hope the great majority, and there are people who may lose, in the sense that they are no longer efficient, modernised, reformed, and perhaps also mentally not prepared enough, to go for change and so may disappear from the marketplace. That is a typical situation whenever you go for structural change. This is also the main reason why in many circumstances structural change does not make the progress which the majority of people would hope for. What is the picture here? In view of the process we have seen over the last four years, my impression is that there is every reason to believe that the process will be achieved, because the advantages in this case are so evident, and the chances of survival for the weaker players by adjustment are also so evident. We have no illusions that there will not be resistance. There already is resistance. All people who have to change their traditional ways of doing things, because the world is changing around them, are reluctant and very often do not like it. My perception, however, is that this process will go ahead, not because it is a total win-win situation but because it is an overwhelming win situation for the participants in the exercise.

(Mr Wright) Could I add one point to what my Director-General has said? It is probably not well known that, in most European Member States, capital markets are quite underdeveloped. They do not have big wholesale capital markets like London. I think that everybody in this business recognises that there is an enormous potential for long-term growth of the capital market. We believe that it will happen anyway because, if you look at the demographic time bomb as just one example, it does not seem to us that you can resolve that long-term pension problem unless you use the capital markets. Many people therefore see trillions of euros of growth in these capital markets in the future. The markets will become more competitive—which is what we want, because that will drive down the cost of capital for all of our 18 million businesses and 500 million consumers—and at the same time we believe that there is tremendous long-term growth potential, which will have positive economic spillovers.

Chairman

315. You open up a Pandora's box and some very important issues, which I am tempted almost immediately to follow up; but let me come back to it later, because we may get sidetracked. I suppose the question then is, who is going to ensure that all these Directives and all this legislation are carried through? There will actually be a lot of resistance. When we hear politicians speaking—all over the place, not just here—they think more readily in terms of retail markets than wholesale markets. They think of, as we put it in England, grandma and her small savings. Of course, grandma is enormously important, but the efficient capital markets which we are trying to achieve here—the wholesale markets, the wider markets—are much more than grandma. Who will drive this through? The record of the Commission in other single market issues is a bit patchy. The record of Member States in implementing things is patchy. It is a great venture, which we wish well, but who will enforce it? Who will make sure that implementation follows?

(Dr Schaub) This is the key problem of the whole exercise. Not the adoption of the rules, which is already difficult enough—as we saw yesterday again in the Council—but the effective transposition and enforcement, which means respect, of these rules. It is clear that this cannot be achieved by the Commission alone. Under the Treaty, as you know, the Commission is the guardian of the Treaty rules. That was a very good idea in the small and cosy European Community family of six Member States, but it is not a very realistic exercise in a union of 25 or 30 Member States. It is simply a non-starter to expect that, out of one central place, you can make sure that the whole of Europe will correctly transpose and, from day to day, apply and enforce these rules. We therefore need a change of culture in relation to this point. We have to explain to the world at large that this is a common responsibility, not only of the Commission in Brussels but a kind of joint venture of the Commission and the public authorities in Member States. These are there not just as the executing arm of Brussels, but also to make sure that the decisions

Chairman *contd.*]

which they have themselves approved in the Council of Ministers—and, in Level 2 and Level 3 committees, via their representatives' contribution—are also a responsibility for the business community as such. It is not just for the public policy people; it is also for the business community. These three levels and the various intermediate institutions in the system—the Level 2 committees, and Level 3 committees in particular, which are a total innovation, and the supervisory institutions working jointly at European level—should all push the process in the same direction. One has to be aware and explain—and you can have a very important role in this and make a key contribution—that this is something which has not happened in the past. We have had regulatory committees, the so-called "comitology" stuff, for the last 40 years—starting with agriculture and in many other areas. In that sense, the Level 2 structures are not at all revolutionary. However, the Level 3 structures are revolutionary because here we are dealing with a sector, the financial services sector, which almost by its nature has a problem that does not exist in agriculture or in veterinary questions, namely the systemic risk. We cannot just be satisfied that there are rules and they will be applied. All countries, in Europe and elsewhere, have authorities, special bodies, with responsibility to watch for the possibility of systemic risk and to intervene if these risks should appear on the horizon. What is essential for national capital markets is also essential for an integrated Europe-wide market. How do we make sure that the consumer, the investor, the people who have saved their money and want to invest it, have the necessary trust in the continued functioning, stability and solidity of this integrated financial market? What has happened in the United States more recently, and to some extent also in Europe, certainly has turned this question into a much more acute one than it was 10 years ago. The credibility of a European supervisory system, therefore, is a key element for success. Here we are in a kind of step-by-step process. Up to now we have the CESR committee, where all the heads of the national supervisory bodies are working together—which they have never done in this way. They are working together not just to have a nice congress on a beautiful island somewhere, but they are working together almost every week on the operational question of what should be the future European rules for ensuring that the system works in a credible way. That causes problems of co-operation amongst people with different backgrounds and cultures, and it is therefore not so evident that it works. However, if we look at how CESR has been working—and David and myself are participating regularly in their meetings in Paris and elsewhere—we are really encouraged by the very professional and responsible approach they have shown. We hope that the Level 3 committees for banks and insurances, and the people who will be dealing with UCITS within CESR in the future, will follow this positive example and contribute to the solidity and credibility of the system. However, it is really something new. Perhaps I may immediately add something here. You know of the debate—in my view, a totally misleading debate—about the so-called single European supervisor. I do not believe that we will ever have, or that we indeed need, a single European supervisor. What we do need, and what we have to some extent, is a European system of supervision. System means that elements at national level have to be combined in an appropriate way with elements at the centre. We have this with CESR which, so to speak, is the European roof over the existing national systems. We believe that this very light system is good enough for the time being. We do not believe that, for the sake of shaking things up all the time, we need revolutionary new bodies, but that a pragmatic process has to be assured. If in real life it were to be discovered that the present light system is not totally satisfactory or sufficient for certain types of transactions—for instance, conglomerate operations or operations which at the same time touch five or ten of the 30 future Member States—then one would have to see what was necessary. That is what people now call the subsidiarity principle: more intense dealing with the business only if the less intense structure we have at present is insufficient. In my view, in all of this the private sector has an absolutely essential role—for two reasons in particular. First, it is important that the private sector people understand this, perhaps too complex—at any rate, highly complex—system. I am a little worried when I listen to debates on Lamfalussy, because it has become a kind of secret sign where only a limited number of "high priests" have fully grasped the system and the rest are bandying terms which are obviously not totally clear to them and where, because of that, they do not feel at ease with these strange things—which, in addition, use a mysterious name like "Lamfalussy". I believe that we have a common responsibility to simplify the explanation and to make sure that the broader public understands what is happening here under the name of Lamfalussy. When people have understood that, they then assume their responsibility and contribute to the development of the system. If we have a system which is driven only by the public authorities, by the legislator, and not also by the positive, or less positive, echo coming from the private sector, which is involved from day to day in the use of the new tools which have been created, then we are in danger of missing important points. I believe that will be our key responsibility in the future.

(*Mr Wright*) May I add one or two tools, which I think will be helpful to reinforce the implementation and enforce the matter you raised? First of all, it is clear that we need resources, and that is a major problem. Second, I think that we can strengthen the monitoring mechanisms by the Commission of all these Acts and how they are being implemented. There we think that it might be useful if Member States actually published how they implement the Acts in concordance tables. Just as we are trying to be more transparent, we think that Member States should explain how they implement Article 1 of the Market Abuse Directive and show exactly the links between our Directives and their Acts. We think that it could be important from an economic point of view to look at market behaviour: looking, for example, at why in certain Member States import penetration of, let us say, UCITS is very low whereas in other states it is very high. Why is that? That will help understand

Chairman *contd.*]

why our Directives may or may not be working. We think that it would be useful to have scoreboards of Member States' performance in terms of implementing and enforcing Community rules. That has not always been very popular with some Member States, but we think that it is quite a good, transparent discipline. A new technique that would be useful in certain circumstances would be for the Commission to publish guidance on how certain provisions of Directives should be implemented, because one of the problems has been that, at the end game of some of these Directives, you sometimes have some ambiguous provisions in order to keep everybody happy, but then there is the problem that the implementation becomes difficult. There we think that it might be useful for us to publish guidance on how the Commission sees provision X or Y—it being understood that Member States can implement in the way they want, but they may then take a legal risk if they do not implement it in the way the Commission has said. Finally, I would just repeat what Alex has said regarding the private sector. The private sector is largely absent from helping the Commission identify where Community law is not being implemented and enforced properly. One of the reasons is that they fear the commercial consequences of doing that. I think that ways have to be found, and the private sector has to be more bold and imaginative in bringing such cases to us. It is quite remarkable how few cases there are in this area and that is the reason: they fear the consequences of bringing that information to the Commission.

Chairman

316. I would like to turn in a moment to some retail issues with Baroness Cohen. On that, however, could I share the same view—both in terms of your approach and the last point you made about the private sector? Do I take it from those remarks that you do intend to publish annually a measured progress report, as it were, on the single market in financial services? That is the intention of the Commission and it would be done by your directorate, presumably?

(*Dr Schaub*) At present we are doing this every six months, but it may become more appropriate to do it once a year. Certainly we will continue that, and we are keen to find the kind of indicators which would help to measure. It is very fashionable these days to talk about indicators. Once you try to develop indicators which are relevant and a real source of useful information for the non-specialised reader, however, it is not so easy to find such indicators. We are working very hard on this question. We have launched a study and I believe that it is of considerable interest to find a set of indicators which, over time, can be an easy indication of the direction in which the process is going. So that is certainly our ambition. Once we start this, we would appreciate it if you could have a critical look at it and give us your advice as to whether or not, from your point of view, the kinds of indicators we will be using are helpful, or whether they are so theoretical that people will only be confused.

Baroness Cohen of Pimlico

317. I should declare that, as well as being a baroness, I am a director of the London Stock Exchange—which makes me either a member of the private sector, or a lobbyist, or whatever, in this instance. One of the things that has just come to light is that we have been told that companies issuing securities under English law may find that their liability to investors is made much wider by the Transparency Directive, as it will apply to all investors and not just those, i.e. the shareholders, to whom the annual accounts are addressed. Do you believe that this concern is well founded? Are all company directors going to have to be liable to all investors? If so, was this an intended effect or does it come under the law of unintended consequences?

(*Dr Schaub*) I am not a technical expert, so I cannot give you a precise answer on specific situations. What one can certainly say, however, is that the question of liability is inevitably posed when you try to put together 15, 20 or 25 national capital markets which have all sorts of different rules on this liability question and where, afterwards, the investors/citizens concerned will ask, "What does that now mean for my rights in the integrated market?". I am almost sure that the rules, which are not yet adopted in relation to this question, will create increased liabilities in some countries, in particular if the obligations for the companies—the stock exchange and other investment houses—were not yet very developed. There will be other countries where nothing new will be added, because perhaps they already have a satisfactory level of responsibility towards their clients. I do not know exactly what it means from the perspective, for instance, of someone working on the London Stock Exchange. Is it your impression that the rules, as they are at present discussed in the Council and the Parliament, would increase the degree of liability?

318. We think on the face of it that, yes, they do increase it. At the moment, doctrine and practice are fairly clear in England. We are responsible to shareholders and only incidentally to the wider market. The people who can sue you—which, as a lawyer, is where I always look—are your shareholders. It looks as if the category of people who can sue you is being widened to anybody who might be a potential shareholder—to investors generally. This would be a great change for us, and I wondered what your perceptions were of whether that is really what is happening—whether that is really the intention?

(*Mr Wright*) I am intrigued by what you say. I have not actually heard that. I have heard a lot of criticism about the Transparency Directive and reporting, but I have not heard that particular point made. Maybe I should have done. What we can do is to note it and we will get back to you.

(*Dr Schaub*) We would be very interested in clarifying this point.

(*Mr Wright*) If either you could write to us with the precise point, or else we can certainly provide you with additional comment on that point.

Baroness Cohen of Pimlico *contd.*]

319. This may be United Kingdom paranoia, you understand, but it does look as if a well-understood convention is being extended quite sharply.

(*Mr Wright*) I am sure that was not the intent, but let us check it.

Lord Fearn

320. I am looking to the future now. One key criterion for success is whether the cost of capital in Europe post-FSAP is equal to or lower than that in the USA and other large markets. Success in this criterion will attract non-EU issuers to Europe's markets. Perhaps I may ask four small questions on that. Do you think that this objective will be achieved? Second, by when? How important is it to Europe to attract more non-EU business? Lastly, will there be sufficient mutual recognition with other large markets such as the US to attract capital, or will political argument lead to more barriers to cross-border activity?

(*Dr Schaub*) All four questions are very pertinent. Let me try to give a considered reply. First of all, we do believe that the objective can be achieved. There is no question about that. It should be the natural result, if we do things right. Whether we do things right will also be proved by the results. If we find that the cost is not reduced and perhaps increased, then we must be doing something wrong, and the earlier we find this out the better. It would be rather hazardous to give an exact date today when that will be possible, but I believe that it should become noticeable at a relatively early stage after the full implementation of the system. When talking about transposition and enforcement, I should perhaps have added that the story there is not yet finished. After the adoption of the rules and then the transposition and correct application, we have a third phase. We then have to find out if the system, correctly implemented, really functions. This is not self-evident. It would not be the first time in the life of legislation or of reform that, even if all the rules are beautifully implemented, one finds that something does not work; that the construction, the architecture, or the technical side of it has weaknesses. We therefore believe that, not just when everything is in place, but already now—in parallel with the finishing of the architecture and adoption and implementation of the rules—we have to see whether it works or whether we already see points of weakness in the construction. Once the whole thing is implemented, I believe that it should quickly lead to a reduction of costs, and we should keep in touch and look at that. The importance of this process with regard to other areas in the world can only increase. I believe that we are only at the beginning of a globalisation process which is not anywhere near its end. Over time, and probably with an accelerating speed, I believe that the main players, and also the less powerful and less important players, will discover the possibilities there are of reducing costs and improving business opportunities in a global system. Therefore, the relative advantage in financing will become more important, because it will be impacting on a much broader market than has traditionally been the case. I believe your last question was whether we will have competition between an integrated, modernised European capital market and the existing, and of course not passive, American market. It seems to me that, yes, obviously we will have that. We will have a kind of competition of systems, and I believe that is a good thing. If it is a fair competition, non-politicised, it can only contribute to improvement on both sides. We want to organise a process of transfer of best practice. To make such a thing work, you need a hopefully conflict-free situation. Once you are in a political conflict it becomes much more difficult, if not impossible, to talk quietly and unemotionally around a table about the question of which is the most efficient, the most successful technique and, if we agreed that one was more successful—whether it is American or whether it is Chinese—we would do it. We do not care who has invented it, as long as it is better than what we are doing. Our experience is that, once we get into a conflict, it becomes much more difficult, if not impossible, to apply rational considerations. It becomes a matter of prestige. People will ask, "Why are you selling out to the Americans?", or whoever, "Why are you applying their rules?". There will also be opponents in our own camp saying, "No, I want to stick with the present rules. I don't believe that the other rules are better. In any case, they are American" or French, or whatever—they are foreign. Therefore it is very important, in parallel with the construction of a convincing European system, to keep a clear eye on the transatlantic angle. In this area it is more evident than anywhere else, because everybody knows that the US and Europe are by far the most important capital markets. You will therefore find very few areas where transatlantic co-operation and partnership are more evident and more necessary than in this area. If we let the internal process develop without keeping a very close eye on it—and more than a very close eye—and without in parallel organising co-operation, then we are in danger of coming into conflict. Sarbanes-Oxley is the most spectacular illustration of the conflict. Simplifying grossly, what is happening in this globalisation process is that the markets become bigger; the sovereign national operators remain in charge of adopting the rules for their sovereign territory; and the enforcement bodies for their national sovereign territory are paid to ensure enforcement. If there is no co-operation, no dialogue, however, the inevitable result is that the rules are different. Nobody can blame anyone that the rules are different, because they are adopting rules for Europe and not for Canada, for Australia or for the US. The enforcement bodies in Washington, in Brussels, in Canberra, in Ottawa, are paid to ensure that the rules of that area are respected. While doing their job honestly and correctly, there is nevertheless a danger of coming into conflict. That is exactly what has happened in Sarbanes-Oxley. What happened in the past in areas like competition policy—for instance, when there was a merger between Boeing and MacDonald-Douglas, two American companies producing outside the European Union but selling the major part of their production in Europe? When they wanted to merge, it was, in the first phase, incompatible with European rules. We were about to

Lord Fearn contd.]

prohibit it—correctly, because it was not compatible with our rules. The Americans had quickly to authorise it—correctly, because it was compatible with their rules. The rules were different. We then found a way out, but it was the first illustration in another sector. With Sarbanes-Oxley, we have a new illustration in our own sector. The lesson to be learned from it is that we have to make sure that we do not ignore the transatlantic/global dimension, but keep one eye on our internal process and, in parallel, work on the international prolongation. What I mean by this is that we have to make sure that, whatever we are reforming, renewing, introducing here, is also discussed with our American partners, so that we see early on what impact it will have. Will it trigger a conflict? The same is true when the Americans are reforming their rules. They did not do it in the case of Sarbanes-Oxley, for reasons which I believe one can understand—and which politicians will understand even better than modest technocrats. If the political pressure is such as it was in that case, they cannot say, "Give us a year or two to have a dialogue". People wanted to see results. The more scandals which broke out, the more they wanted to see results. That led to the incompatibility of some of their rules with our rules in Europe. We are now working hard—next week again in Washington—to find a solution with the new people responsible in the oversight body for auditors, and with the US administration. We believe that it is possible. It will be difficult, but the lesson is—also accepted in Washington—that we should learn from this process, in order to avoid it happening too often in the future. It means that, in a proactive way, we should talk regularly about new projects here and new projects there. The experts should sit together, compare notes, find out whether it creates conflict, and perhaps whether it introduces rules on the other side which are better than our present rules—and, in that case, why not modernise our present rules on their model and the other way round? That has happened in merger control policy over recent years with the Americans. I was in that sphere for eight years and we were sitting together. It was not spectacular—not on page 1 of the *Financial Times* or the *Sun*—but just the day-to-day work of people who were looking for the best possible solution, trying to anticipate potential conflict and to defuse it before it broke out. There again, you could give us major help if you helped us contribute to the understanding of this global angle of the process. It is an inevitable angle. We can close our eyes and try to forget about it, but it is there: the system produces it.

Chairman: Obviously we share that view very much and take a very global view about these things. If anything, some of the things we hear coming from Europe indicate that that global view and that willingness to look at the global view is not as strongly felt as expressed by you, I have to say. Some of the details of some of the Directives have perhaps made matters more difficult rather than easier on occasions. I would just touch on yesterday's matter of the ISD which, as you know, has caused us some concern. It indicates a frame of mind in parts of the Member States that does not necessarily understand the damage that can be done to large wholesale markets, and so on. However, perhaps I may invite Lord Walpole to ask the next question.

Lord Walpole

321. Looking into the future again, we have discussed the implementation, resources, and so on, but do you think that there will be an FSAP II, and what items would you like to have in it? In other words, what are you missing from what you hope to achieve by the end of the year?

(Dr Schaub) We believe that, by then, a major first phase will be finished. We must not expect that there will be a second, third and fourth phase of the same. It will be quite fundamentally different. There will not be a second package of 42 measures for the following five years. Rule-making will be perhaps the last priority. The first priority after that period will be to make the system function. That is the clear first priority. There are two things necessary to make the system function. First, we must make sure that the rules are effectively and correctly transposed and that they are applied. In a Community of 25 or 30 countries, where nothing is stable—where today everything may be fine, but where in two months' time they may have introduced a law in Estonia, for example, which they are not even aware creates a problem—what is necessary is a permanent professional dialogue between the people involved in the process. Second, even if everything is correctly applied, does the system function satisfactorily? There will perhaps be corrections here, or additions there—but that is different to throwing another 42 or more new Directives into the air. In our view, that is by far the most important thing. There may be a number of additions. For instance, people are talking about clearing and settlement and people are talking about retail. We believe that we should not shoot from the hip on these matters but, before coming up with new projects, we should organise a very solid, professional assessment process. I believe that we have sent you some papers about how we want to organise it. We are about to launch four major working groups, where the practitioners will sit together and work out their considered view, their experience up to now, and their advice on the most useful and helpful further steps. We want to organise a major conference in the middle of next year. By chance, it is in the period where lawmaking is not possible in any case and where Commissioners are not sitting here, telling us about the next project to be sold in Parliament or in the Council. There is to be an open, transparent process of assessment, of exchange, of what has been achieved—with its good and not-so-good sides—and what should be the main areas of future development. It would then be the basis for our preparing, if necessary, additional action, which can then be produced in the form of a proposal by the incoming new Commission. That would then come onto the Council's table and to the public at large by probably the end of next year but, for most of it, more likely in the course of 2005. That was a more modest middle piece. I believe that the third piece, of increasing importance, is this regulatory dialogue and the transatlantic/global dimension. That will occupy us in the future much

Lord Walpole *contd.*]

more than most people imagine today, because they are still looking traditionally at what is on their doorstep. They are not so aware that this will be a process where the Brazilians, the Canadians, the Australians, the Chinese, and the Japanese will discover that there are important things happening and, if they do not link their own markets to this process, they are in danger of losing speed and losing market chances.

Chairman

322. That takes me to the last question. What are your views on the relative progress of wholesale and retail markets? Do you not think, in practical terms, that the Commission should be concentrating on wholesale markets and leaving retail for later?

(*Dr Schaub*) In practical terms there is no question but that the wholesale markets are the very first topic for treatment in the creation of a transatlantic capital market.

323. Politicians are often more worried about the retail market, in their mind.

(*Dr Schaub*) The difficulty is that the politicians in different countries have different ideas about retail. We are rather puzzled that, before we have made any serious or deeper analysis, we are already being told by some Member States, "You must do your homework here and come up with something" and, by other Member States, "You keep your fingers out of this. There is no need. Retail is never trans-border". I am not a specialist but I am rather sceptical about the two camps. If I try to look a little deeper—for instance, in my own country—I could tell you outside this meeting some of the real reasons why people are telling us, "Keep off retail". They are not always of such a divine nature as people try to make us believe!

324. We finish on an appropriately realistic note. Thank you very much indeed. You have given us an enormous amount of your time and it has been a pleasure to have met you.

(*Dr Schaub*) We would like to continue to work with you, because you can help us a lot. You speak

with much more credibility and public authority and, if you support our business, it will be seen with different eyes. David and others have already underlined that this is also an exercise which will require resources. It is very unpopular to say this, but you cannot make such a process work with resources which were sufficient at a time when nothing of this sort existed. There will come a time when we will need more resources. At present, we are working on a quite brutal, ruthless exercise of internal reallocation and simply skipping things—things which are not useless but which are not of comparable importance. The time will come, however, when we cannot professionally do this business without the necessary resources. Perhaps you could keep this in mind and try to explain to people that we are not obsessed bureaucrats who want to have a little army round us because it makes us feel better but because this is really necessary and, if we do not do it, there is a danger that things could happen which have happened in competition policy. I went through that process for eight years. When there was uproar in the press that certain judgments were annulled by the court—and in some cases rightly so, I would say—I was prepared to explain to the critics how these decisions had to be taken. These were merger decisions that were at an absolute pinnacle of merger activity which had never ever been seen in Europe in that intensity. Our people had to work under conditions which were simply inhuman, unreasonable, insane. I felt very bad that I had to force them to be here and not to take holidays. I said at the time that it was a miracle that we did not have any dramas or scandals. We had them in modest form—because you cannot easily find other competition authorities which have had so little annulled by the courts than the European Commission. Having gone through this once, I would hate to go through such an exercise again—just because of a lack of professionally necessary resources.

Chairman: I should explain that an early witness before the Committee next is a Treasury minister. I am sure that she will have the text of today's meeting drawn to her attention.

Examination of Witnesses

Mr Richard Desmond, Chairman, Financial Services Working Group, Union of Industrial and Employers' Confederations of Europe, Ms Barbara Stearns-Bläsing, Senior Adviser, Economic and Financial Affairs Department, Unice, and Dr Ralf Fischer Zu Cramburg, *Deutsches Aktieninstitut*, examined.

Chairman

325. Good morning.

(*Mr Desmond*) I am Richard Desmond, Chairman of the Financial Services Working Group of the European employers' federation, UNICE. As such, I appear now and again and chair the working group, perhaps a little more often than some others, and try to keep on top of the topics. The major work of course is handled by the UNICE staff here, which is very ably represented by Barbara Stearns-Bläsing, and the very effective membership we have from all of our member federations. I am delighted

to say that we also have Ralph Fischer with us who, as well as being a member of the Financial Services Working Group, works for the Germany Equity Institute. We have prepared some remarks today and it is entirely up to you as to how you would like us to proceed. We can make our remarks and we thought that, in making our remarks, we would talk first of all about the Financial Services Action Plan and, after talking about it in general, talk about the UK facets of it; then going on to implementation and enforcement as it has been taking place, and then talking a bit about the future, making it a very interactive discussion one would

Chairman *contd.*]

hope, answering all of your questions as they come to your minds, as opposed to waiting for the end of any comments. Would that be an appropriate way to proceed for you?

326. Bearing in mind our limited time, we do have a small number of focussed questions in our mind. By all means go through this as you want. It may mean that we come back to you on one aspect of what you are likely to cover, so I apologise for that. I should first of all say thank you very much for meeting us. We are genuinely appreciative. We very much wanted to hear the views of industry, as it were, and not just the institutions. They are the people who are actually affected by this.

(*Mr Desmond*) The users. Could we briefly do an introduction? We will try to keep it as short as possible.

327. Yes, of course. I suspect that you will find that you will be able to tell us everything you want to.

(*Dr Fischer*) Let me start by saying something about my organisation, which is the German Equity Institute. It is a non-profit organisation, representing the interests of German issuers. In addition, we seek to strengthen the acceptance of shares and encourage continued development of the equity culture in Germany. The German *Aktieninstitut's* members comprise over 200 companies, associations and institutions, which promote the equity culture in Germany and in Europe. As concerns the Financial Services Action Plan, we can state that a significant distance has been travelled since the adoption of the FSAP in 1999. Up to now, 36 of the original 42 measures have been finalised; three are under negotiation, and three proposals have still to be made. I propose that we concentrate on those measures which have been finalised this year. The first was the Directive on insider dealing and market manipulation or market abuse, which was adopted in January 2003. It harmonises the rules on the prevention of insider dealing and market manipulation in both regulated and unregulated markets. It is due to be implemented in October 2004. In fact, this Directive is the first Directive which has to undergo the Lamfalussy Process, which Barbara will outline later. We have now reached the stage of the second set of implementation measures of the CESR—the Committee of European Securities Regulators. Perhaps I may give you an example that the discussion does not end in the Parliament but that there are also different views concerning the implementation measures. CESR advised publishing every transaction of directors and officers in shares of their own company. We think— and I also speak for UNICE and QCA, our British counterpart, the Quoted Company Alliance—that it is advisable not to make every single minor transaction subject to the reporting obligation, because the market will no longer be in a position to filter out the information it needs to make sound investment decisions. For the same reason we think that it is also necessary to introduce a significant threshold over a certain period that triggers the duty to disclose the transaction, and to exempt from the disclosure requirement some transactions such as

transfers by inheritance or donation, where there can be no doubt that there is no insider dealing. In all these cases we believe that these operations are private and of minor interest for market participants. Unfortunately, CESR does not think so. The next Directive to be adopted was the Directive on pension funds. It regulates the operation of employment-related pension schemes across the borders of the European Union. It is based on mutual recognition of home state regulation and establishes a so-called "prudent person" approach in Community law, so that a prudent investment policy can be followed for scheme members in each Member State. It is due to be implemented. Some of you may have read Monday's *Financial Times,* where a headline reads, "Pensions Directive Thumbs-Down". I quote: "Companies appear to doubt the usefulness of the European Union's Pensions Directive which came into effect earlier this year. Bruce Garner, head of pensions at BP, said the company would not establish a pan-European fund while tax discrimination on a national level existed. BP said a pan-European pension fund could lead to internal cost savings up to £28 billion a year". The next Directive was the Prospectus Directive, which was adopted in July. It is designed to provide a single passport for issuers of equity and debt securities so that, once an issue of securities meets prospectus requirements in one country, the securities can be sold in the European Union. It is expected to be implemented by May 2005. So much for the original measures which have been finalised this year. As I have already mentioned, there are now three measures under negotiation, which are takeovers, transparency and investment services. In the Brussels' European Council the heads of states and governments called on the European Parliament and Council to ensure that the adoption of these particularly important proposals should end before the deadline of 2004. The Transparency Directive, which was proposed by the Commission in March of this year, is set to impose an obligation on issuers to meet continuing disclosure requirements after issue. The Directive wants to increase the frequency and content of interim reporting, in particular quarterly reporting, by listed companies. It is hoped that a greater transparency will increase investors' confidence and encourage a more rational and efficient allocation of resources. The Directive is asking for quarterly reporting. We and QCA think that would be an entirely wasteful exercise. We believe that it will add a burden on companies, with little benefit. It has not helped to prevent corporate scandals in the US, like Enron, and there is a risk that mandatory quarterly reports will encourage short-termism as management becomes overly focussed on the next reporting deadline. The Takeover Bids Directive, proposed in October last year in place of an earlier Directive on which agreement was not reached, proposes a minimum framework for the national approval of takeovers, including applicable law, protection of shareholders and disclosure, taking into account the recommendations of the High-Level Group of Company Law Experts—the so-called "Winter Group". It addressed three principal concerns of the

Chairman *contd.*]

European Parliament: the so-called "level playing field"; a definition of an equitable price; and the possibility for a majority shareholder to buy out a minority shareholder, the so-called "squeeze-out". The most controversial point of course is the question whether or not a board should be allowed to take defensive measures against a hostile takeover. We are now discussing a Portuguese proposal that believes that a balanced trade-off between specific corporate structures, cultures and sensibilities of each Member State, and an improvement in common legislation at EU level, requires a system of options which are granted to the parties involved—Member States and companies—with respect to defensive measures applicable in case of takeover bids, while safeguarding transparency and reciprocity. The new model is based on three main axes: Member States' options with respect to their own law; companies' choices within the framework permitted by the Directive and by their own Member State; and transparency of choices and regimes towards markets and other companies—all three accompanied by a rule of reciprocity and, in the case of a regime, derived from choices made by companies. As you can see, this would not really lead to a level playing field but it would be more transparent where the playing field is uneven. Last but not least, the upgrade of the Investment Services Directive. A revision was proposed in November of last year and it is due to replace the 1993 Directive, which regulates the authorisation, behaviour and conduct of business of securities firms and markets, including exchanges. The proposal constitutes the core of a securities rule book for the EU, governing the main types of investment services and the activities of exchanges. The most crucial point is still the question of internalisation and pre-trade transparency. You arrived at the right time, because the *Financial Times* of today has the headline, "Five Countries Outvoted on EU Bank Rules", one of them being the United Kingdom. I quote: "At stake are proposals that would allow investment banks to compete with stock markets throughout the EU but also oblige them to stick to pre-published prices. Britain, the only country in which investment banks already internally match buy and sell orders on a widespread basis, is worried that the draft will increase the risk for banks and consequently push up prices for consumers. The Chief Secretary to the Treasury cited a study that estimated the measures would increase costs in the EU for such internalisation by at least £319 million". I am afraid that I am entering the field that Richard wanted to outline, namely the British point of view—which I am of course not able to deliver.

(*Mr Desmond*) Let me just say that when UNICE talks about the UK interest or the UK financial services industry's interest in the FSAP, we are doing this from the basis of our own brief. Our brief is as the users of financial services. We try as best we can to represent the users and the issuers. That is our position. In that sense, as users of financial services, the United Kingdom, in all sectors of the companies, will benefit from a more efficient pan-European capital market. They will benefit from the developments that have taken place. Even if the developments apparently help other markets, like the rapid deepening of the investment market taking place through the IORP, freedoms of investments that are taking place, and so forth, the vast supply coming into the markets will benefit UK companies. It will benefit UK companies simply because the access to capital will become easier. We have prepared and can send to you our general statement on this. We as UNICE have a natural position, where we are balancing the views of all of our member federations. As such, we have to try to come out and respond to all of these legislative initiatives and Directives with a compromise position. We are balancing views that are not particularly antagonistic views. They are views that have developed from different cultures and different methods, particularly in investment protection. Part of the views are more deeply market orientated—those coming from northern Europe, particularly the Scandinavian countries, the United Kingdom, Ireland, and a few others. Other views are more regulatory-based and they are coming from the historic development of markets elsewhere. We are moving through this and creating compromises as we can. This is what our Financial Services Working Group does. They are the issues we deal with every time we meet. I think that the entire Financial Services Action Plan is doing the same thing, except that it is writ large and it affects all facets of the financial services industry rather than just the users, as we do. We are often able to come back with a simple statement of principle because, as users, we want things to be more transparent and more competitive, particularly on the basis that we as employers are charged with making the entire European Union more competitive under the Lisbon Process. Will the FSAP benefit the UK? From our point of view as users, yes, you will have a much more efficient capital market and it will boost the supply of finance and improve the cost of finance to all of the sectors of the UK market. I can go through that anecdotally in detail or even analytically in detail, but it will do that. Has the position of the UK financial services industry been taken into account in the FSAP? To a great degree, yes—but through this procedure where you have to effect some compromise between natural points of view that, on occasion, will come into opposition on an issue. I think that the Investment Services Directive is a perfect example of that. In general, however, if you look through the complete set of measures that have been done, the UK experience and the UK positions have had a very good hearing. There are procedures that will even enhance those, which Barbara will talk about. As far as both the UK interests overall—and we see those as the interests of the employers—and the UK financial services industry, we think that the Financial Services Action Plan to date has been a benefit to both and will be a benefit to both. I would be happy to take other questions on this, but we are ready to go on and talk about implementation.

328. It is important that we do hear what you want to say rather than just fire questions at you. We do have questions to fire at you, but perhaps you would like to continue in the meantime.

Chairman *contd.*]

(*Ms Stearns-Bläsing*) UNICE has been following quite closely the implementation and working of the Lamfalussy Process. We have participated in the consultation that was launched by the Inter-Institutional Monitoring Group. We have stressed the following points in particular. I have to say that UNICE is not only representing users but also providers of financial services, because some of our member federations do represent banks. Given that the market structures in many of the member countries are very different in financial services, on certain issues we do have a great need for cost-benefit analysis of regulatory alternatives. One of the main points UNICE made in the consultation procedure was that there should be more cost-benefit analysis by the Commission and by independent experts of the regulatory alternatives and their effects, before the Commission proposes a certain instrument at Level 1. That applied particularly in the case of the Investment Services Directive, where UNICE was trying to find a position on, for example, pre-trade transparency requirements—and that was very hard for us. We would therefore have wished for a better analysis of what effect different transparency requirement regimes would have on the stated goals of the regulation, i.e. liquidity provision, better price discovery procedure, and so on. That led to another point. UNICE feels that where continuous evaluation and calibration of rules is necessary in view of fast-paced developments in the financial markets, the standard-setting should be left to Level 2, i.e. to CESR, rather than being predetermined by the Commission. Again, an example from the Investment Services Directive is the pre-trade transparency requirements, where we feel that CESR should have been left with more room in the first place. Instead, the Commission proposal imposed requirements on investment firms, which we feel established a regime that was too rigid, and we would have wished for Level 1 principles to have been restricted to stating the end goal, i.e. better quality of price formulation in this case, rather than the means by which to reach these goals. Other than that, we have called for more feedback statements, which is again linked to the cost-benefit analysis. We would like to have more clarity on why CESR and the Commission proposed a certain regulatory instrument rather than another one; why they proposed regulatory instruments in the first place; whether we could not have done better with market-based solutions and avoided regulation in general. The last important point that we made was that, for Level 3—i.e. for the transposition, because a lot of the Level 2 measures will be in the form of Directives and they require transposition into national law—we feel that there have to be more or better mechanisms for achieving convergence of rules at Level 3, so as not to leave too much room for national discretion which could then move into protectionist biases in that national transposition process. So we have been thinking about the various alternatives and what mechanisms could be added to this. It is a work priority for the Financial Services Working Group and we are planning a position paper on guidance rules for the national implementation of FSAP measures. We feel that the room left for national discretion in these Directives has not always been in accordance with sound economic criteria. Of course there needs to be room for national discretion, but it has to be guided by certain criteria so as not to move into a protectionist style of transposition.

Lord Walpole

329. The FSAP is one of the key deliverables of the Lisbon Process of economic reform to improve EU competitiveness. So presumably serious delays would look like a setback, given that the 2005 implementation deadline is probably one of the most important milestones. However, we have had much evidence stressing that quality rather than quantity is desirable and pointing out the risks of rushed legislation. Do you feel that the balance is being correctly struck at present? Can you point to any specific instances where adverse results have already happened?

(*Mr Desmond*) We have not felt, as the employers' federation, that, in the implementation of the measures to date, any of the compromises that have been made have been more than what was necessary. As I have said, we have to compromise all the time outside our own group. I will take a recent example with which we are very familiar—the IORP Directive. In an ideal world we would eliminate all investment restrictions—all qualitative and quantitative investment restrictions—and would have everyone bound only by the prudent person principle in terms of qualitative investment restrictions. That was not achievable, because of the history and position of Member States, and we have something that is almost as good. It will perhaps be, in a macro economic sense, a small drag on the efficiency of the single market. All we can do is ask that the Commission monitor this and report to us, as we have asked it formally, as to whether it thinks that this is holding back the achievement of the single market. In the end, however, we were totally behind the compromise because it was all that we could achieve. Yes, it was not what we would have liked to have seen, and there are other measures that we will go through where we will have to recognise that ourselves. However, we live in a world of compromise ourselves, not only as an employers' federation but as a working group. It is important that we come back to the basic principles of transparency, the basic principles of feedback, and the basic principles of trying to have these things implemented in the most effective way.

(*Dr Fischer*) I would like to add an example, if I may. There can be no doubt that we aim to achieve the 2005 finishing line. There is a danger, however, that the quality will suffer. Whenever the Parliament is not able to find a compromise, they give it to CESR. Yesterday's compromise on ISD—what is the standard market size? Parliament says, "I don't know. I'll leave it up to CESR". We do not think that is the way to do it, and we think that quality really suffers in this field.

Chairman

330. The difficult Directives, the difficult problems, are still to be resolved.

(*Dr Fischer*) Absolutely.

Chairman: That is why they are there; that is why they have not been resolved. Because they are difficult, getting it right is important. It is Catch 22. There is a danger that at the end of it the difficult ones may be rushed, in order to get solutions. As you know, in the UK we are greatly concerned about what happened yesterday. The pressure is building up, so deals are done. The deals done, however, have nothing much to do with the reality and the best, most efficient way for that Directive to contribute to the ultimate objective. As you put it, it is not the mechanism but what we are trying to achieve. Yesterday was a very good example. If the Italian presidency spends the next few months stitching up deals rather than asking, "What are we trying to do here and what is the best way of doing it?", we are in for a very difficult few months. I would not want you to think for one minute that we are here as "bleating British". We are very supportive of the whole process. We entirely agree with you that the objective of a lower cost of capital for issuers, for borrowers, a wide range of choice and better returns for investors, stronger equity markets, is absolutely right. A stronger international contribution, with a part to play in the international markets—they are very important. However, we have to get these next few things right. If people like you are not saying these things, the politicians, Parliament, and everybody else will stitch up deals that are not the best thing to do. Let us push on with questions, however.

Lord Shutt of Greetland

331. International Accounting Standards—there have been suggestions that the cost and complexity of drawing up accounts under these standards for non-European Union companies will be a major deterrent to using European Union markets. Do you agree with that? Have you seen any examples of companies thinking of shifting their listings, and where might they go where life would be easier?

(*Mr Desmond*) First of all, the application of IAS is and has been a main UNICE theme. It is handled by the Company Affairs Group. They would be happy to give you any detail on that. We have not seen any evidence, either anecdotal or not. On the contrary, I have seen evidence of Swiss companies reaffirming their commitment to IAS, simply to make it easier to move into the market. A major set of issuers in the euro markets nowadays are clearly a range of US corporate and, for that matter, institutional investors. Their position will depend on how the IAS and the US accounting standards are brought together—brought together and compromising. This is clearly the responsibility of the people dealing with accounting standards, to try to create this reciprocity. They are dealing with it on the technical basis of accountants' statements themselves, as far as I can see. If you would like to have more on that, it is the Company Affairs Group and not our ECOFIN group here in UNICE that deals with the International Accounting Standards. We would be happy to put you in touch with them.

Lord Fearn

332. Other issuers have made trenchant criticisms of the costs involved in reporting under IAS 39. These may be administrative costs but, perhaps more significantly, real economic costs by moving away from optimal debt management techniques. However, the International Accounting Standard project is very much a transatlantic, even global, project. The question is, are you in favour of the move to global accounting standards? Do you believe that it is only a governance failure of the standard-setting process that may impose these costs? How could the governance be improved to avoid this in future?

(*Mr Desmond*) I am not sure how these costs are defined. I know that some of the major issues involved in it are the market-to-market recognition of funds. These are issues that I think are accepted now by virtually all the structured accounting standard groups. I think that the IAS bears the burden of being the revision of accounting standards—the only revision of accounting standards taking place at this time, because a lot of other sets of accounting standards have probably stepped back from the process, knowing that IAS is going to become a European standards. If IAS was not out there, then I think that a range of individual structured accounting standards, by market, by country, would probably be changing in the same direction in any case. I think that IAS has absorbed the necessary changes in accounting standards that have to come along to meet the changes in market, the changes in approach to the value of companies, and so forth. Again, I could pass this to our Company Affairs Committee. They do tell us of their progress but, from my understanding of the overall process of the development of accounting standards, I think that IAS is less to blame than people may think, because if it was not there then those costs would be arriving on companies via their own domestic accounting standards.

333. So there should be a single set of standards, should there?

(*Mr Desmond*) The more there is a common set of international standards, the better it is for everyone. The better it is for investors, clearly, and that makes a better market; but the better it is for issuers, because then it gives you an option of wider distribution of the source of funds. It might sound like a very remote issue for small and medium size businesses, but the small and medium size businesses use a range of sources of finance that, in turn, are put onto wider capital markets—factoring bank finance that becomes securitised, and so on. All of these are routes into the international capital markets from any size of company. The more efficient that process becomes—and common accounting standards is one of the marks of increasing efficiency—then the better off we shall be.

Chairman

334. On the one hand, we share the vision of pressure to reduce the cost of raising capital but in reality, within the process of getting there, is a whole set of Directives, many of which actually

Chairman *contd.*]

raise costs. On balance, do you believe that the FSAP, taken as a whole, will actually reduce the cost of capital for issuers? Not the theoretical economic proposition that you and I share, but do you think that it will take account of the other elements that are raising costs?

(*Mr Desmond*) The other elements that are raising costs generally come from arguing their case from the investment protection side. I find that I become very macro when I answer this, because if you have strong investment protection in the market then, in the long term, that will not be an increased cost. It will mean that there will be fewer failures of the market in terms of investors and it will be a more orderly and effective market. Again, this is the compromise that we work with every day in UNICE, including in the Financial Services Working Group. There are different cultures of capital markets. One side defines its approach primarily based on investor protection; the other side defines its approach on self-regulating markets. I hope that we will be able to get to the compromise that keeps costs down overall; but if the costs do go up, they will be based on arguments and positions won by people who are more oriented towards formal investment protection rather than the market self-regulating. That is the underlying theme that will increase costs and I think that it is very difficult to argue against that.

(*Ms Stearns-Bläsing*) It is not just between different markets; it is also within one market and different players in the market. If you take yesterday's agreement on pre-trade transparency requirements and you look at a market like Germany, you have big banks which already practise it; on the other hand, you have small banks which do not. So the costs will be different, depending on whether you are going to practise this or not.

(*Dr Fischer*) You might read that there was a conflict between continental Europe and the United Kingdom. That is a complete nonsense. It was a conflict between German and British banks and the London Stock Exchange and the Frankfurt Stock Exchange on the other side. So there are different interests but these do not just apply to certain nations.

Baroness Cohen of Pimlico

335. I should declare that I am a director of the London Stock Exchange.

(*Dr Fischer*) But you formed a coalition with the Frankfurt Stock Exchange, did you not?

336. Possibly a member of the "enemy" in this respect! However, we are fairly clear that pre-trade notification will be destructive of the kind of market that we have built up. I would now like to ask about the bond market, which has not primarily been one of our areas. The FSAP is now moving towards completion. Its goals included a broader and deeper bond market, to match the cost of capital paid by EU companies with that paid by their global competitors. How much progress do you think has been made since EMU began and over a longer time span? Do we need a few additional measures, or

should we be patient and wait for the FSAP to work through? If we do need more measures, what should they be?

(*Mr Desmond*) I have a little experience in the bond markets—quite a bit, actually. It must be 28 years of issuing—quite a volume. If you look back in history, particularly from a UK base, it was very interesting to try to drive down your bond cost of capital to match US competitors. It was very difficult to do. You had to get over into the US markets to do that, because they had a better market, et cetera. It was only within, I would suggest, the last five years of the last century—1995 onwards, and perhaps even later than that—that you began to see the total of the euro markets becoming as competitive, in terms of the range of products, the access and the consistency of access, that you always had in the United States. At that level, for certain high-level companies directly issuing, you began to be able to raise bond finance in the euro markets competitive to your SEC-registered competitor raising funds in the US markets. Only then did the matching start to take place. It was not there in 1975, obviously. It was not there in 1985; it was not there in 1990. Only recently has that occurred in the offshore euro market. As of yet, I do not see anything that, overall, will diminish the impact of euro markets, European-based markets, that have grown to this level: none of the Directives coming out. The Prospectus Directive will not hold things back. What we are doing is creating a single European capital market and it will be able to build on the levels of efficiency already achieved. The other point to realise is that there is a huge amount of supply of funds pouring into the European capital markets. They will pour in via, if you like, domestic centres. It will be the life insurance companies in Spain; the institutional investors in France, et cetera. They will be the ones bringing all of this new capital into the market. They will bring it into the most competitive and efficient market that they can. If they can, they will bring it into the single capital market. The answer, therefore, is that we are finally getting to that level in the bond markets—not entirely, but at least one large company is able to match its bond-funding costs. The Financial Services Action Plan to date enhances that and continues that. Given other things that are happening in the market—some of them abetted by the Financial Services Action Plan and helped along by Directives like the IORP Directive—the pool of funds will be better and the prospects for better international competitiveness are very good, with the European companies being able to fund in Europe as efficiently as an American company can fund in America. The structures are here to do it. New things are developing; they are developing in the credit derivatives market now, beyond the provisions of the FSAP, but it is strengthened in Europe. They are the types of things that will bring up the competitive level of European bond finance. That might be a particularly sanguine point. As an example, however, the most recent transaction in which I have been involved, in a peripheral advisory function, was all done in Europe. It was a hybrid capital transaction for a major international insurance company with 52 per

Baroness Cohen of Pimlico *contd.*]

cent of its business in the United States, and yet the most efficient sources of funding are euro and sterling for that transaction.

337. That has a good deal to do, I think you are saying, with the development of a very efficient derivatives market.
(*Mr Desmond*) Yes.

338. And perhaps not a whole lot to do with the Financial Services Action Plan.
(*Mr Desmond*) The markets develop their own competitiveness and the markets are always ahead of regulation, and they always will be. What we need is to have regulation that takes account of the market progress. Yes, this is a theme that is very much like the Wicks' paper—market-sensitive regulation. Yes, that is UNICE's position and I think that much of what we have is market-sensitive regulation, but certainly more can be done. That is why I think that the Level 2 processes are very important, and the Level 3 processes are particularly important on this. As Barbara so effectively said, let us not be tied by too many Level 1 restrictions when Level 2 might be a better level at which to make sure this is crafted for efficiency.

339. Is cross-border clearing and settlement also of importance?
(*Mr Desmond*) Yes.

340. I know that it is in equities. Does it matter very much to bonds?
(*Mr Desmond*) It does but, remember, there is an enormous evolution that is already taking place in that. The market has evolved already in this. It is settling down to one or two major competitors. As long as there are competing participants in the market and as long as the regulation and the Directives keep up with the market, then we are okay.

Chairman

341. You came very near in your last remark to the ideal way of finishing the meeting, so I will just pick up that point. In summary, do you think that the FSAP, as it has actually emerged, has provided a framework at Level 1 that does and will enable market forces to have the room for flexibility and

the room for development in the way that you would want? Some concerns were expressed at one stage that Level 1 was becoming too detailed, with too many constraints that would then be a problem lower down the line. Is that now a concern without substance, do you think?
(*Mr Desmond*) I think that you will find strong proponents of the market regulating itself who will say that. I think that what we have to date is the necessary compromise. We will only make further progress if we leave more flexibility at Level 1, because now all of the easy compromises have been made. We now have the difficult ones to deal with.
(*Ms Stearns-Bläsing*) We feel that in some instances there has been too much regulation at Level 1; in other instances there has been too little. There has been a lack of compromise because the Council could not agree on anything, and the problem has just been transferred on to Level 2, to CESR. There we would have wished for a good, sound agreement at Level 1, so that CESR would have a principle by which to work. So for us it does work both ways.
(*Dr Fischer*) That is also my impression. So much was left to CESR that at this stage it is much too early to make a final judgment. There are many crucial points which are not dealt with in the Directive itself, and so we will see what CESR and the ESCB will do with it. There are already rumours on the floors about FSAP II. Nobody really knows what this might be. There is a lot to be done, however.

342. You tempt me! However, thank you very much. It has been a pleasure to learn from you and to hear your views. I am sure that it will be helpful to us in our deliberations, and we are extremely grateful.
(*Mr Desmond*) I do apologise that we were not able to give you complete answers on the accounting standards, but this is an area of another part of UNICE in which they are very active. They would be happy to respond to any questions you have.
Chairman: If there was anything which we would like to follow up, you can be reassured that we shall fire a note off to you. We will try to avoid it, if possible.

Memorandum from the Federation of European Securities Exchanges

The Federation of European Securities Exchanges is the Brussels based organisation representing all regulated securities markets in Europe. For brevity sake I may refer you to the FESE website for further information. Among our Members we count the London Stock Exchange, the International Petroleum Exchange, the London Metal Exchange, the London Clearing House, Euronext/LIFFE, as well as virt-X. Although FESE's primary aim is to represent its Members towards the European Union Institutions, we do take pleasure to submit our views to Britain's House of Lords as well in view of the importance of especially the City of London to Europe's integrated capital markets. We are grateful for the opportunity offered.

For factual data on progress with the FSAP we may refer to the Commission's recent eighth Progress Report which of course reflects the Commission's perspective.

A.

Your primary question relates obviously to the benefits of the FSAP to UK interests. We would like to stress that in view of the past and current role of the City of London and its many varied participants of many different nationalities from the EU and beyond, any substantive steps towards further integration of Europe's capital markets are and must be beneficial, especially if, on the basis of a level playing field, the degree of competition on the markets is enhanced. The current emphasis in the FSAP and in a number of its component parts on the removal of barriers to cross-border trades, can only benefit those service providers, both in the UK and elsewhere, who understand and implement the play of competition better than others.

From an overall European perspective we would dare say that the position and experience of the United Kingdom's financial services industry has indeed been given sufficient and adequate weight in the regulatory and legislative discussions in Brussels. We stress that the UK financial sector, again of whatever nationality, in substance is rather well organised compared to that of some other European countries. This also is an issue of competition. Moreover, the introduction by the Lamfalussy Committee of an extensive and intensive consultation process by the European Commission and by CESR plays into the hands of those who have views worth to be heard. A point of criticism here is for the ECOFIN Council and its sub-committees that essentially work without the transparency that Commission, CESR, and to a very large degree, the European Parliament practice. It is also especially in the Council that we find examples of protectionist tendencies that we believe should not be part of the European legislative process, are often short-sighted and do not bring lasting benefits.

On the second question under A, the main outstanding matters and key issues to be resolved, we would first of all stress as the overarching goal the restoration of confidence of investors in European capital markets and players in such markets. In that respect, it is of crucial importance that Europe, including Britain, should not accept US dictates, (by way of example I mention the Sabarnes-Oxley legislation), but plays into consideration of global expectations on the basis of mutual recognition. We stress here that for such mutual recognition to be effective a difficult change in attitude for our American competitors would be required.

Among the outstanding issues, we believe it is important that the Take-over Directive be enacted, on the basis of advance communication of clear legal competency, an improvement that we supported all along and that has been now accepted by Parliament and Commission, but was not in the earlier text. For capital markets the most important is the Investment Services Directive which should create a level playing field between those willing and able to compete, while taking care not to impose unnecessary requirements affecting investors/participants in predominantly wholesale/professional markets where they are capable of assessing their own risk, exposure, and quality of execution as such an approach could serve to drive business to non-EU financial centres. It should also enable some degree of pre-trade transparency and it should create appropriate conditions for in-house matching and internalisation by intermediaries that do not run Exchanges. It should definitely create a best execution regime for retail business in securities markets. Much progress has been made with International Accounting Standards for which it is crucially important that these be made into global standards including recognition and convergence with the US standards which are traditionally considered the best by our American competitors but have not shown to be so in view of the number of major disasters across the Atlantic.

B.

The Lamfalussy recommendations emphasise also implementation and enforcement but no Directives are yet in that phase or on level 4. The consultation process on the Prospectus and the Market Abuse Directives are under way with CESR. There it is important that CESR learns not to collate to a maximum the existing national rules and that sufficient flexibility be maintained. Enforcement also means, for instance with Market Abuse, that due recognition is given to the clear limitations of official bodies like regulators and official prosecutors and that appropriate scope be extended to the self-regulatory and contractual enforcement mechanisms including Ombudsman, Complaint Committee, and the like. Our Federation has suggested setting up an Ombudsman to provide some degree of protection for professional financial services providers in their contacts and possible disputes with regulators other than their own. We would be very interested in expanding on this concept to your Committee. The very limited resources of the European Commission are simply not enough for infringement success and procedures before the European Court of Justice are simply too complicated to expect adequate enforcement via those channels. More is necessary.

On the issue of the remaining barriers, we would like to mention the 15 barriers in the area of Cross-border Clearing & Settlement as recognised by the Giovannini Committee as well as Taxation issues. The unanimity rule in the Council relating to tax issues although understandable, is not of benefit to the overall integrated market, nor dare we add, to the interests of the United Kingdom.

C.

Looking at the future development of the single market we must not lose out of sight the cultural, linguistic and historical variety in Europe that is not to go away nor should it. Further progress than foreseen in the current plans needs to be made on implementation, on the ground of taxation (eg on tax basis), and on corporate governance. These all seem to be asking for priority. In the process, assistance, not necessarily in money, but in educational terms to the accession countries must not be forgotten.

May we conclude by arguing that in the area of financial services, what is good for Europe and its integrated market is good for the City in its global context. At the same time we should warn and counsel that this will only be felt substantively if the City whole-heartedly embarks to make the process and the outcome productive.

The Federation remains at your disposition to provide more detail on any of these issues. May I as a Dutchman, before I became a European, express the personal hope that one day Britain may decide to join EMU as well?

26 June 2003

Examination of Witnesses

MR PAUL ARLMAN, Secretary General and MR ALEXANDER WIJNBERGEN, Consultant, Federation of European Securities Exchanges, examined.

Chairman

343. Thank you for having us.

(*Mr Arlman*) May I welcome you here? It is not up to me to praise the House of Lords or its Committees, but I very much appreciate your anxiety to get behind some of the major developments in European financial markets. Although my core business is of course aimed at the European Union and all its institutions, plus a sidestep occasionally towards the SEC, we are very desirous to co-operate with you and to provide whatever insights we can possibly offer into the areas that you are most concerned with. I should perhaps add that it is not only the London Stock Exchange, of which institution a director is present here—and may I welcome you?—but literally all the exchanges in London are members of our Federation. In the last five years we have included the derivatives markets and, very recently, the specialised commodities markets. We do believe— and it is the core factor that binds the Federation together—that all regulated markets have a clear interest in appropriate legislation and policy formation in Brussels. At the same time, we have meetings in the morning amongst friends and, in the afternoon, we all go out and compete against each other. I think that may be a fair way of putting it. Also, in the last five years we have accepted as members, after an examination process, the exchanges of the accession countries of eastern Europe. Well before the legal decisions and the accession next year, we felt it important for them to integrate as soon as they can—which is one reason why the examination we did with them is not limited to the exchange itself but spreads to the regulator, to the legislation, and so on. I think that we have had some success, in the sense that these exchanges and their regulators are more prepared for the accession next year than they otherwise would have been. Finally, I express my regrets that you could not come yesterday when, wearing my other hat as chairman of the industry committee of the European Parliamentary Financial Services Group, I had the pleasure of hosting a luncheon with the governor of the central bank of Poland, who reminded us of the importance to stick to the Stability Pact and how important it is that the integration of eastern European countries takes place as soon as possible. You would have been very welcome, but I understand that your programme did not permit it. With that, it is entirely over to you, Chairman.

Chairman

344. Thank you very much indeed. May I repeat more formally what I said to you informally: how grateful we are that you have given us some of your time today? By way of background, and only briefly, our view as a Committee is very much in favour of the move towards a single market in financial services. We see enormous benefits there for European industry in the lower cost of capital and also, ultimately, for savers and investors in greater choice and hopefully better returns too. Our remarks and questions today, therefore, do not imply other than considerable support for the process and the objectives. Inevitably, we will concentrate on some of the problems, because it is the problems that one needs to address but, in context, we are generally very supportive. I was going to start the ball rolling myself with a question about the outstanding Directives and ask, notwithstanding all the agreements to date on 36, is not time getting fairly tight and is there not a danger of rushed legislation and poor decisions? That was before yesterday and ISD. In our view, that confirms some of the fears that have been expressed to us. What is your view about the ISD position as it stands at the moment?

(*Mr Arlman*) The ISD, as you will recognise, is the most crucial Directive for the exchanges. We see it as the constitution, at a European level, of how the exchanges function and the environment in which we function, in a general sense. That certainly applies to ISD. We would rather spend another three or six months discussing the issues involved than rush to judgment. I cannot judge—and I am not accusing you of having done so—the ECOFIN decisions of yesterday, simply because I do not have them. I rely on (1) the various press releases, some of which are confusing to put it mildly, and (2) on your host of this morning, the chairperson of EMAC, Ms Radzio-Plath. She told us yesterday at the luncheon that she had good news by telephone from the ECOFIN, because the ECOFIN was moving in the direction of the Parliament. Looking at this morning's *FT*, I am not quite sure that everyone agrees with that assessment. We are concerned about the quality of the legislation. Let me give you an illustration of one of many factors why we are concerned. If you try to change a European Directive and nobody disagrees with you, it takes three years—and we had that experience a number of years ago—let alone if you need more time because someone does not like it. You do not always get into the 13 years of takeover— and that saga has not ended yet—nor of the *Sociétés*

Chairman *contd.*]

Européennes, which has been taking 30 years. We have taken a view on the ISD—and "we" includes all exchanges, including exchanges in London. I say that because, originally, there was the belief, also amongst ourselves, that there was a London view and there was a view from everybody else. That was not the case, especially not after the London Stock Exchange, as the main spokesman, was very careful to explain how the systems of internalisation actually function in London. Frankly, round our tables, there was no one who objected to that: quite the contrary. So we said if the ISD text were to guarantee that that system could continue, then we would have no problem with it whatsoever. However, there is the other side of it, and let me try to phrase it taking into account the views from various angles. The principal point of view we took is the following. If governments all over the world decide that you need legislation to control financial markets because otherwise they turn into a den of thieves then, once you have done that, you should not say to somebody else, "But you can provide the same functions and I will not supervise you, I will not regulate you. You can do whatever you want"—which is essentially what the American investment banks, primarily in London but also in other places, wanted originally. That is when the Commission came out with the original proposals on the ISD. The reaction has been, "They have their regulation, supervision, and so on, but as banks, not as exchanges". We felt that there should be a level playing field in that area as well. You can take that to the extreme and ask for all kinds of pre-trade transparency, and so on. Frankly, we believed that the compromise—which indeed was a hard-fought compromise—was something that we could support. We understood from our contacts with the "enemy"—for instance LIBA, the London Investment Banking Association—that they could also support it. I believe that the text, as the Parliament had it, provided a compromise in the sense that you would still have flexibility, jurisdiction by jurisdiction—which for the time being, for the decades to come, will remain crucial; that you would have liberty of action within certain limits for national regulators; but that an investment bank could not, without any regulation and without any supervision, internalise. If you do that, it is a licence to steal. Greed is an important factor in financial markets, as I do not need to tell you. So we were reasonably okay with the proposals by the EMAC, which the Parliament accepted. I have not seen the details of what the ECOFIN has done. Some reports suggest that they moved towards the Parliament on some issues and away from the Parliament on others. We have seen that apparently the ECOFIN decided to—"take a vote" is a big word, but the chairman must have noted that a majority was for—but we have not seen a text. I have not seen anyone outside Council circles who has seen the latest text that went into it. That is already a problem because, as you know under the Lamfalussy recommendations, we and others are consulted with great transparency by CESR, by the Commission, by the Parliament, but not by the Council. If I have a Council text, then somebody has lost it—by coincidence of course—just as I was passing by.

Chairman: I think that our inquiry will conclude on 20 October. In the next couple of weeks, if you were able to establish quite what the position was, could you give us a view on that? My understanding at the moment is that there is an enormous gulf between the position and the Parliament. Like you, however, I am wise enough to know that seeing things for oneself and forming a view is always helpful. Some of the tough problems have still to be overcome. That is why they have been left to this stage. If this is an example of how tough problems are going to be dealt with, perhaps because it helps the process to get things through quickly, then I would have said that it is somewhat of a concern.

Lord Fearn

345. While good progress has been made on FSAP, many commentators note that key Directives such as Capital Adequacy, Investment Services, Transparency, and Takeover, are still not agreed and are facing intense political lobbying. Do you regard these Directives as key to achieving the FSAP? Are there key measures within the FSAP which concern you and your organisation's interests? Could failure to agree these Directives fatally damage the FSAP?

(*Mr Arlman*) The very brief answer is yes, yes, and yes. They are quite crucial, if only because of the expectations that have been created. When you look at institutional investors outside the European Union who play a very major role in our capital markets, if we, or whoever, were to announce that the Market Abuse Directive is dead, this would make a terrible impression. Right or wrong is another matter, because I do have my views on the Market Abuse Directive in terms of its quality and what it is going to bring additional to what is currently the case in individual jurisdictions. All the Directives you have mentioned, however, are crucial to creating or to keeping the momentum to create an integrated market—all of them, including the Takeover Directive.

346. And is that momentum slowing down?

(*Mr Arlman*) I do not think that the momentum is slowing down. We do have a major timing problem next year. The members of Parliament are disappearing from the scene on 1 April or 1 May, and they will be campaigning and will be gone for the process here. That is one reason why there is such enormous pressure to get the ISD done at Level 1 of Lamfalussy so that, in the six months that the Parliament will effectively be gone, the other bodies—CESR, the Commission, the consultation process and so on—can proceed with Level 2. That is more crucial for the ISD than for any of the others. There is an enormous amount of secondary work to be done, as we have seen with the Prospectus Directive and as we have seen with MAD—what I call the Market Abuse Directive. All of them are crucial to keep up that momentum but, with the ISD, we have to finish it before the Parliament leaves.

347. That will happen, will it not?

(*Mr Arlman*) I would tend to believe—with the other European who was a Dutchman before he became a European, Mr Bolkestein—that there is sufficient momentum for the ISD to be done and over

Lord Fearn contd.]

with before the Parliament leaves, yes. I think that all parties concerned believe that it has to be done before that break, and then we can work on Level 2. As you mentioned, however, the others are absolutely crucial. Do not forget that, when the European Union introduced the Insider Trading Directive a number of years ago, at that time Germany had no legislation whatsoever. I am not saying that the Directive as such was, from a quality point of view, a brilliant piece of work. No, it was not. As you have seen, there has been legislation since then in both the UK and the Netherlands which vastly improved upon it. However, it forced the Germans to have legislation, and that was the major point. The same with MAD: it will add to it in a very major sense. It will not dramatically change the world of the UK, Holland or France, but it will force a number of others to make progress. So, yes, it is crucial.

Chairman

348. So if any of these slipped into 2005, it would be unfortunate but liveable with?

(*Mr Arlman*) Except for the ISD, my answer is yes, it would be liveable with. If on, say, International Accounting Standards and especially on Basel II, we were to meet with some delay—because of the relationship with the Americans for instance—then I think we can have that, as long as it is quite clear that it is a delay and people are not using the break to break up the entire discussion.

Lord Shutt of Greetland

349. One of the objectives of the FSAP is greater competition, with resulting benefits to users of capital and consumers, in their role as savers. However, the implication of this objective, applied properly, will be the demise of weaker and less efficient players in the financial services industry. Do you agree with this conclusion? If you do, do you think that this outcome will be politically acceptable amongst Member States, or will Member States protect their own industries and thus frustrate one objective of the FSAP?

(*Mr Arlman*) First, I would say that that competition is simply unavoidable. If, as a Member State, you were to try to keep a gate around you, your economy will simply suffer in general and, in the long run, you will probably not save those you were claiming to save. The sentiment of protecting weaker and smaller participants in the financial markets is one you see pronounced in the Council. Not so much with the Commission and not so much in the European Parliament either. It is primarily the Council where such protectionist feelings come out. I think that it is an appropriate body to deal with that. I think that finance ministers understand that it is a lost battle. The competition would create new opportunities for smaller players, if they can find the right niches. An integrated, much larger market of course automatically creates more niches as well. In terms of straight competition, however, yes, that is going to happen and it is a good thing.

Lord Walpole

350. The FSAP has made more progress in harmonising wholesale markets than retail markets, according to some commentators. Do you agree with this statement? Will Member States really open up their markets to retail products from other Member States? Is the FSAP too ambitious in trying to harmonise both markets at the same time anyway?

(*Mr Arlman*) That was the question that most intrigued me, because my brief answer to the first part is no. I do not see any overly great emphasis on retail protection. Actually, one of the areas where I would have some concern is that wholesale and retail markets are often more intertwined than people proclaim. There is an absolute interrelationship between, say, the commodity markets that you have in London, say in oil, and companies that produce oil—and therefore shares in oil companies, and so on. Secondly, there is in Europe a growing network of institutions beyond formal legislation—let me stress that point, I support it very strongly—to protect the individual investor or the individual depositor, and so on. That is the ombudsmen, complaints committees, et cetera. You made the slight mistake in the UK, if I may say so, of having that ombudsman within the FSA. I think that it should be entirely outside and totally independent. Apart from such a detail, however, there is a growing intertwined, interlinked system of ombudsmen all through Europe. This is one of the major advantages we have compared to the United States' markets where, if you have a complaint, you go and see your lawyer first, pay $500, and then see whether he wants to talk to you again. In Europe, you pay euro 50, you get euro 50 back, and you do not have to bring your lawyer. That is a very crucial point, because the effectiveness of the protection of the individual investor, depositor and so on, is much more than in any formal legal system—which, by the way, is a general point I would like to submit to you. That is, formal legislation does not always offer the best and the most effective solutions. Take market abuse, where there is a great emphasis on public prosecution—criminal law and, yes, now also the FSAs of this world—but not a word about codes of conduct, about contractual law, about disciplinary committees, and so on, which have been shown in quite a number of jurisdictions to be far more effective. So I do not believe that the discussions are hampered too much. I do know that, for instance in the area of consumer credit, there is outright protectionism. That, by the way, is beyond the Lamfalussy recommendations, so consumer credit is discussed—full harmonisation—at EU level, which of course will produce a nightmare. However, exchanges are not into consumer credit. If I am too long in my responses, please tell me.

Chairman

351. No, not at all. You keep leading us down intriguing avenues.

(*Mr Arlman*) May I add one intriguing avenue?

352. Yes.

(*Mr Arlman*) It is my own invention and, to my immense surprise, I get a lot of support for it, so why

Chairman *contd.*]

not try to broaden my support? In the area of FSAP implementation, which is crucial under Lamfalussy and which we believe not enough attention is being paid to, I have come forward with the idea of having an ombudsman for professionals only. Nothing to do with private, retail or what-have-you: professionals only. Perhaps an exchange that wants to broaden its scope and finds regulators elsewhere difficult. You can talk to the regulator and you can talk again, and then you get into a row, and then what? Sue them? Forget it. They will not see you for the next six years. There is no mechanism for dealing between a regulator elsewhere—which might be the FSA—and the professional, whether a market, a bank, an insurance company. So my suggestion has been to have a professionals' ombudsman. It does not take away any of the official infringement powers of the European Commission, but that procedure may take years. It is a mechanism—I am not even talking about an institutional person—which would create peer pressure among the regulators in terms of, "Solve this, because you are not behaving according to EU intent", and would harvest complaints from private industry—because private industry will not complain about another regulator. There have been a couple of cases. How would you feel about starting, say, a bank or a brokerage office in Italy or Spain? You may have started three years ago and you would have got nowhere in Spain. In Italy you would have spent euros 250,000 in translation costs alone. Do you call that a passport? I mention those two examples because I have them in my pocket. There are more of them.

353. I cannot comment on your particular proposal, but the issue that you are seeking to resolve there is one of which we are acutely aware. Has that kind of idea been floated with the Commission?

(*Mr Arlman*) It has been floated with the Commission. It has been floated with CESR, and I will see their Chair tomorrow in Amsterdam. It has been floated with the financial industry in a very broad sense. So far, the noises I hear are all extremely positive. The Commission is of course institutionally concerned, as they always are. At the same time, however, the Commission—not only DG Market but also DG Consumer Affairs—have expressed support because they understand that an ombudsman-type procedure is much more effective than a formal procedure ever could be. So there is support for it. At this moment there is a British consultant who is working on a feasibility study for us. Within three or four months we would expect to come forward with a more elaborated proposal—but we will keep up the pressure.

Baroness Cohen of Pimlico

354. I almost had my question answered, but not quite. I will therefore try the rest of it. It is a question of the Lamfalussy Process. Good progress, even if somewhat impeded yesterday, has been made at achieving political agreement at Level 1 of the Lamfalussy Process. The devil is in the detail, which is less advanced. The key processes for implementation and enforcement seem to us to be less clear. Do you agree that implementation and enforcement are the real tests of turning the FSAP into a reality? Are you clear on how we are all going to do this?

(*Mr Arlman*) The first yes; the second no. Implementation is absolutely crucial because, so far, the ISD has not created that implementation process. The Commission, apart from collecting and translating national legislation, has not done anything in terms of "How does this work?". The Commission has promised that they would improve, but they cannot. They simply do not have the resources. When you look at how many people work in DG Market, it is next to nothing. You have much bigger groups working on the beloved Common Agricultural Policy, and so on. There is absolutely no way that they will get far more resources. I believe that one should not even look too much in that direction, but should use implementation and peer pressure on the ground. This is one of the reasons for the ombudsman idea. The second part of your question relates to whether we know how to go forward. No, we do not. We are just at Level 2 with the Prospectus Directive and the MAD, and certainly the Prospectus Directive did not make me overly optimistic. CESR simply added one brick after another—not saying, "This is our set of implementing rules". No, they simply took all the rules of all the countries—and *entassement* is the nicest word. They simply put one brick upon another, and the result is that one cannot carry all one's papers to the meetings. There is therefore some concern about how it will work. At the same time, let me stress that there is no alternative. There is no going back to pre-Lamfalussy. We have to continue to insist on principles at Level 1, and then work it out with CESR, with the Council working group, with the Commission, at a later stage. There is one factor there that you may not appreciate sufficiently. You had and have a certain tradition in the United Kingdom of consultation about financial market legislation. That did not exist anywhere else. Today I see the finance minister of my own former country, Holland, putting out draft proposals for consultation. That is new.

355. It is fairly new for us.

(*Mr Arlman*) But it was already practised, and it is new to many, many others. Thanks also to technology, the process is functioning. We can shoot at everything—and we do.

356. I wanted to go on to ask a bit about the future. We both know that the key criterion for success is whether the cost of capital in Europe after the Financial Services Action Plan is lower than the US and other markets. This is how we are going to attract non-EU issuers to Europe's markets. Do you think that we are going to achieve this objective and that Europe will attract more business than before?

(*Mr Arlman*) It is very hard to predict, especially the future. It will take a bit longer than one might wish, but I am fairly optimistic. Let me give you one illustration of my optimism that may continue in the future. In 1993 professionals in the London inter-bank market were so unkind as to steal away all business in bond trading from quite a number of other people, including from the Dutch. I was the Secretary General of the Amsterdam Stock

Baroness Cohen of Pimlico contd.]

Exchange, and we did not really like this. So we thought of measures how to get the business back. Surprise, surprise! We got the business back by the invention of remote membership. That was three years before the ISD allowed remote membership. Simply by saying, "You stay where you are. This business is electronic. Sign up. We will change all the rules into English anyhow. Join that market", it worked. We got the business back. It shows that a wise use of technology can even create markets where there were not any before. In equity cash markets as well, when you look at the spread of remote membership all round Europe, you see that today a company wishing to raise, say, £5 billion or euro 10 million or whatever, can do so in 24 hours.

357. They can sit down with a telephone.

(Mr Arlman) They have done it. You do not have to go to America because there is wider access to capital markets. No. The Americans are all here, and not only in London but in Frankfurt, Amsterdam, Paris, and so on. You already have the entire market. What you then focus on is eliminating barriers, whether language barriers or tax barriers—and, talking about the future, I do say that tax issues are inescapable—and it is about clearing and settlement issues.

358. Where do you see us going next on clearing and settlement?

(Mr Arlman) The ESCB and CESR have jointly sent out 19 standards for clearing and settlement, which essentially are a translation of current best practices. We will probably all say, "You should change this, that and the other, but that is a good set". In terms of quality, therefore, I would say that it is roughly covered. Then you have the issues of governance, of interconnectivity and of ownership. What we are seeing at the moment is, as you know, a very rapid concentration, and an emphasis—whether it is a spokesman from London, from Clearstream or from wherever—on interconnectivity. There again, my argument would be to let them go and do it. What does interconnectivity mean? It simply means that by being open in my systems I attract more business. That is what they are aiming at—and let them do it. I do know that the former chairman of the London Stock Exchange at a session at Chatham House—so I cannot quote him—made proposals about ownership of clearing and settlement, and so on, that have not found a resounding echo, because he forgot that the devil is in the detail. You have to write a treaty if you want to do that. You have to impose, and a treaty is the only way to impose. The market is already functioning. Due to Taurus, that part of the market was not functioning in the UK, but nevertheless there are very important UK players involved in what the market is currently doing.

359. For the benefit of the Committee, my ex-chairman used to believe that exchanges should not own the clearing and settlement, but there should be a common clearing and settlement not owned by exchanges. As one might have expected, this met with no favour whatsoever with the exchanges who owned clearing and settlement—and we have rather gone off it too.

(Mr Arlman) Dare I say, with good reason. The Americans try to tell us that they are doing everything perfectly, and should we not learn from them? As to CCP—central counterparty in clearing organisations—Americans believe that it is an American invention. Of course, it was invented in Austria in the 1920s. They apply it in quite a number of places. The clearing and settlement systems domestically in Europe are, by and large, very good indeed. Our problem is the connectivity across the borders. I am sorry to mention tax again, but taxation issues and legislative issues are the prime barriers.

Chairman: I will not follow that one through!

Lord Fearn

360. The London Stock Exchange regards the measures of the Prospectus Directive as unhelpful to AIM, which is Europe's most successful SME market. SME companies are vital to Europe's future economic success. Are you happy with the approach taken by the FSAP to smaller and medium size enterprises? What changes would you like to see to ensure this important market sector flourishes?

(Mr Arlman) First, the London Stock Exchange should be complimented on (a) being successful and (b) being successful consistently. I have been involved in some of the new markets in the past and they have been extremely successful for a while and then they disappear, like the Neuer Markt in Germany—which was far more successful than everybody else combined. The FSAP does not pay much more than lip service to issues of smaller and medium companies. When we talk about smaller and medium companies, we are talking about companies that nevertheless are big enough, important enough, public enough, to go public. However, there is ample scope within the variety of jurisdictions, and the implementation in that variety of jurisdictions, to allow adjusting measures for smaller companies. There is absolutely no reason why one should believe that reporting by Royal Dutch Shell—to mention one that you and I know well—should be exactly the same as a company that is one-thousandth of its size. So a certain adjustment to smaller companies, without losing sight of the fundamental transparency that smaller companies also have to provide to the market . Otherwise they cannot trade. The FSAP does not take it into account often enough, and I think that you have a valid point there.

361. Why is that, do you think?

(Mr Arlman) Imagine the situation as a civil servant—I do not know whether you have been, but I have and so need little imagination!—and you are sitting behind your desk, writing the principles for a Directive. You have to take into account a great number of things, and you have to be consistently told also to take into account the fact that the rules should not be the same for different size companies in order to really put it into practice. That is a factor that sometimes comes up in the proposals and sometimes it is, "Sorry, it was forgotten", and then it comes up in the consultation.

Chairman

362. You said in one of your remarks that consumer protection has often been used in practice by some Member States as essentially a protectionist device. Obviously, in different ways, we are politicians here on our side—partisan or otherwise—and we well understand the reason why, quite properly, elected politicians have to be acutely aware of the merits of consumer protection. One is always against sin. Do you think that there is just the danger that the thought processes in the politicians' mind, as it were, when transferred to wholesale markets is not helpful in the operation and development of wholesale markets?

(*Mr Arlman*) I am not quite sure I am getting where you want to go to.

363. When you talk to politicians, and I have certainly experienced it in the European Parliament, time and time again there is a tendency to think, quite understandably, of what we would say in English was "grandma", the small saver and their problems; then to transfer that thinking, what care you have to take and the rules you must have to make sure that nobody is doing anything. When you translate that into the billions in wholesale market dealings, where professionals are dealing, it can lead to a rather constraining and constricting view. The way in which it often turns out at Level 1 is rather more prescriptive, rather than the broader principles one would be trying to achieve. Do you get a sense that there is some kind of restricting or constraining frame of mind there?

(*Mr Arlman*) Yes, I think that plays a role partially, because some voices that should be heard at a European level are not being heard. Major institutional investors have their voice in Europe, in Brussels. Small investors do not have one. Yes, we have a couple of national associations. Yes, they have set up a European body but, to put it mildly, it is rather weak at the moment. That is a complaint by the Commission and by the Parliament equally. There is not yet an organised EU-level voice of the small investor. The result of that, paradoxically, is that you get members of Parliament who see behind them voters—investors, depositors—and they say, "Wait a moment, they must be protected. There is no one to advise me on it, so I will help and protect them myself". Let me give you one example. The Investor Protection Directive that guarantees an investor euro 20,000 in case the broker becomes bankrupt and has not separated the funds or the stock. That is a wonderful thing for those countries that did not have one to begin with, but it considerably decreased the existing arrangements in a number of Member States. It was a wonderful proposal but, in actual practice, it worked out negatively for the investor. So, yes, there is a point that one tries to protect without understanding what impact it will have on a wider market. That is certainly true. It is difficult, in the discussions here in Brussels, to say, "Let them play with each other. They are mature, adult parties. Let them just contract and, if they want to make their mistakes, let them do so". So there is an issue there. At the same time, one might occasionally overshoot. When you look at the Market Abuse Directive, there are a number of exceptions made for professionals that are simply too wide. There is a tendency sometimes in the markets to believe that

organisations are professional and mature, but they are not in all cases. In Holland we have had cases in financial business of, say, other bodies than the top government which were considered professionals but which were not really.

Baroness Cohen of Pimlico

364. The Home Country Regulator Rules prevent companies from listing their equity in another European Member State. There are certain exemptions for debt being offered to professional investors, so that non-EU companies will be able to choose their regulator when they turn up. Do you think that the Home Country Regulator Rules discriminate against the larger and more efficient capital markets, like us and France and Germany? How serious do you regard this measure, in terms of its impact on wholesale markets? We were much distressed by it.

(*Mr Arlman*) I can see your point. I should say that this cannot be recorded, but I believe that that part of the Prospectus Directive should be renamed national regulator protection—because that is what it is.

365. Look After the Regulators' Day?

(*Mr Arlman*) It is looking after the regulators. I admit that some of my exchanges may not have minded too much sitting in shadow of their regulator. It is a very weird one, however, especially as non-EU companies can have their choice when they come in.

366. They had to, did they not, or they would not come?

(*Mr Arlman*) At the same time, however, I believe that if a company has reason to think that they could fairly easily get a couple of listings, instead of only one—there is a tendency to go back to one single listing because, via remote membership, the entire market is there anyway—companies could get a different listing and focus on that other listing, and follow the rules of that other listing more than the rules back home. It is an unsatisfactory situation that we will have to live with for the next four years or so. There is some kind of sunset clause coming up, but we should have bitten the bullet and gone for total liberalisation there.

367. I cannot help feeling that it is rather hard on some of the small companies in the accession countries if you are required to list on the Hungarian Stock Exchange instead of some bigger exchange.

(*Mr Arlman*) I am not paid by the number of members I have—I should make that point. I would never advise a Hungarian company to list in London or New York. I would advise them, "List in your home jurisdiction and list somewhere else if you have big international business—either you sell abroad or have shareholders in such countries". In any case, the function of the Hungarian exchange is the relationship with the national investors. You cannot do that unless you speak Hungarian well enough and have a relationship with listable companies in Hungary. By all means have a listing in Budapest and a co-listing in Frankfurt, London or wherever.

368. I suppose if they can have a co-listing . . .

(*Mr Arlman*) Because the London Stock Exchange, however brilliant they are, cannot serve the local investor and the local small company. The

Baroness Cohen of Pimlico *contd.*]

French have tried it—that is why I am so convinced about it. They have come to a number of companies in Holland and have been transparent enough to tell me in advance that they were going to do that, and I said "Good luck", knowing what the result would be. Do you know what the result was? The companies came back to us at the exchange and said, "There is this funny man with a strange accent in English—and I don't speak English—who was trying to convince me to list in Paris". Of course it did not work. Europe is many jurisdictions and many languages.

Chairman

369. A smaller number of witnesses have said that there is some danger that non-EU companies might shift their listing outside of the EU, given some of the changes proposed and going on. Do you have any view about that?

(*Mr Arlman*) There is a considerable uncertainty and lack of clarity, for instance in the Transparency Directive, about the application of accounting standards—equivalency and so forth. Whether you believe that American accounting standards are equivalent to European ones, I leave to your imagination. I have my doubts, frankly. However, companies need to be sure in advance what are equivalent accounting standards—and whether it is IAS, US or Australian GAAP, I do not care too much. There is indeed concern therefore, especially with companies from farther away than Europe— not with the Swiss, but with the Japanese and so on— that a lack of legal clarity might bother them. They do not know what is going to happen to them and they do not like that.

370. How long do you think it will be before there is clarity?

(*Mr Arlman*) The Transparency Directive—there are three or four issues, but the hot issue is quarterly reporting. Do you make that mandatory for everybody? That is the one thing on which, in the last few years, I have allowed my deputy and myself to disagree in public. He believes it is good and I believe that it is not good. I am supported as of today by Chris Huhne and Peter Skinner, from two different parties of the European Parliament, who have argued that those who have it do not seem to be too enthusiastic and those who do not have it do not seem to be too eager—and what would it add in terms of information dissemination? My view there is entirely in line with Porsche, the German auto company, who are saying that it does not add anything. Frankly, I believe that the battle is already won. No one in the Parliament wants it to be mandatory, so make it clear to everyone concerned what the regime is, and then leave it to individual markets. If I can have a market niche where I advertise with companies that are all doing quarterly reporting and I meet success—wonderful. Competition. It is also competition between regulators.

Lord Shutt of Greetland

371. There is much talk about the desirability and inevitability of a European SEC if Member States do not implement or enforce FSAP measures. What are your views on the pros and cons of that?

(*Mr Arlman*) My federation has written two reports on the subject, known as Kremer I and Kremer II—the then chairman of the Luxembourg Exchange who chaired the group, at the time of the writing of the Lamfalussy report. We used that as input into that committee's deliberations—our conclusion was that the SEC is there because the Americans, by the 1933 and 1934 Acts, made America into one single jurisdiction for securities. If one takes the insurance business in America , there are 52 different regulators. In the securities business, however, their Acts turned it into one single jurisdiction. If you did not have one single jurisdiction, you would have to have a European SEC with, by next year, 25 different bureaux for each and every jurisdiction. Putting it another way, if you did not have the supervisor to the markets very close to them—and the market supervision director in many markets is a former trader—you need a thief to catch a thief!—I have been that as well—

372. We understand what you mean. We will put quotation marks round "thief"!

(*Mr Arlman*) As a supervision director you need to be close to the markets. The further away you move the supervisor, the regulator, from the actual markets, the less effective you will be. It is not a question of our liking no supervision or less supervision and that we feared a European SEC; we simply said, "We want legislation—and regulation, and policymaking, and supervision, and enforcement—to be effective". It is one reason why I insist that, in relation to the Market Abuse Directive, you have other methods of enforcement than only the official one. Effectiveness.

373. You have been extremely generous with your time and absolutely to the point. You said that you wanted to add a point or two?

(*Mr Arlman*) Yes, I would like to bring up one point which has been high on our agenda for, I am afraid to say, the last seven years. That is, transatlantic capital markets. I am tempted to quote Chris Huhne MEP, who yesterday spoke at the conference and scolded the Americans for the total lack of quality of their securities legislation. He was very eloquent. Our point is a slightly different one but it relates to it. The SEC and their by now famous 1997 Draft Concept Release, which related to the securities market structure in the US and changed a couple of things, including regulation of ATSs, ECNs and what-have-you, had a chapter on the access to America of foreign trading screens. We picked that up right away. We had meetings with the SEC, Daniel Hodson then Liffe's CEO and myself, at that time—and got absolutely nowhere. The SEC was totally unwilling to talk shop, to talk business, to talk substance. We offered them an exchange of information on all kinds of issues. They said they knew everything. We then of course showed them that they did not, but that was not particularly liked. We have continued to press the issue with the SEC,

Lord Shutt of Greetland *contd.*]

as it is the crucial body in the US on this, over the last six or seven years. We had a breakthrough. Thanks to SEC chairman Pitt who (1) received us and (2) met with us for a substantive two-hour meeting, we made enormous progress. We wrote a memorandum to Mr Pitt in April 2002, outlining our thoughts. The rest is history. Mr Pitt has gone and Mr Bill Donaldson, former chairman of the New York Stock Exchange, has not seen the light, in the sense that he refuses even to meet us. We will see one of the commissioners next week. We will also see Congressman Oxley next week, and Senator Shelby and possibly Senator Sarbanes, with whom we have had discussions on the subject when they visited us this summer in Brussels. The issue essentially is one of protectionism and one of a total refusal on the part of the Americans to recognise that the FSA is worth anything—or the COB or the Consob or whatever other regulator. They strongly believe, or profess to believe, that their system is superior. If we want to put trading screens in America, then we should register as an American exchange and come entirely under the SEC—as if the SEC has not enough to do. In essence, what we would like to do is take our trading screens, put them with American intermediaries—who are and remain subject to the SEC legislation, regulations and supervision. That allows American investors, via that screen, to trade on our markets. Today, an investor would have to go to two intermediaries: one American intermediary that goes to a European intermediary, and the European intermediary trades. The SEC does not want to discuss the issues seriously. We have a total blockade. We talked to the US Treasury, who express interest—but that is about it. I just wanted to mention that to you. Would we

accept it if American electronic exchanges were to come to Europe? Our answer is yes, we would—on the basis of simple reciprocity. If we can go there, they are welcome here. There is one slight problem. We here are all electronic, whereas the Americans— with two exceptions in the derivatives area—are not electronic markets, so they cannot offer what we can offer. The result is that, with the 300 European companies that are already listed in America on the New York Stock Exchange and the 200 Canadian ones—because we are working with the Canadians and Australians on this—the American investor is bound to trade on the New York Stock Exchange, and we therefore cannot create competition between them and us. Would that be important? Yes. Let me quote you one example only—Daimler Chrysler. Daimler was traded in Frankfurt; Chrysler was traded in New York. Then the two merged and they created a global share: meaning you trade the original in both places. Then all trading was in New York, was it not? The biggest market in the world, the envy of us all? Eighty-five per cent of the trading is in Frankfurt—of global trade. It was a former head of Goldman Sachs who said that the European exchanges are light years ahead compared to the Americans. I am not of that opinion, but we would like the competition. Anything that you could do on that score would be very welcome indeed. Thank you very much for providing this opportunity.

Chairman: Not at all. Again, that is helpful to us. Once more, could I thank you and your colleague? As I have said, you have been more than generous with your time and more than generous with your frankness with us. We do appreciate it.

Examination of Witness

Mr Chris Huhne, Member of the European Parliament, examined.

Chairman

374. Good afternoon. One of the points in our mind over the last few weeks is the piling-up of a small number of unresolved, yet to be sorted-out, Directives, and the voices saying to us, "Time is getting short. This will result in being rushed at the end. It will not be good and some problems will arise", and so on. Then yesterday occurred. What is your view about the practical consequences of Article 25 as it stands at the moment, and the process now? How do you see it?

(*Mr Huhne*) Obviously there is quite a lot of the legislative process still to go through before we get to the final text, but what worries me about this is that this is the first occasion I can think of when the Council has actually, from my perspective—and I suppose our perspective—has actually done damage and gone in the wrong direction, compared with the Commission proposal. Up until now, on almost everything, we have managed to have some rather good amendments accepted in the Council Common Position, which the Parliament has then managed to push even further. On the Prospectus Directive, for example, the Council Common Position was a clear

improvement on the Commission's proposal, and then we introduced further improvements in the Second Reading. This clearly goes backwards. I think that execution-only stockbroking—which avoids your question, but I will come to it—will probably just about be okay. I think that we can probably finesse that one. It does look as if Article 25 is going to be quite a serious obstacle, both to internalisation and to proprietary trading. The essential problem is obviously that a lot of investment banks will be effectively required to make a market for people like us, when actually they only want to deal with Hermes and the big institutional investors. Therefore the potential costs are quite substantial. The name of the game, and what is at stake here, is that basically the southern Europeans—and of course the Italians have their own interests in this, even though they are in the presidency—are trying to reintroduce, through Article 25 and the pre-trade transparency requirements, what they lost in the Commission proposal abolishing concentration rules. Effectively, at the moment they can funnel the vast majority of trading through their stock exchanges—which they want to continue to do. That rule goes with the

Chairman *contd.*]

Investment Services Directive and the battle has been about whether they reintroduce the same effect through the back door, by making the obstacles to competition from the investment banks sufficiently serious that they are not able to do it and therefore trade goes back through the stock exchanges again. That is what is going on, therefore. Politically, it is also rather worrying because it is the first time in my memory when we have had five Member States being outvoted on a Common Position, namely the UK, Luxembourg, Ireland, Sweden and Finland. It is the first time to date on any Financial Services Action Plan Directive when the UK has been outvoted and not been able to come to some compromise.

375. What will be the mood in the Parliament on this?

A. An absolutely key thing now—speaking as a past rapporteur who has been in this position and who has been trying to move a piece of legislation forward in our direction—is that the Council thinks that we have a strong position to amend this in Second Reading. In Second Reading, of course, we need 314 votes to amend the Council Common Position. If we do not amend it, it goes through anyway. So the Council Common Position now becomes the default piece of legislation, and we need 314 votes, a qualified majority, to amend that.

376. When will you get to that voting point?

A. It will be some time early next year. The other strategy is to talk it out, basically. Effectively, if there is not a Second Reading by April, it is dead for this Parliament. We then start again in the new Parliament (i.e. if Parliament makes amendments that the Council cannot accept, then it goes to conciliation. But there is probably not enough time).

Lord Walpole

377. The Takeover Directive is a crucial part of the plan to improve the productivity of the EU's capital stock by introducing an effective market in corporate control, so that corporate assets can be moved into the hands of those who make the most productive use of them. Do you expect a Directive to be enacted that meets this criterion? Will the Commission simply withdraw any proposal that would be an inadequate Directive?

A. Let me start with the second bit, because that is easy. I have never come across the Commission withdrawing a proposal ever—not since 1958. As far as I know, the Commission has never ever withdrawn a proposal in anger as opposed to because they were too ashamed of the drafting. They have withdrawn proposals because they have been shot to pieces and they have come out with a new one, but they have never withdrawn a proposal in anger, in the sense of effectively exercising a veto. I think that we are really in the realms of second, third, fourth best, with the Takeover Directive. I hope that it is possible to get something on the statute book by the end of this Parliament. I am not confident. I have a meeting later today with Klaus-Heiner Lehne, who is the rapporteur in the Legal Affairs Committee, to discuss the latest situation. At the moment, however, we do not even have a German line. As you know, the British line is entirely determined by the German line,

because Downing Street and the *Bundeskanzleramt* have done a rather dirty deal whereby we will tag along and help block anything the Germans do not like in the Takeover Directive, in exchange for the Germans tagging along and blocking anything that we do not like in the Temporary Workers Directive. Effectively, the UK Government position is now entirely determined by the German Government position, and the German Government has not made up its mind yet. So we will have to wait and see. My guess is that, if there is any runner at all, it is the sort of proposal/compromise that has been put forward by the Portuguese and is in the Lehne report in Parliament for First Reading. That basically will not create a level playing field. What it will do is make clearer what are the companies that are applying the provisions that would allow a level playing field and what are the companies that are not. The hope is that the capital markets will be efficient enough and farsighted enough to increase the cost of capital for the companies like *Daily Mail* and General Trust, Volkswagen, the Wallenberg companies in Sweden, which impair shareholder rights, and will reduce the cost of capital for the companies where there is a genuine market and corporate control. It is through that mechanism, of the differentiation in the cost of capital, that this compromise would gradually improve corporate governance and improve the level playing field. But that, I think, is the only game in town this side of the European elections. Post-June—new Commission, new Parliament, maybe new compromises; but this one has been running for 14 years, so do not hold your breath!

Chairman

378. Let me put it on the table—as it were, on this corner of the table. So far, you have mentioned that there is just the possibility that both the ISD and the Takeover Directives will not get through in this Parliament. I do not put it any stronger than that.

A. I think that is absolutely right. We are getting very near the end of the Parliament. Personally, I rather agree with what I think was implicit in your remarks at the beginning: that I would prefer to take a little longer and get it right, rather than get it wrong at speed. That does not worry me enormously. Overall, however—because I think that you are looking at the whole package—the track record, broadly, is pretty good so far. My own personal test of any of these pieces of legislation is, will it open up markets? Will it actually create more competition and give people more choice, and therefore lead to efficiency and so forth? The reality is, if you look at the Occupational Pensions Directive, that is a big move forward in abolishing quantitative limits on asset allocation. The UCITS Directive expands the instruments that can be invested in, and that is quite useful. The Prospectus Directive is pretty dramatic, actually. You can get one approval for a prospectus and you can now sell to investors throughout 25 Member States. You can go through the measures and it does not look too bad. We really are at the tail end of this.

379. There are some big ones left.

Chairman *contd.*]

A. I personally think that the Takeover Directive, from a structural change point of view, is quite significant and important but, remember, there are no federally agreed rules on this in the US at all, and half of US-listed companies are listed under Delaware law, which allows any sort of poisoned pill you like without prior shareholder approval. I think that we can get a little over-the-top on this, but I personally would like to see, at the very least, the provisions on the protection of minority shareholders in there. There are really two Directives struggling to get out of the Takeover Directive. One is the level playing field for takeovers and corporate control; the other is the very important protection of the minority shareholder when a controlling shareholder builds up a position within the company and potentially can do what they want with the company. Take one of your colleagues, Lord Black, and what is happening with Hollinger, controversial things about management fees and so forth. You would not necessarily want to be a minority shareholder in a company where that was happening.

Baroness Cohen of Pimlico

380. I expect you know that I am a director of the London Stock Exchange and therefore *parti pris* in this matter. The Prospectus Directive is something we were not terribly keen on. It is a key part of creating a single capital market. It was fought over intensely and even reissued. It was designed for equities and then bonds were added in as an afterthought. There are issues on accounting questions. They are still worried about that: as to whether people will want to list in the EU. Looking back, do you feel that particular Directive could have been better researched in the first place? It has created an awful lot of hard work.

A. The proposal? Absolutely clearly. Your conversations on this will obviously have been largely with the London Stock Exchange. To my mind, the London Stock Exchange had a slightly eccentric view of that Directive, and particularly as regards the AIM market, for example. That was not shared with a lot of other practitioners within the AIM market—including, for example, the quoted companies. So I think that we sorted out pretty much everything in the Directive which was of serious concern. Obviously we will wait with bated breath to see what the LSE decides to do with the AIM market: whether it is going to continue it as a regulated exchange . . .

381. That is our aim, yes.

A. I hope you do, because I think it would not be in your interests not to do that. But there was a certain amount of huffing and puffing about pulling out of this altogether, ·which I did not think was very sensible.

382. I do not think it was an eccentric view, in the sense that the Prospectus Directive owed a lot to the need of home regulators to hang on to their jobs.

A. No. On the choice of regulator issue, I entirely agree. Obviously it would have been great if we had had choice of regulator for equities as well as for bonds. The compromise that had to be done was a compromise which basically reflects what happens

now. The real issue for the LSE, I suppose, was whether or not we could continue to delegate approval of prospectuses in the AIM market to the nomads. The difficulty there for a lot of other Member States is, can you really give a prospectus, a passport, allowing them to go to any retail investor anywhere amongst 450 million people, on the say-so of an investment banker, who has a clear potential conflict of interest in both approving the contents of the prospectus and bringing the company to the market? You know the arguments.

383. Do you think that the final shape, the way the Directive finally came out, will discourage non-EU companies from seeking to issue securities in the EU?

A. I hope not. I do not think so, no. What are you particularly thinking of in terms of provisions that might do that?

384. The accounting provisions certainly may not help.

A. You mean IAS and the US GAAP?

385. Yes. It has been put to us that people need certainty.

A. Yes, that is always true. Markets always like certainty, although markets are also there to price uncertainty. If there were not uncertainty, most people in the markets would be out of a job. I think that there is a short-term, serious issue. Linklaters have just put out a note, advising Asian clients that they should be wary about issuing in the European bond market because of lack of clarity in the Prospectus Directive and in the Transparency Directive about whether IAS, for example, and whether the Commission would regard US GAAP and Japanese GAAP as being compatible with national accounting standards. The Commission cannot prejudge the discussions on the Transparency Directive, but I think that it could certainly put out some words of comfort about it not having any intention to disrupt the market. I have to say that it only has to think for two minutes—privately I think this is the case—to realise that it would be pretty stupid to do that, because not only would it be reducing deal flow in the European markets—not just London but Frankfurt, Paris and Luxembourg—but also the last thing most euro area countries want at the moment is a further strengthening of the euro. It has now just hit 1.1770 last night—so it is right back to where it began on 1 January 1999. At a point where the euro area economy's recovery is still fairly fragile, to introduce anything which stops people borrowing euros— which is the major form of capital flow out of the euro area to the rest of the world—would push the euro up, and it is the last thing they need. So I suspect that that is all a bit of a storm in a teacup.

386. I acquit people of meaning to do these things: of course they do not. I was just wondering whether it came under the department of unintended consequences.

A. I think that they are aware of that consequence now. That point has been made at official level. I was at dinner with Frits Bolkestein last Thursday and made that point very strongly to him. Hopefully, that particular issue will be tackled. It should not be too much of a problem. There is an ongoing issue which

Baroness Cohen of Pimlico contd.]

London is right to be worried about, which is that there is a long list of rather bad US protectionist practices in financial services which we want to see changed. Inevitably, people worry that the particular stick which we use to beat the Americans with could actually hurt us as well as hurting the Americans. However, I think that the Commission are aware, first of all, that we need to hone the leverage and the instrument fairly carefully, so that they are not hurting us more than they are hurting them. Secondly, they are aware of the limits of this game. As a former financial journalist and having been here years ago for the *Economist*, I covered the Tokyo Round. The stock-in-trade was "Trade War Looms", "Breakdown in Negotiations Between the US and the EU"—start thumping on the table, transatlantic flights and all the rest of it. Then, "Peace Breaks Out: Hopes Rise". This is a fairly regular cycle and it is something which we have known how to live with. I hope that it does not degenerate, but there is quite a long track record in managing that particular *pas de deux*.

Lord Shutt of Greetland

387. Good progress has been made at achieving political agreement at Level 1 of the Lamfalussy Process. However, the devil is in the detail, which is less advanced. Furthermore, the key processes for implementation and enforcement are less clear. Do you agree that implementation and enforcement are the real tests of turning the FSAP into reality? Are you clear on how this is to be achieved, and do you have any suggestions in this regard?

A. Yes, I think that everybody is now saying that and it has become a sort of conventional wisdom—which does not mean that it is wrong, but it causes me to think, "Hang on . . .". Once we have got all this on the statute book, the Commission has to apply it, make sure it is implemented, and of course Level 2 has to come into effect properly. So we are beginning to get a lot of advice coming through from the Committee of European Securities Regulators, CESR. That is beginning to go into the sausage machine. Graham [Bishop] is probably in a better position than anybody else to know about all this, since he is our representative—not your representative—on the Inter-Institutional Monitoring Group. From our point of view, however, one of the things which we have said all the way through this Lamfalussy Process is that one of the key reasons for doing things at Level 2 is that we are not very good with the detail. That is absolutely crucial in the whole process of getting the detail out of Level 1 and Level 2 and getting it out of the hands of politicians, who broadly do not know one end of a securitised bond from another. The key thing that we wanted was to ensure that there was enough openness and transparency in the process that, if something went wrong, there would be people out there who would be able to tell us quickly, and then we could bring in the call-back procedures—not that they are yet formally call-back procedures, but at least the procedures whereby we can review what is going on. We are very open to that. Of course, if the Commission were not either to respect the transparency provisions in the Lamfalussy agreement and bolt it into each of the Lamfalussy directives, or if the Commission were to do something foolish, we have the right not to renew the delegated powers. These are also the first pieces of EU legislation formally to incorporate sunset clauses. So we have four-year sunset clauses, which will remove the powers of the Commission and the Securities Committee, and they have to be voted again. So we have that sword of Damocles there and if Level 2 does not work, and the transparency obligations are not respected and Level 2 is bad quality, there is that there. The incentives are there to make it work, so I very much hope that it will.

Chairman

388. You said in the middle of that that it is up to the Commission to make sure that things are implemented and enforced.

A. On Level 1, yes, in terms of its role as guardian of the Treaty.

389. And in due course, through Level 2 and Level 3, even when it is all done, even when the technical details are all there in place, it still has to be implemented. The track record inevitably on some of the market in different areas has been patchy—UK plc's track record as well as others. In terms of financial markets, despite the theory, there is still a lot of protectionism around—for understandable reasons. In practice, who will make sure that it is implemented? Is the will there to take on vested interests and protectionist interests, and so on?

A. I think there is, but I think that you have to make a very clear distinction between the wholesale markets and the retail markets.

390. Talk us through the two separately.

A. What has happened in the wholesale market, with the creation of the euro and the creation of a common raw material for the financial services industry for 12 Member States, is that not having an integrated financial sector looks so ridiculous that the political pressures have become quite strong to do that. Although there are rearguard actions of the sort that we have had over Article 25 of the ISD, broadly the pressure is very heavily in the direction of opening up and making it a real single market. I think that is therefore happening. It is happening partly because of the euro, partly because of the FSAP. For example, interbank outstandings—the interbank market is completely integrated in the euro area; short-term interest rates are exactly the same throughout the euro area. An example of the political pressures—although not in the wholesale area but in the retail area—was that, as soon as notes and coin were introduced, there was enormous political pressure, for instance, to ask, "What if a Belgian credit card holder goes and shops in northern France and suddenly finds he or she will be charged euro 24 per euro 100 in a cross-border transfer, and he or she thought it was the same currency and the same area?". You can see that the politics of that were an immense problem. So basically we pressured the Commission, the Commission acted, and we put through a regulation which means that the banks have to equalise that. The banks are now putting the

Chairman *contd.*]

structure in place to ensure that actually happens. The euro has created an enormous difference in the way in which this whole thing is perceived. The retail area will go at an entirely different pace, for very good reasons. The retail area is simply much more difficult. I know, from having recently been attempting to explain equity release mortgages to my aged mother, that there are very sound reasons for making sure that people are protected from mis-selling of products that are not appropriate to them. Therefore, although we like to say everything is protectionist and so on, in fact in the financial services area, given the extraordinary evidence taken in the Consumers' Association for how little people actually understand financial products—most people find it very hard to compute a rate of interest, let alone some of the fancy stuff that is going on these days—I think that there are quite strong arguments for making sure that we have consumer redress mechanisms, particularly when they are cross-border; cross-border selling, and so on. I think that it will be intrinsically much more difficult to make progress in the retail area, and also intrinsically there are language barriers, barriers of culture and taste, which are much more significant than they are in the wholesale area. I would therefore expect that to be much more difficult. In fact, it may be so difficult and the benefits may be so relatively small that the Commission decides not to have a major attack on retail. That would be my guess. Obviously that will depend on the new Commission.

391. Ultimately it is the Commission's duty to ensure that the single market is enforced.
A. Yes.

392. Do you think that they will have the resources to do that in financial services?
A. No. The resource issue is a very serious one for the Commission. One of the reasons why the Prospectus Directive—to go back to that conversation—was so appalling was because it was left in the hands of a relatively junior Italian official, who decided that the easiest way of coming up with a proposal was to ring his former colleagues in Rome and to take the way that the Italians did it off the shelf, which I am afraid was not best practice in the EU. The Commission has—the last time I looked at it, but you would need to check this—about 100 people working on financial services. That is probably too small, just in terms of the quality of the proposals. I hasten to add that I am not arguing for an expansion of the Commission overall. However, in those areas where there is a high amount of pressure, often for a short period of time—financial services or, for example, merger controls in the boom years where, suddenly, the merger team was expected to deal with three times as much as it was the previous year—the Commission has to be more fleet of foot in moving resources into the area, and it has not been. So I think that is certainly an issue.

Lord Fearn

393. Some witnesses we have had before us have predicted that the Lamfalussy Process will fail and will be replaced by a "EuroSEC". What are the areas that give you most concern about the future of the

Lamfalussy Process and therefore the ultimate goal of an effective single financial market? What can be done about them?
A. What can be done about . . .? I am sorry?

394. The ultimate goal of an effective single market—what concerns you and what can be done about it?
A. I think that the Commission does not marshal its resources as effectively as it should, partly because it is not moving them round. If I were the Commissioner, I would try to be much more problem-focussed and much less theoretical and Cartesian about the whole thing. I would commission a number of studies on where the price differences are biggest in the single market, benchmark those price differences against the US, and work on those areas where the biggest price differences were, because that is the prima facie evidence that there is a lack of work as a single market going on. That is the way I would do it, therefore. I think that there is pressure in the undergrowth for a EuroSEC to come along behind Lamfalussy.

395. In terms of political will, you mean?
A. I think that it appeals instinctively to a French mind set, certainly, to have a sort of EuroSEC, or a EuroCOB as it probably would be if we were not in the euro area. It seems to me that may come down the track. The financial systems are so different at the moment, and the regulatory systems are so different, that there is quite a long way to go in approximation of the Lamfalussy variety. I am not as pessimistic about it as, say, Ruben Lee on the impossibility of making progress. I think that we can make progress with this approach. Indeed, it is probably a necessary approach, even if you think that in the long run we are going to end up with a EuroSEC—which I do. I think that we will have a EuroSEC in the euro area, simply because I think that, on a 10 or 20-year view, there will be such enormous integration cross-border that having a bank regulator who is responsible for Belgian banks, when the Belgian banks happen to have 80 per cent of their balance sheet outstanding outside Belgium, does not really make a lot of sense. So people will then say, "All of these things are getting so confused" and, effectively, the system will gradually become a system which has to reflect the reality of the much greater degree of integration in the euro area than exists outside it. That is really the problem for us in the long run. It is not that I think anybody is likely—though possible—to come along and try to create a EuroSEC maliciously. A De Gaulle-type situation with the CAP is unlikely. I do think, however, that reality will be changing within the euro area: the reality of this much closer integration. If the raw material is the same for the financial services industry, at some point you wake up and say, "Hang on a minute. Does it really make sense to have all these different national bank regulators? Does it really make sense to have all these different financial market regulators?"—when the integration is as pronounced as it almost certainly will be on a 10 or 20-year view. We have a certain amount of time in the UK, and then we will have to decide which way we are going to get off the little fence that we are sitting on—one way or the other.

Chairman

396. I can promise you that, in our report, we will not try to be certain as to what is going to happen in 10 or 20 years' time—but I am certain that you have

been extremely generous with your time and very helpful in your responses.

A. Thank you. I look forward to reading your report.

Examination of Witness

MR PETER SKINNER, Member of the European Parliament, examined.

Chairman

397. I have done you the discourtesy of not being on time, Mr Skinner, and I apologise for that. In general, as a Sub-Committee of the Select Committee on the European Union, we are very supportive of the underlying drive for the Single Market and the opportunities that offers, and indeed of the process itself. We are going to raise a number of the problem issues today. That is the context. We are looking at the problems, because those are the things we need to get our mind round. We have five short themes we would like to touch on. One of the matters in our mind over the last few weeks has been to look at the way in which everybody, quite rightly, has congratulated themselves on how many Directives have actually gone through. However, there is a little pile of the difficult ones to be sorted out. A number of people are increasingly saying to us, "They are going to have a real problem, getting these things through. If we are not careful there will be pressure to start sorting these things out in haste at the end and it will lead to some problems. Some bad decisions will be taken if we are not careful". Then yesterday, the day before we arrive, the ISD situation occurs. What is your own take on the ISD position, as it stands after yesterday?

(*Mr Skinner*) I was naturally disappointed that the Council decided to push a vote, to force it through, which seems to fly in the face of how the Parliament had arrived at quite a fragile decision to support this as a European law that everyone in the markets could live with. As this is public comment, I will reserve some of my better judgments for maybe a private word later, but I think that "disappointment" is enough at the moment. However, to say that this is all over would be wrong as well. The Parliament still has its opinion. In the First Reading it was not the same as the Council's. It is difficult to see though that we will be able to maintain that position, given the fragility of how we came to it. In that respect, we will have to try to find a new form of words which people will get behind. On the other hand, what has been quite a rewarding experience in the European Parliament is that people do give their word—do stick by it. You will also notice that amongst politicians, I am sure, within your House. People who may not actually benefit from it directly will still feel that preserving the right of the institution to cut a deal in Council is something that they are intent on doing. I am rather hoping that we will be able to do that specifically on the issue of the scope of this Directive and on price improvement—the two issues which we have fallen foul of. The other thing that we still have in

our favour is that the UK is not just London and the City. We are a powerful economic force within the European Union, and so also are Luxembourg, Sweden, Finland and the Irish economies. We still have the Irish presidency to come into, by the way—which is another thing. So I think we should take a step back, see what Britain really wants out of this; see what can work and what cannot work, and then come back to the table, because we do not want to be compromised with the view that all we are doing is just carrying a flag for a certain issue of industrial interest. We have now to play the role of being a government. In that respect, the Chancellor and others are right to take a step back and say, "Okay, move everything else out of the way. Let's get a clear picture on this; let's get some clear thinking. What is the route ahead?". Then I think that we can make some progress. Until we do that, I do not know. The processes within the Parliament will unroll, as they do, very clearly. We have this First Reading and then we will have a Second Reading. There will be changes attempted to the amendments, perhaps to reflect Council's position by some. There will be people peeling off, according to their own national delegation's views. I believe that the vote in the Second Reading— being a bit pessimistic here—will probably reflect those national views. It is up to us to try to stave off too much of a bleeding-away from the current position held by the Parliament.

398. An air of possible optimism?

A. Yes, possible.

Lord Walpole

399. One of the objectives of the FSAP was to lower the cost of raising capital in the EU. One of the consequences of this objective may be to reduce the number of exchanges and intermediaries, as the weaker and less efficient players are driven out of the market as costs come down. Do you accept that for the cost of capital to come down there will have to be a rationalisation in the financial services industry in Europe? Is this politically acceptable? If Member States do not allow their financial services industries to be taken over, will FSAP still be a success?

A. I think that, given what happened yesterday to the ISD, it gives you a direction or a flavour of what some people would like to do—to protect their bourses, their markets. I think that they are mistaken in just doing that. It is a bit like talking about the airline industry and keeping flag-carriers alive and well. It does not bode well for competition and, in the long term, those bourses will shrink

Lord Walpole *contd.*]

down to a few. It is quite clear that is going to happen. However, in the short term I am sure that many Member States will be able to shore up against that happening. That is my problem all the time, with trying to get an integrated financial services market at the European level and facing, day after day, this protectionism which emerges. I guess that even we are guilty of it slightly. We cannot say that we are perfect. There are many nations, however, who want to drag down the players who are most advanced in order to get them to a level where they are. That is just astounding really.

Chairman

400. Can you give us one or two examples there, to make that point concrete? You said that it is astounding—the resistance and the protectionism that comes across. Could you give us one or two concrete examples of that?

A. Yes. Again, we can use ISD as a model, can we not? I think it is fairly clear. The objective behind ISD is to broaden the scope of competition, for the maintenance of internalisation—when investment banks were allowed to continue to do that, to match buyers and sellers internally, and not to have to go through bourses. Of course, primarily in some countries this was their monopoly. These were the funds which they used in order to support their services. This was the way that they explained their existence. You can pick on a few countries. Dare I do that? Perhaps not.

401. You will have an opportunity to review the notes. You are able to edit the notes. It is to help us this afternoon.

A. I think that it is very interesting that one of the beneficiaries of this particular move will be the Milan bourse, and issues relating to the French bourse as well. I noticed that the German bourse was very keen on it. Interestingly enough, the German bourse were interested in expanding their arrangements throughout Europe. So there is a two-edged sword to that one. I do not want to sound too insulting, but it is really two-faced. A lot of what the industry has come up with, a lot of what the Member States have come up with, is literally two-faced. It blows away the competition in order to maintain a monopoly structure in a Member State—in ISD it is very manifest—and at the same time to say, "But we will allow perhaps the Deutsche Bourse and others to start to take over many of these bourses at a later date". Indeed, I have to tell you that companies like Deutsche Bank will be operating internalisation by setting up companies themselves. So it is very two-faced as far as I am concerned. I will put it as directly as that, but I would like to have a look at this record.

402. I do assure you of that. We are all politicians. It is more important that you are frank this afternoon and then to give you the chance to delete what you need to.

A. But not everything is as bad as that!

Lord Fearn

403. The last measure of the FSAP is the Transparency Directive and this seeks to impose quarterly reporting, albeit of a limited extent, on all listed companies. Do you feel that the cost of this requirement has been balanced with the demand from investors for extra protection? Do you think that the Directive will be enacted before the deadline?

A. Taking the last question first—yes. As the rapporteur on this report for the Parliament, the Skinner report, the issue about costing—I would say no, it has not been properly thought out. That is quite clear from where the Commission sits. However, may I answer this as well? They have not done any proper assessment on the impact to the business community. We have discussed this, day in and day out, on the issue of quarterly reporting. Regularity of reporting does nothing to guarantee the security of the investor in a market. It is the material information, simultaneous transmission of that material out to markets and to users who need it at the time when they need to make decisions. It is nothing to do with a 12-week or an eight-week period. That has nothing to do with it. Frankly, I think the Commission is gradually realising that quarterly reporting will be lost from this Directive—not least because the Parliament, in its wisdom, two-thirds of it, are going to vote in favour of the deletion of quarterly reporting. I cannot guarantee that, but I would probably put my last euro on it.

404. So is it pressure that is causing that or incompetence?

A. If I used the word incompetence, I would use it on the basis that I do not think that the necessary skills are there in the Commission to take account of what is really happening. They are pushing forward the Financial Services Action Plan at breakneck speed. That is true. So it is incompetence to a degree and, for some, it sounds quite whimsical what they are trying to do—borrowing what they think is a model from the United States. What they are doing, however, is trying to borrow a regime to fix something which is not broken. If you look at the United States' model on regular reporting, you cannot tell me that that is guaranteed investor security at all. Indeed, it is laid up in favour of the particular rules process which their accountancy procedure is organised for. It has nothing to do with the European Union scene. It is almost alien. In respect to whether quarterly reporting can work, however, yes, it can—but not in all markets where we want to trade and issue stocks.

405. Are you the only one who thinks like that or do you have allies?

A. I have significant allies round the table, and round the Parliament. I have not heard a voice in dissent. There are issues regarding custodians as well, for the ICs. It is very important for them as to whether or not custodians who honour the votes for investors but do not benefit from them should be covered under the same scope in the same way for this Directive. We are clearly trying to mark that up. There are issues about whether or not companies are bothering to locate an issue inside

Lord Fearn *contd.*]

the UK or elsewhere in the EU because it is not becoming a good place to raise capital, because of these burdens which are expected to come in. We do see reports coming out from financial houses suggesting that they issue elsewhere, and that is having a material effect. You hear that the business is going to other countries; you want to stop that. That is not the intention of the FSAP, as Lord Walpole indicated: it is the opposite. If you take the matter of the economic view of the FSAP, marry that against the risk capital action plan, which is actually to promote growth within the European Union and make it a firm knowledge-based economy—the best in the world—then clearly this Directive would be a failure, if the Commission takes [*inaudible*]—but it will not.

Lord Shutt of Greetland

406. We have been told that companies issuing securities under English law may find that their liability to investors is made much wider because of the Transparency Directive, because it will apply to all investors and not just those to whom annual accounts are addressed. Is this concern well founded? If so, is it by design or by accident? If it is by accident, what can be done about it at this stage?

A. The answer is I do not really know. I have a feeling that I am going to be told all about it though!

Chairman

407. When you have had a chance to reflect on the point, it would be useful to hear from you. It is something that has seized us, as it were.

A. Could it be an email exchange? Would that be good?

408. It would be exceptionally helpful, yes. If you could put your mind to it, it would be helpful to us in our deliberations. Obviously we have been looking at a lot of issues.

A. We are at the very early stages, I must say, of this discussion in the Parliament. I am quite sure that other issues will come out later.

Baroness Cohen of Pimlico

409. I was going to ask how you felt about the whole of the Lamfalussy Process. Clearly there has been good progress at Level 1, but the devil is in the detail. None of us can quite see where the key processes for implementation and enforcement are. Do you agree that these are the real tests— implementation and enforcement? Are you, as a member of the European Parliament, clear on how it will be done?

A. I think that implementation and enforcement are absolutely vital to the Lamfalussy Process, and it is the one thing we struggle with. Giving the role to the Parliament, to see how it measures out the concerns and expectations, has been one of the defining points of where we can move ahead with Lamfalussy. We called for call-back where we do not think that the legislation, for example, is

making the mark. I think that is still on the table. We are waiting for the IGC. We had discussions with Council, and they are sympathetic to the idea that the Parliament should have call-back, or some form of call-back, over legislation which is put out that does not perform to the expectation that was laid down. No one has given a role to organisations like CESR to implement this legislation—not in an official way. Whether we would ever want to do that or not is another issue. I sense that there may be some opposition about that. In terms of the legislators, however—we want to see legislation finally implemented and be a judge of what work we have done—I think it is important that we have the right to see . . .

410. To keep on looking at it?

A. Exactly. To revise it, if we need to.

Chairman

411. In your view, whose job is it to ensure that it is implemented and enforced?

A. I would like to see the national state regulatory bodies, as we have now, do this. We are not going to have a single regulatory body, I think, for the European Union in the foreseeable future. We may have one at some time. So it is best, for the UK for example, for the FSA to be led clearly to make that decision, reporting to, one presumes, organisations that are involved within the European Union like the Commission, the Parliament—why not?—and of course CESR. These technicalities, however, I am only loosely aware of. I would still like to see the FSA play that role. I think that they have done a great job. They have shown a way of moving ahead, and I think that it has been a carrot which many people in the European Union are now jumping for themselves in their own countries.

412. In some countries the regulators may also find it difficult always to distinguish between . . .

A. Government and regulator.

413. Yes. Then they are protecting an interest actually.

A. It is a good thing you say that, because I think that the Parliament has been a good driving force in trying to clean up many countries' acts on this. The efficacy of the FSA has been put up there, large. We have been able to use that as quite a bold emblem of the way countries can move forward— without being arrogant in terms of making the claim that it is the be-all and end-all. People do look to the FSA, however, and what the UK has done in terms of that independence, and regard the role that it has been able to play as being unique and one to look to as best practice.

414. You touched there, more than obliquely, on "EuroSEC" as an idea. You said, "If it came about—not for some time". Are there any murmurings in the undergrowth—as somebody put it—anywhere? What is the flavour of the feel about that as an issue?

A. If you went to Paris, I am sure the French would love it! I am really fed-up with the idea that countries just need to steal institutions as prizes. We have got a European Union that has grown so large

Chairman *contd.*]

now—we really have to settle that down before we can even think about that, and whether we do think about it or not. There are murmurings about this, but they are not concrete, they are not formed and, if they are formed, they are on the fringe of the discussion.

415. I raise it because it has been raised with us, but I should say that they have not been enthusiasts for it. As a politician, it seems to me to be so far in the future that we should not lose any sleep about it now.
A. It is rocket science at the moment.

416. Is there anything else? As with Chris, you are enormously experienced in what is going on. You know the mood of the Parliament. Does the Parliament regard a single market in financial services as a really major matter that is going to make a difference to the European economy?
A. It has exploded onto the scene, I would say, in the last two or three years. I joined the committee as a full member in only the last two years—the link member to the Treasury as well—and it is quite pleasing to see the interest which all governments now place upon the Financial Services Action Plan, and of course getting the legislation which suits all European countries, and the flavour of that being very important. I would say, if we were being selfish, that so far the UK has won over an awful lot of European friends on the issue about how we can liberalise our financial instruments and services, and that has made a real impact in changing the scene—which has to be good for the competitive base of the United Kingdom financial services industry. However, if there are glitches—and we need to be earnest about this—we have to re-engage, step back and see whether or not there are things which we need to iron out. Europe is not just happening in one day or just five years. It will be another five years—and you know it from your scrutiny committee work, I am quite sure. I might be experienced but, from what I hear about this particular Committee, you are very experienced at judging the legislation as well. I think that it is very positive and has been very powerful in terms of changing people's minds about what we do in the UK.

Baroness Cohen of Pimlico

417. I think that we feel a little beleaguered, as if nobody is listening to us. It is not true actually, viewed objectively, when you see what has been changed.

A. They are jealous of that, but that is a different matter. Jealousy goes to the point of saying, "We would like to have that too". It is not that they think that we are not doing a good job. They would like to have that share of the market, to have done what we have done. They would like to do it through a shortcut of mechanisms, however, through legislation; but you do not create markets through legislation.

Chairman

418. Some observers have said to us that, when it comes to implementation, there will be quite a reluctance on the part of market players to blow the whistle, as it were. Overcoming that and finding a mechanism—heavily Member State-orientated equivalent FSAs and so on—it will be very difficult to get people to complain, and so on. So, apart from the long-term trends and benchmarking, being focussed on the problems might not be quite as easy as one thinks. How would you react to that?
A. I think that is a broad brush. I think that Europe is moving in a direction which will not allow that to be an issue. We should be pleased with that, considering where we started from. If you measure it in terms of the number of laws that we can effectively pass in any one year, it looks as if it has been pretty timid and pretty slow; but some of those laws are quite landmark laws. For example, the Patents Directive, company law—these have unlocked issues and routes for raising capital, for increasing savings and investment, which have got to be positive and good. If you take the three barriers to the European Union—administrative, legal, cultural—the one that is outstanding and the biggest barrier is cultural.

419. That, of course, is important in retail financial markets. I do apologise again for the late start. Not today, but if, perhaps by phone or otherwise, you could talk about one or two things off the record as well, that would be quite helpful.
A. It will be my pleasure.

THURSDAY 9 OCTOBER 2003

Present:

Cohen of Pimlico, B.　　　　　　　Walpole, L.
Fearn, L.　　　　　　　　　　　　Woolmer of Leeds, L.
Shutt of Greetland, L.　　　　　　　　(Chairman)

Examination of Witnesses

M HERVÉ HANNOUN, Deputy Governor, M ALAIN LAURIN, M NACHBAUR, M COUSSERAN and M VISNOVSKY, Banque de France, examined.

Chairman

420. Good morning.
(*M Hannoun*) If you would allow me just to introduce ourselves here at the Banque de France. We have those people who are in charge of financial stability. We meet periodically and this institution is involved in financial stability through three aspects, I would say. One is banking supervision. We are in charge of the supervision of financial intermediaries in the field of banking and securities firms/investment firms. Here M Visnovsky is part of this supervisory body. Secondly, we are in charge of oversight of the infrastructures in the field of payment systems, settlement systems and gearing systems. We have some legal responsibilities in this field and this is the business of our Directorate General (Operations) And of course we are also part of an operational mission in the field of payment systems. As you know, we are part of the Target system for the high-value payment systems. The last aspect, the third pillar I would say, in the field of financial stability is the aspect of reviewing markets functioning. Of course, I would say the aspects related to market integrity are not our business but the business of the markets regulator, which is now the Autorité des Marchés Financiers, but we are closely monitoring the markets functioning in the other sectors, the market dynamics I would say—the exchange rate markets and also money markets. Of course the Banque de France as part of the Euro-system is one of the national central banks which is operating and, for instance, we are operating the main refinancing operations of the Euro-system for monetary policy. This is just a small presentation and I will stop there.
Chairman: Thank you very much indeed. Before we start could I thank you for making us so welcome and we thank your colleagues for meeting with us too, that is greatly appreciated. We are all busy people and you are very busy and your time is valuable so thank you very much indeed. It may help you if my colleagues very briefly introduce themselves so that you know who is here. I will tell you the principals but then they can introduce themselves. There are five Members of the House of Lords, so five parliamentarians, and two external advisers from the private sector. My head of office will introduce himself (the particular name we use in Britain is different) and a researcher from our office is here too. I wonder if the Members would introduce themselves first.

Lord Walpole: I am Robin Walpole, I am a Member of the House of Lords, and I am an independent cross-bencher, of no political party.
Baroness Cohen of Pimlico: I am Janet Cohen, I am a Member of the House of Lords. I am also, to save saying this later, on the Board of the London Stock Exchange.
Chairman: I am Lord Woolmer and I am Chairman of this particular Committee. I am a member of the Labour Party, as is Lady Cohen.
Lord Fearn: Lord Fearn, I am a Liberal Democrat member of the Committee.
Lord Shutt of Greetland: David Shutt, Lord Shutt of Greetland, Member of the House of Lords and a Liberal Democrat.

Chairman

421. So we all know who we are. I will explain briefly the background to our inquiry but only briefly. We do have a number of specifics that we would like to discuss with you, if we may. I think we are aiming to conclude, if it is agreeable to you, at a quarter to 11. I like to know when we will finish and as I think we are due to leave, unfortunately, at 10.45 we have to be quite brief. The Committee decided a few months ago to look carefully into the processes and the progress of the Financial Services Action Plan and the move towards the single financial market. We have been taking written evidence and also oral evidence for a period of some two or three months now. We visited Brussels yesterday to meet with the various people, including of course the Commission, and discuss matters there and we thought that it would be extremely helpful to us to visit at least one major partner Member State at a senior level to get a feeling of how things feel here and, if I may say so, we thought France was an eminently important country to visit to take the temperature, as it were, and see how things look from France. Our intention in coming to France was to ensure that we are not looking at things from a peculiarly British point of view to see how these things look from a different perspective, are they the same or are they different, and so on. You will know that the House of Lords, although we are from a number of political parties and independents, as the second chamber (certainly in the United Kingdom) is very much non-partisan and we wish to enquire into and look at the issues of substance objectively rather than in a partisan manner. So we do welcome your perspective on these matters. First of all, by

Chairman *contd.*]

way of introductory advice to us we understand that there are some changes going on in the supervision and regulation of the financial services industry in France at the moment. It would be helpful to us to understand what the changes are that are going on, what is the underlying thinking behind those changes and how you think this will help improve or change the way in which the financial service industries are regulated in France in the future, just to get a feel for what is going on.

(*M Hannoun*) Thank you very much. I think this is a key question. From our perspective we make a very clear distinction between market regulation and prudential supervision. In our view these are totally different jobs. I think basically the recent Bill in France, *la loi de sécurité financière*, is based on this distinction. Sometimes it is called the "twin peaks" approach because on the one hand we have the supervisory body, the main body, which is the Commission Bancaire, which is very close to the Banque de France, which is chaired by the Governor of the Banque de France. It is a collegiate body with some high-ranking magistrates, people from the Court de Cassation and Conseil d'Etat and also some other members. The Commission Bancaire is the main body in the field of supervision. It is in charge not only of banks but also in charge of securities firms. We did not merge the prudential supervision in insurance with banks. Again we have a separate body for the insurance companies which is the Commission de Controle des Assurances. In our view, these two types of business are very different in terms of supervision. We could elaborate on this and Mr Visnovsky could elaborate on this. We think that the best way of operating is having specialised bodies—supervision of insurance firms on the one hand and supervision of banking and securities firms on the other hand—but a very close co-operation between both, and this is well organised by the recent law because the new element is a cross-membership of the Commission Bancaire and Commission de Controle des Assurances, the insurance supervisor. I am the Chairman of the Banking Commission by delegation of my Governor and I will be a member of the insurance supervision body. Reciprocally, the President of the insurance supervisor will be a member of the Banking Commission. What is key is not only this cross-membership but the fact that on specific issues we have a close co-operation with the insurance supervisor. Just to give you one important example: we have close co-ordination with the insurance supervisor on credit derivatives and we now have very close co-operation in that area. So this is the supervisory part of the regulation of the financial system. Totally separate is this authority in charge of market regulation which is AMF, the Autorité des Marchés Financiers, which is a new body. I think it is a very positive element to merge two separate bodies. Previously we had the distinction between the Commission des Opérations de Bourse, the equivalent of the SEC, and another body which was the Conseil des Marchés Financiers, and here I think it was not appropriate to have this division. The new law has merged these two elements of market regulation so now we have this twin peaks approach to simplify it and I think this is an appropriate framework. I can elaborate if you wish.

Chairman: That is very helpful and just what we wanted.

Baroness Cohen of Pimlico

422. It is particularly apposite that we are here at this moment when you are slightly altering your system of regulation but clearly, whatever system, the Banque de France is key to it. Can I ask the general question we have been asking everybody. It is clear that in the Financial Services Action Plan good progress has been made at the political agreement level, level one of the Lamfalussy Process, but I think we all know that the devil is going to be in the detail and there is not much detail yet in level two, and that the other place the devil is really going to be is in the key processes for implementation and enforcement, which are not yet very clear to us nor is anybody else in the Commission or Brussels offering any clear answers. What I would like to ask is do you at the Banque de France agree that implementation and enforcement are going to be the real test of turning the FSAP into a reality and what are your plans on how this will work in France and who is going to have the responsibility for doing it all?

(*M Hannoun*) I think our assessment on the Financial Services Action Plan is that much progress has been made to date. I read the list of the 42 FSAP measures and we realise that out of the 42, if we understand correctly, 36 are now completed. Much progress has been made, so I think there is a feeling of acceleration. If we look at the list of the remaining outstanding issues, of course there is this issue of the Investment Services Directive and we will come back to this. In our view, there is a very important point related to accounting standard IAS39 and perhaps we could come back later on and we could explain what our core concerns are in that domain. Taxation of savings income in our view is also an important issue. Of course the Takeover Bids Directive and the Directive on Capital and Basle II are the outstanding issues which have still to be completed. As far as the Lamfalussy Process is concerned, we support this framework and we do think that this distinction between the four levels is very appropriate. Our view is that we should rely on level one because we do think that this level of general principles should not be too vague and we stick to the idea that the rules content of the Directives at level one is key, and we would not be in favour of a process in which with the comitology the main things would go out of this level one. Of course, maybe as a banking supervisor we have got used to the importance of level one with the Banking Directives, Directives on solvency and so on, but this is an important point to us. As far as the comitology is concerned at level two, this level you have only representatives of the ministries of finance. I think this idea of level two is an appropriate idea and, as I said, we support this suggestion by Mr Lamfalussy. As far as level three is concerned, we were very much in favour of having

Baroness Cohen of Pimlico *contd.*]

on board for the banking side both banking supervisors and central banks because there are many aspects in which central banks, even when they are not supervisors, must be around the table in the field of banking. As far as level four is concerned, I think that this idea to have a level at which the consistency of national frameworks or rules is checked is appropriate. Of course, we have not enough experience of this four-level approach and we need time to assess this framework better, but we are confident that this Lamfalussy Process will work. Let me emphasise one point. Sometimes we hear of the idea of having a European regulator or European supervisor. In our view, the key is to work under the principle of subsidiarity. On the one hand, what is very important is the harmonisation of the rules at the European level via the comitology and other ways. Also we are very much in favour of the harmonisation of reporting. For instance, in the European fora we are very much in favour of having the supervisors organised collectively to report so as to avoid different and complex reporting. This is very important and once you have the harmonisation of the rules, the legal framework and harmonisation of reporting to the supervisors, we are very much in favour of a decentralised approach with national supervisors in charge. We do not want to embark into any European regulator or European supervisor because, in our view, the principle of proximity is key. But of course then the key issue is to have very close co-operation between all the national supervisors and here I think the organisation of the co-operation between supervisors has made very much progress. We have cross-sector and cross-border co-operation. I think the cross-border co-operation between supervisors works very well. We may give you some examples. We have close co-operation with the FSA in London and when big French banks are taken over, for example Credit Commercial de France was taken over by the HSBC, we have a memorandum of understanding between the FSA and the French supervisor and all this works very well, and the idea that the supervisor would be segmented is a false idea. Cross-border co-operation, in our view, works very well and we also think cross-sector co-operation is absolutely key and this is what I mentioned with the insurance supervisor in our country. So, harmonisation of the rules at the centre, harmonisation of reporting, and decentralised supervision close to the financial centres with the principle of proximity, we think that is the best framework that we could try to implement, with close co-operation amongst supervisors, with the memoranda of understanding (which is one of the tools we use).

423. Can I come back on this a little. I know that the general supervisory framework can work very well cross-border. I was in fact an employee of Credit Commercial de France. I worked for Charterhouse and we had been owned by Credit Commercial for some years before HSBC came and swept us all off our feet and away into HSBC, at least in the case of the English merchant bank of which I had the honour of being a director. Surely, however, we are going to have to harmonise our

accounting systems in order for this supervision to work and, if not under IAS, what?

(*M Hannoun*) You mean the International Accounting Standards? I totally agree with you.

424. I know that the Banque de France is not keen on this.

(*M Hannoun*) Maybe if we could devote a few minutes on this idea.

Chairman

425. Sure, that is one of our targets.

(*M Hannoun*) I think we totally agree on the idea to have accounting standards by 2005. As we know, the Commission has already accepted all the standards except for the important IAS 39 and IAS 32. Our concern is the following: there are many good things in the accounting standards prepared by the IASB but we have still four concerns which are all related to prudential concerns. The French view is sometimes described as being against volatility in the outcomes. In my view this is not our main concern. The difficulty we have is with the fact that first there was in the last IAS 39 proposal the idea that you can decide to account at fair value whatever you decide to account that way. As you know, in 1997 there was a decision made not to embark into the full fair value. At that time it was agreed that while the trading book in the banks' accounts would be at fair value, marked-to-market, the banking book would not be at fair value and it was decided to keep for the banking book the technique of historical accounting. Then the new thing was a proposal related to IAS 39 where there was the option to decide that you could use fair value on every item or financial instrument you decided and this is, in our view, detrimental to comparability because everybody can choose this fair value accounting. This would not be within the rules and we have tried to make our views understood. We can give one example of what this could produce[1]. I think it could be useful just to look at it and maybe to reflect on it. This is something I tried to discuss. It is a very simple example which shows that if a company is in trouble it could decide with this fair value option to calculate its liabilities, its debts at a fair value and then (and it is of course an absurd example) this company by definition would have a reduction of the accounting value of its debt and then you could have the effect of having an improvement in the net income of this company and an improvement in the value of the equity. So this is one element. The second point we have is on the issues related to deconsolidation. We have some reservations on the IAS39 and this deconsolidation issue, which was very much in the spotlight after the Enron failure. The third point we have is the fact that the provisioning rules in IAS 39 have to be consistent with the Basle II framework. We, at the Banque de France, have strong views on the fact that the provisioning rules should be less cyclical. You cannot have dynamic provisioning in the accounting standards now because only incurred

---

[1] See Annexed Note: Fair Value Measurement Option.

Chairman *contd.*]

losses can be taken into account and not the expected losses, so we have also some reservations on these provisioning rules vis-à-vis the last IAS 39 proposals, and this has to do with the fact that if the losses are taken into account too late then you have a cyclical contribution to the mechanics of provisioning. This is our third point. We have a last point which is very well-known on which the IASB is now working, which is macro-hedging. I think the IASB has accepted changing somewhat its proposal but our banking community still has problems with this hedging accounting technique. These are our concerns. I just mention that these are prudential concerns and some work has to be done. As far as the procedures are concerned, we do think that of course the IASB has the leading role but in Europe, the EFRAG (European Financial Reporting Advisory Group), as you know, has an advisory role vis-à-vis the Commission on accounting rules and our concern is that on IAS 39, this advisory body gave negative advice but it was only at a simple majority and a qualified majority was required to stop the train of the thing. So it is a situation in which I think we have to reflect on IAS 39 on the grounds of financial stability. I think it should be possible to solve the remaining issues but I am not totally reassured at the moment.

Lord Shutt of Greetland

426. Can I just come in on that one. Are other countries bothered about this as an issue? You have gone to a lot of trouble to set out to us that this is of real concern to you. Do you know whether other countries are concerned about this?

(*M Hannoun*) I think it is a very good question because we are somewhat isolated. It is difficult to understand why we are isolated because we are supervisors and we are very close to these accounting issues—"we", ie the Banque de France. This was mentioned by us in a recent Financial Stability Forum and at that time we had no answer to this question. I think the difficulty with these accounting issues is that whereas the Basle Committee has decided to have quantitative impact studies before embarking on Basle II—we have had three quantitative impact studies—in the field of accounting it is a very difficult issue. Very few people are really aware of what is going on and we have no quantitative impact studies. It would be very interesting to know whether the CEOs of the major banks would now be able to say what are the precise consequences of this new accounting framework. It would be interesting. I hope that the response is positive but it has to be checked.

427. How do you believe this will be resolved?

(*M Hannoun*) I think the Commission understood that there was a problem. You have the problems raised by banks for their own reasons, which are not the same as ours. For instance, this is not something that banks are criticising because we are criticising the points on which the prudence is not sufficient, in our view. For instance, we have accepted that the trading book is calculated at marked-to-market value but our traditional view at the Banque de France as supervisor is that unrealised gains should

not be taken recognised in the income statement, and we would like to neutralise such unrealised gains because these are fairly fragile and reversible. However, it is the concern of the supervisor to be more prudent. The principle of prudence is part of the accounting principles but supervisors are maybe even more prudent. To answer your question, the Commission has understood that there were some problems and I would say what is positive is that the train has been stopped to check. I think it would be very important to have a clear agreement between the Basle Committee—because some members of the Basle Committee share our views— and the IASB to have some checking in the field of financial stability so there is a clear consensus and not an implicit consensus without the process of checking.

428. Do you believe that this is something where ultimately it is possible to compromise?

(*M Hannoun*) I think it would be possible to compromise. It would be easy for the IASB not to have this fair value option in their document which is, as I said, a threat to comparability, also it would be easy for the IASB to come back as far as provisioning is concerned. Previously there was a draft that was satisfactory to us but it changed. It was satisfactory because you could account for the expected losses and not the incurred losses, so it offered to have a dynamic provision able to work in a timely manner, but then they withdrew this and they came back to the incurred provisioning mechanism. It is easy to compromise but we are the only ones to raise this issue. My view is that there is a lack of consensus because there was no quantitative impact study and people realised that these are existing issues but maybe too late.

Chairman

429. The lack of quantitative impact studies applies not only to this Directive but there are many Directives where they have not looked carefully at the impact of them, and I am delighted to see you nodding head too. It is often a problem not only, I have to say, in the financial services sector in the Commission but in many others where it is our view that they are not carefully considered. There are one or two matters I would like to pull in. Lord Walpole in a moment would like to touch on banking and insurance again and a particular matter but could I just confirm, I think you said there—and I have to say I agree with you—that the Bank's view is that the desirability of a EuroSEC, a European-wide single regulator is, should I say, very low on the agenda. I think I understood you right. On the harmonisation question, what role do you see that that leaves for subsidiarity or variations? Where do you see balance between harmonisation and, as it were, flexibility and responsiveness within a clear reporting framework? Again, I was greatly encouraged and interested in the views that you expressed there.

(*M Hannoun*) I think harmonisation is related to the rules and regulations, and decentralisation is related to implementation practices and so on. I think if we have the harmonisation of the rules (and,

Chairman *contd.*]

as I said for instance with Basle II we are in a harmonised system) and if we have the harmonisation of the reporting framework also, (and as you know this is the goal of the level three committee for banking, if we have convergence of supervisory practices, because we are embarking with co-operation among supervisors to converge on the supervisory practices, if we have this level three committee and also the group de contact, which is a special body which already exists, then you have a very harmonised framework and you only have national supervisors working under the principle of proximity vis-à-vis the banks which are supervised. Then all these national supervisors are working under the same rules, they apply the same framework, they are exchanging views on the methods on the basis of best practice, we learn from each other (and supervisors have a long tradition of exchanging views on best practices). I think the key to not having this view from the market practitioners that it would be better to have a single supervisor or single regulator is to have a harmonised reporting framework. Of course, we will not be able to solve the problem of different languages but I think it could be easy to have harmonised reporting frameworks. I think this is the challenge for us all in the meetings amongst supervisors. On the instructions of our governors we should insist on the need to harmonise reporting because this is the only way for the professionals to say, "There is complexity because I have to report differently to 15 supervisors," but this is easy to resolve and I think this would be the best way of making progress.

Lord Walpole

430. Chairman, I am very aware of the time and I am wondering whether I could ask the question and perhaps if we cannot deal with it today a written answer might be given. The Lamfalussy Process really only applies to securities market regulation at present. Do you expect this process to be extended into banking and insurance and, if so, what are the implications for those industries. I am sorry, that is far too big a question to ask you because of time constraints, I am well aware of that, but it is a question we particularly wanted to ask you.

(*M Hannoun*) We agreed to have transposition of the same idea for the banking and insurance sectors as for the securities market regulation so I think the process is well advanced. For banking, level one is

the Directive and we will have this Directive in the future on Basle II. On level two the comitology is now organised. Now we are in the process of having established the level three committee. We do not know for the time being where the location of this Committee will be and this is an issue which is not resolved at the moment, but it is very important for us to have a level three committee with both supervisors and central banks around the table and it is very important for us—for instance, in the United Kingdom you have the FSA and the Bank of England—to have this level three committee because, as you know, even when central banks are not in charge of supervision they have major responsibilities in the field of emergency liquidity assistance and systemic risk and so on, so it is very important for us that this level three committee is not only a committee of supervisors but also with all central banks, the 15 central banks. The level three committee will have the mission to make this convergence of supervisory practices between supervisors and it will also be up to the level three committee to look into this issue of the harmonisation of reporting amongst supervisors, so I am very confident that this Lamfalussy approach can work in the field of banking.

431. And insurance?

(*M Hannoun*) We are not competent in that domain at the Banque de France. I would be prudent and I am not an expert in insurance. But as far as banking is concerned we already had this co-operation. We had the Comité Consultatif Bancaire, which was treasuries plus supervisors plus central banks, which was a committee which existed, so we are not starting from scratch and so maybe all this framework looks complicated because you have this architecture of committees which is to some extent impressive and gives an impression of complexity but I think on balance it could work.

Lord Walpole: Thank you.

Chairman

432. Deputy Governor, we could have gone on for a long time but unfortunately, as with age, time catches us up. Thank you so much. You have been generous with your time and helpful with your advice.

(*M Hannoun*) Thank you very much and it was a great honour to have your visit.

Annex

Fair Value Measurement Option

We have serious concerns about the possibility to designate any financial instrument as an instrument that is measured at fair value, with changes in fair value recognised in the income statement. Such designation would enable borrowers to benefit from the fall in the fair value of its own debts. Indeed, by recognising profits when their own credit risk deteriorates, it increases its own funds and thus Tier 1. Such a proposal is both counter-intuitive and contrary to market discipline.

COMPARISON OF THE IMPACT OF THE USE OF THIS PROVISION TO LIABILITIES UNDER IAS AND FRENCH ACCOUNTING STANDARDS

Assumptions

An entity whose equity amount to 200 forecasts that its rating will decrease. It issues a debt security which it decides to state at fair value from the outset. On Y0, the market value of the debt is 1,000. As expected, the entity's rating decreases because of losses which are −100 on Y1 and −200 on Y2 (apart from revaluation of the debt). The market value of its debt falls to 800 on Y1 and 500 on Y2.

Under IFRS (IAS 39), unrealised gains are recognised in the income statement and improve the earnings of the troubled company. Under French standards, the debt remains at historical cost.

	Value of debt in the balance sheet			Annual change in net income		Value of equity		
	Y0	Y1	Y2	Y1	Y2	Y0	Y1	Y2
French GAAP	1,000	1,000	1,000	−100	−200	200	100	−100
IAS	1,000	800	500	+100	+100	200	300	400
				(−100+200)	(−200+300)			

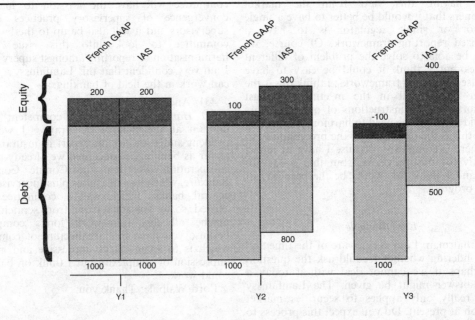

Commission des Operations de Bourse—Evidence withdrawn at Witnesses' request (Q433–Q461)

Memorandum from Euronext

1. INTRODUCTION:

1.1 Euronext welcomes the Inquiry being carried out by Sub-Committee B of the House of Lords Select Committee on the European Union into the European Commission's Financial Services since it closely follows, and is significantly affected by, developments in this field.

1.2 Euronext supports the current reforms that are being carried out in the context of the Financial Services Action Plan. Since it operates cash and derivatives markets across five EU Member States, Euronext has a strong interest in ensuring that there is a proportionate and workable European regulatory regime within which it can provide its services in an efficient manner and meet the needs of investors and other market users.

1.3 The remainder of this submission addresses the specific questions that were posed in Sub-Committee B's Call for Evidence.

2. QUESTIONS POSED IN THE CALL FOR EVIDENCE

A. THE FINANCIAL SERVICES ACTION PLAN

What progress has been made to date? Has this been beneficial or deleterious to UK interests? Has sufficient weight been given to the position and experience of UK financial services industry?

Response:

2.1 A large number of measures have been completed in the framework of the FSAP. As far as we are concerned, the most relevant steps forward have been the following:

(a) UCITS[28]: The widening of the scope of assets in which units of collective investment funds can invest as well as the new framework for management companies (especially the "European passport" and the expansion of the activities which they are allowed to undertake as non-core services) should enhance the cross-border marketing of UCITS. The concept of a simplified prospectus should provide more accessible, comprehensive information to strengthen investor protection

(b) Financial collateral[29]: The adoption of a clear and uniform framework of rules for the use of collateral should boost cross-border transactions, help integrate EU financial markets and create a more competitive European financial market.

(c) IAS[30]: The harmonisation of accounting standards in Europe by the adoption of uniform, high quality financial reporting rules in EU capital markets should enhance overall market efficiency and thereby reduce the cost of capital for companies.

(d) Market Abuse[31]: The adopted framework should contribute to the harmonisation of the rules for market abuse throughout Europe as well as to reinforce market integrity, enhance co-operation and exchange of information between national authorities. It should also foster investor's confidence in European financial markets.

(e) The setting up of the European Securities Committee and the Committee of European Securities Regulators which serve to implement the Lamfalussy process also constitute important steps within the framework of the FSAP.

2.2 Since most of the measures set out above are not yet implemented in practice at national level, it is difficult at this stage to evaluate their results. However, we believe that they should be beneficial, in particular the common accounting rules and the efforts to coordinate and align measures against market abuse.

What are the main outstanding matters that remain to be dealt with under the FSAP and what key issues will need to be resolved?

Response:

2.3 As far as we are concerned, the main outstanding matters are:

(a) the review of the Investment Services Directive (draft directive in first reading);

(b) the adoption of the Directive on Prospectuses (draft directive being finalised);

(c) the elaboration of the Directive on Transparency requirements for issuers (draft directive in first reading);

(d) the European Commission Communication on clearing and settlement (to be issued in the near future);

(e) the reform regarding corporate governance standards (The Commission has issued an action plan which is undergoing public consultation until end of August 2003).

2.4 Regarding the review of the Investment Services Directive, a harmonised implementation of the rules to be set by the proposed Directive is essential in order to achieve a truly integrated European financial market. This main objective should however not exclude the flexibility necessary (i) to foster competition and innovation within the EU, as long as such flexibility does not frustrate the ability to operate on a pan-European basis and (ii) to make appropriate distinctions between the protections needed by professional investors on the one hand and retail investors on the other. Moreover, in order to ensure the completion of the Single Market in financial services, it is crucial that the proposed Directive fosters the active participation of exchange members and customers located outside the EU. Furthermore, the Directive should create an appropriate framework in which regulated markets, Multilateral Trading Facilities ("MTFs") and internalisers can compete effectively, to the ultimate benefit of customers. Finally, Euronext believes that it

---

[28] Directives 2001/107/EC and 2001/108/EC on UCITS adopted on 21 January 2002.

[29] Directive 2002/47/EC on financial collateral arrangements adopted on 6 June 2002.

[30] Regulation (EC) 1606/2002 of the European Parliament and of the Council on the application of international accounting standards adopted on 19 July 2002

[31] Directive 2003/6/EC of 28 January 2003 on Insider Dealing and Market Manipulation.

is important to take into account price formation aspects since in order to build an efficient EU financial market the quality of price formation is key.

2.5 With respect to the Directive on prospectuses, the negotiation is well underway and the second reading in the European Parliament has recently been concluded. As far as we are concerned, the main problems that we see include: the possibility to delegate the vetting of the prospectus to stock exchanges even when issuers seek admission to trading on a foreign regulated market. The fact that issuers have to obtain a green light from their local stock exchange when they seek admission to trading on the exchange of another EU Member State distorts competition between such exchanges. We are also concerned with the language regime with respect to international offering for which translations are still required.

2.6 Concerning the Directive on Transparency requirements for issuers, we are still in the process of finalising our position. The main issues should be the scope of the obligations, which are limited to securities admitted to regulated markets only, whereas in order to protect investors adequately, minimum standards may have to be extended. The fact that the proposed Directive does not identify regulated markets as recipients of the information concerned may also cause problems, especially in the light of the obligations imposed on regulated markets by the draft ISD regarding verification that issuers duly implement transparency requirements.

2.7 The European Commission Communication on clearing and settlement is not yet available but one of the issues will certainly be to ensure that no structure is imposed by public authorities before the market forces have been given the possibility to explore any possible arrangements. In fact, we wish to underline that barriers to effective clearing and settlement (in particular the associated costs related to such barriers in case of cross border transactions within Europe) are key issues that need to be solved if we want to create a competitive single financial market.

2.8 We are currently carrying out an analysis of the European Commission Action Plan on corporate governance and cannot at this stage provide an assessment on the issues to be resolved. We wish, however, to underline that this will be relevant to the Transatlantic dialogue since some of the measures proposed share the same objectives and principles of the Sarbanes-Oxley Act.

B. IMPLEMENTATION AND ENFORCEMENT

The success of setting up a single market in financial services will depend to a considerable degree on the way in which the regulatory Framework is implemented and enforced.

How successful do you expect the Lamfalussy process to be? Are any changes needed?

Response:

2.9 We believe that the instruments that have been negotiated under the Lamfalussy process have greatly benefited from the enhanced consultation developed in this context. It has to be noted that this process requires time. In order to obtain the anticipated benefits, sufficient time should be allocated both to interested parties, to allow for valuable comments to be made, and to the European Commission, to permit a thorough analysis of the advice delivered by the Committee of European Securities Regulators. We also wish to underline that the legal form of the implementing measures may be problematic. For some implementing measures, the Commission envisages to use directives whereas such instrument will not allow reaching the harmonisation of national regulation that is wanted.

Who will be responsible for ensuring effective implementation and enforcement of the single market, after the regulatory Framework is in place? How successful do you expect this process to be? What will be the role of competition regulators at EU and Member State level?

Response:

2.10 The Commission will be responsible for ensuring effective implementation and enforcement of the single market but also Member States through peer pressure. It is difficult to anticipate whether implementation and enforcement will be effectively controlled. However, if there is a political will to do so, it should be possible. Competition regulators at both EU and Member State level will have to ensure that the concentration of activities among a limited number of partners, as a consequence of a more integrated market, does not lead to abuses.

What issues will arise as the single market framework is implemented and enforced?

Response:

2.11 We can anticipate the following issues:

(a) the need for regulatory authorities at Member State level to ensure that the Committee of European Securities Regulators remains an effective forum for co-operation, co-ordination and information sharing;

(b) political concern when some Member States may no longer have a national securities market

(c) the uniform and effective implementation throughout Europe of the Directives' provisions and implementing measures.

What non-regulatory barriers might impede the effective functioning of a single market for financial services?

Response:

2.12 Harmonisation of back office systems will be among the most important ones.

C. THE FUTURE

How do witnesses see the future development of a single market in financial services following implementation of the FSAP? Are additional measures needed?

Response:

2.13 The development of a single market in financial services should foster the concentration of markets and market participants leading to economies of scales and a better image world-wide, making it easier to enhance relationship with third countries.

2.14 It should allow issuers to diversify their pool of investors throughout Europe and allow for a wider access to capital.

2.15 Concerning additional measures, it seems that a single market would benefit from more harmonisation of company laws.

Will the changes resulting from the FSAP proposals have an impact on the competitive position of London and EU markets as a whole in the global environment?

Response:

2.16 The prospectus Directive and the creation of a passport for issuers, which will allow raising capital in all Member States with the same prospectus, should increase competition between European Exchanges. Such competition between markets should in turn increase the quality of Europe's markets. Once the US market is open to European products this may be a considerable advantage in a competition of large operators competing at global level.

2.17 By defining a clear status for European regulated markets, the revised ISD may facilitate the mutual recognition process between Europe and the USA and therefore constitute an important competitive advantage for Europe as a whole.

18 July 2003

THURSDAY 9 OCTOBER 2003

Present:

Shutt of Greetland, L.   Woolmer of Leeds, L. (Chairman)

Examination of Witnesses

M JEAN FRANÇOIS THÉODORE, Chairman, and M OLIVIER LEFEBVRE, Executive Vice-President, Member of the Managing Board, Euronext Nv, examined.

Chairman

462. Thank you for seeing us.

(*M Théodore*) I would like to say that we are very honoured to welcome you to Euronext, Paris. It is our pleasure of course. You know that we have a supervisory body and I am Chairman of the Managing Board and M Lefebvre is a member of the Managing Board, in charge of legal affairs, internal affairs, international affairs, including Investment Services Directive proposal by the European Commission. Maybe the best thing is that you express what you would like to know from us so that we can make some exposé of what we are. It is best if we know your main concerns or fields of interest.

463. Thank you very much indeed, President. First of all, we are scheduled to conclude the meeting around 4.30 if that is agreeable to you, just so we know what time we have. I thought firstly I should explain very briefly why we are here to set a little context and then we do have a number of questions that we would like to talk with you about and to develop in conversation. The Select Committee that I chair is conducting a review of the Financial Services Action Plan and the move towards the single financial market. We are very supportive obviously of the move towards a Single Market in finance. We are very supportive of the Lamfalussy Process but inevitably as an inquiry we are concentrating on areas where there may be difficulties or problems. That does not mean that we are looking for problems but simply that we agree with all the good things, but we would like to look at things where there may be difficulties. We visited Brussels yesterday and met with all the usual people you would expect us to meet and we thought we should visit another major financial centre within the Member States and we thought it would be very useful to visit Paris. Obviously while we are in Paris we thought we really ought to meet you. It would be helpful because we are taking a transcript of our meeting if for the reading into the record you could just say a few words about Euronext, to explain who you are and what you are doing on the European stock market scene and then, if we may, we would like to move onto around six questions in the time we have. Perhaps if you could commence by giving a little picture which, as I say, will be read into the parliamentary record, then that would be helpful.

(*M Théodore*) Thank you very much. As you may know, Euronext is a Dutch company. It is a young Dutch company because we are the result of a merger in September 2000 (so we are only three years old) of the Amsterdam, the Brussels and the Paris Stock Exchanges. Lisbon joined later and in 2001 we combined with LIFFE, as you certainly know. We are a pan-European stock exchange covering four countries of the European Union for cash markets and five countries for derivatives, if you can speak country-by-country in the European Union. In derivatives there are only two major players left. One is EUREX, the first one in Europe, and the second is EURONEX LIFFE, in combining the derivatives from the Continent with LIFFE in London. And in the cash markets our listed companies represent is close to 50 per cent of the market cap of euroland and close to 25 per cent of the whole of Europe. By this criterion we are second in Europe to the LSE. If we look at the number of trades matched in the central order book (because we are much more of a central order book type organisation) we are number one, ahead of the LSE and much ahead of the Deutsche Börse. For cash markets we are probably in between two or three times the size of the Deutsche cash market. We have been a listed company since July 2001. Our market cap is around 2.6 billion euro, which is roughly half the Deutsche Börse but a little bit less than twice LSE, so that is the order of magnitude for the three big listed European Stock Exchanges.

464. Thank you very much, that is extremely helpful. Could I go straight into the questions. There has been a lot of good progress with the Financial Services Action Plan but some key Directives still remain to be resolved. In the timescale that the Council and Commission and European Parliament have set themselves time is getting very short. One of our concerns has been that inevitably some of the difficult problems in Directives have been left until last to resolve and now time is getting very short and we are concerned about the balance with the quality of Directives and legislation as time gets pressured. The decision on ISD earlier this week confirmed, in our view, some of those fears, the pressure to get decisions made, the pressure to speed up processes and not necessarily to take, in our view you will not be surprised to hear, sensible decisions. If ISD, for example, did not get through the processes before 2004-05, do you think that would cause any problems? Is ISD an important Directive?

(*M Théodore*) Maybe I will answer first and then I will give the floor to Olivier. I need to tell you that on our side we were relatively comfortable with the compromise of the European Parliament for the ISD, and not being very close for the time being to what has come out of the Council of Ministers, we are a

Chairman *contd.*]

little bit concerned that it would lead to waiting for weeks or months for a final version of the ISD because we would tend to believe that we need an ISD and Europe's single financial market needs to have it. Maybe we would not have needed to have started but now that we have started it will be a sign of failure and weakness not to have an ISD and I think it would leave a void in the infrastructure of the market. Olivier may have a different view.

(*M Lefebvre*) No, I do not, I would not dare! Just to say that Euronext, as Jean Franois said, is a cross-border exchange. It is really the only one at this stage in Europe (with some exception now in Scandinavia with OMHEX) and so we operate integrated markets because what the technology allows you to do is to create an effective, integrated market but on a cross-border basis which is quite new for an exchange. The traditional view is that an exchange always tries to attract everything to its initial jurisdiction. It is a culture of a floor but now with electronic means we can work differently. So anything that can help harmonise and facilitate the cross-border dimension is of course not only good for Europe, but we believe, which is a very selfish view, it is also good for our business, and so we are extremely supportive of the Financial Services Action Plan in general and we believe that the ISD more specifically is one of the cornerstones of this integration. It is true, as Jean Franois said, that we were confident that the compromise—and I do not like that word because I think compromise has a negative connotation—was a workable balance that was reached in discussion in the Parliament under the leadership of Theresa Villiers. This has now been re-opened to some extent by the Council, which is a source of concern because we supported this compromise, although it is not yet clear to what extent exactly the amendments that are now in the Council text would drift us away from the balance. We are still waiting for that and consulting with banks and members and other exchanges to see what the exact discrepancy is and how we can try to help convergence in the second reading which is the last phase of the legislative process. It would indeed be a big failure for Europe if the entire ISD were blocked and postponed for several years if it is not passed under this legislation.

465. When do you think you might be completing your consideration of the position as it stands? You have said that you are looking in detail at the Council wording. When do you think you will be in a position to . . .

(*M Lefebvre*) That is probably a matter of weeks because we want to be sure. We have some months because, as you know, the process of the second reading will start after this heavy translation work is over. We know that the second reading in the Parliament will take some months so we believe we have some time to consult again with the various associations in London. We have regular meetings with the associations and institutions in London and everywhere where we are active as well as the other exchanges.

466. Are any of the other outstanding Directives significant, to your mind?

(*M Lefebvre*) In the case of our core business the most significant ones on top of the ISD are the Prospectus Directive, the Market Abuse Directive and the Transparency Directives, for example. Generally speaking, as I said, we are extremely supportive of the work of the Commission to go ahead with these texts. It does not mean that we are totally happy with all the ingredients or content of all these things. For example, one difficult point we have with the Prospectus Directive is that you will remember that there has been a long debate between freedom of choice and the monopoly of home market control. There has been a choice, we are not going to challenge that choice again, whatever our own preference is, but there is an inconsistency between the fact that there is a monopoly of the home authority and at the same time there is the possibility for some Member States to delegate from the public authority to the domestic exchange the appproval of the prospectus because this is a distortion of competition between exchanges in Europe. This concern has been flagged up several times but, unfortunately, it is still in the text that has been approved at this stage. We are not going to say that this Dilective should be dropped because we believe the Prospectus Directive is an important milestone in the entire process, so it is not sufficient reason to block it, but this specific point is very unsatisfactory.

Chairman: I think you will find a lot of people agree with that too. Lord Shutt?

Lord Shutt of Greetland

467. Just before I go on to ask you what I was going to ask you about, you did not mention accounting standards in that. Is that one that does not trouble you?

(*M Lefebvre*) Those were not my words!

468. Oh I see, I thought you are telling us that did not trouble you.

(*M Lefebvre*) Sorry, that is obviously an important milestone as well.

469. We have heard about that, you see. Coming on to the point that I wanted to raise with you, there is some concern in the United Kingdom that the investor (or consumer) protection lobby in Europe is gaining too much influence in the development of the FSAP with respect to the effective operation of retail markets and—perhaps unintentionally—the wholesale markets. Are you concerned that too much emphasis on investor protection could be damaging to wholesale capital markets across the European Union?

(*M Lefebvre*) I think that if the devices that should be placed on protecting the retail investor is extended to the wholesale market it could indeed be damaging. It is not totally clear at this stage. One very significant aspect is the definition of "best execution". The definition is largely open at level two so we will see how this is resolved. It is certainly something on which we would be extremely keen to look at a solution but you are right to say that an inadequate spill over from investor protection to the wholesale market could damage the wholesale market potentially. However, we believe there might have been some confusion between two different dimensions of the Directive. One dimension is

Lord Shutt of Greetland *contd.*]

investor protection where a clear distinction should be made between the retail investors and the professional investors or wholesale investors. The other dimension is more the efficiency of the market itself in terms of, for example, price formation and in the debate around transparency, for example, very often there has been confusion between these two dimensions because transparency is required certainly for investor protection but some forms of transparency are also required in price formation. That is not related to the split between retail and wholesale; it is a different matter. We should look at these two dimensions separately and I think it is important to find solutions that could avoid having this perverse result that we altogether fear.

Chairman

470. On a rather different subject, one of the objectives of the FSAP obviously is greater competition, both to reduce the cost of capital to users of capital—borrowers—and hopefully to improve the choice or the net risk return to lenders—savers—which we would all agree are very good objectives. One of the implications of this objective, if it is applied rigorously, will be the demise of weaker and less efficient players in the market-place. Do you think for at least a few years ahead there will be political resistance amongst Member States when they realise the institutional impact on some of the weaker players of the introduction of the single market? Do you think there will be a tendency to try and protect financial service industries in Member States for a while? You have managed to cross borders and congratulations to you. Do you think there is a resistance in some areas?

(*M Lefebvre*) I think it is likely that there will be a resistance, for good and bad reasons. Bad reasons would be claiming a protectionist attitude. There might be some other reasons that we would have to look at to make sure that the integration of the market does not involve negative externalities in some countries. We were just explaining, for example, the model that Euronext has put in place in order to make sure that there is a highly integrated market. If you want to remove the cost of the national segmentation of the European market you have basically two solutions. The first one is to concentrate all the activity in one national jurisdiction. We believe that this, although it appears to be simple, is probably a difficult way and a costly way because you disrupt the economic value that exists in all the national markets. This is particularly important for small and medium-sized listed caps, if you move them around and it creates disruption and cost. That is not the model we are implementing. We believe that taking the benefit of electronic trading and virtually integrating markets and gaining synergies without disrupting these relations is the way to maximise the value of the integration. This is true from a trading point of view and this is also true in various other fields. I think in this national dimension we should clearly separate the plain protectionist attitude, which is certainly to try to avoid it, and the dimension of some true economic values that are there, and we have to take that into account and embody these dimensions into the solutions we create. So that is the answer.

(*M Théodore*) We would tend to think that the conditions of the move have to be studied and adapted, globally speaking. The world and Europe shows us that consolidation is the name of the game, so I am not sure if it is exactly your question but I do not think many people would think that we could stay in a competing environment, an opening up environment, going to a single European financial market at the stage we are now, which has obviously changed to what it was ten years ago, what it was in 1996 when the first Investment Services Directive was implemented. Everybody knows that consolidation is not only the name of the game but a necessity, and I think that we will see how best consolidation could be operated is by making the European financial market a strong and efficient one at the same time but taking out most of the wealth of diversity of players.

471. If you look ten years ahead—because many of these changes will take longer than the market-place might otherwise permit—what kinds of change in terms of consolidation (and I do not mean the individual institutions) do you foresee in the financial service industries? If we looked at the picture of the European financial service industries this year we could take a picture and look at it in ten years' time; how would they differ do you think broadly?

(*M Théodore*) Ten years is a very long period in our business!

472. I am happy to say four or five years but I do not know want to know when your next target is. Five years?

(*M Théodore*) I tend to believe that the landscape will be completely different in five or ten years' time, that we will see fewer players, that they will have consolidated, especially in our field—exchanges and trading related companies. For the time being we speak of trading but it would be the same for clearing, settlement, whatever. For the time being in trading even if we have seen some consultation Europe still has 15 exchanges, most of them being purely national ones, and I do not think in five or ten years' time we will see so many exchanges. We will see cross-border organisations. I would think that at the end there would be two or three groups but not more. Market players will probably also be playing on a wider European range or will be only niche players. On the reverse side, I would tend to believe that Eastern Europe, the new countries that are acceding to the European Union, will play a stronger part than they do for the time being because they will be developing faster and joining the others, so five to ten years' development will be important for them, especially the big ones. On the reverse side we would say that the story in five to ten years' time would be mainly a European one, consolidating into the European landscape. I believe we will not see the development of very strong trans-continental links, not with Asia for obvious reasons but not even trans-Atlantic links because we do not see the US as being ready for those. We believe the story to be happening in Europe. We have to consolidate in Europe before being able to speak on a par with the US.

(*M Lefebvre*) That is in the field of equity. In the field of derivatives it might be different.

Chairman *contd.*]

(*M Théodore*) In derivatives it is different in the economic field but in the political and regulatory field we still have a very heavy US barrier and when European players are competitive with American players, most of the European players, not only us, are more effective than the American ones, but every time there is a difference in competitiveness you find out that there is a some kind of American barrier to entering the American market. So for a European exchange, going for the American market is going for some kind of venture while building on the roots of European consolidation is a more immediate move, I would tend to say.

(*M Lefebvre*) If I may insist on that because that is certainly a concern we have conveyed regularly to the European Commission, this fact that we suffer from the protectionist attitude of the American authorities. There is a clear asymmetry in the fact that Europe is more open to the American markets than the other way around where we are not allowed, the LSE is not allowed the Deutsch Börse is not allowed to put trading screens in the United States. So it is not only frustrating for transaction costs on the European securities but it is also, as Jean François said, a big handicap given the fact that certainly the derivatives market but also the equity market in the US—and I am not mentioning the intermediaries but the operators—are lagging behind the European ones in terms of quality of governance and market model. It is a heavy European handicap that the Europeans should stress and stress and stress again even if we know that the position of US SEC would be hard to move.

Chairman: I am sure you would find a lot of support for that view too, certainly in the House of Lords.

Lord Shutt of Greetland

473. The London Stock Exchange regards the measures of the Prospectus Directive as unhelpful to the alternative investment market. SME companies are vital to Europe's future economic success. Are you happy about the approaches taken by the FSAP to the smaller and medium-sized enterprises? Are there any changes you would like to see to ensure that this important sector flourishes?

(*M Lefebvre*) First of all, we believe that having a very active small and medium sized market is very important and it is clearly part of our economic role in the future of this market. We have to be careful in the way that we differentiate at the moment between the blue chips and the small caps because it is a bit of a potential squabble. At the same time we have to be realistic and accept that some requirements are more difficult to be met by small caps than by big listed companies. On the other hand, creating two very different universes, especially at the risk of giving a passport to the big ones and avoiding giving a similar passport or a passport of a similar standard to the smaller ones, could be counter-productive because there is a natural tendency in the market to create a gap between the blue chips and the other parts of the market. We believe that we should be very, very careful in not enhancing that gap, not creating a barrier between the two because the reality is that

there is a continuum of companies between small caps and blue chips and this is a changing world so let's try to avoid as much as we can creating too many barriers between the two in market structure, in regulation and so on. So it is a very delicate matter and I know that the United Kingdom has taken a relatively strong stance on that. We think that is reasonable but be careful not to go too far because if you go too far in the differentiation between the two then you increase the gap between the two worlds and this could be counter-productive at the end of the day.

(*M Théodore*) I understood that in one of the Directives there was some tedious disposition which was important as a potential threat to the Alternative Investment Market, which is quite a successful compartment of similar jurisdictions, and we understand that this would be of some concern. As Olivier said, we consider that working for small and medium caps is a huge part of our business and is about a social responsibility, I should say, especially because it has not been so easy these last three years. The market has been for blue chips, not so many IPOs, and small and mid caps already listed are struggling to be inside and in favour of investment, so we have to support them. Then having some specific dispositions for small and med caps, as Olivier said, we thought that having this kind of thing, even if it is a positive discrimination at the beginning, would cause a backlash at the end.

Chairman

474. There has been some talk around Europe that a single security regulator might be desirable or might be inevitable. What is your view on the pros and cons of a EuroSEC?

(*M Théodore*) I will maybe start and then give the floor to Olivier and he will elaborate much more on the subject. Personally I would be divided on that issue. On one side we see that more and more we are speaking about Europe as a more united market and then through CESR and so on the Securities Commission has been working together, and you have the intellectual question of regulatory fragmentation, regulatory arbitrage, to which we are rather sensitive being a paneuropean exchange because regulatory fragmentation certainly leads to inefficiency. Then of course you are tempted to have a progress towards unifying regulation and the regulators. We have the example of the United States in which we have one regulator for the cash market and one for derivatives. But on the reverse there is a fear to have in that case too bureaucratic a structure which would prevent market forces from playing their role in the competing game. Even in a country like the United States—and we are speaking rather freely—you can see a tradition where the SEC plays a huge role in the American market in competition. The referee is a player in the game which is rather strange and our counterparts in the American agencies are spending a lot of their time, a sizable part of their time at least, in lobbying the SEC, which I tend to think is not exactly the best example of competition. Olivier might be more careful on this.

Chairman *contd.*]

(*M Lefebvre*) No, I think based on our own experiences – and as I said we are the first cross-border exchange so we do work with several regulators including the FSA in our daily life because are markets are cross-border and we base this co-operation on a memorandum of understanding – obviously in this respect we would be keen to see them working together even more, although we have to be realistic in Europe because it makes no sense to put the horse before the cart because creating from scratch a European SEC would probably be largely counter-productive. There is a process in the Lamfalussy Plan to have more and more co-operation between the national regulators on jurisprudence and on the way these rules are implemented – implementation and enforcement— so we believe that this market will indeed be a unified market not because there will be a new European institution but because the implementation of the rules and enforcement of the rules will be similar and more and more harmonised. So the way it should be done is probably by a step-by-step process where rather than merging together institutions we should have obligations on these institutions to deliver harmonisation of their behaviour in terms of implementation, which is probably more pragmatic as an approach. To some extent I do not want to take your example of creating a new one, but the limited experience we have with five regulators is it is very interesting in this respect because these regulators monitor law enforcement in a market which is organised by several of them where they have to work together. So it is a bottom-up approach, it is not a top-down approach. We have seen how far it can go and indeed we should go further and take action step-by-step rather than in an artificial top-down approach.

(*M Théodore*) I would like to emphasise on the bottom-up approach our experience has been one in which the economic infrastructure has a little bit modelled the regulatory environment. We have created something and then the regulators have adapted themselves to a new reality which was a merger of four exchanges and I think the fact they have been successful in doing so and have not prevented the development of the new company is proof of their capacity to adapt to new challenges.

Lord Shutt of Greetland

475. If this FSAP is a success there should be cheaper capital in Europe. That in its turn may bring non-European Union issuers into Europe. Do you think that is going to happen and, if it is, is this something that is going to be important to your concern?

(*M Théodore*) Yes, I think it should be the case. I think it could be important for the development of European financial markets, especially in London I would say, but not only in London, and I think that based on a stronger single European financial market, Europe could regain the role of being the centre of finance for the companies of emerging countries in the rest of the world from Asia to Latin America, which Europe had until 20 years ago and lost a little bit, mainly because of the New York Stock Exchange, so may be it is an opportunity, at least on our side, to build a single European market which could bring more to European financial centres, and especially to the London market.

Chairman

476. And clearly also global markets—I am sure you take the same view—we in the United Kingdom think it is very important in the development of the Single Market that we do not lose sight of the importance of the global market and our place in that global market in Europe. We have got a lot of strengths between us and that should be an opportunity, not a threat.

(*M Lefebvre*) That is an important point. If you will allow me to come back on your previous question on ISD, another important reason why we need a new ISD now is that it will strengthen the position of the Europeans in their negotiations vis-à-vis the Americans in this respect because if you want to have more open financial markets across the Atlantic it will be much easier if our operation is more harmonised than it is today. We do have a problem of credibility when we negotiate with the Americans because of the fragmentation so having the ISD, for example, is a significant contribution in this respect.

477. And of course accounting standards is a big issue for non-EU issuers. I am delighted to hear that you agree with that. It is an important issue.

(*M Lefebvre*) On international accounting standards we took the initiative, for example, to promote this among the Euronext companies, because it was a way also to effect a direct comparison between Dutch, French and Belgian companies and so on by pushing them and incentivising them to use international accounting standards, so we have created quality labels if they recourse to international accounting standards, for example, so we certainly promote that.

478. What is your view on quarterly reporting?

(*M Théodore*) In this quality segment we have created for mid caps and for those wanting voluntarily to do that we have created a specific marketing segmentation for those going into IA standards and for those there are quarterly reports, so it is the same. Our own thinking speaking to investors would be to be in favour of quarterly reports because we think that six months is a long time for companies and especially for the mid ones. Six months without giving news to the market is rather a long time since the markets internally are looking at the risk of them going out of business and getting out of touch in six months. As a listed company we are in a sense practising IA standards on quarterly reports. We are a big exchange by market cap. but we have only 1,800 people in our company— 600 in London so that is a big centre, 500 in Paris, and 400 in Amsterdam—so it is a huge task especially when you are cross-border to do quarterly reports, but it is rewarding. That being said, I must say that when we speak to listed companies and to the global environment we are maybe ahead of their thinking and the trends of the time.

Chairman *contd.*]

479. Not in line with their thinking, I think.

(*M Théodore*) They would be a little bit afraid of quarterly reporting and even condemn quarterly reporting as being a source of volatility and short-termism and even an accounting mistake because people want to comply on the quarterly reporting what they have promised the market. That being said, being able to speak on a regular basis is quite an advantage if you are not giving a forecast for each quarter by half a pound or half a euro.

Lord Shutt of Greetland

480. Is it not like taking the temperature every morning? If you are doing it every quarter have you got enough time to run a business if you are constantly having to count up the beans every quarter and to give reports and put on press releases and all this sort of stuff that people do?

(*M Théodore*) That is the debate but at the same time you have necessarily when you are running a company a monthly vision of your company. In our case, which might be a specific one, we are publishing our market daily. Everyone can see on a daily basis or if they want, on a monthly basis what the market activity is so the income part of our P&L is rather easy to guess and then we would prefer that people would not be misthinking or guessing wrong on the expenses part. So normally you could say that it is like normal breathing. That being said, it may depend on the company and it has to be accepted by the financial world and investors that you do not make big moves and over-react on the quarterly report.

Chairman

481. In practice the issues of corporate governance have been much more problematical for the markets than where the companies have been reporting every three months or every six months. You can have all the reports in the world—you can have them weekly—but if the corporate governance is wrong it causes problems there. I would have thought, going back to the retail view and consumer protection, if I were the elderly lady with my savings in securities and the stock exchange I would want to be assured about corporate governance before I called for quarterly reporting, I have to tell you, and there is a place where Europe can take a lead as well as overstate. Could I ask one last question. It is a very short answer, I suspect the answer is yes or no. Are there any signs at all of non-EU companies listed in our markets considering delisting from Europe?

(*M Théodore*) No, I do not think so.

(*M Lefebvre*) What we observe is that some non-European companies are rationalising their listing arrangements because many of the listings do not generate any significant volume so it is a sort of cleaning up, but beyond that I do not think that there is any trend.

(*M Théodore*) In the 1980s you had some marketing listings, so for instance it was very common for Japanese companies to be established in every single important European market because it was important for marketing reasons to have a name in France and Spain and so on, and this has been rationalised, but it had never a decisive trading activity. I do not remember anybody delisting from Europe for an economic reason or because they found the European financial market unsatisfactory. Most probably we have lost listings that went into the New York Stock Exchange in the last years because Europe was not able to offer a sufficiently strong and deep market. What we can see these days is that we probably have an opportunity, with the American market being a little bit questionable and even some EU companies considering delisting from the US exchange for different reasons.

482. Thank you, Mr President. You have been outstandingly helpful to us and informative and at all times positive and I do appreciate it. Could I on behalf of my delegation thank you all for your kind reception and cup of tea, which is a first in Paris!

(*M Lefebvre*) Can you give us a rating on that?

(*M Théodore*) It has to be improved. The hot water and tea is most important.

Chairman: Thank you very much indeed.

Examination of Witness

SENATOR M PHILIPPE MARINI, General Rapporteur, Finance Committee, the French Senate, examined.

Chairman

483. Thank you for seeing us.

(*M Marini*) Chairman, ladies and gentlemen, it certainly is a pleasure, in fact I am very flattered to welcome you here in this meeting room of the Finance Committee of the French Senate. This is the regular meeting room of the Finance Committee of the Senate. Perhaps I could start very quickly with just a few words about how we are organised. The Finance Committee is one of the six permanent committees of the Senate and it has responsibility in particular for the budget, for budgetary policy, and for all financial legislation. We of course have a chairperson, namely Mr Jean Arthuis, a former Minister of Economics and Finance of the Republic. Personally I am the Committee's General Rapporteur which I think is a typically French institution, I do not think that exists in parliamentary practice anywhere else. The general rapporteur is entrusted with co-ordinating the work done by the individual rapporteurs who are members of the committee and who are responsible for monitoring the budget of a given part of the administration. I am also responsible for drafting positions of the committee, to then get them approved by the committee and then to present them in plenary sessions of the Senate. That is done systematically for all financial legislation and for budgetary policy but

Chairman *contd.*]

that can also be the case for the examination of individual draft bills, draft laws. For example, this year I was responsible for drafting an opinion on the Financial Security draft law. In 2001 new economic regulations were also covered by a draft on which I wrote an opinion and in 1996 there was a law on the modernisation of economic activity which was nothing but a transposition into domestic law of the first Investment Services Directive. So I believe that, Chairman, gives you a sense of what we do and what I do personally. I have seen that you have a long list of detailed and technical questions. I will try to answer them to the extent I can. If I cannot in fact come up with reasonable and sensible answers on the spot I could perhaps then transmit my answers in writing subsequently.

484. Senator, you are too modest, your reputation tells me that you are more than able to answer our questions. Could I first of all thank you very warmly for welcoming us here this afternoon. Our Committee has been looking at the development of the Financial Services Action Plan. We are most supportive of the move to a Single Market in financial services. We are very supportive of the Lamfalussy Process. In the nature of any inquiry we are concentrating on areas where there may be questions or problems but that does not in any way diminish our support for the objectives. We have, as always, not enough time to discuss all of the issues so we are going to just cover six areas, if we may. Lord Shutt is a colleague on the Committee. I am a member of the Government side on the Committee and I chair the Committee and Lord Shutt is a Liberal Democrat in the House of Lords. A great deal has been achieved in the Financial Service Action Plan. Most Directives have been dealt with but there remain just a few and those few are of course the more difficult few which is why they are still left. Initially it was hoped that everything would be resolved by next year. In your view do you think all of the key Directives will be completed by next year?

A. Well, I have not in fact had any recent information updates from the Commission because it has been several months now since I last went to Brussels. I of course was informed of the progress achieved by the ECOFIN Council last week on the very important issue, in my view, of the internalism of market orders. This is of course a co-decision domain and experience shows that the to-ing and fro-ing between the Commission and the Parliament can take quite some time, but I do hope, given the high expectations of the markets and of the professionals, that the process will not in fact be too long. As you know, there are two subjects in particular about which a lot of ink was spilled in France: These are subjects of a very structural nature, shall I say – the internalisation of stock exchange orders which I have already mentioned, and secondly as a contextual issue of substantial importance the integration of IAS accounting standards, with all of the consequences for the accounting of banks and insurance companies that would result from that. Of course, we are also very interested in the text on information transparency and we very much hope that this financial services package will make it

possible, for instance, to deal with certain subjects dear to our hearts on a European-wide scale such as, for instance, an appropriate framework for financial analysts. But I am sure you could tell me a lot about the process that is underway because you are involved in an investigation or an inquiry that is much more precise than anything that I have done on these issues in recent weeks.

Chairman: We certainly are aware of the current state of developments. You will not be surprised if I told you that the position that has developed on the ISD in the last few days is one that causes us some concern but that is not a matter for us to discuss today. I think one of our concerns more broadly is that there are some difficult issues still to resolve and time is short and we would hope that decisions will still be taken with care, with full consultation and to ensure that the quality of the proposals remains high and that in order to meet a deadline decisions are not taken more hastily than they would have been in earlier times. I hope that in France there is some agreement too that the quality of legislation is often as important as the time it takes. It is probably important to get the quality right. Lord Shutt, do you want to go on from there?

Lord Shutt of Greetland

485. Yes, there is a view that the investor (or the consumer protection lobby) in Europe has had too much influence in the development of the Financial Services Action Plan. Examples include the inflexible approach of the Prospectus Directive on equity markets which applies a one-size-fits-all to the detriment of the junior markets such as the Alternative Investment Market which have enjoyed a more flexible regulatory approach. The current debate from the ISD is over whether to ban "execution only" trading. Do you accept that there has got to be a balance between over-protection of retail investors on the one hand and allowing markets to operate flexibly on the other? Have the present proposals got things right or are they going to damage wholesale markets as some people, particularly in the UK, believe?

A. Well, I do not have the last version of the text to hand, I have not even studied it carefully so I will try to answer but in terms of principle rather than detail. I think that our national legislatures will more and more have to take into consideration the very differing nature of players in the market. On the one hand you have the retail investors, the individual shareholders you are talking about and on the other hand the professional or highly qualified investors who know more what they are doing. Under the Financial Securities Bill in France that I referred to earlier we have set out that difference, we have made the distinction, which is something relatively new in French legislation which up until now tended to treat all investors on an equal footing. Many financial products have seen the light of day over the last few years and they are designed precisely for professional investors for wholesale investment markets. And as a corollary to that we believe that individual shareholders should be given the opportunity or the

Lord Shutt of Greetland *contd.*]

possibility of associating themselves to defend their rights. We are not in favour of the inclusion in the French legal system of mechanisms like the American class action, no, but in that recent Bill we did make available certain means of action, certain means of publicity, of dissemination of information, a common means of defence, which go much further for associations of individual shareholders in order to make it possible for them to defend the collective interests of their members, whereas before that under French law such action was very difficult to carry out. The principle previously was that each individual must defend his own individual interests. So insofar as that distinction to be made between retail and wholesale investors is concerned we are very conscious of that. We have, for instance, redefined the status of financial so-called *démarchage*, which is advertising if you will. It is a specific form of organisation that guarantees individual and non-professional investors and shareholders to give them a protective framework, it is something that they can use to defend themselves. This system of so-called *démarchage,* in our jargon, takes into consideration the fact that there is a disproportionality between the knowledge and information means available to the individual consumer, who is in the contract between him and the share giver the weaker party vis-à-vis the financial network that sells him some financial product or financial operation. On the other hand, we have accepted some amendments in our legislation that make it possible to develop securitisation markets which require some legal innovations compared to the previous legal situation in France, but I think that these are examples that show quite clearly that to an increasing extent we do take segmentation of the investment market into consideration and the fact that there are different levels of product sophistication with, for instance, this explosive growth in credit derivatives. And so in the round we accepted that collective investment organisations should be able to underwrite credit risk, which is something that was already being done in practice for some time before that but it had not been enshrined in law and we did that just recently. In summary, on the one hand you have those segments of the market where the only players who can reasonably act are professional investors anyway and then, on the other hand, you have individual shareholders and consumers of financial products who are needed for good balance on markets but who quite evidently are no longer in a position to be involved in all the different types of transactions that are offered on an individual basis. I think the new European texts may well drive us to mark that distinction even further but in any event that evolution or that change in trend is something that will already have been prepared by us in our most recent bills.

486. So you are saying that in France there is a clear distinction that people understand between where it is *caveat emptor* and where there is investment protection?

A. Absolutely, absolutely. In fact, in the work that we did on this we were quite heavily inspired by British legislation insofar as the organisation of financial investment consultants was concerned, the

various rules that need to be followed, the extent to which a commercial offer has to be explained and the details given before a consumer can accept it, the requirement to provide the consumer with certain types of information, to make offers that are in line with what that consumer really needs, taking into consideration, for instance, the size of his assets. Those are principles and practices that we have tried to strengthen taking advantage of your experience and being inspired by what you have done as we have understood it.

Chairman

487. Senator, you have played a major part in important changes in the framework for regulating and supervising the financial markets in France. The Financial Services Action Plan itself is reaching the point now where implementation and enforcement issues become important. Are you clear on how implementation and enforcement of the Directives and the detailed procedures will be followed through?

A. Well of course once these European texts have had their Is dotted and Ts crossed and once the Directives enter into force, they will have to be transposed rapidly into national legislation. I myself in the financial area have always fought hard to make sure that these transpositions do not take forever and a day because I believe that such waiting periods are very destructive for markets. So we of course have absolutely no problem of principle whatsoever insofar as these future Directives are concerned. No doubt there are a number of points still to be identified on which agreement will have to be reached at the EU level. For my part, I do not see any problems of principle that would result in the French legislature having substantial reservations about the continuation of this process. Let me specify that in our constitution we do have the possibility of voting in resolutions. When a European text is on the verge of being submitted to the Council, the text is then given to us and we of course have only a short period of time but in that period of time we can, in fact, formulate recommendations to the government, either to warn the government or to support its negotiating position. For instance, on a number of occasions the Senate has already adopted the resolutions, as we call them, about the Directive on Public Procurement and Calls for Tenders. We would like that Directive to see the light of day finally because the implementation of those provisions that would make it possible to integrate financial markets in that respect must be based increasingly on bringing stock exchange rules closer together. Insofar as this seems to be a reference to takeovers, that comes under the Takeover Directive. Insofar as transparency is concerned and the control thresholds and the understanding of the concepts of control and of "concert", of course our different markets have their own traditions, their history and culture in all of these respects but we are firmly convinced that if we do not manage to set out the clear, long-term objectives of bringing these various different national institutions we have closer together and of achieving convergence, if we do not manage to do that then we

Chairman *contd.*]

will be depriving Europe of the advantages of high volume and liquidity that should in principle be available to us, and why not?

Lord Shutt of Greetland

488. There seems to have been a swing amongst some market participants away from the concept of maximum market harmonisation towards greater flexibility at the national level. After the process of peer review by these national regulators, this might turn out to be a false choice as the essence of level three is to bring detailed rules into close harmonisation, at least in their impact even if that is not the way it is written in legal form. Do you agree that this national flexibility may turn out to be an illusion?

A. No, I do not think so. I believe that the subsidiarity of nations is a principle that has a very important role but it seems to me that on the main concepts insofar as characteristics of operations are concerned the main market rules, the major market rules, when it comes to, how shall I put it, the terms and conditions of the exercise of the profession—the main professional ethics rules, if you will, for people involved in finance—it seems to me that on all these things we really ought gradually to come to a common core of accepted concepts. And I said progressively, gradually. Insofar as the actual exercise or implementation of regulation is concerned, I would not believe it to be possible or even desirable to set up a sort of supra-regulator, a European monster regulator. I believe that the reciprocal agreements that allow for the free flow of information amongst national regulators and to make sure that common rules are being followed, at least in broad terms, can remain or can continue to be a satisfactory solution probably for a very long period of time. However, let me take the example of the architecture of regulations, it seems to me that our different European states need to bring under one single responsibility or authority prudential control and control of professional ethics, the control of operations and of the professionals involved in them. Personally, and this is my own personal opinion, I am more in favour of the FSA model than in favour of the French model where you have the stock exchange, banking and insurance regulators still separate. I believe that these regulatory approaches need to be integrated, they need to be brought together. So I would like to see everyone adjusting their laws and moving in the direction of convergence especially since it is necessary that the main rules underpinning the markets be the same from one territory to another in order that Europe be an area of financial security easily identifiable as such by outside investors. Gradually we must come to represent or to offer similar options or choices, in other words that we get the same sort of balance in our approaches—and I am talking about the balance between effectiveness and efficiency and total transparency, or somewhere in between. I think it would be very difficult to envisage on these really structural and crucial issues that there continue for a long time to be substantial differences among our markets. So to sum up my answer to your question,

I would say that the role of national regulators will continue to be important in order in particular for the definition of the professional status of the individuals involved, but to my mind none of that is incompatible with the adoption of common principles and with genuine convergence. Well perhaps you do not agree with what I am saying. If that is the case it would be well that you say so. Please tell me if on certain points that I have made you have differing views or opinions. We do not have many opportunities to exchange our ideas on this subject.

Lord Shutt of Greetland: We have been listening to people today who are part of a federation of regulators and most of their discussion has been about how they can agree about the same form of regulation in the different national states and we were wondering in which areas there would still be a national differentiation.

Chairman

489. But I think the way that you expressed it is a view with which we would have a great deal of sympathy. In fact, with great political skill you have answered the next two questions that we were going to ask you on my list! We were going to ask you your view on a single regulator within a country, because we have today been discussing these matters with the Banque de France and with others and noted the more fragmented approach, and I was also going to ask you your views on a single regulator for the whole of the EU, a EuroSEC? As I say, with great prescience you have managed to answer both without me asking the question. What is my next question? Do you know?

A. Well, I think that I did in fact answer those questions, at least in broad terms. In the period 1993-95, about ten years ago, there was a lot of talk about the architecture of financial regulation that time the French authorities and those responsible in the professional associations and organisations in the world of finance were convinced that it was necessary to keep a regulator responsible for operations, for transactions, that is our Conseil des Marchés Financiers (the Financial Markets Council) and the regulator responsible for verifying that appropriate information is divulged to the public, that is the Commission des Opérations de Bourse (the Stock Exchange Operations Commission). They were separate. They were convinced that it was a good idea at the time but I myself suggested that we get rid of one of them and put them together and merge them. It seems that the idea was not ripe then because it was not done until 2003 and as of today the French central bank, the Banque de France, which is very close to the banking regulator, the Commission des Bancaire, considers that it is a good thing to continue to separate out the prudential control of banks as done by the Commission des Bancaire and to separate that out from the verification of information provision and professional ethics and so on which is in the hands of the new AMF, the Autorité des Marchés Financiers. I believe personally that we could speed things up even more and put all of these control and regulatory functions together in one body. That is my personal opinion and I think that it

Chairman *contd.*]

will end up being done in a few years from now because in fact when you look carefully at the transmission of credit risk, the credit derivatives markets, which takes certain categories of assets and circulates them, often across the Atlantic from one side to the other, from banks to insurance companies and from banks and insurance companies into market instruments picked up by investors, and if you look at all of this and you look at how omni-directional the transmission has become, it is clear the regulation must be total and complete, but at the same time I do not believe that it is appropriate to think today in terms of an overall EU regulator because it would become a super-bureaucracy, a monstrous bureaucracy.

490. With great regret we have to finish because we must go but there are three things. First of all, thank you so much. Secondly, I agree with you full-heartedly on your last two points and it has, as we say, whetted my appetite to return and talk further with you. I will fairly soon, if I may, come back personally and talk further with you because, as I did say to you, your reputation goes before you and you have much to tell me and it is of interest.

A. Well, that feeling is certainly reciprocated, Chairman, and I would of course be delighted to be able to continue this conversation with you on another occasion. For those questions that were sent to me I would be prepared to send you written answers.

491. Yes please.

A. And what would be your deadline for them to be useful for you?

492. Two or three weeks.

A. I will note down three weeks and, Chairman, I will send you a written contribution with more precise and detailed answers to your written questions.

Chairman: I do apologise that we have to go. You have been generous with your time and thoughtful and helpful in your advice to us. Thank you very much.

Supplementary evidence from Senator Philippe Marini Paris, Rapporteur General, aux Questions Relatives a la Mise en Œuvre du Plan d'Action Pour les Services Financiers, French Senate.

I—Le Plan D'Action Pour Les Services Financiers

1—*Quels ont été les progrès réalisés à ce jour ? Quel a été l'impact sur le secteur des services financiers en Grande-Bretagne et en Europe ?*

Il convient en premier lieu de rappeler le contexte de mise en œuvre du PASF. Le marché des services financiers s'inscrit dans le champ plus vaste du marché intérieur, dont l'unification constitue un des objectifs principaux de l'Union, et a connu d'importants bouleversements au cours des vingt dernières années, que l'on a coutume de résumer en France par les trois termes **désintermédiation, déréglementation et marchéisation**. Ce nouveau contexte s'est révélé propice à **l'innovation financière**, par anticipation ou par alignement concurrentiel sur les pratiques étrangères : nouveaux compartiments de marché, nouveaux instruments et nouvelles techniques d'utilisation de produits existants, nouvelles stratégies de gestion d'actifs, nouveaux indices boursiers et outils de mesure des risques . . . Toutes ces innovations ont contribué à la structuration, par la concomitance d'une expansion et d'une resegmentation, d'une **véritable industrie financière**, avec ses centres de recherche, ses≫ usines≫, ses ingénieurs, ses gammes de produits, son marketing, son service après-vente . . . L'innovation entretient des rapports ambigus avec la stabilité et la sécurité financières, qu'elle contribue à la fois à renforcer et à menacer, et **appelle dès lors la constitution d'un environnement réglementaire susceptible d'en limiter les risques et propice à l'amélioration de la compétitivité des acteurs européens**.

L'Union européenne a tenu compte de ces évolutions et de l'industrialisation du secteur financier et a mis en oeuvre plusieurs textes importants, en particulier les premières directives OPCVM en 1985 et 1988 et la directive sur les services d'investissement en 1993. Le mouvement était cependant loin d'être achevé, **aussi la Commission a-t-elle adopté le 11 mai 1999 un plan d'action** contenant une série d'objectifs politiques et de mesures spécifiques qui visaient à perfectionner le marché unique des services financiers d'ici 2005. Ce plan d'action propose des priorités indicatives et un calendrier de mesures, notamment législatives, devant permettre d'atteindre **trois objectifs stratégiques** : instaurer un marché unique des services financiers de gros, faire en sorte que les marchés de détail soient accessibles et sûrs, moderniser les règles prudentielles et de surveillance. Le plan d'action préconise également l'adoption par le Conseil de ministres et le Parlement européen, avant fin 1999, des propositions de directives sur les organismes de placement collectif, la vente à distance de services financiers et la monnaie électronique. Le plan s'appuie sur le cadre d'action rendu public par la Commission en octobre 1998 et sur les délibérations du groupe de politique des services financiers, formé de représentants des ministres des finances, qui se sont réunis de janvier à mars 1999 sous la présidence du commissaire chargé des services financiers, M. Mario Monti.

Parmi les objectifs et propositions du PASF, on peut ainsi mentionner :

— **s'agissant des services financiers de gros** : la suppression des obstacles qui empêchent encore de lever des capitaux à l'échelle de l'Union (actualisation de la directive prospectus) ; la mise en place d'un cadre juridique commun pour des marchés intégrés des valeurs mobilières et d'instruments dérivés (directive sur les services d'investissement, directive sur les manipulations du marché) ; l'évolution vers l'élaboration d'un corpus unique de règles d'information financière pour les sociétés cotées en bourse ; l'instauration de la sécurité juridique nécessaire pour soutenir les opérations transfrontalières sur titres ; la création d'un environnement sûr et transparent pour les restructurations transfrontalières (statut de la société européenne, directive concernant les offres publiques d'acquisition . . .) ; l'établissement d'un cadre solide permettant aux gestionnaires d'actifs d'optimiser les performances de leurs portefeuilles dans l'intérêt des détenteurs de fonds ;

— **concernant l'accessibilité des marchés de détail** : l'amélioration de l'information, de la transparence et de la sécurité dans le domaine de la fourniture transfrontalière de services financiers de détail (directive concernant la vente à distance des services financiers, directive sur les intermédiaires d'assurance, plan d'action sur la prévention de la contrefaçon et de la fraude dans les systèmes de paiement) ; la promotion d'un règlement rapide des litiges de consommation à travers des procédures extrajudiciaires efficaces ; la garantie d'une application équilibrée des règles locales de protection des consommateurs ;

— **au titre de la stabilité des marchés financiers de l'Union** : l'alignement de la législation prudentielle des secteurs bancaire, de l'assurance et des valeurs mobilières sur les normes de qualité les plus exigeantes, en tenant compte des travaux réalisés par le Comité de Bâle et le FESCO (directives concernant l'assainissement et la liquidation des banques et des entreprises d'assurance, ainsi que la monnaie électronique ; modification de la directive sur le blanchiment des capitaux, propositions de modification du cadre réglementaire applicable aux fonds propres des banques et des entreprises d'investissement, modification des marges de solvabilité des compagnies d'assurance) ; des travaux sur la surveillance prudentielle des conglomérats financiers ; et des initiatives visant à améliorer le dialogue et la coopération intersectoriels entre autorités sur les questions d'intérêt commun (création d'un comité consultatif sur les valeurs mobilières).

La Commission proposait également de **poursuivre le processus parallèle de coordination fiscale et d'élimination des distorsions de nature fiscale** : directive visant à garantir un minimum d'imposition effective des revenus de l'épargne transfrontalière, application du code de conduite de décembre 1997 sur la fiscalité des entreprises, directive sur la coordination des régimes fiscaux applicables aux retraites complémentaires et aux fonds de pension.

Sur les 42 mesures initialement proposées, 34 ont été finalisées après avoir connu une accélération manifeste en 2002, ce qui témoigne d'un remarquable effort des acteurs de marché et des autorités nationales. Parmi les principales directives adoptées, il convient ainsi de relever les deux directives OPCVM du 21 janvier 2002, la directive du 23 septembre 2002 concernant la commercialisation à distance des services financiers, la directive du 30 septembre 2002 sur les intermédiaires d'assurance, la directive sur les conglomérats financiers adoptée le 20 novembre 2002, la directive du 3 décembre 2002 relative aux opérations d'initié et aux abus de marché, ou la directive prospectus adoptée le 15 juillet 2003. Ces textes constituent des avancées décisives en matière d'accessibilité et de sécurisation des marchés, et permettent en outre aux opérateurs de réduire certains coûts.

La mise en œuvre du PASF a vu sa pertinence croître avec la crise qu'ont connue les marchés financiers entre fin 2000 et début 2003. Le marché des actions fortement baissier a induit une certaine défiance des investisseurs et des doutes au sein des émetteurs, de telle sorte que la rénovation du cadre juridique et l'unification du marché des services financiers, facteur de mutualisation des risques, devenaient une réelle priorité. La dynamique n'est pas encore achevée, et la Commission a indiqué, dans son huitième et dernier rapport intermédiaire sur le PASF publié début juin, qu'il était crucial d'achever la traduction législative du PASF d'ici le changement de législature, **c'est-à-dire avant avril 2004**, ainsi qu'en ont décidé les chefs d'Etat ou de gouvernement lors du Conseil européen de Bruxelles des 20 et 21 mars 2003. Il restera ensuite dix-huit mois aux Etats membres pour mettre en œuvre les dispositions correspondantes.

Néanmoins, on constate que les propositions législatives qui n'ont pas encore été adoptées (cf. question 2) ne sont pas les moins importantes, loin s'en faut ; il est donc nécessaire qu'elles fassent l'objet d'un examen précis et de négociations exhaustives, afin d'arriver à des compromis satisfaisants, et que la qualité du travail ne soit pas sacrifiée du fait de délais très exigeants. Entre l'opportunité politique, qui fait craindre à la Commission que le report de certains textes après les élections européennes ne soit synonyme de retrait *de facto*, et les exigences techniques, qui imposent de prendre le temps nécessaire au compromis, je crois qu'il est possible de trouver une voie médiane : certaines propositions de directives, en particulier la nouvelle directive sur les services d'investissement (DSI) ou celle relative aux offres publiques d'acquisition, ont franchi des étapes décisives de négociation et devraient pouvoir être adoptées dans les prochains mois sans que les parties intéressées aient le sentiment d'avoir ≫ le couteau sous la gorge ≫. **En revanche les textes plus problématiques doivent poursuivre leur cheminement institutionnel avec l'espoir de respecter le délai mais sans que ce dernier ne devienne absolument impératif**. Dans le cas où certains de ces textes ne seraient pas adoptés avant avril 2004, il est probable que de nouvelles discussions enregistreraient un certain retard avec la nouvelle législature, mais il n'est pas évident que ces textes soient pour autant enterrés. **Je considère en effet qu'un report demeure préférable à l'adoption d'un mauvais texte**, résultat d'un compromis bancal alors que l'objectif est bien de parvenir à une harmonisation concertée et consentie. En outre, la multiplication des échéances majeures d'ici avril prochain (Conférence inter-gouvernementale et ultimes préparatifs de l'élargissement) incite à hiérarchiser les priorités et ne pas trop démultiplier des efforts qui seraient contre-productifs.

En ce qui concerne l'impact du PASF sur le secteur des services financiers, il paraît difficile aujourd'hui de l'évaluer précisément, tant sur le plan macro que micro-économique, après seulement trois années de législation communautaire d'intensité croissante. **Un certain nombre d'acquis législatifs du PASF ont néanmoins eu une incidence concrète sur le fonctionnement des services financiers** : absence de frais pour les paiements par carte bancaire et virements transfrontaliers, nouvelles gammes d'OPCVM coordonnés . . . **Les conséquences sur les législations nationales sont en outre immédiates** : en France, la loi de sécurité financière du 1er août 2003 a ainsi été l'occasion de procéder à la transposition de mesures décidées dans le cadre du PASF, concernant en particulier les OPCVM et la vente de services à distance.

Sur le plan économique, il est très vraisemblable que la réalisation du PASF sera un facteur notable de croissance, ne serait-ce que parce qu'il réduira les asymétries informationnelles, les coûts de transaction (notamment sur les marchés d'actions et d'obligations, qui devraient enregistrer une croissance des volumes échangés) **et de couverture du risque juridique, et lèvera certaines incertitudes**—facteur inhibant de la prise de risque et de la confiance, donc de la croissance—tenant aux différences entre les droits nationaux. Ces avantages sont difficiles à chiffrer, mais **la Commission en a néanmoins présenté une évaluation dans son septième rapport intermédiaire du 7 décembre 2002** :

— un marché unique des valeurs mobilières et un meilleur accès au marché pourraient entraîner une hausse de 1,1 % du PIB de l'UE au cours de la prochaine décennie ;

— un mécanisme unique de compensation et de règlement pourrait entraîner une réduction supplémentaire des coûts de 42 à 52 % ;

— la poursuite de l'intégration des marchés financiers de détail pourrait entraîner des gains potentiels en termes de taux d'intérêt de 0,7 % du PIB de l'UE ;

— les virements transfrontaliers seront restés beaucoup plus onéreux pour les consommateurs que les virements nationaux jusqu'en 2003. Le fait de ramener les coûts de ces virements à leur niveau le plus ≫ performant ≫ permettrait de réaliser des économies d'au moins 41 % ;

— les niveaux d'efficience des banques européennes se sont légèrement détériorés. Si elle est importante, une perte d'efficience se traduit par un surcoût du capital. L'élimination des inefficiences qui grèvent actuellement le secteur bancaire pourrait se solder par des gains de 1,4-1,6 % du PIB.

Le PASF constitue donc aujourd'hui davantage une promesse de croissance, dont on peut éventuellement contester le chiffrage, mais il est indéniable qu'il exercera un impact majeur non seulement sur les opérations et la gestion quotidienne des établissements bancaires et financiers, mais encore sur les opportunités stratégiques des acteurs (cf. question 7). J'estime également que l'intégration financière, en renforçant les avantages comparatifs de l'Europe, permettra une **expansion de l'emploi qualifié** dans un secteur qui n'est pas encore soumis à un vaste mouvement de délocalisations vers les pays émergents et dans lequel les entreprises européennes ont démontré un véritable savoir-faire. Enfin, un autre avantage, et non des moindres, pourrait résider dans une **meilleure absorption de la volatilité boursière**, dont on sait qu'elle s'est considérablement accrue au cours des quatre dernières années, pour des raisons à la fois techniques (impact des ventes à découvert et des arbitrages des *hedge funds*, programme de rachats d'actions . . .) que structurelles (emprise des fonds d'investissement sur la capitalisation boursière, incertitudes des intervenants sur les méthodes pertinentes d'évaluation des sociétés, prégnance du court-terme, difficulté d'agréger une information financière devenue omniprésente . . .).

L'analyse de l'impact du PASF sera tributaire de l'évaluation du degré d'intégration des marchés européens de capitaux, que la Commission a récemment initiée en constituant quatre nouveaux groupes d'experts spécialisés dans les secteurs de la banque, de l'assurance, de la gestion de patrimoine et de l'intermédiation en investissement. Une liste des barrières à l'intégration (juridiques, structurelles, réglementaires, fiscales . . .) sera *in fine* établie par ordre décroissant de priorité, et des mesures correctives seront proposées. **Je serai particulièrement attentif aux résultats de cette évaluation**.

2—Quelles sont les principales questions en suspens ?

Les huit mesures du PASF dont les propositions de directive font toujours l'objet de discussions ou qui n'ont pas encore donné lieu à une proposition de directive sont les suivantes : les offres publiques d'acquisition (OPA), la proposition de directive relative à la transparence et à l'information financière, la DSI, le projet de troisième directive sur le blanchiment des capitaux, la contrôle de la réassurance, la future directive sur le nouveau régime des fonds propres applicable aux banques et aux entreprises d'investissement (qui pourrait faire l'objet d'une proposition de directive début 2004, mais dont l'entrée en vigueur ne sera pas effective avant 2006), les propositions relatives à la solvabilité dans le secteur de l'assurance, et un cadre juridique européen applicable aux paiements effectués dans le marché intérieur. Ces sujets font émerger des difficultés plus ou moins grandes et font se confronter des points de vue dont les contours sont variables : on tend ainsi à opposer la vision anglo-saxonne de celle continentale s'agissant des services financiers et plus spécifiquement de l'internalisation des ordres, et la position de l'Allemagne est mise en exergue dans les négociations sur la directive OPA, dont elle a contribué à faire échouer plusieurs projets. Je souhaite me concentrer sur trois sujets en particulier :

Le projet de directive sur les OPA constitue un sujet sensible car il comporte une dimension plus nationale que les autres. Les OPA amicales ou hostiles menées par des entreprises étrangères sont souvent perçues par les observateurs de l'Etat de la société cible sinon comme une agression économique, du moins comme une défaite (cf. Manesmann/Vodaphone ou plus récemment Péchiney/Alcan). La psychologie et la sensibilité citoyenne des acteurs sont donc mobilisées—ce que l'on peut regretter—alors même que les OPA peuvent contribuer à sauver une entreprise nationale et se font également dans l'autre sens. En outre, le régime des OPA comporte de nombreux liens avec des dispositions fiscales et de droit des sociétés parfois fort anciennes, dans lesquelles une forme de ≫ tradition nationale ≫, ou du moins de spécificité, peut s'être progressivement constituée, comme en témoignent les droits de vote multiples et les divers mécanismes anti-OPA. Il est donc difficile de conclure un projet équilibré et de préserver tous les intérêts en présence. **Je crois cependant que l'équité et la libre-circulation des capitaux doivent prévaloir. Sur mon initiative, notre commission des finances avait à ce titre adopté une résolution en 1999, et nous avons adopté une autre résolution en février 2003**, qui avait été proposée par la délégation du Sénat pour l'Union européenne. Cette résolution formulait notamment quatre demandes à l'attention du gouvernement français :

— ≪ *promouvoir un seuil maximum de 50 % des droits de vote pour le déclenchement d'une procédure d'offre obligatoire au sens de la présente proposition de directive ;*

— ≪ *réclamer un encadrement des dérogations pouvant être apportées par les autorités de contrôle à la définition du ≪ prix équitable ≫ proposé par l'offrant aux actionnaires minoritaires ;*

— ≪ *veiller à ce que le respect des pactes d'actionnaires soit garanti jusqu'à la fin de l'offre publique d'acquisition ;*

— ≪ *s'opposer à ce que soient le cas échéant remis en cause, au cours de la négociation de la proposition de directive, les titres à droits de votes multiples.* ≫

Les négociations sur cette directive n'ont pas encore abouti et se révèlent difficiles. **Dans ce contexte, il ne me paraîtrait pas déraisonnable que la directive soit recentrée sur une version** *a minima*, qui tendrait à assurer la meilleure protection possible des actionnaires minoritaires—laquelle a déjà été améliorée dans plusieurs Etats membres par des mesures d'inspiration libérale—sans remettre en cause les éléments les plus importants des législations nationales. Si ce thème ne se révélait effectivement pas encore suffisamment mûr dans les esprits pour donner lieu à une réelle harmonisation, il conviendrait alors de reporter les ambitions initiales de la Commission.

La directive sur les services d'investissement a enregistré de grands progrès au cours des derniers mois, alors que les positions semblaient très antagonistes il y a moins d'un an. La France et la Grande-Bretagne se sont mutuellement accusées de faire pression pour infléchir la proposition de la Commission en fonction des intérêts de leurs établissements financiers. Le fait est que le fonctionnement des marchés repose de part et d'autre sur des principes différents : une préférence continentale pour les marchés régis par la centralisation des ordres, et la logique anglo-saxonne des marchés régis par les prix. Dès lors les principales évolutions apportées par la nouvelle DSI—abandon du principe de concentration au sein de marchés réglementés et autorisation des plates-formes d'internalisation développée par les grands établissements financiers—constituaient un défi plus difficile à relever pour les acteurs continentaux, et pouvait dans leur version initiale conduire à de réelles distorsions de concurrence. **Le débat doit cependant être dépassionné et revenir à des principes simples : le libre choix de l'infrastructure de négociation, le respect d'une concurrence équitable, l'information transparente des investisseurs (en particulier des non professionnels) et la constitution de marchés financiers larges et profonds. Autrement dit, la recherche de l'optimisation des coûts de transaction ne doit pas conduire à une fragmentation excessive des bassins de liquidité** en autant d'infrastructures de traitement des ordres. **Le compromis politique auquel est parvenu le Conseil Ecofin le 7 octobre dernier me paraît acceptable** et de nature à lever une bonne part de mes réserves initiales : la transparence pré-négociation prévue à l'article 25 est ainsi mieux assurée et l'application du ≫ test d'opportunité ≪ inscrite à l'article 18 est modulée selon la nature des prestations (il est par exemple complet pour le conseil en investissement, qui doit effectivement requérir un assentiment explicite et approfondi de l'investisseur). Le processus d'≫ amélioration du prix ≪ après une cotation initiale serait certes limité aux ordres d'une taille importante, mais pourrait sans doute encore fait l'objet de précisions. J'ai cependant bon espoir que ce texte aboutisse à un compromis acceptable pour les sociétés continentales et britanniques avant la fin de l'année.

La proposition de directive sur la transparence financière est à mon sens d'une importance capitale pour le fonctionnement efficient des marchés financiers, auxquels elle permettra de donner des repères cohérents et fiables, propres à limiter les phénomènes de surréaction et de mimétisme auxquels donnent parfois lieu la surveillance et l'exploitation de l'information financière. Comme certains observateurs, notamment britanniques, **je suis toutefois circonspect sur l'obligation d'une information trimestrielle**, même allégée par rapport aux comptes annuels. Certes, la législation française prévoit depuis 1983 la publication d'un chiffre d'affaires trimestriel pour les sociétés cotées, et Euronext vient d'imposer la publication de comptes trimestriels aux sociétés cotées sur son principal compartiment, mais **je crois qu'un tel principe et la description de son contenu ne doivent pas revêtir un caractère trop systématique et relèvent avant tout de la convergence progressive par les pratiques**, si tant est que la périodicité trimestrielle puisse être vraiment considérée comme un gage de pertinence et de crédibilité. L'enjeu du véhicule de transmission de l'information doit également être traité par cette directive. **Quel seraient en effet les media considérés comme fiables** : les informations fournies par Reuters ou Bloomberg, le Bulletin des annonces légales et officielles, la presse financière quotidienne, les sites internet ? Enfin, la directive devrait inclure les éléments fondamentaux d'un code de conduite en matière de communication financière.

Au-delà de ces projets du PASF, il convient également de garder à l'esprit **l'évolution des négociations portant sur les normes IAS 32 et 39**. L'application des normes IAS aux sociétés européennes est considérée comme un acquis du PASF, dans la mesure où elle a fait l'objet du règlement du 19 juillet 2002, et les discussions portant sur l'application de chaque norme ne feront pas l'objet de directives distinctes. Le sujet est d'importance et a soulevé une polémique en France, où les réactions des établissements bancaires sur la valorisation en ≫ *fair market value* ≪ des instruments financiers ont été tardives mais non moins hostiles, et l'IASB n'a pas toujours manifesté une réelle aptitude au dialogue . . . **Mais le refus exprimé par la Commission d'appliquer en l'état les normes IAS 32 et 39 (dont il faut rappeler qu'elles ont été conçues par l'ancien** *Board*) pourrait paradoxalement contraindre les parties prenantes à trouver une issue à la situation, en particulier grâce aux discussions actuelles sur la macro-couverture, que les banques souhaitent pouvoir mettre en œuvre mais qu'il convient d'encadrer afin d'éviter qu'elles ne l'utilisent pour camoufler des pertes. Si les négociations n'aboutissaient pas sur les deux normes précitées, il serait toujours possible à la Commission d'en adopter la plus grande partie mais non l'intégralité, c'est-à-dire en excluant les points les plus problématiques. Une telle solution ne serait toutefois pas totalement satisfaisante car elle conduirait *de facto* à l'établissement de deux normes européennes, dans la mesure où les IAS 32 et 39 originelles seraient perçues négativement, ce qui introduirait une étape supplémentaire dans le cheminement vers des normes comptables harmonisées puis globales, lorsque la compatibilité avec les normes US GAAP sera totale.

II—MISE EN ŒUVRE

3—*Pensez-vous que le processus Lamfalussy sera couronné de succès? Des modifications sont-elles nécessaires?*

Il convient en premier lieu de rappeler l'argumentation qui a présidé à l'introduction de la méthode Lamfalussy. Cette dernière est née du constat que le processus législatif traditionnel européen n'était pas adapté à la création d'un marché unifié de services financiers. Ce processus présente en effet trois types d'inconvénients :

— il peut être **lent**, dans la mesure où il n'est pas rare qu'un délai de trois à quatre ans s'écoule entre la mise en chantier d'une directive et sa transposition au niveau national. Ce délai est tributaire de la réactivité des Etats membres, et il faut bien reconnaître que la France ne s'est jusqu'à récemment pas particulièrement illustrée par sa rapidité dans la transposition des directives relatives au marché intérieur, avant que des mesures d'amélioration n'aient été prises en octobre 2002. Or les marchés et acteurs financiers européens évoluent sans cesse et ont besoin d'un environnement juridique adapté, ce qui suppose que tout changement majeur de la législation s'effectue dans des délais plus restreints ;

— **il est relativement rigide** car il ne connaît pas le système de la loi cadre et des mesures réglementaires d'application, qui existe dans tous les pays européens, de telle sorte que les conventionnels ont été amenés à réfléchir sur une architecture normative similaire lors de l'élaboration du projet de constitution européenne, et ont transcrit cette nouvelle architecture des actes juridiques de l'Union dans les articles 32 à 38 du projet de Traité. Les directives actuelles sont donc parfois très détaillées, ce qui les rend peu lisibles et peut conduire à des divergences d'interprétation lors de la transposition ;

— **il ne prévoit pas de phase de consultation préalable** à l'élaboration d'un texte, même si une telle consultation existe de manière empirique. La construction d'un marché unique des services financiers constitue un chantier de très grande ampleur et qui a trait à des législations et sensibilité nationales parfois très différentes : l'association des professionnels de la finance à l'élaboration des textes est donc absolument déterminante pour assurer le caractère opératoire et l'acceptabilité du PASF.

La méthode Lamfalussy a donc pour vocation, dans la continuité des mesures législatives qui auront été prises dans le cadre du PASF, d'accélérer la prise de décision, de mieux associer les régulateurs nationaux et les représentants professionnels, et d'assurer la cohérence des mesures d'application du PASF. Il s'agit d'aboutir à une norme claire pour tous et qui ne donne pas lieu à des applications trop différenciées, car on sait que de telles divergences peuvent être source de distorsions de concurrence dans le domaine bancaire et financier, par exemple dans l'application des ratios prudentiels. **Fondamentalement, la méthode contribue à déléguer à la Commission l'adoption de la législation secondaire, avec une surveillance a posteriori du Conseil et du Parlement, et donc dans une certaine mesure à modifier la nature des rapports institutionnels.** Cette nouvelle approche constitue un gage d'efficacité en ce que, si l'on considère les choses de manière un peu sommaire, les décisions relatives au domaine très complexe que sont les services financiers sont prises par des techniciens, mais aussi des aspects inacceptables, puisque les dimensions démocratique et intergouvernementale sont édulcorées.

Cette méthode fait donc appel à la ≫ comitologie ≫ et est structurée selon quatre niveaux de décisions :

— **niveau 1** : actes législatifs proposés par la Commission et adoptés en codécision par le Conseil et le Parlement européen ;

— **niveau 2** : adoption des mesures d'exécution et implication des deux nouveaux comités que sont le CEVM/ESC (Comité européen des valeurs mobilières), de nature plus politique puisqu'il est composé des ministres des finances, et le CERVM/CESR (Comité des régulateurs des marchés européens de valeurs mobilières), qui mobilise les professionnels. Le CEVM assiste la Commission dans l'adoption des mesures techniques d'exécution, et le CESR donne des avis techniques à la Commission sur ces mesures, selon un mandat donné par la Commission. Les deux comités déterminent de quel niveau relèvent les mesures proposées : soit des mesures directement annexées à la directive qui constituent le niveau 2, soit des mesures de niveau 3 ;

— **niveau 3** : amélioration de la mise en œuvre des actes législatifs de niveau 1 et 2 par des mesures de transposition nationale. LE CESR détient une responsabilité particulière dans ce domaine ;

— **niveau 4** : application rigoureuse de la législation communautaire par la Commission.

Le processus Lamfalussy répond à une préoccupation que je juge légitime et met en œuvre un mécanisme innovant de concertation en amont de l'application des normes, susceptible de limiter les conflits d'interprétation et de préserver l'exigence d'harmonisation européenne qu'implique le PASF. Pourtant on conçoit bien qu'en dépit de précautions organisationnelles et d'un souci de progressivité que traduit l'architecture en 4 niveaux, **le niveau déterminant de ce système est le niveau 3. C'est bien dans la détermination des mesures de transposition qu'est susceptible d'apparaître l'ambiguïté entre la recherche d'une harmonisation maximale, qui est l'objectif théorique du PASF, et la préservation d'une certaine flexibilité dans l'application nationale, qui constitue une exigence pratique de faisabilité et d'acceptabilité du Plan.** La position du curseur au niveau 2 apparaît plus mouvante qu'escompté : confrontés à la richesse des détails, à la technicité des textes et à de possibles oppositions sur la traduction concrète de tel principe ou exigence législative, les participants peuvent avoir la tentation de s'en remettre à la seule transposition pour régler les difficultés. Dès lors une surcharge du niveau 3 traduirait un certain vice de fonctionnement du processus Lamfalussy, c'est-à-dire l'externalisation au niveau national du règlement des divergences apparues au sein du CEVM ou du CESR, et contribuerait de surcroît à ralentir la mise en place du PASF, ce qui serait précisément contraire à l'objectif. Il s'agit donc d'éviter que l'innovation du processus Lamfalussy n'aboutisse *in fine* à reproduire les inconvénients du processus législatif de droit commun.

De fait, les professionnels constataient voici quelques mois un certain nombre de dysfonctionnements dans la mise en œuvre du processus : des délais trop courts pour les consultations, un manque de moyens humains à la Commission européenne pour engager un vrai dialogue avec les professionnels, une tendance à privilégier les mesures de niveau 3 et donc à laisser trop de place à l'interprétation des textes.

Le ≪ **groupe institutionnel de surveillance des marchés des valeurs mobilières** ≫, composé de six experts, a en outre remis en mai dernier son premier rapport intérimaire sur la mise en œuvre de la méthode Lamfalussy, et a fait les observations suivantes :

— il a constaté que le processus en était encore au stade de ≫ l'apprentissage par la pratique ≫, ce qui me paraît inévitable compte tenu de sa courte existence, et que l'adoption des mesures de niveau 1 nécessitait du temps ;

— il a exprimé sa **préférence pour une utilisation accrue des règlements**, qui sont directement applicables en droit interne, de préférence aux directives, lorsqu'il s'agit d'adopter des mesures de niveau 2. Ce souhait paraît légitime en ce qu'il conduit à une application plus rapide, mais il n'apporte pas la garantie d'une implication et d'un assentiment des professionnels sur des mesures qui les concernent pourtant directement ;

— il a souligné la nécessité de modifier l'article 202 du Traité CE, et **l'importance des travaux de la Convention sur les compétences comitologiques définies par les articles 35 et 36 du projet de Constitution**, qui traitent des deux nouvelles normes juridiques que sont d'une part les ≫ règlements délégués ≫ [1] à la Commission, et d'autre part les ≫ actes d'exécution ≫, qui font appel à la comitologie selon des modalités définies par un règlement européen. **J'estime que ces nouvelles dispositions, susceptibles d'accorder un grand pouvoir à la Commission, méritent un examen attentif des Etats-membres**. La comitologie présente en effet une réelle utilité, mais il convient à mon sens de la circonscrire aux matières les plus techniques. On peut en outre se demander quel serait le critère d' ≪ éléments non essentiels ≫ *auquel l'article 35 fait référence.*

Je prends toutefois acte de ce que la Commission se soit déclarée favorable au souhait du Parlement européen de disposer d'un pouvoir de ≫ *call-back* ≫ à égalité avec le Conseil, **qui permettrait de rétablir un certain équilibre démocratique dans le processus quelque peu ≫ technocratique ≫ de la comitologie**, pour autant que le Parlement use de ce pouvoir avec discernement et mesure. Enfin, il convient de rappeler que la Commission, par la voix de son Président Romano Prodi lors d'une intervention au Parlement européen le 5 février 2002 (sur la mise en œuvre du PASF), avait manifesté son intérêt pour la requête du Parlement tendant à limiter à quatre ans, à compter de l'entrée en vigueur de chaque directive concernée, la durée d'une délégation de compétence d'exécution à la Commission. De même, M. Prodi avait assuré que la Commission respecterait pleinement l'exigence de transparence vis-à-vis du Parlement européen pendant toute la procédure d'adoption des mesures d'exécution pour lui permettre de les examiner et de se prononcer. Il convient donc de garder ces engagements à l'esprit, et au besoin de les rappeler avec force à la Commission ;

— le groupe d'experts s'est également **interrogé sur le degré de détails contenus dans les directives et règlements adoptés en codécision** (niveau 1, cf. infra), en se demandant s'il y avait ≫ *une délégation suffisante pour permettre l'adoption des mesures d'exécution par la Commission* ≫ avec l'aide du CEVM et du CERVM au niveau 2. Ce point est important, car des mesures de niveau 1 doivent plutôt s'en tenir à la définition des principes et règles de portée générale, et un excès de détail tendrait à rompre la logique même de la méthode Lamfalussy. Les experts ont également souligné la nécessité d'éviter des mesures de niveau 2 qui ne soient qu'un amalgame de règles détaillées déjà existantes ;

— enfin, les **experts ont plaidé pour que la procédure d'adoption en une seule lecture pour le niveau 1 (''** *fast track facility* ≫) soit utilisée plus fréquemment. Je ne suis pas favorable à une telle extension, qui outre le fait qu'elle ne permet guère de gagner que quelques mois, pourrait préluder une généralisation et n'est pas conforme aux exigences d'une Union démocratique, c'est-à-dire respectueuse des prérogatives du Parlement européen et des parlements nationaux.

Aussi, bien que le processus présente des imperfections en apparence contradictoires tant à son sommet (permanence de directives trop précises et manque de délégation) qu'à sa base (risque d'extension des mesures de transposition), je ne crois pas pour autant qu'il faille le condamner et l'enterrer. Il est normal que la méthode se cherche et se construise par itérations, et **elle a dans une certaine mesure déjà fait la preuve de son efficacité**, avec un rééquilibrage du contenu des textes entre les niveaux législatif et réglementaire, et un très net raccourcissement des délais d'adoption des directives, notamment parce que le travail des comités s'effectue parfois concomitamment, plutôt que successivement, à la poursuite des négociations politiques au niveau 1 sur les mêmes textes avant leur adoption.

---

[1] Le premier alinéa de l'article 35 dispose que ≪ les lois et les lois-cadres européennes *(c'est-à-dire les directives et règlements actuels)* peuvent déléguer à la Commission le pouvoir d'édicter des règlements délégués qui **complètent ou qui modifient certains éléments non essentiels** de la loi ou de la loi-cadre ≫ ''.

Tout en restant vigilant, je suis donc assez optimiste quant au succès de ce processus, qui pourrait profiter au cadre juridique communautaire et à la convergence des législations nationales s'il était étendu à d'autres secteurs, mais qui ne doit pas pour autant devenir dès aujourd'hui le mode décisionnel de droit commun.

4—*Qui sera effectivement responsable de la mise en oeuvre du marché unique une fois que le cadre réglementaire sera entré en vigueur? Quels succès attendez-vous de ce processus? Quel sera le rôle des autorités de la concurrence au niveau de l'Union européenne et des Etats membres?*

Ainsi que je l'ai souligné, le processus Lamfalussy présente des qualités et devrait être bénéfique à la construction européenne. Dès lors que les mesures d'application du PASF auront été décidées par comitologie, il reviendra aux autorités nationales de régulation et de surveillance prudentielle de les traduire dans leur règlement et de les faire respecter par les intervenants financiers. Ces autorités ne disposeront guère de marge de manœuvre d'interprétation, ce qui est une des finalités du PASF, **mais la réglementation qu'elles appliqueront sera d'autant plus légitime aux yeux des professionnels et aisée à transcrire qu'elles auront été impliquées en amont du processus Lamfalussy**, par l'intermédiaire du comité CESR et grâce aux consultation entreprises par ses membres. On ne pourra donc pas les accuser de se voir imposer, selon une démarche *top-down* aveugle et rigide, des mesures d'application auxquelles ces autorités comme les associations professionnelles n'auraient pas été associés. Ce processus accentuera également la tendance à l'unification des autorités de régulation nationales, et je dois à ce titre souligner l'apport décisif de la loi de sécurité financière adoptée cette année en France, **dont le principal résultat réside dans la constitution d'une autorité unique dénommée Autorité des marchés financiers**, par la fusion de la Commission des opérations de bourse (COB), autorité administrative indépendante de droit public, et du Conseil des marchés financiers (CMF), autorité professionnelle de droit privé. Cet édifice complexe était source de chevauchements de compétences, de concepts juridiques dissemblables compte tenu de cultures différentes, et donnait lieu à un réel problème de frontières entre les deux institutions. J'avais ainsi dès 1994, dans un rapport sur la transposition en droit français de la première directive sur les services d'investissement, souligné ces vices de fonctionnement et souhaité la constitution d'une autorité unifiée, dont il a donc fallu attendre près de dix ans la traduction concrète. Ce mouvement d'unification n'est toutefois pas achevé en France, puisque le secteur des assurances et mutuelles est soumis à une autorité distincte de l'AMF, la Commission de contrôle des assurances, mutuelles et institutions de prévoyance (CCAMIP), et que les banques restent soumises à la Commission bancaire.

S'agissant des autorités de la concurrence, la situation ne devrait pas fondamentalement changer par rapport à celle qui prévaut aujourd'hui. Les autorités nationales devraient continuer d'accorder leur agrément aux opérations de fusions entre entreprises nationales, selon des objectifs parfois distincts (on considère ainsi que l'Allemagne et le Royaume-Uni se fondent plutôt sur des objectifs exclusivement concurrentiels, et la France sur une vision plus large mais aussi plus floue de politique industrielle), et la Commission, en tant que gardienne de la législation communautaire, poursuivrait son contrôle des concentrations reposant sur un test de création ou de renforcement d'une position dominante, selon les nouvelles modalités d'analyse qu'elle a récemment décidées. Les critères de la Commission sont néanmoins parfois contestés, en ce qu'ils traduisent une vision plus réductrice et une méthodologie plus fluctuante que le test dit» SLC» mis en œuvre par les Etats-Unis, consistant à déterminer si la concentration risque de» *porter substantiellement atteinte à la concurrence* ».

En ce qui concerne le secteur bancaire, qui est prioritairement concerné par le PASF, il importe de relever le changement de conception opéré en France, avec mon soutien, à la faveur de la loi de sécurité financière. Le contrôle de la concentration bancaire était auparavant exercé par un comité proche de la Banque de France, qui outre sa qualité de banque centrale assure la surveillance prudentielle des établissements de crédit, sans fondement juridique clair et en appliquant un postulat de spécificité du secteur bancaire au regard du droit de la concurrence. Le secteur bancaire rejoint désormais le droit commun, puisqu'il est soumis au contrôle du Conseil de la concurrence (avec avis consultatif de la Banque de France, qui conserve l'octroi de l'agrément au titre du contrôle prudentiel), qui se prononce déjà sur les concentrations dans les autres secteurs d'activité. Je considère que cette évolution bienvenue pourrait préluder un mouvement similaire dans d'autres Etats membres, et ainsi contribuer à l'unification des marchés et services financiers, qui constituent toujours un secteur spécifique à plusieurs égards mais font l'objet d'un processus d'harmonisation, au même titre que d'autres domaines du marché intérieur.

5—*Quelles sont les questions qui se poseront lors de la mise en oeuvre du marché unique?*

J'ai le pressentiment que la réalisation du marché unique des services financiers posera, à terme plus ou moins long, la question d'une autorité unique de régulation à l'échelle européenne, qui constitue l'étape succédant à la fusion des autorités au niveau national. J'ai souhaité une telle évolution lors de l'examen du projet de loi de sécurité financière que j'ai précédemment évoqué, car elle est nécessaire à au moins deux titres :

— **au plan communautaire, la pratique de chaque autorité de régulation nationale multiplie d'autant les divergences potentielles et les différences de traitement des opérations financières**, bien que le PASF contribue à réduire la marge de manœuvre des régulateurs. On peut ainsi mentionner l'exemple des dérivés de crédit, dont la nature juridique (contrat d'assurance, opération de banque, instrument financier à terme ?) fait l'objet d'intenses débats chez les spécialistes, mais qui a suscité un inégal intérêt de part et d'autre de la Manche. Ainsi l'organe français de contrôle du secteur des assurances, la Commission de contrôle des assurances (qui est depuis juin 2003 devenue la CCAMIP, mentionnée précédemment), a jusqu'en 2002 fait preuve d'une grande discrétion sur cette question importante, tout comme la Fédération française des sociétés d'assurance, qui représente les professionnels, n'avait pas abordé le thème des produits dérivés dans ses rapports annuels antérieurs à 2000. Cet intérêt tardif contraste avec le dynamisme et le pragmatisme de la FSA, qui du fait de la surveillance globale qu'elle exerce sur les marchés financiers, bénéficie de synergies et d'une vision plus complète de sujets de plus en plus transversaux. Au fur et à mesure de l'intégration des marchés européens, la parcellisation et le cloisonnement de la régulation auront moins de justification, et la création d'une autorité européenne s'imposera. A présent que les arbitrages, transferts de risque et investissement de portefeuille sont réellement transnationaux (ainsi, nombre d'institutions de retraite et de sociétés d'assurance ont désormais modifié leur allocation d'actifs pour fondre leur part de titres nationaux dans une classe globale de titres européens), la sphère administrative et juridique doit suivre le même cheminement ;

— **au plan international, il est clair que l'Europe n'est pas encore de taille à faire efficacement valoir ses intérêts auprès de la puissante SEC américaine,** dans un environnement où la mondialisation de la finance constitue une réalité déjà ancienne. L'application de la loi Sarbanes-Oxley en a fourni un exemple, avec le projet initial de soumission des sociétés européennes cotées sur les marchés américains à l'ensemble des règles nationales relatives au contrôle des comptes. Les autorités de régulation européennes doivent se réapproprier certains sujets aujourd'hui débattus dans des enceintes dont ce n'est pas la vocation première (tel le Forum de la stabilité financière du FMI), ou par la SEC qui en détient tacitement l'exclusivité. Je songe en particulier à la surveillance des agences de notation, aux *hedge funds* et aux nouveaux instruments de transfert du risque, sur lesquels l'Europe se doit de construire une position cohérente et harmonisée, et dont la crédibilité serait plus affirmée si elle émanait d'un régulateur européen puissant. Une telle position devrait ensuite être défendue au niveau international, car un nombre croissant de sujets ne peut être efficacement traité qu'à cette échelle. A cet égard, je relève que l'Union européenne s'est récemment engagée dans un dialogue réglementaire UE/Etats-Unis sur les marchés financiers, mené avec le Trésor américain, le Conseil de la FED et la SEC. Ce dialogue pourrait permettre, *ex-ante*, de prévenir de manière informelle certains conflits, et *ex-post*, de garantir l'accès aux marchés boursiers respectifs. A ce titre, **je crois indispensable que la Commission et les autorités de régulation nationales, particulièrement en France, accentuent leurs efforts pour développer la reconnaissance mutuelle des marchés et compartiments**, dont l'étendue est aujourd'hui clairement trop restreinte.

Dans l'attente qu'une telle perspective se précise, les autorités nationales, étant prioritairement concernées par l'achèvement du marché intérieur, **devront veiller à mieux faire converger leurs doctrines et concepts, à renforcer la compatibilité de leurs systèmes de surveillance des marchés et de traitement des données, et à banaliser les échanges d'informations** hors du seul cadre juridique déjà précis de la lutte contre le blanchiment.

Hors de ce que je considère comme un objectif de long terme, la mise en œuvre du marché unique pourrait inciter à intensifier les progrès dans des secteurs connexes. **L'harmonisation du** *back-office* et des systèmes de règlement-livraison, si elle fait aujourd'hui l'objet d'un projet de la Commission, n'a cependant pas constitué une vraie priorité du PASF, attaché à traiter les enjeux plus séduisants du *front office* et du *corporate finance*. Le **crédit à la consommation**, qui ne fait pas partie du PASF mais connaît un développement rapide, doit également faire l'objet d'un examen attentif et d'une relance du processus de négociation sur le projet de directive, aujourd'hui obéré par la fermeté du Parlement européen. Le crédit à la consommation est nécessaire et apporte une contribution à la croissance économique, mais il est également soumis à des abus et effets pervers. J'ai d'ailleurs profité de l'examen du projet de loi de sécurité financière pour améliorer les dispositions législatives relatives à la publicité pour ce type de crédit.

6—Quels sont les obstacles non réglementaires qui pourraient nuire au bon fonctionnement du marché unique des services financiers?

Il est difficile de préjuger des obstacles d'ordre qualitatif et non réglementaire qui pourraient s'opposer à la réalisation effective du marché unique, car ils impliquent de pouvoir anticiper le comportement et les possibles déviances des acteurs. **Il est toutefois possible d'anticiper une possible contradiction entre les logiques de concurrence et d'harmonisation**. Le marché unique et l'harmonisation des législations permettent d'une part d'aplanir certaines distorsions de concurrence et d'inciter les acteurs à développer des avantages comparatifs sur un socle juridique commun (harmonisation ne signifie pas uniformisation des services financiers), mais en facilitant les mouvements transnationaux de concentration, ils étendent d'autre part les possibilités d'ententes et d'abus de position dominante. Certes, la concentration dans le secteur bancaire n'est pas aussi avancée que dans d'autres secteurs industriels matures et de réelles marges existent aux plans national et européen (ainsi en France, un oligopole tend à se construire progressivement mais comporte un champ concurrentiel encore large, du fait de la consolidation des principaux acteurs), mais la recherche de la taille critique et des synergies de coûts dans les différents segments de l'activité bancaire, en particulier dans les activités de réseau à faible rentabilité, sont susceptibles à long terme de conduire à des positions dominantes et de restreindre l'accès et la performance de certains marchés financiers. En outre, **la volonté d'ouverture à la concurrence qui sous-tend la DSI présente**

toujours le risque, même réduit, de fragmenter les bassins de liquidité, de rétrécir les fourchettes de prix et d'introduire une nouvelle segmentation des investisseurs, avec pour conséquence ultime un renchérissement des coûts d'entrée et d'information pour les petits porteurs.

La concrétisation du PASF n'empêchera pas non plus, du moins dans un premier temps, certains **paradis fiscaux** et havres juridiques de perdurer. Néanmoins, il convient de distinguer la justification d'une plus grande vigilance au regard du blanchiment d'un éventuel débat sur l'existence même de ces paradis fiscaux. A mon sens, ces places ne sont pas condamnables en soi et peuvent être comparées aux zones franches industrielles, mais sont critiquables dès lors qu'elles ne s'engagent pas fermement dans la lutte contre le blanchiment. Or c'est bien là que réside l'ambiguïté des paradis fiscaux, car un statut fiscal très privilégié est difficilement compatible avec la traçabilité des fonds.

Enfin **l'innovation financière, dont les rapports avec la stabilité sont ambigus, ainsi que je l'ai évoqué, contribue à la fois à fluidifier les marchés et à en exacerber certains errements**. Elle contribue indéniablement à la sécurité financière, directement ou non, et à l'extension des capacités de financement, mais poursuit également d'autres objets : contournement de la réglementation, externalisation du risque, rendement et optimisation des placements, riposte aux contraintes de la concurrence, exploitation des niches d'inefficience de marché, recherche de nouveaux modes de financement en période de raréfaction des canaux traditionnels (crédit bancaire et introduction en bourse). L'innovation financière est donc aussi facteur d'instabilité en créant de nouveaux risques, en impliquant de nouveaux acteurs ne disposant pas nécessairement des moyens pour évaluer correctement lesdits risques, en biaisant l'arbitrage de certains acteurs au profit de la recherche du rendement absolu et au détriment de la perception du risque (cf. le cas du fonds LTCM, dont le levier était supérieur à 25), voire dans certains cas en facilitant la fraude. Un événement sur un des maillons de la chaîne serait alors susceptible de dégénérer en crise systémique par l'absence de cantonnement du risque à des acteurs bien identifiés. Dès lors, pour limiter l'impact négatif de l'innovation sur le bon fonctionnement du marché unique, il convient de réunir les conditions suivantes :

— **au niveau des législateurs nationaux et européen** : éviter une normativité trop détaillée afin de limiter les effets de contournement, et être conscient des risques des innovations en cours ;

— **au niveau des régulateurs** : observation précise du marché et de la déontologie des acteurs, accroissement des compétences des experts pour une adaptation plus rapide de la réglementation aux nouvelles pratiques. Le nouveau ratio Mc Donnough participe opportunément de ce mouvement, puisqu'il affine considérablement la définition du risque, et partant sa couverture en capital ;

— **au niveau des acteurs** : renforcement du risk-management et du cadre déontologique, accroissement des compétences pour les nouveaux entrants. Il s'agit également d'éviter le dogme du chiffre, tel le retour sur fonds propres (RoE) à 15%, de privilégier le long terme et de respecter les promesses faites au marché.

III—L'AVENIR

7—Comment voyez-vous l'avènement d'un marché unique des services financiers après la mise en oeuvre du PASF? Des mesures complémentaires sont-elles nécessaires?

La mise en œuvre du PASF constitue à la fois un aboutissement et une étape. Son contenu est très ambitieux et je me félicite des progrès déterminants qui ont été réalisés. Le perfectionnement des marchés et services financiers européens constitue toutefois un mouvement perpétuel, et il conviendra dès lors de compléter le PASF, outre les points que j'ai déjà relevés (concertation avec les autorités américaines, évolution vers une régulation européenne unifiée, expertise approfondie sur les innovations financières . . .), par les avancées suivantes :

— **le droit européen des sociétés doit encore progresser, en particulier sur les terrains du gouvernement d'entreprise et de la société européenne**. La modernisation du droit des sociétés et le renforcement du gouvernement d'entreprise vont faire l'objet d'un plan d'action distinct de la Commission, dans la continuité du rapport remis en janvier 2002 par le groupe d'expert présidé par le professeur Jaap Winter, mais sur ce thème de la gouvernance comme en matière d'information financière, je ne crois pas qu'il soit opportun de légiférer de manière trop approfondie. L'organisation des conseils d'administration doit s'aligner progressivement sur les bonnes pratiques, et je suis opposé à toute tentative de définition et à toute disposition contraignante sur les administrateurs indépendants. S'agissant de la société européenne, j'ai déposé voici quelques semaines au Sénat une proposition de loi tendant à adapter la législation française au règlement CE du 8 octobre 2001 ;

— **l'encadrement de la gestion alternative, et plus spécifiquement des dérivés de crédit, doit être précisé**. Il ne s'agit naturellement pas de créer des barrières résolument dissuasives à l'encontre de cette classe d'actifs, qui permet une réelle diversification et contribue à l'optimisation du couple rendement/ risque, mais de compléter les critères d'agrément des *hedge funds*, d'améliorer la prévention du blanchiment et la transparence des comptes, d'exiger de meilleures garanties de professionnalisme et de rigueur sur les processus de gestion (notamment dans le cas des programmes systématiques des gestionnaires *commodity trading advisors* et *hedge macro*), et d'étendre l'information fournie à l'investisseur. En ce qui concerne les dérivés de crédit, chaque autorité de régulation doit en premier lieu s'attacher à en donner une définition juridique claire ;

— **la réflexion sur le rôle des analystes ne doit pas être interrompue dès lors que les marchés boursiers se redressent**, mais conduire à l'établissement d'un corpus de recommandations concrètes, homogènes et pérennes, destiné à prévenir tout conflit d'intérêt et à sécuriser le travail des équipes de recherche. La constitution de pôles de recherche indépendants constitue un objectif louable mais peu opérationnel, car il ne résout pas de manière satisfaisante la question du financement. Là encore, la tentation d'une législation précise sur les analystes ressemble à une≫ fausse bonne idée≫, et la correction des dysfonctionnements doit essentiellement s'opérer par une prise de conscience des professionnels, déjà largement acquise, et par une auto-régulation.

Au-delà de ces initiatives, qui sont le fait des régulateurs, **il est clair que le PASF va inciter les entreprises de services financiers à mettre en place de nouvelles stratégies**. **On peut par exemple anticiper les tendances suivantes** : poursuite du rapprochement entre activités bancaires et assurantielles (après que les assurances ont proposé des services financiers, les banques tendent à leur tour à créer des filiales d'assurance vie et non vie), diminution des exigences en fonds propres pour les activités de banque de détail et de prêts immobiliers du fait de l'application du ratio Mc Donnough, poursuite du développement de la titrisation et du marché des dérivés de crédit afin de réduire l'encours de risque pondéré et de gérer plus activement le bilan, resegmentation de la gestion d'actifs en fonction d'un critère d'aversion au risque (de la gestion indicielle à la gestion≫ absolue≫ utilisant des *hedge funds*), et renforcement des acteurs de niche qui profiteront de l'externalisation de segments jugés non prioritaires par les grandes banques universelles.

8—Est-ce que les changements consécutifs aux propositions du PASF auront un impact sur la situation concurrentielle des places de Londres, Paris et des marchés de l'UE dans leur ensemble?

La concurrence entre places boursières européennes n'est pas une perspective d'avenir mais bel et bien une réalité. Les bourses sont désormais elles-mêmes des sociétés cotées, et les échecs et succès de certains rapprochements au cours des dernières années (*Deutsche Börse / London Stock Exchange*, Euronext / LIFFE) ont illustré l'intensité de la compétition qui caractérise désormais ces marchés. Les opérations récentes ont toutes mis en exergue l'importance de systèmes homogènes de traitement des ordres et de compensation, et donc **la nécessité de ne pas négliger le** *back office*. En revanche, je ne crois pas que la perspective d'une bourse européenne unifiée, et en particulier d'une fusion entre Euronext, le LSE et la Deutsche Börse s'inscrive dans le court ou moyen terme. **Je ne pense pas qu'une telle concentration soit d'ailleurs souhaitable**.

Les dispositions du PASF qui auront l'impact le plus prononcé sur l'intensité concurrentielle des places européennes sont celles de la DSI. Cette directive devrait conduire à une séparation accrue de l'intermédiation du détail et des institutionnels, et peut être à la constitution de partenariats entre les entreprises d'investissement et les bourses ≪ traditionnelles≫, en vue de la création de *multilateral trading facilities*, accessibles aux seuls professionnels et spécialisées par secteur ou par produit. Les marchés réglementés ne sont en effet sans doute pas aussi menacés que certains l'imaginent par la perspective de l'internalisation des ordres, car ils bénéficient d'ores et déjà de solides positions et d'une peut être à la constitution de partenariats entre

A l'échelle internationale, l'avantage concurrentiel des places européennes sera très vraisemblablement renforcé par le PASF, ce qui pourrait conduire à un relatif rééquilibrage des allocations d'actifs en faveur des actions européennes, et de ce fait à un accroissement de la capitalisation des sociétés de l'Union. La remise en cause dont fait aujourd'hui l'objet l'organisation séculaire du *New York Stock Exchange*, suite aux controverses portant sur la gestion de son ancien président, et l'atténuation de l'hégémonie du NASDAQ sur le marché des valeurs de haute technologie, tendent à conforter la validité et la pérennité de l'offre des places européennes.

Philippe Marini

30 octobre 2003

MONDAY 20 OCTOBER 2003

Present:

Cavendish of Furness, L	Shutt of Greetland, L.
Chadlington, L.	Walpole, L.
Fearn, L.	Woolmer of Leeds, L.
Howie of Troon, L	(Chairman)

Memorandum submitted by HM Treasury

EXECUTIVE SUMMARY

The integration of EU financial services markets is a cornerstone of European economic reform, and the Government believes that it holds huge potential, with the UK standing to gain considerably.

The Financial Services Action Plan (FSAP) is the framework intended to deliver the benefits of a single market for financial services. The Government strongly supports its objectives and has been working closely with stakeholders and co-legislators to secure economically beneficial outcomes.

Although too many of the measures adopted under the FSAP have not been as liberalising as the Government had hoped, it has still succeeded in securing significant progress. The institutional realities, and the magnitude of the potential gains, demand that the Government continues to engage constructively so as to influence both strategy and specific dossiers.

Much work remains to be done to complete the single financial services market. The FSAP measures must be effectively implemented and enforced. The Lamfalussy framework must be made to work successfully in the new areas to which it is being extended, and its better regulation principles applied more rigorously. Any new regulatory challenges or gaps in the single market must be carefully analysed and, where official EU action is justified, tackled with the most appropriate policy tool. The Treasury will continue to work with all stakeholders with the aim of delivering the benefits of the single market.

CONTEXT TO THE FINANCIAL SERVICES ACTION PLAN

1. The Government believes that the process of economic reform is necessary if Europe is to meet the strategic goal agreed at the Lisbon European Council and confirmed at the Stockholm and Barcelona European Councils. The reforms of product, labour and capital markets bring benefits to consumers and businesses through lower prices and greater employment opportunities, and promote businesses through deeper and more efficient capital markets.

2. While the Government believes that benefits can be maximised through reform in all three areas, a recent report ordered from London Economics[32] by the European Commission calculated that the creation of a single EU financial services market would, by itself, lead to significant economic benefits. The report suggested that full integration of EU financial markets would reduce the real cost of capital by 50 basis points for EU businesses, and result in a one-off 1.1 per cent increase in GDP over 10 years for the EU as a whole.

3. The Financial Services Action Plan (FSAP) is the vehicle intended to deliver these benefits. The stated objective of the FSAP is to link better the sources of capital—retail savers and wholesale investors—with the firms and individuals seeking to use it, thus:

— reducing the costs of accessing capital and improving the efficiency of its allocation;

— giving retail consumers access to a wider range of more competitively-priced products;

— promoting broader and more liquid equity and bond markets, permitting greater investment diversification and reduced risk; and

— putting the sector in a stronger position to win market share outside the EU.

4. Successful completion of the FSAP is central to the EU's wider economic reform agenda and the long-term economic health of all Member States.

5. The Government's approach to financial services in the EU was set out in a Treasury paper published in July 2000 and reiterated in the February 2002 White Paper. The Government believes that regulation should be market-driven in most cases and supports legislation based on the mutual recognition of home state

---

[32] Quantification of the Macro-Economic Impact of Integration of EU Financial Markets—November 2002—Study by London Economics, in association with PricewaterhouseCoopers and Oxford Economic Forecasting: http://europa.eu.int/comm/internal market/en/finances/mobil/overview.htm.

standards, underpinned by core common standards. This respects the diversity of regulatory approaches and the great variety of financial markets within the EU. It remains the Government's preferred model, especially for capital market integration.

How the Treasury works with others to deliver the FSAP

6. The Treasury puts considerable effort into working effectively with stakeholders to deliver a successful FSAP.

7. As is its right under the Treaty, the European Commission has the sole right of initiation of draft EU legislation. The Treasury influences draft Commission proposals through proactive engagement with the Commission in the drafting process, and extensive consultation with stakeholders. The Council decides FSAP measures on the basis of Qualified Majority Voting[33]. This necessitates coalition building, as unilateral national vetoes are not available. Most FSAP measures are also subject to co-decision with the European Parliament where, again, the Treasury informs MEPs but has no control over the amendments to proposals that are passed.

8. As it is crucial to maximise influence on those decision-making processes, the Treasury seeks to ensure that positions take full account of all stakeholder perspectives and are based on sound arguments. The Treasury works closely with the UK Permanent Representation in Brussels (UKRep), which provides us with particularly valuable assistance in EU intelligence-gathering and lobbying tasks.

9. In order to keep fully informed of UK stakeholder perspectives, the Treasury has been taking a more formalised approach to consultation and information sharing. The core of this approach, along with a number of other initiatives, includes:

Internal:

— Regular trilateral meetings of senior officials of the Treasury, FSA and Bank of England.

— Project teams are now formed for each new proposal. These teams consist of officials from the Treasury, FSA, UKRep, Treasury Legal Advisers and other Government departments as necessary (particularly the DTI).

— A regular European Financial Services Newsletter is widely disseminated across Whitehall to ensure other Government departments are informed about cross-cutting issues and general developments on specific dossiers.

External:

— Strategy discussions between senior Treasury, FSA and Bank of England officials and senior private sector stakeholders.

— For each new proposal, the Treasury now also forms an industry roundtable, whose aim is to share detailed information on specific dossiers. They are open to all interested parties and their proceedings are informal to encourage debate. The roundtables are particularly valuable when gathering information regarding the potential impact of specific proposals for amendments.

— With the FSA, the Treasury hosts regular stocktake meetings for financial services trade associations and consumer bodies to inform them of cross-cutting issues and developments on specific dossiers.

10. The Treasury believes it is crucial to maintain strong relations with the European institutions and other Member States, particularly their Finance Ministries. Regular contact is made with the Commission and Parliament (UKRep plays a significant part here) and Treasury opposite numbers in other Member States.

11. EU enlargement will increase the number of EU Member States from 15 to 25 by next year. Although May 2004 is set as the accession date, the 10 acceding countries have enjoyed active "observer" status since April 2003. This will have a strong impact on financial services legislation through the re-weighting of votes in Council. The Treasury is developing bilateral links with its counterparts within the accession countries. A number of meetings involving senior officials have taken place in recent months.

---

[33] Article 95 of the EC Treaty stipulates that the majority of legal transactions relating to the establishment and functioning of the internal market are adopted in accordance with the co-decision procedure. This provides for the Council to give a qualified majority ruling by co-decision with the European Parliament.

The FSAP and institutional change

12. Although the FSAP predates the Lamfalussy reforms, many of the most important FSAP measures will use the processes proposed in the report. The Lamfalussy report on financial services legislation, published in February 2001, was based on the recommendations of the Committee of Wise Men on the Regulation of European Securities Markets, chaired by Baron Lamfalussy.

13. It advocated a new legislative framework for securities regulation, which would distinguish between core principles and practical implementing measures, thus fostering a faster and more flexible system. The recommendations proposed a new, four-level approach including the creation of a European Securities Committee (ESC) and a Committee of European Securities Regulators (CESR), and greater use of better regulation analysis and procedures:

— Level 1: legislative acts, namely Directives or Regulations, proposed by the Commission following consultation with all interested parties and adopted under the "co-decision" procedure by the Council and the European Parliament.

— Level 2: the ESC, the regulatory committee, to assist the Commission in adopting detailed technical implementing measures, the nature and extent of which should be decided by Level 1 legislation. CESR to provide technical advice to the Commission on these implementing measures following a Commission mandate.

— Level 3: measures with the objective of improving the common implementation of Community legislation (Level 1 and 2 acts) in the Member States. The CESR has particular responsibility for this.

— Level 4: Commission to strengthen the enforcement of Community law.

14. These proposals were approved by the Council and European Parliament, and have been in place since February 2002. Following an initiative by the Chancellor of the Exchequer and the German Finance Minister, the Council agreed in December 2002 to extend the Lamfalussy arrangements to the regulation of banking, insurance and financial conglomerates.

15. The Inter-institutional Monitoring Group (IIMG) for securities markets published its first interim report on the Lamfalussy process in May 2003[34]. The IIMG consists of six experts nominated by the Commission, Council and European Parliament, and is expected to report biannually on the implementation of Lamfalussy. The May report stated that initial indications are that legislation is progressing faster than would otherwise be the case and that there has been positive joint working between all participants, but that it was very early days and a more authoritative assessment would have to wait until more evidence was available.

16. The Government has been a strong supporter of the Lamfalussy proposals and believes they will play an essential part in creating an effective single market for financial services.

17. While the Treasury acknowledges that legislation appears to be trailing market developments, as stressed in one of the Treasury's EMU reports, "EMU and the cost of capital"[35], it also agrees with the IIMG that good progress has been made. Looking forward, the Treasury believes it is important to make legislative texts focus on core, high-level principles, whilst ensuring that levels 2 and 3 continue to work successfully together in defining the supporting detail.

18. Other recent institutional changes should also have a positive impact on regulatory convergence and effective implementation. As part of the December 2002 ECOFIN agreement, the Financial Services Policy Group (FSPG) was recently replaced by the Financial Services Committee (FSC), which comprises the personal representatives of EU Finance Ministers and is chaired by one of them, unlike the FSPG, which was chaired by the Internal Market Commissioner. The FSC's mandate is to provide strategic advice on financial services issues to ECOFIN. Regular meetings are expected to focus on reviewing progress on the FSAP and financial stability.

PROGRESS

19. The Commission's Eighth Progress Report on the FSAP, presented to ECOFIN on 3 June 2003, showed that 34 of the 42 measures were now agreed. A few examples follow to illustrate the mixed results obtained and issues which the Treasury is currently tackling:

— *the "Prospectus" Directive (under negotiation)* is an example of a Directive that has improved since it was initially proposed, thanks to successful outcomes from the negotiation process. Notable successes included:

— opposing new burdens for small firms;

---

[34] First Interim Report—Monitoring the New Process for Regulating Securities Markets in Europe (the Lamfalussy Process): http://europa.eu.int/comm/internal market/en/finances/mobil/docs/lamfalussy/2003-05-monitoring en.pdf.

[35] http://www.hm-treasury.gov.uk/media//DAA7D/adlei03 1234 496.pdf (part I) http://www.hm-treasury.gov.uk/media//132BE/adlei03 567rab 199.pdf (part II)

— distinguishing between professional and retail investors;

— tailoring provisions to the needs of the eurobond market.

The Treasury believes that the current text of the Directive will contribute towards overcoming some obstacles to cross-border capital-raising through the establishment of a true passport system, and that effective disclosure of information by issuers of securities will encourage market confidence and ensure better investor protection;

— **the first and second amending Directives on UCITS (adopted)** have effectively liberalised the asset classes into which harmonised funds can invest (thus extending from equities only to bank deposits and derivatives), and created a harmonised EU-wide marketing document for UCITS;

— **the Collateral Directive (adopted)** affects a huge market in the EU, with the total value of outstanding contracts on the market for repurchase agreements ('repos') alone estimated to be worth around 2 trillion euros. The Directive should help create a clear and uniform EU legal framework to limit credit risk in financial transactions through the provision of securities and cash as collateral. By determining which law governs cross-border collateral arrangements (market participants currently face 15 different legal regimes) and by allowing market participants to set up such arrangements in the same way all over the EU, the Directive is expected to reinforce financial stability and make secured borrowing easier and cheaper;

— **the Pensions Directive (adopted)** represents a highly significant first step towards a single market for occupational retirement provision and the operation of pan-European pension schemes. It anchors the prudent person principle in EU law, delivers some liberalisation of investment rules currently applied in some Member States and equips occupational pension providers with a single passport to offer their products across the EU. This is expected to make the market for occupational pensions more competitive and more efficient, and help break down some of the barriers which UK pension providers may have faced in the past when trying to access potential customers in other Member States.

— the purpose of the proposed **Transparency Obligations Directive (under negotiation)** is to establish ongoing reporting and transparency requirements for issuers of securities that are admitted to trading on a regulated market. The Government is concerned that the proposed approach places a disproportionate emphasis on investor protection, with insufficient attention to the implications for the cost of capital, and is therefore seeking clarifications and changes, in consultation with stakeholders.

— the proposal for a revised **Investment Services Directive (under negotiation)** makes some important steps towards improving investor choice and facilitating competition between trading venues. However, the Commission's initial legislative proposal included several measures that could cause significant difficulties for the financial sector, including the proposed rules on pre-trade transparency and execution-only business. The Treasury is working closely with stakeholders to achieve consensus on more appropriate measures. Discussions have so far been reasonably promising, with the likelihood of some positive change being made to the proposal. However, clear differences of opinion between Member States exist on some of the key issues.

20. However, adoption of liberalising FSAP measures is, by itself, insufficient to deliver the magnitude of economic benefits quantified in the London Economics study. The measures must be effectively implemented and enforced. Government welcomes the fact that, as it has pressed, the Commission's Eighth Progress Report on FSAP takes up these points and commits the Commission to rigorous action.

21. As the process of implementation and enforcement gathers pace, the Commission will be able to collect data allowing it to include more quantitative analysis in its assessment of the costs and benefits of FSAP. The Government therefore strongly supports the Commission's ongoing work on producing "indicators of success". The indicators will be a useful contribution to a rounded assessment of financial integration. The Treasury would like to see the indicators used both to identify potential gaps in the single market that might be tackled by official action, and also to assess the actual benefit of legislation against its cost to the industry.

COMPLETING THE SINGLE MARKET IN FINANCIAL SERVICES

22. The Commission's eighth FSAP progress report shows that there is still a lot to do to create an integrated financial services market. The Government believes that in completing the single market:

— any official action must be carefully targeted to address specific market failures;

— when Community action is necessary, the Commission should use all the policy levers at its disposal and avoid legislation whenever possible;

— all those participating in the decision-making process must act to improve the quality of legislation with rigorous cost-benefit analysis and consultation with all stakeholders;

— there must be effective implementation of FSAP measures by Member States, and effective enforcement of those measures by the Commission; and,

— the global dimension must feature more prominently in our thinking. The EU-US regulatory dialogue is an important first step and the Government welcomes action to develop this as soon as possible.

23. Considerable effort is being put into the identification of barriers to financial market integration. The Treasury is working closely with the industry in attempting to list and categorise reported problems in the cross-border provision of financial services and the establishment of financial services firms throughout the EU. The Association of British Insurers (ABI) and the Investment Managers Association (IMA) have been particularly active on this front, coordinating and carrying out research into barriers, and the proactive behaviour of the British Bankers' Association (BBA) has also been particularly helpful. The Treasury has urged the Commission to follow-up on the information provided by the industry and to take action as necessary.

24. The Government has encouraged the Commission to tackle its task of completing the single market by using all available policy tools. In the 2003 Budget Statement, the Chancellor encouraged the Commission to make more proactive use of its competition powers to investigate financial services markets that appear uncompetitive. The Government is taking forward further work in this field.

25. Although the Lamfalussy report sought to encourage better regulation, attention has focussed heavily on institutional aspects, and the recommendations on processes also need more attention. The Commission has recently improved the quality of its consultations, and is committed to using cost-benefit analysis gradually from 2003 onwards to justify its proposals economically. The Government continues to press the Commission to implement these initiatives rigorously, and encourages co-legislators to give similar thought to the principles of better regulation.

26. Improving the consistency of Member States implementation of EC legislation should make it easier for firms and consumers to reap the rewards of the single market. As noted by the IIMG, the activities of Level 2 and Level 3 Committees should facilitate cooperation and reduce the level of unnecessary inconsistencies between national regulations. More proactive enforcement of EC legislation by the Commission is also necessary. The current reactive process leading from formal complaint to infraction proceedings is time-consuming and crucially dependent upon the willingness of firms to bring forward complaints. The ABI and IMA papers mentioned above are one method for highlighting problems, and the Treasury will continue to explore others.

27. It is also important to bear in mind the global dimension of financial integration. The Government has repeatedly called for closer EU/US economic co-operation and highlighted the benefits of an enhanced regulatory dialogue, calling for a study on the potential benefits on EU/US capital market integration. The objective is to facilitate a better understanding of each other's approach to regulation via a positive, forward-looking dialogue discussing proposals for new regulation and legislation affecting financial services and considering liberalising measures in accordance with the stated aim. This needs to cover issues such as corporate governance, International Accounting Standards, capital markets, banking supervision, insurance and reinsurance. This will remain high up on the Government's agenda.

Conclusion

28. The integration of EU financial services markets is a cornerstone in the economic reform strategy set out at the Lisbon European Council. The Government believes that integration of EU financial services markets holds significant potential benefits for the whole EU.

29. The Government therefore supports the objectives of the FSAP. The Treasury has been working closely with stakeholders and co-legislators to secure economically beneficial outcomes. Although too many of the measures adopted under the FSAP have not been as liberalising as the Government had hoped they would be, it has still succeeded in securing significant progress. The institutional realities, and the magnitude of the potential gains, demand that the Government continues to engage constructively so as to influence both overall strategy and specific dossiers.

30. Much work remains to be done however to complete the single market in financial services. The FSAP measures must be implemented and enforced effectively. The Lamfalussy framework must be made to work successfully in the new areas to which it is being extended, and its better regulation principles applied more rigorously. Any new regulatory challenges or gaps in the single market must be carefully analysed and, where official EU action is justified, tackled with the most appropriate policy tool. The Treasury will continue to work with all stakeholders with the aim of delivering the benefits of the single market.

June 2003

Examination of Witnesses

RUTH KELLY, a Member of the House of Commons, Financial Secretary to the Treasury, and MR JAMES SASSOON, Managing Director, Finance, Regulation and Industry Directorate, HM Treasury, examined.

Chairman

493. Good afternoon, Mrs Kelly. I apologise for having kept you waiting briefly. Thank you very much for coming before us this afternoon, and to Mr Sassoon, your colleague, and thank you for the written evidence to the Committee which we have received. First of all, I repeat, thank you for coming. It is a delight to see you. I think it is the first time you have given evidence, on this subject anyway. Is there anything you would like to say, by way of introductory remarks, or shall we go straight into questions?

(*Ruth Kelly*) I think we should go straight into it.
Chairman: Thank you very much indeed.

Lord Shutt of Greetland

494. Can we talk about the Financial Services Action Plan. There is powerful political pressure to complete this Plan before the elections to the European Parliament next summer, 2004. Thirty-four Directives, out of a total of 42, have been agreed. The most difficult ones have been left to the last: Capital Adequacy, Investment Services, Transparency and Takeover. We see, even from the document which we have got today, at paragraph 17, that this speed is required. Do you believe that this deadline is going to lead to rushed legislation and poor decisions, and will the quality suffer? Indeed, is it possible at this point to have speed and quality?

(*Ruth Kelly*) To go back to the whole initial concept of a deadline, I think there are lots of situations in which having a political deadline is quite useful, because it does concentrate minds and means that people get on with the job. I suppose inevitably it is associated with something as large as the Financial Services Action Plan that if you do not have any sort of deadline or pressure then the thing could drift. Having said that, much more important than meeting a particular deadline is getting a Directive in place, which does open up the single market and liberalise the capital market and reduce the cost of capital. In every particular instance we try to come back to first principles and see whether the Directive in question actually is lowering the cost of capital, and we argue from a point of principle all the time, rather than meeting a deadline. To give you an example of that, in the recent negotiations on the Investment Services Directive, and you point to that, rightly, as one of the Directives for which there is a concerted attempt to meet a deadline, we argued specifically, in fact, we voted against the Directive in Council, that more time should be given to get it right and to make sure that all the benefits of a particular proposal were realised, rather than to try to rush it through. While deadlines do have their uses, we want always to go back to first principles and argue the case in terms of first principles. Some of the Directives, like the Capital Adequacy Directive, which you mentioned, are not part of the Financial Services Action Plan, and therefore do not suffer from that timetable constraint. We are very aware

that it is much more important to get it right than to meet a deadline.

495. Just referring to that Investment Services Directive, we were aware of that decision, which was news when we were in Brussels and Paris, and the speed and deadline argument. Where does this leave the Government's policy on that, and how important is it? Is that now lost for ever?

(*Ruth Kelly*) No, not at all. In fact, there have been important benefits secured through the Investment Services Directive. The abolition of the so-called 'concentration rule', for instance, will allow more competition to take place between regulated exchanges and large investment houses. What we were concerned about really was that the Directive did not go far enough in opening up the market. Particularly, we wanted to see a provision which would not force all investment houses to publish in advance of a trade what the terms of that trade should be, because we think that there should be some narrowing of scope for competition rather than widening it. We lost that vote because it was a qualified majority vote in ECOFIN. What we are doing now is working very, very closely with the other Member States who share our position, there were four others who voted against the proposal in ECOFIN, and working very closely with the rapporteurs and the other Members of the European Parliament. This Directive goes back to them now, to discuss, to see if we can secure further improvements, before it comes back in the spring. So there is still opportunity there for us to improve the Directive. In fact, the European Parliament has taken, from our point of view, a very encouraging stance in the past. We have to keep on the task and work very closely with other Member States and, of course, the City and others who have an interest in this as well, to try to improve it.

Chairman

496. Is it not also important to try to persuade some of the other Member States who voted against our interests that they were wrong in that kind of vote? If the Member States get behind their MEPs and it starts to become an issue of putting together votes, and so on, it may not sit very easily. After all, this is a situation where, apparently, because of a desire to meet the deadline, Member States were persuaded to go for majority voting. If they do that again, on another Directive, they could make a decision which is not the right decision, and, if this is the wrong decision, it is the wrong decision, is it not?

(*Ruth Kelly*) As I say, we did secure amendments, but we do not think those amendments went far enough, so we think there is more to be done to make this a truly liberalising Directive. Of course, that means that we work with those Member States who voted against, alongside us, in ECOFIN. Also it means working with more neutral Member States, such as Germany, for example, and Denmark, to try to secure the backing of their MEPs in the European Parliament. We are now developing a negotiating

Chairman *contd.*]

strategy for the next six months, which will mean, from ministers downwards, there will be a very concerted lobbying effort with individual MEPs, with the rapporteurs and with other Member States' finance ministries, etc., to try to make sure that they see the validity of our arguments and that it can be improved in the European Parliament. Obviously, we have to be pragmatic as well, but we do want to see a Directive which generally liberalises the market.

497. I think the short answer to the question of the Lord Shutt, if I understood you rightly, is that it is possible, in trying to meet these tight deadlines now, on some difficult outstanding Directives, for some hasty decisions to be taken that are not well-judged. I think you would agree with that, that is possible?

(*Ruth Kelly*) I would not want to underemphasise the ability that we have to persuade people intellectually of the case that we have in some of those Directives. In fact, some of those Member States that voted against the ISD at ECOFIN have already come to us and said that they are willing to work with us to improve the Directive, as it goes through the European Parliament. There is an understanding out there that the Directive ought to be made to work. Obviously, I cannot anticipate the outcome of those discussions, but we will be trying very hard to secure those improvements.

Lord Shutt of Greetland

498. Did anything go wrong at ECOFIN, in terms of that decision, and could that happen again between now and when this is to be concluded? Is there anything that can be done to stop it happening again?

(*Ruth Kelly*) I do not think you could say that something went wrong. We were one of four Member States who voted against the Directive as it stood. If we had had another Member State, things may have turned out differently. What we are going to do is try to improve it from here on in. So this is not the end game, in terms of this Directive, there are still many months during which we can negotiate improvements.

Lord Fearn

499. The outstanding draft Directives pose difficulties for many Member States—perhaps you will tell us which Member States—but Capital Adequacy, Transparency, and Takeover are some of the difficult ones. Do you expect them to be resolved by the spring 2004 deadline? If they are not, does it matter? Are some Directives more important than others, I am talking about ISD as opposed to Takeover?

(*Ruth Kelly*) Clearly, ISD is quite a critical Directive, in terms of the Financial Services Action Plan, which is why we are arguing very forcefully that we should make the maximum use of the opportunity provided to us. The Capital Adequacy Directive is not bound by that timetable, so it is very important that we do not act prematurely and that we act in concert with developments on the BASEL front and we have a truly international approach to Capital Adequacy. On some of the other Directives,

Transparency and Takeover, I think you mentioned, it is much, much more important for us to get it right than it is to have them implemented quickly, and we will continue to argue that case from first principles as these Directives come up.

500. You are still aiming at the 2004 deadline?

(*Ruth Kelly*) There will be some Member States, no doubt, and we would count ourselves among them, if we have a liberalising Directive, we would like to see it implemented and implemented quickly. It is more important to have a liberalising Directive than it is to see that deadline met.

501. Which Member States, in particular, apart from us?

(*Ruth Kelly*) We often have a number of allies among other Member States. If you look just at the ISD, we had four other Member States voting alongside us, but our negotiating alliances differ according to the Directive in question, because sometimes it depends on the structure of the financial services industries in those markets. We continue to go back always and argue the case.

(*Mr Sassoon*) Is it worth just adding, Financial Secretary, that the role of the Presidency is always important? The Takeover Directive, for example, the Italian Presidency have surfaced some texts as a possible compromise, which, in fact, may complicate the process of getting that sorted out. I think often it is not a question of who is in favour or who is against, but the Presidency has an important role in organising compromises for the six months that, as it were, they hold the pen.

502. The President is so powerful?

(*Mr Sassoon*) They have an important role for their six months, as well as the other Member States and the Parliament.

Chairman

503. Do you judge that taking a vote on it and pushing something through under qualified majority was, if not unique, extremely unusual, in the way in which the Financial Services Action Plan has been handled?

(*Ruth Kelly*) That is absolutely right, yes.

504. I assume you would agree with us that it is extremely important, if that precedent was one the Italian Presidency felt was a way of dealing with these matters?

(*Ruth Kelly*) We did argue for more time.

Lord Chadlington

505. SMEs are very important to Europe, and the AIM market has been a great success. There are some views that the Prospectus Directive is not very helpful in that regard. Are you happy with the approach that the FSAP takes towards SMEs, in general?

(*Ruth Kelly*) If you look at the overall objectives of the FSAP to lower the cost of capital, you could argue that is particularly important for small firms. Obviously, it is critical that particular obstacles and difficulties faced by small firms are taken into account at every stage, as Directives are formulated,

Lord Chadlington *contd.*]

and so forth. The point about the Prospectus Directive is quite a good one. Personally, I and officials on many, many occasions had meetings with AIM during the development of our negotiation, to clarify the particular stances we would be taking, and so forth. They were engaged fully with that process, and we obtained a result, from AIM's point of view, I think, which was a relatively good result, we did achieve a Directive which was liberalising. How we go forward and implement the Directive as negotiated is another matter that we have to consider, and we try always to take an approach which minimises the burdens on small firms and maximises the benefits, and look at that particularly. AIM is in negotiation with the London Stock Exchange, I think, and they are thinking of deregistering as a regulated exchange so that they can continue to operate the business model precisely as it was before the Prospectus Directive came into being. There is no reason why AIM should not do that, and indeed I think it is a very comfortable outcome.

506. Do you think there are other things we could do, in this context, to improve the contribution that SMEs make? In the general sense that, it is such an important market, are there other things that we could do to make sure the market flourishes?

(*Ruth Kelly*) What we have to do, I think, is try just to minimise the regulatory burdens on SMEs as they comply with European Directives, so they can take full advantage of that. We need to take SMEs into account in developing regulations, but also, as the Directives are implemented and we can see more data is collected, and so forth, the Commission will be in a much better position, further on down the line, to make an assessment of how any particular Directive impacts particularly on SMEs. It is in the course of developing that we ought to think whether the burden on SMEs can be made even lighter. We do this through the FSA, in Britain, who have a duty to undertake a cost/benefit analysis.

Lord Cavendish of Furness

507. I should declare an interest, as being terribly involved in my life with SMEs, and I often wonder, as the regulations pull at us, what machinery you use for finding out what we do feel, what we do need? Who represents us in helping you to reach a view?

(*Ruth Kelly*) We have an outward-looking strategy for negotiating European Directives, in the Treasury, which has been formulated over the past year and made more explicit. We have a number of groups which bring together the major interested stakeholders, where we discuss Directives even at the stage when they are just being dreamed up, rather than before we get into the detailed negotiation. Then they come together on a case-by-case basis and try to work through all the detail, and so forth. That is one way in which we take all of this into consideration. Also, as I say, through the FSA, we have a system which embeds a cost/benefit analysis into the way we implement proposals, and that is a centrepiece of our implementation strategy.

Lord Shutt of Greetland

508. Can I move on to international accounting standards. The Head of the Accounting Standards Board has said it is imperative that common accounting standards for listed companies are in place by 2005. Some of our UK witnesses have expressed concern about aspects of international accounting standards. When we were in Paris, the week before last, the *Banque de France* were totally opposed to IAS 39 in particular on grounds of prudence. We wonder, what is the Government's position on this issue?

(*Ruth Kelly*) We have taken the view always that the adoption of international accounting standards is probably one of the single most important things we can do in completing the European single market, and we have been very proactive in pushing that agenda. There are many reasons for that. From the financial stability point of view, you might argue even that the IAS is the one means we have of incorporating derivatives, for example, into the accounting system, into making them transparent. There are very many arguments, not just from that point of view but also in terms of investors and opportunities in the single market. The *Banque de France* comes at it from a slightly different perspective and argues that there are potential reasons why they are not in favour of the adoption of international accounting standards. Our argument against that is, and financial stability is one area, international accounting standards may have an impact on financial stability but it is certainly not the only way in which their impact would be felt. They have a huge impact on investment opportunities in Europe as well, and it would be wrong to look at just one aspect of their impact without looking at the broader picture. We are very firm on this and we think there are huge opportunities from a consistent application of international accounting standards across Europe, not least, in fact, that it could promote convergence with non-EU countries, and the United States in particular, in the future as well.

509. I may be mistaken, but my perception was that it was not that they did not want standards but they wanted the standards based on their prudential view, particularly with IAS 39. It seems to me that, whatever the standards are, so long as there are the same standards everywhere, everybody knows how to weigh up a company?

(*Ruth Kelly*) We have taken the view always that putting into practice international accounting standards and a common method of production is the way forward. I thought the objections of the *Banque de France* to this were slightly more to do with the adoption of international accounting standards in general, rather than a specific worry about their implementation.

(*Mr Sassoon*) Undoubtedly it is the case that the French are worried that the adoption of IAS in the present proposed form can result in a less stable regulatory framework for banks and insurers. I think the question is the balance between the objectives of IAS, as the Financial Secretary says, in deepening capital markets, because of their benefits for transparency and consistency across markets, and the extent to which actually it is the primary duty of

Lord Shutt of Greetland *contd.*]

prudential regulators, rather than accounting standard setters, to have primary regard for the prudential issues. We had a debate about this precise issue at the Financial Stability Forum last month, in Paris, as it happens. This is the six-monthly gathering of finance ministries, central bankers and securities regulators. The conclusion of that debate in the Financial Stability Forum was that reaching an international consensus on the unresolved issues was critical, and that the larger objectives which motivate the need for convergent accounting standards had to be borne in mind at all times but that financial stability was one of a list of three or four issues, including financial efficiency and transparency, which needed also to guide the process.

510. I am not clear on whether you think that there should be standards which are the same across Europe, or whether this is an area where there should be some flexibility. Which is it?
(*Mr Sassoon*) We believe there should be standards that are the same across Europe, and indeed the same globally.

511. Is it worth thinking through whether what the French are saying is something which ought to be adopted throughout Europe, or taking the different view from that?
(*Mr Sassoon*) I think, at the moment, the issue is not whether different standards should be adopted in different countries, because everybody is working on a set of IAS standards, but a question of whether, in respect of IAS 32 and 39, in particular, there is a more appropriate standard to be adopted.

512. Is this going to be something which comes to voting, in the end?
(*Ruth Kelly*) There is an absolutely huge amount of work going on in the International Accounting Standards Board, trying to develop common accounting standards. It has been going on for a considerable amount of time, and is coming at it, trying to develop as large a degree of consensus as possible, in what is an incredibly complex area. I think the principle that should account on balance-sheet for some areas, such as derivatives, and so forth, is one that we would push very, very strongly as essential to developing an efficient financial single market.

Lord Chadlington

513. This is an area where already there is an enormous amount of support for companies, this is not something which one is trying to push into people's hands. You see them in the insurance market, you see them in embedded value, and things like that. How is it getting hold of that support from those companies which are trying to push this forward as hard as they can?
(*Ruth Kelly*) The development of international accounting standards largely has been taking place through the independent accounting bodies, who are responsible for this agenda, and obviously companies have very close relationships with their stakeholders and they feed into that process. As I say, this is a debate which has been going on for years and a huge amount of detailed work is going into that. I think it is very commonly accepted that this is right up at the top

of the list of priorities for the Financial Services Action Plan and that companies will benefit particularly through induction.

Chairman

514. Certainly, when we discussed this matter with the *Banque de France*, they gave us the impression that they agreed with the approach to the IAS in general, they had the specific concern about IAS 39. Am I right in understanding that the UK does not have concerns relating to prudential aspects with IAS 39, that is not a concern that we share?
(*Ruth Kelly*) We think there are other avenues for dealing with any prudential impact that the adoption of the international accounting standards would have. There may be an impact. That is one of the things that is looked at, and, as James Sassoon said, was discussed recently at the Financial Stability Forum. Clearly, there are very positive impacts to be had in other areas, which we should not lose sight of, but the idea, I suppose, that we would get involved in the discussions of the International Accounting Standards Board, to try to push them in one way rather than another, is not a realistic one. They are a completely independent body, and they are taking forward an agenda which is very high up the list of priorities of companies operating within Europe, and indeed outside.
(*Mr Sassoon*) Both IAS 32 and 39 have been in use by many existing users for a number of years, so it is not that these are new standards, and indeed the US has a very similar standard. Our starting-point is that we recognise these are controversial, but it is very important that these standards are endorsed and adopted as soon as possible.

Lord Cavendish

515. Financial Secretary, turning to something quite different, which is the balance between the retail and wholesale markets. We have heard it said that, important though it is, the investor voice, or consumer protection voice, in Europe has had too much influence in the development of the Action Plan and that excessive concern for consumer protection is often a desire to protect national interests, it is suggested, by different means. Do you accept that there has to be a balance between overly protecting retail investors, on the one hand, and allowing markets, particularly the wholesale capital markets, to operate flexibly, on the other? Has the Action Plan struck that balance, or will the current proposals damage the wholesale markets, do you think?
(*Ruth Kelly*) Clearly, there is a balance to be struck, and we admit that retail investors do need to be protected adequately. I suppose we would argue, more forcibly than some, that there needs to be a clear distinction between a wholesale market which does not need such a degree of investor protection and the retail market, where retail investors need a particular level of trust and confidence to be able to operate in that market. There is a balance to be struck, and I would be the first to admit that there are different views in different parts of the community about where that line should be drawn. We come at these questions

Lord Cavendish *contd.*]

from a point of view which, as I have stressed before, often emphasises the degree to which the cost of capital could be cut, the desirability of a single market in capital operating across the EU and the benefits that would bring. Whereas other Member States argue slightly more from the point of view of retail investor protection across Europe and elevate that to a more considerable degree than we do. Having said that, all heads of state are signed up to the goals of the Financial Services Action Plan, and we are reminding Member States constantly of their obligations, which they have given to us already and made. The ISD, I suppose, is an example of where there is a delicate negotiation going on at the moment as to where that line should be drawn between retail and wholesale and we think the wholesale market definition should be made broader, but we are very mindful of that distinction.

516. Some witnesses have suggested to us that the emerging rules under the Action Plan could prove a disincentive to non-EU issuers on the European commercial markets. What do you think about that, and is there a danger that the Action Plan will diminish the international attraction of EU markets, and in particular those located in London? If so, what do you think can be negotiated?

(*Ruth Kelly*) As a matter of principle, a deeper and broader single market in capital in Europe should be of benefit, not just to EU investors but also to non-EU investors who are using the single passport that is provided within the EU. So there is no reason, in principle, why the Financial Services Action Plan should put us at a disadvantage, in fact the opposite, it should promote competition. We are always on the alert, looking out for potential barriers which may emerge. I suppose we have become much more mindful, not just in this country but across other EU Member States, of the issues which can emerge from instances such as the reaction of Sarbanes-Oxley to corporate governance scandals in the United States, and mindful of the need to have comparable systems and standards, both in the EU and the US. I am pleased to say, however, that, for about 18 months now, there has been a regulatory dialogue going on between the Commission and the United States, trying to resolve some of these more difficult issues, something which we encourage taking place very much. In the UK, we are trying very actively to broaden and deepen that discussion to make it more forward-looking and proactive, rather than merely a reactive discussion involving Member States and all the different stakeholders in the US and the EU, thinking about how we can make that relationship work much better and actually secure even greater opportunities than are provided currently by the Financial Services Action Plan. A few weeks ago, for example, I chaired a seminar at the Treasury which had representatives from the Commission, the political administration in the US, the SEC, others with an interest and financial sector representatives and representatives from the EU Member States, and so forth, to try to think about how we can deepen this dialogue further.

517. Generally, as far as this Action Plan is concerned, I am getting a slight impression that, compared with other issues, why there is an intractable difference of views between Member States is perhaps that we are winning a few arguments. A combination of the institutions in the City and the Treasury and your team are making progress. Is that right, do you think?

(*Ruth Kelly*) I think we are making progress. One of the things which helps us makes progress, which you may want to discuss later, is the operation of the Lamfalussy arrangements in Europe, which means that we can have a better debate about the principles of any particular Directive, rather than getting tied down in detail straightaway. Which gives us an opportunity to get in there, right from the beginning, and argue our case on first principle grounds for the opening up of the single market, induction and the cost of capital. Also, we are involved very closely with the Commission in developing indicators of success. You do not switch, you test individual Directives to see if they have achieved those objectives and really if they did lead to a lower cost of capital, and this is something we want incorporated into the way in which the EU conducts business.

Chairman

518. On that last point, in drawing up many Directives, that indicates a success, where looking at proposals and Directives or, taking one step earlier, cost/benefit, as it were, has not been notable for its presence and its rigour, to date. So you think that at the implementation stage there is more hope and rigour in getting results against costs than there has been in some of the Directives?

(*Ruth Kelly*) I think there is an opportunity, through the implementation process, of returning to some of these points and incorporating principles of good government, basically, and better regulation. Also, we are beginning to think now about what might come after the Financial Services Action Plan and we are pushing forward very much an agenda which suggests that we should move away from using legislation at every opportunity towards an approach which emphasises, as it were, removing barriers to competition, which may lead to non-legislative solutions just as easily as legislative ones, in fact probably much more often. It concentrates also on implementation and embedding these principles of better regulation and cost/benefit analysis, consultation and transparency right at the heart of thinking as the policy develops. We want to move things even further in that direction.

519. In answer to Lord Cavendish, just to get this right, some of our witnesses have suggested that the Action Plan, as it has emerged and is taken forward, does pose some dangers for the position of London in international markets, your view is that, taken overall, the ground is clear, it is an opportunity, not a threat, in your view?

(*Ruth Kelly*) We do have to be very careful in the implementation process that we do not erect barriers unnecessarily between the EU and non-EU markets, and one area in which this comes in is how you define, for example, what an equivalent standard or regulation is elsewhere. We are trying to move away from an interpretation which suggests that an equivalent standard or regulation elsewhere means

Chairman contd.]

one which is identical to that which currently is operating in the EU, towards one which is comparable and equivalent in a different sense, that you have confidence in the alternative system. We are very, very sensitive to those concerns which you are expressing, but we think that we can move the debate in that direction and have a very sensible discussion about how we relate to non-EU markets. This sort of regulatory dialogue and a pool of thinking that I have been outlining are some of the ways in which we are thinking about moving this process forward.

Lord Chadlington

520. Can I ask, Chief Secretary, it is a very interesting thought about the relationship between this and the US, and you said you have put this group together, what is the continuing mechanism by which the check and balance would go forward, so that we are looking always at what happens here and at what happens in the US?
(Ruth Kelly) Personally, I think that this area has been underdeveloped. It is for about only 18 months that there has been a proper, formal regulatory dialogue taking place between the Commission and the US. It is incredibly valuable and it is essential if we are talking through some of the implications of issues such as Sarbanes-Oxley. That is one which emerges from the US and has an impact on us, but there are others that emerge from us and could have an impact on relations with the US and US companies. What we have got to do is not only develop that regulation dialogue but think slightly more broadly about what issues there may be that are not on the table currently because of some crisis, or some issue, that has meant we have been forced into discussion, but how we can think five years, ten years ahead about what sort of market we would like to see operating and what steps we could take along the way to see that develop. That is a hugely ambitious task. I am not saying this is something that is going to develop overnight, but it is something that realistically we can start thinking about. We can try to identify particular priorities which might be more susceptible to that sort of approach, we can look at different strategies for attaining those ends, should it be mutual recognition, should it be harmonisation, in some areas, of standards, etc. We are just beginning to try to get that sort of deeper dialogue developed at the moment.
Lord Chadlington: That is very encouraging.

Lord Howie of Troon

521. A moment or two ago, you touched on the question of implementation of the FSAP, and I would like to carry on that part of the discussion. It seems to us that the manner of implementation is rather unclear. Some Directives require the maximum harmonisation and others seem to require the minimum, which is a fairly broad spectrum. What is the Government's view on this? Does it favour maximum harmonisation, or does it think that there should be more emphasis on mutual recognition?
(Ruth Kelly) I think our view is that most Directives and most issues probably will end up involving a combination both of minimum harmonisation and maximum harmonisation, and we have to be pragmatic about which is appropriate in which situation. I think those who argue for a maximum harmonisation approach, right across the board, are pretty artificial barriers, in a way, to the development of a true, genuine single market in capital. We would much prefer to see progress made along the lines of mutual recognition, of core standards, partly because it is much simpler and partly because we think that if really you want to see a genuine financial services market in operation you just cannot wait until you have exactly the same manner of implementation and approach in each Member State; it is much more efficient. So we argue the mutual recognition approach, but there are areas in which maximum harmonisation makes sense.

522. Is the UK Government alone in this, or are there others who think in much the same way, and are there many of them?
(Ruth Kelly) We have achieved outcomes already, for instance, in the Market Abuse Directive, in which the approach is one which follows almost entirely that model of mutual recognition, with core standards, and then individual Member States can build upon those in the interpretation of the Directive. That is a pretty key Directive, from the point of view of the Financial Services Action Plan. It is an approach where I think we can persuade others of the case for its implementation. There are other areas, such as information requirements in the Prospectus Directive, and so forth, in which the maximum harmonisation approach may well be preferable. It will depend from case to case as to which approach we adopt and argue for, but I think we can persuade others of the case for mutual recognition, when we have a strong case.

523. You say you can persuade them. Are any of them already behind it? You do not need to tell me, if you do not want to.
(Ruth Kelly) I think it is an approach which has validity in these contexts, and people look at the arguments and they can see the benefits of mutual recognition, but generally it depends from Directive to Directive which sort of camp individual Member States fall into. Of course, there are other pressures on individual Member States negotiating these Directives, and it is not always totally just a concern about the cost of capital.

524. In your submission, towards the end, in paragraph 29, you say: "Although too many of the measures adopted under the FSAP have not been as liberalising as the Government had hoped . . ." and you go on after that. Are the numbers successful because of implementation, or is it because they are not terribly good?
(Ruth Kelly) It is almost too early to say, about how some of these Directives are going to be implemented, because the implementation phase is continuing over the years to come. Some of the Directives, I think, have been really genuinely very liberalising, and the UCITS Directive has been welcomed across the board, as the Occupational Pensions Directive, for instance, has been welcomed by the City. The Prospectus Directive is another one which is liberalising. So I do think we have some real

Lord Howie of Troon *contd.*]

achievements which we can be very proud of, but there are issues such as the Investment Services Directive where we have been arguing a case and we do not think that it delivers yet the improvements which we would expect from a centrepiece of the FSAP. We are still in the early days, actually, of seeing how these things translate into action on the ground.

Chairman

525. Actually on the ground, it will soon have to start being pushed forward, will it not? On the implementation phase, there is the Committee of European Securities Regulators, CESR, and then there is the Commission. Do you think the Commission has enough resources to switch into ensuring the implementation is well followed through?

(*Ruth Kelly*) The issue of resource allocation is one for the Commission. Traditionally, I do not think this area has been prioritised in the way that it could have been. We would argue pretty strongly that they should focus more resources on the implementation and enforcement procedure in the future, as well as thinking, as I said, about non-legislative ways of opening up opportunities for businesses across Europe. For example, we are trying to encourage the Commission to adopt an approach that the Competition Directorate of the Commission uses in the financial services area, which is to use competition powers to look at a particular area to see whether barriers to effective competition can be removed. So there are other ways, which are not necessarily as resource-intensive as producing the Directives, which could have actually pretty powerful effects on the ground.

526. Again, you would find a lot of support right here in the Committee, I am sure. Time and again we have the impression, this is not a criticism of the Commission, it is just an observation, that very often the framing of draft Directives, and so on, is not as impressive as it might be. When one visits and tries to talk to people who do these things, it is a remarkably limited amount of resource, quite often, contrary to outside opinion, and those resources will have to be directed, as you say, towards implementation enforcement, at some point. Turning to CESR, do you see CESR as being an effective way of operating?

(*Ruth Kelly*) We have moved back one step to the Lamfalussy Process as a whole. That is one way of overcoming some of these resource constraints in the Commission, to consult, right from the word go, on the principles, and put into the actual wording of the Directive only the high-level objective and then leave to the lower tiers, including CESR, how to implement that particular Directive and make it work in practice. We have argued consistently for a less prescriptive approach from the Commission, more discretion and lower-tier committees carrying out that work. The regulators are in a pretty powerful position to be sensitive to their local conditions, particularly here, obviously, with the FSA, in the City of London, to be responsive. Regulations can be laid which are updated, rather than the whole process having to be renegotiated at Member State level, for example. I do think it is a very welcome development.

527. Do you think that balance of high-level Directives actually has been struck?

(*Ruth Kelly*) We have not had very many Directives go through this process in a fully functional format. We had the Prospectus Directive and the Market Abuse Directive, which were normally under the Lamfalussy arrangements, but they were very early in that process. I suppose the Investment Services Directive is the best example of a Directive going through it, with mixed results. What I would say is that the initial, draft Directive was put out for consultation at a very early stage, and there was a significant degree of engagement with stakeholders, right early on. The problems were run into later in the process. It is an incredibly valuable model for allowing people to get into the debate and engage early on, so I do think it is a very useful way of taking the process forward.

528. Some witnesses have said that the Directives have not stuck to high-level principles and there has been too much detail in some of them, and it would be very difficult to reverse some of those, for some time. Is that a view you have heard expressed or you share?

(*Ruth Kelly*) Early on, they were, absolutely certainly. It is definitely a view I share. There were more encouraging signs initially in the Investment Services Directive, although we thought still it was overprescriptive in the way that it was drafted, but there was much more initial input from stakeholders, and we argued that it should be even more high-level than it was. Looking forward, I think the model is the right one. We have to get it to work in practice.

Lord Chadlington

529. I also want to stay with implementation and think about the resources of companies, particularly as that hits them in 2004 and 2006. Mr McCarthy has suggested that we may look for some phased implementation to reduce that burden. Given that the EU does not have the same insistence on continuing cost/benefit analysis, which is now obligatory for new regulations imposed in the UK, what response do you have to this proposal?

(*Ruth Kelly*) In a way, Callum McCarthy was making some very sensible points about the implementation process. He was arguing, for instance, that the FSA had to be very careful about how it implemented legislation but had to be mindful of the burden of regulation coming from the domestic arena when firms were dealing already with Directives coming from the EU, for example. Firms themselves should be mindful that senior management time needed to be devoted to some of these issues, rather than just the implementation teams within firms, so that they do not over-implement what has been agreed already. He said also that he would take some of these arguments to the Commission to say that they should be mindful of the implementation process as well and not expect too much from companies and firms in any particular six-month period, or a year. A lot of the points he made are extremely sensible ones. The FSA is making them well and arguing them to the Commission directly.

530. How do you feel about this, as the Government, how do we feel about those kinds of proposals? Are you supportive of it?

Lord Chadlington contd.]

(Ruth Kelly) We have legislative obligations, obviously. We are committed to particular Directives to which we have signed up, but obviously we want to see them implemented in a sensitive way, and I think basically that is the point which Callum was making in his speech.

Lord Fearn

531. The Lamfalussy Process applies only to securities market legislation at present. Moreover, the European Parliament has insisted on a limited life span for the Process unless it is given co-decision powers, even at the lower levels of legislation, so that it can exercise a call-back if needed. Do you expect Article 35 will be agreed by all institutions—EP, Council and EC—as the right basis for continuing with the Process?

(Ruth Kelly) As far as I understand it, this particular Article and the amendment to it, there has been an amendment to it negotiated in ECOFIN, which would provide for the call-back power that you identified and the right of the European Parliament to be involved in that process, and will safeguard the Lamfalussy Process as it has been working so far. It is one of a batch of ECOFIN amendments which have emerged and which will be put to the IGC, and we will be arguing that they should be adopted wholesale. They are very sensible amendments. Through this mechanism, we think the Lamfalussy Process will be safeguarded.

532. Will there be any effect on banking, insurance, etc?

(Ruth Kelly) We need to see the Lamfalussy Process extended to the banking and insurance arenas, and still the negotiation continues about the precise make-up of those and where they should be sited, and so forth, but, potentially, there are very valuable gains to be had through the extension of the Process.

533. Is the flow going all right, on that?

(Mr Sassoon) What we are waiting for is, and as the Minister says, it is very important that the two additional committees, on banking and insurance, are set up. We understand that the Commission is nearly ready to propose the legislation which establishes those committees, and then there is work to be done on where they are to be based and just to get them up and running. Progress is being made, to make sure they do get up and running, and in the meanwhile there are other groupings of regulators, through ad hoc committees, which are beginning to do the groundwork, after which the formal, additional Lamfalussy banking and insurance committees will take off. So the Process goes forward.

534. If they have not started, as yet, will they get through by 2004? Obviously, not?

(Mr Sassoon) There is every expectation that they will, because, as I say, the Commission has just about cleared all their lines, I think, to enable the additional committees to be set up, and a lot of work has been going on to make sure that the practicalities are worked out as to how they will operate.

Chairman

535. You mentioned an amendment to Article 35, coming out of ECOFIN, I think you said. Could you tell us more about that?

(Ruth Kelly) Apparently, as I understand it, ECOFIN has proposed an amendment which would allow the Commission to be assisted by a Member State's experts in the development of financial services legislation, which effectively preserves the level two committees in a slightly different form from their operation at the moment. That is a key way in which the Lamfalussy Process will be safeguarded.

536. That would provide the European Parliament with call-back powers, would it?

(Ruth Kelly) The Process would provide a call-back facility for the European Parliament as well.

Lord Walpole

537. We have heard evidence suggesting that the Lamfalussy Process will fail anyway, and that the setting up of a pan-European regulator, in other words EuroSec, is only a matter of time. Other witnesses seem to see this EuroSec as a culmination of the evolution of the CESR process, and others argue very strongly that there is neither the constitutional basis nor the political will for a central regulatory body. Can you tell us where the Government stands on this?

(Ruth Kelly) We have concentrated very, very strongly, so far, on getting the Lamfalussy Process to work and safeguarding the Lamfalussy Process in the IGC. We think it is a bit premature to start talking now about what hypothetically an EU single regulator would look like, what it might do and whether we would support it, when we have pretty core objectives about the Lamfalussy Process, which, as we have just been discussing, has yet to be extended to the banking and insurance sector, as well as the securities. Also, I think, it is quite early in the day to start talking about whether Lamfalussy has delivered effectively or not. There is a formal review of Lamfalussy next year, and I am not even sure, at that point, whether we will be able to make definitive judgments on whether Lamfalussy has worked. Also it is worth bearing in mind, I think, that the concept of an EU single regulator means very different things to different people, when they are talking about it. I do not think there is a real lobby out there arguing for maximum harmonisation and a consistent approach right the way across Europe, driven by a single centralised body, situated somewhere in the EU. Actually, there is quite a strong consensus in favour of a different approach, with mutual recognition in some areas and maximised harmonisation in other areas, and so forth. We are at a very, very early stage in this debate, and we are concentrating very much on making the Lamfalussy Process work.

Lord Walpole: I have been asking these question of several people and I have found everyone's answers absolutely amazing and interesting.

Chairman

538. Taking the Action Plan and its thrust as a whole, do you see this as, in the words I used previously, a major opportunity for British institutions and business, and, of course, savers and investors, or one which still is to be proven, as it were?

(*Ruth Kelly*) It is a major opportunity, and that is why we signed up to the Financial Services Action Plan in the first place. It is why we have been pushing the agenda of a single capital market so forcefully. As you rightly say, it is not just for investors, ultimately it is consumers who will benefit from a fully functioning single market in capital, and industry, with a lower cost of capital, and consumers, with a much wider choice of products at a lower price. Having said that, it is important that the Directives which are negotiated are ones which further this goal, and certainly are not ones which set it back. Which is why we have been so involved in this process of, for example, indicators of success, each time trying to go back to first principles and arguing the case from that level for each Directive, what its objectives should be and what the high-level principles are behind it. Also, why we have been trying to get other Member States signed up on each Directive, yet again, to those goals, as they have signed up, in principle, at a very high level to the whole idea behind the Financial Services Action Plan, where they have to return to it at each point.

539. My last question relates to your submission. The Treasury submission rightly makes quite a number of points about the way in which the Treasury has been working with others to do the Action Plan. The impression we had from the early days of our inquiry was that, in the initial stages of the move towards the single market, the latest move towards the single market in financial services, neither the City and the other financial institutions nor themselves and HMG, as it were, perhaps worked as effectively together as they might. That sounds like a criticism, it is not meant as a criticism, it is simply a question of being faced with a task that actually will get us out of the starting-blocks quickly, and so on. We had an impression perhaps in the early days, across the board, it is not just a Government issue but perhaps the City and institutions where there seems there is a need to think about how to address the issues, and persuade, after all, 14 other countries that the rules of the game should be of a particular kind. Also we have the impression that, latterly, that has been improved enormously, and those kinds of criticisms are long since gone. Are there any lessons from the last year or two, two or three years, looking ahead, to draw from this, in promoting them, looking after and pushing for UK interests, in what is a vital area for us?

(*Ruth Kelly*) I think what it is fair to say, and I do not think anyone in the Commission, for example, would dispute this, is that the UK, on financial services issues, really punches above its weight, or whatever the expression is. We do have a lot of influence in negotiations considering where the starting position is, and some other Member States, and I think that has always been true. We have always achieved really a tremendous amount through the negotiation process, and sometimes have reversed, actually, some Directives which initially were erecting barriers to the operation of the single market, rather than deepening and broadening that single market. I think the lessons that we have learned probably are more about co-ordinating the lobbying approach. If I have one comment from the last two years when I have been Minister for this area, it is that, at the beginning, I think, there was a huge amount of lobbying taking place, but it was not co-ordinated very effectively. There was lobbying from the City, from the various trade associations, from industry, in different ways, a huge amount of lobbying from the Treasury, and the Treasury's consultation process with the City was informal and ad hoc, and I do not think they thought properly about how we could act to make that lobbying process work better. What has happened since then is that we have formalised our strategy and made it more coherent, I think. There are now strategy meetings about the direction of the Financial Services Action Plan, which try to look quite far ahead and think about what negotiating tactics we ought to employ on particular Directives, and so forth, and who is best placed to make them, and whether it is more effective trying to energise and get stakeholders and players and other Member States also to engage in lobbying, which will suit not only our purposes but ultimately their purposes as well. We have a formalised strategy group bringing together key players. Also we have groups formalised, coming together to discuss individual Directives, as and when they emerge, which bring together different people in different situations. Then we have lots of official working groups as well, when we get into the detail of individual Directives. I think my impression is that this has been welcomed very much by the City, and it has improved our negotiation techniques, and it has led to very concrete results.

540. You have been patient and very straight and forthcoming to us. We do appreciate it. Is there anything you would like to add, before we conclude?

(*Ruth Kelly*) No. I think that is fine, thank you very much.

Chairman: Thank you, and also thank you to your colleague, Mr Sassoon.

Memorandum from the Association of British Insurers

Thank you very much for your letter of 4 June inviting me to respond on behalf of the Association of British Insurers to the Committee's call for evidence for their inquiry into the European Commission's Financial Services Action Plan. I attach a note of the ABI's views on the specific questions you listed.

In addition, you may care to be aware that the ABI recently chaired a group of bodies representing companies active across most sectors of the UK retail financial services markets, with the specific aim of considering the success or otherwise of the FSAP in those markets. (This work complements that recently carried out by the Corporation of London's Industry Group chaired by Sir Nigel Wicks, which concentrated, in the main, on the wholesale and commercial markets.)

The work of our retail markets group culminated in a paper whose main conclusions were accepted by the Treasury and the Financial Services Authority (FSA). In March 2003, this paper was sent to Frits Bolkestein, EU Commissioner for the Single Market. I have attached copies of the paper, the covering letter, and the list of participating organisations for ease of reference.* In May 2003, Dr Alexander Schaub, Commission Director-General for the Single Market, publicly supported many of our paper's arguments in a speech to the ABI National Conference. A copy is also attached.*

While the attached papers concentrate on retail market issues, the ABI has equally strong interests in the EU capital markets, and we are actively engaged in dialogue with the Commission on the relevant FSAP measures. We would be very happy to provide further information on those, or on any of the issues raised in the attached papers, and to give oral evidence to the Committee.

INTRODUCTION

1. The Association of British Insurers (ABI) is grateful for the opportunity to submit evidence to the Committee's inquiry, which is very timely. The ABI's nearly 400 members represent around 97 per cent of the UK insurance market, which is itself the largest single component (30 per cent of total premium) of the current EU market. Many of the ABI's members operate in other parts of the EU and are therefore well placed to comment on the progress so far of the Commission's Financial Services Action Plan (FSAP).

PROGRESS TO DATE OF THE FSAP

2. The ABI fully supports the FSAP's aim of achieving a better integrated and more liquid European capital market. As major market investors on behalf of our customers, we are keen to ensure that the EU market in capital is as wide, deep and transparent as possible. While we have concerns about several of the detailed proposals which have emerged under the FSAP umbrella, including aspects of the Prospectus and Takeovers Directives, we remained committed to the ultimate objective of a genuine Single Market in capital. We would be happy to discuss in more detail with the Committee our views on these and other wholesale market issues. The rest of this paper concentrates on the retail markets.

3. The ABI believes that, while considerable progress has been made in the wholesale markets, the FSAP has so far failed to make very much impact on the retail markets. Indeed, participation of UK-based companies in other EU retail markets, while it varies somewhat by sector, remains low. For example, business transacted by ABI member companies in other EU Member States represents only around 10 per cent of net premiums. Only five British insurance companies earn more than 5 per cent of their premiums from the other 14 EU members.

4. The UK has therefore not yet realised the important benefits which ought to flow from a more effective EU market in retail financial services. These include group-wide economies of scale for our companies, a wider customer base, and opportunities for the exploitation of UK expertise in product design and distribution. Consumers across the EU have similarly largely missed out on the benefits of more competition, lower prices, and a wider choice of products.

5. The main reason is that, while many of the formal and legal barriers to establishment in the national markets have been removed, a level playing field for foreign companies does not yet exist in many parts of the EU. Most financial services companies choose to do business in the other national markets of the EU via subsidiaries, but are not yet genuinely free to compete with local firms.

6. The FSAP has not effectively addressed this problem. Instead, it has assumed that an integrated trans-national market in financial services is an achievable short to medium term goal both for the wholesale and the retail markets. Significant cross-border trade in retail products has thefore been its main aim. We believe that, while sensible for the wholesale markets, this does not reflect the reality of the retail markets. It is perhaps not surprising, against this background, that FSAP Directives, while having little impact on cross-border trade, have often had the perverse effect of adding significantly to the regulation of national markets.

What remains to be dealt with under the FSAP?

7. We believe that, as the Commission has itself recognised, new measures should not now be brought forward under the FSAP. Instead, the Commission should concentrate on the cost-effective implementation of existing FSAP measures (several of which have yet to be completed).

---

* Not published with this report.

The Lamfalussy process

8. We support the high-level regulatory principles contained in the report of the group of "Wise Men" chaired by Baron Alexandre Lamfalussy. These reflect the need for proportionate, flexible, pro-competitive and pro-innovatory regulation. But the Brussels institutions have a long way to go to achieve these high aspirations. Experience thus far of the Lamfalussy process in the securities industry (on which the Committee will no doubt have received separate evidence) does not bode well.

9. Nonetheless, we believe that the hierarchical system of committees for the development and implementation of detailed regulation, which Lamfalussy envisaged, can be made to work. There are two main conditions; first, that good quality cost-benefit analysis is built into every stage of the process, starting with the "high-level" Directives and moving right down to the detailed regulations; and second, that the affected communities (companies, customers and others) are consulted in a predictable manner, early enough to influence the substance, and with enough time to respond to the detail, at every stage of the process.

Effective implementation

10. If the Lamfalussy process can be made to work in this way, then the lower-level committees can play a vital part in the continuous monitoring of the effectiveness of implementation and enforcement. This should involve a regular process of retrospective cost-benefit analysis. One important objective is to avoid the tendency to implement Directives differently in different national markets, which is currently widespread. Not only is regulatory "gold-plating" in some markets a competitive problem, the differences—in whatever direction—between markets represent significant extra compliance costs for companies trying to do business in more than one EU Member State.

11. Competition law can certainly become a more effective tool for enhancing the Single Market. A shift in emphasis in this direction, including better co-operation between the relevant different parts of the Commission, would be welcome. We understand that this is something which the Treasury is currently pursuing in Brussels.

Other issues and non-regulatory barriers

12. The EU retail markets in financial services remain very local in character. This is why companies doing business in more than one market tend to favour local distribution, rather than cross-border trade. The social and cultural factors which determine this will not change quickly. But, as indicated above, the removal of remaining regulatory barriers to market entry (eg by better implementation of existing law) remains a crucial objective. Once this is done, the market will move at its own pace, allowing rapid integration in some areas, less rapid in others. Companies and consumers will see the benefits, because it will be easier for newcomers to establish themselves in local markets, so increasing competition.

Future development of the Single Market

13. Any approach to the future development of the retail markets must therefore start by recognising their varied and local nature. It must be built on a pragmatic assessment of areas where change would produce real commercial and consumer benefits, rather than on a theoretical assessment of the scope for market integration. Where a cross-border market has real potential it should be allowed to develop. Where it doesn't, time and effort should not be wasted trying to create it artificially. Second-guessing the market in this way, while superficially attractive, will almost certainly result in the wrong legislative framework. Facilitation, not prescription, should be the EU's watchword.

14. Not all problems need to be solved. Where costs will almost certainly outweigh benefits, action should not be attempted. Retailers in many sectors are familiar with the fact that some local variation (whether of taste, or of custom and practice) is simply part of the cost of doing business. Complete uniformity is neither achievable nor desirable as an objective for regulation.

15. For problems which clearly do need to be addressed, a variety of different approaches may be envisaged. Different solutions will be required for different problems, and one model will not apply to all markets. These will include legal action by the Commission in some cases, action by national governments or by the industry in others, and—perhaps in the majority of cases—better implementation and enforcement of existing regulation. New Directives will rarely be appropriate. The balance of resources in the Commission needs to change to reflect this. We believe the Commission recognises this.

16. As suggested above, far greater efforts should be made in future to ensure that genuine cost-benefit analysis is carried out for all proposals for new EU regulation. This should take place not only in advance of making regulatory proposals, but also after such proposals have been implemented. Retrospective re-examination—with a view to repeal, revision or better implementation—should become a routine part of the EU legislative process. Experience shows that there is a long way to go to achieve this.

17. The industry recognises that it must also set out clearly its own agenda in Brussels. It is not enough simply to respond to (or criticise) others' proposals. A start has been made, based on a preliminary list of the practical problems currently facing the retail markets, which we have shared with the Commission. By prioritising these problems in a realistic way, it should be possible to come to sensible conclusions about appropriate remedial action.

The competitive position of London and of the EU markets globally

18. To sum up, the FSAP has left untouched many of the factors which make it difficult for newcomers to enter the various EU national retail markets in financial services. At the same time, the cost-benefit analysis of existing Directives has been inadequate. The regulatory costs of FSAP measures have therefore frequently far outweighed any benefit to companies or their customers. If this approach were to continue, the EU would increasingly be seen as an unattractively high-cost and over-regulated environment for internationally-mobile capital. This would, of course, have adverse implications for the City of London, the EU's premier financial centre.

19. However, we have reason to believe that the Commission understands these dangers, and is prepared to adopt a different approach once the remaining FSAP measures have been completed. We hope to work closely with them, and with the UK Government, to ensure this is the case.

25 June 2003

Memorandum from the Association of Private Client Investment Managers and Stockbrokers

Thank you for inviting APCIMS to submit evidence to this inquiry.

1. We are the Association of Private Client Investment Managers and Stockbrokers, the trade association for some 240 member firms who, on more than 400 sites, manage the investments of the UK's 12 million individual shareholders. In April 2002 the European Association of Securities Dealers merged into APCIMS, increasing the organisation's ability to represent its members in the European institutions as well as in the UK.

2. Our concerns about the Financial Services Action Plan are detailed in the following pages but can be briefly summarised:

(a) We support the Plan's goal of establishing a more effective single market in financial services. Due to the UK's experience and expertise, we believe this would create significant opportunities for UK investment firms. However we are concerned that other states with less well-developed investment business have seen the Plan as an opportunity to introduce protectionist measures. The UK market is mature, open, innovative and responsive to change. The FSAP may well make the Continental markets more competitive but this may constrain the UK accordingly.

(b) Consumer protection is cited as the reason for a number of measures in the Plan which would in fact disadvantage UK consumers. The threat to UK execution-only business in the Investment Services Directive is a prime example.

(c) The Lamfalussy process has created yet another EU body (CESR) with which we must consult. However, it has yet to develop a culture of effective, open and genuine consultation such as that in the UK.

(d) Implementation will principally be the responsibility of the European Commission, which is largely untested in this role. APCIMS advocates an independent monitoring group to oversee implementation and enforcement Europe-wide.

(e) Competition is the most significant driving force behind the harmonisation of European financial services. The consolidation of Europe's stock exchanges and clearing and settlement systems are key examples of how business is bringing down borders and regulatory barriers—a process which can be encouraged but not led by political institutions.

A THE FINANCIAL SERVICES ACTION PLAN

What progress has been made to date? Has this been beneficial or deleterious to UK interests? Has sufficient weight been given to the position and experience of UK financial services industry?

3. We support the thrust of the Financial Services Action Plan ("FSAP") towards achieving the goal of establishing a more effective single market in financial services. We believe that a truly single market would lead to real benefits for EU citizens across all Member States, and would signifcantly reduce the costs of capital raising for all sizes of companies. We endorse the view of the EU Commission that a single market should result in substantial benefits for the EU economy.

4. It is therefore disappointing that very little progress, if any, has been made to date. Attached at Appendix B is a list of 12 of the key measures affecting retail and wholesale markets in the FSAP which are outstanding. Not one of the measures in the FSAP has been adopted and implemented[36] and the original deadline of 2003 for achieving the goals for wholesale markets is very far from being met. In our view, the reasons for so little progress being made are threefold:

(a) Absence of political understanding: at the highest level, there is a fundamental absence of political understanding on what are the desired outcomes from the FSAP. While the UK has been a driver and supporter of the FSAP, other states with less well developed financial industries have seen the FSAP as a measure to protect their industries. We urge that the international dimension of London as a global leader in financial services be promoted at the highest political levels.

(b) The new Lamfalussy process has been sidetracked and is at risk of being derailed. The very large backlog of legislation and regulations needing attention means that the process is being used in a manner not intended when established by Baron Lamfalussy.

(c) The lack of trust between regulators is also a factor. CESR has been slow to develop as an effective network regulator, and its difficulties in trying to agree a common regulatory approach are either a reflection of different mindsets among the regulators, or may be due to protectionist factors. But it is important to ensure that there is sufficient time to support CESR, and enable it to develop into a sensible quality network regulator.

5. We would like to draw the attention of the Committee to the following parts of the FSAP, which highlights key pieces of legislation and the major difficulties that they present to the UK.

(a) Investment Services Directive ("ISD"): despite intensive lobbying, there may well be an eventual outcome which results in the "execution-only" or no-advice option which is popular with many investors in the UK no longer being available at a reasonable cost.[37] The overall reach of the ISD is still not finally concluded. Whilst its intention is to be the framework legislation for creating a single market in financial services in Europe as has been said earlier all financial firms fall within it. There is now recognition that very small advice only firms, specifically the Independent Financial Adviser ("IFA") community, will be excluded from ISD requirements provided they have professional indemnity insurance which is now notoriously difficult to get. Inevitably there will be large numbers of firms who will have to make changes to current systems and practices to fit with ISD changes even though they will undertake no cross-border business. How such firms are going to be affected/protected from unnecessary change is still undecided.

(b) Capital Adequacy Directive ("CAD"): A financial firm that falls within the Investment Services Directive also falls within the CAD which designates the amount of capital that a firm has to hold if it is to be allowed to operate. The amount of capital varies from type of firm to type of firm, is substantial, and the current arrangements have worked well. The CAD however is being revised (and also renamed) following decisions that are due to be taken in Basel by the banking industry. The Basel Committee is proposing to change the way internationally active banks assess risks and apply capital according to these risks. The European Commission meanwhile proposes to take that work and apply it to every firm that falls within the ISD. Studies to date have shown that this would result in huge increases for investment firms wholly disproportionate to the amount of risk that they run. Whilst there is now some discussion to modify capital as it applies to investment firms there is still resistance to do so. Should this issue remain unresolved and an investment firm or stockbroking firm have to abide by a Directive crafted for major banks then it will result in serious increase in costs and the customer will pay substantially more for exactly the same service. It is important to note that these firms have no systemic risk effect on the market.

The size of the UK market, its culture and openness means that some aspects of Directives which are liberalising for the smaller and more closed markets operating in some European countries are likely to constrain the UK. For example, the Prospectuses Directive is "one size fits all" ie it covers all new issues, and therefore increases costs substantially particularly to small companies and AIM companies. As AIM is the only viable new company market in Europe, and as the UK has almost more listed companies than all other European countries added together, such measures bring the UK particular problems.

(c) Transparency Obligations Directive: is a key objective of the Financial Services Action Plan currently under discussion. Such a directive will require firms to report quarterly to the market. There is undoubtedly a cost associated with quarterly reporting although it is equally true that some of the larger plcs for practical purposes report quarterly at present. It needs to be noted that such

---

[36] The Collateral Directive and the E-Commerce Directive have been cited as successful achievements, but neither has yet been implemented in all member states.

[37] In 2002 there were 19m transactions executed on behalf of private clients. Of this total, 8m were executed on an execution-only basis.

reporting cannot be done without proper auditing as no company could afford to make a financial statement of this sort unless the numbers had been independently checked.

The main issue with quarterly reporting is that it needs to ensure that companies announce material changes to the market. In the UK, this is a requirement placed upon companies right now in that they have to report immediately any information that is material to the share price. Such a requirement is not present in most European countries where the phraseology about reporting to the market is in terms such as "as soon as possible". The real concern therefore is that a transparency obligation that will improve reporting in some countries would actually reduce reporting in the UK.

6. In concluding our remarks on this first section, we would also comment on the costs of implementing the legislation. The changes required at this early stage come at a high price for many small and medium size investment firms for no obvious benefit in either the short or longer term. Many firms are keen to continue with their UK client business, and have no ambition to conduct business into continental Europe. Yet they are required to implement all of the changes and regulations as if they were moving their business to a cross-border basis.

7. By the nature of European parliamentary and regulatory processes, the UK although it has by the largest industry has only one vote. This is not an area where qualified majority voting should apply. There is little doubt that many FSAP initiatives have been significantly influenced by the weight and experience of the well-established UK industry. But it remains a concern that the compromises put into directives in order to enable other countries to raise their standards do undoubtedly harness or constrain well-developed markets such as London. The UK has a real competitive advantage and other EU countries will invariably endeavour to restrain the single market because of the problems of the competitiveness of their own financial industry.

B IMPLEMENTATION AND ENFORCEMENT

The success of setting up a single market in financial services will depend to a considerable degree on the way in which the regulatory framework is implemented and enforced. How successful do you expect the Lamfalussy process to be? Are any changes needed?

9. Clearly the Lamfalussy process is still in its infancy and it is difficult to predict how successful it is likely to be. But already we consider that the Lamfalussy process represents the best way forward to produce flexible, adaptable EU legislation.

10. There was already, before CESR, a very well developed culture in the UK of dialogue between government, regulators and the regulated. The financial industry has long been consulted in an open and transparent manner, enabling rules to be developed which are workable and which will protect customers where appropriate but not stifle good business practices. This has not been the practice either in continental European countries or among the EU institutions.

11. It is only with the emergence of the Lamfalussy process that we are now seeing more attempts on behalf of, for example, the EU Commission, to listen to the issues being raised by industry on Directives that may be sensible in intention but might have damaging consequences if implemented unchanged. There continues to be room for considerable improvement in the Lamfalussy process in terms of genuine consultation. The purpose of consultation must be to ensure that proposed legislation is appropriate and that it will actually work. Consultation must ensure that new requirements being introduced are sensible, cost effective and proportionate in terms of the nature of the business and the business risks being undertaken.

12. We are hugely concerned at the short timetables involved. The ISD has what is known as 24 separate mandates for CESR which means that body is charged with responsibility for developing further 20 of the substantial proposals. Each mandate can result in several hundred pages of "implementing measures". Yet the timetable given to CESR by the policy makers allows them only 120 days to draft, consult, amend and finalise.

Who will be responsible for ensuring effective implementation and enforcement of the single market, after the regulatory framework is in place? How successful do you expect this process to be? What will be the role of competition regulators at EU and member state level?

13. Responsibility for ensuring the effective implementation and enforcement of the single market will rest jointly in terms of process with a number of bodies, including the Council of Ministers, the European Commission and CESR.

14. In practice, we anticipate that the Commission will seek to enhance its authority and responsibility in this area. The Commission is largely untested in this role and we remain sceptical that without adding significantly to its resources it can be effective in implementation and enforcement. But the real difficulty is in the absence of true political will to overcome the protectionist measures created by several Member States, often under the guise of "consumer protection.".

15. We would suggest that a truly independent monitoring group be set up whose findings are legally binding. The role of competition authorities should be strengthened since in many respects, action by competition authorities will open up securities markets much more quickly than action by regulators. Current actions by the Competition Commission in Brussels have tended to focus on issues between multi-national corporations and the achievement of landmark judgements. But we believe that many supposedly smaller issues have been ignored and these could have had really beneficial effects.

What issues will arise as the single market framework is implemented and enforced?

16. Some of the issues that will arise are legal, language, tax, and IT differences which make it difficult to conduct business across borders. Furthermore there is no mechanism for resolving cross-border disputes satisfactorily, and while this may not be a barrier for capital markets, it is a very real obstacle in the retail markets.

What non-regulatory barriers might impede the effective functioning of a single market for financial services?

17. We have already mentioned the absence of a mechanism for dispute resolution. Other non-regulatory barriers include the following:

— differences in national markets and trade execution processes;

— clearing and settlement systems

— differences in tax, corporate actions and financial and accountancy reporting.

C THE FUTURE

How do witnesses see the future development of a single market in financial services following implementation of the FSAP? Are additional measures needed

18. The majority of significant developments will be delivered by competition and consolidation and are likely to be driven by the industry rather than by regulators. Much depends on implementation and enforcement of the FSAP, and only after this will it be possible to see the gaps. The moves towards consolidation among stock exchanges and clearing and settlement agencies are noteworthy in this context. The protectionist measures taken by Member States to preserve their national carriers present a clear unambiguous obstacle.

Will the changes resulting from the FSAP proposals have an impact on the competitive position of London and EU markets as a whole in the global environment?

19. The FSAP proposals should be liberalising and open up to competition the European Markets. As, however the proposals are inevitably a series of compromises, the consequence will be the degree of competition and openness currently enjoyed in the UK is likely to be less because our markets work much more akin to the US model than they do the continental European model. Thus, as a whole we would anticipate the EU markets becoming more competitive but that London may well be constrained.

APPENDIX A

ASSOCIATION OF PRIVATE CLIENT INVESTMENT MANAGERS AND STOCKBROKERS

MEMBERSHIP 2002–03

Ordinary Members

ADM Securities
Abbey National—City Deal
  Services Ltd
Aberdeen Asset Managers
Allenbridge Group Plc
American Express Financial
  Services Europe Limited
Andersen Charnley Ltd
Andrews Gwynne & Associates
Ansbacher & Co Limited
Arbuthnot Fund Managers Ltd
Arnold Stansby
Ashburton (Jersey) Ltd
Astaire & Partners Ltd
Atkins Bland Ltd
Atlantic Wealth Management
  Ltd
BWD Rensburg
Barclays Private Bank Ltd
Barclays Stockbrokers
Barratt & Cooke
Berry Asset Management Plc
Blankstone Sington Ltd
Brewin Dolphin Securities Ltd
Brown Shipley & Co Ltd
Cambridge Investments Ltd
Campbell O'Connor & Co
  Stockbrokers
Carr Sheppards Crosthwaite
  Ltd
Cave & Sons Limited
Cazenove
Charles Schwab Europe
Charles Stanley & Co Ltd
Cheviot Capital Ltd
Chiswell Associates Ltd
Christows Limited
City Asset Management Plc
C. Hoare & Co
Close Fund Management
Close Private Asset
  Management Ltd
Collins Stewart
Comdirect
Credit Suisse (UK) Limited
Cripps Portfolio Limited
Cunningham Coates
Davy Stockbrokers
Deutsche Bank Private Banking
Direct ShareDeal Ltd
Douglas Deakin Young Ltd
Durlacher
Edward Jones Ltd
Ely Fund Managers
E*Trade Securities Ltd
Everys Solicitors
Farley & Thompson
F. H. Manning Financial
  Services Ltd

Fiske Plc
Fyshe Horton Finney Ltd
Generali Portfolio Management
  (UK)
Gerrard Limited
Global Asset Management
Goy Harris Cartwright & Co
  Ltd
Halifax Share Dealing Ltd
Hargreave Hale Ltd
Hargreave Lansdown
Harris Allday
Hedley & Co
Hichens Harrison & Co
Hill Martin (Asset
  Management) Ltd
Hill Samuel Bank (Jersey) Ltd
Hoodless Brennan & Partners
  Plc
HSBC Bank Plc, Stockbrokers
HSBC Investment Management
Iain Nicholson Investment
  Mgmt Ltd
I. A. Pritchard Stockbrokers
  Ltd
idealing.com Limited
iimia Plc
Incapital Europe Ltd
Insinger Townsley
Irwin Mitchell
James Brearley & Sons Ltd
J M Finn & Co
J O Hambro Investment
  Mgmt Ltd
John Scott & Partners
  Investment Mgmt
J P Jenkins Ltd
J P Morgan Private Bank
KAS Bank N.V.
KBC Peel Hunt Ltd
Killik & Co
Kleinwort Benson Private Bank
Laing & Cruickshank
Leopold Joseph & Sons
Lloyds TSB Stockbrokers
London York Group of
  Companies
M. D. Barnard & Co Ltd
Man Securities Limited
MeesPierson
Merrill Lynch Investment
  Managers, Private Investors
Morgan Stanley Quilter
Murray Beith Murray
NatWest Stockbrokers
NCL Smith & Williamson
Nichols Williams Durrant &
  Co Ltd

Noble Asset Managers Ltd
Norwich & Peterborough
Sharedealing Services Ltd
Oaktree Investment
  Management Ltd
ODL Securities Limited
Pershing Limited
Philip J. Milton & Company Plc
Pilling & Co
Principal Investment
  Management Ltd
Prudential-Bache Limited
Ramsey Crookall & Co Ltd
Rathbone Investment
  Management Ltd
Redmayne Bentley
Reyker Securities Plc
Raymond James Investment
  Services Ltd
Rothschild Private Management
  Ltd
Royal Bank of Canada
  Investment Management
  (UK) Ltd
Rowan Dartington & Co Ltd
Ruffer Investment Management
Russell Wood Limited
Savoy Investment Management
  Ltd
S G Investment Management
  Ltd
Selftrade
Seymour Pierce Ltd
Shepherds Group
Shore Capital Stockbrokers
Standard Bank Stockbrokers
  (CI) Ltd
S P Angel
Speirs & Jeffrey Limited
St Andrews Asset Managers
T D Waterhouse
Taylor Young Investment
  Management Ltd
Teather & Greenwood Ltd
The Share Centre Ltd
Thesis Asset Management Plc
Thornhill Investment
  Management Ltd
Tilman Asset Management Ltd
Tilney Investment Management
Truro Stockbrokers
Van Der Moolem UK Ltd
Vartan & Son
W. H. Ireland Limited
Walker, Crips, Weddle, Beck
  Plc
Williams de Broe Plc

Total: 142

Associate Members

1st Software
Advent Europe Ltd
Aitken Campbell & Co Ltd
Archipelago Europe Limited
Bank of Scotland
Barlow Lyde & Gilbert
BNY Securities Limited
BPP Professional Training
Bristol & West Business
   Architects International
Cantor Index Limited
Citigroup Global Markets
   Limited
CityCompass Ltd
City Consultants Ltd
City Index
ComPeer Ltd
Computers in the City
Consort Securities Systems Ltd
Credit Suisse First Boston
CRESTCo Limited
Deloitte & Touche
Depository Trust & Clearing
   Corporation
Dresdner Kleinwort Wasserstein
Evolution Beeson Gregory
Exact Technical Services Ltd

Exchange Data International
Fortis Clearing London Limited
HSBC Investment Bank Plc
Instinet Europe Limited
Investmaster
Investment Sciences Limited
JHC Plc
Knight Securities International
   Ltd
KPMG LLP
Lawshare Limited
Marsh Limited
MBA Systems
Merrill Lynch International
Minnie Business Systems Ltd
Misys Asset Management
   Systems
Monument Securities Ltd
NASDAQ Europe Limited
OFEX Plc
OM
On Bourse Limited
Optima Financial Systems Ltd
Penson Worldwide Settlement
   Ltd
Performa

Peter Evans & Associates Ltd
PricewaterhouseCoopers
Proquote Limited
Pulse Software Systems Ltd
R. A. McLean & Co Ltd
Royal Bank of Scotland City
   Markets Group
S J Berwin
Schroders Private Bank
Securities Institute
Speechly Bircham
The Stuchfield Consultancy
Summerson Goodacre Ltd
Sungard Investment Systems
UK Ltd
SWIFT
Syntegra
Talos Securities
Telekurs (UK) Ltd
Thomson Financial
Trace Datawise
Virt-x Exchange Limited
Wilco International Ltd
Winterflood Securities Ltd

Total: 70

Affiliates

Attorners at Law Borenius &
   Kemppinen
Brook Partners
Brown Rudnick Berlack Israels
   LLP
Chaintrier & Associes
Covington & Burling
Credit Agricole Indosuez
Cheuvreux
De Bandt
Doughty Hanson

Fontana e associati
Fortis Bank
Gomez Acebo & Pombo
Hannes Snellman Attorneys
   at Law Ltd
Houthoff Buruma
Kas Bank
Lombard Odier & Cie
Plesner Svane Gronborg
Prager Dreifuss
Puilaetco

Santilli e Associati
Solidarietá of Finanza
Sullivan & Cromwell
TELFA
Travers Smith Braithwaite
Verband unabhängiger
Vermögensverwatter
Virt-X
Wedlake Bell

Total: 26

LIST OF 12 PROPOSALS IN EU COMMISSION'S FINANCIAL SERVICES ACTION PLAN RELATING TO WHOLESALE AND RETAIL EQUITY MARKETS

Outstanding as at 26 June 2003

Proposal	Original timescale	Current timescale	Comment
1. Prospectuses Directive	Adoption 2002	Target Adoption by EU Parliament July 2003	Continued uncertainty whether EU Parliament will adopt July 2003
2. Transparency Obligations	Adoption 2001	Published March 2003	Suggestion that this cannot be completed in the current EU Parliament and will therefore fall
3. Investment Services	Proposal 2001 for adoption 2002	Published November 2002	400 amendments EU Parliament vote September 2003. Continued uncertainty whether will be completed by April 2004
4. Takeover Bids	Under discussion since 1990, original timescale long forgotten	New proposal October 2002 for adoption 2003	Continued uncertainty, compromise agreement expected which will render proposal meaningless

Outstanding as at 26 June 2003

Proposal	Original timescale	Current timescale	Comment
5. Report on Company Law	Review of Company Law originated in mid 1990s	Final Report November 2002. New proposals due late 2003	Fundamentally different corporate structures across the EU means that any proposals likely to be implemented differently
6. Clearing and Settlement (not part of FSAP)	Various initiatives, EU Commission timescales slipped substantially	Commission report due April 2003 now due September 2003	Competition Commission rulings would assist in resolving key issues of access, ownership and governance
7. Cross-border redress	FIN-NET was set up in 2001	Scheme in operation	Not widely used with several countries believing first course of action should remain in courts
8. Capital Framework for Banks and Investment Firms	Proposal due 2000	Proposal now due 2004 for implementation 2006	Timescales have slipped substantially. Very unlikely to achieve new target timescale
9. Savings Tax Directive	Proposal due for adoption 2000	Now expected adoption date in 2003	
10. Market Abuse Directive (2003/6/EC)	Original publication date delayed	Published in Official Journal in 2003	Member States to implement by October 2004 will not be achieved due to primary legislation required in several states
11. E-Commerce Directive (2000/31/EC)	Very quick adoption by EU institutions	Proposal published 2000	Due implementation in Member States by January 2002, but less than half of Member States have implemented and those that have are inconsistent in interpretation
12. Distance Marketing Directive (2002/65/EC)	Original publication date delayed and with many exemptions (including some financial services)	Published in Official Journal in 2002	Due implementation in Member States in March 2004, but consultations in Member States proceeding very slowly.

26 June 2003

Memorandum from The Bank of England

BACKGROUND

1. A Single Market in financial services has long been an EU objective. Achieving that objective should bring considerable benefits to the EU economy as a whole (eg through a reduction in the cost of capital for business and an increase in choice for consumers).

2. The EU Financial Services Action Plan (FSAP), launched in 1999, comprises 42 measures which are intended by 2005 to fill gaps in, and remove remaining barriers to, a Single Market in financial services. These measures focus on the legal and regulatory environment. It is important to note, however, that integration is unlikely to be achieved solely by implementing regulatory directives; other measures, in areas such as competition policy, insolvency law and general commercial law, are likely to be needed.

3. As a result of the FSAP, considerable progress has nevertheless been made, particularly since the Lamfalussy process was endorsed by the European Council in March 2001. The Lamfalussy process was designed to improve the quality—and speed up the adoption—of legislative measures in the securities markets, through enhanced consultation with market participants and the drafting of framework directives which are better able to accommodate changes in technology or market practice. The process is now being extended to banking and insurance and, in part, to financial conglomerates.

FSAP: SOME ISSUES

4. There are three main reasons why the FSAP measures, on their own, are unlikely to deliver a Single Market in financial services.

5. First, legislation, however well drafted, may not be an effective instrument to secure changes in deep-rooted "custom and practice" eg "home bias" on the part of retail depositors and equity investors, even if the will to make such changes were clear.

6. Second, the original FSAP does not, in any case, cover some measures important to establishing a Single Market in financial services, such as the removal of cross-border constraints on clearing and settlement (although the Commission is now assessing whether additional measures in this area would be helpful).

7. And third, individual FSAP measures have not always lived up to expectations, whether in terms of their formulation or their implementation.

THE WAY AHEAD

8. If or when implementation of the current FSAP programme of measures is completed, what needs to be done to make further progress towards achieving a Single Market in financial services? There appears to be widespread agreement on the following.

9. First, more emphasis should be given to ensuring that FSAP measures are implemented consistently and promptly at national level, and properly enforced. This requires resolution on the part of Member State governments and the resources, especially in the Commission, to undertake effective monitoring. The Lamfalussy processes and structures are explicitly designed as a tool to promote consistent interpretation and to ensure covergence in national supervisory practices.

10. Second, there is no need for another FSAP. New EU legislation should only be introduced in future if no alternatives are available. The costs of new legislation should be weighed objectively against the benefits before introduction, and the costs and benefits should also be analysed afterwards. The Commission's recent proposals reflected in the "Better Regulation Action Plan" for indicators of integration and efficiency are a step in this direction.

11. Third, where legislation is necessary, market participants should be involved through thorough consultation at each stage, as proposed under the Lamfalussy process. To be effective, this requires a genuine dialogue, which cannot be rushed; but by improving the quality of legislation, time and costs will be saved in the longer run.

12. Fourth, national regulators need to be able to use their discretion in adapting quickly and flexibly to market developments, especially in wholesale markets. In designing measures to protect retail investors, particular care needs to be taken not to damage the efficiency of wholesale markets.

13. Fifth, the EU competition authorities have a vital role to play in identifying and investigating barriers to competition in financial services across the EU, and instituting remedial action. This could have more impact on helping to create a level playing field for financial institutions, without discrimination, than a further proliferation of regulatory directives.

14. Sixth, evidence of discrimination needs to be brought to the Commission's attention. Market firms themselves may be discouraged from making such complaints, because of concerns about retaliatory action by national financial authorities, but their market associations and home authorities could take up complaints on their behalf.

15. Seventh, the Lamfalussy process should be given a chance to work, so that coordination between the network of national regulators can be made more effective. This should be the priority, rather than any attempt at this stage to create a central system of European regulation.

CONCLUSION

16. EU Member States share a common interest in achieving a Single Market in financial services. The benefits of open financial markets will accrue not just—or even mainly—to financial centres, such as the City of London, but to the EU economy as a whole. By contrast, if a Single Market in financial services is not achieved, the EU could be handicapped internationally, eg in relation to the US.

8 August 2003

Memorandum from the Corporation of London

A. THE FINANCIAL SERVICES ACTION PLAN—PROGRESS

1. We have long championed the development of a Single Market for Financial Services because the City today is a powerful example of open markets contributing significantly to Europe's Financial Services performance. This is amply demonstrated by the Corporation's annual report "The City's importance to the EU economy" (Annex A). In the experience of the City a more open market could bring positive benefits for both wholesale customers and retail customers by lowering prices and increasing choice. That would in turn enhance prosperity and job creation in the EU.

2. This is why we welcomed in 1999 the launch of the Financial Services Action Plan (FSAP) to complete the Single Market for Financial Services. Since then the City has been actively engaged in this market opening process as Europe's key international financial centre. Although most of the FSAP measures have since been completed, Annex B shows that the implementation date for many directives still lies ahead, so it is not yet possible to determine what their practical impact will be on the City or more widely. Anxieties about slow progress and the uneven nature of implementation of earlier directives have led to a general endorsement by the City of the Lamfalussy proposals to drive the process forward on the securities front. Practical experience of this process so far has been mixed, leading to increased concerns that implementation of the Single Market will be flawed because aspects of these directives may have been watered down and therefore may be compromised and ambiguous, given the need to reach agreement within a tight timescale.

3. This in part led to the setting up of a high-level City group chaired by Sir Nigel Wicks, which produced a report designed to spell out the principles and related practices which should, if properly observed, produce more reliable results in the decision-making process in Brussels and more even implementation across Member States (Executive Summary at Annex C).

4. Some of the most important FSAP directives remain to be settled. Observance of the principles contained in the "Wicks Report" could help to ensure that future decision-making is not only timely, but also fully consultative. The key objective must be to avoid any further cases of ambiguous directives resulting from compromises in the Council of Ministers, leading to difficulty in effectively enforcing imperfect texts.

5. As part of our dialogue with the European Commission we have been encouraged by DG Markt to provide them with examples of where bad EU legislation has been produced in the Financial Services field, and to identify those sectors and markets in which the most significant implementation problems have already arisen. This work is in hand but is not yet complete.

B. IMPLEMENTATION AND ENFORCEMENT

6. We recognise that the economic gains expected from the creation of a Single Market in Financial Services will not be fully achieved unless implementation and enforcement is given much greater attention. This is why the Wicks Group has made specific recommendations regarding surveillance, implementation and enforcement both at the national level and by the Commission. We believe the Commission itself recognises the need to strengthen its role in this area. For this reason Lord Tomlinson (Alternate National Parliamentary Representative to the Convention of the Future of Europe), drawing on the recommendations of the Wicks Group paper, proposed to the Convention that in order to ensure the proper functioning and development of the Single Market the Commission should be required regularly to:

(i)   evaluate through a detailed and systematic process whether Member States' laws and administrative procedures comply with European Union legislation regarding the Single Market, competition and state aids policy and whether it should bring proceedings for infringement for any failure to comply;

(ii) review those sectors in which the Single Market remains to be completed and identify what further Union or Member State action is needed to complete the Single Market in those sectors;

(iii) report to the Council and Parliament on the above; and

(iv) consult in a timely manner with market practitioners and give a reasoned response.

7. We welcome the fact that according to their latest announcements the Commission intends to work more closely with Member State goverments on implementation issues. More adequate resources will be needed to make heightened attention to implementation and enforcement a reality. The economic gains to be achieved should more than justify the provision of additional resources for this purpose.

8. In principle, we welcome the extension of the Lamfalussy process to cover not only securities, but insurance and banking. It will be important to ensure that the lessons so far learnt from the early stages of the process as applied to securities will be fully reflected in the consultative procedures agreed on for these new Lamfalussy areas of regulatory activity.

C. THE FUTURE

9. The future development of the Single Market for Financial Services must depend very much in practice on the effective implementation of the full range of FSAP measures when completed by 2005. A period of consolidation rather than further legislative activity would then recommend itself to most practitioners faced with such a large volume of new regulatory requirements.

10. In order to aid the process of ensuring that there is a more coherent strategy towards the delivery of the economic gains from a Single Market for Financial Services, various City trade associations and the Corporation of London have commissioned surveys of business opinion and research into the ways in which this could be achieved. A survey of City opinions regarding a Single Market in Retail Financial Services has been submitted to the Commission by a Working Group co-ordinated by the Association of British Insurers.

This highlights the fact that there are concerns about obstacles preventing retail products being made available in other Member States, which go beyond the reach of the FSAP itself.

11. A report commissioned by the Investment Management Association with the support of the Corporation of London has recently been launched in Brussels and looks at the way forward for asset management across Europe on a dynamic basis. This helps to show the benefits which could be secured from a Single European Market in this field if the obstacles to cross-border trade were removed.

12. The Corporation has also recently published reports on Financial Services Clustering and its significance for London, on the future of stock exchanges in European Union accession countries and on London's ranking as a financial centre. Such surveys of opinion as well as underlying research reports into market trends are designed to build a more comprehensive picture of the future dynamics of an effective Single Market for Financial Services.

13. Because we are aware of the need to share more readily the City's experience and strategic thinking, and to enter into a fuller dialogue with the European Commission and the European Parliament, we have recently decided to open a City office in Brussels. This will be backed up by a City Advisory Group reflecting the very broad international nature of the UK-based financial services market place located in London, but also spread more widely across the UK.

26 June 2003

List of Annexes

Annex A—Executive summary of "The City's contribution to the EU economy" 2 January 2003.

Annex B—Implementation dates for FSAP measures.

Annex C—Executive Summary of the "Wicks Report" of November 2002.

1. Executive Summary

The city's importance to the European Union economy is an annual report on the contribution of London's investment banking and related sectors to the overall prosperity and economic performance of the UK and the EU.

Throughout this report, we deal with what we call "City-type" activities—international lending, securities issuance and trading, fund management, corporate finance, plus related activities such as insurance and relevant professional services. Most of this activity in London occurs within the City of London, although some is based outside the Square Mile in the West End, the City Fringe, Docklands or elsewhere. We consider the contribution of London as a whole, and the use of the word "City" throughout this report should be taken to include all City-type activities across London.

1.1 *Key findings*

The key findings in this report are:

— London is a financial centre of truly global scale and scope. There were 325,000 people employed in London to do City-type jobs at the peak of the current business cycle in 2000. Even with a decrease to an estimated 305,000 jobs in June 2002, they conduct over half of all EU investment banking and related business.

— The current fall in investment banking and related jobs—what we call City-type employment—in London is set to end by late 2003. The figure should stabilise at around 295,000, but we do not expect to see it rise significantly before 2006.

— London's international position should not be taken for granted. There is a small but nonetheless real danger that the current global economic and market slowdown, and broader international political developments, could prompt the departure of some foreign banks from London. Without this critical mass, London's attractiveness as an international financial centre could be terminally damaged.

— Business with the EU is an essential part of activity in the City. Around a third of London's turnover in international banking, international equities, bonds, corporate finance and derivatives originates from clients in EU Member States other than the UK.

— Around 76,000 City-type jobs in London (23 per cent of total City-type employment) depend on business from the other EU states.

— Many transactions in London are conducted in euros. Over two-fifths (41 per cent) of foreign exchange trading involve the euro and in other areas, such as derivatives, the euro is equally important.

— There is still little evidence to suggest that the launch of the euro in 1999, and the UK's continued non-participation, has harmed London's competitive position in the EU financial services sector. The Bank of England has concluded likewise in its November 2002 publication *"Practical Issues Arising from the Introduction of the Euro"*.

— Just under 100 EU-owned banks have operations in London, where they employ nearly 30,000 people and have assets worth over $1,000 billion.

— Without the cluster of global finance companies in and around the City, City-type operations would be more expensive across the EU. Without this cluster, the EU would lose 18 per cent of its City-type business to competitors on other continents. A further 12 per cent would be lost altogether as higher costs would make some transactions unviable.

— With London operating as a global financial centre, annual EU GDP is €33 billion higher, and employment 193,000 higher, than it would otherwise be.

— If the financial cluster in London did not exist, employment levels in Luxembourg, the Netherlands, Germany, France, Belguim and Italy, as well as in the UK, would be adversely affected.

— Two recently proposed pieces of EU legislation—the amended Investment Services Directive and the Prospectuses Directive—contain elements that may affect some City markets adversely. This possible adverse effect could be especially serious for the over-the-counter equities trading market in London, where annual turnover could decrease by £250 billion, and on the primary market for equity of small companies, which account for more than half of all listed companies on London exchanges.

Annex B

IMPLEMENTATION OF FSAP COMPLETED MEASURES

Issue	Adoption Date	Implementation Date
Title and Number		
Directive 2000/46/EC on the taking up, pursuit of and prudential supervision of the business of electronic money institutions OJ L 275/39, 27.10.2000	September 18, 2000	April 27, 2002
Directive 2000/64/EC to permit information exchange with third countries (Amending Insurance Directives 92/49/EEC and 92/96/EEC and Investment Services Directive 93/22/EEC) OJ L 290/27, 17.11.2000	November 7, 2000	November 17, 2002
Commission Recommendation on pre-contractual information to be given to consumers by lenders offering home loans OJ L 69/25, 10.03.2001	March 1, 2001	September 30, 2002
Directive 2001/17/EC on the Reorganisation and Winding-up of insurance undertakings OJ L 110/28, 20.4.2001	March 19, 2001	April 20, 2003
Directive 2001/24/EC on the Winding-up and Liquidation of Credit Institutions OJ L 125/15, 5.5.2001	April 4, 2001	May 5, 2004
Directive 2001/65/EC amending to the 4th and 7th Company Law Directives to allow fair value accounting OJ L 283/28, 27.10.2001	May 31, 2001	January 1, 2004
Directive 2001/86/EC on supplementing the Statute for a European company with regard to the involvement of employees OJ L 294/22,10.11.2001	October 8, 2001	October 8, 2004
Council Regulation (EC) No 2157/2001 on the Statute for a European company (SE) OJ L 294/1, 10.11.2001	October 1, 2001	October 1, 2001

Issue	Adoption Date	Implementation Date
Directive 2001/97/EC on prevention of the use of the financial system for the purpose of money laundering (Amending Directive 91/308/EC) OJ L 344/76, 28.12.2001	December 4, 2001	June 15, 2003
Directives 2001/107/EC and 2001/108/EC on UCITS OJ L 41/20, 13.2.2002	January 21, 2002	February 13, 2004
Directives 2002/12/EC (life insurance) and 2002/13/EC (non-life insurance) on the solvency margin requirements in the Insurance Directives (Amending Directives 73/239/EC and 79/267/EC) OJ L 77/11, 20.3.2002	March 5, 2002	September 20, 2003
Directive 2002/47/EC on financial collateral arrangements OJ L 168/43, 27.6.2002	June 6, 2002	December 27, 2003
Regulation (EC) 1606/2002 on the application of international accounting standards OJ L 243/1, 11.09.2002	July 19, 2002	January 1, 2005
Directive 2002/65/EC on the Distance Marketing of Financial Services OJ L 271/16, 9.10.2002	September 23, 2002	October 9, 2004
Directive 2002/92/EC on Insurance Mediation OJ L 9/3, 15.1.2003	December 9, 2002	January 15, 2005
Directive 2002/87/EC on the supplementary supervision of credit institutions, insurance undertakings and investment firms in a financial conglomerate (Amending Insurance, Banking, Investment services Directive 73/239/EEC, 79/267/EEC, 92/49/EEC, 92/96/EEC, 93/6/EEC, 93/22/EEC, 98/78/EC, 2000/12/EC) OJ L 35/1, 11.2.2003	December 16, 2002	August 11, 2004
Directive 2003/6/EC on Insider Dealing and Maket Manipulation (Market Abuse) OJ L 96/16, 12.4.2003	January 28, 2003	October 12, 2004
Directive on the annual and consolidated accounts of certain types of companies, banks and other financial institutions and insurance undertakings (Amending Directives 78/660/EEC, 83/349/EEC, 86/635/EEC, 91/674/EEC) Not yet published in the OJ	May 6, 2003	January 1, 2005
Directive on disclosure requirements in respect of certain types of companies	No formal adoption yet	December 31, 2006

Annex C

EXECUTIVE SUMMARY

Creating the Single European Market for Financial Services

This note:

— Recalls the Lisbon Council Conclusions calling for the completion of the single market in financial services, which is one where buyers and sellers of financial services and products may deal with one another throughout the EU, wherever they, their systems or infrastructures may be located:

— Emphasises the benefits, in terms of greater choice and better value for customers, prosperity, jobs and growth, which a single financial services market can bring.

— Describes what the single financial market should look like, including the need to be responsive to users.

— Reminds that financial markets usually work with "other people's money" and that investors expect markets to operate in a stable, responsible and ethical manner and to be subject to higher standards of governance and accountability.

— Explains why such a market does not yet exist.

— Sets out eight Principles and Practices to underpin policy, legislation, consultation, regulation, surveillance, implementation, enforcement, corporate governance and external review which are needed to achieve the objective of a competitive, innovative fully functioning single market.

On the basis of the reasoning in this paper, it is suggested for discussion that the following Principles and practices should be formally enshrined in the most authoritative manner in Community law and practice:

1. Markets are created and developed by market participants not by rules and regulations (paragraph 36).

2. Policy instruments other than legislation should always be considered in preference to the legislative route. If legislation is necessry it should be proportionate, cost effective and address clear market failure (paragraphs 37-38).

3. Consultation with participants is required at all stages, and in a timely manner, and with a reasoned response to practitioner input (paragraphs 39-41).

4. Regulation must be risk based, taking account of the different nature of the risks facing the different types of firms, customers, investors and counterparties (paragraphs 42-43).

5. Surveillance, implementation and enforcement must be effective both at the national level and by the Commission (paragraphs 44-45).

6. Regulation and behaviour of market participants must help build fair and honest markets, while not frustrating or stultifying their innovation and development (paragraph 46).

7. Representatives of market practitioners should provide regular reports to the European Council, ECOFIN, Parliament and Commission on progress towards creating a fully functioning single market (paragraph 47).

8. A European Financial Market Forum should be established to help develop a coherent approach and philosophy for the creation of the Single Market (paragraphs 48-50).

Inquiry into the Financial Services Action Plan: CBI submission to Sub-Committee B of the House of Lords Select Committee on the European Union

The CBI is a membership organisation, which represents UK, EU and other companies based in the UK, including both providers and users of financial services. With direct corporate membership employing over four million and trade association membership representing over six million of the UK workforce, the CBI is the premier organisation speaking for companies in the UK. The CBI is the UK member of UNICE, the European employers' federation.

The following has been written mainly from the viewpoint of user members, since many providers have already made separate submissions, although it is important to stress that, in most cases under the Action Plan, their concerns have been identical.

A. THE FINANCIAL SERVICES ACTION PLAN

What progress has been made to date? Has this been beneficial or deleterious to UK interests? Has sufficient weight been given to the position and experience of UK financial services industry? What are the main outstanding matters that remain to be dealt with under the FSAP and what key issues will need to be resolved?

The concept of a single market in financial services is one supported by CBI members, whether providers or users. Nevertheless, progress towards this has been sketchy and in some cases has threatened UK interests eg prospectus and investment services directives. Since UK legislation in financial services is well suited to the international marketplace, it may stand to lose more from harmonisation than other countries, where both drafting and negotiations may be subject to political compromise between Member States.

The main outstanding measures are the transparency, takeover, capital adequacy and investment services directives. The CBI gave evidence earlier this year to Sub-Committee E of the House on the takeover directive. Particularly on investment services, the feeling of the City is that not enough weight has been given to the position and experience of UK financial services industry. And on the transparency directive, the feeling of users is that not enough weight has been given to their views (and those of others) against quarterly reporting. However, there is great political pressure to complete outstanding legislative measures under the FSAP by April 2004 because of the change of Commission and Parliament elections so that little time is left to influence these. The main issue for this paper is therefore not these individual directives but what will happen to the FSAP measures at national implementation and what lessons can be learned for the future, particularly for the forthcoming Company Law and Corporate Governance Action Plan, where there are already similar warning signs.

B. Implementation and Enforcement

How successful do you expect the Lamfalussy process to be? Are any changes needed?

So far we have not seen much use of the Lamfalussy process (as reported by the Inter-Institutional Monitoring Group) since that was predicated upon proper consultation. The Commission singularly failed to consult on the prospectus and market abuse directives, which could not be said to have been issued under Lamfalussy, and the quality of those proposals reflected this. Nevertheless we believe that the Lamfalussy process, if applied as intended, should be a positive step forward.

There are, however, some misconceptions about the Lamfalussy process and there is a danger that it will be judged only on its ability to speed up legislation rather than on improvements to quality. From the point of view of users of financial services, it is no use having legislation passed quickly if its effect is to increase costs, impede the single market or otherwise fail to achieve its aims. Quality is more important than speed and CBI members would prefer to have no than to have bad legislation.

Although the Lamfalussy process may or may not speed up the initial legislation, it should improve the speed of amending proposals later where flexibility is needed. It should also enable initial legislation to be passed faster, with the need for fewer drafting changes, where time has been taken before issuing formal legislative proposals to examine the different practices in member states, to understand why these are so and then to arrive at consensus as to what needs to be changed.

The failings of the proposals so far have not been the result of the Lamfalussy process. The main failings so far have been:

(i) inadequate consultation of and information for users, including inadequate or misleading regulatory impact assessments, as to the likely outcomes of the various options,

(ii) insufficient expertise and resources at the Commission and CESR, and

(iii) lack of project planning/unrealistic deadlines agreed by the Council and the Commission.

(i) *Consultation and information:* The lack of proper consultation at the outset on some proposals means that no consensus had developed among Member States and industry as to the best way to achieve the desired outcomes. Companies will be reluctant to support radical changes to the systems they know with ensuing costs and internal reorganisations, unless they can be convinced that the changes will represent an improvement on current practices and that they will thereby obtain benefit. Mere assertions by politicians that change represents such an improvement without the evidence to back these up are unlikely to be convincing. And the evidence has been sketchy—the regulatory impact assessment for the transparency directive, for example, could be read as suggesting that all UK companies already have to make mandatory quarterly reports, which is clearly not the case. Again the prospectus directive literature made sweeping assertions about what the proposals would achieve, which were contradicted by CBI members with experience of the markets.

In addition, some of the proposals under the FSAP have not appeared to be intended to develop a single market but rather to assist national protectionism. It is difficult to prove this because of a lack of sufficient research/evidence before proposals are published. For example, on the investment services directive, all members of UNICE were agreed that the desired outcome was one in which the costs were low and liquidity was good, but without clear evidence either way on the likely outcomes of the different options, were split along national lines. More rigorous debate supported by competition arguments might have helped to enable European federations to reach a common view on their best interests. Without this, it is inevitable that they will continue to try to change as little as possible in their national regimes, thus impeding the development of a single market.

(ii) *Insufficient expertise and resources at the Commission and CESR:* while London is a sophisticated financial market used to dealing with many different types of securities, the same is not true of the markets of all other member states. Commission and CESR staff being drawn from a variety of Member States will not necessarily have the necessary background knowledge of the larger wholesale markets. Even those officials from countries with such markets may have no market experience and thus no knowledge of the subject in which they are drafting legislation. While this is not necessarily a disaster where there is adequate and lengthy consultation, with willingness to listen and understanding on the part of officials that matters may be complex, it may be where the legislation is rushed and subject to unrealistic deadlines.

On the question of consultations by CESR, many hold the view that these are too detailed and difficult for companies to follow. The documents are very long and there are no simple summaries of the key issues for companies, which are forced to rely on the detailed work of professional firms or bodies such as the International Primary Market Association, to study the text in detail and draw to users' attention any particularly urgent issues. The reality is, however, that the constant stream of documentation is far too long and detailed to be accessible to users of financial servies, who will be dependent upon the providers to ensure that the final proposals are sensible or to alert them to any really serious issues. In addition, few people within companies are even aware of CESR and its rule making powers in the same way as they are aware of the FSA and the Listing Rules and have not therefore devoted similar resources to its work.

(iii) *Unrealistic deadlines agreed by the Council of Member States and a failure by the Commission to undertake project planning:* the goals for the FSAP were set as part of the Lisbon process to achieve a competitive EU. There is no check on the quality of legislative proposals passed; the Commission's updates on progress focus on the quantity of legislative proposals passed and not on quality or on implementation, which are the key issues for users. The temptation of this approach is to pass as many easy measures as possible at the start and to leave many of the difficult decisions until the end, thus giving rise to poor quality legislation and a difficult legislative passage for many controversial issues, when agreement must be reached regardless of worth because political credibility is at stake. It should be possible for the Commission to reschedule such Action Plans when it becomes clear that the timetable originally envisaged was unrealistic. In this area, there is the danger that the Company Law Action Plan may repeat many of the mistakes of the FSAP.

Nevertheless, there are some indications of change, which we welcome. The Commission published its first working documents on market abuse, thus increasing transparency and allowing companies' advisers to highlight potential areas for concern before the formal legislative process begins so that these can more easily be corrected. We believe that this increased transparency should be welcomed.

The European Parliament has also played a very important role in improving many of the badly drafted proposals emanating from the Commission and we hope that the Committee will recognise the importance of MEPs' work, particularly UK MEPs on the Economic and Monetary Affairs Committee, in this respect. Nevertheless there is no real accountability of the Commission or MEPs to market users for decisions taken, because implementation is at national level, where those responsible for the decisions at EU level are not the ones responsible for explaining them to the electorate. The work of the Convention in giving a role to the national Parliaments may assist.

Who will be responsible for ensuring effective implementation and enforcement of the single market after the regulatory framework is in place? How successful do you expect this process to be? What will be the role of competition regulators at EU and member state level? What issues will arise as the single market framework is implemented and enforced? What non-regulatory barriers might impede the effective functioning of a single market for financial services?

At national level, the questions are whether there will be some continuity in the officials responsible for working on the directives during negotiation and those involved in implementation and whether the lessons of the FSAP can be passed on to others in government who may be faced with similar issues.

At EU level, one advantage of enlargement may be the difficulty in bringing forward legislation with 25 instead of 15 member states, which might lead to more attention being given by the Commission to implementation. The implementation of the prospectus directive will be particularly important since several issues were left unresolved by the Level 1 text; however, many companies have been dismayed by the volume of detail at Level 2.

The Commission and CESR will be responsible for implementation and enforcement but it is not yet certain how well this will work. For example, CESR recently indicated that an action may be market abuse in one Member State and not in another. In which case where is the single market? Companies could perhaps report complaints about market access to their home regulator as well as the Commission. The regulators could then co-ordinate their information with the Commission. Implementation and enforcement thus far in the EU's history have not been particularly successful in achieving the expected results, since many pieces of legislation remove one barrier only to erect others. We would like to see more effective liaison and policy input between DG Competition and DG Internal Market. In some cases, competition has been reduced eg loss of issuer choice in equity securities as part of the prospectus directive. This was opposed by all European companies as users of financial services but was driven through because many Member States wanted to protect their control over their national companies and markets.

C. The Future

How do witnesses see the future development of a single market in financial services following implementation of the FSAP? Are additional measure needed?

The Commission's progress reports on the FSAP were concerned only with a tick-box mentality of whether proposals had been completed, not with whether they would achieve the aims hoped for by those who had supported the FSAP. Once the proposals are complete, the legislators are no longer interested in whether or not they will actually work. Indeed in some cases it has been questionable whether this is of interest to them before completion. For any further proposals it will be essential that quality is a more important measurement then speed and that there is clear recognition of the different markets within the EU eg equity/debt, retail/wholesale.

So far the FSAP approach has been top-down with the Commission deciding what investors and users should want, without proper consideration being given to their views, or even with views when expressed being dismissed on the basis that the Commission knows better than companies and investors what they should want. This approach has led to a waning of support for any future legislation. Companies are struggling to get to grips with the current deluge of legislative measures and have no desire to see a further raft of legislative proposals. For the future, genuine dialogue is needed.

Another area for concern here is the proposal for an EU Company Law and Corporate Governance Action Plan. As with the Financial Services Action Plan, the general aims and intentions of the Plan appear to be generally laudatory etc, and have generally received the support of industry. Nevertheless the concern must be that we should learn the lessons of the FSAP—in particular the tendency of the Council and Commission to agree over-ambitious deadlines without the necessary expertise and resource, the need for consultation at every stage of the process, the need for proper project planning and the tendency for what appear to be initially innocuous proposals which are described as helping companies to mutate into measures threatening companies' interests.

One of the questions asked earlier is whether sufficient weight has been given to the position and experience of UK financial services industry. We would say not but we would also say that not sufficient weight has been given to the users of the financial markets either. Our experience has been that many companies, especially smaller companies, are unaware of the impact that the FSAP will have on them, or are confused as to the effect and quantity of the various directive. Even larger companies and their professional advisers are struggling to keep track of the various directives, especially at Level 2. Some in the UK still do not worry about EU legislation until UK implementation, by which stage it is too late for major change. As a practical suggestion, it might help if the FSA were to publish Commission and CESR consultations on its own website alongside its own consultation papers so that UK firms are more aware of them. As the Better Regulation Task Force has recently pointed out, "to those who are regulated, it makes little difference" where it comes from.

Will the changes resulting from the FSAP proposals have an impact on the competitive position of London and EU markets as a whole in the global environment?

The Lamfalussy process has already improved the overall co-operation and transparency of the European financial regulators. CESR is an improvement of FESCO. With better dialogue and more realistic timetables in the future, CESR may achieve more. While we do have criticisms of CESR, it is only fair to say that many of the criticisms relate to factors outside CESR's control.

Following the publication of the Eurofi and Wicks reports, the CBI as a member of UNICE contributed to a paper on the needs of users of financial markets. The narrow focus thus far on European companies in the EU markets is a failure to consider the goal of making Europe a competitive and dynamic global economy and in working to make European markets globally competitive. Not only European companies raise capital in the EU markets; third country issuers do so as well. This benefits EU companies in increased depth of markets and reduced costs of capital.

Regarding the position of London, LIBA has pointed out that £800 billion of overseas money is managed from here. There is no sentimental reason for this money to remain here; only business reasons will keep it. The FSAP may increase the liberalisation of continental markets but we are unsure whether the same will be true of London which, by being ahead of the game so far, risks being reduced to the common denominator. There are lessons here for corporate governance and company law as well. We therefore see the likely future impact as making non-EU markets more attractive to third country issuers. Depending on how implementation works, the real beneficiaries of the FSAP may be New York, Zurich, Singapore and Hong Kong.

31 October 2003

Memorandum from CRESTCo

1. This letter sets out the response of CRESTCo Ltd to the House of Lords Sub-Committee B inquiry into the European Commission's Financial Services Action Plan (FSAP). CRESTCo, which is at the core of the UK and Ireland's financial infrastructure, operates CREST, the real-time settlement system for UK and Irish equities, corporate and (UK) government bonds and exchange traded funds. Settlement is the transfer of title to securities (such as bonds, gilts, equities and investment funds) usually for value following a trade or other bilateral agreement to transfer.

2. Although the clearing and settlement industry in Europe was not part of the original FSAP (COM(1999) 232), the European Commission, the Council of Ministers, The Committee of European Securities Regulators (CESR) and the European Central Bank (ECB) have all emphasised the need to develop a more integrated and robust settlement infrastructure in Europe as a means of delivering a truly pan-European capital market. The European Commission issued a Communication (COM(2002) 257) in May 2002 asking the market how efficient cross-border clearing and settlement could be delivered in Europe to realise the full benefit of an integrated financial market. A further document identifying what action is needed in this area and what the priorities are, should be published in the summer of 2003, In addition, the Governing Council of the European Central Bank and the Committee of European Securities Regulators (CESR) have set up a joint Working Party composed of the ECB and the EU national central banks and representatives of the CESR to look at establishing standards for securities clearing and settlement systems.

3. INTRODUCTION

3.1 In September 2002, CRESTCo became part of Euroclear, the International Central Securities Depository (ICSD), to create Europe's largest settlement system. The Euroclear Group now operates as the primary Central Securities Depository (CSD) in five markets: Belgium, France, Ireland, the Netherlands and the United Kingdom. Together, the equity markets in these countries comprise over 50 per cent of the Eurotop 300 (Europe's 300 most liquid securities). In addition, the group represents in excess of 50 per cent of the domestic fixed income securities outstanding in Europe and over 60 per cent of Eurobonds held by the Common Depositories.

3.2 The rationale behind the merger is to deliver a domestic market for Europe reducing the high cost and risks of cross-border settlement to the low levels associated with domestic settlement. This merger and the associated business model for European settlement (a description of which is contained in the Appendix to this submission) will offer all investors in the UK (retail and wholesale) the opportunity of low cost settlement in UK, Irish, French , Dutch, and Belgian securities. It is therefore, vital to the development not only of the London capital market but also the single European capital maket as well.

3.3 Euroclear believes that a low cost and low risk settlement infrastructure is essential for the efficient functioning of Europe's capital markets and is therefore, a prerequisite for the delivery of a single market for Financial Services and directly related to each of the four strategic objectives of the FSAP. As a consequence, we believe that the successful implementation of the FSAP is predicated on the continued development of efficient cross-border settlement in Europe.

THE CURRENT SITUATION IN EUROPE

4.1 The infrastructure which supports European settlement has evolved rapidly since the introduction of the euro. The single currency, combined with the financial market deregulation promoted by the European Commission, the European Parliament and national legislators, has made it possible for market participants to conduct their securities trading more efficiently on a sectoral, rather than a national, basis.

4.2 However, the settlement infrastructure is still in the process of adapting to this new reality since it continues to be organised largely along national boundaries. Today there are around 20 separate systems for 15 domestic markets in the European Union, compared to effectively one in the United States for a market of about the same size. The services of these systems (or Central Securities Depositories—CSDs) are largely tailored to domestic settlement needs (ie the settlement of a transaction in a domestic security between two counterparties in the same market using the same system).

4.3 In contrast the vast majority of cross border settlement transactions particularly in equities (ie transactions in a foreign security, or between two counterparties of different markets using different systems) are settled mainly by certain commercial banks (referred to as "agent banks" who maintain relationships with the domestic CSDs.

4.4 The securities markets which this infrastructure supports have two main characteristics.

4.4.1 First, while domestic settlement is cheap and efficient, cross-border settlement is expensive and inefficient. The excess costs generated by these cross border inefficiencies for market participants are estimated to be about EUR 5 billion per year, resulting from high settlement fees and large internal costs in their own back offices caused by dealing with the very fragmented and heterogeneous markets in Europe.

4.4.2 Secondly, the market for settlement services in Europe is largely competitive, with CSDs International CSDs (such as Clearstream and Euroclear) and agent banks all providing settlement services to firms active in the securities markets, such as commercial banks, investment banks, global custodians and central banks.

4.5 These two characteristics will be examined separately.

THE HIGH COST OF CROSS BORDER SETTLEMENT

5.1 Domestic settlement of securities transactions is regarded by the market as very low-cost and highly efficient. In the UK settlement tariffs range from 10p-50p per transaction, depending on the volume of transactions undertaken. The cost of cross-border settlement varies substantially but typically for equities it ranges from around €4 to around €30 per transaction; these costs have an impact on the investment behaviour of, particularly retail, investors in the UK and across Europe, making domestic securities lower cost to purchase or trade than international securities.

5.2 One major reason for these costs is the diversity of cultural, linguistic, legal, regulatory and fiscal frameworks which makes cross-border settlement a complex and therefore expensive activity. Many of these particular inefficiencies have been described in the two reports of the Giovannini Group in November 2001 and April 2003. Co-ordinated action is required from the market and from Member States to ensure that the barriers to the free movement of cross-border capital are removed to the benefit of all European investors. Euroclear, of which CRESTCo is part, is already working with the market to harmonise specific technical and market practice issues across the five countries for which it acts as CSD.

5.3 The fragmentation of settlement infrastructure is also a source of the risks and costs for the market, creating inefficiencies for customers who have to adapt to different practices, rules and IT interfaces to systems. Here the market has already made considerable progress to reduce this fragmentation. A range of market stimulated mergers between systems has already reduced the number of CSDs in Europe from over 30 just before the launch of the single currency to fewer than 20 today. Further consolidation, driven by the market, will be necessary to reduce the costs for the market to low domestic levels and make the European capital markets more efficient and integrated. Such consolidation will reduce the duplication of costs for which all investors pay.

6. DELIVERING A COMPETITIVE PLAYING FIELD FOR SETTLEMENT SERVICES

6.1 Competition must be allowed to operate fairly across all settlement service providers, leading to a reduction in costs and inefficiencies for customers. For this to happen it is necessary to ensure that a competitive playing field is maintained between the various settlement service providers, including CSDs, ICSDs and agent banks. This means the consistent treatment of all firms involved in the settlement process in law, and by competition and regulatory authorities.

6.2 Given the importance of settlement for the successful implementation of the FSAP, we welcome the ongoing efforts of the European Commission and the European System of Central Banks and Committee of European Securities Regulators (ESCB/CESR) in examining the future optimal structure of clearing and settlement in Europe.

6.3 As part of this exercise, DG Internal Market published, in May 2002, a Communication to the European Parliament and European Council on the main policy issues and future challenges of clearing and settlement.

6.4 In its response to this Communication, the European Parliament called on the Commission to intervene in the current organisation of the settlement market in Europe and to impose a directive on the clearing and settlement industry. It also suggested the separation of "core" and "value-added" settlement services when performed by the same organisation, on the grounds of the systemic and competitive risks which may arise from such services being combined within the same entity.

6.5 We are concerned that by forcing entities to separate "core" and "value added" services (however defined) the opportunity and momentum for delivering efficient structures to cope with the demands of cross-border settlement will be lost. Such separation of "core "and "value added" services is a very radical and unnecessary solution to the highly complex issues of cross border clearing and settlement. We believe that the co-existence of "core" and "value added" services should be acceptable providing they are priced transparently and in accordance with the principles which foster fair competition and customer choice which is, indeed, Euroclear's practice.

6.6 Furthermore, we do not believe that the case has been made for a specific directive in this area. We believe that the implementation of the Giovannini recommendations, the work of ESCB/CESR on strengthened and consistent regulatory standards across the clearing and settlement industry and the presence of an active competition regulator shall all help to create an efficient and low-cost market for settlement services in Europe, without further intervention from legislators.

7. We welcome the opportunity to provide evidence to the Sub Committee inquiry and would be delighted to provide oral evidence to the Committee if necessary.

APPENDIX

1. THE EUROCLEAR BUSINESS MODEL

The Euroclear group (described in section 3 below) is building a new model of settlement to reduce the cost of European cross-border settlement. In delivering this model we are committed to:

— consolidating settlement platforms and removing fixed costs from the industry, thereby greatly reducing investment and running costs for the entire market and their clients;

— delivering in 2005 a Single Settlement Engine to provide book-entry settlement for over 50 per cent of European equities and domsetic bonds, and 60 per cent of eurobonds, at low domestic tariffs;

— giving all customers an open choice between a Domestic Service, available directly through accounts with the CSDs within the Group under local law with settlement in central bank funds, and a Full Service provided through Euroclear Bank under Belgian law, with a choice of settlement in commercial bank money or in central bank funds;

— strong user-governance and active market consultation to ensure the proper functioning and development of the infrastructure of settlement;

— promoting fair competition through ensuring that:

— pricing structures are transparent;

— CSDs within the Group charge the same tariff to Euroclear Bank as they charge all other users;

— cross-charging between group entities will be based on a best practice cost allocation methodology;

— a competitive playing field between all providers of settlement services with regulation of the function of settlement applied consistently across all providers of settlement services;

— providing single-purpose, low-risk settlement banking services to customers to facilitate the efficient settlement of their securities transactions; and

— harmonisation of market practices across the markets for which we are responsible in line with the recommendations of the recent Giovannini and Group of Thirty (G30) reports.

2. BACKGROUND TO CRESTCo

CREST was inaugurated on 15 July 1996 and was originally owned and operated by a private sector company, CRESTCo, which itself was owned by a range of CREST users. Following completion of the merger with Euroclear in September 2002, CRESTCo became a wholly owned subisidiary of Euroclear Bank.

The CREST system provides the UK and Irish markets with a delivery versus payment real-time dematerialised settlement system. CREST's portfolio of settlement services includes equities, gilts, unit trusts, shares in open-ended investment companies (OEICs) and, from September 2003, money market instruments. The CREST settlement system also provides domestic settlement services for Isle of Man, Jersey and Guernsey securities.

Membership of CREST is available to corporates and individuals. CREST has over 54,000 members, of which over 50,000 are individuals holding their securities electronically through CREST Personal Memberships (giving the individuals direct legal title to their securities).

CREST also operates direct links to major European countries and to the USA, providing access to a range of international securities to its customers.

CRESTCo, and the CREST system, is subject to the regulation of the FSA, both as a Recognised Clearing House under the Financial Services and Markets Act 2000 and as the Operator of a relevant system under the 2001 Uncertificated Securities Regulations.

3. BACKGROUND TO EUROCLEAR

The Euroclear System is operated by Euroclear Bank SA, a Belgian credit institution with its registered office in Brussels. Euroclear Bank SA is owned by Euroclear plc. Since its creation in 1968, until the end of 2000, the Euroclear System was operated by the New York State bank Morgan Guaranty Trust Company of New York ("MGT"), via the Belgian branch of that establishment, which had a branch of activities ("Euroclear Operations Centre") specially dedicated to the operation of the Euroclear System. MGT transferred this branch of activities to Euroclear Bank, a new Belgian credit institution that was set up in 2000 for the specific purpose of operating the Euroclear System. Euroclear has developed a non-exclusive partnership with Euronext (resulting from the merger of the stock exchanges of Paris, Amsterdam and Brussels), which enabled Euroclear in 2001 to acquire 100 per cent of the capital of Sicovam, the French central depository, and in 2002 100 per cent of the capital of Necigef, the Dutch central depository. On this occasion, Euroclear also took a 20 per cent stake in the capital of Clearnet, the French credit institution responsible for the clearing of Euronext transactions, and in 2004 will acquire most of the settlement and custody business of CIK, the Belgian central securities depository. Since December 2000, Euroclear has also assumed responsibility for the settlement of Irish government bonds (Gilts) following the decision of the Irish government and the Central Bank of Ireland to delegate this activity to Euroclear.

In September 2002, Euroclear plc acquired 100 per cent of the capital of CRESTCo, the British CSD which operates the real-time settlement systems settling UK, Irish and international securities through the CREST system, and money market instruments through the Central Money Markets Office (CMO). These shares were subsequently transferred to Euroclear Bank through a dropdown arrangement

Euroclear Bank provides both international central securities depository and securities settlement services, including new issues distribution. In addition, it provides other services as custody, securities lending and money transfer. Acting as a limited purpose bank, it also provides the system participants with the banking services directly bound to the settlement activity, including credit, securities lending and borrowing and collateral management services.

In 2002, the Euroclear Group handled business transactions in excess of €238 trillion, settling more than 129 million transactions (post-netting). The total value of securities held in custody was almost €11,000 billion. There are over 208,000 different issues of securities accepted in the Euroclear system issued by entities from over 110 different countries.

3 July 2003

Memorandum from the European Investment Bank

The EIB seeks to promote balanced development within the European Union by making long-term loans to financially sound projects in support of EU policy objectives. Normally, a maximum of 50 per cent of a project cost may be financed by EIB, the balance coming from other sources, usually the commercial markets. EIB funds its own lending operations by issuing debt securities in the capital markets. This year EIB has a funding programme equivalent to EUR 41/42 billion.

So far in 2003, 61 per cent of EIB's issuance has been in EU currencies (euro 45 per cent and sterling 16 per cent) with a further 2.5 per cent in the EU acceding country currencies. Clearly, the health and efficiency of the capital markets within the EU is of vital importance to EIB not only in respect of its own funding but also to support the commercial funding of the projects and the objectives we seek to promote.

Many of EIB's bonds are purchased by retail investors, particularly in continental Europe, but increasingly within the UK. EIB therefore has a strong interest in promoting transparency and efficiency in the retail market as well as ensuring that retail investors are not misled about the underlying nature of investments.

Historically, the European markets have been significantly fragmented as compared to the markets in the United States. European Monetary Union has had a significant impact on the new euro market but significant elements of fragmentation remain which leave the Eurozone markets in some respects less efficient than those in the United States. Some of the factors behind this fragmentation can be addressed; for example, diverse regulations, clearing and settlement systems and trading platforms. Even looking beyond the Eurozone there is much that can be done to iron out differences between different currencies and issuing centres. We believe that the broad objectives of the Financial Services Action Plan will do much to reduce the cost of capital within the European Union as well as to ensure a safer investment environment for investors.

We would like to pay tribute to the work of the European Commission in drafting such an enormous range of legislation. The Economic and Monetary Affairs Committee of the European Parliament are to be congratulated for the way they have pushed through the various aspects of the FSAP. The Committee its staff and advisors have made extensive soundings and have worked hard to refine proposals that take account of the views of all parties.

It is against this background that the following comments are made.

It would not be feasible to cover all the areas of the Financial Services Action Plan, much of which has no significant impact on the EIB, and we focus on three areas which we consider to be of particular importance.

1. The Prospectus Directive (adopted last July).

2. Investment Services Directive, which receives its first reading in the European Parliament this month.

3. Directive 2002/47/EC of 6 June 2002 on financial collateral arrangements.

THE PROSPECTUS DIRECTIVE

Under current EU rules, mutual recognition is granted only to prospectuses that are set up in accordance with the Listing Particulars Directive and are approved by the competent authorities. The host country authority, in the case of recognition of the prospectus, is authorised to require additional information related to the domestic market. Regulations and practices vary widely between Member States. As a result EU capital markets have been fragmented and costly.

The intention of the Prospectus Directive is to make it easier and cheaper for companies to raise capital throughout the EU, while reinforcing protection for investors by guaranteeing that all prospectuses, wherever they are issued in the EU, provide them with the clear and comprehensive information they need to make investment decisions. The Directive introduces a new "single passport" for issuers. This means that once approved by the authority in one Member State, a prospectus would then have to be accepted everywhere else in the EU. In order to ensure investor protection, that approval would only be granted if prospectuses meet common EU standards for what information must be disclosed and how.

The Prospectus Directive draws a distinction between (1) equity issues and bond issues where the minimum denomination is lower than EUR 1000 and (2) bond issues where the minimum denomination is equal to or greater than EUR 1000. The basic rule is that the "home" regulator is the supervisor of issues. However, if the minimum denomination is equal to or greater than EUR 1000, the Directive gives flexibility, to the issuer, to select the supervisor. It is the level of the minimum denomination (now fixed at EUR 1000), which caused so much concern in the bond markets. Early drafts of the Directive had a threshold of EUR 50,000. This would have had the effect of imposing the home regulator as supervisor on most bond issues. If, following the transposition of the Prospectus Directive, its application leads to the results as intended (see paragraph above), it would facilitate the raising of funds within the EU significantly.

INVESTMENT SERVICES DIRECTIVE

(a) *Pre and post trade transparency*

The scope of pre and post-trade transparency under the Directive has been limited to share issues. The ECB has published an opinion dated June 2003 arguing that debt issues should be included within the scope of the ISD. EIB is equally concerned to increase transparency within the market and actively encourages traders to do so in respect of its own bonds. Transparency has been improving over time in both the euro and sterling bond markets—with the latter lagging somewhat behind. Market forces and improved technology have been major factors in this improvement. Major investors are able to obtain a high degree of transparency from their dealers but EIB is concerned for smaller investors and in particular individuals who are increasingly investing in bonds rather than equities. One of the principal requirements for transparency is the obligation on retail brokers (we include all intermediaries and bank branches selling directly to retail investors under the heading of broker) to provide best execution. Many dealers now provide automated bond execution services and there should be no reason why for larger bond issues brokers cannot obtain three live quotes— a significantly larger number of dealers will provide quotes most of the time for EIB benchmark bonds in retail size.

The retail bond market, particularly in continental Europe, has developed though branches of major banks that will usually quote prices, inclusive of commission, from their own traders. We recognise that the economics of the bond market has developed in the different way to the equity market and we can understand if not fully agree with, the decision not to enforce the requirement for full price transparency, in the bond market. We have some sympathy with bond dealers not wishing to publicise the size of orders or the size and price of executed trades as this could discourage liquidity. We feel it is essential for the liquidity of the bond markets that dealers are willing to take positions on to their own books, if necessary for extensive periods of time. The fact that dealers face lower capital adequacy requirements for bond holdings than for equity holdings does much to encourage liquidity and to reduce price volatility. Anything that reduced that willingness is likely to reduce market liquidity.

We hope however that the objective of best execution for retail sized trades will be pursued actively and that new legislation will be introduced without too much delay to ensure best execution in the bond market. We believe that, providing dealers are required to make their prices—for stated market size—freely available, a combination of competitive forces and improved technology will push the markets in this direction in any case. EIB already does and will continue to encourage price transparency to investors amongst its dealers.

Large investors do and should have internal rules requiring that a minimum number of market quotes be obtained before executing orders. The rules may usually be overridden where it is in the interest of the investor not to show the order around. If market prices for retail transactions were freely available large investors will be able to make a better judgement of where the price for large orders should be pitched.

(b) *Suitability tests*

Clearly EIB is anxious that brokers do not sell unsuitable investments to individuals who do not have the expertise to analyse the risks. We are equally anxious that the cost of dealing for individuals should be kept as low as possible. While we recognise the need for investor regulations, designed to protect individual investors, we are anxious that they do not serve to restrict their free access to the market to such a degree that individual investors end up worse off than without the regulatory protection. We recognise that certain structured transactions have been extensively sold to individuals without the full nature of the risks being explained but we are also aware that in highly regulated markets investors are frequently sold unsuitable investments. One measure that would protect investors (or at least put them on alert) would be to require disclosure by brokers of commission (soft or otherwise) payable to brokers by third parties (including in-house commissions). The banning of such commissions altogether might seem a sensible course but may not be practicable.

At EIB we have tried to tighten up our arrangements with our underwriting banks in an attempt to ensure that investors, whether retail or institutional, are made aware of risks involved in structured transactions. Nonetheless we feel that for investment grade securities that are not structured in a complex way and where three competitive live prices are available, the requirement for suitability tests could be dispensed with to enable brokers to offer an execution only service.

DIRECTIVE 2002/47/EC OF 6 JUNE 2002 ON FINANCIAL COLLATERAL ARRANGEMENTS

The above Directive has to be implemented by the Member States by 27 December 2003. Its main object is to simplify regimes for the creation of collateral (transfer of title and creation of a security interest [pledge or charge]), to protect collateral arrangements against some rules of national insolvency laws, to resolve possible conflict of laws, to limit all possible administrative burdens and to allow the re-use of collateral received. The application of the national regulations transforming the Directive will considerably increase legal certainty in the field of collateral arrangements throughout the EU, which is of utmost importance in the ever growing derivatives market.

September 2003

Memorandum from Fidelity Investments

The Fidelity International group of companies is the leading independent fund management provider in the UK. We employ over 2,000 staff and offer a variety of fund management services to both private and institutional clients. We have offices in all the main European markets, giving us considerable experience of the Single Market and the range of legal and regulatory issues that arise from the European Commission's Financial Services Action Plan.

The scope of the Committee's inquiry is broad. But as our business is exclusively in the area of fund management and distribution we will focus on those aspects of the Financial Services Action Plan that affect us most directly.

A representative of Fidelity would, of course, be very happy to appear before the Committee to give oral evidence.

Progress to date

In the arena of financial services, the process for passing new directives has been notoriously slow (Takeovers, UCITS etc). In that regard, the Financial Services Action Plan (FSAP) has been successful in focussing minds and speeding up the process. But this in turn has had the additional effect of undermining the quality of the directives produced. Without the deadlines, things can drag on for years, with a deadline things can be done too hastily. There is no easy solution to this. But it emphasises the need for Governments and MEPs to be tenacious in playing their part in the legislative process.

When considering progress in the FSAP it would be wrong to focus simply on the number of directives churned out by the Brussels machinery. The success of any directive depends heavily on how it is transposed into the national legislation of the Members States and how any inconsistencies or problems are dealt with by the Commission and Courts. (For example, the UCITS Directive, first passed in 1985 and perhaps the most important one for our industry, has thrown up many examples of differences in interpretation and enactment in different markets.) So while the Commission can rightly claim success in passing most of the directives and other initiatives envisaged in the FSAP, the Plan's success will depend on whether those directives are enacted consistently across the EU and whether Governments and Regulators allow the market conditions in which they can achieve their goals.

If there is no consistency, then for a pan-European group such as ourselves, a new directive can give rise not to one set of rules, but to 15 variations of them.

An additional but important point that the Committee should consider is the costs that many new directives impose on firms in terms of additional compliance and administration, particularly when national regulators take differing approaches. We have yet to see a directive that genuinely simplified a process in a way that enabled us to reduce our costs.

Beneficial to the UK?

The UK has the largest and most diverse financial services industry in the EU. It should, therefore, benefit significantly from a genuine single market. However, in the case of mutual funds and investment management the EU market continues to be heavily "fragmented" or national in character. So despite the FSAP, any UK firm seeking to trade across borders in the EU will still face a range of tax and other barriers that ought not to exist in a genuine single market. With enlargement next year, there is an obvious danger that this could get worse.

Is weight given to UK position and experience?

Achieving consensus between 15 markets is bound to entail compromise. In general, the UK has fared reasonably well or, at least, no worse than any other market. But there are a few significant exceptions to that judgement. The revised Investment Services Directive which is still under negotiation in Brussels could have very serious implications for the Direct sales and Execution-only brokerage that are more common in the UK by imposing stringent "Suitability" tests for all sales of financial services products even when no advice is offered or asked for. (It could also drive a coach and horses through the Government's "Sandler" initiative for the sale of simpler products.)

How successful has the Lamfalussy process been?

It is perhaps too early to draw definitive conclusions about the Lamfalussy process. Moreover, the most important directive for our industry, UCITS 3, did not fall within the remit of this process. I have already mentioned that the orignal UCITS regime produced a number of inconsistencies in how individual Member States interpreted the directive. From what we have seen of the transposition process in various Member States, it is already clear that the new directive, due to come fully into force in February 2004, will have similar problems.

Hitherto, the Commisson has not had an effective role in monitoring the transposition process and there has been only limited co-ordination between national regulatory authorities. The Lamfalussy process and the creation of CESR should enable the EU to address differences in interpretation and transposition before they become embedded in national legislation or regulations. This will ensure that directives are applied consistently across the EU. Whether it achieves this will be the real measure of its success.

Enforcement?

CESR

In the first instance, we look to our national regulatory authorities to police the market and enforce directives. As already mentioned, there can often be differences between markets in the way directives are applied. In the future, we would expect to see CESR play an increasingly proactive role in ensuring that such differences do not arise in the first place.

National governments

One of the main impediments to the single market is the extent to which national governments are still able to place discriminatory barriers in the way of cross-border trade. Taxation is the method most commonly used—those seeking to invest in non-domestic funds will often find a more punitive rate of taxation on their savings or a more cumbersome process for declaring the earnings. It is a salutary point that despite the rhetoric about the single market all EU states, to some extent, maintain discriminatory measures against cross-border trade in financial services.

The Commission

The European Commission is ultimately the guardian of the Treaties and of the Single Market. During the FSAP the Commission has focused very heavily on the process of piloting directives through their various discussion and consultation stages in Brussels. Up to now, the resources that the Commission has felt able to dedicate to enforcement of directives have been very limited. But more recently we have seen a very welcome determination on their take enforcement action against states that are undermining the Single Market for investment products. We welcome that and hope that it will continue.

Future developments?

The FSAP has focused to a large extent on the Wholesale Market. But the ultimate beneficiary of the exercise should, of course, be the European citizen. More efficient markets should give Europe's savers and investors more choice, better products, lower costs and better long-term outcomes. This is how history will judge the FSAP and so far we have seen little evidence of any real improvement for individual investors as a direct result of the FSAP. We believe the time has come for greater attention to be paid to the retail makets and the needs of individual investors.

I would commend to the Committee the "Heineman Report", commissioned by the Investment Management Association (IMA) earlier this year. This report is described in detail in the IMA's own submission to this inquiry so I will not cover the same ground beyond saying that, for us, the key message of the Report is that it shows the extent of work that still needs to be done, over and above what is envisaged in the FSAP, if we are to achieve a genuine single market in financial services for Europe's citizens.

Like many products, mutual funds can benefit from economies of scale, with larger funds able to pass savings on to their investors. The comparison with the US market, highlighted in the Heineman Report, shows the price Europe's investors are paying for the lack of a genuine single market. The average fund in the US is five or six times the size of its European counterpart and the savings achieved can add up to many thousands of dollars or euros over the life of the investment.

We believe that the completion of the FSAP in 2005 should mark a change in emphasis in the way the Commission goes about its work. The production of over 40 directives and other initiatives in such a short space of time has lead to enormous changes and it will probably take years for the new legislation to bed down and for the full implications of the changes to be appreciated. So, rather than beginning work on a new list of directives, we believe strongly that the Commission should now focus far more on ensuring that the changes produced by the FSAP are implemented fully and consistently. This will mean strengthening the role of CESR. But it will also mean beefing up the Commission's own efforts to enforce the directives and challenge national Governments that continue to frustrate the achievement of the single market.

26 June 2003

Memorandum from The Financial Services Practitioner Panel

1. The Financial Services Action Plan

1.1 *What progress has been made to date?* Progress so far has been fair, making it feasible that the Commission will meet the FSAP implementation deadline. Of the 42 measures in the Plan, 32 have been implemented so far. It should be pointed out that, even though the official deadline for FSAP implementation is 2005, most measures would have to be approved by spring 2004, before Parliament rises, to avoid the disruption of European elections. Pressure to meet the tight deadlines seems to have caused two related problems:

1.1.1 Shorter consultations—while Commission consultations on draft Directives are improved, response periods for comments on Committee of European Securities Regulators (CESR) Level 2 implementing measures are shorter than practitioners think appropriate. There is a danger that quality may end up sacrificed for speed.

1.1.2 Implementation burden on regulators and industry—the rush to meet the deadline places a great burden on national regulators, like the Financial Services Authority (FSA), who have no choice but to implement these measures on top of other national initiatives. This adds up to a considerable compliance burden on firms.

1.1.3 On the other hand it is crucial to complete the FSAP in time, before European Union Parliamentary elections and the voting in of a new Commission. Moreover, once the 10 accession countries get voting rights, in spring 2004, negotiations will become more difficult, as it will be even harder to reach agreement between 25 Member States than between the current 15.

1.2 *Has this been beneficial or deleterious to UK interests?* This is a difficult question to answer at the moment. As mentioned above, the current flurry of regulation from Brussels is adding to the burden on firms, some of which already are suffering from low profitability due to the market downturn. However, a single European market for financial services should eventually prove beneficial to UK interests, especially on the retail side. It remains to be seen whether the Directives and—more importantly—their implementation on a national level will truely remove the major existing barriers to cross border business.

One must remember that, with 15 Member States participating in the negotiations and defending their national interests, Directives coming out of Brussels will be a compromise. The political horse-trading surrounding the negotiations has been destructive of and sometimes deleterious to UK interests. UK Practitioners do not understand why financial services issues at times get bartered for concessions in completely unrelated sectors, such as agriculture.

The UK financial services sector differs significantly from many other European markets and thus on various contentious issues UK negotiators are at odds with their continental counterparts. (For example, the UK mortgage market is quite distinct, compared to the rest of Europe, and could suffer from proposed Directives on consumer credit.) However, as long as compromises are reasonable and the Directives do not inflict outright damage upon UK interests, any step towards greater integration should be advantageous for the UK. One question mark remains over UK relations with the US (see paragraph 3.3).

1.3 *Has sufficient weight been given to the position and experience of the UK financial services industry?* Even though many UK practitioners voice concerns that lower European standards are being imposed on them, it is worth pointing out that their European counterparts believe that the FSAP follows the UK model in many instances, and is influenced by Anglo-Saxon thinking. The Commission recognises the strong reputation of the FSA and increasingly takes into account its principles-based approach to regulation.

Some UK industry representatives feel they have dimished influence in Brussels due to the immediate disadvantage of being seen as dominated by US financial institutions. However, UK lobbying efforts have proved successful, especially when conducted in conjunction with pan-European trade associations, like the Federation Bancaire de l'Union Europeenne (the European Banking Federation).

As stated above, with 15 countries participating in the negotiations and defending their own national— sometimes protectionist—interests, the UK position does not always prevail.

1.4 *What are the main outstanding matters that remain to be dealt with under the FSAP and what key issues will need to be resolved?*

1.4.1 Outstanding matters: Corporate Governance and Company Law; International Accounting Standards; Clearing & Settlement; Money Laundering; Capital Adequacy Requirements; Insurance

Solvency; Reinsurance Supervision; General Duty to Trade Fairly; Take-over Directive; Consumer Credit Directive.

1.4.2 Key Issues: Internalisation; pre-trade transparency; execution-only business (Investment Services Directive); safe harbours for whistleblowers (Money Laundering Directive); operational risk; treatment of asset managers (Capital Adequacy Directive); treatment of mortgages (Consumer Credit Directive). There are many others, but these are some of the most controversial issues.

2. IMPLEMENTATION AND ENFORCEMENT—THE SUCCESS OF SETTING UP A SINGLE MARKET IN FINACIAL SERVICES WILL DEPEND TO A CONSIDERABLE DEGREE ON THE WAY IN WHICH THE REGULATORY FRAMEWORK IS IMPLEMENTED AND ENFORCED

2.1 *How successful do you expect the Lamfalussy process to be?* In principle, the Lamfalussy process is welcome and a definite improvement on the previous situation. It got off to a slow start because practitioners in many continental European countries were unaccustomed to a regulatory consultation process, however, it has much improved since. Its eventual success is difficult to judge two years before completion of the FSAP. One definite advantage is the fact that it firmly embeds consultation of practitioners and transparency into the policy-making process.

On the downside, it can fall victim to political tugs of war between the European Commission, European Parliament, the Council and CESR. This problem will need to be addressed during the ongoing Treaty revision. Also, the impeding deadline for completion of the FSAP runs the risk of emphasising speed over quality.

2.2 *Are any changes needed?* At this point in time, with the implementation process only just begun and enforcement not yet embarked upon, it is difficult to judge what changes are needed, if any. Some improvement suggestions may include:

— greater emphasis on levels 3 and 4 (implementation and enforcement);

— greater use of Fast Track Facility for adoption of Level 1 legislation;

— less detail in Level 1 legislation;

— use of regulations, rather than Directives, at Level 2; and

— greater resources for CESR to cope with Level 2 workload.

2.3 *Who will be responsible for ensuring effective implementation and enforcement of the single market, after the regulatory framework is in place?* CESR in the securities area and its parallel committees in the other financial services sectors (banking and insurance) will work with national regulators to ensure that the FSAP Directives will be implemented and interpreted in a harmonious manner. There are several proposals on the table to monitor and enforce implementation, among them a peer review by fellow regulators.

One problem with this set-up is that CESR and the other Lamfalussy Committees do not have the power to enact binding rules, but only devise non-binding common standards. This may impair CESR's ability to ensure/enforce compliance with the Lamfalussy Directives at the national level. Also, CESR is facing a very heavy workload and is under-resourced.

2.4 *How successful do you expect this process to be?* As long as European institutions and Member States are committed to this process, and willing to punish non-compliant Member States, it should be successful. Uneven implementation will be the greatest threat to the success of the Lamfalussy process.

2.5 *What will be the role of competition regulators at EU and Member State level?* We do not have a view on this issue.

2.6 *What issues will arise as the single market framework is implemented and enforced?* The main challenge will be to prevent protectionist implementation of the Directives to ensure an environment of fair competition. The wording of some of the more controversial issues within the Directives is often vague, resulting from a political compromise to get it ratified, and thus leaves room for interpretation. Similarly, opportunities for regulatory arbitrage will have to be eliminated, especially during the transition period. Tardy, uneven implementation will have to be discouraged through strict penalties.

In the UK, practitioners will have to watch out for super-equivalent implementation by the FSA. While a degree of super-equivalence may be in order to maintain the high standards and quality of the UK regulatory regime, too much of it could seriously damage the competitiveness of UK firms in relation to the rest of Europe.

2.7 *What non-regulatory barriers might impede the effective functioning of a single market for financial services?* Fiscal and legislative barriers on the national level will have to be removed (ie punitive taxation on pension fund investments in non-domestic funds; legal restrictions on fund mergers, such as investor unanimity requirements). In the UK in particular stamp duty has long been a formidable barrier to competition. At present, all EU member states practice some form of discriminatory taxation regime, making it extremely difficult for financial service providers to break into other markets. As long as these barriers are not removed, there will not be a truly pan-European market for financial services.

3. THE FUTURE

3.1 *How do witnesses see the future development of a single market in financial services following implementation of the FSAP?* Not much thought has been given to this issue. Most protagonists are tied up with meeting the current deadline, and thus long-term strategic thinking has not featured very prominently yet. However, there are some issues of importance. Seamless integration of the 10 accession countries' financial services markets and the challenges posed by further expansion should both be on the agenda. Also, a move away from Directives to more flexible regulation may be endorsed, as well as a move towards equivalence, and away from harmonisation.

In terms of impact, wholesale market participants anticipate an increase in competition. On the retail side, the FSAP could create great opportunities in the long-term savings industry (ie asset management, pension fund products).

3.2 *Are additional measures needed?* Hopefully not! Practitioners do not want a second FSAP, once the first one will be completed. Some issues that have not been addressed or resolved in the FSAP Directives may have to be ironed out by the incoming Parliament and Commission, through new Directives or amendments. However, practitioners favour regulation over Directives for future changes to the regime.

3.3 *Will the changes resulting from the FSAP proposals have an impact on the competitive position of London and EU markets as a whole in the global environment?* Again, this is difficult to say at this point. The impact and degree of change will depend on a number of factors, for example, whether further political compromises will render key Directives toothless or whether national regulators will implement Directives in a protectionist manner.

However, even if the FSAP does not meet all of the UK practitioners' expectations it is fair to say that if some, if not all, of the barriers to an integrated financial market are removed, the UK—and the EU markets as a whole—should benefit competitively. Even a partial success of the FSAP should make the European financial services market more efficient and hence competitive in the global environment.

One significant caveat is the impact of the FSAP on UK/US business. At the moment, roughly 70 per cent of transatlantic financial services business between the US and Europe is conducted with the UK and while the US at present generally accepts UK regulation as adequate, it is not certain whether this will also be true for EU regulation, given uneven implementation of Directives in various Member States.

4. OTHER:

More detail on many of these issues can be found in the Inter-Institutional Monitoring Group's First Interim Report Monitoring the New Process for Regulating Securities Markets in Europe *(The Lamfalussy Process)*, published in May 2003[38]. The report can be found on the European Commission's website: http://europa.eu.int/comm/internal_market/en/finances/mobil/docs/lamfalussy/2003-05-monitoring_en.pdf

26 June 2003

Memorandum from the Institute of Chartered Accountants in England and Wales

EXECUTIVE SUMMARY

1. The Institute of Chartered Accountants in England and Wales ((ICAEW) strongly supports the overall objective of the Financial Services Action Plan (FSAP) to develop the deeper, broader and more efficient securities markets as well as more diversified and innovative financial systems with all the subsequent benefits for consumers, prosperity, jobs and growth. We applaud the significant progress achieved, particularly in relation to financial reporting where the EU has provided leadership and impetus to the adoption of international standards on a global basis. In this as in many other areas, such as EU policy on auditor independence, the views of the UK are well reflected in the measures taken and the outcomes have been overwhelmingly positive.

2. While welcoming the progress and benefits of the FSAP overall, the ICAEW has some concerns that the cost of implementing a number of other proposals may be disproportionate to the benefits they will bring. There is also a danger that the implementation in the UK of FSAP measures can have unforeseen consequences that cause firms to either change their current business practices or cause them to cease providing certain services altogether with negative repercussions for consumer choice.

3. The ICAEW is keen to ensure that the momentum for the implementation of approved legislative measures does not wane—particularly with regard to International Financial Reporting Standards (IFRS).[39] We also recognise the critical importance of the effective enforcement of approved FSAP measures which will

---

[39] For the purpose of this submission IFRS is used inter-changeably with IAS, International Accounting Standards. IFRS is the formal title for all approved IAS standards.

require considerable attention. The ICAEW believes that enforcement can be best achieved through national bodies operating in close co-operation across the EU in accordance with an agreed set of common principles.

4. The FSAP has highlighted important resource issues within the European Commission and, more specifically, has drawn attention to the Commission's growing reliance on outside expertise in both the drafting and implementation of measures. The ICAEW applauds this approach but, equally, believes that resource limitations should not delay required policy development.

5. After 2005, a second, modified FSAP is likely to prove necessary which could give further impetus to market participants and the professions to move forward on the integration of EU capital markets.

INTRODUCTION

6. The accountancy profession has a critical role to play in the FSAP. As the largest professional accountancy body in Europe the ICAEW has a major stake, both where financial reporting, auditing and related policy measures are concerned as well as more broadly in the financial services sphere which also concerns many ICAEW members.

7. Since 1993 the ICAEW has had a dedicated European Union Office based in Brussels responsible for liaising with the European Institutions on all EU matters of relevance to the profession and the business community we support. The ICAEW is also a founding member of the Fédération des Experts Comptables Européens (FEE) which represents the European accountancy profession and the International Federation of Accountants (IFAC).

A. THE FINANCIAL SERVICES ACTION PLAN (FSAP)

What progress has been made to date? Has this been beneficial or deleterious to UK interests? Has sufficient weight been given to the position and experience of UK financial services?

FINANCIAL REPORTING

8. Considerable progress has been made in the financial report sphere, a pivotal element of the FSAP. Among the most significant measures are:

— Amendment of 4th and 7th Company Law Directives to allow fair value accounting;

— the Regulation on International Accounting Standards (IAS);

— the Modernisation of the Accounting Directives (in line with IAS principles).

9. The ICAEW has throughout actively supported the IAS Regulation, from engaging extensively with the European Commission in the pre-drafting stage of the legislation to regular dialogue with Members of the European Parliament to facilitate a swift legislative procedure.

10. The decision by the European Union (EU) to adopt a principle-based approach to financial reporting is in keeping with established UK practice. We believe that the adoption of harmonised accounting standards at an EU level will be extremely beneficial to the continued growth of the UK capital market.

11. The ICAEW strongly supports the EU in its aim to promote the global convergence of accounting standards. Within this framework we also welcome the Norwalk Agreement to develop compatible accounting standards between the International Accounting Standards Board and the US Federal Accounting Standards Board. However, this should not detract from the primary objective of introducing IAS in Europe.

12. Every step should be taken to avoid delays in the EU endorsement (through the specific EU mechanism established under the IAS Regulation) of all IASs to ensure their effective introduction in 2005. There is a real risk that the momentum towards global convergence of accounting standards and more transparent and comparable financial reporting in Europe may be lost, and uncertainty for the corporate sector exacerbated, if this endorsement is not delivered in time.

13. Whilst we recognise the widespread controversy in Europe regarding accounting standard IAS 39, "Financial Instruments: Recognition and Measurement" (see *1), we believe that IAS 39 and the related standard IAS 32 should be endorsed along with all existing standards at the earliest opportunity. Doing so will deliver a clear message that a comprehensive set of IASs will be in place for use in 2005.

AUDITING

14. The ICAEW strongly supports the completed FSAP measures relating to auditing. The UK can be particularly satisfied with the European Commission Recommendations on Independence which adopts the "risks and safeguards" approach strongly advocated by the ICAEW and UK as a whole. The fundamental

premise is that principles-based measures encourage the use of informed judgment whereas over-dependence on rules-based measures, as is evidenced in some non-EU jurisdictions, can be counter-productive.

What are the main outstanding matters that remain to be dealt with under the FSAP and what key issues will need to be resolved?

PROSPECTUSES AND TAKE-OVERS

15. Of the uncompleted original proposals in the FSAP, the ICAEW is particularly concerned over the delays in the passage of the Proposals on Take-Overs and Prospectuses, which are critical to the creation of an integrated capital market.

INVESTMENT SERVICES DIRECTIVE

16. There is a need to ensure that FSAP measures do not result in the reduction of consumer choice in the UK over and beyond what is required to protect public interest. The draft Investment Services Directive, for example, poses problems for investment firms providing "execution" only services and their clients, a significant sector in the UK investment field. In other areas too, such as the Insurance Mediation Directive, the implementation of EU measures in the UK may lead to the curtailment of service provision by certain providers who are faced with excessive regulation out of proportion to public interest objectives. In relation to the Investment Services Directive, we have submitted comments to the Treasury and are active in Brussels to seek sensible amendments.

TRANSPARENCY DIRECTIVE

17. Whilst the ICAEW welcomes many of the proposed requirements in the Transparency Directive nonetheless we still have major concerns in some areas. In particular, these centre on the requirements relating to periodic reporting: in our view, a realistic assessment of the costs and benefits of mandatory quarterly reporting has not been provided. Any new requirements in this area need to have demonstrable benefits which can be achieved on a cost-effective basis.

18. The ICAEW also believes that there would be benefits in phasing the new, shorter deadlines for reporting requirements, principally to avoid imposing unacceptable burdens on listed companies in 2005. (The ICAEW's position on this proposal is set out in *2).

"REINFORCING THE STATUTORY AUDIT IN THE EU" / CORPORATE GOVERNANCE

19. The European Commission recently launched a Communication on "Reinforcing the statutory audit in the EU" which, as the Commission observes, is to be seen in the wider context of the FSAP. The Communication sets a number of objectives which are integral to the 2005 deadline for the achievement of the FSAP but also additional policies which need to be implemented over a longer period of time.

20. The Communication was broadly welcomed by the ICAEW and in particular:

— plans to modernise, on a principles basis, the 8th Directive on the education and training of statutory auditors;

— the Commission's support for the adoption of International Standards on Auditing (by 2005); and

— the Commission's decision to research the case for the reform of auditor liability, as a major issue for the global accounting profession.

21. An important aspect of the Audit Communication relates to the extra-territorial reach of the Sarbanes-Oxley legislation in the US. The ICAEW fully supports the European Union's concerns about the extra-territorial impact of the registration requirements of the US Public Company Accounting Oversight Board (PCAOB). (A full analysis of the ICAEW position on the Communication on Audit can be found in *3).

22. The ICAEW also welcomes the European Communication on "Modernising Company Law and Enhancing Corporate Governance in the EU". This builds on the excellent foundations provided by the Jaap Winter Report published in 2002.

B. IMPLEMENTATION AND ENFORCEMENT

How successful do you expect the Lamfalussy process to be?

23. Whilst the provisions relating directly to the accountancy profession set out above are outside of the so-called Lamfalussy process, they have been pursued through a similar conceptual approach. The ICAEW fully recognises that this is the most suitable solution to deliver a regulatory framework capable of adapting to the changing priorities and demands of the marketplace.

24. However, we believe the Lamfalussy process would benefit from more clarity with regard to the specific competencies of Level 2 (remit of EU Legislation) and Level 3 (implementation at national level). For instance, there is at present uncertainty as to the extent to which recommendations made by the Committee of European Securities Regulators (CESR) on Level 2 implementing measures will be accepted.

25. We believe that every effort should be made to avoid unnecessarily bureaucratic requirements while account should be taken of the importance of compliance cultures. Good compliance is fundamental. As noted in the ICAEW response to CESR on the Market Abuse Directive (*4), Level 2 should reflect different needs in different Member States and not lose sight of the overall objective of reducing the costs of, and increasing the access to capital.

26. As the European Union enlarges next year, the benefits of Lamfalussy-style arrangements are likely to become more apparent. However, the need for regular checks on the powers conferred on delegated committes will also remain, as will the need for effective enforcement mechanisms to ensure consistency of application.

Who will be responsible for ensuring effective implementation and enforcement of the single market, after the regulatory Framework is in place? How successful do you expect this process to be? What will be the role of competition regulators at EU and Member State level?

27. The ICAEW believes, in line with the Commission Communication on Audit, that public oversight and other regulatory matters are best undertaken at Member State level. The ICAEW strongly supports the development of common principles to underpin public oversight arrangements within the EU and the effective coordination of these arrangements at EU level. This would promote trust in the effectiveness and comparability of financial reporting and auditing across the EU while also serving a useful purpose where dialogue with regulatory bodies outside the EU is concerned. The ICAEW would not, however, support the concept of registering or monitoring auditors at EU level.

28. The ICAEW believes that this conceptual approach is appropriate where the regulation of financial services as a whole is concerned.

What issues will arise as the single market framework is implemented and enforced?

29. The consistency of application of legislation and standards is a critical issue for the success of a truly integrated financial services market. But it is consistent outcomes within the EU which matter, rather than identical structures and the ICAEW maintains that enforcement should remain within the competence of EU member states. We also believe that account needs to be taken of compliance cultures and the possibility of differentiating procedures in light of this. This would ensure that regulation is always proportionate and not overly bureaucratic while remaining well tailored to public needs.

30. In relation to financial reporting, a study published by FEE (*5) in 2001 revealed that half the countries surveyed in Europe did not possess any institutional oversight system for the enforcement of financial reporting standards. Such enforcement is a pre-requisite of the successful implementation of IAS.

31. The ICAEW has welcomed the prior consultation exercise and publication by CESR of a paper addressing principles for the enforcement of accounting standards in Europe (*6 and *7). In addition to supporting CESR's adoption of a principles-approach to enforcement, we believe that these principles should relate to the fundamental characteristics of the enforcement regime: the national enforcement bodies should be permitted to develop along different forms as befitting national contexts while, of course, fulfilling pan-European criteria. The Financial Reporting Review Panel should have a continuing enforcement role in the UK.

32. In parallel with oversight in the audit sphere, pan-European co-ordination of national enforcement bodies for financial reporting is essential. Effective disciplinary measures need to be put in place in all jurisdictions to ensure that there is no "race to the bottom".

What non-regulatory barriers might impede the effective functioning of a single market for financial services?

33. It is well documented that different market practices, cultures and structures can present obstacles to the effective functioning of the single market. In some instances, the perception alone of such differences can be sufficient to dissuade efforts at market penetration by participants acting across borders. However, such barriers can, and will over time, be overcome as the benefits of greater cross-border activities and integration of the EU financial services sectors are seen by market participants and consumers alike. Increased efforts to promote awareness of the benefits would be welcome.

34. Given that non-regulatory barriers can arise out of "legitimate" legislation, it is necessary to ensure that regulatory measures are strictly proportionate to the desired outcome, unambiguous in their interpretation and based on the principle of authorisation in one EU Member State which permits a service provider to operate throughout the EU.

C. THE FUTURE

How do witnesses see the future development of a single market in financial services following implementation of the FSAP? Are additional measures needed?

35. The FSAP and the Lisbon agenda which underpins it, are necessarily ambitious. They also imply significant resource commitments. The ICAEW applauds the acknowledgement made by the European Commission that effective regulation can only be put into place with the active cooperation of market participants, professions and of course regulators. The use of such "external" expertise has been one of the successful hallmarks of the FSAP. However, there is a danger that resource constraints on the part of the European Commission could result in delays in the FSAP programme. The ICAEW recognises that in areas of considerable regulatory importance, such as in the company law and corporate governance spheres, the European Commission's resources are severely limited.

36. While the European Union must ensure that the 2005 deadline is met for all measures, it is clear that 2005 will not see an abrupt end to EU action in the financial services sphere. Similar to the European Commission's strategy for the development of the Internal Market as a whole, it is likely that the period after 2005 will require a new phase and type of FSAP. In the auditing sphere, for example, the European Commission has already outlined its medium-term priorities which stretch into 2006. These effectively call for the engagement of the accountancy and auditing profession in new ways to take account of a more integrated EU financial market and business environment.

37. Having opened up many new perspectives, the "first" FSAP could lead to a "second" which allows greater room for market participants and professional bodies to develop new initiatives and solutions. For example, the ICAEW is working with six other professional accountancy bodies across the EU to develop a common framework for accountancy qualifications, which will better equip professionals to operate in the integrated European and global economies.

Will the changes resulting from the FSAP proposals have an impact on the competitive position of London and EU markets as a whole in the global environment?

38. The rapid implementation of the FSAP proposals is critical to the maintenance of the competitive position of London and the EU within the dynamic, fast moving global economy. The creation of a consistent yet flexible regulatory environment across the EU, where unnecessary barriers to market entry and competition are eliminated, is essential. For this reason, in relation both to the specific areas of accounting and auditing as well as in the broader development of the FSAP, the ICAEW has consistently supported an EU approach which is as much outward as inward looking.

APPENDIX 1

REPORTS CITED

(1) IAS 39: Adoption in Europe: A Briefing Paper from the Institute of Chartered Accountants in England and Wales.

(2) Draft Transparency Directive: A Briefing Paper from the Institute of Chartered Accountants in England and Wales.

(3) Comment from the Institute of Chartered Accountants in England and Wales on the European Commission Communications issued 21 May 2003.

(4) Market Abuse—Additional Level 2 Implementing Measures (Tech 18/03) Institute of Chartered Accountants in England and Wales.

(5) Enforcement Mechanisms in Europe, Fédération des Experts Comptables Européens.

(6) Memorandum of comment submitted by the Institutue of Chartered Accountants in England and Wales to the Committee of European Securities Regulators concerning the consultation paper, "Proposed Statement of Principles of Enforcement of Accounting Standards in Europe".

(7) Standard No 1 on Financial Information. Enforcement of Standards on Financial Information in Europe.

June 2003

Memorandum from Investment Management Association

IMA represents the UK-based investment management industry. Our Members include independent fund managers, and the investment arms of banks, life insurers, and investment banks. They are responsible for the management of over £2 trillion of funds (based in the UK, Europe and elsewhere), including authorised investment funds, institutional funds (eg pensions and life funds), private client accounts and a wide range of pooled investment vehicles. In particular, our Members represent 99% of funds under management in UK-authorised investment funds (ie unit trusts and open-ended investment companies).

You have invited evidence on a large number of questions. Given the requirement to submit only four pages of written evidence, IMA has focused on your penultimate question about the development of the single market post FSAP (see paragraph 11), because IMA has recently published an independent report that looks at precisely this issue.*

1. *What progress has been made to date?* "Progress" is typically measured in terms of the likelihood of enacting FSAP legislation by 2005. (This deadline was imposed to support the European Union's Lisbon Council objective of becoming the most competitive and dynamic knowledge based economy in the world by 2010.) As things stand, there has been significant progress to date and the majority of FSAP legislation looks likely to be enacted by 2005 or shortly thereafter. However, IMA is concerned that this focuses too much attention on the speed with which legislation is enacted, and insufficient attention on the quality of that legislation. In particular we would not wish the quality of highly sensitive impending legislation to be compromised by an unnecessarily tight deadline (eg the Investment Services Directive, Capital Adequacy Directive, Transparency Obligations Directive and Takeover Directive, Prospectuses Directive).

2. *Has the FSAP been beneficial or deleterious to UK interests?* IMA is fundamentally supportive of the principles behind the FSAP. There are good economic reasons to suppose that an internal market in financial services will be highly beneficial to UK interests (following the logic, for example, of the recent HM Treasury EMU study "The location of financial activity and the euro"), since it will allow UK expertise in financial services provision to be more easily leveraged throughout Europe. However, by no means all of the provisions so far enacted have gone far enough to achieve these objectives and some (for example as regards the country of domicile provisions of the Prospectus Directive) are postively retrograde.

3. *Has sufficient weight been given to the positions and experience of the UK financial services industry?* Not every piece of FSAP legislation reflects the preferred position of the UK. Whilst some pieces of legislation are broadly beneficial to UK interests (eg the old UCITS Directive and old Investment Services Directive), others are neutral (eg the Occupational Pensions Directive) and some add costs without significant benefits (eg the Savings Tax Directive). Certain pieces of draft legislation remain highly controversial (eg the revised Investment Services Directive). The IMA appreciates that the negotiated nature of internal market law makes such trade-offs likely. However, in the round the IMA believes that the UK is increasingly effective at making its position heard in Brussels. In particular, the IMA commends the work of UK MEPs on the EMAC and Legal Affairs committees, and other UK officials involved in financial services negotiations, including the financial services attaché to the UK Representative Office.

4. *What are the main outstanding matters that remain to be dealt with under the FSAP and what key issues will need to be resolved?* Key outstanding legislation includes: the Investment Services Directive; the Capital Adequacy Directive; the Prospectuses Directive; the Transparency Obligations Directive; and the Takeover Directive. We have been particularly concerned that a number of these directives do not properly take account of the needs and concerns of users of markets—of the "buy-side", in an area where attention has traditionally been focused on the needs and concerns of the "sell-side". We recognise that this is partly because the voice of the "buy side" has not been as strong, a situation which we are seeking to redress.

5. *How successful do you expect the Lamfalussy process to be? Are any changes needed?* IMA is a strong supporter of the principles of the Lamfalussy process and believes that it is important to give it a chance to work before making major changes. Nevertheless its effectiveness is likely to be put into question by the amount of detail which is being contained at all levels of the legislative process; the current draft of the Investment Services Directive contains provisions which have no place in "framework" legislation, and there is a serious danger of CESR becoming overloaded.

6. *Who will be responsible for ensuring effective implementation and enforcement of the single market, after the regulatory Framework is in place? How successful do you expect this process to be?* The fact that local regulators are responsible for implementing and enforcing ("transposing") European legislation has three consequences:

6.1 *Complexity.* First, legislation can be transposed in different ways by different regulators in different Member States, increasing the complexity—and therefore the costs—of cross-border business. For example, the Savings Tax Directive leaves such broad interpretative discretion to local regulators and fiscal authorities, that in the absence of coordination between the authorities and agreement on key concepts, costs and levels of bureaucracy are likely to be extremely high.

6.2 *Protectionism.* Second, legislation can be transposed in a protectionist manner. For example, in its consultation on the implementation of the UCITS Directive 2001/107/EC the Irish Financial Services Regulatory Authority proposes to refuse an investment company in one Member State to appoint a management company in another Member State despite the Directive's clear provisions to the contrary.

---

* Not published in this report.

6.3 *Super-equivalence.* Third, legislation can be transposed in a "superequivalent" manner (ie so as to impose higher regulatory standards than was necessarily intended). For example, the UK Financial Services Authority has interpreted certain aspects of the Banking Consolidation Directive, E-Commerce Directive and UCITS (management company) Directive in a super-equivalent manner, potentially putting the UK-based industry at a disadvantage as compared with those elsewhere in Europe.

7. We believe that it is vital that CESR and its proposed equivalents for banking and insurance, together with the Commission, focus seriously on levels 3 and 4, with CESR actively comparing and coordinating approaches to implementation and the Commission, where necessary, taking action against Member States which do not implement appropriately. We welcome the fact that the Commission is mindful of these problems. In its recent Communication "Internal Market Strategies, Priorities 2003–2006" (IP/03/645) it proposes a number of measures intended to increase the speed and consistency of transposition of internal market law, including: an "Internal Market Compatibility Test" to assess whether specific regulations in specific Member States are compatible with internal market law; a recommendation on "best practices" to speed up and improve the quality of transposition of internal market law; and a study on the different options for improving enforcement of internal market law. We welcome these proposals.

8. *What will be the role of competition regulators at EU and Member State level?* IMA is not aware that the FSAP gives rise to any specific new roles for competition regulators at either the EU or Member State level.

9. *What issues will arise as the single market framework is implemented and enforced?* Please see paragraph 6 above.

10. *What non-regulatory barriers might impede the effective functioning of a single maket for financial regulators?* Please see paragraph 11 below.

11. *How do witnesses see the future development of a single market in financial sevices following implementation of the FSAP?* IMA, with generous financial assistance from the Corporation of London, recently commissioned an independent report to assess the future prospects for the single market for asset management.

12. The report was commissioned from Dr Friedrich Heinemann of the Zentrum für Europäische Wirtschaftsforschung (a leading economic research institute) who was instructed: to identify the economic benefits of the provision of investment management products in a single European Market; and to identify the barriers that are preventing those economic benefits from being realised.

13. The Heinemann Report finds that in most countries the market for retail asset management services is still essentially local: British investors buy from British providers, French from French, German from German and so on. Barely 9 per cent of the market for European investment funds can be attributed to genuine third-party cross-border sales. Consequently, Europe is foregoing significant economic benefits (eg increased economies of scale, externalities, competition and risk adjusted returns) in the region of €5 billion per annum. (Alternatively conservatively estimating cost savings from a single market to be approxmamtley 40 basis points (or 0.4 per cent per annum[40], a single market would increase the pension fund of an individual who saved 10 per cent of his salary throughout his working life by €120,000[41]).

14. The Heinemann Report identifies various barriers which are holding back the single market for asset management. IMA has prepared an accompanying 'position paper' which proposes various solutions to those barriers, ie solutions, which, if enacted, would facilitate the development of the single market.

15. Those solutions set out in the IMA position paper include a number of measures which require action by the EU institutions:

15.1 *Tax discrimination.* Member States' fiscal regimes should not discriminate between returns from domestic investment funds and offshore investment funds. IMA supports ongoing work by DG Tax to bring infringement proceedings against such discriminatory regimes.

15.2 *Fund registration.* Once an investment fund has been registered in its home state under the UCITS Directive[42] (which enables investment funds established in one Member State to be marketed in others), there should be no need for further registration in all of the other Member States in which it is marketed. This would require a change to the existing approach established in the UCITS directive.

15.3 *Fund mergers.* Member States' fiscal and regulatory regimes should not discriminate against cross-border fund mergers. Inclusion of investment funds in the forthcoming Tenth Company Law Directive (on cross-border mergers) may be a possible mechanism to achieve this.

---

[40] For example, SEC Report on Mutual Fund Fees and Expenses, 2001

[41] This is based on a 25-year-old earning €45,000, contributing 10 per cent per annum for 40 years, with a salary growth rate of 4 per cent per annum, and a fund growth rate of 7 per cent. Regardless of the assumptions upon which this calculation is based the difference is roughly constant in percentage terms

[42] A Directive on Undertakings for Collective Investment in Transferable Securities 85/611/EEC.

16. Equally, IMA recognise that there are a number of areas in which the industry itself needs to act and where working with an effective European representative body involving practitioners and equivalent associations from elsewhere in Europe is likely to be the best way forward.

    16.1 *Infrastructure.* Infrastructure providers (particularly transfer agents) should standardise the protocols required to process the buying and selling of shares in investment funds, in order to reduce the complexity (and costliness) of cross-order business. IMA proposes to work with interested parties to this end.

    16.2 *Public data.* Asset managers should standardise the calculation and publication of data on fund classification and performance, costs and financial statements, in order to increase the comparability of investment funds. IMA proposes to work with interested parties to this end, including its sister trade associations elsewhere in Euroe.

    16.3 *Financial advice.* The quality of financial advice should be improved by developing an industry-wide code of conduct/professional rules. This will benefit consumers in countries where the quality of advice is currently low. It will also benefit investment funds providers by increasing awareness of their products. IMA supports the work on the International Standards Organisation in this area and sees this as an area in which cooperation through an effective EU representative body for asset management could be fruitful.

17. Please note that none of these solutions are included in the FSAP. However, some of the solutions are included in other legislative initiatives of the European Commission (for example, the Corporate Governance and Company Law Action Plan, and the Internal Market Strategy).

18. The Heinemann Report and our accompanying position paper was officially launched on 20 May in Brussels, at an event well attended by representatives of the European financal services industry, Commission, Parliament, national representative offices and the media. We are planning one-on-one follow-up with specific Members of the European Parliament and the Commission in order to use the Report as the basis for real and positive change.

19. *Will the changes resulting from the FSAP proposals have an impact on the competitive position of London and EU markets as a whole in the global environment?* See paragraph 2 above.

25 June 2003

Memorandum from Lloyds TSB Group

1. Lloyds TSB welcomes the opportunity to comment to the House of Lords Select Committee, and offers the following observations in the order given in the Call for Evidence:

THE FINANCIAL SERVICES ACTION PLAN (FSAP)

2. Some two years ago, it seemed unlikely that the FSAP would be completed by its deadline of 2005. However, the rate of completion of the legislative proposals appears to have improved during the past year in particular. Indeed, Commissioner Bolkestein explained to EMAC on 17 June that, of the initial 42 FSAP measures, 35 had been completed at an EU level, and the remaining ones would be within six-nine months.

3. Lloyds TSB has consistently supported, in principle, the FSAP and the European Commission's overall intentions to create a single market in financial services. If a truly "level playing field" is achieved, properly monitored and enforced, it should be good for UK interests because of the market opportunities it would provide.

4. We have, however, become concerned that certain proposals could disrupt and undermine UK market practices, which have successfully evolved to address the complex, diverse and sophisticated structure of our financial markets. For instance, with regard to the proposed Investment Services Directive, our trade associations (the BBA and the European Savings Banks Group) and the Rapporteur (Theresa Villiers) continue to encounter considerable difficulties in convincing Continental MEPs of the merits of exonerating providers from giving advice for "execution only" business.

5. We believe that Sir Howard Davies, in his speech at a London conference on European regulation on 6 March, represented some broadly-held views when he referred to the "very complex process" and "no requirement for cost benefit analysis to assess the impact of individual directives" in much of the EU regulatory processes. We support his conclusion, that there would be value in "focusing on mutual recognition of regulatory systems based around harmonised core standards" in a greater proportion of cases.

6. We equally support the basic recommendations in the Wicks Report, November 2002, notably that legislation should be "Specific, Measurable, Achievable, Relevant and Timebound (SMART)".

7. Another concern is the poor pre-proposal consultation and, indeed, drafting, in certain proposals. An example is the proposal for a Prospectus Directive, whose initial text did not take account of certain key working elements in existing regimes. The many Amendments put together by the Rapporteur (Chris Huhne)

are evidence of this. Poor drafting in itself leads to confusion and complications in the legislative process, and this is deleterious not only to the UK but to all interested parties.

8. Positive outcomes, on the other hand, can emanate from EU procedures. One instance in which consideration was given to UK financial services was in the recently-completed Occupational Pension Funds Directive: an amendment disallowing "lump sum" payments, with serious consequences for UK insurers, was reversed following a strong lobby by the private sector supported by HMG.

9. Another proposal considered of high potential impact is the Capital Adequacy Directive (re "Basel 2"). We recognise the potential benefits for the Lloyds TSB Group in terms of improved risk management, better informed risk decisions, and prospects of reductions in capital requirements. On the other hand, we have concerns as to the highly complex compliance requirements, and the tight timelines.

10. Although not part of the FSAP, we wish to highlight the Consumer Credit proposal because it too will have a high impact on financial services. The Commission did not consider this proposal as a financial service issue, but as a *consumer protection* issue. As a result, European parliamentarians generally believe this proposal is seriously flawed as it does not acknowledge sufficiently the practicalities of the markets. Apart from numerous "disproportionalities" in areas such as lender advice, documentation requirements and consumer protection, it fails to take account of the highly developed and diverse nature of UK retail financial services. Legislation of that directive in any form close to its original drafting would have serious negative repercussions for retail consumers, for providers of UK retail financial services and, indeed, for UK consumers. It would entail the removal of many flexibilities offered by overdraft facilities, and "instant" self-service channels would not be able to operate. While the legislative process has some way to go we remain concerned about the impact the directive will have on the credit market in the UK and the impact on UK consumers.

11. Overall, we believe it is too soon to judge whether the FSAP will be beneficial or deleterious to UK interests.

IMPLEMENTATION AND ENFORCEMENT

12. It is in our view also too soon to be able to judge whether the Lamfalussy process is likely to be successful: this can only be judged in a longer-term context. As already indicated, consistency in implementation, monitoring and corrective actions will be critical success factors. Intuitively, it should enable the legislative process to be speeded up. From a business perspective, faster process is preferable so long as it is within an agreed framework. A sufficient parliamentary check should also be retained to prevent bad regulation, to allow the private sector to influence, and to ensure sufficient consultation. We are therefore mindful of the continuing concerns of certain parliamentarians, and entirely support the relevant recommendation of the Inter-Institutional Monitoring Group in its report of May 2003.

13. Proper implementation is essential, and will continue to be. The quality of the single market can be no better than the quality of the implementation—at national levels—of the EU directives and regulations. One of the criticisms voiced when the Commission stated its intentions to develop a "FSAP2" to follow the FSAP was the proper completion and implementation of the FSAP should rank higher in importance than writing the next plan. This appears all the more relevant given that many of the measures have yet to be processed at national levels by 2005, and businesses will also need time for the necessary change management.

14. The responsibility for implementation lies with Member State governments, monitored by the Commission under Lamfalussy Level 4. It remains to be seen how successful the implementation process will be. There may be room for improvement in greater transparency, more headline "naming and shaming" of recalcitrant Member States, greater use of the European Court of Justice, more evident interest/public commitment to implementation *and its performance* at Council level. An important recommendation in the Wicks Report, which we endorse, is that enforcement should be effective, both by home state regulators and by the European Commission.

15. Competition regulators should have a supporting role to play, because the freeing of competition is the central objective of the single market. However, care should be taken to leave the prime responsibility for implementation to Member States, and the key monitoring role to the European Commission.

16. We believe that issues to do with "level playing fields" will arise as the single market is implemented and enforced. It is in our opinion unlikely that national interests will subside, and it is possible that the very dynamic of "Europeanisation" may create its own pockets of resistance at certain national levels. In a report prepared earlier this year at HM Treasury's request by the UK financial services industry, to which Lloyds TSB contributed, numerous complications facing providers of cross-border financial services were identified. General ones include multiple regulatory requirements, imposed product design requirements, price controls, complex local rules encountered by banks, insurers and mortgage lenders. Specific impediments feature domestic cartels (Austria), state aid to savings banks (Germany), limitations to rights of establishment (Spain, Greece, Ireland), residency requirements for branch management (Austria, Denmark), various tax breaks favouring domestic providers of life contracts (Austria, Finland, Denmark, the Netherlands, Portugal, France,) and different tax rates for local/non-domestic investment funds (Austria, Denmark, Germany,

Greece, Spain). We believe that specific examples of such "barriers" should continue to be identified, and vigorously exposed.

17. Among the long-term non-regulatory barriers, we would count differences in culture, taste, and a continuing preference for "home grown" or at least "home familiar" products and services. These will abate in the long term, as a result of global branding, cross-border mergers and partnerships, and through the growing convenience and ease offered by internet banking "in the home". These changes will take a long time: they cannot be simply "regulated away".

18. Of special relevance are the continuing barriers to cross-border acquisitions. EU-wide financial institutions will be a critical success factor for effective competitiveness at global levels, a key objective of the Lisbon Summit. It is with this in mind that Lloyds TSB views with considerable disappointment the continuing difficulties the Commission has been encountering in its proposal for a Takeovers Directive, in particular the outlawing of "poison pill" defences.

19. To these ends, LLoyds TSB also remains supportive of the British Government's consistent calls for European market reforms, and the central position, within these, of measures designed to improve labour flexibilities and competitiveness. Our Prime Minister and Chancellor have voiced these on several occasions, the Chancellor in his last budget speech in April, in which he said ". . . because flexibility at a UK level should be matched by flexibility in Europe, we are proposing that Europe's competition authorities pro-actively investigate barriers to competition, starting with financial services" and, more recently, in his Mansion House speech, in which he re-affirmed that "there is now a growing consensus . . . on the need to complete and extend the European single market and for flexibility and structural reform in Europe".

The Future

20. Lloyds TSB has an overarching concern that an ever-broadening series of consumer protection measures will be legislated. This would undermine the "caveat emptor" principle, and subdue the initiatives of providers at a time when the proportion of cross-border retail business remains relatively low. In the future, there will continue to be a need to ensure innovation in products and services, effective competition and transparency, and avoid over-burdening regulation.

21. While additional measures will no doubt be required, we would recommend that these be selective, that future legislative proposals be firmly supported by impact assessments, and that the "mutual recognition" approach—with agreed and harmonised basic standards—be adopted where appropriate to recognise good market practice and nuances at national levels. Otherwise—at least for a period of time—the concentration of the Commission's attentions should be on implementation and enforcement. The FSAP will need a period of consolidation.

22. Relevant to this, and an important factor in determining the long-term success of the FSAP, will be how well it applies to—and is implemented in—candidate member states as enlargement progresses.

23. Another important factor in the view of Lloyds TSB, is the question of 'maximum harmonisation'. The rationale underpinning it is the Commission's policy to promote consumer protection by ensuring that consumers benefit from common rules across the Union. This poses an issue for the UK retail financial services markets, which are more complex, more diversified and more sophisticated than the Continental ones. In a future environment, while the Lamfalussy Process should speed up the legislative process by allowing the revision of existing directives to go through on a "faster track", a maximum harmonisation approach to retail financial services proposals could make consensus at Council level harder to reach. This could be aggravated by the larger number of Member States after enlargement.

24. The FSAP is bound to affect the competitive position of the UK financial markets. The Lisbon Council in 2000 undertook to make the EU the most competitive economy in the world by 2010, ie more competitive than America. However, regulatory changes that entail disproportionate compliance requirements, unnecessary bureaucracy, and excessive process could undermine market efficiencies and go against consumer interests by reducing choice and competitive offerings to them.

27 June 2003

Memorandum from M. Michel Prada, Inspecteur Général des Finances

A. The FSAP

It seems to me that a lot of progress has been made since the FSAP was launched in 1999. One must however recognise that finalising the Commission's proposals is not easy, basically for two main reasons:

— many difficulties did appear only lately, while analysing the practical consequences of the draft directives; market models differ in Europe, and although principles seem to be acceptable at a high level, implementation raises serious concerns and practitioners do resist according to their legitimate interests; building consensus and negotiating consistent compromises takes time and requires a lot of work and good will;

— the decision-making process of the EU is, quite understandably, relatively complex and slow; the so-called Lamfalussy Process has undoubtedly rationalised the procedure and created momentum, but there remain some possible bottlenecks (see the first report by the IIMG).

I hope the progress made will not be too deleterious to continental markets . . . More seriously, I believe that assessment should be made against EU interest globally and, from that point of view, I have the feeling that the decisions taken will have a positive effect on the European capital market which tends to evolve towards the best international standards;

UK financial services industry has certainly played a major role in defining the new framework of EU legislation. I would only mention, for example, the distinction between professionals and retail, or the innovations with regard to ATS and internalisation. Symetrically, I have the feeling that some of the difficulties met in UK markets during the nineties have paved the way to convergence with a traditionally more "consumer oriented" contintental regulation.

The question now is whether the Institutions will be able to adopt the proposed directives (mainly, in the field of securities, the new ISD, the Prospectus Directive, the Directive on Transparency and the Takeover Directive) within the next nine months. If not, institutional difficulties will severely slow down the achievement of the FSAP. I do believe than the price of necessary compromises is much lower, globally, than the price of several years of standstill.

B. Implementation and Enforcement

Having had the honour of chairing the Inter-institutional Monitoring Group, I cannot but be in accordance with our first conclusions, as presented in our first interim report. I am very optimistic on the efficiency and the future of the LP. Only, EU needs to take the necessary measures to perpetuate the so-called "comitology" procedure and to make a good use of "secondary legislation", in my view, rather through the use of regulations than directives.

Besides the normal responsibilities of the Commission and national bodies in the field of implementation and enforcement, I would personally advocate in favour of enhancing the status and capacities of the CESR. In my view, the CESR should progressively play the role of a *"tête de réseau"*, able to solve possible difficulties between its members, to elaborate a sort of jurisprudence and to monitor the way they play their part in the implementation and enforcement of EU regulation. From a practical and technical point of view, the securities regulators are best suited to deal with these issues on a day-to-day basis and with the speed necessary to business activities. I believe that close co-operation between securities regulators is key to a sound development of financial markets, even more so when considering a unified European market.

I have no competence to answer the question on competition regulation. I can only mention the fact that, after the decision by the "Conseil d'Etat" to annul the decision taken by the banking regulator with regard to the takeover of Crédit Lyonnais by Crédit Agricole in the field of competition issues, the Government proposed to Parliament to confirm the competence of competition regulators as for financial activities, in accordance with, if I am well informed, most existing systems in Europe.

It is difficult to foresee issues arising from the implementation of a single market framework: competition, innovation, industrial restructuring will have positive effects from the point of view of the cost of capital, allocation of capital to productive investment and quality of service to issuers and investors. We may have to cope with social or financial consequences of such evolutions but that's the rule of the game.

Apart from linguistic and cultural barriers which may hinder the development of cross border activities within the EU, there is no reason why financial services should suffer from non-regulatory barriers. Unfortunately, most remaining barriers, after a huge effort of regulatory harmonisation, depend on remaining regulatory differences in relation to domains which, although different from the securities and financial domains, may interfere with these activities. This is typically the case with tax issues, but these are clearly of a regulatory nature and have to be dealt with through classical integration or harmonisation procedures.

C. The Future

Although all market participants have intensified their efforts and committed themselves to achieve the objectives of the FSAP, building a truly single market will take time. Experience of the past years shows that, while time goes on, so does innovation. If EU legislation does not keep pace with the innovations which will develop, as they have in the past, within the boundaries of Member States, new FSAP will have to be undertaken again. This is the reason why the LP should become a normal and permanent process and why, on the basis of basic principles, continuous adaptation to then never-ending process of innovation should be dealt with through an extensive and speedy use of secondary legislation. The example of the painful and never-ending lengthy process of renewal of the UCITS directive shows us how to better in the future our capacity to move forward.

Furthermore, the building of an efficient system of supervision has to be speeded up in order to monitor the implementation of EU legislation and to ensure fairness and a level playing field for market participants. As market supervision deals with a huge number of micro-economic decisions made, on a day to day basis, by a huge number of individual and legal entities operating in very different environments, we have, at least for some years, to rely on a network of regulators acting according to the same principles and rules, closely cooperating together and coordinated by a *"tête de réseau"*, accountable, itself, to EU Institutions: this is precisely what securities regulators had in mind when they established "FESCO" on a voluntary basis, in 1997, and then "CESR" in 2001. We should build on this very positive achievement.

The City of London is old, and strong, and rich, and open, and innovative enough not to worry about the consequences of financial integration of Europe. Maybe the City could even profit from the development of a few financial centers on the Continent? To do business, one needs partners . . . in fact, it is quite obvious that building a true single market will have a positive impact on the competitive position of EU markets as a whole in the global environment. And I have no doubt that London, already being a global market place, will profit from the development of a true market economy in Europe.

15 June 2003

Memorandum from PricewaterhouseCoopers

INTRODUCTION

While we have commented on the Financial Services Action Plan (FSAP) as a whole our comments are more focussed towards progress on a genuine single market for wholesale financial services which most directly affects our clients and our own work as a professional services practice.

THE FINANCIAL SERVICES ACTION PLAN

1. *Progress to date:*

The FSAP represents an extremely ambitious agenda and timetable. We applaud the overall objective of creating a single European capital market with the obvious benefits for both EU investors and companies and also further developing the EU as a counter weight to the US capital markets.

The UK represents almost half of the current European capital markets in terms of securities offerings and secondary trading. Against that background it is surprising how little consultation there was with the UK regarding both the overall framework for the new regulatory structure and the first substantive Directive— the Prospectus Directive.

These early proposals represented a sigificant threat to the interests of the UK capital markets. As an example the "one size fits all" proposals in the first draft of the Prospectus Directive would have led to the Eurobond market being fragmented and probably driven offshore. Fortunately, intensive lobbying from the UK and certain other Member States such as Luxembourg have reduced this threat by granting certain opt-outs for the institutional debt market. The proposals continue to threaten the AIM market which is the most successful SME market in Europe and now faces increased regulation as a result of both the Prospectus and Transparency Directives.

In addition, the proposed revisions to the Investment Services Directive could serve both to outlaw execution only trading which represents a significant proportion of UK business in both the retail and wholesale markets, and to limit the opportunities for alternative trading platforms as alternatives to Stock Exchanges which essentially exist only in the UK.

We have the strong impression that the FSAP proposals for the wholesale financial services market have been drafted from the perspective of retail investor protection and as a result that insufficient consideration has been given to the objective of reducing the cost of raising capital particularly for smaller companies. To our knowledge there has been little work done on the cost/benefit analysis of the new proposals.

2. *Outstanding matters*

Much remains to be done on filling in the detail on key Directives. The Takeover Directive is receiving fresh political impetus; however time will tell whether the significant objections of certain Member States to creating a level playing field with regard to takeovers of public companies will be overcome.

One of our key concerns is whether enough work has been done on the interaction of the new Directives both with each other and with existing laws and practices in Member States. There are examples of inconsistencies in definitions between Directives (for example the application of the Prospectus and Transparency Directive to different types of financial instruments differs) which need attention.

IMPLEMENTATION AND ENFORCEMENT

3. *Lamfalussy process*

The Lamfalussy proposal of framework Directives represented a bold objective of establishing high-level principles and keeping the detail to a manageable level. We applaud the objective but note that the volume of detail emerging at level two may not be in line with the ongoing proposal. Furthermore the lack of an overall framework for regulation underpinning the securities market makes it difficult to assess how successful the proposal will be.

We are concerned that the omission from the Directives of the level of detail essential to adequate regulation of Europe's capital markets has meant that significant pressure has been imposed on the process generating the Level 2 implementing measures. This is exacerbated by the extremely short timescales against which these measures are required to be prepared.

4. *Responsibility for implementation and enforcement*

Responsibility for implementation and enforcement will rest partly with central EU bodies and partly with the Committee for European Securities Regulators (CESR). The success of effective implementation and enforcement will depend on how effectively CESR's constituents cooperate and bring a common approach to issues. While there are no current plans for a Euro SEC we question whether a true single market for financial services can be achieved without one in the longer term; however there could be significant disadvantages to UK interests if a Euro SEC set lower standards than those that have earned the UK markets their excellent reputation.

5. *Implementation issues*

The FSAP proposals are wide ranging, complex and not well understood outside of the political and regulatory role. There are significant practical issues for companies and advisers in interpreting and implementing the new regime in a relatively short timescale.

Further, the interconnection of the various proposals may well give rise to contradictory and divergent regulatory obligations. We would support the suggestion that the FSAP be subject to a "fatal flaw" review before implementation and regular reviews post implementation.

6. *Non-regulatory barriers*

The most significant non-regulatory barriers which might impede the effective functioning of a single market for financial services are cultural and language barriers. Although capital markets have become increasingly global in recent years, capital market regulation has tended to remain largely local in nature, with significant differences between markets often reflecting the particular culture and history of the countries concerned.

THE FUTURE

7. *Future development of a single market in financial services*

Regulation is one aspect of a market and is certainly an important driver of behaviour. However, the future development of a single market in financial services is also critically dependent on the participants in the market and how attractive a place Europe is to conduct financial services business. Europe needs to work out how to market itself to the rest of the world.

We do not believe that substantive additional measures are needed to bring into effect the FSAP. However, we would note the absence of proposals to create a new Admissions Directive. We believe that sensible admission criteria, for example as currently applied in the UK, can act as a powerful investor protection tool. Our view is that this omission should be rectified.

8. *Impact of FSAP proposals on London and the EU as a whole*

The comparative study we performed for the Financial Services Authority (FSA) in April 2002 identified London as a high quality market from the perspective of investors. This is reflected in the high proportion of EU capital markets business transacted in London. The FSAP is bringing in regulation to raise standards across the EU as a whole and there remains a risk that London's standards will be diluted as a result. The FSA are currently consulting on whether to retain those parts of the UK regime which are super equivalent (additional) to the existing European Directives. We would caution the FSA not to harmonise all of the UK's rules with Europe until the FSAP is established and proven.

CESR has made significant progress in developing proposals in the areas of conduct of business and market abuse; however, given that the UK's rules in these areas are now well developed the potential application of maximum as well as minimum enforcement requirements on CESR principles could disadvantage UK interests in forcing change to practices which firms have incurred significant costs in developing and which have made the UK an attractive place in which to do business.

As for EU markets as a whole there is a significant opportunity to attract non-EU companies to raise capital in Europe particularly from developing economies such as China. The FSAP raises the profile of the EU as a serious competitor to New York and this is to the benefit of the EU.

June 2003

Memorandum from Prudential plc

Established in 1848, Prudential plc is a leading international financial services company with more than 16 million customers, policyholders and unit holders worldwide.

We are grateful for the opportunity to submit written evidence to the House of Lords Select Committee on the European Union.

A. THE FINANCIAL SERVICES ACTION PLAN

What progress has been made to date?

1. The Financial Services Action Plan (FSAP) established a timetable to benchmark the creation of an integrated EU financial services market by the end of 2005.

2. The FSAP has raised the political profile of financial market integration and liberalisation as an important factor in the creation of an efficient and competitive European economy. The FSAP is part of the wider political project (as established by the Lisbon Summit in March 2000) of making the EU the world's most competitive information-based economy by 2010.

3. The Commission's 8th Progress Report on the FSAP, published on 3 June 2003, underlines both the continuing progress made in the first half of 2003, but also the urgency of achieving results in the next nine months if the overall deadlines are to be achieved. The report argues that if the 2005 deadline is to be realised, Member States need 18 months for implementation. Given the European Parliament elections in June 2004, this means completion of EU legislative processes by April 2004.

4. We are concerned that the emphasis on meeting these deadlines could compromise the quality of the final legislation.

Has this been beneficial or deleterious to UK interests? Has sufficient weight been given to the position and experience of UK financial services industry?

5. Overall, we view the existing FSAP as beneficial. While we fully supported the original "1992" single market initiative which introduced single European passports for banking, insurance and securities business, it has become clear over time that it was not sufficient to bring about a fully functioning single EU market for retail financial services.

6. The FSAP addressed unfinished business in the financial services area arising from the 1992 project and it incorporated many ongoing legislative initiatives, including some of direct commercial interest to Prudential plc, such as UCITS (mutual funds), occupational pension funds, distance marketing and the Investment Services Directive (ISD), adding a new political momentum to these proposals. This was clearly needed in the case of both retail collective investments (updating the 1985 directive) and occupational pensions (first discussed in 1991).

7. The Treasury consultations on EU issues have become more open and frequent in recent years. The Treasury have encouraged consultation on proposals as they develop and have taken an explicit interest in retail financial services. They have also sought to remove red tape to facilitate the use of the cross-border potential of UCITS. This has helped facilitate the cross-border business of our fund management arm, M&G.

What are the main outstanding matters that remain to be dealt with under the FSAP and what key issues will need to be resolved?

8. In its latest progress report the Commission reported that 34 of the 42 measures in the FSAP had been completed, with 5 currently under negotiation (ISD, prospectuses, takeovers, transparency of reporting obligations and savings tax). Three FSAP proposals were still due from the Commission (10th and 14th company law directives, and the Capital Adequacy Directive 3).

9. A number of important items remain outstanding and will take some time to complete, notably the ISD, work on clearing and settlement, and implementation of the Basel Capital Accords. The outlook for adoption of the Takeovers Directive is currently uncertain.

B. IMPLEMENTATION AND ENFORCEMENT

How successful do you expect the Lamfalussy process to be? Are any changes needed?

10. We believe that the Lamfalussy report and its recommendations have added an important new dimension to the legislative process. The new legislative structure and the enhanced consultation process of the specialist committees should give greater opportunity for industry to influence the detail of EU legislation.

11. However, it is too early to say how effective the process will be, particularly as those areas of major commercial concern for Prudential plc are not yet subject to the Lamfalussy process. Therefore, we welcome the decisive political moves by the Finance Ministers to extend Lamfalussy to insurance and pensions, and also to integrate UCITS into the new European Securities Committee.

12. Initial signs are positive, with greater transparency in the case of the ISD. This has also been reflected in open consultation with the Treasury and the Financial Services Authority. Signs are also positive in the case of the important preliminary work being carried out on Solvency II, where the Commission have used their web pages to disseminate early drafts of consultations widely.

Who will be responsible for ensuring effective implementation and enforcement of the single market, after the regulatory framework is in place? How successful do you expect this process to be?

13. The Lamfalussy Group identified that "almost everyone agrees that existing rules and regulation are implemented differently and that therefore inconsistencies occur in the treatment of the same kind of business, which threatens to violate the pre-requisite of the competitive neutrality of supervision."

14. As a business we look to the Commission to police internal market rules. Recent Commission action against discriminatory taxes affecting foreign-based funds in Germany and Austria demonstrates that even the threat of action can be effective.

15. We would suggest that more Commission resources should be moved into this area as the regulatory output declines following the completion of the FSAP.

16. Correct implementation of directives by Member States will be crucial. The Commission and Member State authorities will need to demonstrate that, even if the directives date from pre-Lamfalussy times, the new approach will be applied in practice. This means that Member States' authorities will need to cooperate fully in order to ensure correct implementation (Level 3 measures), while the Commission will undertake enforcement procedures (Level 4 measures).

17. We are encouraged that the FSAP 8th Progress Report indicates that Enforcement and Implementation is a priority for the Commission following the completion of the FSAP. In addition there are positive points in the Commission Communication "Internal Market Strategy (Priorities 2003–2006)" which puts forward a number of ideas including:

— An internal market "Compatability test" to be applied to all legislation adopted at national level.

— Establishing "best practices" to ensure better and faster transposition of directives.

What will be the role of competition regulators at EU and Member State level?

18. In parallel with enforcement we believe that EU Competition rules may have a greater role to play. It is important to deploy a full range of EU policy instruments and we welcome recent comments from DG Competition indicating a growing interest in the financial services sector. In particular the Commission is starting to take action against the important competition law aspects of the financial infrastructure, eg payment systems, clearing and settlement.

What issues will arise as the single market framework is implemented and enforced?

19. There are still question marks over how far the economic and market objectives of the FSAP are being achieved in practice by the EU legislative processes. There is concern that recent negotiations have curtailed the application of the Single Market principle of "mutual recognition" and that regulators are being driven to try to harmonise too many details.

20. In areas familiar to Prudential plc there has been too little consistency in application. The "general good" provisions of the Insurance Directive provide ample scope for interpretation which can be used to restrict the freedoms provided by the Directive.

21. In the case of UCITS, studies by the Investment Management Association have shown inconsistent implementation, while differences in host country marketing and conduct of business regulations have hindered the development of a single market for funds.

22. Some of this is inherent in the nature of directives and we welcome the growing debate over the use of Regulations, which have direct effect.

What non-regulatory barriers might impede the effective functioning of a single market for financial services?

23. Business has to be realistic that not all "barriers" can be addressed through legal measures. There are a number of "natural obstacles" which are costs of doing business in the market. These include consumer preferences such as language, culture, loyalty and trust. There is also a maxim "all business is local" which is particularly relevant in the case of more complex insurance and pension products, where customer preferences tend to be highly biased towards local structures and established channels of distribution.

C. The Future

How do witnesses see the future development of a single market in financial services following implementation of the FSAP? Are additional measures needed?

Will the changes resulting from the FSAP proposals have an impact on the competitive position of London and EU markets as a whole in the global environment?

24. We do not believe that a major new action plan of legislative measures is required (ie a "FSAP 2"). We welcome the Commission's priorities as outlined in the 8th Progress report:

— Enforcement and Implementation.

— Establishing a process for identifying and resolving new challenges.

— Addressing the global, and especially transatlantic, dimensions.

25. One of the major new challenges should be to re-establish the commitment to mutual recognition. This should be facilitated by the closer co-operation between regulators which is set out in the Lamfalussy process. In this respect we share the view of the Treasury as set out in "Completing a Dynamic Single European Financial Services Market: A catalyst for Economic Prosperity for Citizens and Business across the EU", published in July 2000. This outlined the building blocks for mutual recognition:

— "Home state" (or country of origin) regulation combined with mutual recognition.

— Agreement where necessary on a framework of core standards for conduct of business and consumer protection rules.

— Development of effective, cross-border consumer redress mechanisms.

— Better informed consumers.

26 June 2003

Memorandum from Quoted Companies Alliance

1. We welcome the opportunity to submit evidence on this subject. We have worked hard with our members, HM Treasury, the EC, the EU Parliament and others to obtain a satisfactory outcome from the proposals, particularly where they impact on the smaller quoted company market, a UK feature unique in the EU.

2. About the QCA

2.1 The Quoted Companies Alliance (QCA) is a not-for-profit organisation dedicated to promoting the cause of smaller quoted companies ("SQCs")—defined as those quoted companies outside the FTSE 350 (including those on AIM and OFEX) representing 85 per cent of UK quoted companies by number.

QCA believes that the UK's future prosperity depends on business enterprise and is committed to improving the ability of its members to:

— demonstrate value to both capital markets and the wider economy;

— to represent members' interests and requirements; and

— to ensure that the regulatory environment in which they operate effectively balances the interests of members, investors and other legitimate interests.

Together SQCs employ over 2 million people. The recruitment, retention and motivation of high quality management and employees are pre-requisites for success.

3. THE FINANCIAL SERVICES ACTION PLAN

3.1 It is our view that the aims and ambitions of the FSAP were very much in the UK's interests. Our vibrant financial services sector can only benefit from a larger, open, flexible and appropriately regulated market. However, we believe implementation of these laudable objectives has disappointed many practitioners in the UK.

3.2 Our impression is that little weight was given to the UK's experience by the EC in drafting initial proposals under FSAP. In particular, the outcry over the Prospectus Directive, largely written by a secondee from the Milan Bourse, shows how little consultation occurred and how unsatisfactory the outcome can be.

3.3 Despite the UK's vast experience in financial services, we felt that at the EC level, we were just one voice in 15, easily drowned out by countries with vested interests to protect and a different cultural approach to financial services.

3.4 One issue which appeared to drive a lot of thinking behind FSAP is investor protection, more particularly retail investor protection. As a consequence, many proposals stemming from the FSAP seem onerous from a UK perspective, where the conduct of business rules are more embedded and retail clients are better educated to the risks involved—in short the UK has a much stronger capital market culture. Examples of this feeding through FSAP are restrictions on execution only dealing contained in the Investment Services Directive and for mandatory quarterly reporting contained in the Transparency Directive.

3.5 Another issue that sets the UK apart is the role of the State. Financial Services in the UK have a long history of self regulation, through bodies such as the Takeover Panel and "authorised firms". The Continental markets have a much greater involvement from the State, in approving documents for example.

3.6 Once a draft directive is issued, we have strong evidence to suggest that at EC level and in the Council of Ministers, UK views are regarding as "special pleading" by the City. Despite the fact that the City represents many significant European banks, its views are seen to be narrow vested interests of the UK alone. The City is seen to be a UK asset but certainly not a European one!

3.7 Examples of this attitude are:

(i) We have been advised by MEPs to translate our submissions into another EU language and have them submitted in that country as well as from the UK.

(ii) Consultations, for example by CESR, are divided and summarised by country rather than by number of responses. As a result, a consultation exercise may give rise to many responses from the UK and few from other countries, but they are all summarised for discussion by country, again reducing the weight and content of UK opinion.

3.8 A further problem we see is that because only the UK has a significant number of smaller quoted companies, any concessions to this group are seen as a concession to the UK, rather than on size. In the UK it has long been accepted that a "one size fits all" approach is not appropriate. However, virtually all the Directives are written from the perspective of large companies, rather than the 2000 smaller companies (predominantly UK based), which make up 25% of all quoted companies within the EU.

4. IMPLEMENTATION AND ENFORCEMENT

4.1 We would like the Lamfalussy process to be successful but believe it runs the risk of getting bogged down in bureaucracy and detail. For capital markets to work efficiently they need to be dynamic and flexible. The whole process is building in too much rigidity and prescription.

4.2 Baron Lamfalussy recently said that one of the problems with the process was politicians being keen to protect retail investors because they had no "voice" of their own. He conceded that this may have gone too far.

4.3 On the subject of implementation, there is a real fear of "gold plating" by the UK authorities. As a possible consequence of the FSA's superior knowledge of financial markets and products, we are concerned that regulation in the UK will be detailed and specific, but elsewhere will be more broadly applied.

4.4 As yet, there is no effective body to which appeals can be made. As we have seen with competition decisions overturned by the European Court, victory is hollow because the deal has gone and markets moved on. The process needs to be dynamic and real time, like the actions of the Takeover Panel for example.

5. THE FUTURE

5.1 We believe the impact of FSAP will have a mixed result on London's position. Many smaller companies have already indicated that the increasing regulatory burdens imposed by FSAP will cause them to de-list completely. Similarly, the London Stock Exchange's AIM market is actively considering becoming an "un-regulated" market to remove it from compliance with FSAP. This can only have a detrimental effect on London and the vital role played by smaller companies in bridging the often lamented "equity gap".

23 June 2003

Memorandum from Stephen Revell, Partner, Freshfields Bruckhaus Deringer

1. THE FINANCIAL SERVICES ACTION PLAN

1.1 *What progress has been made to date?*
In terms of legislative progress, this is a matter of public record. According to the eighth progress report on the Financial Services Act Plan (FSAP) published by the Commission on 3 June 2003, 34 of the 42 original measures have been "finalised" ("proposed" is possibly a better word as many of these measures are still under discussion/consultation).

However, there is still much to be done before certain FSAP measures (including many among the 34 measures) can be implemented and completed. Moreover, I have concerns about the product of the current legislative process. While important progress hs been made in transparency, consultation and the articulation of regulatory objectives, the current level 2 process (involving both the Committee of European Securities Regulators (SESR) and the Commission) needs to be improved. The regulations are being suggested by too narrowly a constituted and qualified body, there is inadequate consultation (good consultation also includes feedback and discussion of points rejected) and unrealistic timescales[43]. The process also suffers from the absence of disciplines corresponding to those imposed in the UK context by the requirements in the Financial Services and Markets Act 2000 to justify new measures by reference to clear objectives and principles of regulation and to carry out a cost-benefit analysis. As a result, the quality and balance of the measures that are being produced is suffering; the desired goals are not always being achieved and parts of the legislation are unclear and, in some cases, unduly burdensome.

Like the Prospectus Directive, the final text of many of the directives arising out of the FSAP are the product of "horse-trading"; divergent views have meant that compromises have been slow and difficult to achieve. In addition, certain amendments have been agreed at a political level without adequate consideration of the needs of the market. In one case of change proposed in the light of consultation was revised at a late stage without explanation or further consultation.

1.2 *Has this been beneficial or deleterious to UK interests?*

It is too early to judge the overall effect on UK interests. The essential objective of the FSAP should be strongly in the interests of efficient and competitive financial services institutions and markets, provided that the achievement of these objectives is not compromised by inadequacies in implementation—as to which see the concerns explained above. If the stated objectives of the FSAP are achieved, it should be beneficial to the UK financial services industry; whether or not they are depends on how the various measures are implemented by Member States.

1.3 *Has sufficient weight been given to the position and experience of UK financial services industry?*

No. The composition of the Council and CESR as the primary source of advice and ideas on implementing measures has the effect that insufficient weight is given to contributors with first hand experience of sophisticated wholesale markets. This tends to produce proposals for burdensome and detailed measures intended to proctect retail investors and in some cases local and/or national markets without proper appreciation of the effect of such measures on the availability and cost of capital and financial products on

---

[43] For example, the consultation process on level 2 implementing measures under the Prospectus Directive has been subject to particularly tight deadlines (there were 52 business days to digest and respond to the first consultation paper on level 2 measures (168 pages) and only 32 business days for the addendum to the consultation paper (124 pages)).

large scale users and large scale investors. This view is also shared by the Centre for the Study of Financial Innovation (CSFI). In a recent article published in the Financial Times the CSFI is quoted as saying:

> "EU legislation is being tailored for the needs of the retail markets on the Continent, rather than the predominantly wholesale businesses in London".

Not only is UK experience being ignored, it is being subordinated to a regulatory approach driven by predominantly retail/investor-focused lobbying with insufficient emphasis being given to the maintenance and operation of the wholesale markets. The suggestions and reactions of some Member States seem motivated by the wish to reduce the perceived dominance of the UK market. Clearly, if this aim is realised it will damage the UK financial services industry.

Although the Financial Services Authority and HM Treasury have been closely involved in the process and many trade associations have actively participated, there has been no single body championing the cause of the UK financial services industry; the "business" most affected by these directives. Similarly, corporate Britain's voice is not being clearly heard. I believe that there is a leadership gap and that a new role needs to be created for some institutional body (possibly the Bank of England, which is both independent and well respected) to be the champion of the UK financial services industry. In addition to increasing awareness about the FSAP and educating Europe about the UK financial services industry, this body would, if operating properly, be able to identify and solve potential problems at an early stage not least by engaging in the EU process at the very first opportunity.

Clearly co-ordinated leadership is needed to ensure the appropriate involvement of issuers, investors and all aspects of the business community, some sectors of which are either unaware of the changes and/or are, at present, indifferent to them.

1.4 *What are the Main Outstanding Matters that Remain to be Dealt with under the FSAP and what Key Issues will need to be Resolved?*

Neither the core directives (ie the Prospectus Directive, the Transparency Obligations Directive and the Market Abuse Directive) nor the corresponding level 2 implementing measures are yet in a form that is ideal to the UK markets and the interests of the UK financial services industry. There is no immediate ability to change the Market Abuse Directive, limited scope to change the Prospective Directive and only some room for manoeuvre on the Transparency Obligations Directive. This means that the focus must, in practice, be an appropriate level 2 implementing measures.

These directives and the level 2 implementing measures will need to be implemented by all Member States in due course.

Insufficient emphasis is being given to non-EU issuers—core "customers" not only of the UK financial services industry but of the EU markets more generally. Other inadequacies are highlighted by the following examples:

— Should all UK-listed SMEs (small and medium-sized enterprises) be required to incur the cost of quarterly reporting?

— Insufficient allowance has been made in the Prospectus Directive for wholesale market activity; this is illustrated in part by the €50,000 denomination dividing line between the retail and wholesale market—based on present market practice the UK markets believe this amount should be much lower. As you will appreciate this limit is different from, and not connected with, the level at which issuers can choose home Member State which has been reduced from €50,000 to €5,000 and now to €1,000. Although I support the changes made to the freedom of choice limit, I remain concerned about the €50,000 limit which defines the wholesale market.

— The requirement to maintain insider lists under the Market Abuse Directive, as currently proposed by CESR, is unrealistic and unduly onerous.

— The proposals requiring notification of interests in securities are not yet sufficiently clearly drafted to apply only to interests in shares. The requirements relating to custodians also appear unduly onerous and to change present market practice.

2. IMPLEMENTATION AND ENFORCEMENT

2.1 *The success of setting up a single market in financial services will depend to a considerable degree on the way in which the regulatory framework is implemented and enforced*

I agree with this statement but, with regard to enforcement, there is an important omission; under the Treaty none of the directives are able to harmonise liability. The potential problems can be illustrated with the following example. A Spanish investor buys bonds that have been issued by an Italian company listed on the London Stock Exchange and approved by the competent authority in Luxembourg—under what law should the issuer be liable to the investor and in which court does he bring his claim?

2.2 *How successful do you expect the Lamfalussy process to be?*

Although I think that it is too early to opine on the success of the Lamfalussy process, I do have a number of concerns about the way that the process is currently working. As the "horse trading" on the Prospectus Directive demonstrates, framework directives that are prepared under level 1 are too detailed and controversial and are not passing through the level 1 process sufficiently quickly. Furthermore, the level 2 implementing measures that are being produced are too detailed (even for level 2) and do not draw sufficiently on experience in the UK, in particular with respect to wholesale market matters. I also have concerns about the timescales applied to the consultation process (see paragraph 1.1 above) and the overall quality of the consultation and drafting process.

The FSAP deals with highly technical areas and I believe that more should be done to ensure greater involvement of market experts at a Commission and, particularly, CESR level. Failure to do so may result in poorly drafted measures which leads to uncertainty in the law.

2.3 *Are any changes needed?*

I think that the relationship between the technical advice prepared by CESR and the final implementing measures produced by the Commission needs to be clarified. Is CESR's advice, in practice, going to be adopted by the Commission with or without change?[44] Depending on the answer to this question, the constitution and approach of CESR will need to be reviewed.

Although CESR has had some success, it struggles from being under-resourced and unable to consult properly due to time constraints. Furthermore, because it appears to operate on the basis of majority voting (each regulator has one vote), there is a risk (and events so far suggest) that the UK's experience and views are given insufficient weight particularly in the light of the size and importance of the UK market.

In practice, the process is struggling; perhaps better use could be made of appropriately qualified working parties which include strong market representation especially from the UK (for example, the consultative working group for the Prospectus Directive has no UK member).

2.4 *Who will be responsible for ensuring effective implementation and enforcement of the single market, after the regulatory framework is in place?*

The answer to this question is a matter of public record in the text of the directives. In practice, this will come down to co-operation between Member States and the competent authorities. In this regard CESR's role is unclear (but the position appears to be that it will play a role); I have concerns about its constitution and operation (see above).

2.5 *How successful do you expect this process to be?*

Markets within each Member State are very different and it will be extremely difficult to harmonise different practices in the short to medium term. In the words of Baron Lamfalussy:

> "There are still very substantial differences between EU countries' regulatory structures which make it very difficult to put up a single regulator."

The answer to this question also depends, to some extent, on the role of "institutional" players, for example, CESR (see further above). I am also concerned about the apparent aim of some national regulators to preserve their local and national markets; this brings into question their political will to achieve true harmonisation. The desire to preserve national markets is illustrated by the Prospectus Directive. At present, an issuer has freedom to decide where its prospectuses are approved. Under the Prospectus Directive there is no choice where the securities are shares or convertible bonds.

2.6 *What will be the role of competition regulators at EU and Member State level?*

I do not anticipate that, in practice, they will have a role in creating a single market for financial services. They may play an important role in ensuring anti-competitive behaviour eg in a national market which prevents business activity from other countries is not allowed to prevent the creation of a single market.

2.7 *What issues will arise as the single market framework is implemented and enforced?*

Unless changes are made to framework directives and level 2 implementing measures there are many who believe that the markets could be adversely affected, particularly with regard to non-EU issuers. There are likely to be differences in the implementation and enforcement of the various measures by Member States

---

[44] I refer to the changes made by the Commission to CESR's advice on implementing measures under the Market Abuse Directive (in response to the Commission's first mandate).

and it is also possible that certain aspects of the legislative measures will not operate as expected in practice. Therefore, procedures should be put in place now to deal with the possibility that changes may need to be made to certain measures on an expedited basis to minimise market disruption. These procedures are also needed to facilitate changes on an on-going basis to take account of market developments. The triggers for change and the processes for change need to be clarified as between the Commission and CESR to ensure that regulation is dynamically responsive to the market.

As mentioned above (see paragraph 2.5), many markets/parts of markets are very different and it will be difficult, in practice, to harmonise their practices in accordance with the goals of the FSAP.

2.8 *What non-regulatory barriers might impede the effective functioning of a single market for financial services?*

Tax and differences in markets especially in relation to how retail investors like to save/buy products.

C. THE FUTURE

3.1 *How do witnesses see the future development of a single market in financial services following implementation of the FSAP?*

Implementation of the legislative measures will need to be monitored to ensure that necessary changes can be made quickly and efficiently. Co-operation between competent authorities and Member States should be encouraged, as should the need for an effective champion for the UK financial services industry (see paragraph 1.3 above).

3.2 *Are additional measures needed?*

Please see my comments relating to non-EU issuers (at paragraph 1.4 and 2.7 above), the concern raised by the CSFI that EU legislation is being tailored for the needs of the retail markets rather than wholesale businesses (see paragraph 1.3 above) and the need for procedures to deal with the possibility that changes may need to be made to certain measures on an expedited basis (see paragraph 2.7 above).

3.3 *Will the changes resulting from the FSAP proposals have an impact on the competitive position of London and EU markets as a whole in the global environment?*

Yes (see further above). In the short term I am concerned that the London markets could be disrupted and that service providers in London could be disadvantaged. However, in the long term, if the stated objectives of the FSAP are achieved, it should be beneficial to the UK financial services industry.

26 June 2003

Memorandum from the Royal Bank of Scotland

INTRODUCTION

1. The Royal Bank of Scotland Group, founded in 1727, is one of Europe's leading financial services groups. Market capitalisation as at 25 June 2003 totals £50.2 billion, making the bank the second largest in the UK and in Europe and fifth in the world. The Group has more than 20 million UK personal customers, 2,287 UK branches and total assets at 31 December 2002 of £412 billion. The Group employs over 111,000 staff worldwide with offices in the UK, Europe, the US, and Asia.

2. The Group owns nationally and internationally recognised brands including Royal Bank of Scotland, NatWest, Ulster Bank, Coutts, Lombard, Direct Line, and Citizens in the US. It is the leader in many of its chosen markets, including number one in the UK in corporate and commercial banking, number one for small business customers, number one in UK offshore banking, number one in private banking, number one in the UK for asset finance, number one provider of telephone motor insurance, and number two in UK credit cards and retail banking.

3. The Royal Bank of Scotland Group welcomes the opportunity to take part in this exercise.

A. THE FINANCIAL SERVICES ACTION PLAN (FSAP)

What progress has been made to date?

1. Judged simply in terms of the sheer volume of legislation adopted and draft legislation issued, significant progress has been made. It is, however, less clear whether all of the measures put in place will deliver their desired results. We welcome in principle the creation of a genuine single market for financial services, but the details have to be properly thought through and fairly implemented.

Has this been beneficial or deleterious to UK interests?

2. The FSAP has the potential to provide greatly enhanced commercial opportunities. It is too early to be certain whether or not the FSAP will in practice benefit the interests of the UK Financial Services Industry overall. This will depend in large part upon the extent to which implementing measures are evenly applied across member states; and, in particular, whether some measures are applied in the UK on a "super-equivalent" basis as seems likely in certain areas (for instance, as regards the proposed implementation in the UK of the Distance Marketing Directive). Equally, the adoption of EU legislation on a super-equivalent basis in other member states also has the potential to impact adversely on UK interests. Consistency of application is likely to become more difficult still after enlargement.

Has sufficient weight been given to the position and experience of UK Financial Services Industry?

3. Not always. The UK Financial Services Industry has been involved in the relevant consultation processes, individually and through trade and representative bodies. However, the harmonisation process has led in some areas to standards which cut directly across established UK practice and experience, despite the predominant weight the UK frequently has in many parts of the industry. One important example is the likely loss of execution-only facilities in client investment dealing under the Investment Services Directive.

What are the main outstanding matters that remain to be dealt with under the FSAP and what key issues will need to be resolved?

4. A number of significant proposals remain outstanding and at various stages of progress in the legislative cycle. These include the Investment Services Directive, the Risk Based Capital Requirements Directive, the Takeover Directive and the Prospectus Directive. Adequate consultation, debate and deliberation are essential to the process, given the complexity and significance of many of these issues for the whole of the EU Financial Services Industry. For the same reason, rigorous adherence to implementation timetables should not be at the expense of the quality and effectiveness of legislation in these areas.

B. IMPLEMENTATION AND ENFORCEMENT

How successful do you expect the Lamfalussy process to be? Are any changes needed?

1. We broadly support the Lamfalussy principles and their extension to banking and insurance, in particular the emphasis on adopting framework directives backed up by detailed regulation formulated at the level of committees (for instance, CESR, in respect of the Market Abuse Directive). This should make for better and more flexible EU legislation. In the short-term, there may be difficulties in distinguishing between the essential elements best suited to framework directives and the detail which should be left to CESR and other committees. In the longer-term, proper application of the Lamfalussy principles should accelerate the EU legislative process and improve the general quality of the legislation, particularly if the process leads to the greater involvement of industry expertise.

Who will be responsible for ensuring effective implementation and enforcement of the single market, after the regulatory Framework is in place? How successful do you expect this process to be?

2. The Commission will need to be vigilant in ensuring even and consistent implementation by the national parliaments. But local regulators are best placed to continue to carry out detailed supervision of effective compliance. It remains to be seen how effective these processes will be in practice. There must also be effective collaboration between the regulatory bodies of member states.

What will be the role of competition regulators at EU and Member State level? What issues will arise as the single market framework is implemented and enforced?

3. The single market framework should lead to increased competition and downward pressure on margins. In the longer term, lower value-added activities may move to lower cost locations, and less efficient financial companies could be driven out of the market through consolidation (where the regulatory framework permits). Such changes are likely to create critical tests for the single market. For example, embattled

companies may seek to subvert the competitive process; national governments may intervene to protect them; and will barriers to cross-border acquisitions in practice restrict domestic companies' efforts to secure a foothold in other markets? Firm action will be required by the EU Commission to prevent such outcomes.

What non-regulatory barriers might impede the effective functioning of a single market for financial services?

4. Cross-border trade is likely to be impeded by a number of barriers, particularly in the retail market, where demand depends, to a great extent, on the idiosyncrasies of individual countries and on the nature and structure of the products offered. These are in turn shaped by factors such as varying tax regimes, legal systems, the technical infrastructure and cultural traditions.

5. The extension of the single market to incorporate new EU members, and the move by some existing members to join the euro, may divert Commission resources away from overseeing the development of the single market. In addition, the European labour market remains relatively immobile, limiting the cross-border flow of workers within the Financial Services Industry.

C. THE FUTURE

How do witnesses see the future development of a single market in financial services following implementation of the FSAP? Are additional measures needed?

1. There is always the danger of the industry being swamped by regulatory change. Companies are having to adjust their practices to conform with existing measures, and none would welcome at present the burden of large numbers of additional measures. Where additional measures may be needed, a balance needs to be struck, ensuring a "quality, not quantity" approach, and—crucially—sufficient time allowed for proper consultation.

2. A similarly balanced approach is essential in terms of justifying the need for change and in measuring the degree of effectiveness after implementation of particular measures. For example, the UCITS Directive seems so far to have been relatively little used and an analysis of whether a tool was in fact necessary in this area, and whether this Directive was the correct tool in the first place, would be desirable.

Will the changes resulting from the FSAP proposals have an impact on the competitive position of London and EU markets as a whole in the global environment?

3. Yes. The degree of fragmentation in the pan-European capital market still compares unfavourably with the US; the FSAP should encourage greater convergence and integration and, in time, competitiveness. But there is a careful balance to strike in regulating financial services. The FSAP may equally undermine the competitiveness of the pan-European market if, for example, legislation hinders the development of some markets or drives them abroad. The FSAP is largely concerned, by definition, with the internal EU market. Greater account needs to be taken of the impact of the regime on non-EU market participants; the interaction between FSAP and other, global, measures (for instance, Basel II); and the effect of these two factors on the competitive position of EU financial services firms in the wider world.

SUMMARY

There is, in principle, a significant economic prize to be had by the EU, the UK and by the UK Financial Services Industry if the Lamfalussy process is carefully and effectively implemented. But this dividend may be lost in whole or in part if the Commission does not:

— allow sufficient time for complex issues to be fully debated (including engaging the Financial Services Industry in the consultation process), even where this risks delays to pre-set timetables;

— establish before drawing up legislation a properly thought-through case for the necessity and utility of each proposed measure;

— recognise that the key difficulty in practice will be ensuring equivalent implementation given the great variety of contexts across the range of existing and forthcoming Member States; and

— take steps to engage fully with developments outside the EU context, which may affect significantly the effectiveness of the FSAP in the wider world.

June 2003

Memorandum from Mr Luigi Spaventa, Consob

I am not competent, I am afraid, to address the issues regarding the effects of the FSAP on the UK. Moreover I am leaving Consob shortly, as my mandate is about to expire, and I have been exceedingly busy.

I thought, however, that the attached excerpt of a speech I gave to IPMA may be of some use to you. There I deal with some of the matters which are the subject of your inquiry, and in particular with the implementation of the Lamfalussy process, which I contributed to set up as a member of the committee of wise men.

"1. Let me begin by belabouring the obvious. The proposition that important benefits would arise from greater financial integration in Europe has solid theoretical support (though only in the long run, as pointed out by Baron Lamfalussy in a recent presentation[45]). Requested by the European Commission to give quantitative flesh to this accepted qualitative wisdom, a research centre, London Economics, recently produced a report[46] attempting to measure the macroeconomic impact of financial integration. Without discussing numbers, it may be useful to spell out how the wondrous results that are predicted are expected to come about.

Trading costs, measured as percentage effective bid-ask spreads, are the prime, and indeed the only mover; costs other than the spread are not part of the analysis. It is estimated that in an equity market with a capitalisation equal to the sum of European regional markets, such costs would fall susbstantially. This would lower the average cost of capital in Europe by some 37 basis points and by 10 more due to an unspecified reduction in clearance and settlement costs: whence higher investment, higher GDP and all the rest. The benchmarks of such fully integrated single securities market are: freedom of access for issuers, investors, intermediaries and infrastructure suppliers irrespective of their location; and "a seamless web of market supervision which guarantees stringent and effective . . . enforcement of commonly agreed provisions". Its more precise essence is, however, a single Europe-wide trading platform or, at least, a set of interlinked platforms where—it is assumed—all other differences would disappear.

The realisation of these benchmark features requires not only the top-down interventions envisaged by the FSAP as necessary to establish a "seamless web" of commonly agreed provisions, but also a bottom-up initiative that can only originate from the market. It may even be argued that the latter could set the path for the former and present European law-makers and regulators with relevant *faits accomplis*. It is, after all, the first commandment of the City of London that "markets are created and developed by market participants not by rules and regulations"[47]. What could market participants do, without waiting for rules and regulations, to enhance the creation of the single pool of liquidity? What have they actually have done? The two relevant cases here are exchanges and clearing and settlements.

2. Exchanges are nowadays private entities in the whole of Europe. Mergers, take-overs, the setting up of common platforms, though having important regulatory implications, are in the end private decisions. Consider the consequences that the mere announcement of a merger between the LSE and DB had some time ago. The prospect of that merger prompted a French political initiative at the Ecofin and eventually the creation of the Lamfalussy Committee. Second, British and German regulators began to meet in order to solve the regulatory problems posed by the project. Third, the mere threat of a London-Frankfurt axis provided impetus to Euronext, the establishment of which, again, required a strict cooperation of the French, Belgian and Dutch regulatory authorities. Sometimes, when the market takes the lead, *l'intendence suivra*. But, at the moment, nothing seems to move. On the contrary, continental exchanges seem to be strengthening the walls of their citadels, each with its own vertical post-trade structure: which brings me to a second issue which would clearly require a bottom-up approach.

Two points emerged in the hearings with the industry of the Lamfalussy Committee: first the inefficiencies in the cross-border clearing and settlement of securities transactions represent a major obstacle to market integration; second, that was a problem for the private sector, more than for the authorities to solve. It is said in the Giovannini Report[48] that "there is a consensus . . . that the EU clearing and settlement landscape could be significantly improved by market-led convergence . . . across national systems". I doubt that this is happening, at least with the required speed. The G30 report[49] notes that "incentives within the individual clearing and settlement entities tend to support incremental change that strengthens the local franchise, rather than initiatives to facilitate greater competitiveness . . . that could adversely affect the value of the local franchise".

---

[45] Alexandre Lamfalussy, *Creating an integrated European market for financial services*, Cass Business School Seminar on Financial Services, February 19, 2003.

[46] *Quantification of the Macro-Economic Impact of Integration of EU Financial Markets*, Final Report to the European Commission by London Economics, November 2002.

[47] *Creating a single European market for financial services*, a discussion paper produced by a working group in the City of London, November 2002.

[48] *Cross-Border Clearing and Settlement Arrangements in the European Union*, Brussels, November 2001.

[49] *Global Clearing and Settlement: A Plan for Action*, Washington DC, 2003.

We thus have two important cases in which the market solution, being marred by oligopolistic inefficiencies, does not deliver the optimum. Thus, let us by all means "formally embed[. . .]" the first commandment "in the most authoritative manner in Community legislation", as required by the City of London: but do not expect that market participants, left to themselves can always produce an efficient solution irrespective of the existing entrenched interests.

3. It is certainly not the task of legislation and regulation to create and organise markets. Nor can legislation and regulation be the magic wand that removes a persistent home bias. As this may be due also to the specificity of financial regulation, the proper task of Community top-down initiatives, such as those listed in the FSAP, should be that of establishing the necessary (though far from sufficient) conditions for growing integration.

I do not intend to discuss specific pieces of level 1 legislation (to use the Lamfalussy jargon) now under discussions. I prefer to consider what has been and what can be achieved with the suggestions of the Committee of Wise Men as implemented by the Stockholm Council.

The Lamfalussy report was a success story. Unlike other reports, it was accepted with surprising speed at the political level, it was digested, though with some difficulty, by the European Parliament and it was warmly welcomed by the industry and market participants. I now have the feeling that we have entered a season of disenchantment with the past fashion. Neither the recent report of the City of London nor that of Eurofi[50] spend much time on the Lamfalussy procedure. In a recent paper, Professors Gerard Herting and Ruben Lee[51] predict that the Lamfalussy process will not work.

How warranted is this perceivable scepticism? Though, so far, the Lamfalussy approach has not delivered much in terms of new legislation, can we infer from this that the glass is empty, or are instead observers and scholars missing some important development which the process has at least potentially set in motion? I wish to argue that the true seeds of change are to be found in the level 3 tasks attributed to CESR, though it is far from certain that CESR will find the will and the ability to exploit this opportunity. Before discussing this, however, let me take a quick look at what is happening at level 2.

4. When proposing level 2 legislation the Lamfalussy committee had two objectives in mind: speeding the process of primary legislation by removing a host of technical implementing measures from the table; allowing a quick adaptation of such measures to the changing needs of the market. It is not clear to what extent the first objective has been achieved, considering that the Council and especially Parliament have tended to take a rather narrow view of what is to be left to technical implementation. The sunset clause by Parliament has severely limited the scope of the second objective.

The adoption of the implementing measures for the market abuse directive will be the first test for the newly created Securities Committee working in its comitology capacity, so we do not know yet whether the Committee will deliver and avoid the same squabbles that have often paralysed the Council. It may well happen that the consensus reached at the level of national securities commission vanishes at the level of national (political) representatives.

CESR has worked much harder. In its capacity of an advisory group assisting the Commission, it has drafted proposals for the implementing measures of the market abuse directive, is giving advice on the prospectus directive, is responding to the Commission's consultation on the ISD. The work of CESR is accompanied by intensive consultation with the interested parties.

Whatever the outcome of level 2, one thing is sure. The institutional metamorphis of a cosy club of regulators—as essentially FESCO was— into a committee with institutional dignity in the European law-making process is by itself an important step.

5. Potentially, level 3 may become the most relevant area of CESR work, because unco-ordinated and variegated implementation of the directives in national legislation and regulation is a major obstacle to the development of a single market for financial services.

The Stockholm Council endorsed the indications of the Lamfalussy report: at level 3 CESR should produce consistent guidelines for national regulations, issue joint interpretative recommendations and set common standards, compare and review regulatory practices, conduct peer reviews of administrative regulation and regulatory practices in Member States.

Though CESR level 3 recommendations and standards are not legally binding, the Committee could exercise appropriate pressures on its members by asking them to comply or explain. For this to be possible, CESR should have the means, and above all the strength, to conduct regular reviews of its members' compliance. The same is true for the other major level 3 mission: ensuring "more consistent and timely implementation of Community legislation in Member States" in national regulation and in the regulators' practice.

---

[50] Jacques de la Rosire, Daniel Lebegue and Didier Cahen, *An integrated European financial market.* Eurofi preliminary report, *26 November 2002.*

[51] "Four Predictions about the Future of European Securities Regulations", January 2003.

These new tasks assigned to CESR are somewhat delicate because they imply some intrusion in the domestic regulatory activities of its members. No procedure to deal with them has yet been set in place. In comparison with international organisations that conduct independent assessments in various areas, the technical structure of CESR is still weak. More importantly, will CESR members accept to submit to a peer review? It is perhaps telling that the requirement of "peer reviews" present in the Stockholm Council resolution has disappeared in the CESR chart.

The market appears to be discovering the relevance of level 3. In the recent consultation on the implementating measures for the prospectus directive there was a widespread request that some level 2 detailed prescriptions be downgraded to level 3 recommendations: a sensible request in some cases. But market participants should do more to persuade CESR members to submit to collective constraints, by signalling the inconsistencies between the words of legislation and of recommendations and the deeds of regulatory practices.

In the end, developing and strengthening level 3 work could provide a feasible, sensible and gradual solution to the problems that periodically prompt the proposal of pan-European regulatory authority. As has been noted by two legal scholars.[52] "it is striking that, whereas in the area of financial services the idea is mooted of a European financial services authority, one may discern a trend in Community law to move precisely in the opposite direction, away from centralised control". Before engaging into the less obvious option of a single European authority, they add, one should first consider "whether greater co-operation between national authorities combined with the enactment of the Commission's proposal . . . together with the implementation on of the proposals of the Lamfalussy Committee would suffice." It is up to CESR and its members to prove that this flexible but by no means simple model can work.

6. One last, and concluding, word on a more general issue. Underlying the debate on European financial integration I often detect the elements of a philosophical—at times theological—dispute: one between the harmonisers and, if you allow me the term, the mutual recognisers.

There are of course good arguments on both sides. It is true on the one hand, that, as has been said by my eminent colleague Sir Howard Davies, imposing "a one-size fits all approach . . . simply does not reflect the reality of the difference from one member state to another": the different degree of evolution of markets in different Member States, their different legal regimes, the different role played by self-regulatory organisations are all relevant obstacles to an attempt to establish uniformity. It is also true, on the other hand, that insufficient harmonisation has often provided Member States with the opportunity to introduce additional requirements serving the purpose of insulating the domestic market from competition, while consistent implementation of laws and standards is necessary in order to remove the existing obstacles to the single market. (It is perhaps useful to remember in this context that in the United States securities laws, unlike the company law, soon acquired a federal status).

I think it would be unwise to exasperate the ideological differences between the two views. Remembering that harmonisation, mutual recognition, non-discrimination and free movement are all concurrent and complementary tools for the building of the internal market[53], I am inclined to take a middle-of-the-road view on this issue, based on the following lines. First, we must accept that the process towards a single European financial market requires gradually raising the level of harmonisation, even without specifying to the millimetre the size that should fit all. Second, this process can only be gradual. Third, the more uniform model to which this will lead will not necessarily be that prevailing in one jurisdiction, to which all other should conform. Fourth, and as a result, everybody should be ready to contribute to a workable solution, even at some cost for short-term national and sectoral interests: a more level playing field will in the end provide a better opportunity for the fittest to survive."

20 March 2003.

---

[52] David O'Keeffe and Nekius Carey, "Financial Service in the Internal Market, in G Ferrarini, K G Hopt and E Wymeersch eds., *Capital Markets in the Age of the Euro* Kluwer, The Hague 2002.
[53] See O'Keeffe and Carey in note 9 above.